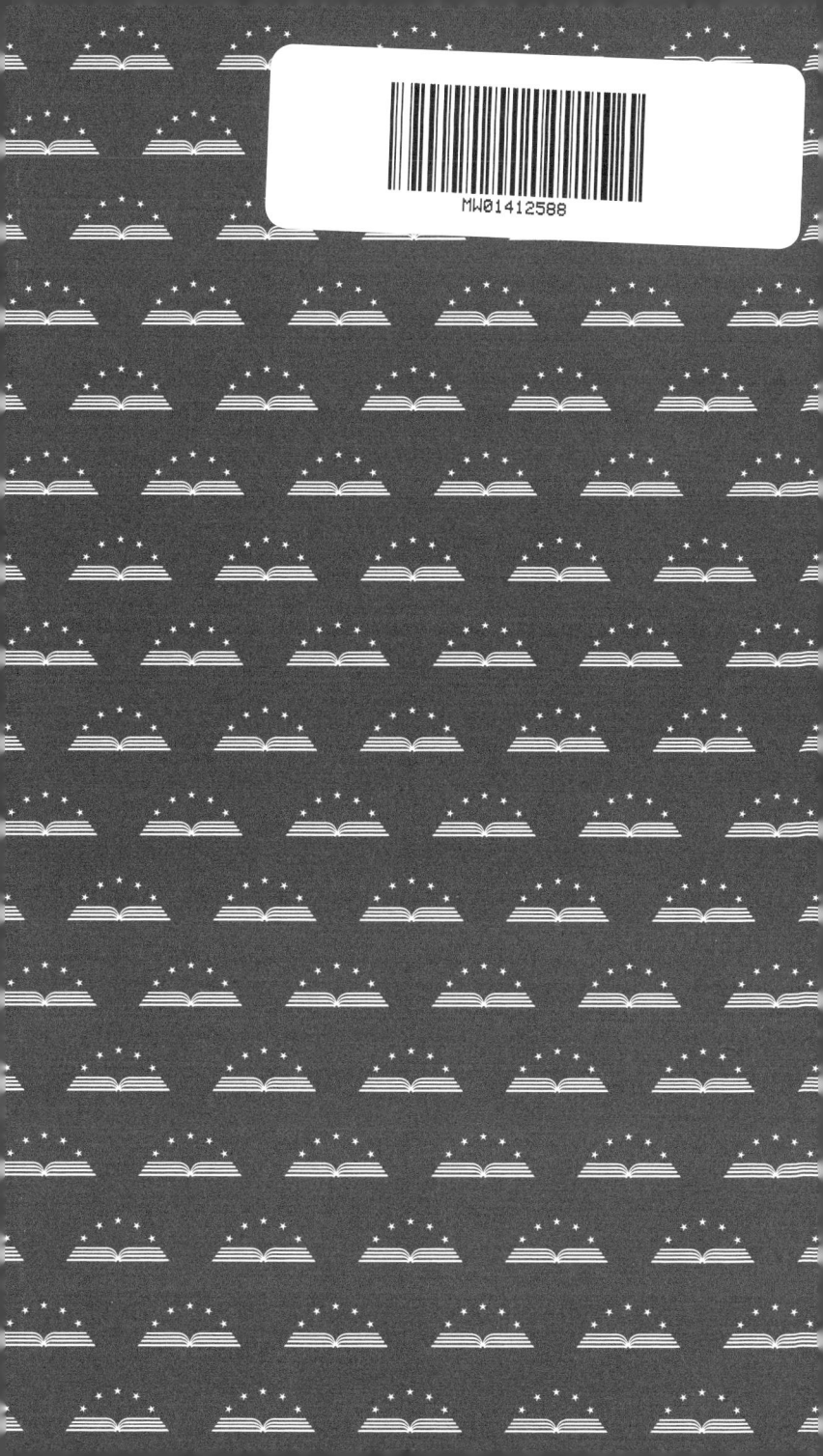

Library of America, a nonprofit organization,
champions our nation's cultural heritage
by publishing America's greatest writing in
authoritative new editions and providing resources
for readers to explore this rich, living legacy.

JOHN QUINCY ADAMS
SPEECHES & WRITINGS

John Quincy Adams

SPEECHES & WRITINGS

David Waldstreicher, *editor*

THE LIBRARY OF AMERICA

JOHN QUINCY ADAMS: SPEECHES & WRITINGS
Volume compilation, introduction, notes,
and chronology copyright © 2025 by
Literary Classics of the United States, Inc., New York, N.Y.
All rights reserved.
No part of this book may be reproduced in any manner whatsoever without
the permission of the publisher, except in the case of brief
quotations embodied in critical articles and reviews.

Visit our website at www.loa.org.

This paper meets the requirements of
ANSI/NISO Z39.48–1992 (Permanence of Paper).

Distributed to the trade in the United States
by Penguin Random House Inc.
and in Canada by Penguin Random House Canada Ltd.

Library of Congress Control Number: 2024943678
ISBN 978–1–59853–808–3

First Printing
The Library of America—390

Manufactured in the United States of America

John Quincy Adams: Speeches & Writings
is published with support from

THE ACHELIS AND BODMAN FOUNDATION

"For more than half a century JOHN QUINCY ADAMS had occupied a prominent position before the American people, and filled a large space in his country's history. His career was protracted to extreme old age. He outlived political enmity and party rancor. His purity of life—his elevated and patriotic principles of action—his love of country, and devotion to its interests—his advocacy of human freedom, and the rights of man—brought all to honor and love him. Admiring legislators hung with rapture on the lips of 'the Old Man Eloquent,' and millions eagerly perused the sentiments he uttered, as they were scattered by the press in every town and hamlet of the Western Continent."

from **William H. Seward,** *Life and Public Services of John Quincy Adams* **(1849).**

Contents

Introduction by David Waldstreicher.........................xi

1. "An Oration, Delivered at the Public Commencement, in the University of Cambridge, in New England, July 18, 1787".........................3

2. Letters of Publicola, June 8–July 27, 1791...............11

3. Letters of Marcellus, April 24–May 11, 1793.............53

4. *An Oration, Pronounced July 4th, 1793, at the Request of the Inhabitants of the Town of Boston, in Commemoration of the Anniversary of American Independence* (Boston, 1793).........................67

5. *An Oration, Delivered at Plymouth, December 22, 1802. At the Anniversary Commemoration of the First Landing of our Ancestors, at that Place* (Boston, 1802)............81

6. Letters of Publius Valerius, October 26–November 16, 1804.........................101

7. *An Inaugural Oration, Delivered at the Author's Installation, as Boylston Professor of Rhetorick and Oratory, at Harvard University, in Cambridge, Massachusetts. On Thursday, 12 June, 1806* (Boston, 1806).........................133

8. *A Letter to the Hon. Harrison Gray Otis, a Member of the Senate of Massachusetts, on the Present State of our National Affairs; with Remarks upon Mr. Pickering's Letter to the Governor of the Commonwealth* (Boston, 1808).........................149

9. The Defence of General Jackson's Conduct in the Seminole War, December 31, 1818.........................181

10. *An Address delivered At the request of a Committee of the Citizens of Washington on the occasion of reading the Declaration of Independence, on the Fourth of July, 1821* (Washington, D.C., 1821).........................205

11.	Inaugural Address. March 4, 1825.	233
12.	First Annual Message. December 6, 1825	243
13.	Message on the Panama Congress. March 15, 1826	269
14.	Speech at the Dedication of the Chesapeake and Ohio Canal. July 4, 1828	287
15.	*An Oration Addressed to the Citizens of the Town of Quincy, on the Fourth of July, 1831, the Fifty-fifth Anniversary of the Independence of the United States of America* (Boston, 1831)	295
16.	*Report of the Minority of the Committee on Manufactures, submitted to the House of Representatives of the United States, February 28, 1833* (Boston, 1833)	325
17.	*Speech of John Quincy Adams, on the Joint Resolution for Distributing Rations to the Distressed Fugitives from Indian Hostilities in the States of Alabama and Georgia. Delivered in the House of Representatives, Wednesday, May 25, 1836.* (Washington, D.C., 1836).	399
18.	*Letters from John Quincy Adams to his Constituents of the Twelfth Congressional District in Massachusetts. To which is Added his Speech in Congress, Delivered February 9, 1837.* (Boston, 1837)	425
19.	*The Jubilee of the Constitution* (New York, 1839)	487
20.	*Mr. Adams' Speech, on War with Great Britain and Mexico; with the Speeches of Messrs. Wise and Ingersoll, to which it is in reply* (Boston, 1842)	567
21.	*Letter from Hon. John Quincy Adams, read at the recent celebration of West India Emancipation in Bangor, (Me.)* [Quincy, MA, 1843]	641

Chronology 657
Note on the Texts. 685
Notes 717
Index. 779

Introduction

BY DAVID WALDSTREICHER

John Quincy Adams is a paradox, which may account for our renewed fascination with him. The sixth president of the United States, he was better prepared and almost certainly more eager to take on the job than any of his predecessors. And yet by the usual measures he was not a great president, becoming just the second to fail to secure reelection. The first, of course, was John Adams. This unhappy distinction wasn't all that Adams had in common with his father. Both were deeply committed to the principles of the American Revolution, but skeptics of democracy. Both rejected the idea of partisanship while being temperamentally unable to resist hard-fought political battles. Both were ardent nationalists, despite a cosmopolitanism born of many years spent abroad in the service of their country. They leaned conservative, except when they were radical. They were against racial slavery—but for a long time had little to say about it.

The Adamses shared one other crucial quality: they led intense inner lives that they committed to paper, leaving prolific records, in the form of diaries and letters, that have informed shifting understandings of their politics, their times, and their legacies.[1] Their often harsh self-criticisms and judgments of others have been visited upon them too—resulting in a focus on personality that sometimes obscures the significance of their more formal principles, their position statements, their eloquence and literary skill.

In the case of the younger Adams, his public writings assume particular value for us as a riveting, ultimately inspiring case study in the long and sustained effort to square the values of the American Revolution with changing political realities in the young nation. For more than fifty years, in one high-stakes political contest after another, John Quincy Adams wrote to and for the American public with insight, passion, and an often lacerating wit. Sometimes he wrote anonymously, for the press; sometimes he wrote for an international audience, as part of his official diplomacy; sometimes he wrote erudite orations for civic celebrations; sometimes he wrote public letters to his constituents in Massachusetts, filled with dramatic transcripts from floor debates to explain what he had done in the Capitol. All were informed attempts to persuade and to make history out of history. By the 1830s he was "Old Man Eloquent": patriot, partisan, and prophet.

Outlasting and frequently outsmarting his political adversaries, scouring the past to make arguments about the present, Adams became our founding revisionist. Over the course of his long career he put America's colonial, revolutionary, and early national history to work in an effort to shape the present and future, with an abiding focus throughout on America's standing in the world and on what might be called the problem of American federalism. Always eager to be, and to be seen as, a man of the whole nation, Adams struggled to frame a national narrative that would transcend the pull of a sectionalism that, as he saw it, was embedded in the very structure of the Constitution. Ironically, it was only after he achieved and lost the presidency, and then in short order returned to public life as the representative of a single congressional district in southeastern Massachusetts, that Adams truly found the voice to match his vision.

It is this late-stage Adams who is the object of our special admiration: the defender of the *Amistad* captives, the antiexpansionist dissenter who foresaw the dire consequences for the union if Texas annexationists like President Andrew Jackson were so foolhardy as to seek a war with Mexico, the vanquisher of the Gag Rule. But the final phase of Adams's career should not overshadow the rest: no one in presidential history, including Jefferson or Jackson, including even his father, can best his half-century of public service or the sheer variety of his contributions as a legislator, executive, diplomat, and secretary of state. Seeing his career in full, following his life in politics from his first public statement as a graduating Harvard senior in 1787 to his forthright denunciations of slavery and other antidemocratic impulses in American life in the 1840s, reminds us that Adams, first and foremost, was a masterful communicator.

In the age of the presidential social media post as weapon, it is important to remember that Adams rose as a writer—a literary craftsman comfortable with both long forms and sound bites mined from them. In the commencement address at Harvard in 1787, he helped define the notion of the 1780s as a "critical period" for the new nation. In his first forays into the art of polemics during the 1790s, he wowed President George Washington with his precociously clear-eyed perspective on European affairs and the young nation's relationship to them. For the next several decades, in published orations on celebratory occasions, he repeatedly digested the trends of the day and provided new words for conceptualizing America's hopes to combine liberty and power. Let us not go abroad "in search of monsters to destroy," he famously cautioned, as part of a long campaign to distance the United States from British-style imperialism that helped justify the American variety, in which expansionists like General Jackson violently displaced Indians by creating new facts on the ground.

He had bitter rivals but for the most part kept personal attacks to his diary, where he also mused on the politics of the possible—especially with respect to slavery's hold on national affairs. From our perspective today, it took him an awfully long time to realize—even longer to go public with—his conviction, as he put it privately during the Missouri Crisis, that "if the dissolution of the Union must come, let it come from no other cause but this."[2] Only after his vexed presidency did he fully or publicly attest that the Constitution's compromises over slavery, and the proslavery drift of national policy under Jackson, were fatally incompatible with his vision of a modern nation dedicated to human improvement and liberty. He would spend much of the remainder of his political career expanding on this theme, in speeches he revised for the newspapers and franked—sent for free—from his desk in Congress.

Adams's story is one of both consistent ideals and of accommodating himself to the politics of persuasion in an emerging democratic society. For those disposed to administer purity tests on historical figures, it may also be instructive to note that Adams's antislavery posture was animated by a mixture of deeply held convictions and less noble or at least more contingent and strategic motives. For those who are looking for creative possibilities in the American political system, it is striking that this supposedly most elitist individual ever to occupy the nation's highest office found in the humbler precincts of the Congress a path out of the partisan mess that had frustrated him as president. He wasn't so much "the professor" the Jacksonians derided in favor of their mythical "ploughman" as he was the son of a conservative yet also democratizing Revolution who looked to different, and better developed, modes of persuasion to promote America's best interests on the world stage and at home.[3] A generation before Lincoln, Adams mostly (but not always) sought to appeal to what the future president, who was his great admirer and one of his congressional pallbearers at his grand state funeral in 1848, would call "the better angels of our nature."

Adams was predisposed to think about politics historically and to conceive of writing as part of his political practice. Perhaps not surprisingly given the extraordinary nature of his upbringing, he also tended to think of his own biography and of the course of American independence as the same story. Over time he developed a tragic as well as triumphalist understanding of the American Revolution and his own era that was deeply bound up in his sense of his relationship with the American people—his "fellow citizens," as he steadfastly referred to them. Grappling with the legacy of the American Revolution ultimately required a reinterpretation of the founding and of subsequent history that would in time form the core of antislavery politics in its Lincolnian mode. The development of that perspective, Adams's answer to what he will call "the great question of human liberty," is the central story line of this volume.

With and through his parents, Adams had close, personal experience of both the most local and the most international dimensions of the American Revolution, witnessing the Bunker Hill battle and its aftermath with his mother and serving as his father's secretary while the elder Adams was representing the American union abroad during and after the Revolutionary War. The deeply rooted nature of his patriotism informed Adams's initial response to the new federal Constitution drafted in 1787: like many antifederalists, at first he feared it meant *giving up* New England traditions of local government—the long-valued past. At the same time in his July 1787 Harvard commencement address he diagnosed the problem of those years as a failure of "union." Economic distress in Massachusetts, in his precocious diagnosis, was a consequence of the erosion of "the bonds of union which connected us with our sister states, [which] have been shamefully relaxed by a selfish and contracted principle," namely, an unwillingness to pay taxes to retire the Revolutionary War debt. Localism was the problem, thinking bigger the solution. When Massachusetts folk abided by their agreements, the "radiant sun of our union" would not only reappear but begin again to protect "the wretched object of tyranny and persecution in every quarter of the globe."

The formative years Adams spent abroad confirmed his sense of American exceptionalism. Years later, when his father, now vice president, was being attacked as a closet monarchist, an old-fashioned Anglophile whose advocacy of a "balanced" constitution struck many Americans as insufficiently democratic, Adams argued that the U.S. Constitution had combined the virtues of both the British and new French constitutions "without the evils of both." Already a trusted adviser to his father, he gained the attention of the rest of the Washington administration with carefully reasoned, pseudonymously published newspaper series—the first and best of these, the "Publicola" letters, was a withering response to Thomas Paine's *Rights of Man*—in which he defended neutrality as the only sure guide against partisanship and "foreign usurpation," which he described, accurately enough, as the bane of past republics. Earlier than most, and more consistently, he defined both British and French influence in the United States as "the shameful fetters of a foreign bondage" and the French Revolution as a tragic rather than heroic story, utterly different from the American Revolution.

Biographers of Adams have tended to focus on what seems to be a series of reverses and vocational crises during these years, as his father lost the election of 1800 and Adams returned from Europe, served in the Massachusetts legislature, and joined the Yankee Federalists' "Augustan" dissent against the Jeffersonian "revolution." He was elected by the Massachusetts legislature to the U.S. Senate to be a bastion of New England Federalism, but became instead a lonely apostate, ultimately forced out of office for supporting the Jefferson administration on the Louisiana Purchase and the Embargo Act. One might, however, view these years as those in which he further developed his intellectual as well as political method: revisiting the classics regularly, keeping a more extensive diary that recorded both political events and his reading, and periodically recalibrating his sense of the relationship between the recent and distant past in writing projects. History, especially ancient history, was an ever-present place of refuge.

Adams consistently positioned the American nation as the sympathetic protagonist of his historical narratives. In his 1802 oration on the anniversary of the Plymouth landing, he highlighted what he saw as the close relationship of New England's founders to the Dutch humanist Hugo Grotius and his influential theories of just international relations. For Adams, no European settlement had ever been kinder and fairer to Native peoples; Indian rights of possession, he concluded, rested "upon a questionable foundation" because Native hunters acted as "lordly savages" wasting land. Plymouth's settlers had providentially landed on the "territory thus free" of a tribe "wasted by disease" and made the most of it. Proof of American virtue lay in expansion itself: in two more centuries American numbers would surely exceed those of Europe. Later Adams wrote in his diary of his pride in this argument "which was afterwards useful to me at Ghent, and which after the lapse of more than twenty years I still think unanswerable."[4]

But if his view of American history began in New England, it did not end there—precisely because he had continental expansion in view. Despite the criticisms of New England Federalists that the Louisiana Purchase would unbalance the union, Adams did not try to argue his way out of the implications of the Purchase, which he was known to have supported. New England's present and future decline in power, he recognized, was inevitable, "founded in nature." The real question was whether southern preponderance would be "enjoyed with moderation." Things had not worked out as anticipated in 1787: slaveholders reaped the representation of three-fifths of the enslaved but without the equivalent federal taxation based on the census that had been part of the deal, since no direct tax had been passed except during the war scare of 1798, during his father's administration. The problem was structural. Adams's 1804 "Publius Valerius" series makes this point clear, offering a stinging historical argument for constitutional change. The compromises of

1787 over representation, taxation, federalism, and slavery were important and understandable at the time but no longer fair. The South was more than safe: it was in the saddle. "Persuaded that the Union is the first of political blessings to every part of these States," Adams felt that planter interest in the union should allow for an adjustment. For his own part, he avoided politicizing slavery with respect to other issues that came before the Senate, including the status of Haiti and the abolition of the slave trade. Impressed by a young Henry Clay's speech against the slave trade, he wrote in his diary that he, nevertheless, "took, and intend to take, no part in the debates on this subject."[5]

Adams's silence on increasingly politicized questions relating to slavery may seem in retrospect surprising. But it is less so when we realize that his thoroughgoing nationalism and his keen sense of history informed both his career strategy and his antipartisan and antisectionalist preferences. Muting the politics of slavery, for Adams, was a good, conservative, nationalist position he had learned at home. His father, notwithstanding a recently acquired reputation as an antislavery figure, had in fact helped tamp down slavery issues in the Continental Congress and never tried to resuscitate them as vice president or president. At a time when sectional and partisan interests dovetailed for many statesmen, John Quincy Adams supported the Virginia-led Democratic-Republican administration, he told a friend, because the nature of the Federalists' opposition, in time of war, could lead to civil war and the subservience of the Atlantic states to Britain.

Adams's subsequent "exile" to Russia as foreign minister under James Madison reinforced his identity as a national statesman, both for himself and in the eyes of the American people. Ultimately, his loyalty and consistency as well as his diplomatic experience earned him the coveted post of secretary of state in James Monroe's administration, a position increasingly seen as a stepping-stone to the presidency. He was the New England man in Monroe's cabinet, there for his manifest skills, to be sure, but also for sectional balance, and thus always in some way suspect; but as a former Federalist he was also a one-man argument for the flourishing of nationalism, and the end of partisanship and sectionalism, in the would-be "era of good feelings."

This had implications for what he did and did not say and do about slavery during the Missouri Crisis. "The fault," he confided to his diary, "is in the Constitution of the United States, which has sanctioned a dishonorable compromise with slavery." The dishonor lay in the conflict with the Declaration of Independence, which had grounded the American Revolution in the consent of the governed—*all* the governed. Yet now it was clearer than ever that "slave representation has governed the Union." Maybe he should not have signed on to the compromise by failing to object in the cabinet meetings. Maybe he should have proposed a constitutional convention.[6]

In public, however, he stayed out of the line of fire. He spoke differently to different colleagues on the matter, dividing himself: as a "servant of the whole union" he had to represent the interests of all, but as an "eastern man" he certainly looked forward to resolutions against slavery in the next wave of territories.[7] It was only the second phase of the Missouri Crisis, over the state's new constitution, that made Adams sure what side he was on, though he was hardly more forthcoming or public about it. The new Missouri constitution that deprived free Blacks of the right to migrate there was unconstitutional and had to be resisted, he said to a congressman privately. His now oft-quoted predictions of "servile war" and the end of slavery date from this period. But war did not come, and three months later he could write that while constitutional conflict would return, this was not the proper time. On a career or policy level, Adams evaded the Missouri Crisis of 1819–21, but it nonetheless shaped the rest of his public life.

In the wake of the crisis, Adams offered his most famous, defining statement of America's exceptional identity. Adams took Fourth of July pieties about the role of the United States in world history very seriously and he seized on the day as an opportunity to think, write, and speak to and for the nation. His Independence Day address in 1821 depicted "conquest and servitude" as "mingled up in every particle of the social existence" of Great Britain. The rebellions of the seventeenth century indexed this British history. By contrast, the settlement of New England, which again stood in for the entire nation, involved the purchase of Indian lands and a social compact "in which conquest and servitude had for part." The Declaration of Independence represented a new epoch in history because it delegitimized empires and states founded "upon conquest." The United States stood for natural and equal rights; "her glory is not *dominion*, but *liberty*." This historical interpretation undergirded the Monroe Doctrine he would later develop: Europe must not interfere in the Americas because the United States "abstained from interference" abroad and refused the "Imperial Diadem."

Adams was framing a sense of the nation's history in which slavery represented a problem needing adjustment by farseeing, historically informed, centrist or non-extremist statesmen like himself. His differences with the National Republican presidents he served, James Madison and James Monroe, seem less important in retrospect than the aid he provided to the "Monrovian" moment.[8] The ascent of Adams epitomized the "shutdown" of formal antislavery politics during the 1820s.[9] During these same years, though, the all too apparent politics of slavery also exposed the limits of his vision. Adams failed to recognize the expropriation of Native lands in the South and Southwest as inherently proslavery because he had become the most prominent exponent of the blame-the-British school. This was a call back to the founding historical narrative of the United States that Jefferson had transcribed in the Declaration of Independence, in which the Americans liberated themselves from a "servitude" about to be imposed by colonial overlords craven enough to set Native peoples (and slaves) against them.

Confronted by the implications of American expansion, Adams found his room for maneuver increasingly narrowed. In the lead-up to the presidential election of 1824, he was suspected of being antislavery—or at least it became useful for planters and their representatives to paint him as such.[10] Nevertheless, as president he refused to see the opposition as particularly southern. That would concede too much. He could not advocate for union and a vigorous, activist national government as president while drawing regional distinctions. Playing the slavery card was what partial, irresponsible politicians did. No redemptive narrative could support it. His speeches and messages during the years of his presidency sought to advance union, "improvement," and good government while carefully stepping over the trip wires of slavery and partisanship. That proved to be, at best, very difficult.

Adams devoted the waning days of his administration and much of his brief retirement to historical writings he neither completed nor published. No doubt his election to Congress in 1830 slowed these ambitious projects. Yet his new position also provided public occasions to try out his revised, experimental versions of U.S. history. By 1831–32, the ex-president had developed an interpretive framework positing the irreducible conflict between slavery and national sovereignty, and he had begun to elaborate its implications on specific public occasions as well as privately with selected interlocutors, such as Alexis de Tocqueville, whom he told that slavery lay at the core of the nation's various and complex woes. He devoted his widely read Fourth of July oration in Boston in 1831 to a historical demolition of "the South Carolina doctrine" of nullification. Union, he insisted, even preceded American independence in 1776; the states were not preexisting entities, as "the Colonies are not named" in the Declaration. The "hallucination of State sovereignty" was based on the same error of undivided sovereignty that had misled the British Parliament into declaring its power to legislate for Americans "in all cases whatsoever" in 1766. Some weeks later in his lengthy eulogy on James Monroe, Adams tried out a new argument about the origins of sectional controversy under the Articles of Confederation, observing that the structure of Confederation government required delegates to the Congress to represent their states, which led to sectional enmities over Mississippi River navigation and "a coldness and mutual alienation between the north and the southern divisions of the Union which is not extinguished to this day."[11]

In the coming years, Adams gradually found in congressional oratory, eulogies, and celebratory occasions something akin to the Ciceronian revival he had trumpeted as the first Boylston Professor of Rhetoric and Oratory at Harvard from 1805 to 1808. His failed postpresidential reinvention as a historian informed his return to national politics as a prophet. A venerable statesman no longer burdened with presidential political ambitions, he could further develop his theory of a slave power perversely resisting the natural rights and nationalist doctrines of the Declaration of Independence and pushing the union toward civil war. Doing the math, Adams highlighted the extent to which minority rule had come to dominate in the national government. These stances were more than theory or even history: in documents like his brilliant *Report of the Minority of the Committee on Manufactures* in 1833, they had distinct policy implications. Where he had once concluded that his nationalist vision could thrive only by isolating and obscuring the divisive issue of slavery, he now became the country's foremost expert at linking it to everything from taxes and tariffs to territorial expansion and wartime refugees.

The gag rule controversy, during which Adams annually objected to the automatic tabling of antislavery petitions and to the suppression of his speeches about them, made a national issue out of Adams's eloquence, experience, and expertise. His mastery of parliamentary tactics and constitutional history was on full display, retailed in the published versions of his speeches (complete with his opponents' outraged objections) like *Letters from John Quincy Adams to his Constituents of the Twelfth Congressional District in Massachusetts* and the *Speech on War with Great Britain and Mexico*. In these vivid writings, he gives the flavor of floor debates and demonstrates his increasing importance to antislavery politics even while he still would not identify publicly with the abolitionist movement. Again and again, he calmly demonstrated that while his adversaries attacked him personally, the real stakes were not only the status of the enslaved and of free Blacks in the District of Columbia or the nation as a whole but also the rights of petitioners and his constituents—women as well as men. What better symbol could there be of enslavers' arrogance and overweening power than the silencing of an ex-president seeking simply to fulfill his constitutional duty to represent the concerns of his people? In these exchanges and the publicity they engendered, Adams did as much as anyone to convince northerners that slavery was a threat to white Americans' liberties. The rights of "mastery" were "incompatible with the inalienable rights of all mankind, as set forth in the Declaration of Independence" and even the "fundamental principles," as opposed to some specific provisions, of the Constitution.

In his role as scourge of the slave power, Adams often returned to narratives about the American Revolution and its role in world history: in his eulogies for Madison and Lafayette; in several

Fourth of July orations; in the remarkable public letter to an assembly of abolitionists in Bangor, Maine, in 1843; in intensive arguments about the course of recent federal policy vis-à-vis Texas and Mexico. The momentous issue of Texas annexation, arising in 1836, successfully quashed by Adams and his allies but then recurring later, required him to bring his intimate knowledge of half a century of diplomatic history—and his own record as a defender of American sovereignty against Britain—to bear on a deeply partisan issue that could no longer be separated from the politics of slavery: "If the national government has no right to interfere with the institution of domestic slavery in any of the states, what right has that same government to hang on your neck the millstone of Texian slavery?" Rejecting the Jacksonian states' rights doctrine and its implications both at home and abroad, he repeatedly went back to 1776 to argue that the Declaration of Independence had founded a nation-state. That union, dedicated to human rights, was a sovereign national government, not "a mere cluster of sovereign confederated States." Because that "heresy" came from the South, it needed to be confronted with an antislavery interpretation of the founding. Nothing else could trump the Jacksonian strict construction of the Constitution that seemed to keep slavery off-limits in politics while repeatedly strengthening the "slave power."

In his later works Adams further developed his account of revolutionary nationalism frustrated in the 1780s and then renewed, with a fatal compromise, in the Constitution. In speeches-turned-pamphlets like *The Jubilee of the Constitution* (1839) he went even further, calling the sovereignty of states established in the Articles of Confederation a "*usurpation* upon the rights of the people of the United States," and extending his narrative into the 1790s and beyond to include the Louisiana Purchase, the most daring initiative the national government had ever undertaken, which, "if not eventually leading to the dissolution of the Union," might yet prove an advance for freedom. As secretary of state, responsible for keeping the nation's papers in order, he had put considerable time into helping to preserve and publish records of the Continental Congress, the very documents that historians rely on today. Combined with the family archive he was reading and cataloging, he had, in other words, unusual access to evidence about the nation's founding. He used this special knowledge to develop a well-honed, revisionist narrative to buttress his appeal to "the fathers." In his public letter celebrating the anniversary of emancipation in the British West Indies, he described an American Revolution that, based on "the rights of human nature," should have ended "two slaveries" everywhere in the United States as it had, he believed, in Massachusetts.

Perhaps most controversially and consequentially, he insisted that the wars that militant slaveholders seemed determined to ignite would be fatal to their class and their very notion of "the South," because they would lead to arming the enslaved, to slave rebellions, and to emancipation under the war powers of Congress, the president, and the military. Adams's reading of history, constitutional limits, and constitutional powers was very hard to refute. It proved prophetic when Republican allies of Lincoln cited his warnings of and justifications for wartime emancipation.

Adams's self-assessment during the congressional years we now see as his heroic era tended to swerve from the grandiose to the tragic and back. The tragic theme was often an antislavery jeremiad, a call to arms. He was winning some battles to define the past and the present and losing others—losing and then finally winning with the gag rule, and not unrelatedly, in the case of Texas annexation during those same years, winning and then losing. We tend to separate his career into successes and failures, or into politics and good intentions, or into doing and writing, and so did he; but he also knew better. Both his historical interpretation of a proslavery republic and his consequently anguished, revisionist quest to square nation-building and empire with America's inspiring opposition to tyranny resonate strongly today, leading to what can only be called an Adams revival. His questions are, again, ours. Did the Revolution make a nation—a people—or merely a federative union? Does the Constitution restrain or advance the cause of human freedom? What is the relationship between the answers to those questions? How might they be applied to the politicized issues of our own time? And so we return to our founding revisionist, the president whose very loyalty to the regime of the fathers first suppressed, and then unleashed, the antislavery nationalism that would lead a generation later to civil war and emancipation, to Lincoln's "new birth of freedom."

1. The Library of America includes a three-volume edition of John Adams's writings and a two-volume edition of selections from John Quincy Adams's diaries. A sixth volume gathers Abigail Adams's letters.

2. David Waldstreicher, ed., *John Quincy Adams: Diaries 1779–1821* (New York: Library of America, 2017), 576.

3. John William Ward, *Andrew Jackson: Symbol for an Age* (New York: Oxford University Press, 1955), 46–78.

4. Worthington C. Ford, ed., *Writings of John Quincy Adams* (New York: The Macmillan Company, 1914), III: 11. Adams led the American delegation that negotiated the Treaty of Ghent in 1814, ending the War of 1812.

5. Waldstreicher, ed., *John Quincy Adams: Diaries 1779–1821*, 138.

6. Ibid., 538, 544.

7. Ford, ed., *Writings of John Quincy Adams,* VII: 53, 191–93.

8. Robert Pierce Forbes, *The Missouri Compromise and Its Aftermath: Slavery and the Meaning of America* (Chapel Hill: University of North Carolina Press, 2007).

9. Donald J. Ratcliffe, "The Decline of Antislavery Politics, 1815–1840," in John Craig Hammond and Matthew Mason, eds., *Contesting Slavery: The Politics of Bondage and Freedom in the New American Nation* (Charlottesville: University of Virginia Press, 2011), 267–90.

10. David P. Callahan, *The Politics of Corruption: The Election of 1824 and the Making of Presidents in Jacksonian America* (Charlottesville: University of Virginia Press, 2022), 99, 141.

11. John Quincy Adams, *An Eulogy on the Life and Character of James Monroe* (Boston, 1831), 37–38.

JOHN QUINCY ADAMS
SPEECHES & WRITINGS

"AT THIS CRITICAL PERIOD"

1. "An Oration, Delivered at the Public Commencement, in the University of Cambridge, in New England, July 18, 1787, by Mr. JOHN QUINCY ADAMS, son of his Excellency JOHN ADAMS, L. L. D. the American Minister at the court of London." *The Columbian Magazine or Monthly Miscellany* I (Philadelphia: September 1787), 625–28.

On July 11, 1787, just one week before he delivered this, his first public address, graduating Harvard senior and future law student John Quincy Adams marked his twentieth birthday in the pages of his diary. "I am good for nothing," he lamented, "and cannot even carry myself forward in the world: three long years I have yet to study in order to qualify myself for business: and then—oh! and then; how many more years, to plod along, mechanically, if I should live; before I shall really get into the world?" Adams was, by any measure, the most accomplished of the young men taking degrees from Harvard that year, having already made two voyages to Europe with his diplomat father, where he enjoyed a range of cultural and educational experiences unknown to many twice his age. Still, he was impatient for something greater, in a hurry to "really get into the world."

Graduation offered a first chance. The faculty of Harvard College designated Adams one of the class orators at the ceremony, always a significant occasion in the civic life of the Commonwealth of Massachusetts, with the governor and other dignitaries usually in attendance. Adams's oration came in the middle of a lengthy program of student presentations that included orations and colloquies in Latin, Greek, and Hebrew; scientific and mathematical demonstrations; and syllogistic and forensic disputations on such topics as "Whether any man be so depraved as to have left all sense of virtue?" His topic, set by the college president, was "The importance and necessity of public faith to the well-being of a Community." "Public faith" here referred not to religion but to the respect for public and private debts and contracts, a subject of paramount importance for the new nation during the "critical period" (a phrase Adams may have coined here) of the framing and ratification of the Constitution.

Nowhere was this issue more urgent than in Massachusetts. The Commonwealth had raised taxes to pay its portion of the national debt in hard coin, aggravating an ongoing currency shortage that hit farmers especially hard. A tax revolt ensued, with Daniel Shays and his followers closing courts in the central and western parts of the state. Shays's insurgents included some of the leading men of Berkshire County, frustrated by policies that threatened dispossession of their neighbors from their farms, seemingly to pay war bonds held by easterners. Ultimately, the state militia, "the hand of patriotism," as Adams calls it, had been called out to crush the "noxious plant" of rebellion, with several of Adams's classmates joining the ranks.

For Adams the issue was bigger than just his home state. Both the debt controversy and the rebellion had national ramifications. The question young Adams asks in his address is the same his father had posed during the protests of the 1760s and early 1770s, and then during the Revolutionary War: Could devotion to the public good be made to last? And more pressingly now, would the present generation take up the task? The answer, for Adams, lay in a renewed commitment to a national compact—"the radiant sun of our union"—and the prompt payment of debts would convey the substance of this renewed nationalism. Local issues would be solved by faith in the union of states. If Americans did not trust each other, why would the foreigners who supported their trade and their outstanding loans? More than just important, public credit was the lifeblood of the social compact. Without it, the nation itself might be of short duration.

Adams's first turn on the public stage was well received. In a July 27 letter to his friend and former comrade-in-arms Henry Knox, David Humphries, who had served as George Washington's aide-de-camp during the war, wrote that "I was present at the Commencement in your University of Cambridge & highly delighted with most of the Academic Exercises, in particular young Mr. Adams distinguished himself by a manly and dignified oration on public credit." Another witness described the event in a Boston newspaper: "The public expectations from this gentleman, being the son of an Ambassador . . . were greatly inflated. The performance justified the preconceived partiality. He is warmly attached to the republican system of his father, and descanted upon the subject of public justice with great energy." Adams was already sensitive to charges of nepotism or favoritism; when clergyman and historian Jeremy Belknap sought permission to publish the address in Philadelphia's *Columbian Magazine*, Adams asked Belknap to publish it anonymously so it could be judged on its own merits. But when the address appeared in the September issue, it carried not only his name, but the additional identifier "son of his Excellency JOHN ADAMS, L. L. D. the American Minister at the court of London." Whatever its billing, the oration fit well with the nationalist sentiments on offer in the magazine, which included the first periodical publication of the U.S. Constitution, under the title "The new plan for a Fœderal Government proposed by the Convention."

Harvard Oration

THE solemnity of the present occasion, the numerous concourse of this brilliant audience, and the consciousness of my own insufficiency, all conspire to fill my breast with terrors hitherto unknown: and although my heart would fondly cherish the hope, that the candor and indulgence, which have ever been the distinguishing characteristics of assemblies on this occasion, will at this time be exerted, yet, this involuntary palpitation expresses fears which cannot be subdued.

Suffer me however, while the united powers of genius and of science, are here displayed by others for your entertainment, to call your attention for a few moments to a subject of the utmost importance to our country, and to every individual as a citizen.

To every reflecting mind, the situation of this commonwealth for some months past, must have appeared truly alarming: on whatever side we turn our anxious eyes, the prospect of public affairs is dark and gloomy: the distressing scarcity of a circulating medium, has been continually increasing: the violent gust of rebellion is scarcely dissipated, and threatening clouds of sullen discontent are still lowering round the horizon: luxury and dissipation, like baneful weeds, have obstructed the growth of all our useful virtues; and although the hand of patriotism has of late been stretched forth to crop the noxious plant, yet, the fatal root still lies lurking beneath the surface: the bonds of union which connected us with our sister states, have been shamefully relaxed by a selfish and contracted principle, and the sails of commerce furled within our ports, witness the lamentable declension of our trade.

At this critical period, when the whole nation is groaning under the intolerable burden of these accumulated evils, and while the most tremendous calamities are suspended by a slender thread over our heads, it is natural to enquire what were the causes which tended to reduce the commonwealth from a state of happiness and prosperity, to the deplorable situation in which we now behold it; and what measures might still be adopted, to realize those happy days of national wealth and honor, which the glorious conclusion of a just and successful war seemed to promise.

In this enquiry, the first question, which will naturally occur, must be, what is the situation of our national credit, and what are the dispositions of our fellow citizens with respect to the fulfilment of those engagements, which in times of difficulty and danger, in times "when then the souls of men were tried," they were under a necessity of contracting? and let me ask, can any man, whose generous soul disdains every base sentiment of fraud or injustice, answer these questions without dropping a tear of shame, or uttering an expression of indignation? Will he not be constrained to acknowledge, that the divine enthusiasm, and the undaunted patriotism which animated the bosoms of our countrymen in their struggle for liberty, have abandoned many so soon as they had attained the darling object of their wishes? but what is liberty, and what is life, when preserved by the loss of honor? would not the most abject state of slavery, to which tyranny and oppression could have reduced a people, have been preferable to standing as an independant nation, exposed to the scorns, the reproach and the derision of mankind:—forbid it heaven that this should be our fate! From the well known honor and integrity of the distinguished patriot, who by the suffrages of a free people, has repeatedly been called to fill the seat of government, and from the present dispositions of the majority of my countrymen, I would still hope, that they will adhere inviolably to every maxim of justice and equity; yet an indolent carelessness, a supine inattention to the solemn engagements of the public, are but too conspicuous among us: numbers indeed, without even assuming the mask of dissimulation, openly avow their desire to evade the fulfilment of those engagements, which they once esteemed supremely sacred.

It is frequently suggested, that nations are not subjected to those laws, which regulate the conduct of individuals: that national policy commands them to consult their own interests, though at the expence of foreigners or of individual citizens; that it is the duty of every government to alleviate the distresses of the people over whom it is placed, and in short, that a violation of the public faith could not subject any individual to censure: but an idea so palpably absurd, can be formed upon no other principle than the probability of escaping the punishment due to the most flagrant enormities: one of the basest principles which can blacken the human heart: the principle which impels the hand of the lawless ruffian, and directs the dagger of the midnight assassin.

Can it be pretended, that there is more than one kind of justice and equity? Or that honor and probity are qualities of such an accommodating nature, that like the venal sycophant of a court, they will suit themselves at all times to the interest of the prevailing party?—Does not the very idea of a *right* imply that of a correspondent *obligation*? And can a nation therefore have a right to form treaties or enter into contracts of any kind, without being held by every bond of justice to the performance?

The contracted bosom which was never expanded by the warm and generous feelings of benevolence and philanthropy, may slight all public engagements, for the sake of a paltry profit, but to a mind not bereft of every virtuous sentiment it must appear, that if any obligation can be more peculiarly solemn than others, they must be those for the performance of which the honor, not of one individual but of *millions* has been pledged; and to a person whose views extend beyond the narrow compass of a day, every breach of public faith must appear equally repugnant to every principle of equity and of policy.—Survey the faithful page of history, peruse the annals of the civilized world, and you will always find that the paths of rectitude and justice, have ever been to a nation the paths of wealth, and greatness, as well as of glory and honor; that public credit has ever been the foundation upon which the fabric of national grandeur has been erected.

So long as the Grecian states adhered inviolably to the bonds by which they were connected, the innumerable armies of the Persian despot, only served as trophies to adorn their victories: when a disregard to their public faith, together with discord, crept in among them, they soon fell, an easy prey to the ambition of a less powerful tyrant.

Rome, the imperial mistress of the world, exhibits to our view the most illustrious example of the grandeur to which a nation may arrive, by a sacred regard to public faith: it was not by the splendor of her victories, it was not by the pageantry of her triumphs that she extended her dominion over the submissive world: but it was by her unalterable attachment to the laws of justice, and her punctilious observance of all the contracts in which she engaged. On the other hand the disastrous fate of Alba, and of Carthage, the faithless rival of the Roman power, displays the melancholy consequences of an unjust system of policy in a nation.

In modern times, Britain attacked at once, by the united power of four mighty nations, and borne down by the load of an enormous debt, exhibits an example of national honour for the admiration of the world, and for the imitation of the American states. The punctual observance of every contract, and the scrupulous fulfilment of every agreement are the only props which have supported the sinking reputation of that ill-fated kingdom. This alone has arrested the progress of threatning conquest, and suspended the uplifted arm of ghastly ruin.

In this country I am persuaded there yet exists a spark of patriotism, which may still rekindle a vivid flame. On you, ye lovely daughters of Columbia, your country calls to revive the drooping public spirit. Without recurring to the examples of distant ages, let me only recommend to you to imitate yourselves: you have already given ample proofs that the patriotic virtues are not confined to man. Nature, it is true, has not formed you to tread the rugged paths of active life; but yours is the nobler influence of the mind. 'Tis yours to encourage by the smiles of applause every virtuous undertaking, and when the warrior returns from the field of battle with the laurel in his hand, 'tis yours to twine it round his head. Oh! may you ever instil into the tender mind the principles of liberty and of patriotism, and remember that the man, who can violate his country's faith, must ever be regardless of his own.

Suffer me, my friends and classmates, to address you, upon this interesting subject. Warmed by that friendship, which will ever be the pride and comfort of my life, I can attest the sentiments of honor and integrity, which I have ever heard you express. To recommend to you a spirit of patriotism and of public zeal, would be needless: I can therefore only exhort you, when you shall be advanced upon the theatre of the world, when your country shall call upon you, to assist in her councils, or to defend her with your fortunes and your lives against the sword of invasion, or against the dagger of oppression, to retain those severe republican virtues, which the pampered minion of a tyrant may deride, which the debilitated slave of luxury may dread, but which alone can effectually support the glorious cause of freedom and of virtue: above all, may your ruling passion ever be to preserve pure and immaculate the reputation of your country! May an insuperable attachment to this, ever shine forth in your actions, ever be the favorite theme of your discourse: for it may be safely asserted, that all the distresses in which the commonwealth is involved, are immediately connected with the loss of our national credit, and that of an invincible resolution to abide by all the agreements to which we have consented, were displayed in the conduct of our citizens in general, we should soon rise superior to every temporary evil: gentle peace and smiling plenty, would again appear, and scatter their invaluable blessings round the happy land: the hands of commerce would recover strength and spread the swelling sail: arts and manufactures would flourish, and soon would vie with those of Europe, and science here would enrich the world with noble and useful discoveries.

The radiant sun of our union, would soon emerge from those thick clouds, which obscure his glory, shine with the most resplendent lustre, and diffuse throughout the astonished world, the brilliant light of science, and the genial warmth of freedom.

Our eagle would soon extend the wings of protection, to the wretched object of tyranny and persecution in every quarter of the globe.

The muses, disgusted with the depravity both of taste and morals, which prevail in Europe, would soon take up their abode in these blissful seats of liberty and peace; here would they form historians, who should relate, and poets who should sing the glories of our country.

And shall we from a sordid motive of self interest forego all these advantages? Shall we draw upon our country the execrations of injured foreigners? Shall we deprive the man who nobly fought and bled to establish our freedom, of that subsistence which he no longer can procure? or shall we reduce his mourning widow and orphan child to beggary, as a reward for his services? Forbid it ye powers who are the protectors of innocence and virtue!—May a detestation of so base a principle be engraved upon the heart of every American! may it be expressed in the first accents of the lisping infant, and the last words pronounced by the faltering voice of age! and may national honor and integrity distinguish the American commonwealths, till the last trump shall announce the dissolution of the world, and the whole frame of nature shall be consumed in one universal conflagration.

"THE UNSUBSTANTIAL FABRICK OF VISIONARY POLITICIANS"

2. Letters of Publicola, I–XI. *Columbian Centinel* (Boston: June 8–July 27, 1791).

About the U.S. Constitution of 1787, drafted behind closed doors in Philadelphia and barely ratified in the state convention of Massachusetts, Adams had originally been skeptical, calling it an aristocratic seizure of power. But as his graduation oration had shown, he had also been concerned about the anarchic drift and "inefficiency" of the Articles of Confederation. By 1789, when his father was elected vice president, Adams had fully reconciled himself to the new federal government. Under the leadership of George Washington, whom the younger Adams revered, it seemed to promise an era of unity and vigor. Events in Europe would soon complicate matters.

The French Revolution came home to many Americans with the publication of Thomas Paine's *Rights of Man*. The first American edition of this controversial book by the author of *Common Sense* had been issued in Philadelphia in May 1791 with a prefatory endorsement by Secretary of State Thomas Jefferson that alluded darkly to "political heresies which have sprung up among us." John Quincy Adams, like many other readers, quickly perceived that the "heresies" Jefferson had in mind included the more balanced—some said more "monarchical" or aristocratic—constitutionalism advanced by John Adams in his "Discourses on Davila," a series of newspaper essays that had recently run in Philadelphia's *Gazette of the United States*. Writing as Publicola, the vice president's son made his debut as a polemicist with this eleven-part response to Paine's book, one of the opening salvos in the emerging partisan contest between the factions that would become known as Federalists and Republicans.

To the extent that that divide would be shaped by perceptions of the French Revolution, the famous debate between Paine and Edmund Burke loomed large, as it does in Publicola's letters. Appalled by the destructive energies unleashed by the Revolution— by the very notion that it was possible or desirable to begin the world over again—Burke in his *Reflections on the Revolution in France* (1790) had urged Britons to take pride in their unwritten constitution, a legacy of centuries that had been, from the perspective of Whigs like Burke, perfected by the Glorious Revolution of 1689. Deeply influenced by the American experience of constitution making in the

1770s and 1780s, Paine responded that any constitution that was not written and directly approved by representatives of the nation was illegitimate, and no constitution at all.

But in framing their written constitutions, Adams points out, Americans had not started from scratch; they had retained English common law, the basis for many of the fundamental rights for which they had fought and died. Confronted now by the more radical and conservative approaches to enlightened government embodied in the French and British models, Adams portrays the American system as a third, middle way, a framing with policy implications that would become more apparent and more important as his career took shape.

Widely believed to have been the work of John Adams, Publicola's letters brought a wave of criticism from nascent Republicans who took the author's defense of the English constitution to be an advocacy of aristocracy and privilege. The response was so intense that younger Adams cut the series short, using the eleventh, now final installment to deny the attribution to his father. James Madison, like Jefferson, felt sure that the vice president must have been "the Friend of the People." When Madison finally learned the truth—it didn't take long for the real authorship to come to light—he professed not to be surprised after all, paying Publicola a backhanded compliment: "There is more of method also in the arguments, and much less of clumsiness and heaviness in the stile, than characterize his [John Adams's] writings."

Letters of Publicola

No. I.

MR. RUSSELL,

THE late Revolution in *France*, has opened an extensive field of speculation to the philosopher and to the politician. An event so astonishing and unexpected in its nature, and so important in its consequences, naturally arrested the peculiar attention of the whole civilized world. The friends of liberty and of man, have seen with pleasure, the temples of despotism, levelled with the ground, and the genius of freedom, rising suddenly, in his collected and irresistible strength, and snapping in an instant all the cords with which for centuries he had been bound. Upon the downfal of the arbitrary system of government in *France*, there appears to have been but one sentiment, and that, a sentiment of exultations; but while the friends of humanity have rejoiced at the emancipation of so many millions of their fellow creatures, they have waited with an anxious expectation to see upon what foundations they would attempt to establish their newly acquired liberty. The proceedings of their Representative Assembly, have been contemplated in very different points of view, by men of names equally illustrious, and of characters equally favourable to the cause of liberty. Among the publications which have appeared upon the subject, two pamphlets founded upon very different principles, appear to have been received with the greatest avidity, and seem calculated to leave the deepest impression. The one, written by Mr. BURKE, which is one continued invective upon almost all the proceedings of the National Assembly since the Revolution, and which passes a severe and indiscriminating censure upon almost all their transactions: The other, the production of Mr. PAYNE, containing a defence of the Assembly, and approving every thing they have done with applause as undistinguishing as is the censure of

Mr. BURKE.—We are told, that the copy from which an edition of this work was reprinted at *Philadelphia*, was furnished by the Secretary of State, and was accompanied by a letter from which the following extract has been published in most of our newspapers. "I am extremely pleased to find, that it is to be reprinted here, and that something is at length to be publickly said, against the *political heresies* which have sprung up among us. I have no doubt our citizens will *rally* a second time round the standard of *Common Sense*."

I confess, Sir, I am somewhat at a loss to determine, what this very respectable gentleman means by *political heresies*. Does he consider this pamphlet of Mr. PAYNE'S as the canonical book of political scripture? As containing the true doctrine of popular infallibility, from which it would be heretical to depart in one single point. The expressions indeed imply more; they seem like the *Arabian* prophet to call upon all true believers in the *Islam* of democracy, to draw their swords, and in the fervour of their devotion to compel all their countrymen to cry out, "There is but one Goddess of Liberty, and Common Sense is her prophet."

I have always understood, sir, that the citizens of these States, were possessed of a full and entire freedom of opinion upon all subjects civil as well as religious; they have not yet established any infallible criterion of *orthodoxy*, either in church or state: Their principles in theory and their habits in practice, are equally averse to that slavery of the mind, which adopts without examination any sentiment that has the sanction of a venerable name. "*Nullius in verba jurare magistri*" is their favourite maxim; and the only political tenet, which they would stigmatize with the name of heresy, would be that which should attempt to impose an opinion upon their understandings, upon the single principle of authority.

I believe also, sir, that the citizens of *America*, are not at present disposed to rally round the standard of any man. In the full possession and enjoyment of all the freedom, for which they have gone through so arduous a conflict, they will not for the poor purpose of extinguishing a few supposed political heresies, return to the horrours of a civil contest, from which they could reap no possible benefit, and which would probably terminate in the loss of that liberty, for which they have been so liberal of their treasure and of their blood.

If however, Mr. PAYNE is to be adopted as the holy father of our political faith, and this pamphlet is to be considered as his Papal bull of infallible virtue, let us at least examine what it contains. Before we determine to join the standard let us inquire what are the articles of war, to which our General requires our submission.—It is the glorious characteristick of truth, at once to invite and bid defiance to investigation. If any opinions which have sprung up among us, have really led us astray from the standard of *truth*, let us return to it, at the call of Mr. PAYNE, or of any other man, who can shew us our errours. But sir, if upon examination, even this testament of orthodoxy, shall be found to contain many spurious texts, false in their principles and delusive in their inferences, we may be permitted, notwithstanding our reverence for the author, at least to expunge the apocryphal doctrine, and to confine our faith to the genuine tenets of real political inspiration.—It is my intention to submit to the publick a few observations which have occured to me upon the perusal of this pamphlet, which has so clear and valid a title to the publick attention.—But I must here observe, that I wish to avoid every appearance of disrespect, either to the real parent of this production, or to the gentleman who has stood its sponsor in this country. Both these gentlemen are entitled to the gratitude of their countrymen; the latter still renders them important services, in a very dignified station. He is a friend to free inquiry upon every subject, and he will not be displeased to see the sentiments which he has made his own, by a publick adoption, canvassed with as much freedom as is consistent with the reverence due to his character.

PUBLICOLA.

No. II.

MR. RUSSELL,

IN that part of Mr. PAINE's pamphlet which he has chosen to call the miscellaneous chapter, he observes that "when a man in a long cause attempts to steer his course by any thing else than some *polar truth or principle*, he is sure to be lost." I have sought for the polar principle to which HIS exertions were directed in this publication, and I must acknowledge, I have sought in vain. His production is historical, political, miscellaneous, satirical and panegyrical. It is an ENCOMIUM upon the National Assembly of *France*. It is a Commentary upon the Rights of Men, inferring questionable deductions from unquestionable principles. It is a severe SATIRE upon Mr. *Burke* and his pamphlet, upon the English Government, upon Kings, upon Nobility, and Aristocracy; it is a narrative of several occurrences, connected with the French Revolution, and it concludes with a kind of prophetical impulse, in the expectation of an "*European Congress to patronize the progress of free government, and promote the civilization of nations with each other.*" The object which he proposed to himself, in this publication, is not so dubious as the principle on which he wrote. His intention appears evidently to be, to convince the people of Great-Britain, that they have neither Liberty nor a Constitution—that their only possible means to procure these blessings to themselves, is to "topple down headlong" their present government, and follow implicitly the example of the French. As to the right, he scruples not to say, "that which a whole nation chooses to do, it has a right to do." This proposition is a part of what Mr. PAINE calls a system of principles in opposition to those of Mr. *Burke*, and it is laid down without any sort of qualification. It is not my intention to defend the principles of Mr. *Burke*—TRUTH is the only object of my pursuit, and I shall without hesitation refuse my assent to every principle inconsistent with that, whether it proceeds from Mr. *Burke*, from Mr. *Paine*, or even from the illustrious *National Assembly* of *France*. This principle that a whole nation has a right to do whatsoever it pleases, cannot in any sense whatever be admitted as true. The eternal and immutable laws of justice and of morality, are paramount to all human legislation. The violation of those laws is certainly within the power, but it is not among the rights of nations. The power of a nation is the collected power of all the individuals which compose it. The rights of a nation are in like manner the collected rights of its individuals; and it must *follow* from thence, that the powers of a nation are more extensive than its rights, in the very same proportion with those of individuals. It is somewhat remarkable that in speaking of the exercise of the particular right of forming a constitution, Mr. *Paine* himself denies to a nation, that omnipotence, which he had before so liberally bestowed. For this same nation, which has a right to do whatever it pleases, has no right to establish a government in *hereditary succession*.—It is of infinite consequence, that the distinction between *power* and *right* should be fully acknowledged, and admitted as one of the fundamental principles of Legislators. A whole nation such as *France, England*, or *America*, can act only by representation; and the acts of the representative body must be considered as the acts of the nation. We must go farther, and say that the acts of the majority in the Representative Assembly are the acts of the whole body, and consequently of the whole nation. If therefore, a majority thus constituted, are bound by no law human or divine, and have no other rule but their sovereign will and pleasure, to direct them; what possible security can any citizen of the nation have for the protection of his unalienable rights? The principles of liberty must still be the sport of arbitrary power, and the hideous form of despotism, must lay aside the diadem and the sceptre, only to assume the party-coloured garments of democracy.

The system of principles upon which Mr. *Paine* advances this assertion is intended to prove that the English nation have a right to destroy their present form of government, and to erect another. I am not disposed to deny this right, nor is it at present necessary to examine whether Mr. *Burke*'s opinions upon this subject, are not directed rather against the expediency than the abstracted rights of such a measure. It may, however, not be improper to trace the origin of Mr. *Paine*'s arguments against the principles maintained by Mr. *Burke*. Doctor *Price* had asserted, that "by the principles of the Revolution, in 1688, the people of *England* had acquired the right, 1. To chuse their own governours. 2. To cashier them for misconduct; and 3. To frame a government for themselves." Mr. *Burke* endeavours to prove that the principles of the Revolution in 1688, so far from warranting any right of this kind, support a doctrine almost diametrically opposite. Mr. *Paine*, in reply, cuts the gordian knot at once, declares the Parliament of 1688 to have been down-right usurpers, censures them for having unwisely sent to *Holland* for a King, denies the existence of a British Constitution, and invites the people of *England*, to overturn their present government, and to erect another upon the "broad basis of national sovereignty, and government by representation."—As Mr. *Paine* has departed altogether from the principles of the Revolution, and has torn up by the roots, all reasoning from the British Constitution, by the denial of its existence, it becomes necessary to examine his work upon the grounds which he has chosen to assume. If we judge of the production from its apparent tendency, we may call it, an address to the English Nation, attempting to prove that they have a right to form a new constitution; that it is expedient for them immediately to exercise that right, and that in the formation of this constitution, they can do no better than to imitate the model set before them by the *French National Assembly.* However immethodical his production is, I believe, the whole of its argumentative part, may be referred to these three points. If the subject were to affect even the British Nation, we might leave them to reason and act for themselves; but, sir, these are concerns equally important to all mankind; and the citizens of *America* are called upon, from high authority to *rally* round the *standard* of this champion of Revolutions. I shall therefore now proceed to examine the reasons upon which he founds his opinions relative to each of these points.—

The people of *England* have in common with every other nation, a natural and unalienable right to form a constitution of government, not because a whole nation has a right to do whatever it chooses to do, but because government being instituted for the common security of the natural rights of every individual, it must be liable to alterations whenever it becomes incompetent for that purpose. The right of a people to legislate for succeeding generations derives all its authority from the consent of that posterity who are bound by their laws, and therefore the expressions of perpetuity used by the Parliament of 1688, contain no absurdity—and expressions of a similar nature may be found, in all the constitutions of the *United States.*

But, sir, when this right is thus admitted in its fullest latitude, it must also be admitted that it ought never to be exercised, but in cases of extreme urgency: Every nation has a right as unquestionable to dissolve the bands of civil society, by which they are united, and to return to that state of individual imbecility in which man is supposed to have existed, previous to the formation of the social compact. The people of *America* have been compelled by an unaccountable necessity, distressing in its operation, but glorious in its consequences, to exercise this right, and whenever a nation has no other alternative but the degradation of slavery, or the formidable conflict of a revolution, the generous spirit of freedom will not hesitate a moment in the choice, whether the people of *France* were at the period of their revolution, reduced to that unhappy situation, which rendered it absolutely necessary to overthrow their whole system to its foundations, is a question, upon which the ablest patriots among themselves have differed, and upon which we are unadequate to decide. Whether the people of *England* are now in that calamitous predicament, is a question, more proper for our discussion, and upon which I shall take the liberty to examine the reasoning of Mr. *Paine.*

PUBLICOLA.

No. III.

MR. RUSSELL,

IN examining the question whether the English nation, have a right, fundamently to demolish their present form of government, it becomes necessary to inquire whether Mr. PAINE's assertion that there is no such thing as an English constitution, be really true? This question may, perhaps, in some measure affect the people of America. For if the government of Great-Britain, is an usurpation, it may be worthy of consideration how far we are bound by treaties, which do not reciprocally bind the inhabitants of that Island.

"A Constitution," says Mr. PAINE, "is not a thing in name only, but in fact. It has not an ideal, but a real existence; and whereever it cannot be produced in a visible form, there is none." Mr. PAINE should have gone further, and told us, whether like a deed it must be written on paper or parchment, or whether it has a larger latitude, and may be engraved on stone, or carved in wood. From the tenor of his argument it should seem, that he had only the American Constitutions in his mind, for excepting them, I believe he would not find in all history, a government which would come within his definition, and of course, there never was a people that had a Constitution, previous to the year 1776. But the word, with an idea affixed to it, had been in use, and commonly understood, for centuries before that period, and therefore Mr. PAINE must, to suit his purpose, alter its acceptations, and in the warmth of his zeal for revolutions, endeavour to bring about, a revolution in language also. When all the most illustrious whig writers in England have contended for the liberty of their country upon the principles of the English Constitution; when the glorious Congress of 1774 declared that "the inhabitants of the English colonies in *North-America* were entitled to certain rights by the immutable laws of nature, *the principles of the English Constitution*, and the several charters or compacts," they knew very well what they meant, and were perfectly understood by all mankind. Mr. *Paine* says that "A constitution is to a government, what the laws, made afterwards by that government are to a court of judicature." But, when the American states, by their constitutions, expressly adopted the whole body of the *common law*, so far as it was applicable to their respective situations, did they adopt nothing at all, because that law cannot be produced in a visible form? No, Sir, the constitution of a country is not the paper or parchment upon which the compact is written, it is the system of fundamental laws, by which the people have consented to be governed, which is always supposed to be impressed upon the mind of every individual, and of which the written or printed copies are nothing more than the evidence.

In this sense, Sir, the British nation have a constitution, which was for many years the admiration of the world; the people of America, with very good reason, have renounced some of its defects, and infirmities. But in defence of some of its principles, they have fought and conquered. It is composed of a venerable *system* of unwritten or customary laws handed down from time immemorial, and sanctioned by the accumulated experience of ages; and of a body of statutes enacted by an authority lawfully competent to that purpose. Mr. *Paine* is certainly mistaken when he considers the British government, as having originated in the conquest of *William* of Normandy. This principle of being governed by an oral or traditionary law prevailed in England eleven hundred years before that invasion. It has continued to this day, and has been adopted by all the American states. I hope they will never abolish a system so excellent, merely because it cannot be produced in a visible form. The constitution of Great-Britain is a constitution of *principles*, not of *articles*, and however frequently it may have been violated by tyrants, monarchial, aristocratical or democratical, the people have always found it expedient to restore the original foundations, while from time to time they have been successful in improving and ornamenting the building.

The people of England are bound therefore by a social compact now existing. And they have no right to demolish their government, unless it be clearly incompetent for the purposes for which it was instituted. They have delegated their whole collective power to a legislature, consisting of a king, lords and commons, and they have included even the power of altering the constitution itself. Should they abuse this power so that the nation itself should be oppressed, and their rights to life, liberty, and property instead of protection, should meet with tyranny, the people would certainly be entitled to appeal in the last resort to themselves, to resume the trust which has been so unworthily betrayed, and (not to do whatever they should choose, but) to form another constitution, which should more permanently secure the natural rights of the whole community. The same may be said of the National Assembly of France, who according to Mr. *Paine*'s idea, are possessed of the whole collective power of the nation, and who seem like him to think they have a right to do whatever they choose. Mr. *Paine* says, that "the authority of the present assembly is different to what the authority of future assemblies will be." But if the present assembly should decree that all future national assemblies should possess the same power with themselves, it would certainly be binding as an article of the constitution. Mr. *Paine*, indeed, will not acknowledge this, and it is the second right which he denies his nation, which at the same time has a right to do every thing. Mr. *Paine*'s ideas upon this subject appear to have been formed by a partial adoption of the principle upon which *Rousseau* founds the social compact. But neither the principle of *Rousseau*, nor that of Mr. *Paine*, is true. *Rousseau* contends that the social compact is formed by a personal association of individuals, which must be unanimously assented to, and which cannot possibly be made by a representative body. I shall not at present spend my time in shewing that this is neither practicable nor even metaphysically true. I shall only observe, that its operation would annihilate in an instant, all the power of the National Assembly, and turn the whole body of the American constitutions (the pride of man, the glory of the human understanding) into a mass of tyrannical and unfounded usurpations. Mr. *Paine* does not go quite so far, but we must examine whether his arguments are not equally wide from the truth. "A government, says he, on the principles on which constitutional governments arising out of society are established, cannot have the right of altering itself. Why not? Because, if it had, it would be arbitrary." But this reason is not sufficient. A nation in forming a social compact may delegate the whole of their collective powers to ordinary legislatures in perpetual succession, and reserve only the right of resisting the abuse of those powers; and every other question relative to the reservation of powers to the nation, must be only a question of expediency. The same power which the present national assembly possess in France, is by the English constitution, constantly vested in the king and parliament of Great-Britain; and the people in both kingdoms have the same right to resist and punish the abuse of that power. Surely, Sir, the people of the United States have a constitution, although they have given the power of making alterations, to those by whom it is administered, in conjunction with the state legislatures. Surely, the people of Massachusetts have a constitution, though it provides for certain alterations by the ordinary legislatures, and though since it was formed, such alterations have accordingly been made. The constitutions of several of the United States, are expressly made alterable in every part by their ordinary legislatures. I think there is not one of them, but admits of alterations without recurring to "the nation in its original character." Yet Mr. *Paine* will surely acknowledge that the American constitution arose *out* of the people and not *over* them. His principle therefore "that a constitutional government cannot have the right of altering itself" is not true. In forming their constitution a nation may reserve to themselves, such powers as they think proper. They may reserve only the unalienable right of resistance against tyranny. The people of England have reserved only this right. The French national assembly have been in session more than two years, to make laws nominally paramount to their future legislatures: I shall hazard some observations upon this subject, when I attempt to follow Mr. *Paine*, through his comparison between the French and English constitutions. But as the English have delegated all their power, I contend they have no right in their original character to change their form of government, unless it has become incompetent for the purposes, for which all governments are instituted. I am aware of the question which will occur here, Who is to judge of this incompetency? and I am aware of the triumphant manner in which it may be asked. But a triumph is not my object, and in the pursuit of truth I shall venture in my next number to consider this subject.

PUBLICOLA.

No. IV.

MR. RUSSELL,

I HAVE assumed for a principle, that the English nation, having delegated all their collective power, have no right in their original character, to change their form of government, unless it has become absolutely inadequate to the purposes for which it was instituted. The people themselves, must from the necessity of the case be the judges of this fact; but if in forming this judgment, and acting in pursuance of it, they proceed from passion and not from principle, if they dissolve their compact from an idea, that "they have a right to do whatever they choose," and break the bands of society, in the forms of despotism, "because such is their pleasure," they may indeed go through the operation by the plenitude of their irresistible power, but the nation will meet with ample punishment, in their own misery, and the leaders who delude them, in the detestation of their own posterity. It is not by adopting the malignity of a political satyrist, by converting the sallies of wit into the maxims of truth or justice, or by magnifying trivial imperfections into capital crimes, that a nation will be justified in resorting to its original strength, to contend against its delegated power. It is not a mechanical horror against the name of a king, or of aristocracy, nor a physical antipathy to the sound of an extravagant title, or to the sight of an innocent ribband, that can authorise a people to lay violent hands upon the constitution which protects their rights, and guards their liberties. They must feel an actual deprivation of their equal rights, and see an actual impossibility for their restoration in any other manner, before they can have a right to lay their hands on their swords, and appeal to Heaven. These are not the principles of slavery; they are the tenets of the only genuine liberty; which consists in a mean equally distant from the despotism of an individual, as of a million. They are sanctioned by our own uniform example, and will, I trust, never be departed from by the most enlightened, and most virtuous people on the globe. For sixteen years, the people of America endured a continual succession of every indignity, which the pride of dominion, the insolence of power, and the rapacity of avarice, could inflict upon them, before they could resolve to renounce an authority, three thousand miles distant from them; and even then, they were so far from thinking they had a right to do whatever they chose, that by the very act, which renounced their connexion with Great-Britain, they exposed to the world their own sufferings, and the various acts of tyranny, which had compelled them to "acquiesce in the necessity which denounced the separation," and "appealed to the Supreme Judge of the world for the rectitude of their intentions." No, Sir, the venerable character who drew up this declaration, never could believe that the rights of a nation, have no other limits, than its powers.—Since the revolution, the people of the United States, have again been compelled to form a national government, and in its formation proceeded in the same spirit. The confederation was found totally incompetent for the purposes for which it was instituted; not from an abuse of the delegated powers, in those by whom it was administered, but because scarcely any powers at all had been given. The inefficiency of that system had long been fully demonstrated, and had reduced us to extreme distress. The States, United but in name, were upon the verge of general bankruptcy. Their credit sunk to the lowest ebb, was upon the point of expiring, and their exhausted treasury, gave perpetually the lie to their publick faith so often and so solemnly pledged. The forcible ties of a common interest directed to one great object during the war, were greatly loosened by the accomplishment of that object, and the seeds of mutual hostility were sown, by the partial commercial regulations of the respective states. The revenue laws which had been enacted in several of the states, were not able to support their credit, and yet were so unequal in their operation, that numerous bodies of men in more than one of the states appeared in open rebellion against the mildest governments that ever were instituted. Instead of the glorious reward which the people had expected for their virtuous exertions, internal discord, and infamy abroad presented themselves in dreary perspective before them. At that critical period, when the system to be annihilated, was an empty name, and there was only a government to be formed, the national constitution was presented to the people of America "in their original character," and even then its existence was to depend upon the assent of nine states, that is of two thirds of the people. Very fortunately it has at length been freely adopted by all the members of the union; but the extreme difficulty which impeded the progress of its adoption, and the various amendments, which in many of the states were in a manner made the condition of their assent, exhibit the fullest evidence, what a more than Herculean task it is, to unite the opinions of a free people upon any system of government whatever.

Under the sanction of such authority, I venture to assert that the people of England have no right to destroy their government, unless in its operation the rights of the people are really oppressed, and unless they have attempted in vain every constitutional mode of obtaining redress. These principles ought to operate with peculiar force upon the people of England, because in the certain and hazardous event of a revolution, they have more to lose, and less to gain, than any other European nation, and because whatever they may acquire, must in all probability be purchased at the expense of a civil war. When provision is made for the alteration of a constitution, otherwise than by the common legislative power, it may be done comparatively without difficulty or danger; but where this power is already delegated, with the other powers of legislation, the people cannot use it themselves, except in their original, individual, unrepresented character, and they cannot acquire the right to act in that capacity, until the power which they have thus conveyed in trust, has been abdicated by the extreme abuses of its administration.

When Mr. PAINE invited the people of England to destroy their present government and form another constitution, he should have given them sober reasoning, and not flippant witticisms. He should have explained to them the nature of the grievances by which they are oppressed, and demonstrated the impossibility of reforming the government in its present organization. He should have pointed out to them some possible method for them to act in their original character, without a total dissolution of civil society among them; he should have proved, what great advantages they would reap as a nation from such a revolution, without disguising the great dangers and formidable difficulties, with which it must be attended.

The principal and most dangerous abuses in the English government, arise less from the defects inherent in the constitution, than from the state of society;—the universal venality and corruption which pervades all classes of men in that kingdom, and which a change of government could not reform. I shall consider this subject more largely hereafter; but at present, with respect to the expediency of a revolution in England, I must inquire how the nation can be brought to act in their original character? Mr. PAINE, perhaps from the delicacy of his situation, has said nothing openly upon this very important point. Yet in two different parts of his work he seems obscurely to hint two methods for the accomplishment of this object. When he compares the situation of the citizens of *London*, to that of the inhabitants of *Paris*, just before the taking of the Bastile, it seems as if it was with an intention to recommend a similar insurrection for the purpose of dispersing the parliament, and expelling the king, which would leave the nation without any government at all, and compel them at all events to act in their original character. When he advises "Revolutions by accommodation," he must probably mean that a convention should be called by act of parliament to regenerate their constitution.—I cannot imagine any other method of answering his purpose. Mr. PAINE seems to think it as easy for a nation to change its government, as for a man to change his coat; but I confess both the modes of proceeding which he suggests, appear to me to be liable to great objections.

PUBLICOLA.

No. V.

MR. RUSSELL,

"THERE are in all European countries," says Mr. PAINE, "a large class of people of that description, which in *England* are called the *mob.*" It was by the people of this description that the Bastile in *Paris* was destroyed. In *London* there is no Bastile to demolish; but there is a government to overturn; and there is a king and parliament, who must either be put to flight, or compelled to call a convention for the purpose of forming a constitution. "In the commencement of a revolution those men are rather the followers of the *camp* than of the *standard* of liberty, and have yet to be instructed how to reverence it." As these men were made instrumental to the accomplishment of the revolution in *France*, Mr. PAINE appears to intimate that they may be employed for a similar purpose in *England*.—I am as little disposed as Mr. PAINE can be, to reproach either the whole nation to which they belong, or that unhappy class of human beings themselves for the devastation which they commit. They cannot be considered as free agents, and therefore are neither the subjects of praise or blame; but the friend of humanity will be extremely cautious how he ventures to put in action a tremendous power, which is competent only to the purposes of destruction, and totally incapable either to create or to preserve. This class of men of whom it is the happiness of Americans, scarcely to be able to form an idea, can be brought to act in concert upon no other principles than those of a frantick enthusiasm and ungovernable fury; their profound ignorance and deplorable credulity, make them proper tools for any man who can inflame their passions, or alarm their superstition; and as they have nothing to lose by the total dissolution of civil society, their rage may be easily directed against any victim which may be pointed out to them. They are altogether incapable of forming a rational judgment either upon the principles or the motives of their own conduct; and whether the object for which they are made to contend, be good or bad, the brutal arm of power is all the assistance they can afford for its accomplishment. To set in motion this inert mass, the eccentrick vivacity of a madman, is infinitely better calculated than the sober coolness of phlegmatick reason. They need only to be provoked and irritated, and they never can in any other manner be called into action. In the year 1780, they assembled at *London*, to the number of 60,000, under the direction of Lord GEORGE GORDON, and carrying fire and slaughter before them, were upon the point of giving the whole city of *London* to one undistinguished devastation and destruction: And this, because the parliament had mitigated the severity of a sanguinary and tyrannical law of persecution, against the Roman Catholicks. Should these people be taught, that they have a right to do every thing; and that the titles of kings and nobles, and the wealth of bishops are all usurpations and robberies committed upon them, I believe it would not be difficult to rouse their passions, and to prepare them for every work of ruin and destruction. But, Sir, when they are once put in motion, they soon get beyond all restraint and controul. The rights of man, to life, liberty and property, oppose but a feeble barrier to them; the beauteous face of nature and the elegant refinements of art, the hoary head of wisdom, and the enchanting smile of beauty, are all equally liable to become obnoxious to them; and as all their power consists in destruction, whatever meets with their displeasure must be devoted to ruin. Could any thing but an imperious, over-ruling necessity justify any man or body of men, for using a weapon like this to operate a revolution in government? Such indeed was the situation of the French national assembly, when they directed the electric fluid of this popular frenzy, against the ancient fabrick of their monarchy. They justly thought that no price could purchase too dearly the fall of arbitrary power in an individual, but perhaps even *they* were not aware of all the consequences which might follow from committing the existence of the kingdom, to the custody of a lawless and desperate rabble.

But do the people of *England* labour under such intolerable oppression, as would authorise any of their patriots to employ an arm like this for their relief? Suppose sixty thousand men should again assemble round *Westminster hall*, and with clubs and firebrands for their sole arguments, should compel the parliament to call a convention to make a constitution, what would be the probable consequences? Is it clear that so large a majority in the people of *England*, have lost all their attachment to their constitution, as to insure an acquiescence in the measure throughout the kingdom? Is it certain that one quarter part of the people would obey an act extorted by such violence as that? Would not all the friends of the present government rally round the standard of the constitution, and would not their duty compel them to defend it with their lives and fortunes? If it should soon appear that they were decidedly the strongest party, would not the insurrection be extinguished in the blood of its leaders? If the parties should prove to be nearly equal, would not the nation be involved in all the horrors of a long and bloody civil war?—In whatever point of view, the effects of this scheme are contemplated, they present nothing but prospects at which every friend of mankind must shudder, nor can I possibly believe that Mr. PAINE, who is certainly a benevolent man, would deliberately recommend this method, though in his ardent zeal for the honour of the French nation, and the propagation of their doctrines, he has incautiously suggested it.

But he recommends revolutions by accommodation; which applied to *England*, must mean that a convention be called by a free and deliberate act of parliament, to alter the constitution; but this plan appears to be equally dangerous with the other, and more impracticable; while by a singular fatality an act of this kind would be the completest evidence of its own inutility, it would be equally dangerous, because by a formal act of competent authority it would expose the kingdom to all the evils of anarchy and of war, which in the other case would result from a popular convulsion. It would be less practicable, because it is contrary to nature, that any body of men should venture to perform the most transcendent act of power of which human beings are capable, for the single purpose of divesting themselves of all power whatever. It would prove its own inutility, because no man will presume that they ought to take such a measure, unless the wishes of a clear and decided majority of the people are favorable to an alteration of the government. If they are disposed to act in conformity with the desires of the people, the very same power which would authorise them to dissolve the government, would likewise justify them in making any alterations which should meet with the wishes of the nation, and would render a recurrence to them "in their original character" perfectly unnecessary.

Whatever Mr. PAINE's opinion may be with respect to the existence of an English constitution, it is certain that every member of the British parliament, who gives his vote in the making of a new law, or the alteration of an old one, must suppose that he acts by virtue of a constitutional *right*, vested in him; but the same right which authorises him to give his suffrage in the most trifling object of legislation, has vested in the parliament of which he is a member, the whole power of the British nation, and he cannot possibly deny their right without utterly destroying his own. The right of the *individual* depends altogether upon the right of the *corporation*, and his right to vote for the regulation of a turn-pike or the toll of a bridge, is the same with their's to make every necessary and convenient alteration in the constitution of the kingdom itself. While they are thus convinced of their right to exercise these great powers, would it not be the summit of extravagance, and folly in them, nay, would it not be the most flagrant breach of the trust reposed in them, of which they could possibly be guilty, to abdicate an authority lawfully committed to them, to declare themselves altogether incompetent to a wise and prudent use of a constitutional power, and to commit the peace, the welfare, the very existence of the nation, to the uncertain and hazardous event of a revolution?

If, however, we can suppose that the parliament should finally accede to the idea, that they are mere tyrants without the shadow of a right to the authority which they have hitherto exercised, the only act which they could agree to, would be a vote to dissolve themselves, and leave the vessel of the state without either a pilot or a rudder. For the very act of calling a convention would be an usurpation, and from the importance of its consequences, an usurpation of the most daring nature: It would be assuming the right to dissolve the ties of society; and at the same instant acknowledging that this assumed right, was without any sort of foundation. In short, this plan of calling a convention to alter the constitution, by act of parliament, appears to me in whatever light it is considered, to involve an absurdity.

But, as there is unquestionably somewhere in England, a combination of the right and of the power to alter the constitution of the country, and as that constitution is indubitably liable to be improved, we may be permitted to enquire, whether a blind imitation of the French national assembly would probably promote *the happiness of the people*; the only object for which all governments were instituted, or which can authorise their alteration.

PUBLICOLA.

No. VI.

MR. RUSSELL,

MR. PAINE affirms that the *French* nation have a Constitution, and that the *English* have none. I have already offered a few observations upon the latter part of this assertion, but as a preliminary to some remarks, which I propose to make upon his comparison, I must premise that directly the reverse of his opinion upon this subject is the truth, and that in reality the *English* nation have a Constitution, and the *French* as yet have none. The *National Assembly* have indeed been constantly sitting these two years, to form a Constitution, and at the ceremony of the Federation about eleven months since, they swore themselves and their King to the observance of a Constitution, *to be made*. But as they are still possessed of the whole power of the nation, they may repeal any article upon which they have hitherto agreed, by virtue of the same authority, which enabled them to pass the decree, and therefore, according to Mr. *Paine*'s own ideas, the *French* cannot be said to have a Constitution, until the *National Assembly* shall please to dissolve themselves and to put their whole system into full operation.

I have endeavoured to show that it is not absolutely essential to the existence of a Constitution, that it should be producible "in a visible form." The period of time, when the foundations of the present *English* government were laid by the association of the people in "their original character" cannot indeed be ascertained. Many of the laws which are in use to this day in *Great-Britain*, and from thence have been adopted by the *American Republicks* may be traced back to the remotest period of antiquity, and the origin even of the institution of Juries, an institution so congeniel to the genuine spirit of freedom, is lost in the obscurity of the fabulous ages. Many of the fundamental principles of the *English* Constitution, are known to have existed long before the invention of printing, and even before the inhabitants of *Britain* were acquainted with the use of letters, and it would therefore be an absurdity to require that the original articles should be produced "in a visible form." But "*ex nihilo, nihil fit*," the very existence of these principles proves the formation of a social compact previous to that existence, and the spirit of liberty which is their distinguishing characteristick, affords internal evidence, that they did not originate in the merciless despotism of a conqueror, but in the free and unrestrained consent of a manly and generous people. It will not be said that an original compact was never formed because it is not recorded in the page of history; as well might it be pretended that the pyramids of *Egypt* arose self-created from the earth, because the time of their erection, and the names of their builders, have been consigned to that oblivion, in which all human labours are destined to be overwhelmed.

William of *Normandy*, to whom Mr. *Paine* always refers the origin of the *English* government, was the conqueror only of *Harold*. He obtained the crown of *England* by popular election, upon the express condition that he would govern the nation according to her ancient laws and customs; he took the same oath at his coronation which had been taken by his predecessors, and by his last will, after bequeathing the province of *Normandy* to his eldest son *Robert*, he expressly acknowledged that he did not possess the kingdom of *England* as an inheritence, and only recommended his son *William*, as his successor. It would be altogether unnecessary at this time to discuss the question whether the crown of *England* was originally hereditary or elective, but the facts which I have here stated, and which are warranted by all the most ancient and most authentick *English* historians, fully demonstrate that the *English* government did not originate in the *Norman* conquest. "If the succession runs in the line of the conquest, *the nation* runs in the line of being conquered, and it ought to rescue itself from this reproach," says Mr. *Paine*. "The victory obtained at *Hastings* not being a victory over *the nation collectively*, but only over the person of *Harold*, the only right that the conqueror could pretend to acquire thereby, was the right to possess the crown of *England*, not *to alter the nature of the government*," says Judge *Blackstone*, (1. Comm. 199.) Upon a question of fact relative to the *English* Constitution, *Blackstone* is, I believe, as good an authority as Mr. *Paine*, but I wish not to rest the question upon any authority whatever: I venture to affirm that any man who will coolly and impartially examine the subject and appeal to the original sources of information, will acknowledge that those who derive the origin of the *English* government from *William* the conquerer, can do it upon no other principle than that of supporting a system.

It is not however necessary upon the present occasion to revive a question, which has been discussed among the *English*, with all the acrimony of faction. Mr. *Paine* has chosen the ground, which was not found tenable by the slavish supporters of passive obedience and the divine right of Kings. They took it originally because it was necessary to them for the support of their system, and they were driven from it, by the friends and supporters of equal liberty. Mr. *Paine* found it necessary, to support a doctrine of a very different nature; and adopting the maxim that it is lawful to learn, even from our enemies, he has freely borrowed from them the practice of accommodating the facts of history to his political purposes.

Be that however as it may, the *Parliament* of *Great-Britain* from time to time have enacted certain laws which from their superiour importance have been denominated constitutional; the acquiescence of the people, to whom most of those laws have been extremely satisfactory, gives them at least as good a sanction, as the constitution of *France* has obtained. The *National Assembly* were not originally chosen to form a constitution. They were called together as *States General*, under the authority of another Constitution, such as it was. They assumed the power to dissolve the old Constitution, and to form another, and the acquiescence of the people, has confirmed that assumption. At all events therefore their Constitution stands upon no better ground than the acts of the *British Parliament*.

If then the *Parliament* of *Great-Britain* have a right to declare, what shall be the supreme law of the land, they will be able to produce a system of constitutional law, even according to Mr. *Paine*'s wish, "in a visible form." This system is contained in a number of statutes, enacted not at one time, or by one body of men, but at divers times, according to the occasional convenience of the people, and by a competent authority. These statutes contain the principles upon which the *English* government is founded, and are therefore proper objects of comparison with the Constitution which is to be the supreme law of the land in *France*. The comparisons which Mr. *Paine* has drawn are not partially favourable to his native country. We shall inquire whether they are perfectly consistent with truth.

PUBLICOLA.

No. VII.

MR. RUSSELL,

BY the English Constitution, the whole collective power of the nation is delegated, and the constitution itself is alterable by the same authority which is competent to the common purposes of legislation.

The *French* are to have a constitution, every part of which will be nominally beyond the controul of their common Legislatures, and which will be unalterable in all parts, except by the nation in its "original character." At least Mr. *Paine* has undertaken to answer for them that it will be so: Although I have not seen any such article in the constitution, and though perhaps it has not yet been decreed, I am willing to take Mr. *Paine*'s word for the fact, and to consider the subject, as if it were already determined.

I have made some observations upon Mr. *Paine*'s arguments, as they respect the right of a nation to delegate all their power. As a question of expediency, it may perhaps be more difficult to determine, which of these two schemes contains the least evil. Both of them are supported by the example of several among the American States, and can therefore boast the sanction of authorities equally respectable.

The fundamental principle upon which society is formed, appears to be, in order that the power of the whole may be rendered subservient to the interests of the whole. The problem to solve is, in what manner the power shall be distributed, so as most effectually to answer that purpose. Considering the extreme difficulty with which a whole nation can be brought to act in their original character, it should seem, that wisdom must dictate to them the necessity of delegating their whole power, in such a manner as that it may be rendered beneficial to the nation, because whatever power is retained, by the people, cannot be exercised for their advantage, any more than to their injury. The question therefore occurs, why a nation should not delegate all its powers? Mr. *Paine* has bestowed very little consideration upon this subject; I find that although he gives his own opinion very freely, he offers only two reasons to support it. One, because "such a government would be arbitrary;" The other because "there is a paradox in the idea of vitiated bodies reforming themselves." In the sense in which the word arbitrary is here used, the first argument attacks the foundation of civil society itself; for whenever a number of individuals associate together and form themselves into a body-politick, called a nation, the possession and the *use* of the whole power, (which is not however arbitrary power,) is the very object of their association. This power must exist somewhere, and I cannot see the reason why it should not exist for the benefit of the people.—But whenever a constitution is made unalterable by the common legislative authority, the nation do in reality abdicate all the powers which they are said to retain, and declare that very important powers shall at all events be useless to them, from an apprehension that they might possibly be abused to their injury.—It is as if a man should bind himself never to wear a sword, lest he should turn it against his own breast.—The only reason why the whole power of a nation should not be delegated, must arise from the danger of its being abused: And a melancholy experience has always shown that when the whole power has been thus delegated to one man, or to one body of men, it has invariably been grossly abused, and the sword of the people has been turned into a dagger against them. From the pressure of those evils, many nations have been induced expressly to forbid their governments the use of certain powers, without considering that the impotence of their supreme authority, would certainly be very prejudicial to them, and perhaps as fatal, as the abuse of power. This experiment has repeatedly been made; it has frequently failed; and I believe that after several more experiments shall fully demonstrate the ill policies of thus annihilating the power of the nation, it will be clearly seen, that all the powers of the people ought to be delegated for their benefit, and that their true interest consists in the distribution of those powers in such a manner as shall in its own operation guard against the abuses which alone are dangerous to the people.

The Constitution of the *United States*, appears to me to unite all the advantages both of the *French* and of the *English*, while it has avoided the evils of both. By that constitution, the people have delegated the power of alteration, by vesting it in the Congress, together with the State Legislatures; while at the same time it has provided for alterations by the people themselves in their original character, whenever it shall evidently appear to be the wish of the people to make them. This article appears to be replete with wisdom; I believe it will stand the test of the severest examination, though according to the ideas emanating from Mr. *Paine,* and coming to us at the same time by reflection from the Secretary of State, it contains a very dangerous political heresy.

It is a maxim which will not I trust, be disputed, that no government of which the people is not a constituent part, can secure their equal rights; but where this is the case, to cramp the operations of their own government, with unnecessary restrictions, and forbid themselves to enact useful laws, what is it but to defeat the purposes of society, by the very act, which gives it a permanent existence; to tie their own hands from an imaginary apprehension that if left at liberty they would administer poison to the body which nourishes them?

It is in the distribution of the national powers, it is in the independent spirit of the people, and not in the manuscript limitation of the Legislative authority, that a nation is to secure the protection of its liberties.—In this Commonwealth we have a constitution, most parts of which are unalterable by our ordinary Legislatures; it has existed but ten years; and already its operation has convinced us all that several alterations in the system would be highly expedient. Our Legislative body would be fully competent to the purpose, and if they had the power would readily make such alterations as might suit the convenience of the people; but they have no authority to act in these cases for the benefit of the people, and as the inconveniencies to which this injudicious jealousy have subjected us, are not at this time of such importance as to render the alterations, of immediate or absolute necessity, we must wait our appointed time, and patiently submit to the operation of bad laws, because we have not chosen to invest our Legislature with the power of making good ones.—Let us not be frightened, however, from the pursuit of our common interest by the words *arbitrary power*. Distribute the whole of your power in such a manner, as will necessarily prevent any one man, or body of men, or any possible combination of individual interests, from being arbitrary, but do not encumber your own representatives with shackles, prejudicial to your own interests; nor suffer yourselves like the Spanish Monarch, of ridiculous memory, to be roasted to death, by denying to your servants the power of removing the fire from before you.

But although a constitution, professedly unalterable by the common legislative authority, is of weight sufficient to prevent the enacting of many good laws, yet it will not always operate as a check upon your legislature. Such is the poverty of all human labours, that even a whole nation cannot express themselves upon paper, with so much accuracy and precision, as not to admit of much latitude of explanation and construction. The Legislature must always be allowed to judge of the intentions with which the instrument was formed, and to construe and explain accordingly the expressions which it contains. They sometimes think proper to violate the letter of the constitution by adhering to its spirit, and at other times they sacrifice the spirit by adhering strictly to the letter. But when your Legislature undertake to decide that the spirit of the constitution, is directly contrary to its express letter, where is the power in the nation that should controul them? The same power, which will always be sufficient to controul a Legislature, of which the people are a constituent part; it is, the *spirit of the people.*—Let your Legislative and Executive authorities be so constituted, as to prevent every essential, or dangerous abuse of the powers delegated, but depend upon the honest and enlightened spirit of the people for a security which you never will obtain, by merely withholding your powers, unless that spirit should be constantly kept up. Divide your power so that every part of it may at all times be used for your advantage, but in such a manner, that your rights may never depend upon the will of any one man or body of men, entrust even the power of altering your constitution itself, because occasions may arise, when the use even of that power, may be absolutely necessary, for your own welfare, when at the same time it may be impossible for you to act in your original character, with the expedition necessary for your salvation; but reserve to yourselves a concurrent power of altering the constitution in your own persons, because by the decay to which all the works of man are liable, it is possible that your Legislature, may become incompetent to make such alterations as may be necessary. But, when the people are constantly represented in the Legislature, I believe they will never find it necessary to recur to their original character, in order to make any alterations which they may deem expedient, unless they deny the power of making them to their Legislature.

"But," says Mr. PAINE, "there is a paradox in the idea of vitiated bodies reforming themselves." This must depend altogether upon the coincidence of the part vitiated, with the part which is to apply the remedy; for unless the defect itself necessarily precludes the possibility of applying the power of reformation, the paradox ceases, and no more involves an absurdity, than that a physician should use his own prescriptions to cure himself of a disorder.

The very act by which septennial Parliaments were established in *England*, affords sufficient proof that the power of altering the constitution itself ought to be delegated, and even exercised by the government upon certain critical occasions. That act was made at a time when the kingdom was threatened with an immediate invasion, when a rebellion had but just been quelled, and when, the peace and safety of the nation, depended upon the use of this power by the Parliament; such was the opinion of the people at that time, and the act met with general approbation, from the general conviction of its necessity. Such occasions may happen in the history of every free people, and it is therefore proper that the power should be delegated. Upon the principles of equal liberty, upon the principles of publick happiness, and therefore of political expediency, I think it may be fairly concluded that Mr. *Paine*'s preference of the *French* to the *English* Constitution, so far as it relates to this article, is not founded in truth.

PUBLICOLA.

No. VIII.

MR. RUSSELL,

MR. PAINE has undertaken to compare the English and French constitutions, upon the article of representation. He has of course admired the latter, and censured the former. This is unquestionably the most defective part of the English constitution—but even the most essential of those defects appear to flow from the natural order of things which a revolution in government could not reform; from a state of society, when every principle of religion or of morality has lost its influence, and where the only shadow of virtue, publick or private, remaining among a great majority of the people, is founded upon an imaginary point of honour, the relict of the exploded age of chivalry. Such at present is the situation of the national character both in *England* and in *France*. To attempt to govern a nation like this, under the form of a democracy, to pretend to establish over such beings a government, which according to *Rousseau* is calculated only for a republick of Gods, and which requires the continual exercise of virtues beyond the reach of human infirmity, even in its best estate; it may possibly be among the dreams of Mr. PAINE, but it is what even the *National Assembly* have not ventured to do; their system will avoid some of the defects, which the decays of time and the mutability of human affairs have introduced into that of the English, but I do not hesitate to affirm that they have departed much further from the essential principles of popular representation, and that however their attachment to republican principles may have been celebrated, the *theory* of their *National Assembly* is more remote from the spirit of democracy than the *practice* of the English House of Commons.

The grounds upon which Mr. PAINE acknowledges his approbation of the French constitution are that they have limited the number of their representatives, in proportion to the numbers of citizens who pay a tax of 60 sous per annum, and the duration of the assembly to two years. It is certainly essential to the principles of representation that there should be a frequent recurrence to the constituent body for election, because it is the only security of the constituent for the fidelity of the agent: It is the only practical responsibility by which the representative is bound. The term of seven years for which the House of Commons is elected, weakens the responsibility too much, and is a proper object of constitutional reform; but by the French constitution, there is no responsibility at all; no connexion between the representative and his constituent: The *people* have not even once in seven years an opportunity to dismiss a servant who may have displeased them, or to re-elect another who may have given them satisfaction. There is upon the French system less dependence of the representative upon his constituent than in *England,* and the mode of election renders the biennial return of the choice almost wholly nugatory. It is not true that the French constitution allows the privilege of voting for a representative in the *National Assembly* to every man who pays a tax of 60 sous per annum. Mr. PAINE has mistaken the fact, for it is impossible that he should have intentionally misrepresented it; though it differs almost as much from his principles as from those of a real popular representation. It is as follows. Every Frenchman born or naturalized, of 25 years of age, who pays a tax equal to three days labour, is not a hired servant, nor a bankrupt, nor the son of a deceased bankrupt (a very unjust qualification) shall be allowed to vote for—what? A representative to the *National Assembly?*—By no means. Yet one would think the exclusions sufficiently severe, for a government founded upon the equal rights of all men; but he shall vote for members of a certain assembly: This assembly is allowed to choose, not the representatives of the nation, but another body of electors, who are to be the immediate constituents of the legislative assembly. Thus the supreme legislative council of the nation, are to be the representatives of a representative body, whose constituents are the representatives of the people; and at every stage of this complicated representation, the free citizens of the state, are excluded from their natural rights, by additional qualifications in point of property.—Yet this is the system which we are told is to abolish aristocracy.

In the formation of the legislative body, the *National Assembly*, contemplated three different objects of representation, the *persons* of the people, their *property*, and the *territory*, which they inhabit: They have endeavoured to establish a proportion compounded from the three, but in the refinement of their metaphysicks and mathematicks, they have lost the primary object itself, and the people are not represented.

But setting aside their calculations, what is the *essential* principle upon which the representation of the people in the legislature is grounded? It is, that a Freeman, shall never be bound by any law unless he has consented to it. It is impossible, except in a very small state, that every individual should personally give his voice, and therefore this practice of voting by representation was invented. In its most perfect state it cannot fully answer the purpose of its institution, because every representative is actuated by several powerful motives, which could not operate upon his constituents. It is an *artificial democracy*, which never can perform completely the functions of the natural democracy; but imperfect as it always must be, no other contrivance has been hitherto devised, which could so effectually give their operation to the opinions of the people. In the theory of representation it is a *personal* trust, by which a thousand individuals may authorise one man to express their sentiments upon every law which may be enacted for the benefit of the whole people: And therefore in theory every representative ought to be elected by the unanimous vote of his constituents; for how can a man be said to have been consulted in the formation of a law, when the agent authorised to express his opinion was not the man of his choice? every pecuniary qualification imposed either on the electors or as a condition of eligibility, is an additional restriction upon the natural democracy, and weakens the original purpose of the institution. Thus far the people of *America* have submitted to necessity in the constitution of their popular assemblies. But when the principle is abandoned so completely, that the individual citizen, even in the pretended exercise of his infinitesimal fragment of sovereignty cannot possibly form an opinion, who will be the elector of the representative that is to be the depositary of his opinion in the acts of legislation. The assembly thus formed may indeed assume the name of a democracy, but it will no more be entitled to the appellation than an ill drawn miniature portrait, to that of the animated original which it may profess to represent.

It is obvious that the reason why the *National Assembly* have chosen to refine their representation through so many strainers was to avoid the violence, the tumults, the riots which render almost all the populous towns in *England* a scene of war and blood at the period of Parliamentary Elections. Time alone will inform us what the success of their system will be, even in this particular. Their elections however must be extremely expensive, and must open a thousand avenues to every sort of intrigue and venality. The *National Assembly* as a body, will be in theory an aristocracy without responsibility. This aristocracy thus constituted are to possess the supreme power of the nation, limited only by a printed constitution, subject to their own construction and explanation.

Happy, thrice happy the people of *America!* whose gentleness of manners, and habits of virtue are still sufficient to reconcile the enjoyment of their natural rights, with the peace and tranquillity of their country—whose principles of religious liberty did not result from an indiscriminate contempt of all religion whatever, and whose equal representation in their legislative councils was founded upon an equality really existing among them, and not upon the metaphysical speculations of fanciful politicians, vainly contending against the unalterable course of events, and the established order of nature.

PUBLICOLA.

No. IX.

MR. RUSSELL,

FROM the existence of game laws and of monopolies in *England*, Mr. PAINE infers the wisdom of the National Assembly, who have decreed, that there shall be none in *France*. I shall not defend the game laws or the monopolies allowed in

England: Mr. PAINE's comparisons are made with the professed intention of showing the superiority of the French Constitution, and he has therefore always chosen his own ground of comparison. He might have pursued a system more consistent with truth and candour, but it would not have answered his purpose so effectually. The true drift of Mr. PAINE's argument in this instance is this, *The English Parliament have enacted game laws that operate unequally. They have allowed more monopolies than are advantageous to the people; therefore the Legislature of a nation ought not to have the power to make any laws at all relative either to game, or to monopolies.* This is Mr. PAINE's principle, and it is the real ground upon which he prefers the French constitution, not merely to that of *England,* but to those of every State in the American Union. He infers that the English constitution is bad, because under that constitution certain bad laws have been enacted, and are not yet repealed. And he concludes that the French constitution is excellent, because the universal freedom of the chace, and the universal freedom of trade are placed beyond the controul of their Legislature.—But the preservation of game is an object of publick concern, and the Legislature of every country ought to have the power of making game laws for the benefit of the publick. Whether the English Parliament have exerted unwisely this power which has been delegated to them or not, is a question altogether foreign to the purpose; we know that bad laws exist in every country under Heaven, but it is strange reasoning, to infer from thence, that there ought not to exist in the nation a power to make good ones. All the Legislatures in the *United States* have the power to enact game laws and to allow monopolies. They all of them exercise this power. We have game laws and monopolies in this Commonwealth, and yet no man complains that they are destructive to his liberty. If the French constitution has placed the regulation of those objects beyond the reach of their ordinary legislative authority, they will soon find by their experience of inconveniences that the goodness of a constitution, does not depend upon the impotence of the Legislature.

In examining the next article it is utterly impossible for me to do justice to the wit of Mr. PAINE. The charge which he has so often repeated against Mr. BURKE's book cannot be made against this production. You find here nothing of the "spouting rank of high-toned exclamation:" You do not even find the delicate sallies of elegant comedy. His own words must be quoted: "The French constitution says, that to preserve the National Representation from being corrupt, no member of the National Assembly shall be an officer of the government, a placeman or a pensioner—What will Mr. BURKE place against this? I will whisper his answer; *Loaves* and *Fishes*." And then he proceeds to show that the answer which he whispers for Mr. BURKE is very ridiculous. There is, it must be acknowledged, something pleasant in this mode of managing an argument; but it is rather unfortunate that Mr. PAINE should complain as an abuse of the English government, that it is "themselves accountable to themselves," so near to a passage which is most assuredly "himself undertaking to answer himself." Every person will acknowledge that this answer of *Loaves* and *Fishes* is very absurd; it is even too absurd for Mr. BURKE in his original character; and the only circumstance that renders it perfectly accountable is, that it comes from Mr. BURKE by his representative, who certainly never had from him any authority to misrepresent him so palpably.

Mr. PAINE has seldom thought proper to answer even the few arguments contained in the book which is so obnoxious to him: Easy as it might have been to refute Mr. BURKE's reasoning, he probably thought it easier to refute his own: He has hunted for epigrams where he ought to have sought arguments: In the pursuit of those epigrams he has been sometimes not unsuccessful in exposing the absurdity of his own reasoning, but a less passionate or more generous political polemick, would not have chosen to place his own inconsistencies to the account of his antagonist.

Mr. PAINE has not however grounded his preference to the French constitution, upon truth, in this instance any more than in the other. The principle of excluding placemen, pensioners and executive officers from the national representation is acknowledged by the laws under the English constitution as well as in that of *France*. The only possible advantage which the French can pretend to, is, that they have been more successful in its application. Mr. PAINE might have said that it was not sufficiently extended by the English laws, and that it was by the French; and his opinion would have had its weight; but this would not answer his purpose: The French constitution must at all events have a triumph; and a system so odious as the English government, was not entitled to the benefits of common truth and justice. There are however several acts of Parliament, expressly excluding a great variety of placemen, pensioners and officers dependent upon the executive authority, from holding seats in the house of commons. With respect to pensioners their principle is more equitable than the total exclusion of the French. Every person holding a pension at the pleasure of the king, or for a term of years is excluded, because such a man may be too liable to be under the influence of the executive power; but if a man has received a pension for life, as a reward for services rendered his country, a pension which carries no dependence, and which can have no effect upon the legislative conduct of the person entitled to it, neither the English nor the Americans think that former services are a regular disqualification for the future; nor are they disposed to deprive any man of an invaluable privilege, merely because they have paid him for hazarding his life perhaps, or his fortune in their service.

But, says Mr. PAINE, by the English constitution "those who vote the supplies are the same persons who receive the supplies when voted, and are to account for the expenditure of those supplies to those who voted them; it is themselves accountable to themselves." This to be sure is very ingenious, but it is not in any sense true. The persons who vote the supplies are the house of commons, the representatives of the nation: To them the king's ministers (and principally the Chancellor of the Exchequer) are accountable for the expenditure of the monies voted. The ministers may indeed be at the same time members of the House of Commons, and the system is perhaps defective in allowing a few individuals to be members of the body to whom they are accountable. It may be inconvenient, but is not at all absurd, and is purposely authorised by the English constitution, because they consider its advantages as more than a balance for its inconveniences. The minister of the supreme executive office, states to the representatives of the nation, the sums necessary to defray the annual expenses of the kingdom. These representatives vote the assessment of such sums as they think necessary, and make the appropriations. The ministers then become accountable for the expenditures according to the previous appropriations, to that body of which they are indeed individual members, but of which they do not compose an hundredth part. Upon what principle then are we told that it is themselves accountable to themselves. They have indeed in *France* taken great pains to secure the independence of the legislative upon the executive authority; but they have not been equally cautious on the other side. Their executive is left totally at the mercy of the legislature, and must infallibly soon fall a sacrifice to their ambition.

The discussion of this subject would lead me far beyond my present intention. I have shown that the constitution of *England* has adopted the principle of excluding citizens dependent upon the executive power, from the House of Commons; the French constitution has done no more; and if they have carried the application of the principle further, that circumstance does not warrant the decided preference which Mr. PAINE has so liberally bestowed: Since it is only a difference of opinion upon the expediency of particular exclusions.

PUBLICOLA.

No. X.

MR. RUSSELL,

THE next article upon which Mr. PAINE has pronounced the superiority of the *French* constitution, is upon the subject of making war and peace. The right he says, is placed where the expense is; that is in the nation. Whereas "in *England*, the right is said to reside in a *metaphor*, shewn at the Tower for six pence or a shilling a piece." He answers himself again in this passage, and shows the folly of placing such a formidable right in a metaphor; but in this instance as in the former, there is much wit and no truth; and I must take the liberty to affirm in contradiction to Mr. *Paine,* that the *French* constitution has not, nor could not place the right of declaring war, where the expense must fall; and that the English constitution has not placed this right in a metaphor.

The expense of supporting wars must in all countries be defrayed by the nation, and every individual must bear his proportion of the burthen. In free countries that proportion must always be determined by the representatives of the people; but the right of deciding when it may be expedient to engage in a war cannot possibly be retained by the people of a populous and extensive territory, it must be a delegated power; and the French constitution has vested it in the *National Assembly*. By the English constitution it is vested in the supreme executive officer; but to guard against the abuse of this formidable power, it has given to the representatives of the people, the exclusive right of providing for the support of the war, and of withholding the supplies, "the sinews of war," if it should ever be declared contrary to the sense of the people themselves. Mr. *Paine* supposes a perplexity, which is warranted neither by theory nor by the experience of history "if the one rashly declares war" says he, "as a matter of right; and the other peremptorily withholds the supplies as a matter of right, the remedy becomes as bad or worse than the disease." But every war in *England* must be the war of the people: The King is in reality no more than the organ of the nation, and must be more than an idiot to declare a war, upon which he must depend altogether upon them for its support, without being certain of that support. Imaginary conclusions drawn by reasoning against the inevitable order of things, are unworthy of a politician, and should be left as a feeble resource for the satyrist. To have given his objection even an appearance of plausibility, Mr. *Paine* should have mentioned an instance, when this clashing of the rights of the King and of the Commons has ever been productive of the ill effects which his fancy has sagaciously drawn from them.

Indeed Mr. *Paine* himself, upon further reflection acknowledges the futility of his objection, and says "that in the manner the English nation is represented, it signifies not where this right resides, whether in the Crown or in the Parliament." But I apprehend, if the representation in *England* were as perfect as human wisdom could devise, their present system with respect to peace and war, would comprise all the advantages of the French system, and at the same time be free from many inconveniences, to which that must be liable.

It must be clear to every one that the French have not, as Mr. *Paine* pretends, united the *right* and the *expense*: The impracticability of such an union, must be equally evident; and the only question which can establish a fair ground of comparison, between the two constitutions is, *Whether it is expedient to delegate to the legislative, or whether to the executive authority, the right of declaring war.*

As I am not yet a convert to Mr. *Paine*'s opinion that a nation has a right to do what it pleases, I must be allowed to say that they have no right to make war upon their neighbours, without provocation. The people by their representatives must judge, when the provocation is sufficient to dissolve them from all the obligations of morality and humanity, by which nations are bound to preserve the blessings of peace. But when they have determined that the great law of self-preservation, to which all other laws must give way, or that the laws which they have enacted in consequence of the primative contract which united all their power for the benefit of every individual, compel them to appeal for justice to the God of battles, then, the declaration of war, the formal act, by which they announce to the world their intention to employ the arm of power in their own defence, seems to be the proper attribute of the executive power. The difference therefore, between the English and French constitutions, considered in this light, can involve only a question of propriety, and as such the English appears to me to deserve the preference.

If this idea should be considered as heretical, I must beg leave to call to my assistance the authority of ROUSSEAU, a name still more respectable than that of Mr. *Paine,* because death has given the ultimate sanction to his reputation. "The act of declaring war" says he in his social compact "and that of making peace have been considered as acts of sovereignty, which is not the case; for either of those acts is not a law, but only an application of the law; a particular act which determines the operation of the law, as will be clearly perceived when the idea annexed to the word *law* shall be ascertained." The spirit of the English constitution is perfectly agreeable to this idea.

But let us consider this subject a little further. Whenever a difference arises between two nations which may terminate in a war, it is proper and customary, that previous negotiations should be held, in order to use every possible means of settling amicably the dispute. These negotiations, the appointment of the agents, by whom they are to be conducted, and the communication of the proposals for accommodation, which are respectively offered by either of the parties, are all appropriated to the executive department. When the restoration of peace becomes expedient in the opinion of the people, agents must again be appointed, and proposals of pacification must again be made. It is obvious to every man, that in the management of these concerns the utmost secrecy and dispatch are frequently of essential necessity to the welfare of the people; but what secrecy can ever be expected, when every instruction to an Ambassadour, every article of a proposed treaty, and every circumstance of information from the Minister, in the progress of his operations, must be known to twelve hundred men assembled in the capital of the republick; what probability of dispatch, when all these things must be debated in this Assembly of 1200 men; where every thing must in the necessary order of events be opposed, by interested individuals, and irritated factions, who may protract the discussion for months or years at their pleasure.

By the constitution of the *United States,* it is true, the right of declaring war is vested in the Congress, that is, in the legislative power. But it is in the point of form that it agrees with the constitution of *France*; it has wisely placed the management of all negociations and treaties, and the appointment of all agents and ministers in the executive department; and it has so thoroughly adopted in this instance the *principles* of the English constitution, that although it has given the Congress the right of declaring war, which is merely a difference of form, it has vested in the President, with the advice of the Senate as his executive council, the right of making peace, which is implied in that of forming treaties.—This is not the first instance in which Mr. *Paine*'s principles attack those of the constitutions of his country.—Highly as we may revere however the principles which we are under every obligation to support, we may without irreverence acknowledge that they partake of the human imperfection from which they originated, and if Mr. *Paine*'s principles in opposition to them, are in any instance founded upon eternal truth, we may indulge the hope, that every necessary improvement will be adopted in a peaceable and amicable manner by the general consent of the people. But if the principles of Mr. *Paine*, or those of the French *National Assembly*, would lead us by a vain and delusive pretence of an impracticable union, between the right of declaring, and the expense of supporting a war, to the sacrifice of principles founded in immutable truth, if they could persuade us, by establishing in the legislative body all negociations with foreign nations relative to war and peace, to open a thousand avenues for base intrigue, for furious faction, for foreign bribery, and domestick treason, let us remain immovably fixed at the banners of our constitutional freedom, and not desert the impregnable fortress of our liberties, for the unsubstantial fabrick of visionary politicians.

PUBLICOLA.

No. XI, AND LAST.

MR. RUSSELL,

THE papers under the signature of PUBLICOLA, have called forth a torrent of abuse, not upon their real author nor upon the sentiments they express, but upon a supposed author, and supposed sentiments.

With respect to the author, not one of the conjectures that have appeared in the publick prints has been well grounded. The VICE-PRESIDENT neither wrote nor corrected them; he did not give his sanction to an individual sentiment contained in them, nor did they "go to the press under the assumed patronage of his son."

With respect to the sentiments, to those who have read the pieces with attention, it is needless to say, that they are simply an examination of certain principles and arguments contained in a late pamphlet of Mr. PAINE's, which are supposed to be directly opposite to principles acknowledged by the constitutions of our country. And the author challenges all the writers who have appeared in support of Mr. PAINE's infallibility, to produce a single passage in these publications which has the most distant tendency to recommend either a monarchy or an aristocracy to the citizens of these States.

The writer never had the intention to defend the corruptions of the English constitution; nor even its principles in theory, except such as were adopted in our own. Mr. PAINE has drawn a comparison between certain parts of the English and French Constitutions, in which are contained principles of government, that are not acknowledged by our own constitutions. So far as the principles of the English constitution, have been adopted by the Americans, I have defended them, and I am firmly convinced, that we cannot renounce them, without renouncing at the same time the happy governments with which we are favoured.—The question of superiority between the French and English constitutions, has no connection with a question relative to monarchy. If this be true, it must apply equally to the admirers of the French constitution, and Mr. PAINE himself is chargeable with having supported a monarchical institution.—It is well known that by the French constitution, a standing army of near 300,000 men is established, and placed beyond the annihilating arm of legislature. Is it impossible that Mr. PAINE should admire this constitution, without being a friend to standing armies?—The argument is the same, and the assertion might be made, with just as much truth, as that PUBLICOLA is an advocate for monarchy or for aristocracy.

When Mr. PAINE says that a whole nation (by which it is admitted that he means a majority of the nation) have a right to do what it chooses, and when he says that before the formation of civil society every man has a natural right to judge in his own cause, it appears to me that he resolves all *right* into *power*; it is this opinion which I have combated, because it appears to me to be of the most pernicious tendency, and if it is not really contained in the pamphlet, I confess myself greatly mistaken. But the *enlightened* writers, who have defended the principle of Mr. PAINE, differ so essentially in the ground they have taken, that the one or the other would certainly have been charged with propogating *detestable heresies*, had not the end sanctified the means, and the object of defending Mr. PAINE, reconciled the inconsistency of their reasonings. One writer supports the principle through thick and thin; and tells you that the *will* of the contracting parties, is the only circumstance that makes treaties obligatory. Another tells you that I have grossly misrepresented Mr. PAINE, and that the national omnipotence which he establishes relates only to the internal concerns of the community. He agrees however that the will of the majority must be taken for the will of the whole nation, and that with respect to the formation of a government, a majority have a right to do what they please. So that it is no longer the "rights of men," but the rights of the majority which alone are unalienable.

Upon the question whether a constitution government can be made alterable otherwise than by the people in their original character, I have defended the constitution of the *United States* against the principle of Mr. PAINE, though in the republication of the paper in several of the southern papers, the passage which supports my opinion by the authority of the Constitution, is omitted.

Upon the article of representation, I have contended that the French representation is no representation of the people at all. Is there a man in the *United States* who would recommend it as a model to us? I have contended that our representation of the people is infinitely superiour both to the French and the English; and this is said to be an abominable heresy.

Upon the subject of monopolies, of game laws, and of exclusions from the legislature, I have defended the *principles* adopted by our own constitutions, and not the abuses of the English Government. Upon that of war and peace I have done the same, and wherever Mr. PAINE's observations have appeared to be founded upon any other foundation than truth I have endeavoured to show their fallacy. But a defence of monarchy or aristocracy was no more in my intention, than the defence of the Salic Law of descents was to that of Mr. PAINE.

I shall now conclude these papers with requesting that those only who read them would judge upon their principles; and I am well persuaded, that the candour of the public will not take misrepresentation for reason, nor invective for argument.

PUBLICOLA.

"A DAGGER AT THE HEART OF THE COUNTRY"

3. Letters of Marcellus, I–III. *Columbian Centinel* (Boston: April 24–May 11, 1793).

By the spring of 1793, France and Britain were at war, and whether the U.S. should aid its former mother country or respect its treaties with France was becoming a partisan issue. The default, some argued, should be to aid France, if only because the treaty of 1778, which had done as much as anything to secure American independence, provided for mutual aid in times of war. Edmond-Charles Genêt, the new French minister to the United States, took this case directly to the public and encouraged American citizens to outfit privateers to attack British ships. This was all much to the consternation of the Washington administration, which was formulating a policy of strict neutrality on general principle and on strategic grounds. Getting involved risked war; American shipping would be particularly vulnerable to either side.

Yet the French revolutionaries pointedly cited the American Revolution, its assertion of popular sovereignty and its overthrowing of a king, as precedent for their own actions. And the French Revolution continued to inspire tremendous enthusiasm in the United States even after its violence became well-known. Those who advocated for more democracy, and a more transparent style of government than the Federalists seemed to favor, publicly celebrated the revolutions that seemed poised to spread all over Europe, including in England. Foreign affairs and domestic politics began to merge. A national political opposition took shape around the entwined issues of democracy and policy toward France and England.

Into this controversy Adams ventured with these three letters, written under a pseudonym evoking an illustrious Roman consul. Like the Publicola letters, they were published in the *Columbian Centinel*, the leading pro-administration paper in Boston, where Adams had established himself, not very contentedly, as a lawyer. As Marcellus, Adams, like Washington, seeks to make neutrality an expression of national independence and strength, portraying it as a long-term strategy. He also emphasizes the high risks of any policy other than trying to preserve neutral rights in time of war, not least to the young nation's commercial prospects. As was often the case in such public letters, Adams begins in an objective, nonpartisan tone, but by the third letter his suspicions of France tip his hand.

Though Thomas Paine is not mentioned by name in this series, he is present by extension in Adams's reference in the second letter to "the revised declaration of rights of the National Convention in France," which Paine had a hand in drafting. After the enormous success of *Rights of Man*—Paine completed the book with a second part in February 1792 and more than 200,000 copies of the combined work were sold by year's end—the French National Assembly conferred honorary citizenship on Paine and in September he was elected to the newly formed National Convention, where he promptly voted with the majority to abolish the monarchy and establish the French Republic. On October 11 he was appointed to a nine-man committee charged with writing a republican constitution, along with the new iteration of the declaration of rights, the second of three issued over the course of the French Revolution. As factionalism within the Convention grew more volatile, especially in the wake of the execution of Louis XVI in January 1793, Paine's influence quickly receded and before the year was out he had fallen out of favor and was imprisoned in the former Luxembourg Palace. His release would eventually be secured in November 1794 by future president James Monroe, then the American minister in Paris. Of the nine members of the committee to draft the new French constitution, only Paine and two others would survive the Terror.

Letters of Marcellus

MR RUSSELL,

AT a period, when all the European powers, with whom we have any considerable commercial intercourse, are involved in war, it becomes an interesting question to every American, what line of conduct ought to be pursued by the *United States* as a nation, and by their citizens as individuals, in relation to the contending parties. The individual must follow the dictates of his own discretion, and the path to be pursued by the nation, must be pointed out by the wisdom of the National Legislature: But upon a subject in which all are so deeply interested, it is the right, and in some measure the duty of every citizen, to express his opinions with decency, but with freedom and sincerity.

The solution of the question as it respects the country, involves in itself an answer to that which relates to individuals. There have indeed been certain suggestions in the public papers, and in private circles something similar has been heard, of an intention among some of our fellow citizens to arm privateers, and commit depredations upon the commerce of one of the parties under the authority of another. It is to be hoped, that this violation of the laws of nature and nations, this buccaneering plan of piratical plunder, may not in any instance be carried beyond the airy regions of speculation, and may never acquire the consistency of practical execution. If the natural obligations of justice are so feeble among us, that avarice cannot be restrained from robbery, but by the provisions of positive law, if the statute book is to be our only rule of morality to regulate the observance of our duties towards our fellow creatures, let those whose ideas of equity are so very subservient to their private interests, consult the treaties between the *United States*, and the several powers now at war, which by the constitution of the *United States*, are declared to be "the supreme law of the land," and in the 21st, the 19th and the 20th articles of the several treaties of commerce with *France*, *Holland*, and

Prussia, they will find, that by taking letters of marque or arming privateers with commissions under either of those powers against either of the others, they would subject themselves to the punishment of pirates. There can be no doubt but that a similar act of hostility, against any subject of the King of *Great-Britain*, would be a direct violation of the 7th. article of the treaty of peace. If we were not bound by any treaty whatever, with either of the nations, the natural obligation of neutrality would operate upon us individually, unless the nation should take a decisive part in favour of one of the parties. Every citizen would be legally responsible for all the property which he might seize with violence under a commission to which he could not be entitled, and if he should preserve himself from the punishment of piracy, he would be liable to make entire satisfaction for all the damage he might occasion, and to restore his ill-acquired plunder.

It is indeed of material importance to the commercial interest of this country, that our merchants should show a peculiar degree of circumspection in their conduct, because the country becomes at a season so critical as this, in some measure responsible for them. In the just and honourable pursuit of their legitimate interest, it is the duty of the nation to support them with all its force and all its authority. In time of war, the subjects of all belligerent powers are frequently disposed to violate the rights of neutral nations. The master and the crew of a privateer, fitted out and cruising for the sole purpose of seizing upon defenceless wealth, and stimulated by the prospect of a valuable spoil, often feel the full force of disappointed rapaciousness, when after a long chase they discover that the ship, upon the plunder of whose cargo they had already feasted their imaginations, is rescued from their violence by the protection of a neutral flag. They are not apt to be nice in their distinctions of morality. Their disappointed passions often seek a vent against the unarmed opulence which eludes their grasps, and they are frequently guilty of insolence, and sometimes of oppression towards those who are not in a condition to resent their injustice.—In such case the individuals of the neutral nation, who suffer in consequence of such lawless proceedings, have no remedy but to call upon the sovereign of their own country to support them in their demand for satisfaction: Should any complaints arising from causes like this, become a subject of negociation, between the *United States* and either of the contending parties, it behoves us all, as we value our interests, or our reputation, that no occasion to retort a complaint that the neutrality was first violated on our part, should be given. In order to obtain justice, for any citizen who may suffer by the iniquity of a foreigner, we must disavow in the most decisive manner, all acts of iniquity committed by our own citizens, and our government can never have an expectation of gaining a compensation for the *injured* individual, unless they can compel the *injuring* individual to make compensation in his turn.

To expatiate upon the natural injustice and wickedness of privateering under a foreign commission against a nation at peace with us, would be as idle, as an attempt "to add a perfume to the violet."—The practice of privateering even in its most excusable form, between nations formally at war, has been condemned by the most amiable and virtuous moralists. In the treaty between the United States and the King of Prussia, it is provided that in case war should arise between the contracting parties, "All merchant and trading vessels employed in exchanging the products of different places, and thereby rendering the necessaries, conveniences and comforts of human life more easy to be obtained, and more general, shall be allowed to pass free and unmolested; and neither of the contracting powers shall grant or issue any commission to any private armed vessel, empowering them to take or destroy such trading vessels or interrupt such commerce." This clause in the treaty, which was I believe the first instance in which two great nations have adopted this system of benevolence and humanity, has been justly admired and applauded; it was adopted by the late French National Assembly, when they declared war against the Emperor of Germany, and the real friends of mankind, must regret that the policy is abandoned at this time, when the war extends to all the great commercial nations of Europe. For, if as the poet, with more than poetical truth, has said, "War is murder," the plunder of private property, the pillage of all the regular rewards of honest industry and laudable enterprize, upon the mere pretence of a national contest, to the eye of reason and justice, can appear in no other light than that of highway robbery. If however, some apology for the practice is to be derived from the uncontroulable laws of necessity, or from the iniquitous law of war, certainly there can be no possible excuse for those who incur the guilt without being able to plead the palliation; for those who by violating the rights of nations in order to obtain a licence for rapine, manifestly shew, that it is only the lash of the executioner that binds them to the observance of their civil and political duties.

MARCELLUS.

No. II.
"NON NOSTRUM, TANTAS COMPONERE LITES."

MR. RUSSELL,

HAVING attempted, in a late paper, to shew that a rigid adherence to the system of Neutrality between the European nations now at war, is equally the dictate of justice and of policy, to the individual citizens of the United States, while the Nation remains neutral, the question recurs, what is the line of conduct prescribed to the nation itself, at this delicate juncture, by those immutable laws of justice and equity, which are equally obligatory to sovereigns and to subjects, to republicks and to kings. I shall not make any consideration of general policy a separate subject of enquiry, because I hold it to be one of the most undeniable principles of government, that the truest policy of a nation consists in the performance of its duties. The rights of nations are nothing more than an extension of the rights of individuals to the great societies, into which the different portions of mankind have been combined; and they are all mediately or immediately derived from the fundamental position which the author of christianity has taught us as an article of religion, and which the revised declaration of rights of the National Convention in France have declared, to contain the essence of liberty. "*Liberty*," says the new Declaration of Rights, "*consists in the power of doing whatever is not contrary to the rights of others.*" "*Whatsoever*," says the Saviour of mankind, "*you would that men should do to you, do ye even so to them.*" Let us therefore be cautious to do nothing contrary to the rights of others, and we shall continue to enjoy and to deserve the blessings of freedom. Let us do as we should chuse others might do to us, and we shall deserve the favours of Heaven.

If these are the principles upon which our national conduct is to be grounded, it will follow, that an impartial and unequivocal neutrality between the contending parties is prescribed to us as a duty, unless we are bound by some existing contract or stipulation, to make a common cause with one of them.

I have already said it: The natural state of all nations, with respect to one another, is a state of peace—"*damus petimusque vicissim:*" It is what we have a right to expect *from* them, and for the same reason it is our duty to observe it *towards* them. In addition to this natural obligation, we are bound by express treaties with *France*, *England*, *Holland* and *Prussia*, to observe the laws of peace with the subjects of their different governments, and we have no right to interfere in their contentions. Whatever may be the current of our sentiments, or of our opinions—whatever may be the language suggested by our passions, or the wishes inspired by our affections, we are not constituted judges of the respective merits of their cause. From a feeling of gratitude towards a nation which assisted us in the days of our own calamity, we may be disposed to throw a veil over their own errors and crimes, and wish them that success which their frantic enthusiasm has rendered so improbable. As the descendants of Englishmen, we may be willing to lose the memory of all the miseries they inflicted upon us in our just struggle against them, and even the relics of their resentment, which still refuse the complete fulfilment of the treaty of peace, and we may wish them still to retain their reputation for successful courage and conduct in war—as men, we must undoubtedly lament the effusion of human blood, and the mass of misery and distress which is preparing for the great part of the civilized world; but as the citizens of a nation at a vast distance from the continent of Europe—of a nation whose happiness consists in a real independence, disconnected from all European interests and European politicks, it is our duty to remain, the peaceable and silent, though sorrowful spectators of the sanguinary scene.

With the reasons for neutrality suggested by these considerations of natural duty and of positive stipulation, a forcible argument concurs, derived from our interest. In the general conflict of all the commercial European Nations, the advantages which will be thrown into our hands, and the activity and vigour which will be given to every branch of our commerce, are too obvious to need any discussion. As the natural consequence of War, the necessities of all the belligerent powers must increase in proportion as their means of supply will diminish, and the profits, which must infallibly flow to us from their wants, can have no other limitation than the extent of our capacity to provide for them.

With all these inducements to a decided neutrality, let us look at the other side of the medal, and see what would be the consequence of our making ourselves partizans in the contest.—First, we should be engaged in a quarrel, with the laws of nations against us. It would be a violation of our political duties; a departure from the principles of national justice, and an express breach of the positive stipulations of peace and friendship with the several belligerent powers, contained in the treaties which I have already mentioned. An act of partiality in favour of either party would be an act of perfidy to the other.

I have so full a confidence in the equity and virtue of my countrymen, that I should rest the argument on this point alone, if I had not perceived that a contrary system of policy, is avowed by men of some influence among us, and openly recommended in some of the public prints of the day. A system, which professing to arise from an extraordinary attachment to the cause of Liberty and Equality, may in reality be traced to the common sources of private avarice, and private ambition, perhaps at once the cause and effect of an implicit devotion to *France*, and an antipathy to *England*, exceeding the limits of a national resentment.

To men of this description, arguments derived from the obligations of natural justice, or of written contract will be perfectly nugatory. "The Rights of Man," will be their answer to the one, and "Liberty and Equality," to the other. I apply therefore to a principle of more efficacious operation in their minds, if their own interest is in any degree connected with that of their country, and ask them what would be the inevitable consequence of a war with all Europe, excepting only the present prevailing power in *France*? The experience of the late war, would perhaps, discourage an attempt on the part of *Great-Britain* to conquer this Continent, but we have a sea-coast of twelve hundred miles every where open to invasion—and where is the power to protect it? We have a flourishing commerce, expanding to every part of the Globe, and where will it turn when excluded from every market of the Earth? We depend upon the returns of that commerce for many necessaries of life, and when those returns shall be cut off, where shall we look for the supply? We are in a great measure destitute of the defensive apparatus of War, and who will provide us with the arms and ammunition that will be indispensible? We feel severely at this moment, the burden of our public debt, and where are the funds to support us in the dreadful extremity to which our own madness and iniquity would reduce us?—Not to mention the infallible destruction of our Finances, and the national bankruptcy, which the friends of the system I am combating, would perhaps welcome as a blessing.—Are these, Sir, imaginary apprehensions, or are they objects of trivial moment? Our national existence may depend upon the event of our Councils in the present crisis, and to advise us to engage voluntarily in the War, is to aim a dagger at the heart of the country.

MARCELLUS.

No. III.
"OMNIUM PRIMUM RATUS TUERI PUBLICAM FIDEM."
LIV.

MR. RUSSELL,

IT has been enquired by citizens anxious for the welfare of the country, and aware of the distress to which it must inevitably be reduced by an European war, whether we have not already pledged our faith so far as to preclude us from any present consideration of convenience or inconvenience, and whether we are not by our own voluntary engagement bound to take the part of the present government in *France*, especially in case the West-India islands should be attacked by *Great-Britain*.

By the eleventh article of the Treaty of Alliance with *France*, the *United States* "guaranty to his most Christian Majesty, the possessions of the crown of *France* in *America*."—But the course of human events has either totally absolved us, or at least suspended the obligation of this clause, and it cannot be made even a plausible pretext for involving us in the present war. My reasons for this opinion are,

1. That the guaranty is *to his most Christian Majesty, of the possessions of the crown of France*. I ask, who is at this time *his most Christian Majesty*? A part of the French nation, and all the other powers of *Europe* will answer, he is the son or the brother of the late LOUIS the XVIth. The National Convention, and the present Republick of *France* will say there is no such man. The office and all its powers have been extinguished in the blood of the person with whom your contract was made. If the article binds us to either of the parties, the question, which of the two is entitled to claim the performance, is now a question to be settled by the event of a civil War, and neither party can call upon us to decide it for them.

2. That supposing the revolutions of *France*, are now completed, and a Republick firmly established, it may be doubtful, whether they have not by their change of government, dissolved this clause of the Treaty: I know it is a general principle of the laws of nations, that the rights and obligations of Treaties survive the internal revolutions of government, and therefore that the Republick of *France* may be entitled to the benefits of engagements contracted with the former Monarch. But to this rule there are many exceptions; the first Constituent Assembly were so fully of this opinion that they thought the nation absolved from all such Treaties previously made, as might be injurious to their interests, and the present government have extended the principle much further, when a justification for opening the *Scheldt*, contrary to the positive and express stipulation of many Treaties, they have formally denied the obligation of any compact, which was contrary to *the natural Rights of Men*. Upon speculative principles it may be very questionable how far the sovereign controul of a French Republick, over islands at three thousand miles distance from them is consistent with such natural rights, and it would be difficult to mark the distinction which should prohibit every act of jurisdiction exercised by one nation over a river flowing through the territories of another, and at the same time allow a supreme authority over colonies placed by the hand of nature

at so wide a distance from the metropolis.—The *possessions of the crown of France*, as guaranteed by our Treaty *to his most Christian Majesty*, appear to me to have formed a part of that Constitution of government which then existed in *France*; they were a part of the monarchy, and under the new government they can no longer be considered as *possessions*, in the same sense in which they were understood when the United States bound themselves to the guaranty.

3. Should both these grounds for the opinion I am supporting be considered as erroneous, and the clause in question be held as binding us to the French Republick, in the same manner as it formerly did to the King, it remains to enquire what was intended by the guaranty, and what are the duties which it has prescribed to us?—During the administration of the royal government, had the authority of the sovereign been guided by the maxims of speculative freedom or of practical tyranny; had he provoked a rebellion in the islands, by oppressing the planters or by liberating their slaves; the guaranty in the treaty would not have bound us to assist him with our blood and treasures, in enforcing an absurd and unnatural Government against the perpetual resistances which it would necessarily provoke. Had the late King of *France*, like other Kings of whom we read in history, veiling his insatiate ambition, under some specious pretence of glory, of dignity or of safety, declared a wanton and unjustifiable war against any or all of the commercial nations in Europe, and had his possessions in *America* been conquered by his enemies in the course of such a war, he never could have called upon the United States by virtue of this guaranty, to repair the injuries of his folly, and to sacrifice themselves in support of his pernicious projects. It is unnecessary to fatigue the public with the pedantry of quotations from the writers upon natural and political Law, but it may be laid down as an universal principle, that no stipulation contained in a treaty, can ever oblige one nation to adopt or support the folly or injustice of another.—In applying this principle, it becomes necessary to observe, that the administration of the French government over their colonies, since the first revolution of 1789 has been such as to keep almost all their islands in a constant state of rebellion and civil War; by the former of these calamities the slaves have been united against their masters; by

the latter the masters have been divided against each other. From the chaotic mass of human passions, a collection of all the most violent and inflammable elements has been selected and combined together; the torch of the furies has been applied to the composition; and the miserable islanders have been the victims of the fatal explosion.

To such a state of desperation have these devoted colonies been reduced, that a formal deputation as we are informed by the publick papers, have solicited for them the protection of the British government; and we are now told that this protection has been promised; that the King of *Great-Britain*, has agreed to take possession of these colonies and to hold them in trust *for his Most Christian Majesty*, the power to whom the letter of our guaranty has promised the assistance of the United States. An arbitrary and oppressive system of administration compelled us to renounce the authority of *Great-Britain,* and *France* assisted us to maintain our honourable warfare. A similar evil, has driven some of the French colonies to a similar remedy; one of them has even attempted a Declaration of Independence, and all the others would doubtless have done the same, were they not profoundly sensible that the time is not yet come, for the Lion to lie down with the Lamb, and that the justice of their cause would avail them but little against the powerful injustice of their oppressors. But surely there would be something singularly, absurd and iniquitous, to see the United States support the French in a plan of oppressive administration over their colonies, as a reward, for rescuing them from the oppression of *Great-Britain*. It would be such a total subversion of all moral and political consistency, such a covenant between virtue and vice, such a coalition of liberal freedom with despotick tyranny, as can scarcely be imagined without a confusion of ideas, or expressed without an absurdity of language.

4. The last ground upon which I consider this guaranty as dissolved or at least suspended, is, that by the act of the French Government, it has been rendered impracticable. They have declared war against all the naval powers of *Europe*. What the event of that war will be, it is not given to man to foretel; but we cannot take a part with the French Republic, without uniting all the rest of *Europe* against us; which upon every rational

calculation of probability, would be dooming ourselves to inevitable ruin and destruction. We are therefore commanded by a law, which supercedes all others, by that uncontroulable law of nature, which is paramount to all human legislation, or compact, to remain at peace, and to content ourselves with wishing that laureled Victory may sit upon the sword of justice, and that smooth success may always be strewed before the feet of virtuous Freedom.

                                                MARCELLUS.

"WE WILL PROVE OURSELVES NOT
UNWORTHY OF THE PRIZE"

4. *An Oration, Pronounced July 4th, 1793, at the Request of the Inhabitants of the Town of Boston, in Commemoration of the Anniversary of American Independence* (Boston: Benjamin Edes & Son, 1793).

Adams's authorship of the Marcellus letters soon became widely known and the town fathers of Boston honored the vice president's son with an invitation to deliver the annual Independence Day oration. Boston had been a major stage for patriotic anniversary addresses even before 1776, with March 5, the date of the Boston Massacre, serving as the occasion for more solemn observances during the early 1770s. Fourth of July orations became significant civic events during the early republic, a centerpiece of town-based festivities in which citizens expressed their feelings for the nation, rehearsed the history of the American Revolution, and heard speeches and toasts that grappled with the issues of the day. These speeches, like the toasts given at banquets after the public festivities and later published in newspapers, were carefully crafted to ennoble more or less political agendas with the aura of patriotism, and to link local and state matters to national and international events.

Delivered before a capacity crowd in Boston's Old South Meeting House, Adams's first July Fourth oration is an early exemplar of the genre, notable for broaching the theme of gratitude to the generation of revolutionary leaders, his parents' generation. He begins here to articulate his strong belief in what later generations would call "American exceptionalism." The American Revolution might be an inspiration to the French and others who claimed to fight to preserve liberty, but it was already apparent to Adams that it was unique among revolutions for its conservative character, preserving traditional English freedoms from the English themselves while creating something new, a postcolonial nation-state. Even as he, like other Federalists, grew increasingly uncomfortable with some of the bloody results of revolution in France, he was nevertheless very much in tune with his audience: in 1793, even supporters of the Washington administration could hold the "delightful expectation" that all the monarchies of Europe would be toppled by popular movements. All of Europe (except for England), it was still possible to imagine, "shall hail *your* country, Americans! as the youngest daughter of Nature, and the first-born offspring of Freedom."

Taking to his diary on the evening of the Fourth, Adams wrote that his oration had been "well received.—for which I feel grateful as I ought." He also noted that he had met with the printer Benjamin Edes, "who was very solicitous to print." Thirty-five years later, he recalled that his speech had been greeted "with a warmth and admiration which gave me cheering encouragement at the threshold of life. It has dwelt like a charm upon my memory ever since." Indeed, Adams's early published works had been noticed approvingly by many, not least by President Washington. On May 19, 1794, Vice President John Adams, writing to Abigail Adams from the seat of the national government, revealed that their son's "Writings have given him a greater Consideration in this Place than he is aware of." That consideration would translate, just days later, into John Quincy Adams's first diplomatic appointment, beginning his career as one of the nation's best-informed and most skilled foreign officers. He was really into the world at last.

AN

ORATION,

PRONOUNCED

JULY 4th, 1793,

AT THE

REQUEST OF THE INHABITANTS

OF THE

TOWN of *BOSTON*,

IN COMMEMORATION

OF THE

ANNIVERSARY OF
AMERICAN INDEPENDENCE.

BY JOHN QUINCY ADAMS,

O NOMEN DULCE LIBERTATIS! *Cic.*

YE ſhades of ancient heroes! Ye who toil'd,
Through long ſucceſſive ages to build up
A labouring plan of ſtate; behold at once
The wonder done! THOMSON.

B O S T O N :
PRINTED by BENJAMIN EDES & SON, *in Kilby-Street.*
M,DCC,XCIII.

AT a Meeting of the Freeholders and other Inhabitants of the Town of BOSTON, *duly qualified and legally warned, in publick Town-Meeting, aſſembled at* FANEUIL HALL, *on Thurſday the 4th of July, A. D.* 1793:

VOTED,

THAT the SELECTMEN be and hereby are appointed a Committee to wait on JOHN QUINCY ADAMS, Eſq. and in the Name of the Town to thank him for the ſpirited and elegant ORATION, this Day delivered by him, at the requeſt of the Town, upon the ANNIVERSARY OF THE INDEPENDENCE OF THE UNITED STATES OF AMERICA—in which, according to the Inſtitution of the Town, he conſidered the feelings, manners, and principles which led to that great National Event—and to requeſt of him a Copy thereof for the Preſs.

Atteſt,
       WILLIAM COOPER, *Town-Clerk.*

GENTLEMEN,

IN compliance with the polite Requeſt of my Fellow-Citizens, the O R A T I O N *yeſterday delivered, again ſolicits the Indulgence of the Public.*

 I am,

  Gentlemen,

   With ſincere Reſpect,

    Your very humble Servant,

     JOHN Q. ADAMS.

BOSTON, JULY 5th, 1793.

Fourth of July Oration

It has been a custom, sanctioned by the universal practice of civilized Nations, to celebrate with anniversary solemnities, the return of the days which have been distinguished by events the most important to the happiness of the people. In countries where the natural dignity of mankind, has been degraded by the weakness of bigotry, or debased by the miseries of despotism, this customary celebration has degenerated into a servile mockery of festivity upon the birth day of a sceptered tyrant, or has dwindled to an unmeaning revel, in honour of some canonized fanatic, of whom nothing now remains but the name, in the calendar of antiquated superstition. In those more fortunate regions of the earth where Liberty has condescended to reside, the cheerful gratitude of her favoured people has devoted to innocent gaiety and useful relaxation from the toils of virtuous industry the periodical revolution of those days which have been rendered illustrious by the triumphs of freedom.

AMERICANS! Such is the nature of the institution which again calls your attention to celebrate the establishment of your national Independence. And surely since the creation of the heavenly orb which separated the day from the night, amid the unnumbered events which have diversified the history of the human race, none has ever occurred more highly deserving of celebration by every species of ceremonial, that can testify a sense of gratitude to the DEITY, and of happiness, derived from his transcendent favours.

It is a wise and salutary institution, which forcibly recalls to the memory of freemen, the principles upon which they originally founded their labouring plan of state. It is a sacrifice at the altar of Liberty herself;—a renewal of homage to the Sovereign, who alone is worthy of our veneration;—a profession of political fidelity, expressive of our adherence to those maxims of liberal submission and obedient freedom, which in these favoured climes, have harmonized the long-contending claims of liberty and law. By a frequent recurrence to those sentiments and actions upon which the glory and felicity of the Nation rest supported, we are enabled to renew the moments of bliss which we are not permitted to retain; we secure a permanency to the exaltation which the Constitution of Nature has rendered fleeting, and a perennial existence to enjoyments which the lot of humanity has made transitory.

The "feelings, manners and principles" which led to the Independence of our Country; such, my friends and fellow-citizens is the theme of our present commemoration. The field is extensive; it is fruitful: but the copious treasures of its fragrance have already been gathered by the hands of genius; and there now remains for the gleaning of mental indigence, nought but the thinly scattered sweets which have escaped the vigilance of their industry.

They were the same feelings, manners and principles, which conducted our venerable forefathers from the unhallowed shores of oppression; which inspired them with the sublime purpose of converting the forests of a wilderness into the favourite mansion of Liberty; of unfolding the gates of a new world, as a refuge for the victims of persecution in the old. The feelings of injured freedom, the manners of social equality, and the principles of eternal justice.

Had the Sovereigns of England pursued the policy prescribed by their interest, had they not provoked the hostilities of their Colonists against the feeble fortress of their authority they might perhaps have retained to this day an Empire which would have been but the more durable, for resting only upon the foundation of immemorial custom, and national affection.

Incumbered however with the oppressive glory of a successful war, which had enriched the *pride* of Britain, with the spoils of her own oppulence, and replenished the arrogance in proportion as it had exhausted the resources of the nation; an adventurous ministry, catching at every desperate expedient to support the ponderous burden of the national dignity, and stimulated by the perfidious instigations of their dependents in America, abandoned the profitable commercial policy of their predecessors, and superadded to the lucrative system of monopoly, which we had always tolerated as the price of their protection, a system of internal taxation from which they hoped to derive a fund for future corruption, and a supply for future extravagance.

The nation eagerly grasped at the proposal.—The situation, the condition, the sentiments of the colonies, were subjects upon which the people of Britain were divided between ignorance and error. The endearing ties of consanguinity, which had connected their ancestors, with those of the Americans, had been gradually loosened to the verge of dissolution, by the slow but ceaseless hand of time. Instead of returning the sentiments of fraternal affection, which animated the Americans, they indulged their vanity with preposterous opinions of insulting superiority: they considered us, not as fellow-subjects equally entitled with themselves to every privilege of Englishmen; but as wretched outcasts, upon whom they might safely load the burden, while they reserved to themselves the advantages of the national grandeur. It has been observed, that the nations the most highly favoured with freedom, have not always been the most friendly to the liberty of others. The people of Britain, expected to feel none of the oppression which a parliamentary tyranny might impose upon the Americans; on the contrary, they expected an alleviation of their burden, from the accumulation of ours, and vainly hoped that by the stripes inflicted upon us, their wounds would be healed.

The King—Need it be said, that he adopted as the offspring of his own affections, a plan so favourable to the natural propensity of royalty towards arbitrary power. Depending upon the prostituted valour of his mercenary legions, he was deaf to the complaints, he was inexorable to the remonstrances of violated freedom. Born and educated to the usual prejudices of hereditary dominion, and habitually accustomed to the syren-song of adulation, he was ready to believe what the courtly tribe about his throne did not fail to assure him; that complaint was nothing more than the murmur of sedition, and remonstrance the clamour of rebellion.

But they knew not the people with whom they had to contend. A people, sagacious and enlightened to discern, cool and deliberate to discuss, firm and resolute to maintain their rights. From the first appearance of the system of parliamentary oppression under the form of a stamp-act, it was met, by the determined opposition of the whole American Continent. The annals of other nations have produced instances of successful struggles to break a yoke previously imposed; but the records of History did not perhaps furnish an example of a people whose penetration had anticipated the operations of tyranny, and whose spirit had disdained to suffer an experiment upon their liberties. The ministerial partizans had flattered themselves with the expectation that the Act would execute itself; that before the hands of Freedom could be raised to repel the usurpation, they would be loaded with fetters; that the American Samson would be shorn of his locks while asleep; and when thus bereaved of his strength, might be made their sport with impunity.—Vain illusion!—Instantaneous and forceful, as an electric spark, the fervid spirit of resistance pervaded every part of the country; and at the moment, when the operation of the system was intended to commence, it was indignantly rejected, by three millions of men; high-minded men, determined to sacrifice their existence, rather than resign the Liberty, from which, all its enjoyments were derived.

It is unnecessary to pursue the detail of obstinacy and cruelty on the one part; of perseverance and fortitude on the other, until the period when every chord which had bound the two countries together, was destroyed by the violence of reciprocal hostilities, and the representatives of America, adopted the measure, which was already dictated by the wishes of their constituents; they declared the United Colonies free, sovereign and independent States.

AMERICANS! let us pause for a moment to consider the situation of our country, at that eventful day when our national existence commenced. In the full possession and enjoyment of all those prerogatives for which you then dared to adventure upon "all the varieties of untried being," the calm and settled moderation of the mind, is scarcely competent to conceive the tone of heroism, to which the souls of freemen were exalted in that hour of perilous magnanimity. Seventeen times has the sun, in the progress of his annual revolutions, diffused his prolific radiance over the plains of Independent America. Millions of hearts which then palpitated with the rapturous glow of patriotism, have already been translated to brighter worlds; to the abodes of more than mortal freedom. Other millions have arisen to receive from their parents and benefactors, the inestimable recompense of their atchievements. A large proportion of the audience, whose benevolence is at this moment listening to the speaker of the day, like him were at that period too little advanced beyond the threshold of life to partake of the divine enthusiasm which inspired the American bosom; which prompted her voice to proclaim defiance to the thunders of Britain; which consecrated the banners of her armies; and finally erected the holy temple of American Liberty, over the tomb of departed tyranny. It is from those who have already passed the meridian of life; it is from you, ye venerable assertors of the rights of mankind, that we are to be informed, what were the feelings which swayed within your breasts and impelled you to action, when, like the stripling of Israel, with scarce a weapon to attack, and without a shield for your defence, you met, and undismayed, engaged with the gigantic greatness of the British power. Untutored in the disgraceful science of human butchery; destitute of the fatal materials which the ingenuity of man has combined, to sharpen the scythe of death; unsupported by the arm of any friendly alliance, and unfortified against the powerful assaults of an unrelenting enemy, you did not hesitate at that moment, when your coasts were infested by a formidable fleet, when your territories were invaded by a numerous and veteran army, to pronounce the sentence of eternal separation from Britain, and to throw the gauntlet at a power the terror of whose recent triumphs was almost co-extensive with the earth—The interested and selfish propensities which in times of prosperous tranquility have such powerful dominion over the heart, were all expelled, and in their stead, the public virtues, the spirit of personal devotion to the common cause, a contempt of every danger in comparison with the subserviency of the country, had assumed an unlimited controul. The passion for the public, had absorbed all the rest; as the glorious luminary of heaven extinguishes in a flood of refulgence the twinkling splendor of every inferior planet. Those of you my countrymen, who were actors in those interesting scenes, will best know, how feeble, and impotent is the language of this description to express the impassioned emotions of the soul, with which you were then agitated: yet it were injustice to conclude from thence, or from the greater prevalence of private and personal motives in these days of calm serenity, that your sons have degenerated from the virtues of their fathers. Let it rather be a subject of pleasing reflection to you, that the generous and disinterested energies, which you were summoned to display, are permitted by the bountiful indulgence of Heaven to remain latent in the bosoms of your children. From the present prosperous appearance of our public affairs, we may admit a rational hope that our country will have no occasion to require of us those extraordinary and heroic exertions which it was your fortune to exhibit. But from the common versatility of all human destiny, should the prospect hereafter darken, and the clouds of public misfortune thicken to a tempest; should the voice of our country's calamity ever call us to her relief, we swear by the precious memory of the sages who toiled, and of the heroes who bled in her defence, that we will prove ourselves not unworthy of the prize, which they so dearly purchased; that we will act as the faithful disciples of those who so magnanimously taught us the instructive lesson of republican virtue.

Seven years of ineffectual hostility, an hundred millions of treasure fruitlessly expended, and uncounted thousands of human lives sacrificed to no purpose, at length taught the dreadful lesson of wisdom to the British Government, and compelled them to relinquish a claim which they had long since been unable to maintain. The pride of Britain, which should have been humbled, was only mortified. With sullen impotence, she yielded to the pressure of accumulated calamity, and closed with reluctance an inglorious war, in which she had often been the object, and rarely the actor of a triumph.

The various occurrences of our national history, since that period, are within the recollection of all my hearers. The relaxation and debility of the political body, which succeeded the violent exertions it had made during the war: the total inefficacy of the recommendatory federal system, which had been formed in the bosom of contention; the peaceable and deliberate adoption of a more effectual national constitution by the people of the union, and the prosperous administration of that government, which has repaired the shattered fabric of public confidence, which has strengthened the salutary bands of national union, and restored the bloom and vigour of impartial justice, to the public countenance, afford a subject of pleasing contemplation to the patriotic mind. The repeated unanimity of the nation has placed at the head of the American councils, the heroic leader, whose prudence and valour conducted to victory the armies of freedom; and the two first offices of this Commonwealth, still exhibit the virtues and employ the talents of the venerable patriots, whose firm and disinterested devotion to the cause of Liberty, was rewarded by the honourable distinction of a British proscription. Americans! the voice of grateful freedom is a stranger to the language of adulation. While we wish these illustrious sages to be assured that the memory of their services is impressed upon all our hearts, in characters, indelible to the latest period of time, we trust that the most acceptable tribute of respect which can be offered to their virtues, is found in the confidence of their countrymen. From the fervent admiration of future ages, when the historians of America, shall trace from their examples the splendid pattern of public virtue, their merits will receive a recompense of much more precious estimation than can be conferred by the most flattering testimonials of contemporaneous applause.

The magnitude and importance of the great event which we commemorate, derives a vast accession from its influence upon the affairs of the world, and its operation upon the history of mankind. It has already been observed that the origin of the American Revolution bears a character different from that of any other civil contest, that had ever arisen among men. It was not the convulsive struggle of slavery to throw off the burden of accumulated oppression, but the deliberate, tho' energetic effort of freemen, to repel the insidious approaches of tyranny. It was a contest involving the elementary principles of government, a question of right between the sovereign and the subject which in its progress had a tendency to introduce among the civilized nations of Europe, the discussion of a topic the first in magnitude, which can attract the attention of mankind, but which for many centuries, the gloomy shades of despotism had overspread with impenetrable darkness. The French nation cheerfully supported an alliance with the United States, and a war with Britain, during the course of which a large body of troops and considerable fleets were sent by the French government, to act in conjunction with their new allies.

The union which had at first been formed by the coalescence of a common enmity, was soon strengthened by the bonds of a friendly intercourse, and the subjects of an arbitrary prince, in fighting the battles of freedom, soon learnt to cherish the cause of Liberty itself. By a natural and easy application to themselves of the principles upon which the Americans asserted the justice of their warfare, they were led to inquire into the nature of the obligation which prescribed their submission to their own sovereign; and when they discovered that the consent of the people is the only legitimate source of authority, they necessarily drew the conclusion that their own obedience was no more than the compulsive acquiescence of servitude, and they waited only for a favourable opportunity to recover the possession of those enjoyments, to which they had never forfeited the right. Sentiments of a similar nature, by a gradual and imperceptible progress, secretly undermined all the foundations of their government; and when the necessities of the sovereign reduced him to the inevitable expedient of appealing to the benevolence of the people, the magic talisman of despotism was broken, the spell of prescriptive tyranny was dissolved, and the pompous pageant of their monarchy, instantaneously crumbled to atoms.

The subsequent European events which have let slip the dogs of war, to prey upon the vitals of humanity; which have poured the torrent of destruction over the fairest harvests of European fertility; which have unbound the pinions of desolation, and sent her forth to scatter pestilence and death among the nations; the scaffold, smoking with the blood of a fallen monarch; the corpse-covered field, where agonizing nature struggles with the pangs of dissolution; permit me my happy countrymen, to throw a pall over objects like these, which could only spread a gloom upon the face of our festivity. Let us rather indulge the pleasing and rational anticipation of the period, when all the nations of Europe shall partake of the blessings of equal liberty and universal peace. Whatever issue may be destined by the will of Heaven to await the termination of the present European commotions, the system of feudal absurdity has received an irrecoverable wound, and every symptom indicates its approaching dissolution. The seeds of Liberty are plentifully sown. However severe the climate, however barren the soil of the regions in which they have been received, such is the native exuberance of the plant, that it must eventually flourish with luxuriant profusion. The governments of Europe must fall; and the only remaining expedient in their power, is to gather up their garments and fall with decency. The bonds of civil subjection must be loosened by the discretion of civil authority, or they will be shivered by the convulsive efforts of slavery itself. The feelings of benevolence involuntarily make themselves a party to every circumstance that can affect the happiness of mankind; they are ever ready to realize the sanguine hope, that the governments to rise upon the ruins of the present systems will be immutably founded upon the principles of freedom, and administered by the genuine maxims of moral subordination and political equality. We cherish with a fondness which cannot be chilled by the cold unanimated philosophy of scepticism, the delightful expectation that the cancer of arbitrary power will be radically extracted from the human constitution; that the sources of oppression will be drained; that the passions which have hitherto made the misery of mankind, will be disarmed of all their violence, and give place to the soft controul of mild and amiable sentiments, which shall unite in social harmony the innumerable varieties of the human race. Then shall the nerveless arm of superstition no longer interpose an impious barrier between the beneficence of Heaven, and the adoration of its votaries: then shall the most distant regions of the earth be approximated by the gentle attraction of a liberal intercourse: then shall the fair fabric of universal Liberty rise upon the durable foundation of social equality, and the long-expected æra of human felicity, which has been announced by prophetic inspiration, and described in the most enraptured language of the Muses, shall commence its splendid progress—Visions of bliss! with every breath to Heaven we speed an ejaculation that the time may hasten, when your reality shall be no longer the ground of votive supplication, but the theme of grateful acknowledgment: when the choral gratulations of the liberated myriads of the elder world, in symphony, sweeter than the music of the spheres, shall hail *your* country, Americans! as the youngest daughter of Nature, and the first-born offspring of Freedom.

"THE DESTINIES OF THIS EMPIRE"

5. *An Oration, Delivered at Plymouth, December 22, 1802. At the Anniversary Commemoration of the First Landing of our Ancestors, at that Place* (Boston: Russell and Cutler, 1802).

In the annual calendar of civic observances, Forefathers' Day, December 21/22, was the day when Americans, especially New Englanders, celebrated the landing of the Pilgrims in 1620. The first "official" Forefathers Day speech was given, significantly, in 1769, when Boston was occupied by British soldiers, and beleaguered colonists looked to their earliest origins for inspiration and, inevitably, to give vent to provincial pride. The tradition continued more or less annually until the Civil War; Daniel Webster would memorably use the platform to catapult himself to greater national prominence in 1820. In the wake of the Republican triumph with the election of Thomas Jefferson to the presidency in 1801, which brought John Adams's political career to an end, sectional and partisan tensions were on the rise, and celebrations of New England history took on a distinctly political charge.

In 1802, when Adams was tapped to give the address, he was back at his law books in Boston after seven years of distinguished service abroad. (He was also serving in the Massachusetts Senate and he had almost been elected to Congress, losing by just 59 out of 3,739 votes.) Adams took up the assignment with gusto. Unlike other empires and nations, including the Roman, which had been built on blood and conquest, Adams posits that New England (and, by extension, America) had innocent origins, characterized by "the gentle temper of christian virtue—the rigorous observance of reciprocal justice—the unconquerable soul of conscious integrity." However idealized from our vantage, this is a theme Adams would develop with considerable energy throughout his career as a writer, diplomat, and politician, and it was key to his vision of the United States as a continental nation, a vision he would do more than any other American of his generation to realize.

Adams's budding expansionism is on display in what he came to regard as the most original and important contribution of his speech—one that builds on his argument in favor of private property and his unmistakable sense of New England's cultural superiority. American Indian rights of possession rested "upon a questionable foundation," he argues, because Native hunters acted as "lordly savages," wasting land, underpopulating the continent. Proof of American virtue thus lay in American fecundity: at then current rates, Adams extrapolates that America's population will exceed that of Europe in two more centuries, in the process consigning the continent's native inhabitants to irrelevance. Many years later, referring to his key role in negotiating the Treaty of Ghent, which brought an end to the War of 1812 without making any concessions to British territorial demands on behalf of their Indian allies, Adams would write with pride in his diary of this articulation of the *res nullius*, or empty land, argument, "which was afterwards useful to me at Ghent, and which after the lapse of more than twenty years I still think unanswerable."

AN

ORATION,

DELIVERED

AT

PLYMOUTH,

DECEMBER 22, 1802.

AT THE

ANNIVERSARY COMMEMORATION

OF THE

FIRST LANDING OF OUR ANCESTORS,

AT THAT PLACE.

BY **John Quincy Adams.**

[Publifhed at the requeft of the Hon. Joshua Thomas, James Thacher, and William Jackson, Efquires, the Committee of the town of *Plymouth*, by whofe defire it was publifhed.]

Ad illa mihi pro fe quifque acriter intendat animum quæ vita, qui mores fuerint ; per quos viros, quibufque artibus et partum et auctum imperium fit—Hoc illud eft præcipue in cognitione rerum falubre ac frugiferum, omnis te exempli documenta in illuftri pofita monumento intueri : inde tibi tuaeque reipublicæ quod imitere, capias.——Livy.

BOSTON,
PRINTED BY RUSSELL AND CUTLER,
1802.

ADVERTISEMENT.

THE historical facts, relative to the first settlers of the Plymouth Colony, noticed in this Discourse, are collected from the narratives in Purchas, from Prince's Chronology—from the Appendix to the second volume of Hutchinson's History, and above all from the second volume of Dr. Belknap's American Biography—a work which no American, interested in the honour of his country, can peruse without keenly feeling, as a national calamity, the stroke of death which arrested the author in the midst of his labours upon its continuation. I cannot forbear expressing here the hope, that some of the living ornaments of our literature will take up the plan which he had so successfully commenced, and make all the distinguished characters of past times on this continent, more intimately known to their posterity, than they have been hitherto.

Plymouth Oration

Among the sentiments of most powerful operation upon the human heart, and most highly honorable to the human character, are those of veneration for our forefathers, and of love for our posterity. They form the connecting links between the selfish and the social passions. By the fundamental principle of christianity the happiness of the individual is interwoven by innumerable and imperceptible ties with that of his cotemporaries: by the power of filial reverence and parental affection, individual existence is extended beyond the limits of individual life, and the happiness of every age is chained in mutual dependence upon that of every other. Respect for his ancestors excites in the breast of man, interest in their history, attachment to their characters, concern for their errors, involuntary pride in their virtues. Love for his posterity spurs him to exertion for their support, stimulates him to virtue for their example, and fills him with the tenderest solicitude for their welfare. Man, therefore, was not made for himself alone—No! He was made for his country by the obligations of the social compact: he was made for his species, by the christian duties of universal charity: he was made for all ages past by the sentiment of reverence for his forefathers; and he was made for all future times by the impulse of affection for his progeny. Under the influence of these principles, "Existence sees him spurn her bounded reign." They redeem his nature from the subjection of time and space: he is no longer a "puny insect shivering at a breeze;" he is the glory of creation—Form'd to occupy all time and all extent: bounded during his residence upon earth, only by the boundaries of the world, and destined to life and immortality in brighter regions, when the fabric of nature itself shall dissolve and perish.

The voice of history, has not in all its compass a note, but answers in unison with these sentiments. The barbarian chieftain who defended his country against the Roman invasion, driven to the remotest extremity of Britain, and stimulating his followers to battle by all that has power of persuasion upon the human heart, concludes his exhortation by an appeal to these irresistible feelings*—"Think of your forefathers and of your posterity." The Romans themselves, at the pinnacle of civilization, were actuated by the same impressions, and celebrated in anniversary festivals every great event which had signalized the annals of their forefathers. To multiply instances, where it were impossible to adduce an exception would be to waste your time and abuse your patience: but in the sacred volume which contains the substance of our firmest faith and of our most precious hopes, these passions, not only maintain their highest efficacy, but are sanctioned by the express injunctions of the Divine legislator to his chosen people.

The revolutions of time furnish no previous example of a nation, shooting up to maturity and expanding into greatness with the rapidity which has characterized the growth of the American people. In the luxuriance of youth and in the vigor of manhood it is pleasing and instructive to look backwards upon the helpless days of infancy: but in the continual and essential changes of a growing subject, the transactions of that early period would be soon obliterated from the memory, but for some periodical call of attention to aid the silent records of the historian. Such celebrations arouse and gratify the kindliest emotions of the bosom. They are faithful pledges of the respect we bear to the memory of our ancestors and of the tenderness with which we cherish the rising generation. They introduce the sages and heroes of ages past to the notice and emulation of succeeding times: they are at once testimonials of our gratitude, and schools of virtue to our children.

These sentiments are wise—they are honorable—they are virtuous—their cultivation is not merely innocent pleasure, it is incumbent duty. Obedient to their dictates, you my fellow-citizens have instituted and paid frequent observance to this annual solemnity. And what event of weightier intrinsic importance or of more extensive consequences was ever selected for this honorary distinction?

In reverting to the period of their origin, other nations have generally been compelled to plunge into the chaos of

---

* Proinde ituri in aciem, et majores vestros et posteros cogitate. *Galgacus* in Vita Agricolae.

impenetrable antiquity, or to trace a lawless ancestry into the caverns of ravishers and robbers. It is your peculiar privilege to commemorate in this birth-day of your nation, an event ascertained in its minutest details: an event of which the principal actors are known to you familiarly as if belonging to your own age: an event of a magnitude before which Imagination shrinks at the imperfection of her powers. It is your further happiness to behold in those eminent characters who were most conspicuous in accomplishing the settlement of your country, men upon whose virtues you can dwell with honest exultation. The founders of your race are not handed down to you, like the father of the Roman people, as the sucklings of a wolf. You are not descended from a nauseous compound of fanaticism and sensuality, whose only argument was the sword, and whose only paradise was a brothel. No Gothic scourge of God—No Vandal pest of nations—No fabled fugitive from the flames of Troy—No bastard Norman tyrant appears among the list of worthies who first landed on the rock, which your veneration has preserved as a lasting monument of their atchievement. The great actors of the day we now solemnize were illustrious by their intrepid valor, no less than by their christian graces; but the clarion of conquest has not blazon'd forth their names to all the winds of Heaven. Their glory has not been wafted over oceans of blood to the remotest regions of the earth. They have not erected to themselves, colossal statues upon pedestals of human bones, to provoke and insult the tardy hand of heavenly retribution. But theirs was "the better fortitude of patience and heroic martyrdom." Theirs was the gentle temper of christian kindness—the rigorous observance of reciprocal justice—the unconquerable soul of conscious integrity. Worldly Fame has been parsimonious of her favors to the memory of those generous champions. Their numbers were small—their stations in life obscure—the object of their enterprize unostentatious—the theatre of their exploits remote: how could they possibly be favorites of worldly Fame? That common crier, whose existence is only known by the assemblage of multitudes—That pander of wealth and greatness so eager to haunt the palaces of fortune, and so fastidious to the houseless dignity of virtue—that parasite of pride, ever scornful to meekness, and ever obsequious to insolent power—that heedless trumpeter, whose ears are deaf to modest merit, and whose eyes are blind to bloodless distant excellence.

When the persecuted companions of *Robinson*, exiles from their native land, anxiously sued for the privilege of removing a thousand leagues more distant to an untried soil, a rigorous climate and a savage wilderness, for the sake of reconciling their sense of religious duty with their affections for their country, few, perhaps none of them formed a conception of what would be within two centuries the result of their undertaking. When the jealous and niggardly policy of their British sovereign, denied them even that humblest of requests, and instead of liberty would barely consent to promise connivance, neither he nor they might be aware that they were laying the foundations of a power, and that he was sowing the seeds of a spirit, which in less than two hundred years would stagger the throne of his descendants, and shake his united kingdoms to the centre. So far is it from the ordinary habits of mankind to calculate the importance of events in their elementary principles, that had the first colonists of our country ever intimated as a part of their designs, the project of founding a great and mighty nation, the finger of scorn would have pointed them to the cells of bedlam, as an abode more suitable for hatching vain empires than the solitude of a transatlantic desert.

These consequences, then so little foreseen, have unfolded themselves in all their grandeur, to the eyes of the present age. It is a common amusement of speculative minds, to contrast the magnitude of the most important events with the minuteness of their primeval causes, and the records of mankind are full of examples for such contemplations. It is however a more profitable employment to trace the constituent principles of future greatness in their kernel; to detect in the acorn at our feet the germ of that majestic oak, whose roots shoot down to the centre, and whose branches aspire to the skies. Let it be then our present occupation to enquire and endeavour to ascertain, the causes first put in operation at the period of our commemoration, and already productive of such magnificent effects.—To examine with reiterated care and minute attention, the characters of those men who gave the first impulse to a new series of events in the history of the world.—To applaud and emulate those qualities of their minds which we shall find deserving of our admiration.—To recognize with candour those features which forbid approbation or even require censure, and finally, to lay alike their frailties and their perfections to our own hearts either as warning or as example.

Of the various European settlements upon this continent which have finally merged in one independent nation, the first establishments were made at various times, by several nations and under the influence of different motives. In many instances the convictions of religious obligation formed one and a powerful inducement of the adventurers; but in none, excepting the settlement at Plymouth, did they constitute the sole and exclusive actuating cause. Worldly interest and commercial speculation entered largely into the views of other settlers: but the commands of conscience were the only stimulus to the emigrants from Leyden. Previous to their expedition hither they had endured a long banishment from their native country. Under every species of discouragement they undertook the voyage—they performed it in spite of numerous and almost insuperable obstacles: they arrived upon a wilderness bound with frost and hoary with snow, without the boundaries of their charter: outcasts from all human society; and coasted five weeks together in the dead of winter, on this tempestuous shore, exposed at once to the fury of the elements, to the arrows of the native savage, and to the impending horrors of famine.

Courage and perseverance have a magical talisman, before which difficulties disappear and obstacles vanish into air. These qualities have ever been displayed in their mightiest perfection as attendants in the retinue of strong passions. From the first discovery of the western hemisphere by *Columbus*, until the settlement of Virginia, which immediately preceded that of Plymouth, the various adventurers from the antient world had exhibited, upon innumerable occasions, that ardor of enterprize and that stubbornness of pursuit, which set all danger at defiance and chain the violence of nature at their feet. But they were all instigated by personal interests—Avarice and ambition had tuned their souls to that pitch of exaltation—Selfish passions were the parents of their heroism. It was reserved for the first settlers of New-England to perform atchievements equally arduous, to trample down obstructions equally formidable to dispel dangers equally terrific under the single inspiration of conscience. To them, even liberty herself was but a subordinate and secondary consideration. They claimed exemption from the mandates of human authority, as militating with their subjection to a superior power. Before the voice of Heaven they silenced even the calls of their country.

Yet, while so deeply impressed with the sense of religious obligation, they felt in all its energy the force of that tender tie which binds the heart of every virtuous man to his native land. It was to renew that connection with their country which had been severed by their compulsory expatriation, that they resolved to face all the hazards of a perilous navigation, and all the labors of a toilsome distant settlement. Under the mild protection of the Batavian Government, they enjoyed already that freedom of religious worship for which they had resigned so many comforts and enjoyments at home: but their hearts panted for a restoration to the bosom of their country. Invited and urged by the open-hearted and truly benevolent people who had given them an asylum from the persecution of their own kindred, to form their settlement within the territories then under their jurisdiction; the love of their country predominated over every influence save that of conscience alone, and they preferred the precarious chance of relaxation from the bigoted rigor of the English Government to the certain liberality and alluring offers of the Hollanders. Observe, my countrymen, the generous patriotism, the cordial union of soul—the conscious yet unaffected vigour which beam in their application to the British Monarch—"They were well weaned from the delicate milk of their mother country, and inured to the difficulties of a strange land. They were knit together in a strict and sacred bond, to take care of the good of each other and of the whole. It was not with them as with other men, whom small things could discourage or small discontents cause to wish themselves again at home." Children of these exalted Pilgrims! Is there one among you, who can hear the simple and pathetic energy of these expressions without tenderness and admiration? Venerated shades of our forefathers! No! ye were indeed not ordinary men! That country which had ejected you so cruelly from her bosom, you still delighted to contemplate in the character of an affectionate and beloved mother. The sacred bond which knit you together was indissoluble while you lived—and oh! may it be to your descendents the example and the pledge of harmony to the latest period of time! The difficulties and dangers which so often had defeated attempts of similar establishments were unable to subdue souls tempered like yours. You heard the rigid interdictions—you saw the menacing forms of toil and danger, forbidding your access to this land of promise: but you heard without dismay—you saw and disdained retreat. Firm and undaunted in the confidence of that sacred bond—Conscious of the purity, and convinced of the importance of your motives, you put your trust in the protecting shield of Providence, and smiled defiance at the combining terrors of human malice and of elemental strife. These, in the accomplishment of your undertaking, you were summoned to encounter in their most hideous forms: these you met with that fortitude, and combated with that perseverance which you had promised in their anticipation: these you completely vanquished in establishing the foundations of New-England, and the day which we now commemorate is the perpetual memorial of your triumph.

It were an occupation, peculiarly pleasing, to cull from our early historians and exhibit before you, every detail of this transaction. To carry you in imagination on board their bark at the first moment of her arrival in the bay—to accompany *Carver*, *Winslow*, *Bradford* and *Standish*, in all their excursions upon the desolate coast—to follow them into every rivulet and creek where they endeavoured to find a firm footing, and to fix with a pause of delight and exultation the instant when the first of these heroic adventurers alighted on the spot where you, their descendants, now enjoy the glorious and happy reward of their labors. But in this grateful task, your former orators on this Anniversary have anticipated all that the most ardent industry could collect, and gratified all that the most inquisitive curiosity could desire. To you, my friends, every occurrence of that momentous period is already familiar. A transient allusion to a few characteristic incidents which mark the peculiar history of the Plymouth settlers, may properly supply the place of a narrative, which to this auditory must be superfluous.

One of these remarkable incidents is the execution of that instrument of Government by which they formed themselves into a body-politic, the day after their arrival upon the coast, and previous to their first landing. This is perhaps the only instance, in human history, of that positive, original social compact, which speculative philosophers have imagined as the only legitimate source of government. Here was a unanimous and personal assent by all the individuals of the community, to the association by which they became a nation. It was the result of circumstances and discussions, which had occurred during their passage from Europe, and is a full demonstration that the nature of civil government, abstracted from the political institutions of their native country, had been an object of their serious meditation. The settlers of all the former European Colonies had contented themselves with the powers conferred upon them by their respective charters, without looking beyond the seal of the royal parchment for the measure of their rights, and the rule of their duties. The founders of Plymouth had been impelled by the peculiarities of their situation to examine the subject with deeper and more comprehensive research. After twelve years of banishment from the land of their first allegiance, during which they had been under an adoptive and temporary subjection to another sovereign, they must naturally have been led to reflect upon the relative rights and duties of allegiance and subjection. They had resided in a city, the seat of an university, where the polemical and political controversies of the time were pursued with uncommon fervour. In this period they had witnessed the deadly struggle between the two parties, into which the people of the United Province, after their separation from the crown of Spain, had divided themselves. The contest embraced within its compass not only theological doctrines, but political principles, and *Maurice* and *Barnevelt* were the temporal leaders of the same rival factions, of which *Episcopius* and *Polyander*, were the ecclesiastical champions. That the investigation of the fundamental principles of government was deeply implicated in these dissensions is evident from the immortal work of *Grotius*, upon the rights of war and peace, which undoubtedly originated from them. *Grotius* himself had been a most distinguished actor and sufferer in those important scenes of internal convulsion, and his work was first published* very shortly after the departure of our

---

* In 1625.

forefathers from Leyden. It is well known, that in the course of the contest, Mr. *Robinson* more than once appeared, with credit to himself as a public disputant against *Episcopius*; and from the manner in which the fact is related by Governor *Bradford*, it is apparent that the whole English church at Leyden took a zealous interest in the religious part of the controversy. As strangers in the land it is presumable that they wisely and honorably avoided entangling themselves in the political contentions involved with it. Yet the theoretic principles, as they were drawn into discussion, could not fail to arrest their attention, and must have assisted them to form accurate ideas concerning the origin and extent of authority among men, independent of positive institutions. The importance of these circumstances will not be duly weighed without taking into consideration the state of opinions then prevalent in England. The general principles of government were there little understood and less examined. The whole substance of human authority was centered in the simple doctrine of royal prerogative, the origin of which was always traced in theory to divine institution. Twenty years later the subject was more industriously sifted, and for half a century became one of the principal topics of controversy between the ablest and most enlightened men in the nation. The instrument of voluntary association executed on board the *Mayflower*, testifies that the parties to it had anticipated the improvement of their nation.

Another incident from which we may derive occasion for important reflections, was the attempt of these original settlers to establish among them that community of goods and of labor which fanciful politicians, from the days of *Plato* to those of *Rousseau*, have recommended as the fundamental law of a perfect republic. This theory results, it must be acknowledged, from principles of reasoning most flattering to the human character. If industry, frugality and disinterested integrity, were alike the virtues of all, there would apparently be more of the social spirit, in making all property a common stock, and giving to each individual a proportional title to the wealth of the whole. Such is the basis upon which *Plato* forbids in his republic the division of property. Such is the system upon which *Rousseau* pronounces the first man who enclosed a field with a fence and said *this is mine*, a traitor to the human species. A wiser and more useful philosophy however directs us to consider man, according to the nature in which he was formed; subject to infirmities, which no wisdom can remedy; to weaknesses which no institution can strengthen; to vices which no legislation can correct. Hence it becomes obvious, that separate property is the natural and indisputable right of separate exertion—that community of goods without community of toil is oppressive and unjust; that it counteracts the laws of nature, which prescribe, that he only who sows the seed shall reap the harvest: that it discourages all energy by destroying its rewards; and makes the most virtuous and active members of society, the slaves and drudges of the worst. Such was the issue of this experiment among our forefathers, and the same event demonstrated the error of the system in the elder settlement of Virginia. Let us cherish that spirit of harmony, which prompted our forefathers to make the attempt, under circumstances more favorable to its success than perhaps ever occurred upon earth. Let us no less admire the candor with which they relinquished it, upon discovering its irremediable inefficacy. To found principles of government upon too advantageous an estimate of the human character, is an error of inexperience, the source of which is so amiable, that it is impossible to censure it with severity. We have seen the same mistake, committed in our own age, and upon a larger theatre. Happily for our ancestors their situation allowed them to repair it, before its effects had proved destructive. They had no pride of vain philosophy to support, no perfidious rage of faction to glut, by persevering in their mistakes until they should be extinguished in torrents of blood.

As the attempt to establish among themselves the community of goods was a seal of that sacred bond which knit them so closely together, so the conduct they observed towards the natives of the country, displays their stedfast adherence to the rules of justice, and their faithful attachment to those of benevolence and charity.

No European settlement ever formed upon this continent has been more distinguished for undeviating kindness and equity towards the savages. There are indeed moralists, who have questioned the right of the Europeans to intrude upon the possessions of the aboriginals in any case, and under any limitations whatsoever. But have they maturely considered the whole subject? The Indian right of possession itself stands with regard to the greatest part of the country, upon a questionable foundation. Their cultivated fields; their constructed habitations; a space of ample sufficiency for their subsistence, and whatever they had annexed to themselves by personal labor, was undoubtedly by the laws of nature theirs. But what is the right of a huntsman to the forest of a thousand miles over which he has accidentally ranged in quest of prey? Shall the liberal bounties of Providence to the race of man be monopolized by one of ten thousand for whom they were created? Shall the exuberant bosom of the common mother, amply adequate to the nourishment of millions, be claimed exclusively by a few hundreds of her offspring? Shall the lordly savage not only disdain the virtues and enjoyments of civilization himself, but shall he controul the civilization of a world? Shall he forbid the wilderness to blossom like the rose? Shall he forbid the oaks of the forest to fall before the axe of industry, and rise again, transformed into the habitations of ease and elegance? Shall he doom an immense region of the globe to perpetual desolation, and to hear the howlings of the tyger and the wolf, silence for ever the voice of human gladness? Shall the fields and the vallies, which a beneficent God has formed to teem with the life of innumerable multitudes, be condemned to everlasting barrenness? Shall the mighty rivers poured out by the hands of nature, as channels of communication between numerous nations, roll their waters in sullen silence and eternal solitude to the deep? Have hundreds of commodious harbours, a thousand leagues of coast, and a boundless ocean been spread in the front of this land, and shall every purpose of utility to which they could apply be prohibited by the tenant of the woods? No, generous philanthropists! Heaven has not been thus inconsistent in the works of its hands! Heaven has not thus placed at irreconcileable strife, its moral laws with its physical creation! The Pilgrims of Plymouth obtained their right of possession to the territory on which they settled by titles as fair and unequivocal as any human property can be held. By their voluntary association they recognized their allegiance to the government of Britain; and in process of time received whatever powers and authorities could be conferred upon them by a Charter from their Sovereign. The spot on which they fixed had belonged to an Indian tribe, totally extirpated by that devouring pestilence which had swept the country, shortly before their arrival. The territory thus free from all exclusive possession, they might have taken by the natural right of occupancy. Desirous however of giving ample satisfaction to every pretence of prior right, by formal and solemn conventions with the chiefs of the neighboring tribes, they acquired the further security of a purchase. At their hands the children of the desert had no cause of complaint. On the great day of retribution, what thousands, what millions of the American race will appear at the bar of judgment to arraign their European invading conquerors! Let us humbly hope that the fathers of the Plymouth Colony will then appear in the whiteness of innocence. Let us indulge the belief that they will not only be free from all accusation of injustice to these unfortunate sons of nature, but that the testimonials of their acts of kindness and benevolence towards them will plead the cause of their virtues as they are now authenticated by the records of history upon earth.

Religious discord has lost her sting: the cumbrous weapons of theological warfare are antiquated: the field of politics supplies the alchymists of our times, with materials of more fatal explosion, and the butchers of mankind no longer travel to another world for instruments of cruelty and destruction. Our age is too enlightened to contend upon topics, which concern only the interests of eternity; and men who hold in proper contempt all controversies about trifles, except such as inflame their own passions, have made it a common-place censure against your ancestors, that their zeal was enkindled by subjects of trivial importance; and that however aggrieved by the intolerance of others, they were alike intolerant themselves. Against these objections, your candid judgment will not require an unqualified justification; but your respect and gratitude for the founders of the state may boldly claim an ample apology. The original grounds of their separation from the church of England, were not objects of a magnitude to dissolve the bonds of communion—much less those of charity, between christian bretheren of the same essential principles. Some of them however were not inconsiderable, and numerous inducements concurred to give them an extraordinary interest in their eyes. When that portentous system of abuses, the Papal dominion, was overturned, a great variety of religious sects arose in its stead, in the several countries which for many centuries before had been screwed beneath its subjection. The fabric of the reformation, first undertaken in England upon a contracted basis, by a capricious and sanguinary tyrant, had been successively overthrown and restored, renewed and altered according to the varying humours and principles of four successive monarchs. To ascertain the precise point of division between the genuine institutions of christianity, and the corruptions accumulated upon them in the progress of fifteen centuries, was found a task of extreme difficulty throughout the christian world. Men of the profoundest learning, of the sublimest genius, and of the purest integrity, after devoting their lives to the research, finally differed in their ideas upon many great points both of doctrine and discipline. The main question, it was admitted on all hands, most intimately concerned the highest interests of man, both temporal and eternal. Can we wonder, that men who felt their happiness here and their hopes of hereafter, their worldly welfare and the kingdom of Heaven at stake, should sometimes attach an importance beyond their intrinsic weight to collateral points of controversy, connected with the all-involving object of the reformation? The changes in the forms and principles of religious worship, were introduced and regulated in England by the hand of public authority. But that hand had not been uniform or steady in its operations. During the persecutions inflicted in the interval of Popish restoration under the reign of Mary, upon all who favored the reformation, many of the most zealous reformers had been compelled to fly their country. While residing on the continent of Europe, they had adopted the principles of the most complete and rigorous reformation, as taught and established by *Calvin*. On returning afterwards to their native country they were dissatisfied with the partial reformation, at which, as they conceived, the English establishment had rested, and claiming the privileges of private conscience, upon which alone any departure from the church of Rome could be justified, they insisted upon the right of adhering to the system of their own preference, and of course upon that of non-conformity to the establishment prescribed by the royal authority. The only means used to convince them of error, and reclaim them from dissent, was force, and force served but to confirm the opposition it was meant to suppress. By driving the founders of the Plymouth Colony into exile, it constrained them to absolute separation from the church of England, and by the refusal afterwards to allow them a positive toleration even in this American wilderness, the council of *James the First* rendered that separation irreconcileable. Viewing their religious liberties here, as held only upon sufferance, yet bound to them by all the ties of conviction, and by all their sufferings for them, could they forbear to look upon every dissenter among themselves with a jealous eye? Within two years after their landing they beheld a rival settlement* attempted in their immediate neighbourhood; and not long after the laws of self preservation compelled them to break up a nest of revellers,† who boasted of protection from the mother country, and who had recurred to the easy but pernicious resource of feeding their wanton idleness by furnishing the savages with the means, the skill and the instruments of European destruction. Toleration in that instance would have been self-murder, and many other examples might be alledged in which their necessary measures of self-defence have been exaggerated into cruelty, and their most indispensible precautions distorted into persecution. Yet shall we not pretend that they were exempt from the common laws of mortality, or entirely free from all the errors of their age. Their zeal might sometimes be too ardent, but it was always sincere. At this day religious indulgence is one of our clearest duties, because it is one of our undisputed rights. While we rejoice that the principles of genuine christianity have so far triumphed over the prejudices of a former generation, let us fervently hope for the day when it will prove equally victorious over the malignant passions of our own.

In thus calling to your attention some of the peculiar features in the principles, the character, and the history of your forefathers, it is as wide from my design, as I know it would be from your approbation, to adorn their memory with a chaplet plucked from the domain of others. The occasion and the day are more peculiarly devoted to them, but let it never be dishonored with a contracted and exclusive spirit.

---

* *Weston's* Plantation at Wessagusset.
† *Morton,* and his party at Mount Wollaston.

Our affections as citizens embrace the whole extent of the Union, and the names of *Raleigh, Smith, Winthrop, Calvert, Penn,* and *Oglethorpe,* excite in our minds recollections equally pleasing, and gratitude equally fervent with those of *Carver* and *Bradford.* Two centuries have not yet elapsed since the first European foot touched the soil which now constitutes the American union—Two centuries more and our numbers must exceed those of Europe herself. The destinies of this empire, as they appear in prospect before us, disdain the powers of human calculation. Yet, as the original founder of the Roman State is said once to have lifted upon his shoulders the fame and fortunes of all his posterity, so let us never forget that the glory and greatness of all our descendants is in our hands. Preserve in all their purity, refine if possible from all their alloy, those virtues which we this day commemorate as the ornament of our forefathers—Adhere to them with inflexible resolution, as to the horns of the altar; instill them with unwearied perseverance into the minds of your children; bind your souls and theirs to the national union as the chords of life are centred in the heart, and you shall soar with rapid and steady wing to the summit of human glory. Nearly a century ago, one of those rare minds* to whom it is given to discern future greatness in its seminal principles, upon contemplating the situation of this continent, pronounced in a vein of poetic inspiration,

"Westward the Star of empire takes its way."

Let us all unite in ardent supplications to the founder of nations and the builder of worlds, that what then was prophecy may continue unfolding into history—that the dearest hopes of the human race may not be extinguished in disappointment, and that the last may prove the noblest empire of time.

---

* Bishop *Berkeley.*

Erratum.—In the title page, the last word of the notice, respecting the request of the Committee of the town of Plymouth, should be *delivered*, instead of "published."

"THE DEEPEST AND MOST DANGEROUS MATTER"

6. "Serious Reflections, Addressed to the Citizens of Massachusetts" (Letters of Publius Valerius, I–V) *The Repertory* (Boston: October 26–November 16, 1804).

Federalists in Massachusetts led an opposition to the Jefferson administration that was both partisan and sectional. Their disaffection was intensified dramatically by the Louisiana Purchase, which threatened to dilute the weight of New England (frequently referred to as "the commercial states") in the national councils. Adams, who had been elected to the U.S. Senate by the Massachusetts legislature in 1803, did not arrive in Washington in time to vote on the Purchase itself, but he was the lone Federalist senator to vote both for admitting the territory and against limiting slavery in Louisiana. Adams's anxious fellow Federalists quickly perceived that his attitudes dovetailed with Jeffersonian expansionism. And they weren't much consoled by his repeated assertions that a U.S. senator should seek to represent the interests of entire nation as well as those of his state.

Asked by the Massachusetts legislature to sponsor a constitutional amendment (the Ely amendment, named for a member of that body) to eliminate the three-fifths clause, which would lessen the rising advantage that slave states could count on in the House of Representatives, Adams wrote a speech but did not actually deliver it on the Senate floor. Instead, he developed it into this highly charged series of letters, published under the name Publius Valerius in the Boston *Repertory*, and timed to influence the fall elections. He comes out swinging, with a partisan attack on the slim achievements of the Jefferson administration and the corrupt motives of its supporters in the Commonwealth, which he calls "the Virginian faction." Adams ridicules these Bay Staters (particularly Boston Republican Perez Morton) who heaped adulation on Jefferson and gave him credit for achievements that rightly belonged to the administration of Jefferson's predecessor.

Adams then weighs the effects of the Louisiana Purchase in the sectional balance, as he does a scheme to change the mode of choosing presidential electors to employ district voting so that Jefferson would reap some electors in the state. All these actions, designed to consolidate the Republicans' hold on power, raise the central question for Adams: "whether this excessive southern preponderance will be enjoyed with moderation, or used with generosity." These installments set up the final, and not coincidentally the longest, of the letters, which is a structural analysis of slaveholders' political power, and an argument for constitutional adjustment in a union designed to be permanent. By seeking an end to the proportional representation of enslaved people and positing it in terms of fairness and the original intentions of the founders of the republic to preserve sectional balance, Adams seeks a middle ground between partisanship and nationality. A constitutional amendment restoring balance to taxation as well as representation, he argues, is the key to preserving the union.

This series reveals Adams's developing thinking about the politics of slavery, and his increasing ambivalence about partisanship, something that was not going unnoticed. As a senator, he wasn't really pleasing anyone. By year's end, Adams would conclude in his diary, not without some reason, that "my political Prospects, have been daily declining."

Letters of Publius Valerius

No. I.

As the time is approaching when the People of this Commonwealth will be called to give their suffrages for electors of President and Vice President of the United States, and also of members for the National House of Representatives, it is of importance to them to fix the principles which ought to govern them in their choice. Candidates of various descriptions and of militating political sentiments will be held up to their view, and recommended to their suffrages, by the friends of the past and the partizans of the present administration of the General Government. It is not my intention to advocate or to oppose the election of any individual, but as a sincere friend to the interests of my country, to submit some observations to my fellow citizens, concerning the principles to which I believe their own interest directs them, for the determination of their votes, between the several claimants to their favour.

The government of the United States is to be considered in a two fold view. First as an association of the People, and Secondly as a confederation of the States which constitute the North American Union. The representation of the States is in the Senate, and that of the People in the House of Representatives. The duties of the members of those respective branches of the general Legislature are correspondent to the stations in which they are placed. And consequently it behoves every Senator to support and maintain the interests of the State, by which he is delegated; as it is incumbent on the Representatives to promote with a warm and honest zeal those of the People by whom he was elected. I shall not be understood as meaning to say that the Senator for any State, or the Representative from any section of the People, ought so exclusively to pursue the interests of his immediate Constituents, as to wish that those of the whole union or of any other part of it should be sacrificed to them; but that he should so far be devoted to those from whom he derives his powers, as on no consideration whatsoever to suffer their just interests to be sacrificed to the partial views and purposes of others. Addressing then the People of Massachusetts, I trust they will feel the force of the argument, when I say; fellow citizens, in choosing your Representatives, be sure to choose men, who will support your own Interests. Those of other parts of the Union, you may be assured will be sufficiently represented and supported without your assistance. The People of Virginia will not choose Representatives, who will abandon their interests for the sake of advancing yours; you cannot expect or wish that they should; let it be your care on your part to elect men, who shall have no bias on their minds, the tendency of which will be to prostrate your legitimate rights at the feet of Virginian policy.

Since the first association of the United Colonies, at the dawn of the American Revolution, there never has been a time, when it so essentially imported to the People of Massachusetts to make reflections like these, and to act conformably to them. During the war of the revolution and the first confederation, Massachusetts was among the first in support of the common cause. The treasures and the blood of her citizens freely flowed for the benefit of the Union, while afflicted with the miseries of War. After the Peace, she exhibited in an eminent degree, the same enlarged and liberal spirit. She readily complied with the requisitions of Congress for raising funds to discharge the obligations of the publick faith, and actually taxed herself by commercial regulations, until she found she was only raising rival, and less generous neighbours upon her own ruins. At the formation and adoption of the present or rather the *late* National Constitution, her conciliatory spirit, and willingness to yield much for the general good was equally conspicuous— Equally conspicuous have they been during the administration of that government, and while she has uniformly borne, more than her proportion of all the burdens, she has been content to share, at most, her equal part of the blessings derived from it. But neither under the old confederation, nor under the Constitution of 1787, had she ever, until very recently, a formidable party within her own bosom, whose systematick policy it was to make her peculiar interests a sacrifice to those of another quarter of the Union. The members of her own Legislature, and her delegations to the national Councils have been Massachusetts Men, who felt it their duty to support by all fair and honourable means the measures most favourable to her interests, and who would have thought it treachery of the deepest dye to make themselves the servile instruments of a policy, directly hostile to their own constituents—now, however, this singular phenomenon has appeared: and at the late session of the General Court, the most unequivocal proof has been exhibited, of a strong party, who build all their hopes of success upon the basis of unlimited devotion to a system, the first feature of which, is the annihilation of New England's weight and influence in the Union.

It is painful to be under the necessity of stating this fact.—It is painful to remark to what extremes faction and ambition have already proceeded in this Country—But it cannot be disguised and ought not to be concealed. It is not possible to believe that this subserviency to foreign views, and this immolation of their own interests have reached the mass of the People—The mass of the People have no private and selfish purposes to answer by recommending themselves to the favour of the National Executive—They have no offices to obtain from the removal of honest able and faithful federalists—They have no reward in prospect from the prostration of personal or political antagonists—They therefore have no motive to betray themselves.—If then it be made manifest to them, that a numerous and closely combined party of the men in whom they have placed their confidence, have, whether from personal or from factious motives, surrendered themselves up without reserve to a political system in direct hostility to the fair and just interests of the people, whom they represent, the danger that impends will be fully disclosed, and the effectual guard against it will be seasonably applied—The confidence which has been betrayed will be transferred, from hollow professions, to solid merit; from fawning flattery, to honest zeal; from selfish faction, to pure patriotism; and Massachusetts will recover that weight and influence in the Union, which some of her own sons have unblushingly attempted to wrest from her.

I am aware that assertions like these ought not to be made on light grounds. In the ardour of political controversy it is but too common to see men entertain unjust and unwarrantable suspicions of their adversaries, and impute to them motives, which are not theirs. So long as the party in this Commonwealth, in opposition to the present administration of its government kept within the bounds of decency and moderation, nay, so long as they were gratified, by the arts of popular courtship to blazon their own pretensions to favour, and to run down opponents, whose publick merits and private virtues could never suffer by comparison with their own, however ungenerous and censurable their procedure, its effects were not immediately pernicious and dangerous to their country. When at one of our annual periods of election, their heaviest engine of detraction, against the Governour of the Commonwealth, was a charge of carriage hire for attendance at a funeral; when at another their most elaborate topick of reproach, was *the rent of the Province House*, their patriotick economies were estimated at their just value; their slanders were even productive of good effects, for when complaints like these were dwelt upon, with the choicest of their bitterness, the evidence was irresistible, that no reasonable ground for complaint existed. But when from the circulation of petty calumny against the Governour, they proceeded to hold assault upon the clearest and most important interests of the State, when after spending their most envenomed arrows, in fruitless efforts against individual virtue, they selected their last shaft to aim at the vitals of their country, it became the duty of every real friend to that country to resist, and expose them.

At the late session of the Legislature, three occasions happened when the party in opposition to the present Administration of the Commonwealth, discovered their unqualified devotion to the interests of Virginia, or rather to the views of Mr. Jefferson. The first, was a motion for making certain additions to the answer of the House to the Governour's Speech. The object of this was personal adulation to the President of the United States. The second was the vehement opposition and indecent protests against the choice of electors, for President, and Vice President, by a General Ticket. And the third was the struggle against the motion of Mr. Ely, for instructing the Senators of the Commonwealth in Congress, to propose an amendment to the National Constitution, for the purpose of correcting that humiliating inequality which gives a representation to the slave-holding Southern Planters, nearly double to that of the Massachusetts Farmer. On each of these transactions I shall submit to the publick, remarks, which will tend to elucidate the motives in which the conduct of the opposition party originated. I shall examine the arguments alledged by themselves, and endeavour to point out the difference between their outward practice, and their real purposes.—After the lessons of experience which have so recently been taught to all true Republicans by the terrible example of the French Revolution and its last catastrophe, the people of Massachusetts, turning an eye upon themselves, have the deepest interests to inquire, what are the real designs of that party, which has always held up the Revolution as the theme of their highest admiration and applause.

PUBLIUS VALERIUS.

No. II.

WHEN the answer of the House of Representatives of the Commonwealth, to the Governour's speech, at the opening of the last session, was in debate before the House, a long panegyrick upon the present administration of the National Government was moved by Mr. Perez Morton, of Dorchester, to be inserted in the answer, by way of amendment.—Mr. Morton both in the motion upon which I am about to remark, and in the other party measures of the session assumed exclusively the lead in the House of Representatives; the stability of his political opinions, their character and their tendency, are of no small importance as indications of the views which actuate him and his followers.

Mr. Morton, of late years has been a very ardent partizan, of that political denomination among us who by a manoeuvre borrowed from France, the prototype of all their party tacticks, and suggested to them in the famous intercepted letter of Fauchet the minister of Robespierre in this country, affect exclusively to style themselves *Republicans.*

Mr. Morton is of course a profound admirer of the sublime virtues and stupendous talents of Mr. Jefferson, whose tender sympathies for the French Revolution have been so perfectly congenial with his own—this admiration he has more than once anxiously endeavoured to communicate to the Legislature of Massachusetts. In the January session of 1802, he laboured with the burden of his admiration so much, that he attempted to bring it forth in the form of an *Address,* to the President of the United States—and not having at that time any of the topicks for approbation which he has now chosen to specify, he was at no loss for others equally well founded—at that time the principal atchievements of Mr. Jefferson's administration had been, the repayment of Callender's fine; the nolle prosequi, to screen Duane from punishment—the squandered thousands upon the Berceau; the dismission of numerous honest, capable, and faithful servants of the publick, to make way for their counterparts of an opposite sect; and above all the comment upon the inaugural speech, in the answer to the merchants of New Haven—the destruction of the federal Judiciary was resolved, but not then accomplished. Still Mr. Morton, had no dearth of materials for his address, and could he have persuaded a majority of his fellow legislators, to participate in his zeal, was even then, no less than at present, ready

"To crook the pregnant hinges of the knee.
Where thrift might follow fawning."—

The two succeeding winters, Mr. Morton has past at the city of Washington, as a humble solicitor to Mr. Jefferson and his administration, for simple justice, in a private concern, without being able to obtain it—he is personally interested in what has been called the Yazoo purchase of Georgia Lands; and has been employed by the other proprietors as their agent to support their claims upon the Government of the United States.—The last winter, after having been fed with airy promises year after year, and after a majority of the National House of Representatives had decided that these claimants ought to be indemnified, behold, Mr. John Randolph came out with a string of Resolutions, the purpose of which was to declare that no such indemnity should be given, and Mr. Thomas Randolph,

Mr. Jefferson's son in law, in a speech highly celebrated for its eloquence, the only speech he made during the whole session, supported the principles of his namesake.

It was observed by Voltaire, that in his time, the Parisian Courtiers were in the constant practice, of riding Post haste to Versailles, to receive buffetings, which, Post haste, they went back to return at Paris—just so it appears to be with Mr. Morton, he goes annually to Washington, to ask justice for himself and others—he implores it as a favour, and it is denied; but he abates not a jot of heart and hope. Mr. Jefferson he knows favours his claim, though Mr. Jefferson's son in law, reserves all the thunders of his eloquence to oppose it; another winter Mr. John Randolph's influence may be diminished in the House of Representatives; or perhaps his docility to private lessoning may become such that he will withdraw his opposition—so Mr. Morton comes home; perseveres in his admiration of Mr. Jefferson, with unabating fervour; and returns the buffetings he received at the Federal city, in offencive reflections upon the majority in the Massachusetts Legislature.

Let us now turn from the mover to the motion. As in the former we find certain sources of devotion to Mr. Jefferson and a Virginian policy, other than those of publick spirit, so in the latter we shall find causes of admiration alledged distinguishable by a similar remoteness from the fountains of truth—in short Mr. Morton appears to be gifted with the endowment of the great Mc'Fingal—he sees what is not to be seen.

The first assertion which evinces this sharpness of his opticks, is that which he has chosen to place in the front of his commendations. "That the general government, without the aid of direct taxes and burthensome excises have effected an important diminution of the publick debt by the appropriation of seven million of dollars annually to that object."

1. It is not true that the general government has appropriated seven millions of dollars annually to the diminution of the publick debt.

2. It is not true that the portion of the old debts of the United States which they have discharged was paid off by them without the aid of direct taxes and excise.

3. It is not true that the general government, under the present administration, has effected *any* diminution of the publick debt. On the contrary they have effected a very great addition to it.

Here then are no less than three mistakes in point of fact committed by Mr. Morton at the threshold of his *plausive tale*. Mistakes which it is much easier for me than for him to account for his having committed.

I know very well that in all the newspapers and party publications of the faction, for these two years, the falsehood has been perpetually repeated in the teeth of detection, that seven millions annually were appropriated to pay off the principal of the publick debt. It is also known that on the 29th of April 1802, an act of Congress passed, the *title* of which affirmed that it made provision for the payment of the *whole* of the publick debt; but if Mr. Morton in the heat of his affection for the present national order of things, will take upon trust, newspaper falsehoods, or the titles of acts of Congress, he must not expect that the people of Massachusetts will be equally credulous or equally obsequious.

By the act of 29th April 1802. The annual sum of seven millions three hundred thousand dollars was vested in the commissioners of the sinking fund, "to be applied by them to the payment of *interest* and charges, and to the reimbursement or redemption of the principal of the publick debt." and in this sum are included all the appropriations which had before that time been made towards effecting the same purpose.

Now in the first place, appropriations had been made under the former administrations for the regular payment of all the interest and for the reimbursement of the greater part of the principal of the debt. The repayment for example of the old six per cents, and deferred stock, had been going on for years before this act of 29th April was made. The appropriation of seven millions then, was little or nothing else than renewing provisions which had already been made.

And secondly, of this appropriation, a large portion being applied to pay the *interest* of the debt, could have no effect to diminish the debt itself; since the interest might be paid to the end of time without any diminution of the debt.

If seven millions annually, had been appropriated to the *diminution* of the publick debt, it must of course have followed that in the course of two years since the appropriation was made, fourteen millions of dollars would have been paid off.

But the President of the United States in his message to Congress at the opening of their last session, states that the amount of debt paid in one year preceding was "about three millions one hundred thousand dollars," and in two years "more than eight millions and an half." A great part of this had been paid before the act of 29th April 1802, and consequently was provided for before the pretended annual appropriation of seven millions.

And by the report of the commissioners of the sinking fund, made on the 6th day of February last, it appears that of these boasted seven millions, nearly five millions during each of the years 1802 and 1803 were paid "on account of the reimbursement and interest of the *domestick funded debt*," under provisions enacted long before Mr. Jefferson's administration commenced.

With what face then can it be said that under his administration, the general government has appropriated seven millions annually to the diminution of the publick debt?

But whatever the amount may be of the national debt, discharged by the present Administration, it has not been effected *without the aid of direct taxes or excise.*

As a proof of this, Mr. Morton, please to look to the official account of receipts and expenditures of the United States for the year 1802, and you will find upwards of six hundred thousand dollars in the course of that year received into the Treasury from the produce of the internal taxes, the principal part of which were excises, and upwards of two hundred thousand dollars from the direct tax.—Here then is nearly a million of dollars, which in the year 1802 aided towards the payment of the national debt. Will you tell us, that you only meant to say the present Administration had renounced the aid of excise and direct taxes *for the future*? Then I reply that you meant one thing and said another.—Your assertion was, that the general government *had*, without the aid of direct taxes or excise effected an important diminution of the publick debt— But they have not even renounced this aid for the future. In the last report of the Secretary of the Treasury to Congress on the finances, made the 24th of October last, he estimates the arrears of the direct tax then due at two hundred and fifty thousand, and the outstanding internal duties, at near four hundred thousand dollars; here then is upwards of half a million, depended upon as future aid from excise and direct tax to discharge the debt. I appeal to official documents, and I defy you Mr. Morton to point out any sense in which this part of your assertion was founded in truth.

But further—It is not true that the present Administration has effected any diminution of the national debt at all—On the contrary they have added largely to it.

Let us take the President's statement as correct, and set down eight millions and an half of the debt existing when he came into office as paid—But of new debt contracted we must charge nearly three millions, payable by a convention with Great Britain, and fifteen millions for the Louisiana purchase. So for eight millions and an half redeemed, we have nearly eighteen millions of accumulation, and the whole debt of the United States, which at the accession of Mr. Jefferson amounted to about seventy-five, now exceeds eighty-five millions of dollars. We shall find Mr. Morton soon making this very purchase of Louisiana, one of his motives for applause; *his* willing admiration flies with equal alacrity to greet the aggravation or the aleviation of the publick burden.—The value or the hardness of the bargain has however no relation whatever to the relative amount of publick debt. That subject will be separately treated. Mr. Morton very well knew that Louisiana had saddled this Union with fifteen millions of additional debt—He knew or ought to know, that to pay the *interest*, on a part of it, seven hundred thousand dollars a year, *raised from the duties on imports and tonnage*, are appropriated, and vested in those very Commissioners of the sinking fund, who are the Trustees of his glorious seven millions; and he is now requested in support of his own credit, to show any possible sense in which it can consistently with truth be said that the present Administration has *effected a diminution* of the publick debt.

PUBLIUS VALERIUS.

No. III.

FROM the peculiar stress with which Mr. Morton dwelt upon the first article of his intended panegyric in upon the general government, it is fair to presume that he considered the others as less important in themselves, or less calculated to produce the impression he intended; and I shall therefore bestow less time in commenting upon them. The reduction of the army to a peace establishment, was indeed a thing which on the complete restoration of peace, would have followed, of course, under any administration. The work had been chiefly accomplished before Mr. Jefferson's elevation, and in all probability this subject would have slept in peace, but for the opportunity it afforded of hoisting in that ingenious execration against standing armies in time of peace, a *sentiment,* the justice of which I shall not contest, any more than the propriety of its expression in any commendation of Mr. Jefferson.

But when the disposition of our naval force, and the Barbary War are held up as objects of glory to our general government, whatever our candour or our desire to approve may be, we struggle to applaud in vain, and however reluctantly, must say, that in the sycophant we lose sight, utterly lose sight of the American. What can be meant by the assertion that we have *dictated* terms of peace to *some* of the Barbary powers, and *rendered harmless* the hostility of others? I say not, to what some, but to what *one* of the Barbary powers have we dictated terms of peace. The treaty between us and the Emperour of Morocco, was broken by one of his cruisers, which captured an American vessel. By a fortunate accident, and not by any previous disposition by the government of our naval force, one of our frigates met and captured the Moorish cruiser and her prize. The Emperour of Morocco, disavowed the act of hostility committed by his cruiser; we restored to him, without indemnity or satisfaction, two of his ships which we had in our possession, and are taxed to pay the captors of those same ships their prize money, for taking them, amounting to one half their value.

The statement is not made for the purpose of censuring any part of the proceedings of the general government in relation to the Emperour of Morocco. Our Seamen were very justly entitled to the prize money for their captures. But the simple fact is that the people of the United States have paid many thousand dollars, and restored two armed ships; for what? why, for the Emperour of Morocco to disavow the violation of his Treaty with us? Is this dictating terms of Peace?

But further—The whole of these transactions, excepting the provision for the payment of the prize money, took place without a single disposition of the general government concerning it. The violation of the treaty, the capture of the Moorish ships, the disavowal of the Emperour, and the restoration of his cruisers to him, all took place before the government had a suspicion of a rupture with Morocco. Undoubtedly the most honourable credit is due to the Captains Bainbridge and Rogers and their gallant companions, for the capture of the Moorish ships; and their restoration by the Consul, Mr. Simpson, to obtain the recognition of the old Treaty, was as the President justly styles it "temperate and correct conduct." But it must be a braggart temper indeed which can boast of *such* an accommodation, as dictating terms of peace.

If this idle rodomontade is a reflection upon the modesty of the nation, the other part of the assertion, that the general government has *rendered harmless* the hostility of other Barbary powers, is an insult upon the calamities of our countrymen. What! when by the hostilities of the very meanest of those powers we have lost one of the best frigates in the navy. When her brave commander, and four hundred of our fellow citizens are languishing in captivity at Tripoli, are we to be told that their chains are rivetted by harmless hostilities? When nearly a million of dollars a year have just been added to the burdens upon our commerce, for a *Mediterranean fund*, to support the dispositions now first made of an efficient armament against those paltry pirates, is it a time to talk of having rendered their hostilities harmless? We read of the Emperour Caligula, that he made a triumphal entry at Rome, because he had picked up cockle shells on the beach of the German ocean; Mr. Morton improves upon the ideas of Caligula, and goes to the dungeons of Africa, to pluck laurels for the brows of Mr. Jefferson.

Of the purchase of Louisiana, I shall not now undertake to discuss the policy. That it is a great and important feature of Mr. Jefferson's administration is unquestionably true. Whether it will prove a blessing or a curse to this Union, it is only future time that can determine. Thus much we know, that the price of the purchase will be paid almost entirely by the Eastern and Atlantick states—thus much we know that when admitted as members of the Union, the whole weight and power of the purchased territories will be thrown into the scale of southern and western influence. In the relative situation of the United States, New England and the Maritime States, have been constantly declining in power and consequence; they must continue to decline in proportion as the growth of the southern and western parts shall be more rapid than theirs—This vibration of the centre of power, being founded in nature cannot be resisted, and as good citizens it is our duty to acquiesce in the event; but to this increasing ascendency of the south and west, the acquisition of Louisiana adds an immense force, never contemplated in the original compact of these states. We are still to learn whether this excessive southern preponderance will be enjoyed with moderation or used with generosity—should it prove otherwise, and the present symptoms are by no means favourable, the people of America will have no cause to thank Mr. Jefferson for his Louisiana bargain. New England particularly, the dupe of her own good nature, will find that she has been made to bear the charge of aggrandizing a rival interest, for the degradation of her own. We are willing to hope for better things; but while the cost of the Louisiana purchase hangs like a mill stone upon the neck of our commerce; and while all its advantages are in fallacious hope, and precarious conjecture, it is not a time for New England-men especially to celebrate as an atchievement deserving their gratitude, a measure of so very problematical an issue.

In arriving at the last specifick item of Mr. Morton's eulogium, which speaks of our Government's "desire to remain in peace with all the belligerent nations of Europe and their *firmness* to vindicate the rights of our citizens against the aggressions of any," we are at a loss to imagine to what solitary fact his words can possibly bear an allusion. The desire to remain at peace with all the nations of Europe *but one* has indeed been conspicuous enough; but their firmness to vindicate our rights! where has it ever been manifested.—There is but one way of accounting for Mr. Morton's inferences from facts, and that may be called, the rule of *inverse* deduction; or the rule of making inferences in direct contradiction to their premises. Or to adopt the words of Hudibras,

> "As by the way of inuendo
> Lucus is made a *non* lucendo."

Thus when Mr. Livingston in a publick memorial, formally proposes that France and the United States, should make a *common cause* against Great Britain, Mr. Morton thinks it an indisputable proof of our government's desire to remain at peace with all the world. Mr. Monroe, as far as any part of his negociations is known to the publick, is constantly giving similar proofs of a pacifick disposition. The treatment of the British Minister at Washington has been exactly conformable to such indications, and Mr. Livingston, to place this desire of peace beyond all question, has recently repeated an outrageous insult upon the British government.

On the other hand what rights of our citizens has the government vindicated against any aggressions. Mr. Morton says our commerce is *less interrupted*, and says it at the very moment when foreign armed ships both English and French have violated our own territorial rights, and taken men from our merchant vessels, men within our own harbours. Never since the United States have been an Independent nation, never have they been so grossly insulted; and what satisfaction has our government obtained; What satisfaction could they ask? When every article of complaint they could advance might be retorted with ten fold recrimination upon themselves.

We have waded through the sickening detail of Mr. Morton's praises, and shall have but little to remark when he comes to generalize. It is so easy to say that the objects and pursuits of the government have been *one continued effort,* to promote the faith, justice and honour of the nation, and the peace, security and happiness of all its citizens; it is so easy to say all this without conveying or even forming any fixed or determinate idea, that we may consider the object of those words to be rather to round a period, than to have any meaning. To all general encomium on this administration, the destruction of the Judiciary, and the system of political *removals* from office, must forever remain insuperable objections. The first has overthrown all confidence in the stability of Justice, and the second, has given the pernicious example of setting up the government as the prize and the instrument of faction. These two corrupted streams issuing from the same fountain, will spread their pestilence over this Union, beyond the lapse of ages to purify. They have entailed a curse upon our posterity, which the blessings of a thousand Louisianas will never compensate.

Such then being the materials of which Mr. Morton's motion consisted, it is not at all surprizing that when its accuracy was once becoming a subject of discussion he should have shrunk from the test and withdrawn it from the scrutiny of his opponents—But it still remains for him to account for having produced a rhapsody so grossly variant from the truth, and so abhorrent to the sentiments of the Legislature and People of Massachusetts. It appears that he withdrew the motion on consultation with some members of his own party. This is thus far honourable to them; since it shows that they were not prepared to go with him into the rapturous regions of romance, for the purpose of daubing Mr. Jefferson with unmerited flattery; but why did he produce it? Was it to operate as a letter of recommendation for himself; as a passport to office from which some honest man must be turned out? or was it to propitiate the evil genius of Mr. John Randolph, to the Yazoo claimants of Georgia Lands? If the former was his motive, he may perhaps have reason for his hopes. We have seen services of a similar character very lately rewarded by the office of Commissioner of Loans; and there are still a few federalists of unimpeachable worth, who may be thrown breadless upon the world to accommodate candidates of such exemplary fervour; but as to the Yazoo purchasers, they may rest assured that ferocity will give as little, or less aid to their cause than its Justice. Mr. John Randolph's opposition is not thus to be appeased or overpowered, and the next Winter as the last, their agents will have the most indisputable proofs of Mr. Jefferson's favouring their claims; but it will so happen that they will again be set aside. Desirous as Mr. Jefferson may be to have Justice done, severe as his *one* continued effort may be for their relief, it can only be obtained by the vote of both houses of Congress, and the world knows how little influence he has over them. Mr. John Randolph knows very well when to oppose a motion "from whatever quarter of the House it may come," and if on any improper occasion, Mr. Jefferson's influence should be in hazard of weighing too much in the House, his own sons in law will take care to restore the balance. The sins of a first purchaser, will be visited upon all the subsequent assignees, and the corruptions of a Georgia legislature, will be punished by the spoils of New-England claimants. Grant however that the issue should be more favourable to their claim, grant that the services of so zealous a partizan should find favour in the sight of the national rulers, it is obvious that the motives which led to such flaming panegyrics as those of Mr. Morton's motion are partial, are private, are personal, that they relate only to particular interests, and are in unequivocal hostility to the interests of the people.   PUBLIUS VALERIUS.

No. IV.

THE second occasion upon which the Virginian faction in the late session of the State Legislature displayed their determination to sacrifice the interests of the State to the purposes of Mr. Jefferson, was in their conduct respecting the mode of choosing Electors of President, and Vice President.— That the choice should be made by the People, was agreed on all sides; but whether by a General Ticket, where the whole People should vote for the whole electoral body of the State, or whether by separate Districts, conformably to the mode of choosing members for the National House of Representatives, was made a question upon which one would have thought the faction deemed their whole salvation to depend.

The difference in point of principle, between the two modes of election was not worth a cavil—But the difference in the result was obvious—Had the choice by districts prevailed, it was contemplated that a proportion of partizans of Mr. Jefferson would be chosen among the electors, perhaps nearly equal to that he has in the House of Representatives. The body would be divided against itself and the voice of Massachusetts in the choice of President of the United States would be annihilated—A General Ticket they knew would give the clear, full, and unequivocal voice of the State, and that voice the faction knew was not in their favour. They dreaded to hear it, and they struggled with all their violence and all their cunning to evade it. Hence, after attempting in every shape and form to defeat the Resolution for choosing by a General Ticket, they concluded their career of opposition by offering in each House a *protest*, against it—assigning no less than *nine* reasons for their preference of District elections over a General Ticket. That this measure was concerted by the leaders of the faction in both Houses is apparent from the sameness of their pretended reasons; but so extreme was the violence and indecency of the language used in the protest offered to the House, that many of the members, who by a misplaced confidence had signed the paper without knowing its contents, declared their approbation of them when they discovered what they were, and although the signatures amounted to 101, only 53 voted for inserting the protest on the Journals of the House.

As the reasons alledged, were not the real operative reasons, their weakness makes it almost superfluous to refute them. Let us however, as briefly as possible notice the arguments which are given to the world in justification of these intemperate protests.

First—It is said that the elector ought to know the character and sentiments of the candidate for whom he votes—which is impossible in so extensive a territory as this State; and then the protest of the Senate goes on to define the boundaries of the Commonwealth, and tells the good People, how many original Colonies, judiciary Districts, Counties, Towns, and individual souls it contains.

But there can be no imaginary difficulty in the selection of nineteen persons, throughout the Commonwealth, whose character and sentiments, will be sufficiently known to all the electors for every necessary purpose of such an election as this. If the office elected to were of a nature to require particular talents, or the exertion of a peculiar character, as of a Representative, a Senator, a County Treasurer, or a Selectman, there would be some colour for this objection—But in this case the persons chosen have but one act to perform, and that is to vote. They are merely the proxies of the People to deliver the suffrage which they cannot conveniently give themselves, and the only quality which the primary elector is interested to know of the candidate is, *for whom he will vote?*—Now I do not hesitate to say, that this will in the general course of things, be at least as well, and perhaps better ascertained by a General Ticket, than by a choice in Districts. In the first formation of the Tickets recommended by the parties, each of them will undoubtedly select such men as will be known to possess the weight and influence proper to promote the success of the Ticket in his District, and at the same time men, whose opinions have been so clearly pronounced as to leave no doubt of the complexion of their votes. The unity of object and of exertion throughout the State, will give a more pointed energy to the support of every individual candidate. The protesters themselves will find none of the difficulty which they alledge, nor will their adherents have any of that ignorance of the character and sentiments of those candidates for whom they will vote, which they so pathetically deplore. If their Ticket should fail of success, it will not be for want of certain knowledge, how their candidates would discharge the duties assigned them.

Second—Election by a General Ticket is said to be repugnant to the habits and usages of the People. But the National Constitution itself under which this election first originated is so recent in date, that no usage can be predicated upon it.—The election has hitherto occurred but four times, and has not been uniform in mode. The whole People have always voted in this manner for the two highest Executive Officers of the State, and in one instance for a member of Congress. Every County annually chooses its Senators by a General Ticket. So that this mode of election is perfectly familiar to the People throughout the Commonwealth, and there can be no more difficulty in forming or delivering a Ticket of nineteen names selected from the whole State, than a Ticket of five or six names selected from a whole County.

Third—"Because this mode is calculated to open the door to intrigue and imposition on the People."

The protesters have not explained their grounds for this assertion, which is merely matter of *opinion*—Without contesting their skill and experience on this head, it may be observed that this mode of election has been sanctioned by all the principal States, in which their party predominates. The doors of intrigue and imposition will be open in every mode of election, to a People that will tolerate them; but on general principles it is more natural to infer, that these corrupt engines lose their efficacy in proportion as the number of voters is increased.

Fourth—This mode of election is fallacious, because the candidate selected from any given District, may vote contrary to the wishes of a majority in that District.

The selection of a candidate from each of the seventeen Districts which elect a member to Congress, must have been for the purpose of distributing equally throughout the Commonwealth, the honours of an important appointment. An example which the General Government, in their *one continued effort* for the happiness of all, have yet to learn. As each elector will be an elector for the whole Commonwealth, undoubtedly the partial majorities of single Districts will merge in the General majority of the whole State. It will not array the vote of one County against the vote of another, and thus reduce the influence of the Commonwealth to a level with that of the smallest State in the Union—but will give to Massachusetts her full Constitutional weight. This is no fallacy. The fallacy would be in such a difference of the modes of election, that while all the Southern States take care to give unanimous votes, the People of Massachusetts should be amused with a mere show of voting and in fact have no voice at all.

Fifth—This objection included so gross and pointed an insult upon the majority of the Legislature, that it was finally disavowed by many of the signers themselves; nor have they chosen to publish it with the rest.

Sixth—This is a repetition in other words of the fourth objection. A complaint that one party, meaning their own party, will be deprived of their due weight in the election. But that party will have much more than its due weight, by securing to themselves the whole weight of such States as Virginia, Pennsylvania and New-York—The language of those Gentlemen is, where we are the minority we must have our full proportion, and where we are the majority we will have all.

Seventh—This mode of election, it is supposed will have a tendency to excite heats and animosities; and to disturb the harmony and tranquillity of the State.

This is another conjectural objection. It is just as easy and much more agreeable to anticipate that it will be productive of more harmony and lead to unanimity. It seems much more probable that an obstinate and persevering attempt to degrade the State, to destroy its influence in the Union, and to reduce its condition in the political orb, from that of a primary planet, to that of the meanest of satellites, should produce discord and irritation.

Then come the two reasons why the protesters prefer the election by Districts. These are only repetitions of some of those before adduced as objections against the mode which prevailed.

Such are the arguments, if arguments they can be called, by which a large minority in both branches of your Legislature, fellow citizens of Massachusetts, varnished the attempt to deprive you of your Constitutional suffrage, at the approaching election of President and Vice President. For this was the undoubted real motive and design in this attempt. They know that if your opinion should be fully and fairly taken it would be against their party measures, party projects and party candidates. They wished therefore to drown your voice altogether. It was impossible for them to give a more convincing proof that *their attachment to their faction overpowers their attachment to the Commonwealth.*

In order to set this observation in its true light and to shew its full importance, we must again remark, that if the mode of choosing electors by single districts were established throughout the Union, Mr. Jefferson and his administration would lose so many Electors, that his re-election would be doubtful in the highest degree. It is at least certain that they dared not make the experiment. For when the amendment to the Constitution, which was carried through Congress last winter to secure this re-election was under discussion, Mr. Huger, a warm federalist moved, on the 20th of October, at the very commencement of the Session, as a further amendment to be sent out to the State Legislatures with the other.

"That the State Legislatures shall from time to time, divide *each* State into districts, equal to the whole number of Senators and Representatives from such State in the Congress of the United States; and shall direct the mode of choosing *an Elector* of President and Vice-President in *each* of the said districts, who shall be chosen by citizens having the qualifications requisite for electors of the most numerous branch of the State Legislature: and that the districts so to be constituted shall consist, as nearly as may be, of contiguous territory and of equal proportion of population, except where there may be any detached portion of territory, not of itself sufficient to form a district, which then shall be annexed to some other portion nearest thereto; which districts, when so divided, shall remain unalterable until a new census of the United States shall be taken."

Here we see this very measure of voting for electors by single Districts, proposed as a general measure to operate throughout the United States—but observe, it was brought forward by a federalist; for although the Legislature of New York had expressly instructed their Senators to propose this very amendment with the other, those Senators had only obeyed one half of their instructions. They brought forward the discriminating amendment—and passed over the other in total silence.

Mr. Huger's motion was committed to the same committee who had the other under consideration but they did not act upon it at all; and although Mr. Huger, pressed the subject as often as he could during the session, he never could prevail upon the majority in the House of Representatives, so much as to discuss his motion; and on the 2d of March, when he moved that it might be referred to a committee of the whole, his request though supported by all the federal members, *was negatived*.

I intreat you, fellow citizens to compare this conduct of the same faction so nearly at the same time, in the National House of Representatives, and in your state Legislature—the only manner possible whereby a choice of electors by single Districts, can be made to operate fairly and equally throughout the Union, is that it should be *uniformly* established—yet when this is proposed in an assembly, where Mr. Jefferson's majority is all powerful, a member of the most respectable character, backed by the instructions of one of the first Legislatures in the Union, is refused even the discussion of the proposal; and at the same time your own Legislature cannot secure to you the very same advantage, to which Mr. Jefferson's partizans so tenaciously adhere where they hold it, they cannot place you on the same footing with your Virginian fellow citizens, without being grossly insulted, and without protests of your own servants, against this your enjoyment of equal rights.

PUBLIUS VALERIUS.

No. V.

To an impartial spectator of passing events, the movements of political factions in a free government are always objects of curious and interesting speculation. In countries approaching so near a democracy as these United States, it must ever be the primary object for the leaders of party to court the favour of the people. There are two modes of accomplishing this with success, one of which consists in rendering real service to the publick, and the other by professing extraordinary solicitude for the people, by flattering their prejudices, by ministering to their passions, and by humouring their transient and changeable opinions. These two processes for the attainment of the same object, are scarcely ever combined together, and as the ambitious and aspiring must universally be impelled to aim at the end, so the choice of the means takes its complexion from the individual character of every candidate for power through popularity. In times of national difficulty and distress, when the service of the publick is a service of danger and of toil, when *deeds* are the only test of attachment to the Country, and mere words are estimated at their proper worth, the *patriot by action*, generally obtains the ascendency; but in days of peace and tranquillity, when the duties of publick life, are little more than a routine, when honour without peril, and profit without sacrifice is the result of publick employment, then the *patriot by profession* takes his turn, and often bears away the palm from his more reserved and unassuming competitor.

This distinction between the patriot by *profession* and the patriot by *action*, could not better be illustrated than in the contrast between the struggle for a General Ticket, upon which in my late numbers I have animadverted, and the effort of the same party in opposition to Mr. Ely's motion. We have seen on the former occasion, great professions of regard for the *people*. We have seen a minority in the Legislature, undertaking to say that the people, prefered election by Districts, because they prefered it themselves, and formally assigning this preference of the people, as one of the conclusive reasons for their's, when the people had never manifested, and probably never entertained any such a sentiment. This was patriotism by profession. The protesters take for granted, that the people like their project best, and then make a merit of advocating it, for that reason. When Mr. Ely brought forward his motion, the object of which was to render the people a real service, a great and important service, then these flaming *wordy* patriots, lost all their zeal, and instead of supporting it with that genuine devotion to the interests of the people, which they had so recently trumpeted abroad, either slunk from the discharge of their duty, and their vote as Legislators, or attempted to check by insidious amendment, or by open opposition a measure of the deepest moment to the welfare of the people. The reasons upon which are grounded the instruction, for which Mr. Ely moved, are so clear, so strong and so indisputable, that no direct answer to them has been attempted either in the Legislature, or in the newspaper speculations which have appeared on the subject. The rule of representation prescribed by the Constitution of the United States is universally admitted to be *unequal*, and when combined with the practice under the Constitution is oppressive on all the States holding few or no slaves. At present the people of the United States, consist of two classes. A privileged order of slave-holding Lords, and a race of men degraded to a lower station, merely because they are not slave-holders.— Every planter South of the Potomack, has one vote for himself, and 3 votes in effect for every 5 slaves he keeps in bondage; while a New England farmer, who contributes tenfold as much to the support of the government, has only a single vote—our share of representation is only proportionate to numbers, their share is in the same proportion of numbers, and their property is represented besides. At the time when the Constitution was formed this provision was submitted to on the ground that the burden of taxation should be apportioned to the benefit of representation. The experience of fifteen years however has proved the errour of these calculations. The experience of fifteen years has proved that four fifths of the burdens of this government must be supported by the States, which have no representation for slaves. The benefit pledged to us, as compensation for inadequate taxation is not secured to us;—we are doubly taxed, and they are doubly represented.

The necessary consequence of this has been the loss of all our weight and influence in the Councils of the Union. It is a fact well ascertained that this excess of Southern Representation decided the fate of the last election for President and Vice President of the United States; the same event must inevitably follow every contest in which the interests of the North and those of the South shall be at variance. While the present system of representation continues, an even balance in the National Councils must not be expected. The slave representation like the sword of Brennus, will forever be thrown into the Southern scale, and must forever make our's kick the beam.

In a moral and political view, this representation of slaves is alike objectionable. The number of those miserable beings already existing in some States is such as to occasion the most serious alarm in all humane and thinking minds. Mr. Jefferson has said that the populace of large cities, no more add strength to the body politick, than sores to the body natural. If this comparison be just the slaves of our Southern neighbours are abscesses of the deepest and most dangerous matter to our national body. Instead of strength they are distemper, deadly distemper, which if it cannot be eradicated, ought at least not to be fostered and stimulated. By allowing representation for slaves, we encourage and reward the infamous traffick of human flesh; and accordingly we find that although at one period this traffick was prohibited in all our states, yet the temptation to allow it has already overpowered every other consideration in South Carolina, and she has opened all her ports to that disgraceful trade.

It will not be necessary at this day to prove that in the eye of morality this purchase and sale of man, is criminal. The laws of the United States have long since declared it so, and as such it is prohibited to every citizen of the United States on the severest penalties. Thus the Constitution instigates and urges the Southern States to that which the laws punish as a crime. It makes the highest privilege of freemen, the purchase of accumulated slavery. It says to the Northern and navigating States, you shall not trade in slaves. If you do your ships and their cargoes shall be confiscated, your estates shall be ruined by fines, and your persons shall be buried in dungeons, and at the same breath it says to the Southern States deal in slaves—multiply the fetters of your bondage, and for every five victims of avarice and cruelty, you import within your territories, you shall have an increase of three votes towards composing the legislative and executive authorities of the nation. For in the very same act it offers a bounty to one citizen, while it brandishes the scourge over another. Can any thing be more inhuman? Can any thing be more absurd?

Thus in whatever point of view we contemplate this provision in the Constitution, whether as moralists, as politicians, or as citizens, it calls aloud for amendment. Yet in the legislature of Massachusetts itself were found men, who made the most formal and pointed opposition against a fair, and Constitutional attempt to obtain this amendment. And what were the arguments they alledged? They were worthy of the cause in which they were advanced.

They said, that it might perhaps give offence to Virginia, and the slave-holding States, and thus endanger the existence of the Union.

But surely propositions of amendment to the Constitution can give no offence to those States whose most influential characters have been and still are clamorous for amendments much more calculated to strike at the existence of the Union—who are continually telling us that the Constitution not only permits, but invites proposals of amendment—who have just accomplished one, which they deemed essential to the increase of their own power, and who have announced their determination to accomplish others, still more contrariant to the principles upon which that compact was originally settled.

This fear of giving offence, by the exercise of an indisputable right, under the sanction of every inducement which justice, humanity and liberty can inspire, is a motive which ought not to be urged upon freemen. It is an appeal to weakness—a plea to cowardice—an argument fit only for slaves to utter and to hear. It discovers a mind prepared for every degree of submission. It is language of a negro driver on a plantation, to the wretches, who tremble under his lash—but it can find no accessible corner in the heart of a New England farmer.

The pretence of danger to the Union, cannot be credited by those who raise it. The amendment when proposed in Congress, will be adopted or rejected. If adopted, it will have a greater tendency to cement and perpetuate the Union than any thing that has occurred since the adoption of the Constitution itself. If rejected, its friends will undoubtedly submit to the Constitutional decision, and wait until the progress of reason shall produce a state of things more favourable to the purposes of Justice. Of the seventeen States there are only five whose representation is increased by the slaves they hold. Twelve States therefore have a permanent and decisive interest, which must unite them eventually in wiping away this national scandal. Of the five whose number of members would be reduced by the amendment, Georgia would lose but one member and North Carolina only two. The *relative* weight of these two States would therefore rather be raised than depressed by the exchange, and their interest will concur with that of the twelve. Even in Virginia, the inhabitants beyond the mountains, who constitute a majority of the freemen, in that Commonwealth, would gain rather than lose in their proportion of the representation; so that when once the voice of solid and undeniable *interest*, concurring with those of honour, and Republican principle shall cease to be stilled by the deafening din of party spirit, there can be no doubt but that the amendment will prevail. This consideration will naturally lead the friends of the measure to pursue it at once with temper and perseverance. Persuaded that the Union is the first of political blessings to every part of these States, they will never be inclined to hazard it for any subordinate consideration, at the same time, assured that the more firmly its foundations are fixed on the foundations of freedom and equal rights, the more solid and durable will be the fabrick, they will not relax their mild but determined exertions until the honourable object for which they contend shall be attained.

But it was asserted that when the Constitution was debated in the State Convention this very article was warmly advocated by the most distinguished character, in that body, who advocated its adoption.

It must be remembered that the Constitution was then an untried experiment, every one of the important States in the Union, was divided almost equally, on the propriety of adopting it at all. In the Massachusetts convention the vote of adoption was carried only by a majority of eighteen in three hundred and seventy members. Those who on the main question were for the rejection of the instrument, of course, raised every possible objection of detail which their ingenuity could devise; and they who conceived it of the utmost importance upon the whole that it should be adopted were often called upon to justify or palliate sections which separately considered might have been highly objectionable to themselves. How the government would operate in practice was necessarily conjectural; and they whose hopes were chiefly founded upon the result of the *whole* system, naturally became sanguine in their expectation of advantages from particular parts.

The ground upon which this paragraph was supported by the federalists in the Massachusetts Convention was, that it sanctioned the principle of making representation and taxation go hand in hand. The objections against it were that the negroes would not be taxed enough, for this proportion, and it was compared with the mode established in the old confederation of raising quotas in proportion to the lands surveyed and improvements. The inequality of representation, resulting from this article, was not foreseen; no objection of that nature was raised. It has arisen from the non-execution of that part of it which favours us—*the taxation*, while the part which favours our Southern States, *the representation*, is carried into full effect.— Both parties took it for granted that as we should be represented, so should we be taxed. The practice of the Constitution has proved otherwise. In the course of fifteen years the direct tax has been resorted to only once, and then was paid ineffectually or not at all by the Slave-holding States. The Treasury has not received a dollar of this tax from South Carolina or Georgia, and several others of those States are great defaulters in that payment.

This amendment then, thus reasonable in itself, thus urged by every moral and political consideration, and thus required by the unequivocal *interest* of a proportion of those States abundantly sufficient to carry it through, can be resisted effectually, only by the operation of a single cause; the undue influence of the National Executive. The President of the United States, belongs to that part of the State of Virginia, which by the effect of the iniquitous mode of representation now established, sends, at least, two representatives to Congress, where upon principles of equal rights, they ought to send but one. His personal and local interests are of course in opposition to the proposed amendment, and there is no doubt but all his influence will be exerted against it. If we judge of the party which now governs this Union by their acts, it will appear that their whole political system centres in personal attachment to him and his views, while on the other part his system consists in substituting them instead of the Nation. The destruction of the Judiciary Independence; the persevering system of turning out honest men from office to introduce partizans in their place; and the amendment to the Constitution, carried through with such extreme precipitation, and at such heavy expence to the people of this country, for the sole purpose of securing his re-election, are all explained by this solution and can be explained by no other. It is this consideration which makes it of the utmost importance to the people of Massachusetts to mark the conduct of that faction here. Let us not deceive ourselves with fallacious hopes. So long as a formidable party *among ourselves*, shall oppose our restoration to equal rights, we shall certainly never obtain it. They who derive the benefit from exclusive privileges will not readily relinquish them, and while the cause of freedom is paralyzed by defection in its own ranks, it can meet with nothing but defeat.

An anxious concern for the liberties and interests of my fellow citizens has been the sole inducement to these remarks which I shall now bring to a conclusion. On three important occasions, in the Legislature of the State we have seen the leaders of a party running counter to the manifest and momentous interest of the State. It was conceived an injunction of public duty to show first—that the arguments and pretended facts alledged for this strange dereliction of principle were not founded in truth and secondly—That those party leaders, were under the influence of certain partial and personal inducements, different from, and in opposition to the interests of their constituents. The singularity of their conduct necessarily led to an investigation of its motives, and the discovery of the motives furnishes a clear elucidation of the conduct.—It is with the most cordial satisfaction, I have observed, that on every one of those occasions, many individuals of the party, in the house of Representatives, refused to go the lengths to which the leaders would have impelled them. The motion for a panegyrick on Mr. Jefferson, was hence withdrawn. The insult upon the majority of the Legislature was disavowed by many of those who in an unguarded hour had signed it—and on the final question upon Mr. Ely's motion, the small number of those who dared to vote against it, was a proof that all were not equally prepared to abandon their country, to please their patron. I am sorry to have seen no such signs of compunction in the minority of the Senate. To those who thus staggered at the sacrifice of duty required of them, and started back from the threshold of guilt to which they had been drawn, the present recess of the Legislature gives a favourable opportunity for the reflection. Let us fervently hope that they will see the precipice into which interested and artful men have been struggling to push them, and by their future conduct will prove that they are determined to pursue the path of their duty, and cling to the true interest of their country.

PUBLIUS VALERIUS.

"GOVERNMENT ITSELF HAS NO ARMS
BUT THOSE OF PERSUASION"

7. An Inaugural Oration, Delivered at the Author's Installation, as Boylston Professor of Rhetorick and Oratory, at Harvard University, in Cambridge, Massachusetts. On Thursday, 12 June, 1806 (Boston: Munroe & Francis 1806).

A sense of his rapidly declining "political prospects" led Adams to accept an appointment as the first Boylston Professor of Rhetoric and Oratory at his alma mater in 1805. Because he was a sitting U.S. senator, this was something of a celebrity appointment, but it was also a recognition of his larger family's status: the Boylstons were cousins on his mother's side, and they had insisted he be invited to be the first holder of the chair, a part-time position more akin to an endowed lectureship than to a full-time professorship. This enabled him to negotiate special terms about when his lecturing duties would be fulfilled—between sessions of the Senate, if he were to remain there.

The professorship also recognized his achievements as a persuasive and learned speaker with an appreciation for Greek and Roman classics and the arts as well as history and politics. Harvard took its duty to train young men for public service—religious and secular—very seriously, and in Adams they had a true believer in the importance of higher education for statesmanship. He began the lectures on his thirty-ninth birthday, reflecting in his diary with the usual gravity on this "undertaking of magnitude and importance, for the *proper* accomplishment of which, I pray, for patience, perseverance, and that favour from above, without which no human industry can avail; but which without persevering Industry, it is presumption to ask."

Adams announces at the outset of the lectures that both rhetoric and oratory have not always been given the respect or attention they deserve. He insists that they are the core elements of "reason" and essential to public life. Originally, among the Mediterranean ancients, rhetoric and oratory had been co-extensive with politics itself, in "deliberative assemblies" where matters were not pre-decided or subject primarily to powerful external forces. When Adams the committed neoclassicist called these arts "ancient," he meant it as the greatest of compliments. At their best, rhetoric and oratory had spoken Greek and Latin.

His introduction to his lectures, then, had to be an act of translation, even for Harvard students who were studying those ancient languages. His appeal is ultimately not to those students who went to Harvard to become ministers, but rather those who sought to be lawyers and politicians, "under governments purely republican, where every citizen has a deep interest in the affairs of the nation." The lectures were well received by the students and, initially, by others in the Boston area who dropped in to listen, though by the time he finished the lecture series, intensifying political differences led some of his former friends and classmates to stay away.

AN

INAUGURAL ORATION,

DELIVERED AT

THE AUTHOR's INSTALLATION,

AS BOYLSTON PROFESSOR OF

RHETORICK AND ORATORY,

AT

HARVARD UNIVERSITY, IN CAMBRIDGE, MASSACHUSETTS.

ON THURSDAY, 12 JUNE, 1806.

BY **JOHN QUINCY ADAMS.**

. . . .ἵνα τ᾽ἄνδρες ἀριπριπέες τελέθουσι.

Published at the request of the Students.

B O S T O N :

PRINTED AT THE ANTHOLOGY OFFICE,

By Munroe & Francis.

1806.

Cambridge, June 17, 1806.

SIR,

The students of Harvard University having expressed an unanimous desire that a copy of the Inaugural Discourse of the Boylston Professor of Rhetorick and Oratory be requested for the press ; the subscribers, their committee for that purpose, would make known to you their request. With sentiments of sincere respect, we remain,
Sir, your humble servants,
JOSEPH G. COGSWELL.
WILLIAM SMITH, JUN.
S. M. A. STORROW.
THEODORE EAMES.

HON. JOHN QUINCY ADAMS, ESQ.

Boston, 17 *June,* 1806.

GENTLEMEN,

In compliance with the request of the students of Harvard University, which you have communicated to me, I shall with pleasure furnish you a copy of the Inaugural Discourse, and with the assurance of my best wishes for your and their happiness, and improvement in every laudable pursuit, remain,
Gentlemen, your friend and very humble servant,
JOHN QUINCY ADAMS.

Messrs. Joseph G. Cogswell, William Smith, junior, S. M. A. Storrow, Theodore Eames, Committee of the Students of Harvard University.

Boylston Oration

IT is the fortune of some opinions, as well as of some individual characters, to have been, during a long succession of ages, subjects of continual controversy among mankind. In forming an estimate of the moral or intellectual merits of many a person, whose name is recorded in the volumes of history, their virtues and vices are so nearly balanced, that their station in the ranks of fame has never been precisely assigned, and their reputation, even after death, vibrates upon the hinges of events, with which they have little or no perceptible connexion. Such too has been the destiny of the arts and sciences in general, and of the art of rhetorick in particular. Their advancement and decline have been alternate in the annals of the world. At one period they have been cherished, admired, and cultivated; at another neglected, despised, and oppressed. Like the favourites of princes, they have had their turns of unbounded influence and of excessive degradation. Now the enthusiasm of their votaries has raised them to the pinnacle of greatness; now a turn of the wheel has hurled them prostrate in the dust. Nor have these great and sudden revolutions always resulted from causes seemingly capable of producing such effects. At one period, the barbarian conqueror destroys, at another he adopts, the arts of the vanquished people. The Grecian Muses were led captive and in chains to Rome. Once there, they not only burst asunder their own fetters, but soon mounting the triumphal car, rode with supreme ascendancy over their victors. More than once have the Tartars, after carrying conquest and desolation over the empire of China, been subdued in turn by the arts of the nation, they had enslaved; as if by a wise and equitable retribution of nature the authors of violence were doomed to be overpowered by their own prosperity, and to find in every victory the seeds of defeat.

On the other hand the arts and sciences, at the hour of their highest exaltation, have been often reproached and insulted by those, on whom they had bestowed their choicest favours, and most cruelly assaulted by the weapons, which themselves had conferred. At the zenith of modern civilization the palm of unanswered eloquence was awarded to the writer, who maintained, that the sciences had always promoted rather the misery, than the happiness of mankind; and in the age and nation, which heard the voice of Demosthenes, Socrates has been represented as triumphantly demonstrating, that rhetorick cannot be dignified with the name of an art; that it is but a pernicious practice . . . the mere counterfeit of justice. This opinion has had its followers from the days of Socrates to our own, and it still remains an inquiry among men, as in the age of Plato, and in that of Cicero, whether eloquence is an art, worthy of the cultivation of a wise and virtuous man. To assist us in bringing the mind to a satisfactory result of this inquiry, it is proper to consider the art, as well in its nature, as in its effects; to derive our inferences, not merely from the uses, which have been made of it, but from the purposes, to which it ought to be applied, and the end, which it is destined to answer.

The peculiar and highest characteristick, which distinguishes man from the rest of the animal creation, is REASON. It is by this attribute that our species is constituted the great link between the physical and intellectual world. By our passions and appetites we are placed on a level with the herds of the forest; by our REASON we participate of the divine nature itself: formed of clay, and compounded of dust, we are, in the scale of creation, little higher than the clod of the valley; endowed with reason, we are little lower than the angels. It is by the gift of reason, that the human species enjoys the exclusive and inestimable privilege of progressive improvement, and is enabled to avail itself of the advantages of individual discovery. As the necessary adjunct and vehicle of reason, the faculty of speech was also bestowed as an exclusive privilege upon man: not the mere utterance of articulate sounds; not the mere cries of passion, which he has in common with the lower orders of animated nature; but as the conveyance of thought; as the means of rational intercourse with his fellow-creature, and of humble communion with his God. It is by the means of reason, clothed with speech, that the most precious blessings of social life are communicated from man to man, and that supplication, thanksgiving, and praise are addressed to the Author of the universe. How justly then, with the great dramatick poet may we exclaim,

> "Sure, he that made us with such *large discourse*,
> Looking before and after, gave us not
> That capability and God-like reason
> To rust in us, unus'd."

A faculty thus elevated, given us for so sublime a purpose, and destined to an end so excellent, was not intended by the supreme Creator to be buried in the grave of neglect. As the source of all human improvements it was itself susceptible of improvement by industry and application, by observation and experience. Hence, wherever man has been found in a social state, and wherever he has been sensible of his dependance upon a supreme disposer of events, the value and the power of publick speaking, if not universally acknowledged, has at least been universally felt.

For the truth of these remarks let me appeal to the testimony of history, sacred and profane. We shall find it equally clear and conclusive from the earliest of her records, which have escaped the ravages of time. When the people of God were groaning under the insupportable oppressions of Egyptian bondage, and the Lord of Hosts condescended by miraculous interposition to raise them up a deliverer, the want of ELOQUENCE was pleaded by the chosen object of his ministry, as an argument of his incompetency for the high commission, with which he was to be charged. To supply this deficiency, which, even in the communication of more than human powers, Eternal Wisdom had not seen fit to remove, another favoured servant of the Most High was united in the exalted trust of deliverance, and specially appointed, for the purpose of declaring the divine will, to the oppressor and the oppressed: to the monarch of Egypt and the children of Israel. "Is not Aaron the Levite thy brother? I know that he can SPEAK WELL. And he shall be thy spokesman unto the people: and he shall be, even he shall be to thee instead of a mouth, and thou shalt be to him instead of God."

It was not sufficient for the beneficent purposes of divine Providence, that the shepherd of his flock should be invested with the power of performing signs and wonders to authenticate his mission, and command obedience to his words. . . . the appropriate instrument, to appal the heart of the tyrant upon his throne, and to control the wayward dispositions of the people, was an eloquent speaker; and the importance of the duty is apparent in the distinction, which separated it from all the other transcendent gifts, with which the inspired leader was endowed, and committed it as a special charge to his associate. Nor will it escape your observation, that when the first great object of their joint mission was accomplished, and the sacred system of laws and polity for the emancipated nation was delivered by the voice of heaven from the holy mountain, the same ELOQUENT SPEAKER was separated from among the children of Israel, to minister in the priest's office; to bear the iniquity of their holy things; to offer up to God, their creator and preserver, the publick tribute of their social adoration.

In the fables of Greece and Egypt the importance of eloquence is attested by the belief, that the art of publick speaking was of celestial origin, ascribed to the invention of a God, who, from the possession of this faculty, was supposed to be the messenger and interpreter of Olympus. It is attested by the solicitude, with which the art was cultivated, at a period of the remotest antiquity.

With the first glimpse of historical truth, which bursts from the oriental regions of mythological romance, in that feeble and dubious twilight, which scarcely discerns the distinction between the fictions of pagan superstition and the narrative of real events, a school of rhetorick and oratory, established in the Peloponnesus, dawns upon our view. After the lapse of a thousand years from that time, Pausanias, a Grecian geographer and historian, explicitly asserts, that he had read a treatise upon the art, composed by the founder of this school, a cotemporary and relative of Theseus, in the age preceding that of the Trojan war. The poems of Homer abound with still more decisive proofs of the estimation, in which the powers of oratory were held, and of the attention, with which it was honoured as an essential object of instruction in the education of youth.

From that æra, through the long series of Greek and Roman history down to the gloom of universal night, in which the glories of the Roman empire expired, the triumphs and the splendour of eloquence are multiplied and conspicuous. Then it was that the practice of the art attained a perfection ever since unrivalled, and to which all succeeding times have listened with admiration and despair. At Athens and Rome a town-meeting could scarcely be held, without being destined to immortality; a question of property between individual citizens could scarcely be litigated, without occupying the attention, and engaging the studies of the remotest nations and the most distant posterity.

There is always a certain correspondence and proportion between the estimation in which an art is held, and the effects which it produces. In the flourishing periods of Athens and Rome, eloquence was POWER. It was at once the instrument and the spur to ambition. The talent of publick speaking was the key to the highest dignities: the passport to the supreme dominion of the state. The rod of Hermes was the sceptre of empire: the voice of oratory was the thunder of Jupiter. The most powerful of human passions was enlisted in the cause of eloquence, and eloquence in return was the most effectual auxiliary to the passion. In proportion to the wonders she atchieved, was the eagerness to acquire the faculties of this mighty magician. Oratory was taught as the occupation of a life. The course of instruction commenced with the infant in the cradle, and continued to the meridian of manhood. It was made the fundamental object of education, and every other part of instruction for childhood, and of discipline for youth, was bent to its accommodation. Arts, science, letters, were to be thoroughly studied and investigated, upon the maxim, that an orator must be a man of universal knowledge. Moral duties were inculcated, because none but a good man could be an orator. Wisdom, learning, Virtue herself were estimated by their subserviency to the purposes of eloquence, and the whole duty of man consisted in making himself an accomplished publick speaker.

With the dissolution of Roman liberty, and the decline of Roman taste, the reputation and the excellency of the oratorical art fell alike into decay. Under the despotism of the Cæsars the end of eloquence was perverted from persuasion to panegyrick, and all her faculties were soon palsied by the touch of corruption, or enervated by the impotence of servitude. Then succeeded the midnight of the monkish ages, when with the other liberal arts she slumbered in the profound darkness of the cloister.

At the revival of letters in modern Europe, eloquence, together with her sister muses awoke, and shook the poppies from her brow. But their torpors still tingled in her veins. In the interval, her voice was gone; her favourite languages were extinct; her organs were no longer attuned to harmony, and her hearers could no longer understand her speech. The discordant jargon of feudal anarchy had banished the musical dialects, in which she had always delighted. The theatres of her former triumphs were either deserted, or they were filled with the babblers of sophistry and chicane. She shrunk intuitively from the forum, for the last object she remembered to have seen there, was the head of her darling Cicero, planted upon the rostrum. She ascended the tribunals of justice; there she found her child, Persuasion, manacled and pinioned by the letter of the law; there she beheld an image of herself, stammering in barbarous Latin, and staggering under the lumber of a thousand volumes. Her heart fainted within her: she lost all confidence in herself: together with her irresistible powers, she lost proportionably the consideration of the world, until, instead of comprizing the whole system of publick education, she found herself excluded from the circle of sciences, and declared an outlaw from the realms of learning. She was not, however, doomed to eternal silence. With the progress of freedom and of liberal science in various parts of modern Europe, she obtained access to mingle in the deliberations of their parliaments. With labour and difficulty she learned their languages, and lent her aid in giving them form and polish. But she has never recovered the graces of her former beauty, nor the energies of her ancient vigour.

The immeasurable superiority of ancient over modern oratory is one of the most remarkable circumstances, which offer themselves to the scrutiny of reflecting minds, and it is in the languages, the institutions, and the manners of modern Europe, that the solution of a phenomenon, so extraordinary, must be sought. The assemblies of the people, of the select councils, or of the senate in Athens and Rome were held for the purpose of real deliberation. The fate of measures was not decided before they were proposed. Eloquence produced a powerful effect, not only upon the minds of the hearers, but upon the issue of the deliberation. In the only countries of modern Europe, where the semblance of deliberative assemblies has been preserved, corruption, here in the form of executive influence, there in the guise of party spirit, by introducing a more compendious mode of securing decisions, has crippled the sublimest efforts of oratory, and the votes upon questions of magnitude to the interest of nations are all told, long before the questions themselves are submitted to discussion. Hence those nations, which for ages have gloried in the devotion to literature, science, and the arts, have never been able to exhibit a specimen of deliberative oratory, that can bear a comparison with those, transmitted down to us from antiquity.

Religion indeed has opened one new avenue to the career of eloquence. Amidst the sacrifices of paganism to her three hundred thousand gods, amidst her sagacious and solemn consultations in the entrails of slaughtered brutes, in the flight of birds, and the feeding of fowls, it had never entered her imagination to call upon the pontiff, the haruspex, or the augur, for discourses to the people, upon the nature of their duties to their maker, their fellow-mortals, and themselves. This was an idea, too august to be mingled with the absurd and ridiculous, or profligate and barbarous rites of her deplorable superstition. It is an institution for which mankind are indebted to christianity; introduced by the Founder himself of this divine religion, and in every point of view worthy of its high original. Its effects have been to soften the tempers and purify the morals of mankind; not in so high a degree as benevolence could wish, but enough to call forth our strains of warmest gratitude to that good being, who provides us with the means of promoting our own felicity, and gives us power to stand, though leaving us free to fall. Here then is an unbounded and inexhaustible field for eloquence, never explored by the ancient orators, and here alone have the modern Europeans cultivated the art with much success. In vain should we enter the halls of justice, in vain should we listen to the debates of senates for strains of oratory worthy of remembrance, beyond the duration of the occasion which called them forth. The art of embalming thought by oratory, like that of embalming bodies by aromaticks, would have perished but for the exercises of religion. These alone have in the latter ages furnished discourses, which remind us, that eloquence is yet a faculty of the human mind.

Among the causes, which have contributed thus to depress the oratory of modern times, must be numbered the indifference, with which it has been treated, as an article of education. The ancients had fostered an opinion, that this talent was in a more than usual degree the creature of discipline; and it is one of the maxims, handed down to us as the result of their experience, that men must be born to poetry and bred to eloquence; that the bard is always the child of nature, and the orator always the issue of instruction. The doctrine seems to be not entirely without foundation, but was by them carried in both its parts to an extravagant excess.

The foundations for the oratorical talent, as well as those of the poetical faculty, must be laid in the bounties of nature; and as the Muse in Homer, impartial in her distribution of good and evil, struck the bard with blindness, when she gave him the powers of song, her Sister not unfrequently, by a like mixture of tenderness and rigour, bestows the blessing of wisdom, while she refuses the readiness of utterance. Without entering however into a disquisition, which would lead me far beyond the limits of this occasion, I may remark, that the modern Europeans have run into the adverse extreme, and appear, during a considerable period, in their system of publick education, to have passed upon eloquence a sentence of proscription. Even when they studied RHETORICK as a theory, they neglected ORATORY as an art; and while assiduously unfolding to their pupils the bright displays of Greek and Roman eloquence, they never attempted to make them eloquent themselves. Of the prevailing indifference to this department of human learning, no stronger evidence could be offered, than the circumstances under which we are assembled.

Nearly two centuries have elapsed since the foundation of this university. There never existed a people more anxious to bestow upon their children the advantages of education, than our venerable forefathers; and the name of Harvard is coeval with the first settlement of New-England. Their immediate and remote descendants down to this day have inherited and transmitted the same laudable ardour, and numerous foundations of various kinds attest their attachment to science and literature: yet so far have rhetorick and oratory been from enjoying a pre-eminence in their system of education, that they are now, for the first time, made a separate branch of instruction; and I stand here to assume the duties of the first instructor. The establishment of an institution for the purpose was reserved to the name of BOYLSTON: a name, which, if publick benefits can impart a title to remembrance, New-England will not easily forget: a name, to the benevolence, publick spirit, and genuine patriotism of which, this university, the neighbouring metropolis, and this whole nation have long had, and still have, many reasons to attest: a name, less distinguished by stations of splendour, than by deeds of virtue; and better known to this people by blessings enjoyed, than by favours granted: a name, in fine, which, if not encircled with the external radiance of popularity, beams, brightly beams, with the inward lustre of beneficence. The institution itself is not of a recent date. One generation of mankind, according to the usual estimates of human life, has gone by, since the donation of Nicholas Boylston constituted the fund for the support of this professorship. The misfortunes which befel the university, unavoidably consequent upon our revolution, and other causes, have concurred in delaying the execution of his intentions until the present time; and even now they have the prospect of little more than honest zeal for their accomplishment.

In reflecting upon the nature of the duties I undertake, a consciousness of deficiency for the task of their performance, dwells upon my mind; which, however ungraciously it may come from my lips, after accepting the appointment with which I am honoured, I yet cannot forbear to express. Though the course of my life has led me to witness the practice of this art in various forms, and though its theory has sometimes attracted my attention, yet my acquaintance with both has been of a general nature; and I can presume neither to a profound investigation of the one, nor an extensive experience of the other. The habits of instruction too, are not familiar to me; and they constitute an art of little less difficulty and delicacy, than that of oratory itself: yet as the career must necessarily be new by whomsoever it should here be explored, and as it leads to a course of pleasing speculations and studies, I shall rely upon the indulgence of the friends and patrons to this seminary towards well-meant endeavours, and assume with diffidence the discharge of the functions allotted to the institution. In the theory of the art, and the principles of exposition, novelty will not be expected; nor is it perhaps to be desired. A subject, which has exhausted the genius of Aristotle, Cicero, and Quinctilian, can neither require nor admit much additional illustration. To select, combine, and apply their precepts, is the only duty left for their followers of all succeeding times, and to obtain a perfect familiarity with their instructions is to arrive at the mastery of the art. For effecting this purpose, the teacher can do little more than second the ardour and assiduity of the scholar. In the generous thirst for useful knowledge; in the honourable emulation of excellence, which distinguishes the students of this university, I trust to find an apology for the deficiencies of the lecturer. The richness of the soil will compensate for the unskilfulness of the tillage.

Sons of Harvard! you who are ascending with painful step and persevering toil the eminence of science to prepare yourselves for the various functions and employments of the world before you, it cannot be necessary to urge upon YOU the importance of the art, concerning which I am speaking. Is it the purpose of your future life to minister in the temples of Almighty God, to be the messenger of heaven upon earth, to enlighten with the torch of eternal truth the path of your fellow-mortals to brighter worlds? remember the reason assigned for the appointment of Aaron to that ministry, which you purpose to assume upon yourself. . . . I KNOW THAT HE CAN SPEAK WELL; and, in this testimonial of Omnipotence, receive the injunction of your duty. Is your intention to devote the labours of your maturity to the cause of justice; to defend the persons, the property, and the fame of your fellow citizens from the open assaults of violence, and the secret encroachments of fraud? fill the fountains of your eloquence from inexhaustible sources, that their streams, when they shall begin to flow, may themselves prove inexhaustible. Is there among you a youth, whose bosom burns with the fires of honourable ambition; who aspires to immortalize his name by the extent and importance of his services to his country; whose visions of futurity glow with the hope of presiding in her councils, of directing her affairs, of appearing to future ages on the rolls of fame, as her ornament and pride? let him catch from the relicks of ancient oratory those unresisted powers, which mould the mind of man to the will of the speaker, and yield the guidance of a nation to the dominion of the voice.

Under governments purely republican, where every citizen has a deep interest in the affairs of the nation, and, in some form of publick assembly or other, has the means and opportunity of delivering his opinions, and of communicating his sentiments by speech; where government itself has no arms but those of persuasion; where prejudice has not acquired an uncontroled ascendency, and faction is yet confined within the barriers of peace, the voice of eloquence will not be heard in vain. March then with firm, with steady, with undeviating step, to the prize of your high calling. Gather fragrance from the whole paradise of science, and learn to distil from your lips all the honies of persuasion. Consecrate, above all, the faculties of your life to the cause of truth, of freedom, and of humanity. So shall your country ever gladden at the sound of your voice, and every talent, added to your accomplishments, become another blessing to mankind.

"THE LAST REFUGE OF OUR VIOLATED PEACE"

8. *A Letter to the Hon. Harrison Gray Otis, a Member of the Senate of Massachusetts, on the Present State of our National Affairs; with Remarks upon Mr. Pickering's Letter to the Governor of the Commonwealth* (Boston: Oliver and Munroe, 1808).

Though they were ostensibly both members of the same party, Massachusetts senators John Quincy Adams and Timothy Pickering were, as the axiom goes, strange bedfellows. Pickering had been John Adams's secretary of state, in which role he had proven himself more loyal to Alexander Hamilton than to the president, and as senators Pickering and the younger Adams disagreed on Louisiana and many other issues. It was the so-called *Chesapeake* affair that triggered what would be a final rupture.

On June 22, 1807, HMS *Leopard*, having been dispatched by British Vice Admiral Sir George Berkeley to the Virginia coast in pursuit of Royal Navy seamen believed to have deserted, attacked the USS *Chesapeake* without warning after the American captain refused to permit a British search for the fugitives. Three crew members of the American frigate were killed and four others were seized, and the nation erupted in outrage and condemnation. When Federalists in Boston, for whom opposition to the Jefferson administration and an affinity for the British went hand in glove, initially refused to call a town meeting in protest, the town's Republicans filled the breach and called a meeting of their own. Adams crossed party lines to attend, drafting resolutions in support of the administration.

When the British government finally disavowed the *Leopard*'s attack, it forfeited any goodwill by almost simultaneously issuing new "Orders in Council" that stripped Americans of their neutral shipping rights in Europe and in the West Indies. In response, at the request of the president, Congress on December 18 passed the Embargo Act of 1807, shutting off American commerce to the world. Adams was the only Federalist to vote for the act. Then, a month later, to the astonishment and dismay even of his mother, Adams attended a Republican congressional nominating caucus meeting in Boston. This was too much for Timothy Pickering and the Boston Federalists, including Adams's long time friend, Harrison Gray Otis, president of the Massachusetts Senate, who engineered the public letter to which Adams responds here. Some 70,000 copies of the Pickering pamphlet were circulated throughout New England and beyond, warning readers of "the imminent danger of an unnecessary and ruinous war" with Great Britain and calling for the "interposition" of the commercial state legislatures against the embargo, effectively nullification by another name.

For Adams, acceding to Britain, and taking at face value its claims of principle, as Pickering did, "would have degraded us to the condition of colonies": "If we yield the principle, we abandon all pretence to national sovereignty." His public response put Massachusetts on notice: if his colleagues didn't already know, Adams was resolute in considering himself a man of his country, not of a party, region, or state. In May, though Adams had months left in his term, the state legislature named his replacement well ahead of schedule, which led him immediately to resign his Senate seat. He proclaimed himself finished politically in Massachusetts, but his advocacy on foreign policy made him a trusted expert again nationally, for the party in power. It would be at the call of newly elected Republican president James Madison that he would return to the diplomatic service in 1809.

A

LETTER

TO THE

HON. HARRISON GRAY OTIS,

A MEMBER OF THE SENATE OF MASSACHUSETTS,

ON THE

PRESENT STATE OF OUR NATIONAL AFFAIRS;

WITH REMARKS

UPON

MR. PICKERING'S LETTER

TO THE

GOVERNOR OF THE COMMONWEALTH.

....

BY JOHN QUINCY ADAMS.

....

BOSTON:
PUBLISHED BY OLIVER AND MUNROE.

1808.

Letter to Harrison Gray Otis

WASHINGTON, MARCH 31, 1808.

Dear Sir,

I HAVE received from one of my friends in Boston a copy of a printed pamphlet, containing a letter from Mr. Pickering to the Governor of the Commonwealth, intended for communication to the Legislature of the State, during their Session, recently concluded. But this object not having been accomplished, it appears to have been published by some friend of the writer, whose inducement is stated, no doubt truly, to have been the importance of the matter discussed in it, and the high respectability of the author.

The subjects of this letter are the embargo, and the differences in controversy between our Country and Great-Britain—Subjects upon which it is my misfortune, in the discharge of my duties as a Senator of the United States to differ from the opinions of my Colleague. The place where the question upon the first of them, in common with others of great national concern, was between him and me, in our official capacities a proper object of discussion, was the Senate of the Union—There, it was discussed, and, as far as the constitutional authority of that body extended, there it was decided—Having obtained alike the concurrence of the other branch of the national Legislature, and the approbation of the President, it became the Law of the Land, and as such I have considered it entitled to the respect and obedience of every virtuous citizen.

From these decisions however, the letter in question is to be considered in the nature of an appeal; in the first instance, to our common constituents, the Legislature of the State—and in the second, by the publication, to the people. To both these tribunals I shall always hold myself accountable for every act of my public life. Yet, were my own political character alone implicated in the course which has in this instance been pursued, I should have forborne all notice of the proceeding, and have left my conduct in this, as in other cases, to the candour and discretion of my Country.

But to this species of appeal, thus conducted, there are some objections on Constitutional grounds, which I deem it my duty to mention for the consideration of the public. On a statement of circumstances attending a very important act of national legislation, a statement which the writer undoubtedly believed to be true, but which comes only from one side of the question and which, I expect to prove in the most essential points erroneous, the writer with the most animated tone of energy calls for the *interposition* of the commercial States, and asserts that "nothing but their sense, clearly and emphatically expressed, will save them from ruin." This solemn and alarming invocation is addressed to the Legislature of Massachusetts, at so late a period of their Session, that had it been received by them, they must have been compelled either to act upon the views of this representation, without hearing the counter statement of the other side, or seemingly to disregard the pressing interest of their constituents, by neglecting an admonition of the most serious complexion. Considering the application as a precedent, its tendency is dangerous to the public. For on the first supposition, that the Legislature had been precipitated to act on the spur of such an instigation, they must have acted on imperfect information, and under an excitement, not remarkably adapted to the composure of safe deliberation. On the second they would have been exposed to unjust imputations, which at the eve of an election might have operated in the most inequitable manner upon the characters of individual members.

The interposition of one or more State Legislatures, to controul the exercise of the powers vested by the general Constitution in the Congress of the United States, is at least of questionable policy. The views of a State Legislature are naturally and properly limited in a considerable degree to the particular interests of the State. The very object and formation of the *National* deliberative assemblies was for the compromise and conciliation of the interests of all—of the whole nation. If the appeal from the regular, legitimate measures of the body where the whole nation is represented, be proper to one State Legislature, it must be so to another. If the commercial States are called to interpose on one hand, will not the agricultural

States be with equal propriety summoned to interpose on the other? If the East is stimulated against the West, and the Northern and Southern Sections are urged into collision with each other, by appeals from the acts of Congress to the respective States—*in what are these appeals to end*?

It is undoubtedly the right, and may often become the duty of a State Legislature, to address that of the Nation, with the expression of its wishes, in regard to interests peculiarly concerning the State itself. Nor shall I question the right of every member of the great federative compact to declare its own sense of measures interesting to the nation at large. But whenever the case occurs that this sense should be "clearly and emphatically" expressed, it ought surely to be predicated upon a full and impartial consideration of the whole subject—not under the stimulus of a one sided representation—far less upon the impulse of conjectures and suspicions. It is not through the medium of personal sensibility, nor of party bias, nor of professional occupation, nor of geographical position, that *the whole Truth* can be discerned, of questions involving the rights and interests of this extensive Union. When their discussion is urged upon a State Legislature, the first call upon its members should be to cast all their feelings and interests as the Citizens of a single State into the common Stock of the National concern.

Should the occurrence upon which an appeal is made from the Councils of the Nation, to those of a single State be, one, upon which the representation of the State had been divided, and the member who found himself in the minority, felt impelled by a sense of duty to invoke the interposition of his Constituents, it would seem that both in justice to them, and in candour to his colleague, some notice of such intention should be given to him, that he too might be prepared to exhibit his views of the subject upon which the difference of opinion had taken place; or at least that the resort should be had, at such a period of time as would leave it within the reach of possibility for his representations to be received, by their Common Constituents, before they would be compelled to decide on the merits of the case.

The fairness and propriety of this course of proceeding must be so obvious, that it is difficult to conceive of the propriety of any other. Yet it presents another inconvenience which must necessarily result from this practice of appellate legislation—When one of the Senators from a State proclaims to his constituents that a particular measure, or system of measures which has received the vote and support of his colleague, are pernicious and destructive to those interests which both are bound by the most sacred of ties, with zeal and fidelity to promote, the denunciation of the measures amounts to little less than a denunciation of the man. The advocate of a policy thus reprobated must feel himself summoned by every motive of self-defence to vindicate his conduct: and if his general sense of his official duties would bind him to the industrious devotion of his whole time to the public business of the Session, the hours which he might be forced to employ for his own justification, would of course be deducted from the discharge of his more regular and appropriate functions. Should these occasions frequently recur, they could not fail to interfere with the due performance of the public business. Nor can I forbear to remark the tendency of such antagonizing appeals to distract the Councils of the State in its own Legislature, to destroy its influence, and expose it to derision, in the presence of its sister States, and to produce between the colleagues themselves mutual asperities and rancours, until the great concerns of the nation would degenerate into the puny controversies of personal altercation.

It is therefore with extreme reluctance that I enter upon this discussion. In developing my own views and the principles which have governed my conduct in relation to our foreign affairs, and particularly to the Embargo, some very material differences in point of fact as well as of opinion, will be found between my statements, and those of the letter, which alone can apologize for this. They will not, I trust, be deemed in any degree disrespectful to the writer. Far more pleasing would it have been to me, could that honest and anxious pursuit of the policy best calculated to promote the honour and welfare of our Country, which, I trust, is felt with equal ardour by us both, have resulted in the same opinions, and have given them the vigour of united exertion. There is a candour and liberality of conduct and of sentiment due from associates in the same public charge, towards each other, necessary to their individual reputation, to their common influence, and to their public usefulness. In our republican Government, where the power of the nation consists alone in the sympathies of opinion, this reciprocal deference, this open hearted imputation of honest intentions, is the only adamant at once attractive and impenetrable, that can bear, unshattered, all the thunder of foreign hostility. Ever since I have had the honour of a seat in the National Councils, I have extended it to every department of the Government. However differing in my conclusions, upon questions of the highest moment, from any other man, of whatever party, I have never, upon suspicion, imputed his conduct to corruption. If this confidence argues ignorance of public men and public affairs, to that ignorance I must plead guilty. I know, indeed, enough of human nature to be sensible that vigilant observation is at all times, and that suspicion may occasionally become necessary, upon the conduct of men in power. But I know as well that confidence is the only cement of an elective government—Election is the very test of confidence—and its periodical return is the constitutional check upon its abuse; of which the electors must of course be the sole judges. For the exercise of power, where man is free, confidence is indispensable—and when it once totally fails— when the men to whom the people have committed the application of their force, for their benefit, are to be presumed the vilest of mankind, the very foundation of the social compact must be dissolved. Towards the Gentleman whose official station results from the confidence of the same Legislature, by whose appointment I have the honour of holding a similar trust, I have thought this confidence peculiarly due from me, nor should I now notice his letter, notwithstanding the disapprobation it so obviously implies at the course which I have pursued in relation to the subjects of which it treats, did it not appear to me calculated to produce upon the public mind, impressions unfavourable to the rights and interests of the nation.

Having understood that a motion in the Senate of Massachusetts was made by you, requesting the Governor to transmit Mr. Pickering's letter to the Legislature, together with such communications, relating to public affairs, as he might have received from me, I avail myself of that circumstance, and of the friendship which has so long subsisted between us, to take the liberty of addressing this letter, intended for publication, to you. Very few of the facts which I shall state will rest upon information peculiar to myself—Most of them will stand upon the basis of official documents, or of public and undisputed notoriety. For my opinions, though fully persuaded, that even where differing from your own, they will meet with a fair and liberal judge in you, yet of the public I ask neither favour nor indulgence. Pretending to no extraordinary credit from the authority of the writer, I am sensible they must fall by their own weakness, or stand by their own strength.

The first remark which obtrudes itself upon the mind, on the perusal of Mr. Pickering's letter is, that in enumerating all the *pretences* (for he thinks there are no causes) for the Embargo, and for a War with Great Britain, he has totally omitted the British orders of Council of November 11, 1807, those orders, under which millions of the property of our fellow citizens, are now detained in British hands, or confiscated to British captors, those orders, under which tenfold as many millions of the same property would have been at this moment in the same predicament, had they not been saved from exposure to it by the Embargo, those orders, which if once submitted to and carried to the extent of their principles, would not have left an inch of American canvass upon the ocean, but under British licence and British taxation. An attentive reader of the letter, without other information, would not even suspect their existence. They are indeed in one or two passages, faintly, and darkly alluded to under the justifying description of "the orders of the British Government, *retaliating* the French imperial decree:" but as causes for the Embargo, or as possible causes or even *pretences* of War with Great Britain, they are not only unnoticed, but their very existence is by direct implication denied.

It is indeed true, that these orders were not officially communicated with the President's Message recommending the Embargo. They had not been officially received—But they were announced in several paragraphs from London and Liverpool Newspapers of the 10th, 11th and 12th of November, which appeared in the National Intelligencer of 18th December, the day upon which the Embargo Message was sent to Congress. The British Government had taken care that they should not be authentically known before their time—for the very same newspapers which gave this inofficial notice of these orders, announced also the departure of Mr. Rose, upon a special mission to the United States. And we now know that of these all-devouring instruments of rapine, Mr. Rose was not even informed.—His mission was professedly a mission of conciliation and reparation for a flagrant—enormous—acknowledged outrage.—But he was not sent with these orders of Council in his hands.—His text, was the disavowal of Admiral Berkley's conduct—The Commentary was to be discovered on another page of the British ministerial policy—On the face of Mr. Rose's instructions, these orders of Council were as invisible, as they are on that of Mr. Pickering's letter.

They were not merely without official authenticity. Rumours had for several weeks been in circulation, derived from English prints, and from private correspondences, that such orders were to issue; and no inconsiderable pains were taken here to discredit the fact. Assurances were given that there was reason to believe no such orders to be contemplated. Suspicion was lulled by declarations equivalent nearly to a positive denial: and these opiates were continued for weeks after the Embargo was laid, until Mr. Erskine received instructions to make the official communication of the orders themselves, in their proper shape, to our Government.

Yet, although thus unauthenticated, and even although thus in some sort denied, the probability of the circumstances under which they were announced, and the sweeping tendency of their effects, formed to my understanding a powerful motive, and together with the papers sent by the President, and his express recommendation, a decisive one, for assenting to the Embargo. As a precautionary measure, I believed it would rescue an immense property from depredation, if the orders should prove authentic. If the alarm was groundless, it must very soon be disproved, and the Embargo might be removed with the danger.

The omission of all notice of these facts in the pressing enquiries "why the Embargo was laid?" is the more surprising, because they are of all the facts, the most material, upon a fair and impartial examination of the expediency of that Act, when it passed—And because these orders, together with the subsequent "retaliating decrees" of France and Spain, have furnished the only reasons upon which I have acquiesced in its continuance to this day. If duly weighed, they will save us the trouble of resorting to jealousies of secret corruption, and the imaginary terrors of Napoleon for the real cause of the Embargo. These are fictions of foreign invention—The French Emperor had *not* declared that he would have no neutrals—He had *not* required that our ports should be shut against British Commerce—but the orders of Council if submitted to would have degraded us to the condition of Colonies. If resisted would have fattened the wolves of plunder with our spoils. The Embargo was the only shelter from the Tempest—The last refuge of our violated Peace.

I have indeed been myself of opinion that the Embargo, must in its nature be a temporary expedient, and that preparations manifesting a determination of resistance against these outrageous violations of our neutral rights ought at least to have been made a subject of serious deliberation in Congress. I have believed and do still believe that our internal resources are competent to the establishment and maintenance of a naval force public and private, if not fully adequate to the protection and defence of our Commerce, at least sufficient to induce a retreat from these hostilities and to deter from a renewal of them, by either of the warring parties; and that a system to that effect might be formed, ultimately far more economical, and certainly more energetic than a three years Embargo. Very soon after the closure of our Ports, I did submit to the consideration of the Senate, a proposition for the appointment of a committee to institute an enquiry to this end. But my resolution met no encouragement. Attempts of a similar nature have been made in the House of Representatives, but have been equally discountenanced, and from these determinations by decided majorities of both houses, I am not sufficiently confident in the superiority of my own Wisdom to appeal, by a topical application to the congenial feelings of any one—not even of my own native Section of the Union.

The Embargo, however, is a restriction always under our own controul. It was a measure altogether of defence, and of experiment—If it was injudiciously or over-hastily laid, it has been every day since its adoption open to a repeal: if it should prove ineffectual for the purposes which it was meant to secure, a single day will suffice to unbar the doors. Still believing it a measure justified by the circumstances of the time, I am ready to admit that those who thought otherwise may have had a wiser foresight of events, and a sounder judgment of the then existing state of things than the majority of the National Legislature, and the President. It has been approved by several of the State Legislatures, and among the rest by our own. Yet of all its effects we are still unable to judge with certainty. It must still abide the test of futurity. I shall add that there were other motives which had their operation in contributing to the passage of the act, unnoticed by Mr. Pickering, and which having now ceased will also be left unnoticed by me. The orders of Council of 11th Nov. still subsist in all their force; and are now confirmed, with the addition of *taxation*, by act of Parliament.

As they stand in front of the real causes for the Embargo, so they are entitled to the same pre-eminence in enumerating the causes of hostility, which the British Ministers are accumulating upon our forbearance. They strike at the root of our independence. They assume the principle that we shall have no commerce in time of war, but with her dominions, and as tributaries to her. The exclusive confinement of commerce to the mother country, is the great principle of the modern colonial system; and should we by a dereliction of our rights at this momentous stride of encroachment surrender our commercial freedom without a struggle, Britain has but a single step more to take, and she brings us back to the stamp act and the tea tax.

Yet these orders—thus fatal to the liberties for which the sages and heroes of our revolution toiled and bled—thus studiously concealed until the moment when they burst upon our heads—thus issued at the very instant when a mission of atonement was professedly sent—in these orders we are to see nothing but a "retaliating order upon France"—in these orders, we must not find so much as a cause—nay not so much as a pretence, for complaint against Britain.

To my mind, Sir, in comparison with those orders, the three causes to which Mr. Pickering explicitly limits our grounds for a rupture with England, might indeed be justly denominated *pretences*—in comparison with them, former aggressions sink into insignificance. To argue upon the subject of our disputes with Britain, or upon the motives for the Embargo, and keep them out of sight, is like laying your finger over the *unit* before a series of noughts, and then arithmetically proving that they all amount to nothing.

It is not however in a mere omission, nor yet in the history of the Embargo, that the inaccuracies of the statement I am examining have given me the most serious concern—it is in the view taken of the questions in controversy between us and Britain. The wisdom of the Embargo is a question of great, but transient magnitude, and omission sacrifices no national right. Mr. Pickering's object was to dissuade the nation from a war with England, into which he suspected the administration was plunging us, under French compulsion. But the tendency of his pamphlet is to reconcile the nation, or at least the commercial States, to the servitude of British protection, and war with all the rest of Europe. Hence England is represented as contending for the common liberties of mankind, and our only safe-guard against the ambition and injustice of France. Hence all our sensibilities are invoked in her favour, and all our antipathies against her antagonist. Hence too all the subjects of differences between us and Britain are alledged to be on our part mere *pretences*, of which the *right* is unequivocally pronounced to be *on her side*. Proceeding from a Senator of the United States, specially charged as a member of the executive with the maintenance of the nation's rights, against foreign powers, and at a moment extremely critical of pending negotiation upon all the points thus delineated, this formal *abandonment* of the American cause, this summons of unconditional surrender to the pretensions of our antagonist, is in my mind highly alarming. It becomes therefore a duty to which every other consideration must yield to point out the errors of this representation. Before we strike the standard of the nation, let us at least examine the purport of the summons.

And first, with respect to the impressment of our seamen. We are told that "the taking of British seamen found on board our merchant vessels, by British ships of war, is agreeably to a *right*, claimed and exercised for ages." It is obvious that this claim and exercise of ages, could not apply to us, as an independent people. If the right was claimed and exercised while our vessels were navigating under the British flag, it could not authorize the same claim when their owners have become the citizens of a sovereign state. As a relict of colonial servitude, whatever may be the claim of Great Britain, it surely can be no ground for contending that it is entitled to our submission.

If it be meant that the right has been claimed and exercised for ages over the merchant vessels of other nations, I apprehend it is a mistake. The case never occurred with sufficient frequency to constitute even a practice, much less a right. If it had been either, it would have been noticed by some of the writers on the laws of nations. The truth is, the question arose out of American Independence—from the severance of one nation into two. It was never made a question between any other nations. There is therefore no right of prescription.

But, it seems, it has also been *claimed and exercised*, during the whole of the three Administrations of our national Government. And is it meant to be asserted that this claim and exercise constitute a right? If it is, I appeal to the uniform, unceasing and urgent remonstrances of the three administrations—I appeal not only to the warm feelings, but cool justice of the American People—nay, I appeal to the sound sense and honourable sentiment of the British nation itself, which, however, it may have submitted at home to this practice, never would tolerate its sanction by law, against the assertion. If it is not, how can it be affirmed that it is on our part a mere pretence?

But the first merchant of the United States, in answer to Mr. Pickering's late enquiries has informed him that since the affair of the Chesapeake there has been no cause of complaint—that he could not find a single instance where they had taken one man out of a merchant vessel. Who it is, that enjoys the dignity of first merchant of the United States we are not informed. But if he had applied to many merchants in Boston as respectable as any in the United States, they could have told him of a valuable vessel and cargo, totally lost upon the coast of England, late in August last, and solely in consequence of having had two of her men, native Americans taken from her by impressment, two months after the affair of the Chesapeake.

On the 15th of October, the king of England issued his proclamation, *commanding* his naval officers, to impress his subjects from neutral vessels. This proclamation is represented as merely "requiring the return of his subjects, the seamen especially, from foreign countries," and then "it is an acknowledged principle that every nation has a right to the service of its subjects in time of war." Is this, Sir, a correct statement either of the Proclamation, or of the question it involves in which *our* right is concerned? The king of England's right to the service of his subjects in time of war is nothing to us. The question is, whether he has a right to seize them forcibly on board of our vessels while under contract of service to our citizens, within our jurisdiction upon the high seas? And whether he has a right expressly to command his naval officers so to seize them—Is this an acknowledged principle? certainly not. Why then is this Proclamation described as founded upon uncontested principle? and why is the command, so justly offensive to us, and so mischievous as it might then have been made in execution, altogether omitted?

But it is not the taking of British subjects from our vessels, it is the taking under colour of that pretence our own, native American citizens, which constitutes the most galling aggravation of this merciless practice. Yet even this, we are told is but a pretence—for three reasons.

1. Because the number of citizens thus taken, is *small*.

2. Because it arises *only* from the impossibility of distinguishing Englishmen from Americans.

3. Because, such impressed American citizens are delivered up, on duly authenticated proof.

1. Small and great in point of numbers are relative terms. To suppose that the native Americans form a small proportion of the whole number impressed is a mistake—The reverse is the fact. Examine the official returns from the Department of State. They give the names of between four and five thousand men impressed since the commencement of the present War. Of which number, not one fifth part were British Subjects— The number of naturalized Americans could not amount to one tenth,—I hazard little in saying that more than three fourths were native Americans. If it be said that some of these men, though appearing on the face of the returns American Citizens, were really British subjects, and had fraudulently procured their protections; I reply that this number must be far exceeded by the cases of Citizens impressed, which never reach the Department of State. The American Consul in London estimates the number of impressments during the War at nearly three times the amount of the names returned. If the nature of

the offence be considered in its true colours, to a people having a just sense of personal liberty and security, it is in every single instance, of a malignity not inferior to that of murder. The very same act, when committed by the recruiting officer of one nation within the territories of another, is by the universal Law and usage of nations punished with death. Suppose the crime had in every instance, as by its consequences it has been in many, deliberate murder. Would it answer or silence the voice of our complaints to be told that the number was small?

2. The impossibility of distinguishing English from American seamen is not the only, nor even the most frequent occasion of impressment. Look again into the returns from the Department of State—you will see that the officers take our men without pretending to enquire where they were born; sometimes merely to shew their animosity, or their contempt for our country; sometimes from the wantonness of power. When they manifest the most tender regard for the neutral rights of America, they lament that they *want* the men. They regret the necessity, but they *must* have their complement. When we complain of these enormities, we are answered that the acts of such officers were unauthorized; that the commanders of Men of War, are an unruly set of men, for whose violence their own Government cannot always be answerable, that enquiry shall be made—A Court Martial is sometimes mentioned—And the issue of Whitby's Court Martial has taught us what relief is to be expected from that. There are even examples I am told, when such officers have been put upon the yellow list. But this is a rare exception—The ordinary issue when the act is disavowed, is the promotion of the actor.

3. The impressed native American Citizens however, upon *duly authenticated proof* are delivered up. Indeed! how unreasonable then were complaint! how effectual a remedy for the wrong! an American vessel, bound to a European port, has two, three or four native Americans, impressed by a British Man of War, bound to the East or West Indies. When the American Captain arrives at his port of destination he makes his protest, and sends it to the nearest American Minister or Consul. When he returns home, he transmits the duplicate of his protest to the Secretary of State. In process of time, the names of the impressed men, and of the Ship into which they

have been impressed, are received by the Agent in London. He makes his demand that the men may be delivered up—The Lords of the Admiralty, after a reasonable time for enquiry and advisement, return for answer, that the Ship is on a foreign Station, and their Lordships can therefore take no further steps in the matter—Or, that the ship has been taken, and that the men have been received in exchange for French prisoners—Or, that the men had no protections (the impressing officers often having taken them from the men)—Or, that the men were *probably* British subjects. Or that they have entered, and taken the Bounty; (to which the officers know how to reduce them.) Or that they have been married, or settled in England. In all these cases, without further ceremony, their discharge is refused. Sometimes, their Lordships, in a vein of humour, inform the agent that the man has been discharged as *unserviceable*. Sometimes, in a sterner tone, they say he was *an imposter*. Or perhaps by way of consolation to his relatives and friends, they report that he has fallen in Battle, against nations in Amity with his Country. Sometimes they cooly return that there is *no such man on board the ship;* and what has become of him, the agonies of a wife and children in his native land may be left to conjecture. When all these and many other such apologies for refusal fail, the native American seaman is discharged—and when by the charitable aid of his Government he has found his way home, he comes to be informed, that all is as it should be—that the number of his fellow-sufferers is *small*—that it was impossible to distinguish him from an Englishman—and that he was delivered up, on *duly authenticated proof.*

Enough, of this disgusting subject—I cannot stop to calculate how many of these wretched victims are natives of Massachusetts, and how many natives of Virginia—I cannot stop to solve that knotty question of national jurisprudence whether some of them might not possibly be slaves, and therefore not Citizens of the United States—I cannot stay to account for the wonder, why, poor, and ignorant and friendless as most of them are, the voice of their complaints is so seldom *heard* in the great navigating States. I admit that we have endured this cruel, indignity, through all the administrations of the General Government.—I acknowledge that Britain claims the right of seizing her subjects in our merchant vessels, and that even if we could acknowledge it, the line of discrimination would be difficult to draw. We are not in a condition to maintain this right, by War, and as the British Government have been more than once on the point of giving it up of their own accord, I would still hope for the day when returning Justice shall induce them to abandon it, without compulsion. Her subjects we do not want. The degree of protection which we are bound to extend to them, cannot equal the claim of our own citizens. I would subscribe to any compromise of this contest, consistant with the rights of sovereignty, the duties of humanity, and the principles of reciprocity: but to the right of forcing even her own subjects out of our merchant vessels on the high seas I never can assent.

The second point upon which Mr. Pickering defends the pretentions of Great Britain, is her denial to neutral nations of the right of prosecuting with her enemies and their colonies, any commerce from which they are excluded in time of peace. His statement of this case adopts the British doctrine, as sound. The *right*, as on the question of impressment, so on this, it surrenders at discretion—and it is equally defective in point of fact.

In the first place, the claim of Great Britain, is not to "a right of imposing on this neutral commerce *some limits and restraints*"—but of interdicting it altogether, at her pleasure, of interdicting it without a moment's notice to neutrals, after solemn decisions of her courts of admiralty, and formal acknowledgments of her ministers, that it is a lawful trade—And, on such a sudden, unnotified interdiction of pouncing upon all neutral commerce navigating upon the faith of her decisions and acknowledgments, and of gorging with confiscation the greediness of her cruizers—This is the right claimed by Britain—This is the power she has exercised—What Mr. Pickering calls "limits and restraints," she calls relaxations of her right.

It is but little more than two years, since this question was agitated both in England and America, with as much zeal, energy and ability, as ever was displayed upon any question of national Law. The British side was supported by Sir William Scott, Mr. Ward, and the author of War in Disguise. But even in Britain their doctrine was refuted to demonstration by the Edinburg reviewers. In America, the rights of our country were maintained by numerous writers profoundly skilled in the science of national and maritime Law. The *Answer* to War in Disguise was ascribed to a Gentleman whose talents are universally acknowledged, and who by his official situations had been required thoroughly to investigate every question of conflict between neutral and belligerent rights which has occurred in the history of modern War. Mr. Gore and Mr. Pinckney, our two commissioners at London, under Mr. Jay's Treaty, the former, in a train of cool and conclusive argument addressed to Mr. Madison, the latter in a memorial of splendid eloquence from the Merchants of Baltimore, supported the same cause; memorials, drawn by lawyers of distinguished eminence, by Merchants of the highest character, and by statesmen of long experience in our national councils came from Salem, from Boston, from New-Haven, from New-York and from Philadelphia together with remonstrances to the same effect from Newburyport, Newport, Norfolk and Charleston. This accumulated mass of legal learning, of commercial information and of national sentiment from almost every inhabited spot upon our shores, and from one extremity of the union to the other, confirmed by the unanswered and unanswerable memorial of Mr. Munroe to the British minister, and by the elaborate research and irresistible reasoning of the *examination* of the British doctrine, was also made a subject of full, and deliberate discussion in the Senate of the United States. A committee of seven members of that body, after three weeks of arduous investigation, reported three Resolutions, the first of which was in these words "Resolved that the capture and condemnation, under the orders of the British government, and adjudications of their courts of admiralty of American vessels and their cargoes, on the pretext of their being employed in a trade with the enemies of Great Britain, prohibited in time of peace, is an unprovoked aggression upon the property of the citizens of these United States, a violation of their neutral rights, and *an encroachment upon their national Independence.*"

On the 13th of February, 1806, the question upon the adoption of this Resolution, was taken in the Senate. The yeas and nays were required; but not a solitary *nay* was heard in answer. It was adopted by the unanimous voice of all the Senators present. They were twenty-eight in number, and among them stands recorded the name of Mr. Pickering.

Let us remember that this was a question most peculiarly and immediately of *commercial*, and not *agricultural* interest; that it arose from a call, loud, energetic and unanimous, from all the merchants of the United States upon Congress, for the national interposition; that many of the memorials invoked all the energy of the Legislature, and pledged the lives and properties of the memorialists in support of any measures which Congress might deem necessary to vindicate those rights. Negotiation was particularly recommended from Boston, and elsewhere— negotiation was adopted—negotiation has failed—and now Mr. Pickering tells us that Great-Britain has claimed and maintained her *right*! He argues that her claim is just—and is not sparing of censure upon those who still consider it as a serious cause of complaint.

But there was one point of view in which the British doctrine on this question was then only considered incidentally in the United States—because it was not deemed material for the discussion of *our* rights. We examined it chiefly as affecting the principles as between a belligerent and a neutral power. But in fact it was an infringement of the rights of War, as well as of the rights of Peace. It was an unjustifiable enlargement of the sphere of hostile operations. The *enemies* of Great Britain had by the universal Law of Nations a right to the benefits of neutral Commerce within their dominions (subject to the exceptions of *actual* blockade and contraband) as well as neutral nations had a right to trade with them. The exclusion from that commerce by this new principle of warfare which Britain, in defiance of all immemorial national usages, undertook by her single authority to establish, but too naturally led her enemies to resort to new and extraordinary principles, by which in their turn they might retaliate this injury upon her. The pretence upon which Britain in the first instance had attempted to colour her injustice, was a miserable *fiction*—It was an argument against fact. Her reasoning was, that a neutral vessel by mere admission in time of war, into Ports from which it would have been excluded in time of peace, became thereby deprived of its national character, and ipso facto was transformed into enemy's property.

Such was the basis upon which arose the far famed rule of the war of 1756—Such was the foundation upon which Britain *claimed and maintained* this supposed right of adding that new instrument of desolation to the horrors of war—It was distressing to her enemy—yes! Had she adopted the practice of dealing with them in poison—Had Mr. Fox accepted the services of the man who offered to rid him of the French Emperor by assassination, and had the attempt succeeded, it would have been less distressing to France than this rule of the war of 1756; and not more unjustifiable. Mr. Fox had too fair a mind for either, but his comprehensive and liberal spirit was discarded, with the Cabinet which he had formed.

It has been the struggle of reason and humanity, and above all of christianity for two thousand years to mitigate the rigours of that scourge of human kind, war. It is now the struggle of Britain to aggravate them. Her rule of the war of 1756, in itself and in its effects, was one of the deadliest poisons, in which it was possible for her to tinge the weapons of her hostility.

In itself and in its effects, I say—For the French decrees of Berlin and of Milan. The Spanish and Dutch decrees of the same or the like tenor, and her own orders of January and November—these alternations of licenced pillage, this eager competition between her and her enemies for the honour of giving the last stroke to the vitals of maritime neutrality, all are justly attributable to her assumption and exercise of this single principle. The rule of the War of 1756 was the root, from which all the rest are but suckers, still at every shoot growing ranker in luxuriance.

In the last decrees of France and Spain, her own ingenious fiction is adopted; and under them, every neutral vessel that submits to English search, has been carried into an English port, or paid a tax to the English Government is declared *denationalized*, that is to have lost her national character, and to have become English property. This is cruel in execution; absurd in argument. To refute it were folly, for to the understanding of a child it refutes itself. But it is the reasoning of British Jurists. It is the simple application to the circumstances and powers of France, of the rule of the war of 1756.

I am not the apologist of France and Spain; I have no national partialities; no national attachments but to my own country. I shall never undertake to justify or to palliate the insults or injuries of any foreign power to that country which is dearer to me than life. If the voice of Reason and of Justice could be heard by France and Spain, they would say—you have done wrong to make the injustice of your enemy towards neutrals the measure of your own. If she chastises with whips do not you chastise with Scorpions.—Whether France would listen to this language, I know not. The most enormous infractions of our rights hitherto committed by her, have been more in menace than in accomplishment. The alarm has been justly great; the anticipation threatening; but the amount of actual injury small. But to Britain, what can we say? If we attempt to raise our voices, her Minister has declared to Mr. Pinckney that she will not hear. The only reason she assigns for her recent orders of Council is, that France proceeds on the same principles. It is not by the light of blazing temples, and amid the groans of women and children perishing in the ruins of the sanctuaries of domestic habitation at Copenhagen, that we can expect our remonstrances against this course of proceeding will be heard.

Let us come to the third and last of the causes of complaint, which are represented as so frivolous and so unfounded—"the unfortunate affair of the Chesapeake." The orders of Admiral Berkley, under which this outrage was committed, have been disavowed by his Government. General professions of a willingness to make reparation for it, have been lavished in profusion; and we are now instructed to take these professions for *endeavours;* to believe them sincere, because his Britannic Majesty sent us a special envoy; and to cast the odium of defeating these endeavours upon our own government.

I have already told you, that I am not one of those who deem suspicion and distrust, in the highest order of political virtues. Baseless suspicion is, in my estimation, a vice, as pernicious in the management of public affairs, as it is fatal to the happiness of domestic life. When, therefore, the British Ministers have declared their disposition to make ample reparation for an injury of a most atrocious character, committed by an officer of high rank, and, as they say, utterly without authority I should most readily believe them, were their professions not positively contradicted by facts of more powerful eloquence than words.

Have such facts occurred? I will not again allude to the circumstances of Mr. Rose's departure upon his mission at such a precise point of time, that his Commission and the orders of Council of 11th November, might have been signed with the same penful of ink. The subjects were not immediately connected with each other, and his Majesty did not chuse to associate distinct topics of negotiation. The attack upon the Chesapeake was disavowed; and ample reparation was withheld only, because with the demand for satisfaction upon that injury, the American Government had coupled a demand for the cessation of others; alike in kind, but of minor aggravation. But had reparation really been intended, would it not have been offered, not in vague and general terms, but in precise and specific proposals? Were any such made? None. But it is said Mr. Munroe was restricted from negotiating upon this subject apart; and therefore Mr. Rose was to be sent to Washington; charged with this single object; and without authority to treat upon or even to discuss any other. Mr. Rose arrives— The American government readily determine to treat upon the Chesapeake *affair*, separately from all others; but before Mr. Rose sets his foot on shore, in pursuance of a pretension made before by Mr. Canning, he connects with the negotiation, a subject far more distinct from the butchery of the Chesapeake, than the general impressment of our seamen, I mean the Proclamation, interdicting to British ships of war, the entrance of our harbours.

The great obstacle which has always interfered in the adjustment of our differences with Britain, has been that she would not acquiesce in the only principle upon which fair negotiation between independent nations can be conducted, the principle of reciprocity, that she refuses the application to us of the claim which she asserts for herself. The forcible taking of men from an American vessel, was an essential part of the outrage upon the Chesapeake. It was the ostensible purpose for which that act of war unproclaimed, was committed. The President's Proclamation was a subsequent act, and was avowedly founded upon many similar aggressions, of which that was only the most aggravated.

If then Britain could with any colour of reason claim that the general question of impressment should be laid out of the case altogether, she ought upon the principle of reciprocity to have laid equally out of the case, the proclamation, a measure so easily separable from it, and in its nature merely defensive. When therefore she made the repeal of the Proclamation an indispensible preliminary to all discussion upon the nature and extent of that reparation which she had offered, she refused to treat with us upon the footing of an independent power. She insisted upon an act of self-degradation on our part, before she would even tell us, what redress she would condescend to grant for a great and acknowledged wrong. This was a condition which she could not but know to be inadmissible, and is of itself proof nearly conclusive that her Cabinet never intended to make for that wrong any reparation at all.

But this is not all—It cannot be forgotten that when that atrocious deed was committed, amidst the general burst of indignation which resounded from every part of this Union, there were among us a small number of persons, who upon the opinion that Berkley's orders were authorized by his Government, undertook to justify them in their fullest extent—These ideas probably first propagated by British official characters, in this Country, were persisted in until the disavowal of the British Government took away the necessity for persevering in them, and gave notice where the next position was to be taken. This patriotic reasoning however had been so satisfactory at Halifax, that complimentary letters were received from Admiral Berkley himself highly approving the spirit in which they were inculcated, and remarking how easily *Peace*, between the United States and Britain might be preserved, if *that* measure of our national rights could be made the prevailing standard of the Country.

When the news arrived in England, although the general sentiment of the nation was not prepared for the formal avowal and justification of this unparalleled aggression, yet there were not wanting persons there, ready to *claim and maintain* the right of searching national ships for deserters—It was said at the time, but for this we must of course rest upon the credit of inofficial authority to have been made a serious question in the Cabinet Council; nor was its determination there ascribed to the eloquence of the gentleman who became the official organ of its communication—Add to this a circumstance, which without claiming the irrefragable credence of a diplomatic note, has yet its weight upon the common sense of mankind; that in all the daily newspapers known to be in the ministerial interest, Berkley was justified and applauded in every variety of form that publication could assume, excepting only that of official Proclamation.—The only part of his orders there disapproved was the reciprocal offer which he made of submitting his own ships to be searched in return—that was very unequivocally disclaimed—The ruffian right of superior force, was the solid base upon which the claim was asserted, and so familiar was this argument grown to the casuists of British national Jurisprudence, that the right of a British man of war to search an American frigate, was to them a self-evident proof against the right of the American frigate to search the British man of war. The same tone has been constantly kept up, until our accounts of latest date, and have been recently further invigorated by a very explicit call for war with the United States, which they contend could be of no possible injury to Britain, and which they urge upon the ministry as affording them an excellent opportunity to accomplish a *dismemberment of this Union*.—These sentiments have even been avowed in Parliament, where the nobleman who moved the address of the house of Lords in answer to the king's speech, declared that the right of searching national ships, ought to be maintained against the Americans, and disclaimed only with respect to European sovereigns.

In the mean time Admiral Berkley, by a court martial of his own subordinate officers, hung one of the men taken from the Chesapeake, and called his name Jenkin Ratford.—There was, according to the answer so frequently given by the Lords of the Admiralty, upon applications for the discharge of impressed Americans, *no such man on board the ship.* The man thus executed had been taken from the Chesapeake by the name of Wilson. It is said that on his trial he was identified by one or two witnesses who knew him, and that before he was turned off he confessed his name to be Ratford and that he was born in England—But it has also been said that Ratford is now living in Pennsylvania—and after the character which the disavowal of Admiral Berkley's own government has given to his conduct, what confidence can be claimed or due to the proceedings of a court martial of his associates held to sanction, his proceedings.—The three other men had not even been demanded in his orders—They were taken by the sole authority of the British searching lieutenant, after the surrender of the Chesapeake.—There was not the shadow of a pretence before the court martial that they were British subjects, or born in any of the British dominions. Yet by this court martial they were sentenced *to suffer death*. They were reprieved from execution, only upon condition of renouncing their rights as Americans by voluntary service in the king's ships—They have never been restored.—To complete the catastrophe with which this bloody tragedy was concluded, Admiral Berkley himself in sanctioning the doom of these men—thus obtained—thus tried—and thus sentenced, read them a grave moral lecture on the enormity of their crime, in its tendency to provoke a war between the United States and Great Britain.

Yet amidst all this parade of disavowal by his government—amidst all these professions of readiness to make reparation, not a single mark of the slightest disapprobation appears ever to have been manifested to that officer. His instructions were executed upon the Chesapeake in June—Rumours of his recall have been circulated here—But on leaving the station at Halifax in December, he received a complimentary address from the colonial assembly, and assured them in answer, that he had no official information of his recall.—From thence he went to the West Indies; and on leaving Bermuda for England in February was addressed again by that colonial government, in terms of high panegyric upon his energy, with manifest allusion to his atchievement upon the Chesapeake.

Under all these circumstances, without applying any of the maxims of a suspicious policy to the British professions, I may still be permitted to believe that their ministry never seriously intended to make us honourable reparation, or indeed any reparation at all for that "unfortunate affair."

It is impossible for any man to form an accurate idea of the British policy towards the United States, without taking into consideration the state of parties in that government; and the views, characters and opinions of the individuals at their helm of State—A liberal and a hostile policy towards America, are among the strongest marks of distinction between the political systems of the rival statesmen of that kingdom—The liberal party are reconciled to our Independence; and though extremely tenacious of every right of their own country, are systematically disposed to preserve *peace* with the United States. Their opponents harbour sentiments of a very different description—Their system is coercion—Their object the recovery of their lost dominion in North America—This party now stands high in power—Although Admiral Berkley may never have received written orders from them for his enterprize upon the Chesapeake, yet in giving his instructions to the squadron at Norfolk, he knew full well under what administration he was acting. Every measure of that administration towards us since that time has been directed to the same purpose—To break down the spirit of our national Independence. Their purpose, as far as it can be collected from their acts, is to force us into war with them or with their enemies; to leave us only the bitter alternative of their vengeance or their protection.

Both these parties are no doubt willing, that we should join them in the war of their nation against France and her allies—The late administration would have drawn us into it by treaty, the present are attempting it by compulsion. The former would have admitted us as allies, the latter will have us no otherwise than as colonists. On the late debates in Parliament, the lord chancellor freely avowed that the orders of Council of 11th. November were intended to make America *at last* sensible of the policy of joining England against France.

This too, Sir, is the substantial argument of Mr. Pickering's letter.—The suspicions of a *design* in our own administration to plunge us into a war with Britain, I never have shared. Our administration have every interest and every motive that can influence the conduct of man to deter them from any such purpose. Nor have I seen any thing in their measures bearing the slightest indication of it. But between a design of war with England, and a surrender of our national freedom for the sake of war with the rest of Europe, there is a material difference. This is the policy now in substance recommended to us, and for which the interposition of the commercial States is called. For this, not only are all the outrages of Britain to be forgotten, but the very assertion of our rights is to be branded with odium.— *Impressment—Neutral trade—British taxation*—Every thing that can distinguish a state of national freedom from a state of national vassalage, is to be *surrendered at discretion*. In the face of every fact we are told to believe every profession—In the midst of every *indignity*, we are pointed to British protection as our only shield against the universal conqueror. Every phantom of jealousy and fear is avoked—The image of France with a scourge in her hand is impressed into the service, to lash us into the refuge of obedience to Britain—insinuations are even made that if Britain "with her thousand ships of war," has not destroyed our commerce, it has been owing to her indulgence, and we are almost threatened in her name with the "destruction of our fairest cities."

Not one act of hostility to Britain has been committed by us, she has not a pretence of that kind to alledge—But if she will wage war upon us, are we to do nothing in our own defence? If she issues orders of universal plunder upon our commerce, are we not to withhold it from her grasp? Is American pillage one of those rights which she has claimed and exercised until we are foreclosed from any attempt to obstruct its collection? for what purpose are we required to make this sacrifice of every thing that can give valour to the name of freemen? this abandonment of the very right of self-preservation? is it to avoid a war?—Alas! Sir, it does not offer even this plausible plea for pusillanimity—For, as submission would make us to all substantial purposes British colonies, her enemies would unquestionably treat us as such, and after degrading ourselves into voluntary servitude to escape a war with her, we should incur inevitable war with her enemies, and be doomed to share the destinies of her conflict with a world in arms.

Between this unqualified submission, and offensive resistance against the war upon maritime neutrality waged by the concurring decrees of all the belligerent powers, the Embargo was adopted, and has been hitherto continued. So far was it from being dictated by France, that it was calculated to withdraw, and has withdrawn from within her reach all the means of compulsion which her subsequent decrees would have put in her possession. It has added to the motives both of France and England, for preserving peace with us, and has diminished their inducements to war. It has lessened their capacities of inflicting injury upon us, and given us some preparation for resistance to them—It has taken from their violence the lure of interest—It has dashed the philter of pillage from the lips of rapine. That it is distressing to ourselves—that it calls for the fortitude of a people, determined to maintain their rights, is not to be denied. But the only alternative was between that and war. Whether it will yet save us from that calamity, cannot be determined, but if not, it will prepare us for the further struggle to which we may be called. Its double tendency of promoting peace and preparing for war, in its operation upon both the belligerent rivals, is the great advantage, which more than outweigh all its evils.

If any statesman can point out another alternative, I am ready to hear him, and for any practicable expedient to lend him every possible assistance. But let not that expedient be, submission to trade under British licences, and British taxation. We are told that even under these restrictions we may yet trade to the British dominions to Africa and China, and with the colonies of France, Spain, and Holland. I ask not how much of this trade would be left, when our intercourse with the whole continent of Europe being cut off would leave us no means to purchase, and no market for sale?—I ask not, what trade we could enjoy with the colonies of nations with which we should be at war? I ask not how long Britain would leave open to us avenues of trade, which even in these very orders of Council, she boasts of leaving open as a special indulgence? If we yield the principle we abandon all pretence to national sovereignty—To yearn for the fragments of trade which might be left, would be to pine for the crumbs of commercial servitude—The boon which we should humiliate ourselves to accept from British bounty would soon be withdrawn. Submission never yet set boundaries to encroachment. From pleading for half the empire we should sink into supplicants for life—We should supplicate in vain. If we must fall, let us fall, freemen—If we must perish, let it be in defence of our RIGHTS.

To conclude, Sir, I am not sensible of any necessity for the extraordinary interference of the commercial States, to controul the general Councils of the nation.—If any interference could at this critical extremity of our affairs have a kindly effect upon our common welfare, it would be interference to promote union and not a division—to urge mutual confidence, and not universal distrust—to strengthen the arm and not to relax the sinews of the nation. Our suffering and our dangers, though differing perhaps in degree, are universal in extent.—As their causes are justly chargeable, so their removal is dependent not upon ourselves, but upon others. But while the spirit of

Independence shall continue to beat in unison with the pulses of the nation, no danger will be truly formidable—Our duties are, to prepare with concerted energy, for those which threaten us, to meet them without dismay, and to rely for their issue upon Heaven.

> I am, with great respect and attachment,
> Dear Sir, your friend and humble servant,
> JOHN QUINCY ADAMS.

Hon. Harrison Gray Otis.

"THIS NARRATIVE OF DARK AND
COMPLICATED DEPRAVITY"

9. The Defence of General Jackson's Conduct in the Seminole War, December 31, 1818.

After eight years abroad as minister to Russia, leader of the U.S. delegation at Ghent, and, like his father before him, minister to the Court of St. James's in London, Adams returned to the United States in 1817 to become secretary of state in the administration of the newly elected president, James Monroe. Unlike his predecessors, Jefferson and Madison, who often engaged in direct communications with foreign ministers, Monroe announced that all such exchanges would be directed to and through Adams. With his unparalleled experience in the foreign service, Adams was positioned to be the most influential secretary of state in the young nation's history.

Among the first hotspots that commanded his attention was Spanish Florida, where American filibusters on Amelia Island and cross-border raids into Georgia by Seminole and Creek Indians complicated Adams's negotiations with the Spanish minister in Washington, Don Luis de Onís, to secure both East and West Florida for the United States and to establish a western boundary for Louisiana, as far to the west of the Mississippi River as possible. On December 23, 1817, President Monroe instructed Secretary of War John C. Calhoun to issue an order to fifty-year-old General Andrew Jackson, the hero of the battle of New Orleans and a seasoned and brutal Indian fighter, "to repair with as little delay as practicable, to Fort Scott [in southwest Georgia], and assume the immediate command of the forces, in that quarter, of the southern division." Jackson's orders, relayed through his commanding officer, Major General Edmund P. Gaines, were to pursue the Indian raiding parties and ensure that they could no longer threaten American settlements, "unless they shelter themselves under a Spanish fort. In the last event, you will immediately notify this department." When the fleeing Indians did precisely that, Jackson disregarded his orders, and occupied the Spanish fort at St. Marks, executing not only the Indians sheltering there, but also two British subjects, Robert Chrystie Ambrister and Alexander Arbuthnot, who he believed had been fomenting the Indian raids. He then occupied Pensacola, establishing his command there.

All of this provoked a firestorm, not only in Washington and Madrid, but also in London, where the British foreign secretary,

Lord Castlereagh, informed the U.S. minister, Richard Rush, that public opinion was so agitated that war would have resulted "if the Ministry had but held up a finger." On July 15, 1818, the president convened his cabinet. As Adams recorded in his diary, "the subject of deliberation was General Jackson's late transactions in Florida; particularly the taking of Pensacola. The President and all the members of the Cabinet except myself are of opinion that Jackson acted not only without, but against his Instructions— That he has committed War upon Spain, which cannot be justified, and in which if not disavowed by the Administration, they will be abandoned by the Country." Adams convinced his colleagues and his chief that Jackson's actions were supportable as self-defense under international law, or at least natural law, and that the onus was properly on Spain for its inability to police its territory. He then issued the following combative letter to George Erving, the American minister in Madrid, which was promptly published, complete with marginal references to supporting documents in possession of the State Department. Jefferson, in retirement at Monticello, thought that of all the state papers he had written or read, it was "the most important and . . . among the ablest compositions I have ever seen, both as to logic and style." Widely circulated in pamphlet form, Adams letter soon became known popularly as "Mr. Adams' Defence of General Jackson," and it quickly righted his negotiations with Onis. Just weeks later, on February 22, 1819, Washington's birthday, Adams signed the Transcontinental Treaty with Spain, acquiring Florida and establishing a boundary between the Viceroyalty of New Spain and the United States that extended, for the first time, to the Pacific.

Mr. Adams' Defence of General Jackson's Conduct in the Seminole War

---

Department of State,
Washington, 28th November, 1818

SIR:
Your despatches, to No. 92, inclusive, with their enclosures, have been received at this Department. Among these enclosures, are the several notes addressed to you by Mr. Pizarro, in relation to the transactions during the campaign of General Jackson against the Seminole Indians and the banditti of Negroes combined with them, and particularly to his proceedings in Florida, without the boundaries of the United States.

In the fourth and last of those notes of Mr. Pizarro, he has given formal notice that the King, his master, has issued orders for the suspension of the negotiation between the United States and Spain, until satisfaction shall have been made by the American government to him for these proceedings of Gen. Jackson, which he considers as acts of unequivocal hostility against him, and as outrages upon his honor and dignity; the only acceptable atonement for which, is stated to consist in a disavowal of the acts of the American General, thus complained of—the infliction upon him of a suitable punishment for his supposed misconduct, and the restitution of the posts and territories taken by him from the Spanish authorities, with indemnity for all the property taken, and all damages and injuries, public or private, sustained in consequence of it.

Within a very few days after this notification, Mr. Pizarro must have received, with copies of the correspondence between Mr. Onis and this Department, the determination which had been taken by the President, to restore the place of Pensacola, with the fort of Barrancas, to any person properly authorized, on the part of Spain, to receive them, and the Fort of St. Marks to any Spanish force adequate to its protection against the

Indians, by whom its forcible occupation had been threatened, for purposes of hostility against the United States. The officer commanding at the post, has been directed to consider 250 men as such adequate force; and, in case of their appearance, with proper authority, to deliver it up to their commander accordingly.

From the last mentioned correspondence, the Spanish government must likewise have been satisfied that the occupation of these places in Spanish Florida, by the commander of the American forces, was not by virtue of any order received by him from this government to that effect, nor with any view of wresting the province from the possession of Spain; nor in any spirit of hostility to the Spanish government—that it arose from incidents which occurred in the prosecution of the war against the Indians—from the imminent danger in which the Fort of St. Marks was of being seized by the Indians themselves, and from the manifestations of hostility to the United States, by the commandant of St. Marks and the Governor of Pensacola, the proofs of which were made known to Gen. Jackson, and impelled him, from the necessities of self-defence, to the steps of which the Spanish government complains.

It might be sufficient to leave the vindication of these measures upon those grounds, and to furnish, in the enclosed copies of General Jackson's letters, and the vouchers by which they are supported, the evidence of that hostile spirit on the part of the Spanish commanders, but for the terms in which Mr. Pizarro speaks of the execution of two British subjects, taken, one at the Fort of St. Marks, and the other at Suwany, and the intimation that these transactions may lead to a change in the relations between the two nations, which is doubtless intended to be understood as a menace of war.

It may be, therefore, proper to remind the government of His Catholic Majesty of the incidents in which this Seminole war originated, as well as of the circumstances connected with it, in the relations between Spain and her ally, whom she supposes to have been injured by the proceedings of General Jackson, and to give to the Spanish cabinet some precise information of the nature of the business, peculiarly interesting to Spain, in which these subjects of her allies, in whose favor she takes this

DEFENCE OF GENERAL JACKSON | 1818   185

interest, were engaged, when their projects of every kind were terminated, in consequence of their falling into the hands of General Jackson.

In the month of August, 1814, while a war existed between the United States and Great Britain, to which Spain had formally declared herself neutral, a British force, not in the fresh pursuit of a defeated and flying enemy—not overstepping an imaginary and equivocal boundary between their own territories and those belonging, in some sort, as much to their enemy as to Spain, but approaching by sea, and by a broad and open *invasion* of the Spanish province, at a thousand miles, or an ocean's distance from any British territory, landed in Florida, took possession of Pensacola and the Fort of Barrancas, and invited, by public proclamations, all the runaway Negroes—all the savage Indians—all the pirates, and all the traitors to their country, whom they knew or imagined to exist within reach of their summons, to join their standard, and wage an exterminating war against the portion of the United States immediately bordering upon this neutral, and thus violated territory of Spain. The land commander of this British force, was a certain Col. Nicholls, who, driven from Pensacola by the approach of General Jackson, actually left, to be blown up, the Spanish Fort of Barrancas, when he found it could not afford him protection, and, evacuating that part of the province, landed at another, established himself on the Appalachicola river, and there erected a Fort, from which to sally forth with his motley tribe of black, white, and red combatants, against the defenceless borders of the United States, in that vicinity. A part of this force consisted of a corps of colonial marines, levied in the British colonies, in which George Woodbine was a Captain, and Robert Chrystie Ambrister was a Lieutenant. [II.–2.]

As between the United States and Great Britain, we should [LIX.] be willing to bury this transaction in the same grave of oblivion [LX.] with other transactions of that war, had the hostilities of Col. Nicholls terminated with the war. But he did not consider the peace which ensued between the United States and Great Britain, as having put an end either to his military occupations or to his negotiations with the Indians, against the United States. Several months after the ratification of the treaty of

Ghent, he retained his post and his party-colored forces, in military array.

[II.–2.] By the 9th article of that treaty, the United States had stipulated to put an end, immediately after its ratification, to hostilities with all the tribes or nations of Indians with whom they might be at war at the time of the ratification, and to restore to them all the possessions which they had enjoyed in the year 1811. This article has no application to the Creek nation, with whom the United States had already made peace, by a treaty concluded on the 9th day of August, 1814, more than four months before the treaty of Ghent was signed. Yet, Colonel Nicholls not only affected to consider it as applying to the Seminoles of Florida, and the outlawed Red Sticks, whom he had induced to join him there, but actually persuaded them that *they* were entitled, by virtue of the treaty of Ghent, to all the lands which had belonged to the *Creek* nation, within the United States, in the year 1811, and that the government of Great Britain would [II.i, III.] support them in that pretension. He asserted also this doctrine in a correspondence with Col. Hawkins, then the Agent of the United States with the Creeks, and gave him notice, in their name, with a mockery of solemnity, that they had concluded a treaty of Alliance, offensive and defensive, & a treaty of Naviga-[IX.] tion & Commerce with Great Britain, of which more was to be heard after it should be ratified in England. Col. Nicholls then evacuated his Fort, which, in some of the enclosed papers, is called the Fort at Prospect Bluff, but which he had denominated the *British* post on the Appalachicola; took with him the white portion of his force, and embarked for England, with several of the wretched savages whom he was thus deluding to their fate—among whom was the Prophet Francis, or Hillis Hadjo—and left the Fort amply supplied with military stores and ammunition, [IV.v.] to the Negro department of his allies. It afterwards was known by the name of Negro Fort. Col. Hawkins immediately communicated to this government the correspondence between him and Nicholls, here referred to, (copies of which, marked No. 1 to 5, are herewith enclosed,) upon which Mr. Monroe, [x.] then Secretary of State, addressed a letter, (copy marked G,) to Mr. Baker, the British Chargé d'Affaires, at Washington, complaining of Nicholls's conduct, and shewing that his pretence that the 9th article of the treaty of Ghent, could have any

application to his Indians, was utterly destitute of foundation. [XI.]
Copies of the same correspondence were transmitted to the
Minister of the United States, then in England, with instructions to remonstrate with the British government against these
proceedings of Nicholls, and to shew how incompatible they
were with the peace which had been concluded between the [XII.a.b.]
two nations. These remonstrances were accordingly made, first
in personal interview with Earl Bathurst and Lord Castlere- [XIII.a.b.]
agh, & afterwards in written notes, addressed successively to
them, (copies of which, together with extracts from the despatches of the American Minister to the Secretary of State,
reporting what passed at those interviews, are enclosed.)
Lord Bathurst, in the most unequivocal manner, confirmed
the facts, and disavowed the misconduct of Nicholls; declared
his disapprobation of the pretended treaty of Alliance, offensive and defensive, which he had made; assured the American
Minister that the British government had refused to ratify that
treaty, and would send back the Indians whom Nicholls had
brought with him, with advice to make their peace on such
terms as they could obtain. Lord Castlereagh confirmed the
assurance that the treaty would not be ratified; and if, at the
same time that these assurances were given, certain distinctions
of public notoriety, were shown to the Prophet Hillis Hadjo,
and he was actually honored with a commission, as a British
officer, it is to be presumed that these favors were granted him
as rewards of past services, and not as encouragement to expect
any support from Great Britain, in a continuance of savage
hostilities against the United States, all intention of giving any
such support having been repeatedly and earnestly disavowed.

The Negro fort, however, abandoned by Col. Nicholls,
remained on the Spanish territory, occupied by the banditti to
whom he had left it, and held by them as a post, from whence
to commit depredations, outrages and murders, and as a receptacle for fugitive slaves and malefactors, to the great annoyance [XIV.]
both of the United States and of Spanish Florida. In April, 1816,
General Jackson wrote a letter to the Governor of Pensacola,
calling upon him to put down this common nuisance to the
peaceable inhabitants of both countries. That letter, together [XV.]
with the answer of the Governor of Pensacola, have already
been communicated to the Spanish Minister here, and by him,

doubtless, to his government. Copies of them are, nevertheless, [XXIII.] now again enclosed; particularly as the letter from the Governor, explicitly admits—that this fort, constructed by Nicholls, in violation both of the territory and neutrality of Spain, was still no less obnoxious to his government than to the United States; but, that he had neither sufficient force, nor an authority, without orders from the Governor-General of the Havanna, to destroy it. It was afterwards, on the 27th July, 1816, destroyed by a cannon shot from a gun vessel of the United States, which, in its passage up the river, was fired upon from it. It was blown up, with an English flag still flying as its standard, and immediately after the barbarous murder of a boat's crew, belonging to the navy of the United States, by the banditti left in it by Nicholls.

In the year 1817, Alexander Arbuthnot, of the Island of New-Providence, a British subject, first appeared, as an Indian trader in Spanish Florida; and as the successor of Colonel Nicholls, in the employment of instigating the Seminole and outlawed Red Stick Indians to hostilities against the United States, by reviving the pretence that they were entitled to all the lands which had been ceded by the Creek Nation to the United States, in August, 1814. As a mere Indian trader, the intrusion of this man, into a Spanish province, was contrary to the policy observed by all the European Powers in this hemisphere, and by none more rigorously than by Spain, of excluding all foreigners from intercourse with the Indians, within their territories. It must be known to the Spanish government, whether Arbuthnot had a Spanish license for trading with the Indians in Spanish Florida or not; but they also know that Spain was bound by treaty, to restrain by force all hostilities on the part of those Indians, against the citizens of the United States, and it is for them to explain how, consistently with those engagements, Spain could, contrary to all the maxims of her ordinary policy, grant such a license to a foreign incendiary, whose principal, if not his only object, appears to have been, to stimulate those hostilities which Spain had expressly stipulated by force to [XLIX.] restrain. In his infernal instigations he was but too successful. No sooner did he make his appearance among the Indians, [L.] accompanied by the Prophet Hillis Hadjo, returned from his expedition to England, than the peaceful inhabitants on the borders of the United States, were visited with all the horrors of savage war; the robbery of their property, and the barbarous and indiscriminate murder of woman, infancy and age.

After the repeated expostulations, warnings and offers of a peace, through the summer and autumn of 1817, on the part of the United States, had been answered only by renewed outrages, and after a detachment of forty men, under Lieutenant. Scott, accompanied by seven women, had been waylaid and murdered by the Indians, orders were given to General Jackson, and an adequate force was placed at his disposal, to terminate the war. It was ascertained that the Spanish force in Florida was inadequate for the protection even of the Spanish territory itself, against this mingled horde of lawless Indians and Negroes; and, although their devastations were committed within the limits of the United States, they immediately sought refuge within the Florida line, and there only were to be overtaken. The necessity of crossing the line was indispensable; for it was from beyond the line that the Indians made their murderous incursions within that of the United States. It was there that they had their abode, and the territory belonged in fact to them, although within the borders of the Spanish jurisdiction. There it was that the American commander met the principal resistance from them; there it was, that were found the still bleeding scalps of our citizens, freshly butchered by them; there it was that he released the only *woman,* who had been suffered to survive the massacre of the party under Lieutenant Scott. But it was not anticipated by this government that the commanding officers of Spain, in Florida, whose especial duty it was, in conformity to the solemn engagements contracted by their nation, to restrain, by force, those Indians from hostilities against the United States, would be found encouraging, aiding and abetting them, and furnishing them with supplies, for carrying on such hostilities. The officer in command, immediately before General Jackson, was, therefore, specially instructed to respect, as far as possible, the Spanish authority, wherever it was maintained, and copies of those orders were also furnished to General Jackson, upon his taking the command. In the course of his pursuit, as he approached St. Marks, he was informed, direct from the Governor of Pensacola, that a party of the hostile Indians had threatened to seize that Fort, and that he apprehended the Spanish Garrison there was not in strength sufficient to defend it against them. This information was confirmed from other sources, and by the evidence produced upon the trial of Ambrister, it proved to have been exactly true. By all the laws of neutrality and of war, as well as of prudence and humanity, he was warranted in anticipating his enemy, by the amicable, and that being refused, by the forcible occupation of the Fort.—There will be no need of citations from printed treatises on international law, to prove the correctness of this principle. It is engraved in adamant on the common sense of mankind; no writer upon the laws of nations ever pretended to contradict it; none of any reputation or authority ever omitted to assert it.

[XXXIV.] At Fort St. Marks, Alexander Arbuthnot, the British Indian trader from beyond the seas, the firebrand, by whose torch this Negro Indian war against our borders had been rekindled, was found an inmate of the commandant's family; and it was also found that, by the commandant himself, councils of war had been permitted to be held within it, by the savage chiefs and warriors; that the Spanish store-houses had been appropriated to their use; that it was an open market for cattle, known to have been robbed by them from citizens of the United States, and which had been contracted for and purchased by the officers of the garrison. That information had been afforded from this fort by Arbuthnot, to the enemy, of the strength and movements of the American army; that the date of the departure of express had been noted by the Spanish Commissary, and ammunition, munitions of war, and all necessary supplies furnished to the Indians.

The conduct of the Governor of Pensacola was not less marked by a disposition of enmity to the United States, and by an utter disregard to the obligations of the treaty, by which he was bound to restrain, by force, the Indians from hostilities against them. When called upon to vindicate the territorial rights and authority of Spain, by the destruction of the Negro fort, his predecessor had declared it to be not less annoying and pernicious to the Spanish subjects in Florida, than to the United States, but had pleaded his inability to subdue it. He, himself, had expressed his apprehensions that Fort St. Marks would be forcibly taken by the savages, from its Spanish garrison:

DEFENCE OF GENERAL JACKSON | 1818   191

yet, at the same time, he had refused the passage up the Escambia river, unless upon the payment of excessive duties, to provisions destined as supplies for the American army, which, by the detention of them, was subjected to the most distressing privations. He had permitted free ingress and egress at Pensacola, to the avowed savage enemies of the United States. Supplies of ammunition, munitions of war and provisions had been received by them from thence. They had been received and sheltered there, from the pursuit of the American forces, and suffered again to sally thence, to enter upon the American territory and commit new murders. Finally, on the approach of General Jackson to Pensacola, the Governor sent him a letter, [XXXIII.] denouncing his entry upon the territory of Florida, as a violent outrage upon the rights of Spain, commanding him to depart and withdraw from the same, and threatening, in case of his non-compliance, to employ force to expel him.

It became, therefore, in the opinion of General Jackson, indispensably necessary to take from the Governor of Pensacola [LIV.] the means of carrying his threat into execution. Before the forces under his command, the savage enemies of his country had disappeared. But he knew that the moment those forces should be disbanded, if sheltered by Spanish fortresses, if furnished with ammunitions and supplies by Spanish officers, and if aided and supported by the instigation of Spanish encouragement, as he had every reason to expect these would be, they would reappear, and fired, in addition to their ordinary ferociousness, with revenge for the chastisement they had so recently received, would again rush with the war hatchet and scalping knife, into the borders of the United States, and mark every foot-step with the blood of their defenceless citizens. So far as all the native resources of the savages extended, the war was at an end, and General Jackson was about to restore to their families and their homes, the brave volunteers who had followed his standard, and who had constituted the principal part of his force. This could be done with safety, leaving the regular portion of his troops to garrison his line of forts, and two small detachments of volunteer cavalry, to scour the country round Pensacola, and sweep off the lurking remnant of savages, who had been scattered and dispersed before him. This was sufficient to keep in check the remnant of the banditti, against whom he had marched, so long as they should be destitute of other aid and support. It was, in his judgment, not sufficient, if they should be suffered to rally their numbers under the protection of Spanish forts, and to derive new strength from the importance or the ill will against the United States of the Spanish authorities.

He took possession, therefore, of Pensacola, and of the Fort of Barrancas, as he had done of St. Marks, not in spirit of hostility to Spain, but as a necessary measure of self-defence; giving notice that they should be restored whenever Spain should place commanders and a force there, able and willing to fulfil the engagements of Spain towards the United States, of restraining, by force, the Florida Indians from hostilities against their citizens. The President of the United States, to give a signal manifestation of his confidence in the disposition of the King of Spain, to perform with good faith this indispensable engagement, and to demonstrate to the world that neither the desire of conquest nor hostility to Spain, had any influence in the councils of the United States, has directed the unconditional restoration to any Spanish officer, duly authorized to receive them, of Pensacola and the Barrancas, and that of St. Marks to any Spanish force adequate for its defence against the attack of the savages. But the President will neither inflict punishment, nor pass a censure upon general Jackson for that conduct, the motives for which were founded in the purest patriotism, of the necessity for which he had the most immediate and effectual means of forming a judgment, and the vindication of which is written in every page of the law of nations, as well as in the first law of nature, self-defence. He thinks it, on the contrary, due to the justice, which the United States have a right to claim from Spain; and you are accordingly instructed to demand of the Spanish government, that enquiry shall be instituted into the conduct of Don Jose Mazot, governor of Pensacola, and of Don Francisco C. Luengo, commandant of St. Marks, and a suitable punishment inflicted upon them for having, in defiance and violation of the engagements of Spain with the United States, aided and assisted these hordes of savages in those very hostilities against the United States, which it was their official duty to restrain. This enquiry is due to the character of those officers themselves, and to the honor of the Spanish government. The obligation of Spain to restrain, by force, the Indians of Florida from hostilities against the United States and their citizens, is explicit, is positive, is unqualified. The fact, that for a series of years they have received shelter, assistance, supplies and protection, in the practice of such hostilities from the Spanish commanders in Florida, is clear and unequivocal. [XXXII.] If, as the commanders both at Pensacola and St. Marks have [XLII.] alleged, this has been the result of their weakness, rather than of their will, if they have assisted the Indians against the U. States to avert their hostilities from the province, which they had not sufficient force to defend against them, it may serve, in some measure, to exculpate, individually, those officers, but it must carry demonstration irresistible to the Spanish government that the right of the United States can as little compound with impotence as with perfidy, and that Spain must immediately make her election, either to place a force in Florida adequate at once to the protection of her territory and to the fulfilment of her engagements, or cede to the United States a province, of which she retains nothing but the nominal possession; but which is, in fact, a derelict open to the occupancy of every enemy, civilized or savage, of the United States, and serving no other earthly purpose than as a post of annoyance to them.

That the purposes, as well of the Negro Indian banditti, with whom we have been contending, as of the British invaders of Florida, who first assembled and employed them, and of the British intruding and pretending traders, since the peace, who have instigated and betrayed them to destruction, have been not less hostile to Spain than to the United States, the proofs contained in the documents herewith enclosed, are conclusive. Mr. Pizarro's note of 29th of August, speaks of His Catholic Majesty's profound indignation at the "sanguinary executions, on the Spanish soil, of the subjects of powers in amity with the King"—meaning Arbuthnot and Ambrister. Let Mr. Pizarro's successor take the trouble of reading the enclosed documents, and he will discover who Arbuthnot and Ambrister were, and what were their purposes: That Arbuthnot was only the suc- [XLIX.] cessor of Nicholls, and Ambrister the agent of Woodbine, and [LVIII.] the subaltern of McGregor. Mr. Pizarro qualifies Gen. Jackson's necessary pursuit of a defeated savage enemy beyond the Spanish Florida line, as a *shameful invasion of His Majesty's territory*—yet, that territory was the territory also of the savage enemy, and Spain was bound to restrain them, by force, from hostilities against the United States—and it was the failure of Spain to fulfil this engagement, which had made it necessary for general Jackson to pursue the savages across the line. What then was the character of Nicholls's invasion of His Majesty's territory; and where was his Majesty's profound indignation at that? Mr. Pizarro says, his Majesty's forts and places have been violently seized on by general Jackson. Had they not been seized on, nay, had not the principal of his forts been blown up by Nicholls, and a British fort on the same Spanish territory been erected during the war, and left standing as a Negro fort, in defiance of Spanish authority, after the peace? Where was His Majesty's profound indignation at that? Has His Majesty suspended formally all negotiation with the sovereign of colonel Nicholls, for the shameful invasion of his territory without color of provocation, without pretence of necessity, without the shadow or even avowal of a pretext? Has His Majesty given solemn warning to the British government, that these were incidents "of transcendent moment capable of producing an essential and thorough change in the political relations of the two countries"? Nicholls and Woodbine, in their invitations and promises to the slaves to runaway from their masters and join them, did not confine themselves to the slaves of the U. States—they received with as hearty a welcome, and employed with equal readiness, the fugitives from their masters, in Florida, as those from Georgia. Against this special [xxv.] injury the governor of Pensacola did earnestly remonstrate with the British Admiral Cockburn (see the document marked XXV.) but against the *shameful invasion* of the territory—against the violent seizure of the forts and places—against the blowing up of the Barrancas, and the erection and maintenance under British banners, of the Negro fort on Spanish soil—against the negotiation by a British officer in the midst of peace, of pretended treaties, offensive and defensive, and of navigation and commerce upon Spanish territory, between Great Britain and Spanish Indians, whom Spain was bound to control and restrain—if a whisper of expostulation was ever wafted from Madrid to London, it was not loud enough to be heard across the Atlantic, nor energetic enough to transpire beyond the walls of the palaces from which it issued, and to which it was borne.

The connexion between Arbuthnot and Nicholls, and between Ambrister and McGregor, is established beyond all question, by the evidence produced at the trials before the court martial. I have already remarked to you on the very extraordinary circumstance, that a British trader from beyond the sea should be permitted, by the Spanish authorities, to trade with the Indians of Florida. From his letter to Hambly, dated 3d May, 1817, (see the documents marked G in the proceedings of the court martial) it appears that his trading was but a pretence; and that his principal purpose was to act as the agent of the Indians of Florida, and outlaws from the Creeks, to obtain the aid of the British government, in their hostilities against the United States. He expressly tells Hambly there, that the chief of those outlaws was the principal cause of his, Arbuthnot's, being in the country; and that he had come with an answer from Earl Bathurst, delivered to him by Governor Cameron, of New Providence, to certain Indian talks, in which this aid of the British government had been solicited. Hambly, himself, had been left by Nichols, as the agent between the Indians and the British government; but having found that Nicholls had failed in his attempt to prevail upon the British government to pursue this clandestine war, in the midst of peace; and that they were not prepared to support his pretence, that half a dozen outlawed fugitives from the Creeks were the Creek nation:—when Arbuthnot, the incendiary, came, and was instigating them, by promises of support [XLVII.B.] from Great Britain, to commence their murderous incursions into the U. States, Hambly, at the request of the Creeks themselves, wrote to him, warning him to withdraw from among that band of outlaws, and giving him a solemn forboding of the doom that awaited him, from the hand of justice, if he persevered in the course that he pursued. Arbuthnot, nevertheless, persisted; and while he was deluding the wretched Indians with [XLIX.] promises of support from England, he was writing letters for b. them to the British minister in the United States, to Gover- c. nor Cameron of New Providence, to Colonel Nichols; to be d. laid before the British government: and even to the Spanish e. go vernor at St. Augustine, and the governor general of the f.

Havana, soliciting, in all quarters, aid and support, arms and ammunition, for the Indians, against the United States; bewailing the destruction of the Negro fort, and charging the British government with having drawn the Indians into war with the United States, and deserting them after the peace.

You will remark among the papers produced on his trial, [XLIX. NO. I.] a power of attorney, dated 17th June, 1817, given him by twelve Indians, partly of Florida, and partly of the fugitive outlaws from the United States. He states that this power, [Compare and his instructions, were, to memorialize the British government, and the governor general of the Havana. These papers are not only substantially proved, as of his hand writing, on the trial, but in the daily newspapers of London, [XLVII.c.] of the 24th and 25th of Aug. last, his letter to Nicholls [Compare is published, (somewhat garbled) with a copy of Hambly's XLVII.c and above mentioned letter to him, & a reference to this Indian XLIX. NO. 1] power of attorney to him, *approved by the Commandant* [XLVII.] *of St. Marks, F. C. Luengo.* Another of the papers is a letter, written in the name of the same chiefs, by Arbuthnot, to the governor general of the Havana, asking of him permission for Arbuthnot to establish a ware-house on the Appalachicola; bitterly and falsely complaining that the Americans had made settlements on their lands, within the Spanish lines, and calling upon the governor general to give orders to displace them, and send them back to their own country. In this letter they assign, as a reason for asking this license for Arbuthnot, the want of a person to put in writing for them their talks, of grievances against the Americans. And they add, "the commander of the fort of St. Marks has heard all of our talks and complaints. He approves of what we have done, and what we are doing; and it is by his recommendation we have thus presumed to address your excellency." You will find these papers in the printed newspaper enclosed, and in the proceedings of the court martial, and will point them out to the Spanish government, not only as decisive proofs of the unexampled compliances of the Spanish officers in Florida, to foreign intrusive agents and instigators of Indian hostilities against the United States, but as placing, beyond a doubt, that participation of this hostile spirit in the commandant of St. Marks, which General Jackson so justly complains of, and of which we have so well founded a right to demand the punishment. Here is the commandant of a Spanish fort, bound by the sacred engagement of a treaty to restrain, by force, the Indians within his command from committing hostilities against the United States, conspiring with those same Indians, and deliberately giving his written approbation to their appointment of a foreigner, a British subject, as their agent, to solicit assistance and supplies from the governor general of Havana, and from the British government, for carrying on these same hostilities.

Let us come to the case of Ambrister—He was taken in arms; leading and commanding the Indians, in the war against the American troops; and to that charge, upon his trial, pleading guilty. But the primary object of his coming there, was still more hostile to. Spain, than to the United States. You find that [LVIII.] he told three of the witnesses, who testified at his trial, that he had come to this country upon Mr. Woodbine's business at Tampa Bay—to see the Negroes righted; and one of them, that *he had a commission in the Patriot army, under McGregor*; and that he had expected a captaincy. And what was the intended business of McGregor and Woodbine, at Tampa Bay? It was the conquest of Florida from Spain, by the use of those very Indians and Negroes, whom the commandant of St. Marks was so ready to aid and support in the war against the United States. The chain of proof that establishes this fact, is contained in the documents communicated by the President to Congress at their last session, relating to the occupation of the Amelia Island by [LVI.] McGregor. From these documents you will find, that while McGregor was there, Woodbine went from New Providence, in a schooner of his own, to join him: That he arrived at Amelia Island, just as McGregor, abandoning the companions of his achievement there, was leaving it: That McGregor, quitting the vessel in which he had embarked at Amelia, went on board that of Woodbine, and returned with him to New Providence: That Woodbine had persuaded him they could yet accomplish the conquest of Florida, with soldiers to be recruited at Nassau, from the corps of Colonial Marines, which had served under Nicholls during the late war with the United States, which corps had been lately disbanded; and with Negroes to be found at Tampa Bay, and 1500 Indians, already then engaged to Woodbine, who pretended that they had made a grant of all [LVII.a.b.] their lands there to him. Among the papers, the originals of which are in our possession, in McGregor's own hand writing, instructions for sailing into Tampa Bay, with the assertion [d.] that he calculated to be there by the last of April or first of May, of the present year; a letter dated 27th December last, to [c.] one of his acquaintance in this country, disclosing the same intention; and the extract of a proclamation which was to have been issued at Tampa Bay, to the inhabitants of Florida, by the person charged with making the settlement there, before his arrival, announcing his approach, for the purpose of liberating them from the despotism of Spain, and of enabling them to form a government for themselves. He has persuaded those who would listen to him here, that his ultimate object was to sell the Floridas to the United States. There is some reason to suppose that he had made indirect overtures, of a similar nature, to the British government. This was Ambrister's busi- [XLIX.] ness in Florida. He arrived there in March, the precursor of McGregor and Woodbine, and, immediately upon his arrival, he is found seizing upon Arbuthnot's goods, and distributing them among the Negroes and Indians; seizing upon his vessel, and compelling its master to pilot him, with a body of armed Negroes, towards the fort of St. Marks, with the declared purpose of taking it by surprize, in the night. Writing letters to Governor Cameron, of New Providence, urgently calling for supplies of munitions of war, and of cannon, for the war against the Americans; and letters to Col. Nicholls, renewing the same demands of supplies; informing him, that he is with 300 Negroes, 'a few of our Bluff people,' who had *stuck to the cause*, and were relying upon the faith of Nicholls's promises. Our Bluff people were the people of the Negro fort, collected by Nicholls's and Woodbine's proclamations, during the American and English war; and the *cause* to which they stuck, was the savage, servile, exterminating war against the United States.

Among the agents and actors of such virtuous enterprizes as are here unveiled, it was hardly expected that there would be found remarkable evidences of their respect, confidence and good faith towards one another. Accordingly, besides the violent seizure and distribution, by Ambrister, of Arbuthnot's property, his letters to Governor Cameron, and to Nicholls, are filled with the distrust and suspicions of the Indians, that they were deceived and betrayed by Arbuthnot; while in Arbuthnot's letters to the same Nicholls, he accuses Woodbine [XLIX.f.] of having taken charge of poor Francis, the prophet, or Hillis Hadjo, upon his return from England to New Providence, and under pretence of taking care of him and his affairs—of having defrauded him of a large portion of the presents which had been delivered out from the king's stores to him, for Francis's use. This is one of the passages of Arbuthnot's letter to Nicholls, [XLVII.a.] *omitted* in the publication of it last August, in the London newspapers.

Is this narrative of dark and complicated depravity; this creeping and insidious war, both against Spain and the United States; this mockery of patriotism; these political philters to fugitive slaves and Indian outlaws; these perfidies and treacheries of villains incapable of keeping their faith even to each other, all in the name of South American liberty, of the rights of runaway Negroes, and the wrongs of savage murderers—all combined and projected to plunder Spain of her provinces, and to spread massacre and devastation along the borders of the United States? Is all this sufficient to cool the sympathies of his Catholic Majesty's government, excited by the execution of these two "subjects of a power in amity with the king." The Spanish government is not this day to be informed that, cruel as war in its mildest forms must be, it is, and necessarily must be, doubly cruel, when waged with savages; that savages make no prisoners, but to torture them; that they give no quarter; that they put to death without discrimination of age or sex; that these ordinary characteristics of Indian warfare have been applicable, in their most heart-sickening horrors, to that war, left us by Nicholls, as his legacy, reinstigated by Woodbine, Arbuthnot and Ambrister, and stimulated by the approbation, encouragement, and the aid of the Spanish commandant at St. Marks. Is proof required? Intreat the Spanish minister of state, for a moment, to overcome the feelings which details like these must excite, and to reflect, if possible, with composure, upon the facts stated in the following extracts from the documents enclosed:

Letter from sailing master Jairus Loomis to Commodore Daniel T. Patterson, 13th August, 1816, reporting the destruction [XXIII.] of the Negro Fort.

"On examining the prisoners, they stated that Edward Daniels, O.S. who was made prisoner in the boat, on the 17th July, *was tarred and buried alive.*"

Letter from Archibald Clarke to Gen. Gaines, 26th Feb. 1817. (Message of the President of the U. States to Congress, 25th March, 1818, p. 9.)

"On the 24th inst. the house of Mr. Garrett, residing in the upper part of this county, near the boundary of Wayne county, (Georgia) was attacked, during his absence, near the middle of the day, by this party, (of Indians) consisting of about fifteen, who shot Mrs. Garret, in two places, and then dispatched her by stabbing and scalping. Her two children, one about three years, and the other two months, were also murdered and the eldest scalped: the house was then plundered of every article of value, and set on fire."

[LXI.] Letter from Peter B. Cook (Arbuthnot's clerk) to Eliz. A. Carney, at Nassau, dated Suwahnee, 19th Jan. 1818, giving an account of their operations with the Indians, against the Americans, and their massacre of Lieut. Scott and his party.

"There was a boat that was taken by the Indians, that had in it thirty men, seven women, four small children. There were six of the men got clear, and one of the women saved, and all the rest of them got killed. The children were took by the leg, and their brains dashed out against the boat."

If the bare recital of scenes like these cannot be perused without shuddering, what must be the agonized feelings of those whose wives and children are, from day, to day, and from night to night, exposed to be the victims of the same barbarity? Has mercy a voice to plead for the perpetrators and instigators of deeds like these? Should enquiry hereafter be made, why, within three months after this event, the savage Hamathli Micco, upon being taken by the American troops, was, by order of their commander, immediately hung, let it be told that that savage was the commander of the party by which those women were butchered, and those helpless infants were thus dashed against the boat. Contending with such enemies, although humanity revolts at entire retaliation upon them, and spares the lives of their feeble and defenceless women and children, yet mercy herself surrenders to retributive justice the lives of their leading warriors taken in arms—and still more the lives of the foreign, white incendiaries, who, disowned by their own governments, and disowning their own natures, degrade themselves beneath the savage character, by voluntarily descending to its level. Is not this the dictate of common sense? Is it not the usage of legitimate warfare? Is it not consonant to the soundest authorities of national law? "When at war, (says Vattel,) with a ferocious nation, which observes no rule and grants no quarter, they may be chastised in the persons of those of them who may be taken; they are of the number of the guilty; and by this rigor the attempt may be made of bringing them to a sense of the laws of humanity." And again; "As a general has the right of sacrificing the lives of his enemies to his own safety or that of his people, if he has to contend with an inhuman enemy, often guilty of such excesses, he may take the lives of some of his prisoners, and treat them as his own people have been treated." The justification of these principles is found in their salutary efficacy, for terror and for example. It is thus only that the barbarities of Indians can be successfully encountered. It is thus only that the worse than Indian barbarities of European imposters, pretending authority from their governments, but always disavowed, can be punished and arrested. Great Britain yet engages the alliance and co-operation of savages in war. But her government has invariably disclaimed all countenance or authorization to her subjects to instigate them against us in time of peace. Yet so it has happened, that from the period of our established independence to this day, *all* the Indian wars with which we have been afflicted have been distinctly traceable to the instigation of English traders or agents, always disavowed, yet always felt, more than once detected, but never before punished. Two of them, offenders of the deepest dye, after solemn warning to their government, and individually to one of them, have fallen, *flagrante delicto*, into the hands of an American general: and the punishment inflicted upon them has fixed them on high as an example, awful in its exhibition, but, we trust, auspicious in its results, of that which awaits unauthorized pretenders of European agency, to stimulate, and interpose in wars between the United States and the Indians, within their control.

This exposition of the origin, the causes, and the character of the war with the Seminole Indians and part of the Creeks, combined with M'Gregor's mock patriots and Nicholls's Negroes, which necessarily led our troops into Florida, and gave rise to all those incidents of which Mr. Pizarro so vehemently complains, will, it is hoped, enable you to present other and sounder views of the subject to his Catholic Majesty's government. It will enable you to show that the occupation of Pensacola and St. Marks was occasioned neither by a spirit of hostility to Spain, nor with a view to extort, prematurely, the province from her possession; that it was rendered necessary by the neglect of Spain to perform her engagements of restraining the Indians from hostilities against the United States, and by the culpable countenance, encouragement, and assistance given to those Indians, in their hostilities, by the Spanish governor and commandant at those places: That the United States have a right to demand, as the President does demand, of Spain the punishment of those officers for this misconduct; and he further demands of Spain a just and reasonable indemnity to the United States for the heavy and necessary expenses which they have been compelled to incur, by the failure of Spain to perform her engagement, to restrain the Indians, aggravated by this demonstrated complicity of her commanding officers with them, in their hostilities against the United States: That the two Englishmen executed by order of Gen. Jackson were not only identified with the savages, with whom they were carrying on the war against the United States, but that one of them was the mover and fomentor of the war, which, without his interference and false promises to the Indians of support from the British government, never would have happened—that the other was the instrument of war against Spain as well as the United States, commissioned by M'Gregor, and expedited by Woodbine, upon their project of conquering Florida with these Indians and Negroes: That, as accomplices of the savages, and, sinning against their better knowledge, worse than savages, Gen. Jackson, possessed of their persons and of the proofs of their guilt, might, by the lawful and ordinary usages of war, have hung them both without the formality of a trial: That, to allow them every possible opportunity of refuting the proofs or of showing any circumstance in extenuation of their crimes, he gave them the benefit of a trial by a court martial, of highly respectable officers: That the defence of one consisted, solely and exclusively, of technical cavils at the nature of part of the evidence against him, and the other confessed his guilt. Finally, that, in restoring Pensacola and St. Marks to Spain, the President gives the most signal proof of his confidence, that hereafter her engagement to restrain, by force, the Indians of Florida from all hostilities against the United States, will be effectually fulfilled; that there will be no more murders, no more robberies within our borders, by savages prowling along the Spanish line, and seeking shelter within it, to display in their villages the scalps of our women and children, their victims, and to sell, with shameless effrontery, the plunder from our citizens in Spanish forts and cities; that we shall hear no more apologies from Spanish governors and commandants, of their inability to perform the duties of their office and the solemn contracts of their country—no more excuses for compliances to the savage enemies of the United States from the dread of their attacks upon themselves—no more harboring of foreign imposters, upon compulsion; that a strength sufficient will be kept in the province to restrain the Indians by force, and officers empowered and instructed to employ it effectually to maintain the good faith of the nation, by the effective fulfilment of the treaty. The duty of this government to protect the persons and property of our fellow citizens, on the borders of the United States is imperative—it *must* be discharged—& if, after all the warnings that Spain has had—if, after the prostration of all her territorial rights and neutral obligations, by Nicholls and his banditti, during war, and of all her treaty stipulations, by Arbuthnot and Ambrister, abetted by her own commanding officers, during peace, to the cruel annoyance of the United States—if the necessities of self-defence should again compel the United States to take possession of the Spanish forts and places in Florida, declare, with the candor and frankness that becomes us, that another unconditional restoration of them must not be expected; that even the President's confidence in the good faith and ultimate justice of the Spanish government will yield to the painful experience of continual disappointment; and that, after unwearied and almost unnumbered appeals to them, for the performance of their stipulated duties, in vain, the United States will be reluctantly compelled to rely, for the protection of their borders, upon themselves alone.

You are authorized to communicate the whole of this letter and the accompanying documents, to the Spanish government. I have the honor, &c. &c.

JOHN QUINCY ADAMS.

"SHE GOES NOT ABROAD, IN SEARCH OF MONSTERS TO DESTROY"

10. *An Address delivered At the request of a Committee of the Citizens of Washington on the occasion of reading the Declaration of Independence, on the Fourth of July, 1821* (Washington, D.C.: Davis and Force, 1821).

With a vestigial Federalist party failing even to field a candidate, James Monroe won reelection in 1820 with the largest majority since George Washington. The final tally in the electoral college was 228 to 1. (The lone dissenting vote went to John Quincy Adams, to the great embarrassment of the secretary of state.) No sooner had the votes been counted than the members of Monroe's cabinet began jockeying to succeed him, Washington having established the custom of presidents stepping down after two terms. The major aspirants were Secretary of the Treasury William H. Crawford, Secretary of War John C. Calhoun, and Adams himself, though even in the privacy of his diary he had trouble explicitly acknowledging the extent of his ambition. Outside the administration, Andrew Jackson and Speaker of the House Henry Clay were also likely candidates. At this ebb tide of national political partisanship in American history, all were nominally members of the same party, the National Republicans.

Adams had certain advantages among the five. The first was sectional: while Jackson (Tennessee) and Clay (Kentucky) could be expected to divide support in the western states, and Crawford (Georgia) and Calhoun (South Carolina) in the southern, Adams faced no significant rivals among the northern. The second was his position at State, which many saw as a stepping-stone to the presidency. Jefferson, Madison, and Monroe had each been the nation's chief diplomat, and the latter two had moved directly from State to the Executive Mansion. If Adams had a disadvantage as a candidate, it was his reluctance to actively be one. "I had made up my mind," he wrote in his diary on February 25, 1821, "I would take no one step to advance or promote pretensions to the Presidency — If that office was to be the prize of cabal and intrigue, of purchasing newspapers, bribing by appointments or bargaining for foreign missions, I had no ticket in that Lottery. . . . I can do nothing, either to canvass for myself, or to counteract the canvassing of others." In 1823, writing in response to a supporter who sought to help him, Adams would call this the

"Macbeth policy," quoting from Shakespeare's tragedy: "If chance will have me king, why chance may crown me / Without my stir."

For all that, Adams did accept the invitation to deliver this Fourth of July oration in the chamber of the House of Representatives, before the assembled ranks of the national government and the diplomatic corps, the closest he ever came to advancing himself for consideration as the next president. The occasion, as always, was a welcome one for Adams, reinforcing by its very nature his sense of himself as a man of the nation. In this instance, the speech afforded him an opportunity to speak forcefully if obliquely to pressing issues bearing on America's role in the world: Should the United States actively support democratic revolutions in Greece and Latin America? Should it join with Great Britain in forming a liberal counterbalance to the reactionary influence of the Holy Alliance? Primed for patriotic flourish, for some well-placed jabs at the former mother country, and for a better sense of this man who seemed poised to be the next president, the audience was rapt as he approached the rostrum. Dressed in his professorial robes, holding the original copy of the Declaration of Independence in his hand—glancing, perhaps, at his father's signature there on the nation's founding charter—Adams delivered what many regard as his finest speech, addressing a question that remains as fundamental today as it was then: What is the relationship between liberty and power?

AN

ADDRESS

DELIVERED

At the request of a Committee of the Citizens of Washington;

ON THE OCCASION OF READING

THE DECLARATION OF INDEPENDENCE,

ON THE

FOURTH OF JULY, 1821.

BY

JOHN QUINCY ADAMS.

CITY OF WASHINGTON:

PRINTED BY DAVIS AND FORCE, PENNSYLVANIA AVENUE.

1821.

Washington, *July* 4, 1821.

SIR:

The Committee of Arrangements for the celebration of this day, in presenting to you their unfeigned thanks for the patriotic and able Address which you have obliged them by delivering, solicit the favor of you to furnish them with a copy of it, for publication in a form suited to its merits.

        J. P. VAN NESS,
        FONTAINE MAURY,
        JOSEPH GALES, Jr.
        JAMES M. VARNUM,
        ARCH. HENDERSON.

Hon. J. Q. Adams.

To the Committee of Arrangements for the
 Celebration of the Anniversary of Independence at the City of Washington.

        Washington, 5 *July*, 1821.

GENTLEMEN :

  In placing at your disposal a copy of the Address yesterday delivered in compliance with your invitation, I avail myself of the occasion of expressing through you, to my Fellow-Citizens, the assurance of my gratitude for the indulgence with which it was received.

     I have the honor to be,
       With great respect, Gentlemen,
         Your very obedient servant,
           JOHN QUINCY ADAMS.

Fourth of July Address

FELLOW-CITIZENS:

UNTIL within a few days preceding that which we have again assembled to commemorate, our Fathers, the people of this Union, had constituted a portion of the British nation; a nation renowned in Arts and Arms, who, from a small Island in the Atlantic Ocean, had extended their dominion over considerable parts of every quarter of the Globe. Governed themselves by a race of kings, whose title to sovereignty had originally been founded in *conquest*, spell-bound for a succession of ages under that portentous system of despotism and of superstition which in the name of the meek and humble Jesus had been spread over the Christian world, the history of this nation had, for a period of seven hundred years, from the days of the conquest till our own, exhibited a conflict almost continual, between the oppressions of power and the claims of right. In the theories of the Crown and the Mitre man had no rights. Neither the body nor the soul of the individual was his own. From the impenetrable gloom of this intellectual darkness, and the deep degradation of this servitude, the British nation had partially emerged. The martyrs of religious freedom had consumed to ashes at the stake: the champions of temporal liberty had bowed their heads upon the scaffold; and the spirits of many a bloody day had left their earthly vesture upon the field of battle, and soared to plead the cause of Liberty before the throne of Heaven. The people of Britain, through long ages of civil war, had extorted from their tyrants not *acknowledgements*, but *grants*, of right. With this concession they had been content to stop in the progress of human improvement. They received their freedom as a donation from their sovereigns; they appealed for their privileges to a sign manual and a seal; they held their title to liberty, like their title to lands, from the bounty of a man; and in their moral and political chronology, the great charter of Runny Mead was the beginning of the world.

From the earliest ages of their recorded history, the inhabitants of the British Islands have been distinguished for their intelligence and their spirit. How much of these two qualities, the fountains of all amelioration in the condition of men, was stifled by these two principles of subserviency to ecclesiastical usurpation, and of holding *rights* as the donation of kings, this is not the occasion to inquire.

Of their tendency to palsy the vigor and enervate the faculties of man, all philosophical reasoning, and all actual experience, concur in testimony.

These principles, however, were not peculiar to the people of Britain. They were the delusions of all Europe, still the most enlightened and most improvable portion of the earth. The temporal chain was riveted upon the people of Britain by the conquest. Their spiritual fetters were forged by subtlety working upon superstition. Baneful as the effect of these principles was, they could not for ever extinguish the light of reason in the human mind. The discovery of the Mariner's Compass was soon followed by the extension of intercourse between nations the most distant, and which, without that light beaming in darkness to guide the path of man over the boundless waste of waters, could never have been known to each other. The invention of Printing, and the composition of Gunpowder, which revolutionized at once the art and science of war, and the relations of peace; the revelation of India to Vasco de Gama; and the disclosure to Columbus of the American hemisphere, all resulted from the incompressible energies of the human intellect, bound and crippled as it was by the double cords of ecclesiastical imposture and political oppression. To these powerful agents in the progressive improvement of our species, Britain can lay no claim. For them the children of men are indebted to Italy, to Germany, to Portugal, and to Spain. All these improvements, however, consisted in successful researches into the properties and modifications of external nature. The religious reformation was an improvement in the science of mind; an improvement in the intercourse of man with his Creator, and in his acquaintance with himself. It was an advance in the knowledge of his *duties* and his *rights*. It was a step in the progress of man in comparison with which the Magnet and Gunpowder, the wonders of either India; nay, the Printing Press itself, were but the paces of a pigmy to the stride of a giant. If to this step of human advancement Germany likewise lays claim in the person of Martin Luther, or in the earlier but ineffectual martyrdom of John Huss, England may point to her Wicliffe as a yet more primitive vindicator of the same righteous cause, and may insist on the glory of having contributed her share to the improvement of the moral condition of man.

The corruptions and usurpations of the Church were the immediate objects of these reformers; but, at the foundation of all their exertions, there was a single, plain, and almost self-evident principle—that man has a right to the exercise of his own reason. It was this principle which the sophistry and rapacity of the Church had obscured and obliterated, and which the intestine divisions of the same Church itself first restored. The triumph of reason was the result of inquiry and discussion. Centuries of desolating wars have succeeded, and oceans of human blood have flowed for the final establishment of this principle; but it was from the darkness of the Cloister that the first spark was emitted, and from the arches of an University that it first kindled into day. From the discussion of religious rights and duties, the transition to that of the political and civil relations of men with one another, was natural and unavoidable; in both, the reformers were met by the weapons of temporal power. At the same glance of reason, the tiara would have fallen from the brow of priesthood, and the despotic sceptre would have departed from the hand of royalty, but for the sword by which they were protected—that sword which, like the flaming sword of the Cherubim, turned every way to debar access to the tree of life.

The double contest against the oppressors of the Church and State was too appalling for the vigor, or too comprehensive for the faculties of the reformers of the European Continent. In Britain alone was it undertaken, and in Britain but partially succeeded.

It was in the midst of that fermentation of the human intellect which brought right and power in direct and deadly conflict with each other, that the rival crowns of the two portions of the British Island, were united on the same head. It was then that, released from the manacles of ecclesiastical domination, the minds of men began to investigate the foundations of civil government. But the mass of the nation surveyed the fabric of their institutions as it existed in fact. It had been founded in conquest; it had been cemented in servitude, and so broken and moulded had been the minds of this brave and intelligent people to their actual condition, that instead of solving civil society into its first elements in search of their rights, they looked back only to conquest as the origin of their liberties, and claimed their rights but as donations from their kings.

This faltering assertion of freedom is not chargeable indeed upon the whole nation. There were spirits capable of tracing civil government to its foundation in the moral and physical nature of man; but conquest and servitude were so mingled up in every particle of the social existence of the nation, that they had become vitally necessary to them, as a portion of the fluid, itself destructive of life, is indispensably blended with the atmosphere in which we live.

Fellow-Citizens, it was in the heat of this war of moral elements, which brought one Stuart to the block, and hurled another from his throne, that our forefathers sought refuge from its fury, in the then wilderness of this Western World.

They were willing exiles from a country dearer to them than life.—But they were the exiles of liberty and of conscience, dearer to them even than their country. They came too with *Charters* from their kings: for even in removing to another hemisphere, they "cast longing, lingering, looks behind," and were anxiously desirous of retaining ties of connexion with their country, which, in the solemn compact of a charter, they hoped by the corresponding links of allegiance and protection to preserve.

But to their sense of right, the charter was only the ligament between them, their country, and their king. Transported to a new world, they had relations with one another, and relations with the aboriginal inhabitants of the country to which they came, for which no royal charter could provide. The first settlers of the Plymouth colony, at the eve of landing from their ship, therefore, bound themselves together by a written covenant; and, immediately after landing, purchased from the Indian natives the right of settlement upon the soil.

Thus was a social compact formed upon the elementary principles of civil society, in which conquest and servitude had no part. The slough of brutal force was entirely cast off: all was voluntary; all was unbiassed consent; all was the agreement of soul with soul.

Other colonies were successively founded, and other charters granted, until, in the compass of a century and a half, thirteen distinct British Provinces peopled the Atlantic shores of the North American continent with two millions of freemen; possessing by their charters the rights of British Subjects, and nurtured by their position and education, in the more comprehensive and original doctrines of human rights. From their infancy they had been treated by the parent state with neglect, harshness, and injustice. Their charters had often been disregarded and violated; their commerce restricted and shackled; their interests wantonly or spitefully sacrificed; so that the hand of the parent had been scarcely ever felt, but in the alternate application of whips and scorpions.

When in spite of all these persecutions, by the natural vigor of their constitution, they were just attaining the maturity of political manhood, a British Parliament, in contempt of the clearest maxims of natural equity, in defiance of the fundamental principle upon which British freedom itself had been cemented with British blood; on the naked unblushing allegation of absolute and uncontrollable power, undertook by their act, to levy, without representation and without consent, *taxes* upon the people of America, for the benefit of the people of Britain. This enormous project of public robbery was no sooner made known, than it excited throughout the colonies one general burst of indignant resistance. It was abandoned, reasserted and resumed, until fleets and armies were transported, to record in the characters of fire, famine, and desolation, the transatlantic wisdom of British legislation, and the tender mercies of British consanguinity.

Fellow-citizens, I am speaking of days long past. Ever faithful to the sentiment proclaimed in the paper* which I am about to present once more to your memory of the past and to your forecast of the future; you will hold the people of Britain, as you hold the rest of mankind, Enemies in war; in peace Friends. The conflict for Independence is now itself but a record of history. The resentments of that age may be buried in oblivion. The stoutest hearts which then supported the tug of war are cold

---

* The Declaration of Independence; read, on this occasion, from the *original*, which is in the office of the Department of State.

under the clod of the valley. My purpose is to rekindle no angry passion from its embers: but this annual solemn perusal of the instrument which proclaimed to the world the causes of your existence as a nation, is not without its just and useful purpose.

It is not by the yearly reiteration of the wrongs endured by your fathers, to evoke from the Sepulchre of Time, the shades of departed Tyranny; it is not to draw from their dread abode the frailties of an unfortunate monarch who now sleeps with his fathers, and the sufferings of whose latter days may have atoned at the bar of Divine Mercy, for the sins which the accusing Angel will read from *this scroll* to his charge; it is not to exult in the great moral triumph by which the Supreme Governor of the world crowned the cause of your country with success. No, the purpose for which you listen with renewed and never-languishing delight to the reading of this paper is of a purer and more exalted cast. It is sullied with no vindictive recollection. It is degraded by no rankling resentment. It is inflated with no vain and idle exultation of victory. The Declaration of Independence in its primary purport was merely an *occasional* state paper. It was a solemn exposition to the World, of the *causes* which had *compelled* the people of a small portion of the British empire to cast off the allegiance and renounce the protection of the British king; and to dissolve their social connexion with the British people. In the annals of the human race, the separation of one people into two, is an event of no uncommon occurrence. The successful resistance of a people against oppression, to the downfall of the tyrant and of tyranny itself, is the lesson of many an age, and of almost every clime. It lives in the venerable records of Holy Writ. It beams in the brightest pages of profane history. The names of Pharaoh and Moses, of Tarquin and Junius Brutus, of Geisler and Tell, of Christiern and Gustavus Vasa, of Philip of Austria and William of Orange, stand in long array through the vista of Time, like the Spirit of Evil and the Spirit of Good, in embattled opposition to each other, from the mouldering ages of antiquity, to the recent memory of our fathers, and from the burning plains of Palestine, to the polar frost of Scandinavia. For the Independence of North America, there were ample and sufficient causes in the laws of moral and physical nature. The tie of colonial subjection, is compatible with the essential purposes of civil government, only when the condition of the subordinate state is from its weakness incompetent to its own protection. Is the greatest moral purpose of civil government the administration of justice? And if justice has been truly defined the constant and perpetual will of securing to every one his *right*, how absurd and impracticable is that form of polity, in which the dispenser of justice is in one quarter of the globe, and he to whom justice is to be dispensed is in another; where "moons revolve and oceans roll between the order and its execution;" where time and space must be annihilated to secure to every one his right. The tie of colonial subjection may suit the relations between a great naval power, and the settlers of a small and remote Island in the incipient stages of society: but was it possible for British intelligence to imagine, or British sense of justice to desire, that through the boundless ages of time, the swarming myriads of freemen, who were to civilize the wilderness, and fill with human life the solitudes of this immense continent, should receive the mandates of their earthly destinies from a council chamber at St. James's, or bow forever in submission to the omnipotence of St. Stephen's Chapel? Are the essential purposes of civil government, to administer to the wants, and to fortify the infirmities of solitary man? To unite the sinews of numberless arms, and combine the councils of multitudes of minds, for the promotion of the well-being of all? The first moral element then of this composition is sympathy between the members of which it consists; the second is sympathy between the giver and the receiver of the Law. The sympathies of men begin with the affections of domestic life. They are rooted in the natural relations of husband and wife, of parent and child, of brother and sister; thence they spread through the social and moral propinquities of the neighbor and friend, to the broader and more complicated relations of countryman and fellow-citizen; terminating only with the circumference of the globe which we inhabit, in the co-extensive charities incident to the common nature of man. To each of these relations, different degrees of sympathy are allotted by the ordinances of nature. The sympathies of domestic life are not more sacred and obligatory, but closer and more powerful, than those of neighborhood and friendship. The tie which binds us to our country, is not more holy in the sight of God, but it is more deeply seated in our nature, more tender and endearing, than that looser link which merely connects us with our fellow mortal man.

It is a common Government that constitutes our *Country*. But in THAT association, all the sympathies of domestic life and kindred blood, all the moral ligatures of friendship and of neighborhood, are combined with that instinctive and mysterious connexion between man and physical nature, which binds the first perceptions of childhood in a chain of sympathy with the last gasp of expiring age, to the spot of our nativity, and the natural objects by which it is surrounded. These sympathies belong and are indispensable to the relations ordained by nature between the individual and his country. They dwell in the memory and are indelible in the hearts of the first settlers of a distant colony. These are the feelings under which the Children of Israel "sat down by the rivers of Babylon, and wept when they remembered Zion." These are the sympathies under which they "hung their harps upon the willows," and instead of songs of mirth, exclaimed, "If I forget thee, O Jerusalem, let my right hand forget her cunning." But these sympathies can never exist for a country, which we have never seen. They are transferred in the breasts of the succeeding generations, from the country of human institution, to the country of their birth; from the land of which they have only heard, to the land where their eyes first opened to the day. The ties of neighborhood are broken up, those of friendship can never be formed, with an intervening ocean; and the natural ties of domestic life, the all-subduing sympathies of love, the indissoluble bonds of marriage, the heart-riveted kindliness of consanguinity, gradually wither and perish in the lapse of a few generations. All the elements which form the basis of that sympathy between the individual and his country are dissolved.—Long before the Declaration of Independence the great mass of the People of America and of the People of Britain, had become total strangers to each other. The people of America were known to the people of Britain only by the transactions of trade; by shipments of lumber and flaxseed, indigo and tobacco. They were known to the government only by half a dozen colonial agents, humble, and often spurned suitors at the feet of power, and by royal governors, minions of patronage, sent, from the footstool of a throne beyond the seas, to rule a people of whom they knew nothing; as if an inhabitant of the moon should descend to give laws to the dwellers upon earth. Here and there, a man of letters and a statesman, conversant with all history, knew something of the colonies, as he knew something of Cochin-China and Japan. Yet even the prime minister of England, urging upon his omnipotent Parliament laws for grinding the colonies to submission, could talk, without amazing or diverting his hearers, of the Island of Virginia: even Edmund Burke, a man of more ethereal mind, *apologizing* to the people of Bristol for the offence of sympathizing with the distresses of our country, ravaged by the fire and sword of Britons, asked indulgence for his feelings on the score of general humanity, and expressly declared that the Americans were a nation utter strangers to him, and among whom he was not sure of having a single acquaintance. The sympathies therefore most essential to the communion of country were, between the British and American people, extinct.—Those most indispensable to the just relation between sovereign and subject, had never existed and could not exist between the British Government and the American People. The connexion was unnatural; and it was in the moral order, no less than in the positive decrees, of Providence, that it should be dissolved.

Yet, Fellow-Citizens, these are not the causes of the separation assigned in the paper which I am about to read. The connexion between different portions of the same people, and between a people and their government, is a connexion of *duties* as well as of *rights*. In the long conflict of twelve years which had preceded and led to the Declaration of Independence, our fathers had been not less faithful to their *duties*, than tenacious of their *rights*. Their resistance had not been rebellion. It was not a restive and ungovernable spirit of ambition bursting from the bonds of colonial subjection, it was the deep and wounded sense of successive wrongs, upon which complaint had been only answered by aggravation, and petition repelled with contumely, which had driven them to their last stand upon the adamantine rock of human rights.

It was then, fifteen months after the blood of Lexington and Bunker's Hill, after Charlestown and Falmouth, fired by British hands, were but heaps of ashes, after the ear of the adder had been turned to two successive supplications to the throne; after two successive appeals to the people of Britain, as *Friends, Countrymen*, and *Brethren*, to which no responsive voice of sympathetic tenderness had been returned—

> "Nought but the noise of drums and timbrels loud,
> Their children's cries unheard that passed thro' fire
> To the grim idol."

Then it was, that the Thirteen United Colonies of North America, by their delegates in Congress assembled, exercising the first act of sovereignty by right ever inherent in the people, but never to be resorted to, save at the awful crisis when civil society is solved into its first elements, declared themselves free and independent States, and two days afterwards, in justification of that act, issued this Unanimous Declaration of the Thirteen United States of America.

IN CONGRESS, JULY 4, 1776.

The Unanimous Declaration of the Thirteen United States of America.

WHEN, in the course of human events, it becomes necessary for one people to dissolve the political bands which have connected them with another, and to assume, among the powers of the earth, the separate and equal station to which the laws of nature and of nature's God entitle them, a decent respect to the opinions of mankind requires that they should declare the causes which impel them to the separation.

We hold these truths to be self-evident—that all men are created equal; that they are endowed by their Creator with certain unalienable rights; that among these are life, liberty, and the pursuit of happiness. That to secure these rights, governments are instituted among men, deriving their just powers from the consent of the governed; that whenever any form of government becomes destructive of these ends, it is the right of the people to alter or to abolish it, and to institute new government, laying its foundation on such principles, and organizing its powers in such form, as to them shall seem most likely to effect their safety and happiness. Prudence, indeed, will dictate, that governments long established should not be changed for light and transient causes; and accordingly all experience hath shown, that mankind are more disposed to suffer while evils are sufferable, than to right themselves by abolishing the forms to which they are accustomed. But when a long train of abuses and usurpations, pursuing invariably the same object, evinces a design to reduce them under absolute despotism, it is their right, it is their duty, to throw off such government, and to provide new guards for their future security. Such has been the patient sufferance of these colonies; and such is now the necessity which constrains them to alter their former systems of government. The history of the present king of Great Britain, is a history of repeated injuries and usurpations, all having in direct object the establishment of an absolute tyranny over these States. To prove this, let facts be submitted to a candid world.

He has refused his assent to laws the most wholesome and necessary for the public good.

He has forbidden his governors to pass laws of immediate and pressing importance, unless suspended in their operation, till his assent should be obtained; and when so suspended, he has utterly neglected to attend to them. He has refused to pass other laws for the accommodation of large districts of people, unless those people would relinquish the right of representation in the legislature—a right inestimable to them, and formidable to tyrants only.

He has called together legislative bodies at places unusual, uncomfortable, and distant from the repository of their public records, for the sole purpose of fatiguing them into compliance with his measures.

He has dissolved representative houses repeatedly, for opposing, with manly firmness, his invasions on the rights of the people.

He has refused for a long time after such dissolutions, to cause others to be elected; whereby the legislative powers, incapable of annihilation, have returned to the people at large, for their exercise, the State remaining, in the mean time, exposed to all the dangers of invasion from without, and convulsions within.

He has endeavored to prevent the population of these States; for that purpose obstructing the laws for naturalization of foreigners; refusing to pass others to encourage their migration hither, and raising the conditions of new appropriations of lands.

He has obstructed the administration of justice, by refusing his assent to laws for establishing judiciary powers.

He has made judges dependent on his will alone, for the tenure of their offices, and the amount and payment of their salaries.

He has erected a multitude of new offices, and sent hither swarms of officers, to harass our people, and eat out their substance.

He has kept among us, in times of peace, standing armies, without the consent of our legislatures.

He has affected to render the military independent of, and superior to, the civil power.

He has combined with others to subject us to a jurisdiction foreign to our constitution, and unacknowledged by our laws; giving his assent to their acts of pretended legislation:

For quartering large bodies of armed troops among us:

For protecting them, by a mock trial, from punishment for any murders which they should commit on the inhabitants of these States:

For cutting off our trade with all parts of the world:

For imposing taxes on us without our consent:

For depriving us, in many cases, of the benefits of trial by jury:

For transporting us beyond seas to be tried for pretended offences:

For abolishing the free system of English laws in a neighboring Province, establishing therein an arbitrary government, and enlarging its boundaries, so as to render it at once an example and fit instrument for introducing the same absolute rule into these colonies:

For taking away our charters, abolishing our most valuable laws, and altering, fundamentally, the forms of our governments:

For suspending our own legislatures, and declaring themselves invested with power to legislate for us in all cases whatsoever.

He has abdicated government here, by declaring us out of his protection, and waging war against us.

He has plundered our seas, ravaged our coasts, burnt our towns, and destroyed the lives of our people.

He is at this time transporting large armies of foreign mercenaries to complete the works of death, desolation, and tyranny, already begun with circumstances of cruelty and perfidy, scarcely paralleled in the most barbarous ages, and totally unworthy the head of a civilized nation.

He has constrained our fellow-citizens, taken captive on the high seas, to bear arms against their country, to become the executioners of their friends and brethren, or to fall themselves by their hands.

He has excited domestic insurrections amongst us, and has endeavored to bring on the inhabitants of our frontiers the merciless Indian savages, whose known rule of warfare is an undistinguished destruction of all ages, sexes, and conditions.

In every stage of these oppressions we have petitioned for redress in the most humble terms: our repeated petitions have been answered only by repeated injury. A prince, whose character is thus marked by every act which may define a tyrant, is unfit to be the ruler of a free people.

Nor have we been wanting in attention to our British brethren. We have warned them, from time to time, of attempts by their legislature to extend an unwarrantable jurisdiction over us. We have reminded them of the circumstances of our emigration and settlement here. We have appealed to their native justice and magnanimity, and we have conjured them by the ties of our common kindred to disavow these usurpations, which would inevitably interrupt our connexions and correspondence. They too have been deaf to the voice of justice and of consanguinity. We must, therefore, acquiesce in the necessity which denounces our separation, and hold them as we hold the rest of mankind, enemies in war, in peace friends.

We, therefore, the representatives of the United States of America, in general congress assembled, appealing to the Supreme Judge of the world, for the rectitude of our intentions, do, in the name and by the authority of the good people of these colonies, solemnly publish and declare, that these united colonies are, and of right ought to be, free and independent States; that they are absolved from all allegiance to the British crown, and that all political connexion between them and the state of Great Britain, is, and ought to be, totally dissolved; and that as free and independent States, they have full power to levy war, conclude peace, contract alliances, establish commerce, and to do all other acts and things which independent States may of right do. And for the support of this declaration, with a firm reliance on the protection of Divine Providence, we mutually pledge to each other our lives, our fortunes, and our sacred honor.

JOHN HANCOCK.

Josiah Bartlett,	John Witherspoon,	Charles Carroll, of
William Whipple,	Francis Hopkinson,	Carrollton.
Matthew Thornton.	John Hart,	
	Abraham Clark.	George Wythe,
Samuel Adams,		Richard Henry Lee,
John Adams,	Robert Morris,	Thomas Jefferson,
Robert Treat Paine,	Benjamin Rush,	Benjamin Harrison,
Elbridge Gerry.	Benjamin Franklin,	Thomas Nelson, jun.
	John Morton,	Francis Lightfoot Lee,
Stephen Hopkins,	George Clymer,	Carter Braxton.
William Ellery.	James Smith,	
	George Taylor,	William Hooper,
Roger Sherman,	James Wilson,	Joseph Hewes,
Samuel Huntington,	George Ross.	John Penn.
William Williams,		
Oliver Wolcott.	Cesar Rodney,	Edward Rutledge,
	George Read,	Thomas Heyward, jr.
William Floyd,	Thomas M'Kean.	Thomas Lynch, jr.
Philip Livingston,		Arthur Middleton.
Francis Lewis,	Samuel Chase,	
Lewis Morris.	William Paca,	Button Gwinnett,
	Thomas Stone,	Lyman Hall,
Richard Stockton,		George Walton.

It is not, let me repeat, fellow-citizens, it is not the long enumeration of intolerable wrongs concentrated in this Declaration; it is not the melancholy catalogue of alternate oppression and entreaty, of reciprocated indignity and remonstrance, upon which, in the celebration of this anniversary, your memory delights to dwell. Nor is it yet that the justice of your cause was vindicated by the God of Battles; that in a conflict of seven years, the history of the war by which you maintained that Declaration, became the history of the civilized world; that the unanimous voice of enlightened Europe, and the verdict of an after age, have sanctioned your assumption of sovereign power; and that the name of your Washington is enrolled upon the records of time, first in the glorious line of heroic virtue. It is not that the monarch himself, who had been your oppressor, was compelled to recognise you as a sovereign and independent people, and that the nation, whose feelings of fraternity for you had slumbered in the lap of pride, was awakened in the arms of humiliation to your equal and no longer contested rights. The primary purpose of this Declaration, the proclamation to the world of the causes of our Revolution, is "with the years beyond the flood." It is of no more interest to us than the chastity of Lucretia, or the apple on the head of the child of Tell. Little less than forty years have revolved since the struggle for independence was closed; another generation has arisen; and, in the assembly of nations, our Republic is already a matron of mature age. The cause of your independence is no longer upon trial; the final sentence upon it has long been passed upon earth and ratified in Heaven.

The interest, which in this paper has survived the occasion upon which it was issued; the interest which is of every age and every clime; the interest which quickens with the lapse of years, spreads as it grows old, and brightens as it recedes, is in the principles which it proclaims. It was the first solemn declaration by a nation of the only *legitimate* foundation of civil government. It was the corner stone of a new fabric, destined to cover the surface of the globe. It demolished at a stroke the lawfulness of all governments founded upon conquest. It swept away all the rubbish of accumulated centuries of servitude. It announced in practical form to the world the transcendent truth of the unalienable sovereignty of the people. It proved that the social compact was no figment of the imagination; but a real, solid, and sacred bond of the social union. From the day of this Declaration, the people of North America were no longer the fragment of a distant empire, imploring justice and mercy from an inexorable master in another hemisphere. They were no longer children appealing in vain to the sympathies of a heartless mother; no longer subjects leaning upon the shattered columns of royal promises, and invoking the faith of parchment to secure their rights. They were a *nation*, asserting as of right, and maintaining by war, its own existence. A nation was born in a day—

> "How many ages hence
> Shall this, their lofty scene, be acted o'er
> In states unborn, and accents yet unknown?"

It will be acted o'er, fellow-citizens, but it can never be repeated. It stands, and must for ever stand, alone, a beacon on the summit of the mountain, to which all the inhabitants of the earth may turn their eyes for a genial and saving light till time shall be lost in eternity, and this globe itself dissolve, nor leave a wreck behind. It stands for ever, a light of admonition to the rulers of men, a light of salvation and redemption to the oppressed. So long as this planet shall be inhabited by human beings, so long as man shall be of social nature, so long as government shall be necessary to the great moral purposes of society, and so long as it shall be abused to the purposes of oppression, so long shall this Declaration hold out to the sovereign and to the subject the extent and the boundaries of their respective rights and duties, founded in the laws of nature, and of nature's God. Five and forty years have passed away since this Declaration was issued by our fathers; and here are we, fellow-citizens, assembled in the full enjoyment of its fruits, to bless the author of our being for the bounties of his providence, in casting our lot in this favored land; to remember with effusions of gratitude the sages who put forth, and the heroes who bled for the establishment of this Declaration; and, by the communion of soul in the reperusal and hearing of this instrument, to renew the genuine Holy Alliance of its principles, to recognise them as eternal truths, and to pledge ourselves, and bind our posterity, to a faithful and undeviating adherence to them.

Fellow-Citizens, our fathers have been faithful to them before us. When the little band of their Delegates, "with a firm reliance on the protection of Divine Providence, for the support of this declaration, mutually pledged to each other their *lives*, their *fortunes*, and their *sacred honor*," from every dwelling, street, and square, of your populous cities, it was re-echoed with shouts of joy and gratulation! And if the silent language of the heart could have been heard, every hill upon the surface of this continent which had been trodden by the foot of civilized man, every valley in which the toil of your fathers had opened a paradise upon the wild, would have rung, with one accordant voice, louder than the thunders, sweeter than the harmonies of the heavens, with the solemn and responsive words, "*We swear.*"

The pledge has been redeemed. Through six years of devastating but heroic war, through forty years of more heroic peace, the principles of this declaration have been supported by the toils, by the vigils, by the blood of your fathers, and of yourselves. The conflict of war had begun with fearful odds of apparent human power on the part of the oppressor. He wielded at will the collective force of the mightiest nation in Europe. He with more than poetic truth asserted the dominion of the waves. The power to whose unjust usurpation your fathers hurled the gauntlet of defiance, baffled and vanquished by them, has even since, stripped of all the energies of this continent, been found adequate to give the law to its own quarter of the globe, and to mould the destinies of the European world. It was with a sling and a stone, that your fathers went forth to encounter the massive vigor of this Goliath. They slung the heaven-directed stone, and

> "With heaviest sound, the giant monster fell."

Amid the shouts of victory, your cause soon found friends and allies in the rivals of your enemies. France recognised your Independence as existing in fact, and made common cause with you for its support. Spain and the Netherlands, without adopting your principles, successively flung their weight into your scale. The Semiramis of the North, no convert to your doctrines, still conjured all the maritime neutrality of Europe in array against the usurpations of your antagonist upon the seas. While some of the fairest of your fields were ravaged; while your towns and villages were consumed with fire; while the harvests of your summers were blasted; while the purity of virgin innocence, and the chastity of matronly virtue, were violated; while the living remnants of the field of battle were reserved for the gibbet, by the fraternal sympathies of Britons throughout your land, the waters of the Atlantic ocean, and those that wash the shores of either India, were dyed with the mingled blood of combatants in the cause of North American Independence.

In the progress of time, that vial of wrath was exhausted. After seven years of exploits and achievements like these, performed under the orders of the British king; to use the language of the treaty of peace, "it having pleased the Divine Providence to dispose the hearts of the most serene and most potent Prince, George the III, by the Grace of God, King of Great Britain, France, and Ireland, Defender of the Faith, Duke of Brunswick and Luneburg, Arch Treasurer and Prince Elector of the Holy Roman Empire, and so forth—and of the United States of America to"—what? "To forget all past misunderstandings and differences that have unhappily interrupted the good correspondence and friendship which they mutually wish to restore"—what then? Why—"His Britannic Majesty ACKNOWLEDGES the said United States, viz: New Hampshire, Massachusetts Bay, Rhode Island and Providence Plantations, Connecticut, New-York, New-Jersey, Pennsylvania, Delaware, Maryland, Virginia, North-Carolina, South-Carolina, and Georgia, to be *Free*, *Sovereign*, and *Independent* States; that he treats with them as such; and for himself, his heirs, and successors, relinquishes all claims to the Government, proprietary and territorial rights of the same, and every part thereof."

Fellow-Citizens, I am not without apprehension that some parts of this extract, cited to the word and to the letter, from the treaty of peace of 1783, may have discomposed the *serenity* of your temper. Far be it from me, to *dispose your hearts* to a levity unbecoming the hallowed dignity of this day. But this treaty of peace is the *dessert* appropriate to the sumptuous banquet of the Declaration. It is the epilogue to that unparalleled drama of which the Declaration is the prologue. Observe, my countrymen and friends, how the rules of unity, prescribed by the great masters of the fictive stage, were preserved in this tragedy of pity and terror in real life. Here was a beginning, a middle, and an end, of one mighty action. The beginning was the Declaration which we have read: the middle, was that sanguinary, calamitous, but glorious war, which calls for deeper colors, and a brighter pencil, than mine to pourtray: the end was the disposal by Divine Providence, that same Divine Providence upon whose protection your fathers had so solemnly and so effectually declared their firm reliance, of the heart of the most serene and most potent prince to acknowledge your Independence to the precise extent in which it had been declared. Here was no great charter of Runny Mead, yielded and accepted as a grant of royal bounty. That which the Declaration had asserted, which seven years of mercy-harrowing war had contested, was here, in express and unequivocal terms, *acknowledged*. And how? By the mere disposal of the heart of the most serene and most potent prince.

The Declaration of Independence pronounced the irrevocable decree of political separation, between the United States and their People on the one part, and the British King, Government and Nation on the other. It proclaimed the first principles on which civil government is founded, and derived from them the justification before Earth and Heaven, of this act of sovereignty: but it left the people of this Union collective and individual without *organized* Government. In contemplating this state of things, one of the profoundest of British statesmen, in an ecstacy of astonishment, exclaimed "Anarchy is found tolerable!" But there was no Anarchy. From the day of the Declaration, the people of the North American Union and of its constituent States, were associated bodies of civilized men and christians, in a state of nature; but not of Anarchy. They were bound by the laws of God, which they all, and by the laws of the Gospel, which they nearly all, acknowledged as the rules of their conduct. They were bound by all those tender and endearing sympathies, the absence of which in the British Government and Nation towards them was the primary cause of the distressing conflict into which they had been precipitated. They were bound by all the beneficent laws and institutions which their forefathers had brought with them from *their* mother Country, not as servitudes, but as rights. They were bound by habits of hardy industry, by frugal and hospitable manners, by the general sentiments of social equality, by pure and virtuous morals, and lastly they were bound by the grappling hooks of common suffering under the scourge of oppression. Where then, among such a people, were the materials for Anarchy? Had there been among them no other Law, they would have been a law unto themselves.

They had before them in their new position, besides the maintenance of the Independence which they had declared, three great objects to attain: the first, to cement and prepare for perpetuity, their common union, and that of their Posterity; the second, to erect and organize civil and municipal Governments in their respective States; and the third, to form connexions of friendship and of commerce with foreign Nations. For all these objects, the same Congress which issued the Declaration, and at the same time with it, had provided. They recommended to the several States to form civil governments for themselves. With guarded and cautious deliberation they matured a confederation for the whole Union; and they prepared treaties of commerce, to be offered to the principal maritime nations of the world. All these objects were in a great degree accomplished, amid the din of arms, and while every quarter of our country was ransacked by the fury of invasion. The states organized their governments, all in republican forms; all on the principles of the Declaration. The confederation was unanimously adopted by the thirteen States, and treaties of commerce were concluded with France and the Netherlands, in which, for the first time, the same just and magnanimous principles, consigned in the Declaration of Independence, were, so far as they could be applicable to the intercourse between nation and nation, solemnly recognised.

When experience had proved that the Confederation was not adequate to the national purposes of the country, the people of the United States, without tumult, without violence, by their delegates, all chosen upon principles of equal right, formed a more perfect Union, by the establishment of the Federal Constitution. This has already passed the ordeal of one human generation. In all the changes of men and of parties through which it has passed, it has been administered on the same fundamental principles. Our manners, our habits, our feelings, are all republican; and if our principles had been, when first proclaimed, doubtful to the ear of reason or the sense of humanity, they would have been reconciled to our understandings, and endeared to our hearts by their practical operation. In the progress of forty years since the acknowledgement of our Independence, we have gone through many modifications of internal government, and through all the vicissitudes of peace and war, with other powerful nations. But never, never for a moment have the great principles, consecrated by the Declaration of this day, been renounced or abandoned.

And now, friends and countrymen, if the wise and learned philosophers of the elder world; the first observers of nutation and aberration, the discoverers of maddening ether and invisible planets, the inventors of Congreve rockets and Shrapnel shells, should find their hearts disposed to enquire what has America done for the benefit of mankind? Let our answer be this:

America, with the same voice which spoke herself into existence as a nation, proclaimed to mankind the inextinguishable rights of human nature, and the only lawful foundations of government. America, in the assembly of nations, since her admission among them, has invariably, though often fruitlessly, held forth to them the hand of honest friendship, of equal freedom, of generous reciprocity. She has uniformly spoken among them, though often to heedless and often to disdainful ears, the language of equal liberty, of equal justice, and of equal rights. She has, in the lapse of nearly half a century, without a single exception, respected the independence of other nations while asserting and maintaining her own. She has abstained from interference in the concerns of others, even when the conflict has been for principles to which she clings, as to the last vital drop that visits the heart. She has seen that probably for centuries to come, all the contests of that Aceldama the European world, will be contests of inveterate power, and emerging right. Wherever the standard of freedom and Independence, has been or shall be unfurled, there will her heart, her benedictions and her prayers be. But she goes not abroad, in search of monsters to destroy. She is the well-wisher to the freedom and independence of all. She is the champion and vindicator only of her own. She will recommend the general cause by the countenance of her voice, and the benignant sympathy of her example. She well knows that by once enlisting under other banners than her own, were they even the banners of foreign Independence, she would involve herself beyond the power of extrication, in all the wars of interest and intrigue, of individual avarice, envy, and ambition, which assume the colors and usurp the standard of freedom. The fundamental maxims of her policy would insensibly change from *liberty* to *force*. The frontlet upon her brow would no longer beam with the ineffable splendor of Freedom and Independence; but in its stead would soon be substituted an Imperial Diadem, flashing in false and tarnished lustre the murky radiance of dominion and power. She might become the dictatress of the world. She would be no longer the ruler of her own spirit.

Stand forth, ye champions of Britannia, ruler of the waves! Stand forth, ye chivalrous knights of chartered liberties and the rotten borough! Enter the lists, ye boasters of *inventive* genius! Ye mighty masters of the palette and the brush! Ye improvers upon the sculpture of the Elgin marbles! Ye spawners of fustian romance and lascivious lyrics! Come and enquire what has America done for the benefit of mankind! In the half century which has elapsed since the Declaration of American Independence, what have *you* done for the benefit of mankind?

When Themistocles was sarcastically asked by some great musical genius of his age, whether he knew how to play upon the lute, he answered, No! but he knew how to make a great city of a small one. We shall not contend with you for the prize of music, painting, or sculpture. We shall not disturb the extatic trances of your Chemists, nor call from the heavens the ardent gaze of your Astronomers. We will not ask you who was the last President of your Royal Academy. We will not enquire by whose mechanical combinations it was, that your Steam-Boats stem the currents of your rivers, and vanquish the opposition of the winds themselves upon your seas. We will not name the inventor of the Cotton-Gin, for we fear that you would ask us the meaning of the word, and pronounce it a provincial barbarism. We will not name to you him, whose graver defies the imitation of forgery, and saves the labor of your executioner, by taking from your greatest geniuses of robbery the power of committing the crime. He is now among yourselves: and since your philosophers have permitted him to prove to them the compressibility of water, you may perhaps claim him for your own. Would you soar to fame upon a rocket, or burst into glory from a shell? we shall leave you to enquire of your naval heroes their opinion of the Steam Battery and the Torpedo. It is not by the contrivance of agents of destruction, that America wishes to commend her inventive genius to the admiration or the gratitude of after times; nor is it even in the detection of the secrets, or the composition of new modifications of physical nature.

"Excudent alii spirantia mollius æra,"

Nor even is her purpose the glory of Roman ambition; nor "Tu regere *Imperio* populos"—her memento to her sons. Her glory is not *dominion*, but *liberty*. Her march is the march of mind. She has a spear and a shield: but the motto upon her shield is, *Freedom, Independence, Peace*. This has been her

Declaration: this has been, as far as her necessary intercourse with the rest of mankind would permit, her practice.

My Countrymen, Fellow-Citizens, and Friends, could that spirit which dictated the Declaration we have this day read; that spirit, which "prefers before all temples the upright heart and pure," at this moment descend from his habitation in the skies, and within this Hall, in language audible to mortal ears, address each one of us here assembled, our beloved Country, Britannia ruler of the waves, and every individual among the sceptred lords of human kind; his words would be

GO THOU, AND DO LIKEWISE.

"A PRECIOUS INHERITANCE"

11. "Inaugural Address." *National Intelligencer — Extra*. (Washington, [D.C.], Friday, March 4, 1825).

Almost four years after his Fourth of July address, Adams returned to the chamber of the House of Representatives to deliver this, his inaugural address as the sixth president of the United States. The election of 1824 had been markedly different from that of 1820. John C. Calhoun, who had run on both the Adams and Jackson tickets, was easily elected vice president, but no candidate received the requisite number of electoral votes to secure the presidency, and it fell to the House of Representatives, voting as states, to choose from among the top three contenders: Andrew Jackson, with 99 electoral votes, John Quincy Adams, with 84, and William Crawford, with 41. It was widely expected that Speaker of the House Henry Clay, who had just missed the cut with 37 electoral votes, would be influential in the outcome. In terms of policy, Clay was most closely aligned with Adams, his former fellow commissioner at Ghent. They shared a vision of the nation bound together by a vigorous federal government, using tariffs to protect and promote industry, a national bank to foster commerce, and federal subsidies for "internal improvements" to link agricultural centers with markets at home and abroad, the three mutually reinforcing components of the so-called American System. But Clay, who was both literally and figuratively an expert horse trader, would expect something in return for his support, and it was no secret that he had his eye on the State Department.

On February 11, 1825, two days after the House elected Adams on the first ballot, with a bare majority of thirteen out of twenty-four states, he had a lengthy conversation with former New Hampshire congressman George Sullivan, which he recorded in his diary: "He said he would tell me what the Calhounites said — That if Mr. Clay should be appointed Secretary of State a determined opposition to the Administration would be organized from the outset — That the opposition would use the name of General Jackson as its head — That the Administration would be supported only by the New-England States. New-York being doubtful." For Adams, this conversation jibed with several others he had had, all revealing "the system of opposition" designed to make Jackson the next president. "To this end, the Administration must be rendered unpopular and odious; whatever its acts and measures may be." "I am at least forewarned," he concluded ruefully. Undeterred, Adams did offer Clay the position of secretary of state, and the predicted recriminations flew.

Dealing with the anxiety induced by accusations of a "corrupt bargain" with Clay and with his wife's sudden and severe fever, Adams did not sleep for two nights before his inauguration. He might then have been forgiven for approaching the rostrum with some trepidation. "Fellow-citizens, you are acquainted with the peculiar circumstance of the recent election," he will tell the assembled audience. "Less possessed of your confidence, in advance, than any of my predecessors, I am deeply conscious of the prospect that I shall stand, more and oftener, in need of your indulgence." But the speech he delivers is notable for its optimism, framing a postpartisan future in which, thanks to the genius of the federal system, "the harmony of the nation is promoted, and the whole Union is knit together by sentiments of mutual respect, the habits of social intercourse, and the ties of personal friendship, formed between the Representatives of its several parts, in the performance of their service at this Metropolis." The address is further notable for Adams's reference to the United States as a "Representative Democracy," making him the first American president to publicly avow democracy, a term that has since become synonymous with the nation's political ethos but which for his father and the Founders generally had been a byword for disorder and popular excess.

His address delivered, Adams took the oath of office from Chief Justice John Marshall, whose long tenure on the Supreme Court constituted perhaps the greatest legacy of John Adams's presidency. And then, as he recalled in his diary, "after exchanging salutations with the late President, and many other persons present, I retired from the Hall."

Inaugural Address

THIS DAY, at the appointed hour, JOHN QUINCY ADAMS took the Oath of Office as President of the United States, at the Capitol, and, on the occasion, delivered the following INAUGURAL ADDRESS:

In compliance with an usage coeval with the existence of our Federal Constitution, and sanctioned by the example of my predecessors in the career upon which I am about to enter, I appear, my fellow citizens, in your presence, and in that of Heaven, to bind myself by the solemnities of religious obligation, to the faithful performance of the duties allotted to me in the station to which I have been called.

In unfolding to my countrymen the principles by which I shall be governed, in the fulfillment of those duties, my first resort will be to that Constitution, which I shall swear, to the best of my ability, to preserve, protect, and defend. That revered instrument enumerates the powers, and prescribes the duties, of the Executive Magistrate; and, in its first words, declares the purposes to which these, and the whole action of the Government, instituted by it, should be invariably and sacredly devoted:—to form a more perfect union, establish justice, ensure domestic tranquility, provide for the common defence, promote the general welfare, and secure the blessings of liberty to the people of this Union, in their successive generations. Since the adoption of this social compact, one of these generations has passed away. It is the work of our forefathers. Administered by some of the most eminent men who contributed to its formation, through a most eventful period in the annals of the world, and through all the vicissitudes of peace and war, incidental to the condition of associated man; it has not disappointed the hopes and aspirations of those illustrious benefactors of their age and nation. It has promoted the lasting welfare of that country so dear to us all; it has, to an extent, far beyond the ordinary lot of humanity, secured the freedom and happiness of this people. We now receive it as a precious inheritance from those to whom we are indebted for its establishment, doubly bound by the examples which they have left us, and by the blessings which we have enjoyed, as the fruits of their labors, to transmit the same, unimpaired, to the succeeding generation.

In the compass of thirty-six years since this great national covenant was instituted, a body of laws, enacted under its authority, and in conformity with its provisions, has unfolded its powers, and carried into practical operation its effective energies. Subordinate departments have distributed the Executive functions in their various relations, to foreign affairs, to the revenue and expenditures, and to the military force of the Union, by land and sea. A co-ordinate department of the Judiciary has expounded the Constitution and the laws; settling, in harmonious coincidence with the Legislative will, numerous weighty questions of construction, which the imperfection of human language had rendered unavoidable. The year of Jubilee, since the first formation of our Union, has just elapsed; that of the Declaration of our Independence, is at hand. The consummation of both was effected by this Constitution.

Since that period, a population of four millions has multiplied to twelve; a territory bounded by the Mississippi, has been extended from sea to sea; new states have been admitted to the Union, in numbers nearly equal to those of the first Confederation; treaties of peace, amity and commerce, have been concluded with the principal dominions of the earth; the people of other nations, inhabitants of regions acquired, not by conquest, but by compact, have been united with us in the participation of our rights and duties, of our burdens and blessings; the forest has fallen by the axe of our woodsmen; the soil has been made to teem by the tillage of our farmers; our commerce has whitened every ocean; the dominion of man over physical nature has been extended by the invention of our artists; Liberty and Law have marched hand in hand; all the purposes of human association have been accomplished as effectively, as under any other Government on the globe; and at a cost little exceeding, in a whole generation, the expenditure of other nations in a single year.

Such is the unexaggerated picture of our condition, under a constitution founded upon the republican principle of equal rights. To admit that this picture has its shades, is but to say that it is still the condition of men upon earth. From evil, physical, moral, and political, it is not our claim to be exempt. We have suffered, sometimes by the visitation of Heaven, through disease; often, by the wrongs and, injustice of other nations, even to the extremities of war; and, lastly, by dissensions among ourselves—dissensions, perhaps, inseparable from the enjoyment of freedom, but which have, more than once, appeared to threaten the dissolution of the Union, and, with it, the overthrow of all the enjoyments of our present lot, and all our earthly hopes of the future. The causes of these dissensions have been various: founded upon differences of speculation in the theory of Republican Government; upon conflicting views of policy, in our relations with foreign nations; upon jealousies of partial and sectional interests, aggravated by prejudices and prepossessions which strangers to each other are ever apt to entertain.

It is a source of gratification and of encouragement to me, to observe that the great result of this experiment, upon the theory of human rights, has, at the close of that generation by which it was formed, been crowned with success, equal to the most sanguine expectations of its founders. Union, justice, tranquility, the common defence, the general welfare, and the blessings of liberty—all have been promoted by the Government under which we have lived. Standing at this point of time; looking back to that generation which has gone by, and forward to that which is advancing, we may, at once, indulge in grateful exultation, and in cheering hope. From the experience of the past, we derive instructive lessons for the future. Of the two great political parties which have divided the opinions and feelings of our country, the candid and the just will now admit, that both have contributed splendid talents, spotless integrity, ardent patriotism, and disinterested sacrifices, to the formation and administration of this Government; and that both have required a liberal indulgence for a portion of human infirmity and error. The Revolutionary wars of Europe, commencing precisely at the moment when the Government of the United States first went into operation under this Constitution, excited a collision of sentiments and of sympathies, which kindled all the passions, and embittered the conflict of parties, till the nation was involved in war, and the Union was shaken to its centre.

This time of trial embraced a period of five and twenty years, during which, the policy of the Union, in its relations with Europe, constituted the principal basis of our political divisions, and the most arduous part of the action of our Federal Government. With the catastrophe in which the wars of the French Revolution terminated, and our own subsequent peace with Great Britain, this baneful weed of party strife was uprooted. From that time, no difference of principle, connected either with the theory of government, or with our intercourse with foreign nations, has existed, or been called forth, in force sufficient to sustain a continued combination of parties, or to give more than wholesome animation to public sentiment, or legislative debate. Our political creed is, without a dissenting voice, that can be heard—That the will of the people is the source, and the happiness of the people the end, of all legitimate Government upon earth—That the best security for the beneficence, and the best guaranty against the abuse, of power, consists in the freedom, the purity, and the frequency of popular elections—That the General Government of the Union, and the separate governments of the States, are all sovereignties of limited powers; fellow servants of the same masters; uncontrolled within their respective spheres; uncontrollable by encroachments upon each other—That the firmest security of peace is the preparation, during peace, of the defences of war—That a rigorous economy, and accountability of public expenditures, should guard against the aggravation, and alleviate, when possible, the burden, of taxation—That the military should be kept in strict subordination to the civil power—That the freedom of the press and of religious opinion should be inviolate—That the policy of our country is peace, and the ark of our salvation, union, are articles of faith upon which we are all now agreed. If there have been those who doubted whether a confederated representative democracy were a government competent to the wise and orderly management of the common concerns of a mighty nation, those doubts have been dispelled. If there have been projects of partial confederacies to be erected upon the ruins of the Union, they have been scattered to the winds—If there have been dangerous attachments to one foreign nation and antipathies against another, they have been extinguished. Ten years of peace, at home and abroad, have assuaged the animosities of political contention, and blended into harmony the most discordant elements of public opinion. There still remains one effort of magnanimity, one sacrifice of prejudice and passion, to be made by the individuals throughout the nation, who have heretofore followed the standards of political party.—It is that of discarding every remnant of rancour against each other; of embracing, as countrymen and friends, and of yielding to talents and virtue alone, that confidence which, in times of contention for principle, was bestowed only upon those who bore the badge of party communion.

The collisions of party spirit, which originate in speculative opinions, or in different views of administrative policy, are, in their nature, transitory. Those which are founded on geographical divisions, adverse interests of soil, climate, and modes of domestic life, are more permanent, and therefore perhaps more dangerous. It is this which gives inestimable value to the character of our Government, at once federal and national. It holds out to us a perpetual admonition to preserve alike, and with equal anxiety, the rights of each individual State in its own government, and the rights of the whole nation in that of the Union. Whatsoever is of domestic concernment, unconnected with the other members of the Union, or with foreign lands, belongs exclusively to the administration of the State Governments. Whatsoever directly involves the rights and interests of the federative fraternity, or of Foreign Powers, is of the resort of this General Government. The duties of both are obvious in the general principle, though sometimes perplexed with difficulties in the detail. To respect the rights of the State Governments, is the inviolable duty of that of the Union; the government of every state will feel its own obligation to respect and preserve the rights of the whole. The prejudices, every where too commonly entertained against distant strangers, are worn away, and the jealousies of jarring interests are allayed, by the composition and functions of the great National Councils, annually assembled from all quarters of the Union, at this place. Here the distinguished men from every section of our country, while meeting to deliberate upon the great interests of those by whom they are deputed, learn to estimate the talents, and do justice to the virtues, of each other. The harmony of the nation is promoted, and the whole Union is knit together, by the sentiments of mutual respect, the habits of social intercourse, and the ties of personal friendship, formed between the Representatives of its several parts, in the performance of their service at this metropolis.

Passing from this general review of the purposes and injunctions of the Federal Constitution, and their results, as indicating the first traces of the path of duty in the discharge of my public trust, I turn to the administration of my immediate predecessor, as the second. It has passed away in a period of profound peace; how much to the satisfaction of our country, and to the honor of our country's name, is known to you all. The great features of its policy, in general concurrence with the will of the Legislature, have been—to cherish peace, while preparing for defensive war; to yield exact justice to other nations, and maintain the rights of our own; to cherish the principles of freedom and of equal rights, wherever they were proclaimed; to discharge, with all possible promptitude, the national debt; to reduce, within the narrowest limits of efficiency, the military force; to improve the organization and discipline of the army; to provide and sustain a school of military science; to extend equal protection to all the great interests of the nation; to promote the civilization of the Indian tribes; and, to proceed in the great system of internal improvements, within the limits of the constitutional power of the Union. Under the pledge of these promises, made by that eminent citizen, at the time of his first induction to this office, in his career of eight years, the internal taxes have been repealed; sixty millions of the public debt have been discharged; provision has been made for the comfort and relief of the aged and indigent among the surviving warriors of the Revolution; the regular armed force has been reduced, and its constitution revised and perfected; the accountability for the expenditure of public moneys has been made more effective; the Floridas have been peaceably acquired, and our boundary has been extended to the Pacific Ocean; the independence of the southern nations of this hemisphere has been recognized and recommended by example and by counsel, to the potentates of Europe; progress has been made in the defence of the country, by fortifications and the increase of the navy; towards the effectual suppression of the African traffic in slaves; in alluring the aboriginal hunters of our land to the cultivation of the soil and of the mind; in exploring the interior regions of the Union; and in preparing, by scientific researches and surveys, for the further application of our national resources to the internal improvement of our country.

In this brief outline of the promise and performance of my immediate predecessor, the line of duty, for his successor, is clearly delineated. To pursue, to their consummation, those purposes of improvement in our common condition, instituted or recommended by him, will embrace the whole sphere of my obligations. To the topic of internal improvement, emphatically urged by him at his inauguration, I recur with peculiar satisfaction. It is that from which I am convinced that the unborn millions of our posterity, who are, in future ages, to people this continent, will derive their most fervent gratitude to the founders of the Union; that, in which the beneficent action of its Government will be most deeply felt and acknowledged. The magnificence and splendor of their public works are among the imperishable glories of the ancient Republics. The roads and aqueducts of Rome have been the admiration of all after ages, and have survived, thousands of years, after all her conquests have been swallowed up in despotism, or become the spoil of Barbarians. Some diversity of opinion has prevailed with regard to the powers of Congress for Legislation upon objects of this nature. The most respectful deference is due to doubts, originating in pure patriotism, and sustained by venerated authority. But nearly twenty years have passed since the construction of the first National Road was commenced. The authority for its construction was then unquestioned. To how many thousands of our countrymen has it proved a benefit? To what single individual has it ever proved an injury? Repeated liberal and candid discussions in the Legislature have conciliated the sentiments, and approximated the opinions of enlightened minds, upon the question of Constitutional power. I cannot but hope that, by the same process of friendly, patient, and persevering deliberation, all Constitutional objections will ultimately be removed. The extent and limitation of the powers of the General Government, in relation to this transcendently important interest, will be settled and acknowledged, to the common satisfaction of all; and every speculative scruple will be solved by a practical public blessing.

Fellow citizens, you are acquainted with the peculiar circumstances of the recent election, which have resulted in affording me the opportunity of addressing you, at this time. You have heard the exposition of the principles which will direct me in the fulfilment of the high and solemn trust imposed upon me in this station. Less possessed of your confidence, in advance, than any of my predecessors, I am deeply conscious of the prospect that I shall stand, more and oftener, in need of your indulgence. Intentions, upright and pure; a heart devoted to the welfare of our country, and the unceasing application of all the faculties allotted to me, to her service, are all the pledges that I can give, for the faithful performance of the arduous duties I am to undertake. To the guidance of the Legislative councils; to the assistance of the Executive and subordinate Departments; to the friendly co-operation of the respective State Governments; to the candid and liberal support of the People, so far as it may be deserved by honest industry and zeal, I shall look for whatever success may attend my public service; and knowing, that, except the Lord keep the City, the watchman waketh but in vain, with fervent supplications for his favor, to his overruling Providence I commit, with humble but fearless confidence, my own fate, and the future destinies of my country.

"THE SPIRIT OF IMPROVEMENT IS ABROAD
UPON THE EARTH"

12. "President's Message." December 6, 1825. *National Journal* (Washington, D.C., Thursday, December 8, 1825).

Adams brought the same scrupulosity that had hobbled his campaign, such as it was, to his presidency. Despite having been forewarned about the prospect of an inveterate opposition against his administration—one led by his own vice president, no less—he would not dismiss any currently serving federal officeholder without specific cause, nor would he use open positions to reward supporters. Tabulating his appointments in his diary at the close of his first full day as president, Adams noted that "efforts had been made by some of the Senators to obtain different nominations, and to introduce a principle of change, or rotation in office, at the expiration" of an administration. This, Adams feared, "would make the Government a perpetual, and unintermitting scramble for Office. — A more pernicious expedient could scarcely have been devised." As one historian has written, "the message became clear: nothing would be lost by opposing the Adams administration, and little could be gained by supporting it."

Adams's cabinet was acutely aware of the political headwinds the administration faced in Congress. When the time came for the president to deliver this, his first annual message on the state of the union, in December 1825, they advised caution. Adams labored over the message for weeks and it reflected the same spirit of optimism expressed in his inaugural address. He seeks here to make that hopeful vision for America programmatic, to lay out for Congress the ways and means to achieve it, and to reassure the strict constructionists among them of their constitutional authority to do so. Whereas internal improvements had heretofore been undertaken on a piecemeal basis—the most notable public work to that period, the famous Cumberland Road, took more than twenty-five years to construct—Adams calls for a concerted program of development of roads and canals. But he goes a step further: "I cannot close," he tells Congress, "without recommending to [your] calm and persevering consideration the general principle in a more enlarged extent." Improvement of the nation's physical infrastructure is vital, he argues, but so are "moral, political, intellectual improvement." He then lays out a remarkably bold plan for federal funding of everything from voyages of exploration to astronomical observatories to a greatly expanded executive branch.

At almost every turn, as he took pains to record in his diary, Adams's cabinet—led by his secretary of state, who as former speaker knew the temperature of Congress better than most—had urged him to rein in the ambition on display here. "Mr. Clay wished to have the recommendations of a National University; and of a new Executive Department struck out — almost everything related to the Patent Office; and the final enumeration of all the purposes of internal improvements for which I asserted that Congress have powers. . . . The University Mr. Clay said was entirely hopeless — and he thought there was something in the Constitutional objection to it." As Adams recalled the conversation, "I concurred entirely in the opinion, that no projects absolutely impracticable ought to be recommended — but I would look to a practicability of a longer range than a single Session of Congress." In other words, he would give voice to his vision for the nation, whatever the cost: "thus situated, the perilous experiment must be made. Let me make it with full deliberation and be prepared for the consequences."

First Annual Message

*F*ELLOW CITIZENS *of the Senate, and of the House of Representatives:*

In taking a general survey of the concerns of our beloved country, with reference to subjects interesting to the common welfare, the first sentiment which impresses itself upon the mind, is, of gratitude to the Omnipotent Dispenser of All Good, for the continuance of the signal blessings of his Providence, and especially for that health which, to an unusual extent, has prevailed within our borders; and for that abundance which, in the vicissitudes of the seasons, has been scattered with profusion over our land. Nor ought we less to ascribe to Him the glory, that we are permitted to enjoy the bounties of His hand in peace and tranquillity—in peace with all the other nations of the earth, in tranquillity among ourselves. There has, indeed, rarely been a period in the history of civilized man, in which the general condition of the Christian Nations has been marked so extensively by peace and prosperity.

Europe, with a few partial and unhappy exceptions, has enjoyed ten years of peace, during which all her Governments, whatever the theory of their constitutions may have been, are successively taught to feel that the end of their institution is the happiness of the people; and that the exercise of power among men can be justified only by the blessings it confers upon those over whom it is extended.

During the same period our intercourse with all those nations has been pacific and friendly—it so continues. Since the close of your last session, no material variation has occurred in our relations with any one of them. In the commercial and navigation system of Great Britain, important changes of municipal regulation have recently been sanctioned by acts of Parliament, the effect of which, upon the interests of other nations, and particularly upon ours, has not yet been fully developed. In the recent renewal of the diplomatic missions on both sides, between the two governments, assurances have been given and received of the continuance and increase of that mutual confidence and cordiality by which the adjustment of many points of difference had already been effected, and which affords the surest pledge for the ultimate satisfactory adjustment of those which still remain open, or may hereafter arise.

The policy of the United States, in their commercial intercourse with other nations, has always been of the most liberal character. In the mutual exchange of their respective productions, they have abstained altogether from prohibitions; they have interdicted themselves the power of laying taxes upon exports, and whenever they have favored their own shipping, by special preferences, or exclusive privileges in their own ports, it has been only with a view to countervail similar favors and exclusions granted by the nations with whom we have been engaged in traffic, to their own people or shipping, and to the disadvantage of ours. Immediately after the close of the last war, a proposal was fairly made by the act of Congress of the 3d of March, 1815, to all the maritime nations, to lay aside the system of retaliating restrictions and exclusions, and to place the shipping of both parties to the common trade, on a footing of equality in respect to the duties of tonnage and impost. This offer was partially and successively accepted by Great Britain, Sweden, the Netherlands, the Hanseatic Cities, Prussia, Sardinia, the Duke of Oldenburg, and Russia. It was also adopted, under certain modifications, in our late commercial convention with France. And, by the act of Congress of the 8th January, 1824, it has received a new confirmation, with all the nations who had acceded to it, and has been offered again to all those who are, or may hereafter be, willing to abide in reciprocity by it. But all these regulations, whether established by treaty, or by municipal enactments, are still subject to one important restriction. The removal of discriminating duties of tonnage and of impost, is limited to articles of the growth, produce, or manufacture, of the country to which the vessel belongs, or to such articles as are most usually first shipped from her ports. It will deserve the serious consideration of Congress, whether even this remnant of restriction may not be safely abandoned, and whether the general tender of equal competition, made in the act of 8th January, 1824, may not be extended to include all articles of merchandise not prohibited, of what country soever they may be the produce or manufacture.

Propositions to this effect have already been made to us by more than one European government, and it is probable, that if once established by legislation or compact with any distinguished maritime State, it would recommend itself by the experience of its advantages, to the general accession of all.

The Convention of Commerce and Navigation between the United States and France, concluded on the 24th of June, 1822, was, in the understanding and intent of both parties, as appears upon its face, only a temporary arrangement of the points of difference between them, of the most immediate and pressing urgency. It was limited, in the first instance, to two years, from the 1st of October, 1822, but with a proviso, that it should further continue in force till the conclusion of a general and definitive treaty of commerce, unless terminated by a notice six months in advance, of either of the parties to the other. Its operation, so far as it extended, has been mutually advantageous; and it still continues in force, by common consent. But it left unadjusted several objects of great interest to the citizens and subjects of both countries, and particularly a mass of claims, to considerable amount, of citizens of the United States upon the Government of France, of indemnity for property taken or destroyed under circumstances of the most aggravated and outrageous character. In the long period during which continual and earnest appeals have been made to the equity and magnanimity of France, in behalf of these claims, their justice has not been, as it could not be, denied. It was hoped that the accession of a new Sovereign to the throne would have afforded a favorable opportunity for presenting them to the consideration of his Government. They have been presented and urged, hitherto, without effect. The repeated and earnest representations of our Minister at the Court of France, remain as yet even without an answer. Were the demands of nations upon the justice of each other susceptible of adjudication by the sentence of an impartial tribunal, those to which I now refer would long since have been settled, and adequate indemnity would have been obtained. There are large amounts of similar claims upon the Netherlands, Naples, and Denmark. For those upon Spain, prior to 1819, indemnity was, after many years of patient forbearance, obtained; and those upon Sweden have been lately compromised by a private settlement, in which the claimants themselves have acquiesced. The Governments of Denmark and of Naples have been recently reminded of those yet existing against them; nor will any of them be forgotten while a hope may be indulged of obtaining justice by the means within the constitutional power of the Executive, and without resorting to those means of self-redress, which, as well as the time, circumstances, and occasion, which may require them, are within the exclusive competency of the Legislature.

It is with great satisfaction that I am enabled to bear witness to the liberal spirit with which the Republic of Colombia has made satisfaction for well established claims of a similar character. And among the documents now communicated to Congress, will be distinguished a Treaty of Commerce and Navigation with that Republic, the ratifications of which have been exchanged since the last recess of the Legislature. The negotiation of similar treaties with all the independent South American States, has been contemplated, and may yet be accomplished. The basis of them all, as proposed by the United States, has been laid in two principles: the one, of entire and unqualified reciprocity; the other, the mutual obligation of the parties to place each other permanently upon the footing of the most favored nation. These principles are, indeed, indispensable to the effectual emancipation of the American hemisphere from the thraldom of colonizing monopolies and exclusions—an event rapidly realizing in the progress of human affairs, and which the resistance still opposed in certain parts of Europe to the acknowledgment of the Southern American Republics as independent States, will, it is believed, contribute more effectually to accomplish. The time has been, and that not remote, when some of those States might, in their anxious desire to obtain a nominal recognition, have accepted of a nominal independence, clogged with burdensome conditions, and exclusive commercial privileges granted to the nation from which they have separated, to the disadvantage of all others. They are all now aware that such concessions to any European nation, would be incompatible with that independence which they have declared and maintained.

Among the measures which have been suggested to them by the new relations with one another, resulting from the recent changes in their condition, is that of assembling, at the

Isthmus of Panama, a Congress, at which each of them should be represented, to deliberate upon objects important to the welfare of all. The Republics of Colombia, of Mexico, and of Central America, have already deputed Plenipotentiaries to such a meeting, and they have invited the United States to be also represented there by their Ministers. The invitation has been accepted, and Ministers on the part of the United States will be commissioned to attend at those deliberations, and to take part in them, so far as may be compatible with that neutrality from which it is neither our intention, nor the desire of the other American States, that we should depart.

The Commissioners under the Seventh Article of the Treaty of Ghent have so nearly completed their labors, that, by the Report recently received from the Agent on the part of the United States, there is reason to expect that the Commission will be closed at their next session, appointed for the twenty-second of May of the ensuing year.

The other Commission, appointed to ascertain the indemnities due for slaves carried away from the United States, after the close of the late war, have met with some difficulty, which has delayed their progress in the inquiry. A reference has been made to the British Government on the subject, which it may be hoped, will tend to hasten the decision of the Commissioners, or serve as a substitute for it.

Among the powers specifically granted to Congress by the Constitution, are those of establishing uniform laws on the subject of bankruptcies throughout the United States, and of providing for organizing, arming, and disciplining the militia, and for governing such part of them as may be employed in the service of the United States. The magnitude and complexity of the interests affected by legislation upon these subjects, may account for the fact, that, long and often as both of them have occupied the attention, and animated the debates of Congress, no systems have yet been devised for fulfilling, to the satisfaction of the community, the duties prescribed by these grants of power. To conciliate the claim of the individual citizen to the enjoyment of personal liberty, with the effective obligation of private contracts, is the difficult problem to be solved by a law of bankruptcy. These are objects of the deepest interest to society; affecting all that is precious in the existence of multitudes of persons, many of them in the classes essentially dependent and helpless; of the age requiring nurture, and of the sex entitled to protection, from the free agency of the parent and the husband. The organization of the militia is yet more indispensable to the liberties of the country. It is only by an effective militia that we can at once enjoy the repose of peace, and bid defiance to foreign aggression. It is by the militia that we are constituted an armed nation, standing in perpetual panoply of defence, in the presence of all the other nations of the earth. To this end, it would be necessary, so to shape its organization, as to give it a more united and active energy. There are laws for establishing an uniform militia throughout the United States, and for arming and equipping its whole body. But it is a body of dislocated members, without the vigor of unity, and having little of uniformity but the name. To infuse into this most important institution the power of which it is susceptible, and to make it available for the defence of the Union, at the shortest notice, and at the smallest expense of time, of life, and of treasure, are among the benefits to be expected from the persevering deliberations of Congress.

Among the unequivocal indications of our national prosperity, is the flourishing state of our finances. The revenues of the present year, from all their principal sources, will exceed the anticipations of the last. The balance in the Treasury, on the first of January last, was a little short of two millions of dollars, exclusive of two millions and a half, being the moiety of the loan of five millions, authorized by the act of 26th May, 1824. The receipts into the Treasury from the first of January to the thirtieth of September, exclusive of the other moiety of the same loan, are estimated at sixteen millions five hundred thousand dollars; and it is expected that those of the current quarter will exceed five millions of dollars; forming an aggregate of receipts of nearly twenty-two millions, independent of the loan. The expenditures of the year will not exceed that sum more than two millions. By those expenditures, nearly eight millions of the principal of the public debt have been discharged. More than a million and a half has been devoted to the debt of gratitude to the warriors of the Revolution; a nearly equal sum to the construction of fortifications, and the acquisition of ordnance, and other permanent preparations of national defence: half a million to the gradual increase of the Navy: an equal sum for purchases of Territory from the Indians, and payment of annuities to them: and upwards of a million for objects of Internal Improvement, authorized by special acts of the last Congress. If we add to these, four millions of dollars for payment of interest upon the public debt, there remains a sum of about seven millions, which have defrayed the whole expense of the Administration of Government, in its Legislative, Executive, and Judiciary Departments, including the support of the Military and Naval Establishments, and all the occasional contingencies of a Government co-extensive with the Union.

The amount of duties secured on merchandise imported, from the commencement of the year, is about twenty-five millions and a half; and that which will accrue during the current quarter, is estimated at five millions and a half; from these thirty-one millions, deducting the drawbacks, estimated at less than seven millions, a sum exceeding twenty-four millions will constitute the revenue of the year; and will exceed the whole expenditures of the year. The entire amount of public debt remaining due on the first of January next, will be short of eighty-one millions of dollars.

By an act of Congress of the third of March last, a loan of twelve millions of dollars was authorized at four and a half per cent. or an exchange of stock to that amount of four and a half per cent. for a stock of 6 per cent. to create a fund for extinguishing an equal amount of the public debt, bearing an interest of six per cent. redeemable in the year one thousand eight hundred and twenty-six. An account of the measures taken to give effect to this act will be laid before you by the Secretary of the Treasury. As the object which it had in view has been but partially accomplished, it will be for the consideration of Congress, whether the power with which it clothed the Executive should not be renewed at an early day of the present session, and under what modifications.

The act of Congress of the third of March last, directing the Secretary of the Treasury to subscribe, in the name and for the use of the United States, for one thousand five hundred shares of the capital stock of the Chesapeake and Delaware Canal Company, has been executed by the actual subscription for the amount specified; and such other measures have been adopted by that officer, under the act, as the fulfillment of its intentions requires. The latest accounts received of this important undertaking authorize the belief that it is in successful progress.

The payments into the Treasury from the proceeds of the sales of the Public Lands, during the present year, were estimated at one million of dollars. The actual receipts of the first two quarters have fallen very little short of that sum; it is not expected that the second half of the year will be equally productive; but the income of the year from that source may now be safely estimated at a million and a half. The Act of Congress of eighteenth May, 1824, to provide for the extinguishment of the debt due to the United States by the purchasers of public lands, was limited, in its operation of relief to the purchaser, to the tenth of April last. Its effect at the end of the quarter during which it expired, was to reduce that debt from ten to seven millions. By the operation of similar prior laws of relief, from and since that of second March, 1821, the debt had been reduced, from upwards of twenty-two millions, to ten. It is exceedingly desirable that it should be extinguished altogether; and to facilitate that consummation, I recommend to Congress the revival, for one year more, of the act of 18th May, 1824, with such provisional modification as may be necessary to guard the public interests against fraudulent practices in the resale of the relinquished land. The purchasers of public lands are among the most useful of our fellow citizens; and, since the system of sales for cash alone has been introduced, great indulgence has been justly extended to those who had previously purchased upon credit. The debt which had been contracted under the credit sales had become unwieldy, and its extinction was alike advantageous to the purchaser and the public. Under the system of sales, matured, as it has been, by experience, and adapted to the exigencies of the times, the lands will continue, as they have become, an abundant source of revenue; and when the pledge of them to the public creditor shall have been redeemed by the entire discharge of the national debt, the swelling tide of wealth with which they replenish the common Treasury may be made to reflow in unfailing streams of improvement from the Atlantic to the Pacific Ocean.

The condition of the various branches of the public service resorting from the Department of War, and their administration during the current year, will be exhibited in the Report of the Secretary of War, and the accompanying documents herewith communicated. The organization and discipline of the Army are effective and satisfactory. To counteract the prevalence of desertion among the troops, it has been suggested to withhold from the men a small portion of their monthly pay, until the period of their discharge; and some expedient appears to be necessary, to preserve and maintain among the officers so much of the art of horsemanship as could scarcely fail to be found wanting, on the possible sudden eruption of a war, which should overtake us unprovided with a single corps of cavalry. The Military Academy at West-Point, under the restrictions of a severe but paternal superintendence, recommends itself more and more to the patronage of the Nation; and the number of meritorious officers which it forms and introduces to the public service, furnishes the means of multiplying the undertakings of public improvements, to which their acquirements at that institution are peculiarly adapted. The school of Artillery practice, established at Fortress Monroe, is well suited to the same purpose, and may need the aid of further legislative provision to the same end. The Reports of the various officers at the head of the administrative branches of the military service, connected with the quartering, clothing, subsistence, health, and pay of the Army, exhibit the assiduous vigilance of those officers in the performance of their respective duties, and the faithful accountability which has pervaded every part of the system.

Our relations with the numerous tribes of aboriginal natives of this country, scattered over its extensive surface, and so dependent, even for their existence, upon our power, have been, during the present year, highly interesting. An act of Congress of twenty-fifth May, one thousand eight hundred and twenty-four, made an appropriation to defray the expenses of making Treaties of trade and friendship with the Indian Tribes beyond the Mississippi. An act of third March, one thousand eight hundred and twenty-five, authorized Treaties to be made with the Indians for their consent to the making of a road from the frontier of Missouri to that of New Mexico. And another act, of the same date, provided for defraying the expenses of holding Treaties with the Sioux, Chippeways, Menomenees, Sauks, Foxes, &c. for the purpose of establishing boundaries and promoting peace between said tribes. The first and the last objects of these acts have been accomplished, and the second is yet in a process of execution. The treaties which, since the last session of Congress, have been concluded with the several tribes, will be laid before the Senate for their consideration, conformably to the Constitution. They comprise large and valuable acquisitions of territory; and they secure an adjustment of boundaries, and give pledges of permanent peace between several tribes which had been long waging bloody wars against each other.

On the twelfth of February last, a Treaty was signed at the Indian Springs, between Commissioners appointed on the part of the United States, and certain Chiefs and individuals of the Creek Nation of Indians, which was received at the Seat of Government only a few days before the close of the last Session of Congress and of the late Administration. The advice and consent of the Senate was given to it on the third of March, too late for it to receive the ratification of the then President of the United States: it was ratified on the seventh of March, under the unsuspecting impression that it had been negotiated in good faith, and in the confidence inspired by the recommendation of the Senate. The subsequent transactions in relation to this Treaty, will form the subject of a separate Message.

The appropriations made by Congress, for public works, as well in the construction of fortifications, as for purposes of Internal Improvement, so far as they have been expended, have been faithfully applied. Their progress has been delayed by the want of suitable officers for superintending them. An increase of both the Corps of Engineers, Military and Topographical, was recommended by my predecessor at the last session of Congress. The reasons upon which that recommendation was founded, subsist in all their force, and have acquired additional urgency since that time. It may also be expedient to organize the Topographical Engineers into a corps similar to the present establishment of the Corps of Engineers. The Military Academy at West Point will furnish, from the cadets annually graduated there, officers well qualified for carrying this measure into effect.

The Board of Engineers for Internal Improvement, appointed for carrying into execution the act of Congress of 30th of April, 1824, "to procure the necessary surveys, plans, and estimates on the subject of roads and canals," have been actively engaged in that service from the close of the last session of Congress. They have completed the surveys necessary for ascertaining the practicability of a Canal from the Chesapeake Bay to the Ohio River, and are preparing a full Report on that subject; which, when completed, will be laid before you. The same observation is to be made with regard to the two other objects of national importance upon which the Board have been occupied: namely, the accomplishment of a National Road from this City to New Orleans, and the practicability of uniting the waters of Lake Memphramagog with Connecticut River, and the improvement of the navigation of that River. The surveys have been made, and are nearly completed. The Report may be expected at an early period during the present session of Congress.

The Acts of Congress of the last Session, relative to the surveying, marking, or laying out, roads in the Territories of Florida, Arkansas, and Michigan, from Missouri to Mexico, and for the continuation of the Cumberland Road, are, some of them, fully executed, and others in the process of execution. Those for completing or commencing fortifications, have been delayed only so far as the Corps of Engineers has been inadequate to furnish officers for the necessary superintendence of the works. Under the act confirming the statutes of Virginia and Maryland, incorporating the Chesapeake and Ohio Canal Company, three Commissioners on the part of the United States have been appointed for opening books and receiving subscriptions, in concert with a like number of Commissioners appointed on the part of each of those States. A meeting of the Commissioners has been postponed to await the definitive Report of the Board of Engineers. The light-houses and monuments for the safety of our commerce and mariners; the works for the security of Plymouth Beach, and for the preservation of the Islands in Boston Harbor; have received the attention required by the laws relating to those objects respectively. The continuation of the Cumberland Road, the most important of them all, after surmounting no inconsiderable difficulty in fixing upon the direction of the road, has commenced under the most promising auspices, with the improvements of recent invention in the mode of construction, and with the advantage of a great reduction in the comparative cost of the work.

The operation of the laws relating to the Revolutionary Pensioners may deserve the renewed consideration of Congress. The Act of 18th March, 1818, while it made provision for many meritorious and indigent citizens who had served in the War of Independence, opened a door to numerous abuses and impositions. To remedy this, the Act of 1st May, 1820, exacted proofs of absolute indigence, which many really in want were unable, and all, susceptible of that delicacy which is allied to many virtues, must be deeply reluctant to give. The result has been, that some among the least deserving have been retained, and some in whom the requisites both of worth and want were combined, have been stricken from the list. As the numbers of these venerable relics of an age gone by diminish; as the decays of body, mind, and estate, of those that survive, must, in the common course of nature, increase; should not a more liberal portion of indulgence be dealt out to them? May not the want, in most instances, be inferred from the demand, when the service can be proved; and may not the last days of human infirmity be spared the mortification of purchasing a pittance of relief only by the exposure of its own necessities? I submit to Congress the expediency of providing for individual cases of this description by special enactment, or of revising the Act of the 1st May, 1820, with a view to mitigate the rigor of its exclusions, in favor of persons to whom charity now bestowed can scarcely discharge the debt of justice.

The portion of the Naval force of the Union in actual service, has been chiefly employed on three stations: The Mediterranean, the coasts of South America bordering on the Pacific Ocean, and the West-Indies. An occasional cruiser has been sent to range along the African shores most polluted by the traffic of slaves; one armed vessel has been stationed on the coast of our eastern boundary, to cruise along the fishing grounds in Hudson's Bay, and on the coast of Labrador, and the first service of a new frigate has been performed in restoring to his native soil, and domestic enjoyments, the veteran hero whose youthful blood and treasure had freely flowed in the cause of our Country's Independence, and whose whole life has been a series of services and sacrifices to the improvement of his fellow-men. The visit of General Lafayette, alike honorable to himself and to our Country, closed, as it had commenced, with the most affecting testimonials of devoted attachment on his part, and of unbounded gratitude of this People to him in return. It will form, hereafter, a pleasing incident in the annals of our Union, giving to real history the intense interest of romance, and signally marking the unpurchasable tribute of a great Nation's social affections to the disinterested champion of the liberties of human-kind.

The constant maintenance of a small squadron in the Mediterranean is a necessary substitute for the humiliating alternative of paying tribute for the security of our commerce in that sea, and for a precarious peace, at the mercy of every caprice of four Barbary States, by whom it was liable to be violated. An additional motive for keeping a respectable force stationed there at this time, is found in the maritime war raging between the Greeks and the Turks; and in which the neutral navigation of this Union is always in danger of outrage and depredation. A few instances have occurred of such depredations upon our merchant vessels by privateers or pirates wearing the Grecian flag, but without real authority from the Greek or any other Government. The heroic struggles of the Greeks themselves, in which our warmest sympathies as Freemen and Christians have been engaged, have continued to be maintained with vicissitudes of success adverse and favorable.

Similar motives have rendered expedient the keeping of a like force on the coasts of Peru and Chile on the Pacific. The irregular and convulsive character of the war upon the shores, has been extended to the conflicts upon the ocean. An active warfare has been kept up for years, with alternate success, though generally to the advantage of the American Patriots. But their naval forces have not always been under the control of their own governments. Blockades, unjustifiable upon any acknowledged principles of international law, have been proclaimed by officers in command; and though disavowed by the supreme authorities, the protection of our own commerce against them has been made cause of complaint and erroneous imputations upon some of the most gallant officers of our Navy. Complaints equally groundless have been made by the commanders of the Spanish Royal forces in those seas; but the most effective protection to our commerce has been the flag, and the firmness of our own commanding officers. The cessation of the war, by the complete triumph of the Patriot cause, has removed, it is hoped, all cause of dissension with one party, and all vestige of force of the other. But an unsettled coast of many degrees of latitude, forming a part of our own Territory, and a flourishing commerce and fishery, extending to the Islands of the Pacific and to China, still require that the protecting power of the Union should be displayed under its flag, as well upon the ocean as upon the land.

The objects of the West India squadron have been to carry into execution the laws for the suppression of the African Slave Trade: for the protection of our commerce against vessels of piratical character, though bearing commissions from either of the belligerent parties: for its protection against open and unequivocal pirates. These objects, during the present year, have been accomplished more effectually than at any former period. The African Slave Trade has long been excluded from the use of our flag; and if some few citizens of our country have continued to set the laws of the Union, as well as those of Nature and Humanity, at defiance, by persevering in that abominable traffic, it has been only by sheltering themselves under the banners of other nations, less earnest for the total extinction of the trade than ours. The irregular privateers have, within the last year, been in a great measure banished from those seas; and the pirates, for months past, appear to have been almost entirely swept away from the borders and the shores of the two Spanish islands in those regions. The active, persevering, and unremitted energy of Captain Warrington, and of the officers and men under his command, on that trying and perilous service, have been crowned with signal success, and are entitled to the approbation of their country. But experience has shown, that not even a temporary suspension or relaxation from assiduity can be indulged on that station, without re-producing piracy and murder in all their horrors; nor is it probable that, for years to come, our immensely valuable commerce in those seas can navigate in security, without the steady continuance of an armed force devoted to its protection.

It were indeed a vain and dangerous illusion to believe, that, in the present or probable condition of human society, a commerce so extensive and so rich as ours, could exist and be pursued in safety, without the continual support of a military marine—the only arm by which the power of this confederacy can be estimated or felt by foreign nations, and the only standing military force which can never be dangerous to our own liberties at home. A permanent Naval Peace Establishment, therefore, adapted to our present condition, and adaptable to that gigantic growth with which the nation is advancing in its career, is among the subjects which have already occupied the foresight of the last Congress, and which will deserve your

FIRST ANNUAL MESSAGE | 1825

serious deliberations. Our Navy, commenced at an early period of our present political organization, upon a scale commensurate with the incipient energies, the scanty resources, and the comparative indigence of our infancy, was, even then, found adequate to cope with all the powers of Barbary, save the first, and with one of the principal maritime powers of Europe. At a period of further advancement, but with little accession of strength, it not only sustained with honor the most unequal of conflicts, but covered itself and our country with unfading glory. But it is only since the close of the late war, that, by the numbers and force of the ships of which it was composed it could deserve the name of a Navy. Yet, it retains nearly the same organization as when it consisted only of five frigates. The rules and regulations by which it is governed earnestly call for revision, and the want of a Naval School of Instruction, corresponding with the Military Academy at West Point, for the formation of scientific and accomplished officers, is felt with daily increasing aggravation.

The act of Congress of 26th May, 1824, authorizing an examination and survey of the harbor of Charleston, in South Carolina, of St. Mary's, in Georgia, and of the coast of Florida, and for other purposes, has been executed so far as the appropriation would admit. Those of the 3d of March last, authorizing the establishment of a Navy Yard and Depot on the Coast of Florida, in the Gulf of Mexico, and authorizing the building of ten sloops of war, and for other purposes, are in the course of execution, for the particulars of which, and other objects connected with this Department, I refer to the Report of the Secretary of the Navy, herewith communicated.

A Report from the Postmaster General is also submitted, exhibiting the present flourishing condition of that Department. For the first time for many years, the receipts for the year ending on the 1st of July last, exceeded the expenditures during the same period, to the amount of more than forty-five thousand dollars. Other facts, equally creditable to the administration of this Department, are, that, in two years from the first of July, 1823, an improvement of more than one hundred and eighty-five thousand dollars in its pecuniary affairs has been realized; that in the same interval the increase of the transportation of the mail has exceeded one million five hundred thousand miles, annually; and that one thousand and forty new post offices have been established. It hence appears, that, under judicious management, the income from this establishment may be relied on as fully adequate to defray its expenses; and, that by the discontinuance of post roads, altogether unproductive, others of more useful character may be opened, till the circulation of the mail shall keep pace with the spread of our population; and the comforts of friendly correspondence, the exchanges of internal traffic, and the lights of the periodical press, shall be distributed to the remotest corners of the Union, at a charge scarcely perceptible to any individual, and without the cost of a dollar to the public treasury.

Upon this first occasion of addressing the Legislature of the Union, with which I have been honored, in presenting to their view the execution, so far as it has been effected, of the measures sanctioned by them, for promoting the internal improvement of our country, I cannot close the communication without recommending to their calm and persevering consideration the general principle in a more enlarged extent. The great object of the institution of civil government, is the improvement of the condition of those who are parties to the social compact. And no government, in whatever form constituted, can accomplish the lawful ends of its institution, but in proportion as it improves the condition of those over whom it is established. Roads and Canals, by multiplying and facilitating the communications and intercourse between distant regions, and multitudes of men, are among the most important means of improvement. But moral, political, intellectual improvement, are duties assigned, by the author of our existence, to social, no less than to individual man. For the fulfillment of those duties, governments are invested with power; and, to the attainment of the end, the progressive improvement of the condition of the governed, the exercise of delegated power, is a duty as sacred and indispensable, as the usurpation of power not granted is criminal and odious. Among the first, perhaps the very first instrument for the improvement of the condition of men, is knowledge; and to the acquisition of much of the knowledge adapted to the wants, the comforts, and enjoyments, of human life, public institutions and seminaries of learning are essential. So convinced of this was the first of my predecessors in this office, now first in the memory, as, living, he was first in the hearts of our country, that, once and again, in his addresses to the Congresses, with whom he cooperated in the public service, he earnestly recommended the establishment of seminaries of learning, to prepare for all the emergencies of peace and war—a national university, and a military academy. With respect to the latter, had he lived to the present day, in turning his eyes to the institution at West Point, he would have enjoyed the gratification of his most earnest wishes. But, in surveying the city which has been honored with his name, he would have seen the spot of earth which he had destined and bequeathed to the use and benefit of his country, as the site for an university, still bare and barren.

In assuming her station among the civilized nations of the earth, it would seem that our country had contracted the engagement to contribute her share of mind, of labor and of expense, to the improvement of those parts of knowledge, which lie beyond the reach of individual acquisition; and particularly to geographical and astronomical science. Looking back to the history only of the half century since the Declaration of our Independence, and observing the generous emulation with which the governments of France, Great Britain, and Russia, have devoted the genius, the intelligence, the treasures of their respective nations, to the common improvement of the species in these branches of science, is it not incumbent upon us to inquire, whether we are not bound, by obligations of a high and honorable character, to contribute our portion of energy and exertion to the common stock? The voyages of discovery, prosecuted in the course of that time, at the expense of those nations, have not only redounded to their glory, but to the improvement of human knowledge. We have been partakers of that improvement, and owe for it a sacred debt, not only of gratitude, but of equal or proportional exertion in the same common cause. Of the cost of these undertakings, if the mere expenditures of outfit, equipment, and completion of the expeditions, were to be considered the only charges, it would be unworthy of a great and generous nation to take a second thought. One hundred expeditions of circumnavigation, like those of Cook and La Perouse, would not burden the exchequer of the nation fitting them out, so much as the ways and means of defraying a single campaign in war. But, if we take into the account the lives of those benefactors of mankind, of which their services in the cause of their species were the purchase, how shall the cost of those heroic enterprises be estimated? And what compensation can be made to them, or to their countries for them? Is it not by bearing them in affectionate remembrance? Is it not still more by imitating their example? by enabling countrymen of our own to pursue the same career, and to hazard their lives in the same cause?

In inviting the attention of Congress to the subject of Internal Improvements, upon a view thus enlarged, it is not my design to recommend the equipment of an expedition for circumnavigating the globe for purposes of scientific research and inquiry. We have objects of useful investigation nearer home, and to which our cares may be more beneficially applied. The interior of our own territories has yet been very imperfectly explored. Our coasts, along many degrees of latitude upon the shores of the Pacific ocean, though much frequented by our spirited commercial navigators, have been barely visited by our public ships. The River of the West, first fully discovered and navigated by a countryman of our own, still bears the name of the ship in which he ascended its waters, and claims the protection of our armed national flag at its mouth. With the establishment of a military post there, or at some other point of that coast, recommended by my predecessor, and already matured, in the deliberations of the last Congress, I would suggest the expediency of connecting the equipment of a public ship for the exploration of the whole northwest coast of this continent.

The establishment of an uniform standard of Weights and Measures was one of the specific objects contemplated in the formation of our Constitution, and to fix that standard was one of the powers delegated by express terms, in that instrument, to Congress. The governments of Great Britain and France have scarcely ceased to be occupied with inquiries and speculations on the same subject, since the existence of our Constitution, and with them it has expanded into profound, laborious, and expensive researches into the figure of the earth, and the comparative length of the pendulum vibrating seconds in various latitudes, from the Equator to the Pole. These researches have resulted in the composition and publication of several works highly interesting to the cause of science. The experiments are yet in the process of performance. Some of them have recently been made on our own shores, within the walls of one of our own colleges, and partly by one of our own fellow citizens. It would be honorable to our country if the sequel of the same experiments should be countenanced by the patronage of our government, as they have hitherto been by those of France and Britain.

Connected with the establishment of an University, or separate from it, might be undertaken the erection of an astronomical observatory, with provision for the support of an astronomer, to be in constant attendance of observation upon the phenomena of the heavens, and for the periodical publication of his observations. It is with no feeling of pride, as an American, that the remark may be made, that, on the comparatively small territorial surface of Europe, there are existing upwards of one hundred and thirty of these light-houses of the skies; while throughout the whole American hemisphere, there is not one. If we reflect a moment upon the discoveries, which, in the last four centuries, have been made in the physical constitution of the universe, by the means of these buildings, and of observers stationed in them, shall we doubt of their usefulness, to every nation? And while scarcely a year passes over our heads without bringing some new astronomical discovery to light, which we must fain receive at second hand from Europe, are we not cutting ourselves off from the means of returning light for light, while we have neither observatory nor observer upon our half of the globe, and the earth revolves in perpetual darkness to our unsearching eyes?

When, on the 25th of October, 1791, the first President of the United States announced to Congress the result of the first enumeration of the inhabitants of this Union, he informed them that the returns gave the pleasing assurance that the population of the United States bordered on four millions of persons. At the distance of thirty years from that time, the last enumeration, five years since completed, presented a population bordering upon ten millions. Perhaps, of all the evidences of a prosperous and happy condition of human society, the rapidity of the increase of population is the most unequivocal. But the demonstration of our prosperity rests not alone upon this indication. Our commerce, our wealth, and the extent of our territories, have increased in corresponding proportions; and the number of independent communities, associated in our Federal Union, has, since that time nearly doubled. The legislative representation of the States and People, in the two Houses of Congress, has grown with the growth of their constituent bodies. The House, which then consisted of sixty-five members, now numbers upwards of two hundred. The Senate, which consisted of twenty-six members, has now forty-eight. But the Executive and, still more the Judiciary Departments, are yet in a great measure confined to their primitive organization, and are now not adequate to the urgent wants of a still growing community.

The naval armaments, which, at an early period, forced themselves upon the necessities of the Union, soon led to the establishment of a Department of the Navy. But the Departments of Foreign Affairs, and of the Interior, which, early after the formation of the Government had been united in one, continue so united to this time, to the unquestionable detriment of the public service. The multiplication of our relations with the nations and Governments of the old world, has kept pace with that of our population and commerce, while, within the last ten years, a new family of nations, in our own hemisphere, has arisen among the inhabitants of the earth, with whom our intercourse, commercial and political, would, of itself, furnish occupation to an active and industrious Department. The constitution of the Judiciary, experimental and imperfect as it was, even in the infancy of our existing Government, is yet more inadequate to the administration of national justice at our present maturity. Nine years have elapsed since a predecessor in this office, now not the last, the citizen who, perhaps, of all others throughout the Union, contributed most to the formation and establishment of our Constitution, in his valedictory address to Congress immediately preceding his retirement from public life, urgently recommended the revision of the Judiciary, and the establishment of an additional Executive Department. The exigencies of the public service, and its unavoidable deficiencies, as now in exercise, have added yearly cumulative weight to the considerations presented by him as persuasive to the measure; and in recommending it to your deliberations, I am happy to have the influence of his high authority, in aid of the undoubting convictions of my own experience.

The laws relating to the administration of the Patent Office are deserving of much consideration, and, perhaps, susceptible of some improvement. The grant of power to regulate the action of Congress upon this subject, has specified both the end to be attained, and the means by which it is to be effected—to promote the progress of science and useful arts, by securing for limited times to authors and inventors the exclusive right to their respective writings and discoveries. If an honest pride might be indulged in the reflection, that on the records of that office are already found inventions, the usefulness of which has scarcely been transcended in the annals of human ingenuity, would not its exultation be allayed by the inquiry, whether the laws have effectively insured to the inventors the reward destined to them by the Constitution, even a limited term of exclusive right to their discoveries?

On the 24th of December, 1799, it was resolved by Congress that a marble monument should be erected by the United States, in the Capitol, at the City of Washington; that the family of General Washington should be requested to permit his body to be deposited under it; and that the monument be so designed as to commemorate the great events of his military and political life. In reminding Congress of this resolution, and that the monument contemplated by it remains yet without execution, I shall indulge only the remarks, that the works at the Capitol are approaching to completion; that the consent of the family, desired by the resolution, was requested and obtained; that a monument has been recently erected in this city, at the expense of the Nation, over the remains of another distinguished patriot of the Revolution, and that a spot has been reserved within the walls where you are deliberating for the benefit of this and future ages, in which the mortal remains may be deposited of him whose spirit hovers over you, and listens with delight to every act of the Representatives of his Nation which can tend to exalt and adorn his and their Country.

The Constitution under which you are assembled is a charter of limited powers. After full and solemn deliberation upon all or any of the objects, which, urged by an irresistible sense of my own duty, I have recommended to your attention, should you come to the conclusion, that, however desirable in themselves, the enactment of laws for effecting them would transcend the powers committed to you by that venerable instrument which we are all bound to support; let no consideration induce you to assume the exercise of powers not granted to you by the people. But, if the power to exercise exclusive legislation in all cases whatsoever over the District of Columbia; if the power to lay and collect taxes, duties, imposts, and excises, to pay the debts, and provide for the common defense and general welfare of the United States; if the power to regulate commerce with foreign nations and among the several States, and with the Indian tribes; to fix the standard of weights and measures; to establish post-offices and post-roads; to declare war; to raise and support armies, to provide and maintain a navy; to dispose of and make all needful rules and regulations respecting the territory or other property belonging to the United States; and to make all laws which shall be necessary and proper for carrying these powers into execution: If these powers, and others enumerated in the Constitution, may be effectually brought into action by laws promoting the improvement of Agriculture, Commerce, and Manufactures, the cultivation and encouragement of the Mechanic and of the elegant Arts, the advancement of Literature, and the progress of the Sciences, ornamental and profound, to refrain from exercising them for the benefit of the People themselves, would be to hide in the earth the talent committed to our charge—would be treachery to the most sacred of trusts.

The spirit of improvement is abroad upon the earth. It stimulates the heart, and sharpens the faculties, not of our fellow citizens alone, but of the nations of Europe, and of their rulers. While dwelling with pleasing satisfaction upon the superior excellence of our political institutions, let us not be unmindful that Liberty is Power; that the nation blessed with the largest portion of liberty, must, in proportion to its numbers, be the most powerful nation upon earth; and that the tenure of power by man, is, in the moral purposes of his Creator, upon condition that it shall be exercised to ends of beneficence, to improve the condition of himself and his fellow men. While foreign nations, less blessed with that freedom which is power, than ourselves, are advancing with gigantic strides in the career of public improvement; were we to slumber in indolence, or fold up our arms and proclaim to the world that we are palsied by the will of our constituents, would it not be to cast away the bounties of Providence, and doom ourselves to perpetual inferiority? In the course of the year now drawing to its close, we have beheld, under the auspices, and at the expense of one State of this Union, a new university unfolding its portals to the sons of science and holding up the torch of human improvement to eyes that seek the light. We have seen under the persevering and enlightened enterprise of another State, the waters of our Western lakes mingle with those of the ocean. If undertakings like these have been accomplished in the compass of a few years, by the authority of single members of our Confederation, can we, the Representative Authorities of the whole Union, fall behind our fellow-servants in the exercise of the trust committed to us for the benefit of our common Sovereign, by the accomplishment of works important to the whole, and to which neither the authority nor the resources of any one State can be adequate?

Finally, fellow-citizens, I shall await with cheering hope, and faithful co-operation, the result of your deliberations; assured that, without encroaching upon the powers reserved to the authorities of the respective States, or to the People, you will, with a due sense of your obligations to your country, and of the high responsibilities weighing upon yourselves, give efficacy to the means committed to you for the common good. And may He who searches the hearts of the children of men, prosper your exertions to secure the blessings of peace, and promote the highest welfare of our country.

JOHN QUINCY ADAMS.
Washington, December 6, 1825.

"THE DESIGN IS GREAT, IS BENEVOLENT,
IS HUMANE"

13. Message on the Panama Congress. March 15, 1826. *The National Intelligencer* Special Supplement (Washington, D.C., Saturday, March 18, 1826).

The consequences Adams had braced himself for were not long in coming. Opposition in Congress quickly coalesced around a range of issues, including the election of a new speaker, a disputed land cession treaty involving Creek Indians in Georgia, and new restrictions on U.S. trade in the British West Indies. But one subject provided the administration's foes with their sharpest wedge: relations with the newly independent states of Central and South America. On December 25, 1825, Adams formally advised Congress of his intention to accept the invitation of Simón Bolívar (alluded to in his Annual Message) to send a U.S. delegation to a congress of the American states to be convened in Panama, nominating Richard C. Anderson of Kentucky, already serving as U.S. minister to Colombia, and John Sergeant of Pennsylvania as ministers plenipotentiary, to be accompanied by William B. Rochester of New York, as their secretary.

As speaker, Henry Clay had been an early and steadfast advocate for recognition of the former Spanish colonies' independence, often to the irritation of Secretary of State Adams. Now, both he and the president saw the conference as an opportunity to strengthen hemispheric ties and, per Bolívar's stated aims, to address such long-standing U.S. concerns as the rights of neutral shipping in times of war and the suppression of the international slave trade. In making the announcement, Adams affirmed his right, as the chief executive, to accept the invitation, but acknowledged that the Senate had to consent to his nominations and the House had to appropriate the funds to support the mission.

The Jacksonian/Calhounite coalition pounced, tying up the nominations in the Senate, making repeated demands for documents and papers related to the invitation to the congress and appointing a select committee to debate whether the executive had the constitutional authority to join in what some called a backdoor alliance in violation of the spirit of Washington's Farewell Address. (In his diary Adams wrote that "these resolutions are the fruit of the ingenuity of Martin Van Buren, and bear the impress of his character.") In the House, meanwhile, debate on the matter consumed session after session, with members, particularly from the South, objecting to the very idea that U.S. policy might be shaped in consultation with, as they viewed them, the culturally alien and racially inferior peoples of Latin America. Never far beneath these objections lay concerns about slavery, as Senator Robert Y. Hayne of South Carolina soon made clear enough: "With nothing connected with slavery can we consent to treat with other nations, and least of all ought we to touch the question of the independence of Hayti in conjunction with Revolutionary Governments, whose own history affords an example scarcely less fatal to our repose."

Adams defended the mission with the following message, the pithiest encapsulation of his foreign policy of his presidency. Near its end, he quotes the famous passage from his predecessor's annual message of December 2, 1823, that articulated what became known as the Monroe Doctrine, which Adams himself had done more than anyone else to conceive. Rising to a patriotic pitch, he avers that the Panama Congress "is congenial with that spirit which prompted the declaration of our independence . . . [and] which filled the hearts and fired the souls of the immortal founders of our Revolution."

The Senate approved the nominations on March 14, 1826, the day before Adams transmitted this message to the House. The House Ways and Means Committee reported a bill funding the mission on March 26, and on April 22, after narrowly voting down amendments designed to limit the mission's remit, the House passed an appropriation of $40,000 by a vote of 134 to 60. On May 3, the Senate endorsed the appropriation, finally enabling the mission to proceed. It was a rare victory for the administration, but a Pyrrhic one: the protracted debates had succeeded in delaying the departure of the ministers until it was too late. Anderson, en route to the congress, died near Cartagena on July 24, 1826. Sergeant meanwhile refused to travel to Panama during the summer, when tropical diseases were most dangerous, and would not arrive until well after the congress had concluded.

Message on the Panama Congress

WASHINGTON, *March 15, 1826.*
To the House of Representatives of the United States:

In compliance with the resolution of the House of the 5th ultimo, requesting me to cause to be laid before the House, so much of the correspondence between the Government of the United States, and the new States of America or their ministers, respecting the proposed Congress, or meeting of Diplomatic Agents at Panama, and such information respecting the general character of that expected Congress, as may be in my possession, and as may, in my opinion, be communicated without prejudice to the public interest; and also, to inform the House, so far as in my opinion the public interest may allow, in regard to what objects the Agents of the United States are expected to take part in the deliberations of that Congress: I now transmit to the House, a report from the Secretary of State, with the correspondence and information requested by the resolution.

With regard to the objects in which the Agents of the United States are expected to take part in the deliberations of that Congress, I deem it proper to premise, that these objects did not form the only, nor even the principal motive for my acceptance of the invitation. My first and greatest inducement was to meet, in the spirit of kindness and friendship, an overture made in that spirit by three sister Republics of this hemisphere. The great revolution in human affairs which has brought into existence, nearly at the same time, eight sovereign and independent nations in our own quarter of the globe, has placed the United States in a situation not less novel, and scarcely less interesting, than that in which they had found themselves, by their own transition from a cluster of colonies to a nation of sovereign States. The deliverance of the Southern American Republics from the oppression, under which they had been so long afflicted, was hailed with great unanimity by the People of this Union, as among the most auspicious events of the age. On the 4th of May, 1822, an act of Congress made an appropriation of one hundred thousand dollars "for such missions to the Independent Nations on the American continent, as the President of the United States might deem proper."

In exercising the authority recognized by this act, my predecessor, by and with the advice and consent of the Senate, appointed, successively, Ministers Plenipotentiary to the Republics of Colombia, Buenos Ayres, Chili, and Mexico. Unwilling to raise among the fraternity of freedom, questions of precedency and etiquette, which even the European Monarchs had of late found it necessary in a great measure to discard, he dispatched these Ministers to Colombia, Buenos Ayres, and Chili, without exacting from those Republics, as by the ancient principles of political primogeniture he might have done, that the compliment of a Plenipotentiary mission, should have been paid *first* by them to the United States. The instructions prepared under his direction to Mr. Anderson, the first of our Ministers to the Southern continent, contain, at much length, the general principles, upon which he thought it desirable that our relations, political and commercial, with these our new neighbors, should be established, for their benefit and ours, and that of the future ages of our posterity. A copy of so much of these instructions as relates to these general subjects, is among the papers now transmitted to the House. Similar instructions were furnished to the Ministers appointed to Buenos Ayres, Chili, and Mexico; and the system of social intercourse which it was the purpose of those missions to establish from the first opening of our Diplomatic relations with those rising nations, is the most effective exposition of the principles upon which the invitation to the Congress at Panama, has been accepted by me, as well as of the objects of negotiation at that meeting in which it was expected that our Plenipotentiaries should take part.

The House will perceive that, even at the date of these instructions, the first treaties between some of the Southern Republics had been concluded, by which, they had stipulated among themselves this Diplomatic assembly at Panama. And it will be seen with what caution, so far as it might concern the policy of the United States, and at the same time, with what frankness and good will toward those nations, he gave countenance to their design of inviting the United States to this high assembly for consultation upon *American interests*.

It was not considered a conclusive reason for declining this invitation, that the proposal for assembling such a Congress had not first been made by ourselves. It had sprung from the urgent, immediate, and momentous common interests of the great communities struggling for independence, and, as it were, quickening into life. From them the proposition to us appeared respectful and friendly; from us to them, it could scarcely have been made, without exposing ourselves to suspicions of purposes of ambition, if not of domination, more suited to rouse resistance and excite distrust, than to conciliate favor and friendship. The first and paramount principle, upon which it was deemed wise and just to lay the corner stone of all our future relations with them, was *disinterestedness*; the next, was cordial good will to them; the third was a claim of fair and equal reciprocity. Under these impressions, when the invitation was formally and earnestly given, had it even been doubtful, whether *any* of the objects proposed for consideration and discussion at the Congress, were such as that immediate and important interests of the United States would be affected by the issue, I should nevertheless have determined, so far as it depended upon me, to have accepted the invitation, and to have appointed ministers to attend the meeting. The proposal itself implied that the Republics by whom it was made, *believed*, that important interests of ours or of theirs, rendered our attendance there desirable. They had given us notice, that, in the novelty of their situation, and in the spirit of deference to our experience, they would be pleased to have the benefit of our friendly counsel. To meet the temper with which this proposal was made, with a cold repulse, was not thought congenial to that warm interest in their welfare, with which the People and Government of the Union had hitherto gone hand in hand, through the whole progress of their Revolution. To insult them by a refusal of their overture, and then invite them to a similar assembly, to be called by ourselves, was an expedient which never presented itself to the mind. I would have sent ministers to the meeting, had it been merely to give them such advice as they might have desired, even with reference to *their own interests*, not involving ours. I would have sent them had it been merely to explain and set forth to them our reasons for *declining* any proposal of specific measures to which they might desire our concurrence, but which we might deem incompatible with our interests or our duties. In the intercourse between nations, temper is a missionary, perhaps more powerful than talent.—Nothing was ever lost by kind treatment. Nothing can be gained by sullen repulses and aspiring pretensions.

But objects of the highest importance, not only to the future welfare of the whole human race, but bearing directly upon the special interests of this Union, *will* engage the deliberations of the Congress of Panama whether we are represented there or not. Others, if we are represented, may be offered by our Plenipotentiaries, for consideration, having in view both these great results, our own interests and the improvement of the condition of man upon earth. It may be, that, in the lapse of many centuries, no other opportunity, so favorable, will be presented to the Government of the United States, to subserve the benevolent purposes of Divine Providence; to dispense the promised blessings of the Redeemer of mankind; to promote the prevalence in future ages of Peace on earth and good will to man, as will now be placed in their power, by participating in the deliberations of this Congress.

Among the topics enumerated in official papers, published by the Republic of Colombia, and adverted to in the correspondence now communicated to the House, as intended to be presented for discussion, at Panama, there is scarcely one in which the *result* of the meeting will not deeply affect the interests of the United States. Even those in which the belligerent states alone will take an active part, will have a powerful effect upon the state of our relations with the American, and probably with the principal European, States. Were it merely that we might be correctly and speedily informed of the proceedings of the Congress, and of the progress and issue of their negotiations, I should hold it advisable, that we should have an accredited agency with them, placed in such confidential relations with the other members, as would insure the authenticity and the safe and early transmission of its reports. Of the same enumerated topics, are the preparation of a manifesto, setting forth to the world the justice of their cause, and the relations they desire to hold with other Christian powers; and to form a convention of Navigation and Commerce, applicable both to the Confederated States and to their allies.

It will be within the recollection of the House, that immediately after the close of the war of our Independence, a measure closely analogous to this Congress of Panama, was adopted by the Congress of our Confederation, and for purposes of precisely the same character. Three Commissioners, with Plenipotentiary powers, were appointed to negotiate Treaties of Amity, Navigation and Commerce, with all the principal powers of Europe. They met and resided for that purpose about one year at Paris; and the only result of their negotiations at that time, was the first Treaty between the United States and Prussia, memorable in the diplomatic annals of the world, and precious as a monument of the principles, in relation to Commerce and Maritime warfare, with which our country entered upon her career as a member of the great family of Independent nations. This Treaty, prepared in conformity with the instructions of the American Plenipotentiaries, consecrated three fundamental principles of the foreign intercourse, which the Congress of that period were desirous of establishing. First, equal reciprocity, and the mutual stipulation of the privileges of the most favored nation in the commercial exchanges of Peace. Secondly, the abolition of private war upon the ocean; and, thirdly, restrictions favorable to neutral commerce, upon belligerent practices, with regard to contraband of war and blockades. A painful, it may be said a calamitous, experience, of more than forty years, has demonstrated the deep importance of these same principles, to the peace and prosperity of this nation, and to the welfare of all maritime States, and has illustrated the profound wisdom with which they were assumed as cardinal points of the policy of the Union.

At that time, in the infancy of their political existence, under the influence of those principles of liberty and of right, so congenial to the cause in which they had just fought and triumphed, they were able but to obtain the sanction of one great and philosophical, though absolute, Sovereign in Europe, to their liberal and enlightened principles. They could obtain no more. Since then, a political hurricane has gone over three-fourths of the civilized portions of the earth, the desolation of which, it may with confidence be expected, is passing away, leaving at least the American atmosphere purified and refreshed—And now, at this propitious moment, the new-born nations of this hemisphere, assembling by their Representatives, at the Isthmus, between its two continents, to settle the principles of their future international intercourse with other nations and with us, ask, in this great exigency, for our advice, upon those very fundamental maxims, which we from our cradle at first proclaimed and partially succeeded to introduce into the code of National Law.

Without recurring to that total prostration of all neutral and commercial rights, which marked the progress of the late European wars, and which finally involved the United States in them, and adverting only to our political relations with these American Nations, it is observable that while in all other respects, those relations have been uniformly, and without exception of the most friendly and mutually satisfactory character, the only causes of difference and dissension between us and them, which ever have arisen, originated in those neverfailing fountains of discord and irritation: discriminations of commercial favor to other nations, licentious privateers, and paper blockades. I cannot, without doing injustice to the Republics of Buenos Ayres and Colombia, forbear to acknowledge the candid and conciliatory spirit, with which they have repeatedly yielded to our friendly representations and remonstrances on these subjects: In repealing discriminative laws which operated to our disadvantage, and in revoking the commissions of their privateers. To which Colombia has added the magnanimity of making reparation for unlawful captures by some of her cruisers, and of assenting, in the midst of War, to treaty stipulations favorable to neutral navigation. But the recurrence of these occasions of complaint has rendered the renewal of the discussions, which result in the removal of them, necessary, while in the mean time injuries are sustained by merchants, and other individuals of the United States, which cannot be repaired, and the remedy lingers in overtaking the pernicious operation of the mischief. The settlement of general principles, pervading with equal efficacy all the American States, can alone put an end to these evils, and can alone be accomplished at the proposed Assembly.

If it be true that the noblest treaty of peace, ever mentioned in history, is that by which the Carthagenians were bound to abolish the practice of sacrificing their own children, *because it was stipulated in favor of human nature*, I cannot exaggerate to myself the unfading glory, with which these United States will go forth in the memory of future ages, if, by their friendly counsel, by their moral influence, by the power of argument and persuasion alone, they can prevail upon the American nations at Panama to stipulate, by general agreement among themselves, and so far as any of them may be concerned, the perpetual abolition of private war upon the ocean. And if we cannot yet flatter ourselves, that this may be accomplished, as advances toward it, the establishment of the principle, that the friendly flag shall cover the cargo, the curtailment of contraband of war, and the proscription of fictitious paper blockades, engagements which we may reasonably hope will not prove impracticable, will, if successfully inculcated, redound proportionally to our honor and drain the fountain of many a future sanguinary war. The late President of the United States, in his Message to Congress, of the 2d of December, 1823, while announcing the negotiation then pending with Russia, relating to the North West coast of this continent, observed, that the occasion of the discussions to which that incident had given rise, had been taken for asserting as a principle, in which the rights and interests of the United States were involved, that the American continents, by the free and independent condition which they had assumed and maintained, were thenceforward not to be considered as subjects for future colonization, by any European Power. The principle had first been assumed in that negotiation with Russia. It rested upon a course of reasoning equally simple and conclusive. With the exception of the existing European colonies, which it was in nowise intended to disturb, the two continents consisted of several sovereign and independent nations, whose territories covered their whole surface. By this, their independent condition, the United States enjoyed the right of commercial intercourse with every part of their possessions. To attempt the establishment of a colony in those possessions would be to usurp, to the exclusion of others, a commercial intercourse, which was the common possession of all. It could not be done without encroaching upon existing rights of the United States. The Government of Russia has never disputed these positions, nor manifested the slightest dissatisfaction at their having been taken. Most of the new American Republics have declared their entire assent to them; and they now propose, among the subjects of consultation at Panama, to take into consideration the means of making effectual the assertion of that principle, as well as the means of resisting interference from abroad, with the domestic concerns of the American Governments.

In alluding to these means, it would obviously be premature, at this time, to anticipate that which is offered merely as matter for consultation; or to pronounce upon those measures which have been, or may be suggested. The purpose of this Government is, to concur in none which would import hostility to Europe, or justly excite resentment in any of her States. Should it be deemed advisable to contract any conventional engagement on this topic, our views would extend no further than to a mutual pledge of the parties to the compact, to maintain the principle in application to its own territory, and to permit no colonial lodgments or establishment of European jurisdiction upon its own soil; and, with respect to the obtrusive interference from abroad, if its future character may be inferred from that which has been, and perhaps still is, exercised in more than one of the new States, a joint declaration of its character and exposure of it to the world, may be probably all that the occasion would require. Whether the United States should or should not be parties to such a declaration, may justly form a part of the deliberation. That there is an evil to be remedied, needs little insight into the secret history of late years to know, and that this remedy may best be concerted at the Panama meeting, deserves at least the experiment of consideration. A concert of measures, having reference to the more effectual abolition of the African slave trade, and the consideration of the light in which the political condition of the Island of Hayti is to be regarded, are also among the subjects mentioned by the Minister from the Republic of Colombia, as believed to be suitable for deliberation at the Congress. The failure of the negotiations with that Republic, undertaken during the late Administration, for the suppression of that trade, in compliance with a resolution of the House of Representatives, indicates the expediency of listening with respectful attention to propositions which may contribute to the accomplishment of the great end which was the purpose of that resolution, while the result of those negotiations will serve as admonition to abstain from pledging this Government to any arrangement which might be expected to fail of obtaining the advice and consent of the Senate, by a constitutional majority to its ratification.

Whether the political condition of the Island of Hayti shall be brought at all into discussion at the meeting, may be a question for preliminary advisement. There are in the political constitution of Government of that People, circumstances which have hitherto forbidden the acknowledgment of them by the Government of the United States, as sovereign and independent. Additional reasons for withholding that acknowledgment have recently been seen in their acceptance of a nominal sovereignty by the *grant* of a foreign prince; under conditions equivalent to the concession by them, of exclusive commercial advantages to one nation, adapted altogether to the state of colonial vassalage, and retaining little of independence but the name. Our Plenipotentiaries will be instructed to present these views to the Assembly at Panama: and should they not be concurred in, to decline acceding to any arrangement which may be proposed upon different principles.

The condition of the islands of Cuba and Porto Rico is of deeper import and more immediate bearing upon the present interests and future prospects of our union. The correspondence herewith transmitted will show how earnestly it has engaged the attention of this Government. The invasion of both those Islands by the United forces of Mexico and Colombia, is avowedly among the objects to be matured by the belligerent States at Panama. The convulsions to which, from the peculiar composition of their population, they would be liable, in the event of such an invasion, and the danger therefrom resulting of their falling ultimately into the hands of some European Power, other than Spain, will not admit of our looking at the consequences to which the Congress at Panama may lead, with indifference. It is unnecessary to enlarge upon this topic, or to say more than that all our efforts in reference to this interest, will be to preserve the existing state of things, the tranquillity of the Islands, and the peace and security of their inhabitants.

And, lastly, the Congress of Panama is believed to present a fair occasion for urging upon all the new nations of the South, the just and liberal principles of religious liberty. Not by any interference whatever in their internal concerns, but by claiming for our citizens, whose occupations or interests may call them to occasional residence in their territories, the inestimable privilege of worshipping their Creator according to the dictates of their own consciences. This privilege, sanctioned by the customary law of nations, and secured by treaty stipulations in numerous national compacts; secured even to our own citizens in the treaties with Colombia and with the Federation of Central America, is yet to be obtained in the other South American States and Mexico. Existing prejudices are still struggling against it, which may, perhaps, be more successfully combated at this general meeting than at the separate seats of Government of each Republic.

I can scarcely deem it otherwise than superfluous, to observe, that the Assembly will be in its nature diplomatic, and not legislative. That nothing can be transacted there obligatory upon any one of the States to be represented at the meeting, unless with the express concurrence of its own Representatives, nor even then, but subject to the ratification of its constitutional authority at home. The faith of the United States to foreign Powers can not otherwise be pledged. I shall, indeed, in the first instance, consider the Assembly as merely *consultative*; and although the Plenipotentiaries of the United States will be empowered to receive and refer to the consideration of their Government, any proposition from the other parties to the meeting, they will be authorized to conclude nothing, unless subject to the definitive sanction of this Government, in all its constitutional forms. It has, therefore, seemed to me unnecessary to insist, that every object to be discussed at the meeting, should be specified with the precision of a judicial sentence, or enumerated with the exactness of a mathematical demonstration. The purpose of the meeting itself is to deliberate upon the great and common *interests* of several new and neighboring nations. If the measure is new and without precedent, so is the situation of the parties to it. That, the purposes of the meeting are somewhat indefinite, far from being an objection to it, is among the cogent reasons for its adoption. It is not the establishment of principles of intercourse with one, but with seven or eight nations at once. That, before they have had the means of exchanging ideas, and communicating with one another in common upon these topics, they should have definitively settled and arranged them in concert, is to require that the effect should precede the cause. It is to exact as a preliminary to the meeting, that for the accomplishment of which the meeting itself is designed.

Among the inquiries which were thought entitled to consideration before the determination was taken to accept the invitation, was that, whether the measure might not have a tendency to change the policy hitherto invariably pursued by the United States, of avoiding all entangling alliances, and all unnecessary foreign connexions.

Mindful of the advice given by the Father of our Country, in his Farewell Address, that the great rule of conduct for us in regard to foreign Nations, is in extending our commercial relations, to have with them as little political connection as possible; and faithfully adhering to the spirit of that admonition, I cannot overlook the reflection, that the counsel of Washington, in that instance, like all the counsels of wisdom, was founded upon the circumstances, in which our country and the world around us were situated, at the time, when it was given. That the reasons assigned by him for his advice were, that Europe had a set of primary interests, which to us had none, or a very remote relation. That hence she must be engaged in frequent controversies, the causes of which were essentially foreign to our concerns. That our *detached* and *distant* situation invited and enabled us to pursue a different course. That by our union and rapid growth, with an efficient government, the period was not far distant, when we might defy material injury from external annoyance, when we might take such an attitude as would cause our neutrality to be respected; and with reference to belligerent nations, might choose peace or war, as our interests, guided by justice, should counsel.

Compare our situation and the circumstances of that time, with those of the present day; and what, from the very words of Washington, then, would be his counsels to his countrymen now? Europe has still her set of primary interests, with which we have little, or a remote relation. Our distant and detached situation with reference to Europe remains the same. But, we were then the only Independent Nation of this hemisphere; and we were surrounded by European Colonies, with the greater part of which we had no more intercourse, than with the inhabitants of another planet. Those Colonies have now been transformed into eight Independent Nations, extending to our very borders. Seven of them Republics, like ourselves; with whom we have an immensely growing commercial, and *must* have, and have already important political, connexions. With reference to whom our situation is neither distant nor detached. Whose political principles and systems of government, congenial with our own, must and will have an action and counteraction upon us and ours, to which we cannot be indifferent if we would.

The rapidity of our growth, and the consequent increase of our strength, has more than realized the anticipations of this admirable political legacy. Thirty years have nearly elapsed since it was written, and in the interval, our population, our wealth, our territorial extension, our power, physical and moral, has nearly trebled. Reasoning upon this state of things from the sound and judicious principles of Washington, and must we not say, that the period which he predicted as then not far off has arrived? That *America* has a set of primary interests, which have none or a remote relation to Europe. That the interference of Europe therefore in those concerns should be spontaneously withheld by her upon the same principles, that we have never interfered with hers; and that if she should interfere, as she may, by measures which may have a great and dangerous recoil upon ourselves, we might be called in defence of our own altars and firesides, to take an attitude which would cause our neutrality to be respected, and choose peace or war, as our interest, guided by justice, should counsel.

The acceptance of this invitation therefore, far from conflicting with the counsel or the policy of Washington, is directly deducible from and conformable to it; nor is it less conformable to the views of my immediate predecessor, as declared in his annual message to Congress, of the 2d of December, 1823, to which I have already adverted, and to an important passage of which I invite the attention of the House. "The citizens of the United States," said he, "cherish sentiments the most friendly in favor of the liberty and happiness of their fellowmen on that (the European) side of the Atlantic. In the wars of the European powers, in matters relating to themselves, we have never taken any part, nor does it comport with our policy so to do. It is only when our rights are invaded, or seriously menaced, that we resent injuries, or make preparation for our defence. With the movements in this hemisphere, we are, of necessity, more immediately connected, and by causes which must be obvious to all enlightened and impartial observers. The political system of the Allied Powers, is essentially different in this respect from that of America. This difference proceeds from that which exists in their respective governments. And to the defence of our own, which has been achieved by the loss of so much blood and treasure, and matured by the wisdom of their most enlightened citizens, and under which we have enjoyed unexampled felicity, this whole nation is devoted. We owe it, therefore, to candor, and to the amicable relations subsisting between the United States and those Powers, to declare, that we should consider any attempt on their part, to extend their system to any portion of this Hemisphere, as dangerous to our peace and safety. With the existing colonies or dependencies of any European Power, we have not interfered, and shall not interfere. But with the governments who have declared their Independence and maintained it, and whose independence we have, on great consideration, and on just principles, acknowledged, we could not view any interposition, for the purposes of oppressing them, or controlling in any other manner their destiny, by any European Power, in any other light than as the manifestation of an unfriendly disposition towards the United States. In the war between those new Governments and Spain, we declared our neutrality at the time of their recognition; and to this we have adhered, and shall continue to adhere, provided no change shall occur, which, in the judgment of the competent authorities of this Government, shall make a corresponding change on the part of the United States indispensable to their security."

To the question which may be asked, whether this meeting and the principles which may be adjusted and settled by it as rules of intercourse between the American Nations, may not give umbrage to the Holy League of European Powers, or offence to Spain, it is deemed a sufficient answer, that our attendance at Panama can give no *just cause* of umbrage or offence to either—and that the United States will stipulate nothing there which can give such cause. Here the right of inquiry into our purposes and measures must stop. The Holy League of Europe itself was formed without inquiring of the United States whether it would or would not give umbrage to them. The fear of giving umbrage to the Holy League of Europe was urged as a motive for denying to the American nations the acknowledgment of their independence. That it would be viewed by Spain as hostility to her, was not only urged, but directly declared by herself. The Congress and Administration of that day consulted their rights and duties, and not their fears. Fully determined to give no needless displeasure to any foreign power, the United States can estimate the probability of their giving it, only by the right which any foreign State could have, to take it from their measures. Neither the representation of the United States at Panama, nor any measure to which their assent may be yielded there, will give to the Holy League, or any of its members, nor to Spain, the right to take offence. For the rest, the United States must still, as heretofore, take counsel from their duties, rather than their fears.

Such are the objects in which it is expected that the Plenipotentiaries of the United States, when commissioned to attend the meeting at the Isthmus, will take part; and such are the motives and purposes, with which the invitation of the three Republics was accepted. It was, however, as the House will perceive from the correspondence, accepted only upon condition that the nomination of Commissioners for the mission, should receive the advice and consent of the Senate. The concurrence of the House to the measure, by the appropriations necessary for carrying it into effect, is alike subject to its free determination, and indispensable to the fulfilment of the intention.

That the congress at Panama will accomplish all, or even any of the transcendent benefits to the human race, which warmed the conceptions of its first proposer, it were, perhaps, indulging too sanguine a forecast of events to promise. It is, in its nature, a measure speculative and experimental. The blessing of Heaven may turn it to the account of human improvement. Accidents unforeseen, and mischances not to be anticipated, may baffle all its high purposes and disappoint its fairest expectations. But the design is great, is benevolent, is humane. It looks to the melioration of the condition of man. It is congenial with that spirit which prompted the Declaration of our Independence; which inspired the preamble of our first treaty with France; which dictated our first treaty with Prussia, and the instructions under which it was negotiated: which filled the hearts and fired the souls of the immortal founders of our Revolution.

With this unrestricted exposition of the motives by which I have been governed, in this transaction, as well as of the objects to be discussed, and of the ends, if possible, to be attained by our representation at the proposed Congress, I submit the propriety of an appropriation, to the candid consideration, and enlightened patriotism of the Legislature.

JOHN QUINCY ADAMS.

"THE EMPIRE OF LEARNING AND THE ARTS"

14. Speech at the Dedication of the Chesapeake and Ohio Canal, July 4, 1828. *National Journal* (Washington, D.C., Tuesday, July 8, 1828).

By the summer of 1828 the presidential electoral contest that seemed to have begun even before Adams took office was nearing its conclusion. He had little doubt about its outcome. In his diary entry for December 17, 1827, Adams surveyed the unending electioneering against him—a morass of "infamous Slander" put forward by a "base and profligate combination"—and concluded bitterly that "General Jackson will therefore be elected. But it is impossible that his Administration should give satisfaction to the people of this Union. He is incompetent both by his ignorance, and by the fury of his Passions — He will be surrounded and governed by incompetent men, whose ascendency over him will be secured by their servility, and who will bring to the Government of the Nation, nothing but their talent for intrigue." Always susceptible to dark moods, Adams approached the end of his presidency with grim resolution to return to private life for good.

The Fourth of July once again afforded him a chance to escape, for a moment, from the gloom of politics and reconnect with the optimism that was also central to his character. At the invitation of the president and directors of the Chesapeake and Ohio Canal Company, Adams ventured forth from the Executive Mansion to deliver these remarks at the groundbreaking for one of the relatively few internal improvements that had been supported by Congress, in this case with the subscription of $1 million in public funds. It was an unseasonably mild summer day, with "a kindly sky," as one observer noted. It was also the twenty-fifth birthday of Adams's son John, who was his personal secretary, and who accompanied him to the construction site in Maryland, just beyond the District's border. This would be one of just two public addresses the president would deliver during his entire term in office (the other being the farewell speech he had made three years earlier at the end of the Marquis de Lafayette's grand tour of the United States) and the closest thing to a reelection campaign speech he ever gave.

After the president of the Canal Company delivered brief remarks, he presented to "the chief magistrate of the most powerful republic on earth" a spade, "this humble instrument of rural labor," with which to break ground on the great work. "As soon as he had ended," according to the newspaper account from which the text below is taken, "the president of the United States . . . stepped forward, and, with animation of manner and countenance, which showed that his whole heart was in the thing, thus addressed the assembly of his fellow citizens," a crowd estimated to be around two thousand strong. The speech itself, a forceful one that bears all the hallmarks of Adams's style, would be somewhat overshadowed that day, and in historical memory, by what happened when the president, midway through his speech, went to work with the shovel. Adams's recollection of the moment in his diary expands on the parenthetical account supplied by the newspaper reporter below: "It happened that at the first stroke of the Spade, it met immediately under the surface a large stump of a tree; after repeating the stroke three or four times without making any impression, I threw off my coat, and resuming the Spade, raised a shovel full of the Earth, at which a general shout burst forth from the surrounding multitude, and I completed my Address, which occupied about fifteen minutes. . . . As has happened to me whenever I have had a part to perform in the presence of multitudes, I got through awkwardly, but without gross and palpable failure. The incident that chiefly relieved me was the obstacle of the stump, which met and resisted the Spade, and my casting off my coat to overcome the resistance — It struck the eye and fancy of the Spectators, more than all the flowers of Rhetoric in my Speech, and diverted their attention from the stammering and hesitation of a deficient memory."

Such interactions with the public were a rare thing for President Adams, and for the First Lady, that was more the shame. "If only he would lend himself a little to the usages and manner of the people without hiding himself and too modestly rejecting their civilities," Louisa Catherine Adams had written to their son Charles Francis Adams in 1827, "no man would be more popular because his manners are simple, unostentatious, and unassuming."

Chesapeake and Ohio Canal Dedication

FRIENDS AND FELLOW CITIZENS: It is nearly a full century since Berkeley, Bishop of Cloyne, turning towards this fair land, which we now inhabit, the eyes of a prophet, closed a few lines of poetical inspiration with this memorable prediction—

"Time's noblest empire is the last."

A prediction which, to those of us whose lot has been cast by Divine Providence in these regions, contains not only a precious promise, but a solemn injunction of duty, since, upon our energies, and upon those of our posterity, its fulfilment will depend. For, with reference to what principle could it be, that Berkeley proclaimed this, the last, to be the noblest empire of time? It was, as he himself declares, on the transplantation of *learning and the arts* to America. Of learning and the arts—the four first acts—the empires of the old world and of former ages—the Assyrian, the Persian, the Grecian, the Roman empires, were empires of conquest, dominions of man over man. The empire which his great mind, piercing into the darkness of futurity, foretold in America, was the empire of learning and the arts—the dominion of man over himself, and over physical nature, acquired by the inspirations of genius, and the toils of industry—not watered with the tears of the widow and the orphan—not cemented in the blood of human victims—founded, not in discord, but in harmony—of which the only spoils are the imperfections of nature; and the victory achieved is the improvement of the condition of all. Well may this be termed nobler than the empire of conquest, in which man subdues only his fellow man.

To the accomplishment of this prophecy, the first necessary step was the acquisition of the right of self-government by the people of the British North American colonies, achieved by the Declaration of Independence, and its acknowledgment by the British nation. The second was the union of all those colonies under our general confederated Government; a task more arduous than that of the preceding separation, but at last effected by the present constitution of the United States.

The third step, more arduous still than either, or both the others, was that which we, Fellow Citizens, may now congratulate ourselves, our country, and the world of man, that it is taken: It is the adaptation of the powers, physical, moral, and intellectual, of this whole Union, to the improvement of its own condition—of its moral and political condition, by wise and liberal institutions—by the cultivation of the understanding and the heart—by academies, schools, and learned institutes—by the pursuit and patronage of learning and the arts—of its physical condition, by associated labor to improve the bounties, and to supply the deficiencies of nature—to stem the torrent in its course; to level the mountain with the plain; to disarm and fetter the raging surge of the ocean. Undertakings of which the language I now hold is no exaggerated description, have become happily familiar, not only to the conceptions, but to the enterprise of our countrymen. That for the commencement of which we are here assembled, is eminent among the number. The project contemplates a conquest over physical nature, such as has never yet been achieved by man. The wonders of the ancient world, the pyramids of Egypt, the Colossus of Rhodes, the Temple of Ephesus, the Mausoleum of Artemisia, the Wall of China, sink into insignificance before it. Insignificance in the mass and momentum of human labor required for the execution. Insignificance in the comparison of the purposes to be accomplished by the work when executed.

It is therefore a pleasing contemplation to those sanguine and patriotic spirits who have so long looked with hope to the completion of this undertaking, that it unites the moral power and resources—first, of numerous individuals; secondly, of the corporate cities of Washington, Georgetown, and Alexandria; thirdly, of the great and powerful States of Pennsylvania, Virginia, and Maryland; and lastly, by the subscription authorised at the recent session of Congress, of the whole Union.

Friends and Fellow-laborers—we are informed by the Holy Oracles of Truth, that at the creation of man, male and female, the Lord of the Universe, their maker, blessed them and said unto them, be fruitful, and multiply, and replenish the earth, *and subdue it.* To subdue the earth was, therefore, one of the first duties assigned to man at his creation; and now in his fallen condition it remains among the most excellent of his occupations. To subdue the earth is pre-eminently the purpose of the undertaking, to the accomplishment of which the first stroke of the spade is now to be struck. That it is to be struck by this hand I invite you to witness—[Here the stroke of the spade*]—and in performing this act I call upon you all to join me in fervent supplication to Him from whom that primitive injunction came, that he would follow with his blessing this joint effort of our great community, to perform his will in the subjugation of the earth for the improvement of the condition of man. That he would make it one of his chosen instruments for the preservation, prosperity and perpetuity of our Union. That he would have in his holy keeping all the workmen by whose labors it is to be completed. That their lives and their health may be precious in his sight; and that they may live to see the work of their hands contribute to the comforts and enjoyments of millions of their countrymen.

Friends and brethren, permit me further to say, that I deem the duty now performed at the request of the President and Directors of the Chesapeake and Ohio Canal Company, and of the Corporations of the District of Columbia, one of the most fortunate incidents of my life. Though not among the functions of my official station, I esteem it as a privilege conferred upon me by my fellow-citizens of the District. Called in the performance of my service heretofore as one of the Representatives of my native commonwealth in the Senate, and now as a member of the Executive Department of the Government, my abode has been among the inhabitants of the District longer than at any other spot upon earth. In availing myself of this occasion to

---

*Attending this action was an incident which produced a greater sensation than any other that occurred during the day. The spade which the President held struck a root, which prevented its penetrating the earth. Not deterred by trifling obstacles from doing what he had deliberately resolved to perform, Mr. ADAMS tried it again, with no better success. Thus foiled, he threw down the spade, hastily stripped off, and laid aside his coat, and went seriously *to work*. The multitude around, and on the hills and trees, who could not *hear*, because of their distance from the open space, but could *see* and understand, observing this action, raised a loud and unanimous cheering, which continued for some time after Mr. ADAMS had mastered the difficulty.

return to them my thanks for the numberless acts of kindness that I have experienced at their hands, may I be allowed to assign it as a motive operating upon the heart, and superadded to my official obligations, for taking a deep interest in their welfare and prosperity. Among the prospects of futurity which we may indulge the rational hope of seeing realized by this junction of distant waters, that of the auspicious influence which it will exercise over the fortunes of every portion of the District, is one upon which my mind dwells with unqualified pleasure. It is my earnest prayer that they may not be disappointed.

It was observed that the first step towards the accomplishment of the glorious destinies of our country was the Declaration of Independence. That the second was the union of these States under our Federative Government. The third is irrevocably fixed by the act upon the commencement of which we are now engaged. What time more suitable for this operation could have been selected than the Anniversary of our great National Festival? What place more appropriate from whence to proceed than that which bears the name of the citizen warrior who led our armies in that eventful contest to the field, and who first presided as the Chief Magistrate of our Union? You know that of this very undertaking he was one of the first projectors; and if, in the world of Spirits, the affections of our mortal existence still retain their sway, may we not without presumption imagine that he looks down with complacency and delight upon the scene before and around us?

But, while indulging a sentiment of joyous exultation, at the benefits to be derived from this labor of our friends and neighbors, let us not forget that the spirit of Internal Improvement is catholic and liberal. We hope and believe that its practical advantages will be extended to every individual in our Union. In praying for the blessing of Heaven upon our task, we ask it with equal zeal and sincerity upon every other similar work in this confederation; and particularly upon that which on this same day, and perhaps at this very hour, is commencing from a neighboring city. It is one of the happiest characteristics in the principle of Internal Improvement, that the success of one great enterprise, instead of counteracting, gives assistance to the execution of another. May they increase and multiply, till, in the sublime language of inspiration, every valley shall be exalted, and every mountain and hill shall be made low—the crooked straight, the rough places plain. Thus shall the prediction of the Bishop of Cloyne be converted from prophecy into history, and in the virtues and fortunes of our posterity the last shall prove the noblest Empire of Time.

"THE PILLARS OF OUR UNION ARE TOTTERING"

15. *An Oration Addressed to the Citizens of the Town of Quincy, on the Fourth of July, 1831, the Fifty-fifth Anniversary of the Independence of the United States of America* (Boston: Richardson, Lord and Holbrook, 1831).

As Adams and most everyone else expected, Andrew Jackson soundly defeated him in the 1828 election. It felt like a repudiation not only of his leadership but, more painfully, of his hopes for the nation. If Adams's inaugural address had been expansive and far-sighted, envisioning the national government as an agent of progress, Jackson's was brief to the point of being taciturn, with an emphasis on "the limitations as well as the extent of the Executive power trusting thereby to discharge the functions of my office without transcending its authority." Decentralization would be the new order of the day. Jackson came in promising a wave of unspecified "reform," which translated in practice into a wholesale turfing of federal officeholders at every level of the government, and their replacement by party loyalists, precisely the type of politics Adams loathed. "Every thing looks to decay and not to improvement," he wrote wearily in his diary. "Every thing has an aspect of pulling down, and not of building up."

Adams's postpresidential retirement was a difficult period in his life—including as it did the tragic death of his eldest son, George Washington Adams, most probably by suicide—but it would not be a long one. Even before he left office, he was entertaining inquiries about whether he might consider this or that position. Per the self-imposed restrictions of the Macbeth Policy, Adams insisted that while he would not seek office, neither would he refuse the call of the people for his service. So, when he was visited at the family home in Quincy, Massachusetts, on September 18, 1830, by a delegation of local National Republicans and asked if he, as an ex-president, would condescend to stand for election to the House of Representatives from Massachusetts's 11th District, Adams reply was cagey but also clear. "I had in that respect no scruple whatever — No person could be degraded by serving the people as a Representative in Congress — Nor in my opinion," he added for good measure, "would an Ex-President of the United States be degraded by serving as a Selectman of his town, if elected thereto by the People." The delegation wisely took that as a yes, and on October 12 Adams was duly nominated, winning election the next month with more than three-quarters of the vote.

He confided to his diary that "No election or appointment conferred upon me ever gave me so much pleasure."

It was as their representative-elect, then, that John Quincy Adams stood before his Quincy neighbors to deliver this Fourth of July address. Mindful, perhaps, of his earlier speeches on the occasion, Adams begins by asking rhetorically what new there might be to say about the nation and its founding. The looming threat of nullification would provide him with his theme, and with the palpable urgency of this address. Near the end of his presidency Adams had signed an unusual bill into law, an extreme tariff measure that had been engineered by Martin Van Buren and antitariff Democrats with a schedule so unpalatable that even protectionist New Englanders would vote against it. When to the surprise of almost everyone "the Tariff of Abominations" passed nonetheless, southerners, especially Vice President Calhoun, howled in protest. Writing anonymously in a December 1828 pamphlet entitled *Exposition and Protest*, Calhoun argued that state legislatures could "interpose" themselves against federal statutes they deemed unconstitutional, reviving the theory of nullification espoused first by Republicans in the late 1790s in the Virginia and Kentucky Resolves and later by Federalists during the controversy over the embargo. "The Constitution has formed the States into a community only to the extent of their common interests," Calhoun wrote, "leaving them distinct and independent communities as to all other interests." Making clear that "nullification is the provocative to that brutal and foul contest of force," that is, to civil war, Adams offers here a strikingly different reading of the nation's founding.

AN

ORATION

ADDRESSED TO THE

CITIZENS OF THE TOWN OF QUINCY,

ON THE

FOURTH OF JULY, 1831,

THE

FIFTY-FIFTH ANNIVERSARY

OF THE

INDEPENDENCE

OF THE

UNITED STATES OF AMERICA.

BY JOHN QUINCY ADAMS.

BOSTON:
RICHARDSON, LORD AND HOLBROOK.

1831.

Quincy, July 6, 1831.

Hon. John Q. Adams.

SIR,—Agreeably to a vote passed on the 4th inst. at the Town Hall, by those who listened to your learned and eloquent address, and in behalf of the Committee of Arrangements, chosen by the citizens of Quincy, we present to you our united thanks therefor, and respectfully request a copy for the press.

> TH. PHIPPS,
> NOAH CURTIS, } *Sub-committee.*
> WILLIAM SEAVER,

Messrs. THOMAS PHIPPS,
NOAH CURTIS, and }
WILLIAM SEAVER.

Quincy, 13th July, 1831.

GENTLEMEN,

A copy of the address, prepared at the request of the citizens, inhabitants of Quincy, on the occasion of their recent celebration of our national anniversary, is, in compliance with your request, submitted to your disposal. It may be proper to apprize you, that, to avoid too great prolixity, some passages of it were omitted in the delivery.

> I am, with great respect, gentlemen,
> your friend and fellow citizen,
> JOHN QUINCY ADAMS.

Fourth of July Oration

Friends, Countrymen, and Fellow Citizens—
The celebrations of this anniversary have been so frequent and multiplied throughout the Union, for a period now largely stretching upon a second half century, that a speaker, far more competent to borrow for support in his flight the wings of imagination, than he who now addresses you, might well open his discourse, by entreating your indulgence, and deprecating your censure. Even the powers of speech, the special prerogative of man, as a member of the animal creation, are not unlimited. The discourse of reason, though looking before and after, is bounded in its vision by an horizon; and Eloquence herself perhaps best performs her appropriate office by silence upon exhausted topics.

The independence of the North American Union is, however, susceptible of being considered under a great variety of points of view. The contemplation of its causes must indeed ever remain the same; but that of its consequences varies from year to year. A speaker, on the first anniversary after the Declaration, in the midst of the terrific conflict to maintain it, and while its expediency, if not its justice, was yet pending upon the issues of war, had a far different theme from him who now, after the lapse of nearly two generations of men, is called to review the progress of principles then proclaimed, as their influence has expanded upon the mind of civilized man. The test of all principle is time; and that which when first announced as truth, may be treated by the almost unanimous voice of mankind as pernicious paradox or hateful heresy, when scrutinized by long observation, and felt in practical results, may become an axiom of knowledge, or an article of uncontroverted faith. The astronomer, who in his nightly visitation of the heavens perceives a ray of light before unobserved, discovers no new phenomenon in nature. He is only the first to discern the beam which has glowed from the creation of the world. After-observation and the calculations of science, will disclose whether it proceeded from a star fixed in the firmament from the birth of time, from a planet revolving around the central luminary of our own system, or from a comet, "shaking from its horrid hair, pestilence and war."

The Declaration of Independence was a manifesto issued to the world, by the delegates of thirteen distinct, but UNITED colonies of Great Britain, in the name and behalf of their people. It was a united declaration. Their union preceded their independence; nor was their independence, nor has it ever since, been separable from their union. Their language is, "We the Representatives of the *United* States of America, in General Congress assembled, do, in the name and by the authority of the good PEOPLE of these Colonies, solemnly publish and declare that these *United Colonies*, are, and of right ought to be, free and independent States." It was the act of one people. The Colonies are not named; their number is not designated; nor in the original Declaration, does it appear from which of the Colonies any one of the fifty-six Delegates by whom it was signed, had been deputed. They announced their constituents to the world as one people, and unitedly declared the Colonies to which they respectively belonged, united, free and independent states. The Declaration of Independence, therefore, was a proclamation to the world, not merely that the United Colonies had ceased to be dependencies of Great Britain, but that their people had bound themselves, before GOD, to a primitive social compact of union, freedom and independence.

The parties to this compact were the people of thirteen Colonies of Great Britain, located upon the continent of North America, occupying territories contiguous to each other, and holding a political existence founded upon charters derived from successive sovereigns of that island. These charters were of various import, nor was there any link of union, or even of connexion between them; but in all, the rights of British subjects had been solemnly secured to the settlers under them, and among the first of those rights, was that of freedom from arbitrary taxation. The first of the charters had been granted by James the First of England and Sixth of Scotland, the first British monarch of the House of Stuart. The most recent of them had emanated from George II., of the House of Hanover, a family, which, by a revolution in the maternal island, had supplanted that of the Stuarts on the British throne. That revolution itself had been the result of a long and sanguinary conflict between the primary principles of human authority and of human freedom. In the preceding ages, England had been, for nearly one hundred years, the theatre of desolating civil wars upon a question in the theory of government, as insignificant to the people of the realm, as if it had been upon the merits of the badges respectively assumed by the parties to the strife.

If an historian or an orator should affirm, that one of the most spirited and intelligent nations upon earth had inflicted upon itself, for a term little short of a century, all the horrors and desolations of a civil war, to ascertain and settle which, of a White Rose or a Red Rose, breathes the sweetest fragrance—the assertion might not be literally, but it would be more than figuratively true. The question between the Houses of York and Lancaster, was, whether upon the death of a King of England, childless, the right to his crown devolved upon the son of a brother, previously deceased, but who had been next to himself by birth, or to his own surviving younger brother. This is a question which could not possibly arise under any government, other than a hereditary monarchy, and in which the people who were the victims of the controversy, had, abstracted from the respective personal qualities of the pretenders to the crown, no more interest than in the dissensions in the kingdom of Lilliput on the question whether an egg should be broken at the big or at the little end. But the civil wars of the British nation in the seventeenth century were of a very different character. The question then was, not who had the right *to* the throne, but what were the rights *of* the throne; not, upon whose head the polished perturbation and golden care of the crown should descend, but what was the lawful extent of power in him who wore it; what the extent of obligation upon the people to yield obedience to him; what their right and duty to defend themselves against his encroachments; and what their just and lawful remedy against the abuses of his authority. It was the question between right and might, between liberty and power;—a question the most solemn and momentous of any that can be agitated among men;—a question upon the issues of which war becomes the most imperious of human obligations, and the field of battle the sublimest theatre of heroic martyrdom and patriotic achievement.

In the progress of this controversy, the British nation had been twice brought to the decision, that the individual at the head of their government, had, by his usurpations and oppressions, forfeited his right to the crown; and in the first of these instances, his life. In the exasperation of feelings, stimulated by a long and cruel civil war, they had tinged the scaffold with the blood of their king; and then, by one of those reactions of popular sensibility, which never fail to follow the violation of the laws of humanity, they had passed from one extreme to another, and worshipped as a saint and martyr him whom they had beheaded as a tyrant. Proceeding in the second instance with more caution, they had suffered the offender to escape, and then construed his flight for life, as a voluntary abdication of his power. This they declared he had done, *by breaking the original contract between king and people.* And thus, by the deliberate and solemn determination of the British nation, it had been settled, that the supreme powers of government, under their political constitution, were possessed and exercised by virtue of an original contract with the people.

The charters of the thirteen North American Colonies were also original contracts between the king and the people to whom they had been granted. It was a right exercised by most of the European monarchs in those ages, and also by the republican government of the Netherlands. By long usage and common consent it had become an acknowledged attribute of colonizing power; and in Great Britain was a royal prerogative in which the Parliament had no agency. The existence of the Colonies, therefore, was from the beginning *independent* of the authority of Parliament. Their contract was with the king.

In the reign of George III., when, by a succession of wars commenced after the final downfall of the House of Stuart, the British nation had become heavily burthened with debt, and consequently with taxation, an English Chancellor of the Exchequer conceived the ingenious idea of recommending himself to the people of his own island, by casting off a portion of their burdens upon the people of the Colonies; as the Knight of La Mancha was disposed to propitiate the lady of his affections, by scourging the back of his Squire: and as it had been well ascertained, since the days of John Hambden and ship-money, that the royal authority, however competent to the grant of charters, did not extend to the arbitrary levy of money by taxation, the minister undertook to perform by act of Parliament, that which he did not dare to attempt by the mere authority of the king.

By their original constitution, the Colonies were independent of the Parliament. They were not represented in that body. They had no share in the election of the House of Commons. The levying of taxes upon them by Parliament was precisely the same usurpation, as the levying of ship-money had been in Charles I. It was the privilege of British subjects, that no part of their property could be taken from them but by an authority in which they were represented. To this principle the Colonies appealed in their first remonstrances and resistance against the Stamp Act. It was not the burden of tax to which they objected. It was to the inherent servitude of the principle.

Alarmed at the vehemence and unanimity with which the first attempt at arbitrary taxation was resisted in the Colonies, the ministers of George III. prevailed upon Parliament to repeal the tax, but at the same time to *declare* their right to make laws for the Colonies in all cases whatsoever.

This declaration of right, was a mere declaration of power. The judges of England had declared that Charles I. had the right to levy ship-money; and that declaration was neither more unjust nor more absurd than this. In either case the mere question whence the right was derived must be fatal to its assertion. In both cases the claim was founded upon an erroneous first principle of government, very far from being eradicated even at this day, in our own age, and our own country; a principle under which the pillars of our Union are tottering while I speak, and which, if once permitted to prevail, will leave us a monumental ruin,

"To point a moral, or adorn a tale."

The British Parliament derived their claim of right to make laws for the Colonies in all cases whatsoever, from a principle of government which is stated by the great commentator upon the laws of England thus;—"There is, and *must be*," says he, "in all forms of government, however they began, or by what right soever they subsist, a supreme, irresistible, absolute, uncontrolled authority, in which the *jura summi imperii* or the *rights of sovereignty,* reside." These are his words, which he further explains by saying, that by the *sovereign* power is meant the making of laws. And in treating of the power of Parliament, he adds;—"This is the place where that absolute despotic power, which must in all governments reside *somewhere*, is entrusted by the constitution of the British kingdoms." These are again his words.

Behold, my fellow citizens, the cause of the North American Revolution! Look at that cold exanimate flint, which, clashing with the steel of your fathers' hearts, struck out the spark and kindled the flame which reduced to ashes the British dominion in these United States;—nor ceasing there, its burning brands have floated on the wings of the winds back to Europe, instinct with unextinguishable fire, and spreading at once light and conflagration throughout the regions inhabited by civilized man,—a false definition of the term *sovereignty;* an erroneous estimate of the extent of *sovereign* power!

It is not true that there *must* reside in all governments an absolute, uncontrolled, irresistible, and despotic power: nor is such power in any manner essential to sovereignty. The direct converse of the proposition is true. Uncontrollable power exists in no government upon earth. The sternest despotisms, in every region and every age of the world, are and have been under perpetual control; compelled, as Burke expresses it, to truckle and to huckster. Unlimited power belongs not to the nature of man; and rotten will be the foundation of every government leaning upon such a maxim for its support. Least of all can it be predicated of any government professing to be founded upon an original compact. The pretence of an absolute, irresistible, despotic power, existing in every government *somewhere*, is incompatible with the first principle of natural right. Take for example the right to life. The moment an infant is born, it has a right to the life which it has received from the Creator. Amiable and benevolent moralists have sometimes denied that this right can be forfeited to human laws, even by the commission of crime. Without concurring in that sentiment, we may safely affirm, that no human being, no combination of human beings, has the power, I say not the physical, but the moral power, to take a life not so forfeited, unless in self-defence or by the laws of war. No power in government exists to take it without a cause; none, surely none, in the British Parliament. Nor let me be told that governments have exercised and do exercise this power; that the ancient Romans and the modern Chinese hold it no wrong in the parent to expose his new-born child, and leave it to perish in its own helplessness.—Fathers! MOTHERS! is this the law of nature? Christians! is this the law of your Redeemer? Americans! ask the Declaration of Independence, and that will tell you that its authors held for self-evident truth, that the right to life is the first of the unalienable rights of man, to *secure*, and not to destroy which, governments are instituted among men, and that the *sovereignty* which would arrogate to itself absolute, unlimited power, must appeal for its sanction to those illustrious expounders of human rights, Pharaoh of Egypt, and Herod the Great of Judea.

Yet upon this false position, and upon this alone, rested the claim of the British Parliament to tax the Colonies, and to make laws for them in all cases whatsoever. Take away this imaginary attribute of sovereignty, and the Stamp Act and the Tea Tax were no better than highway robbery. Take it away, and the British Parliament had no more right to tax the Colonies, than the Parliament of Paris, or the Sultan of Constantinople.

The power of Parliament to tax the Colonies, was denied in America, from the first appearance of the Stamp Act, with a vigor and energy, characteristic of a just claim of right. But the *independence* of the Colonies upon Great Britain, was neither pretended nor contemplated by the great body of the people. The relations between a parent state and her colonies, are founded upon the laws of nature and nations, modified by the civil constitution of the colonizing state. In the administration of human affairs, there is, in all countries, a reluctance at recurring to the first principles of government. Practical men are apt to entertain the opinion that they have little influence upon the conduct of nations, and theoretic men are often wild and fanciful in their application of them. The first British colonies upon this continent were settled precisely at the time when the English nation were in the very fever of controversy preceding the civil wars. Those of New England were settled by the Puritans, a conscientious, intrepid and persecuted race of men, whom David Hume, the Atheist Jacobite, at once their reviler and their eulogist, acknowledges to have been the sole and exclusive founders of all the freedom of the British islands. This record is true, and oceans of calumny will never wash it out.

In their emigration from Europe, they had well considered the rights to which they would be entitled in the land of their new habitation, and the obligations by which they would be bound to the land of their nativity. They retained their affection for their country, and acknowledged their allegiance to the sovereign from whom they had received their charters. It was impossible, however, that the sentiment of local patriotism should be transmitted to their descendants, with the same intenseness with which they had felt it themselves; and the ties of allegiance to a sovereign beyond the seas, changing in rapid succession from a Stuart to a Commonwealth, from a Commonwealth back to a Stuart, then to a William of Orange, to the wife of a Prince of Denmark, and finally to a family and native of Germany, however strong as political ligaments, by the unchangeable laws of nature, could not have a very tenacious hold upon the heart. The Scottish poet, who has emblazoned *his* country with such a resplendent crown of glory, and has arrayed in the gorgeous coloring of imagination this sentiment of patriotism, supposes it to burn only in the bosom of him who in colloquy with himself can exclaim,

"This is *my own,* my *native* land."

But to what land would this exclamation, so natural, so affecting, so pathetic, have applied upon the lips of Carver and Bradford, of Endicott and Winthrop? Their *native* land indeed was England: but *this* might more emphatically be termed their *own* land, for it had become their own by sacrifices, dangers, and toils. And what, five generations later, would have been the purport of the same impressive line,

"This is my own, my native land,"

upon the lips of your Quincy, and your Hancock, patriots, if ever the name existed in other than poetical imagery, one born in the metropolis within reach of your eyes, and the other within hearing distance of the voice, which now joys in recalling him to your memory, as your native townsman and his own.

The *dependence*, then, of the Colonies upon Great Britain, at the time when the British Parliament declared its own right to make laws for them in all cases whatsoever, and undertook to give effect to this declaration by taxation, was a dependence of parchments and of proclamations, unsanctioned by the laws of nature, disavowed by the dictates of reason. To this condition, however, the Colonies submitted as long as they were suffered to enjoy the rights of Englishmen. The attempt to tax them by a body in which they had and could have no representative, was in direct violation of those rights. The acts of Parliament were encountered by remonstrance, deprecated by petition, and resisted by force. Ten years of controversy, and more than one of civil war, preceded the Declaration, "that these United Colonies are, and of right ought to be, free and independent states; that they are absolved from all allegiance to the British crown, and that all political connexion between them and the state of Great Britain, is, and ought to be totally dissolved."

The union of the Colonies had preceded this Declaration and even the commencement of the war. The Declaration was joint, that the United Colonies were free and independent states, but not that any one of them was a free and independent state, separate from the rest. In the Constitution of this Commonwealth it is declared, that the body politic is formed by a voluntary association of individuals; that it is a social compact, by which the whole people covenants with each citizen, and each citizen with the whole people, that all shall be governed by certain laws, for the common good. The body politic of the United States was formed by the voluntary association of the people of the United Colonies. The Declaration of Independence was a social compact, by which the whole people covenanted with each citizen of the United Colonies, and each citizen with the whole people, that the United Colonies were, and of right ought to be, free and independent states. To this compact, union was as vital as freedom or independence. From the hour of that Declaration, no one of the States whose people were parties to it, could, without violation of that primitive compact, secede or separate from the rest. Each was pledged to all, and all were pledged to each by a concert of souls, without limitation of time, in the presence of Almighty God, and proclaimed to all mankind. The Colonies were not declared *sovereign* states. The term sovereign is not even to be found in the Declaration; and far, very far was it from the contemplation of those who composed, or of those who adopted it, to constitute either the aggregate community, or any one of its members, with absolute, uncontrollable or despotic power. They are united, free and independent States. Each of these properties is equally essential to their existence. Without union the *covenant* contains no pledge of freedom or independence; without freedom, none of independence or union; without independence, none of union or freedom.

In the history of the world, this was the first example of a self-constituted nation proclaiming to the rest of mankind the principles upon which it was associated, and deriving those principles from the laws of nature. It has sometimes been objected to the paper, that it deals too much in abstractions. But this was its characteristic excellence; for upon those abstractions hinged the justice of the cause. Without them, our revolution would have been but successful rebellion. Right, truth, justice, are all abstractions. The Divinity that stirs within the soul of man is abstraction. The Creator of the universe is a spirit, and all spiritual nature is abstraction. Happy would it be, could we answer with equal confidence another objection, not to the Declaration, but to the consistency of the people by whom it was proclaimed! Thrice happy, could the appeal to the Supreme Judge of the World for rectitude of intention, and with firm reliance on the protection of Divine Providence for support, have been accompanied with an appeal equally bold to our own social institutions to illustrate the self-evident truths which we declared!

The Declaration of Independence was not a declaration of liberty newly acquired, nor was it a form of government. The people of the Colonies were already free, and their forms of government were various. They were all Colonies of a monarchy. The king of Great Britain was their common sovereign. Their internal administrations presented great varieties of form. The proprietary governments were hereditary monarchies in miniature. New York and Virginia were feudal aristocracies. Massachusetts Bay was an approximation to the complex government of the parent state. Connecticut and Rhode Island were little remote from democracies. But as in the course of our recent war with Great Britain, her gallant naval warriors made the discovery that the frigates of the United States were line of battle ships in disguise, so the ministers of George III., when they brought their king and country into collision with these transatlantic dependencies, soon found to their astonishment, that the United American Colonies were republics in disguise. The spirit of the people, throughout the Union, was republican; and the absurdity of a foreign and a royal head to societies of men thus constituted, had remained unperceived, only because until then that head had been seldom brought into action.

The Declaration of Independence announced the severance of the thirteen United Colonies from the rest of the British Empire, and the existence of their people from that day forth as an independent nation. The people of all the Colonies, speaking by their representatives, constituted themselves one moral person before the face of their fellow men. Frederic I., of Brandenburg, constituted himself king of Prussia, by putting a crown upon his own head. Napoleon Bonaparte invested his brows with the iron crown of Lombardy, and declared himself king of Italy. The Declaration of Independence was the crown with which the people of United America, rising in gigantic stature as one man, encircled their brows, and there it remains; there, so long as this globe shall be inhabited by human beings, may it remain, a crown of imperishable glory!

The Declaration of Independence asserted the rights, and acknowledged the obligations of an independent nation. It recognised the laws of nations, as they were observed and practised among Christian communities. It considered the state of nature between nations as a state of peace; and, as a necessary consequence, that the new confederacy was at peace with all other nations, Great Britain alone excepted. It made no change in the laws—none in the internal administration of any one of the confederates, other than such as necessarily followed from the dissolution of the connexion with Great Britain. It left all municipal legislation, all regulation of private individual rights and interests, to the people of each separate Colony; and each separate Colony, thus transformed into a State of the Union, wrought for itself a constitution of government.

There remained to be formed a confederate government for the whole Union; and of this, an abortive experiment was made by the co-operation of Congress with the State Legislatures, without recurrence to the fountain of power, the people. This error proved well nigh fatal to the Union, and to the liberties of the whole. It palsied in a great degree the subsequent operations of the war; it prostrated the faith and energy of the nation in peace; it became a source of impotence in all the relations of the country with foreign powers; of mutual irritation, discord and anarchy at home. It disabled the nation from the performance of its engagements to others, and from the means of exacting the fulfilment of theirs in return. It degraded the country in the eyes of the world, and disgraced the glorious cause in which our national independence had been achieved. It embittered the hearts, and armed the hands of our citizens against one another, till our judicial tribunals were sullied with trials for treason, and our legislative records blackened with proclamations of rebellion.

In our own Commonwealth, the blood of her citizens was shed by each other, on the field of battle, and the scaffold thirsted for that of her children. Never, even during the gloomiest moments of the revolutionary war, had the condition of the country been so calamitous as in the years immediately succeeding the peace, in the very triumph of our cause, and in the full and undisputed enjoyment of our independence.

The primary cause of all these misfortunes and all these crimes, was the same mistaken estimate of sovereignty which the British Parliament had made, when they undertook to levy money upon the Colonies by taxation. The separate States of the Union, using a term which appears to have been studiously avoided in the Declaration of Independence, declared themselves, not only free and independent, but *sovereign* States;— and then their lawyers, adopting the doctrine of Blackstone, the oracle of English law, inferred that *sovereign* must necessarily be uncontrollable, unlimited, despotic power. Assuming, like the eminent commentator, that in all governments this power must exist *somewhere*, and that it is inherent in the very definition of sovereignty, with about as much plausibility as he deposits it in the British Parliament, they made no hesitation to entrust it to the governments of the separate States.

It were an abuse of your time and patience, fellow citizens, to recall to your memory all the vagaries into which this political sophism of identity between *sovereign* and *despotic* power, has led, and continues to lead, some of the Statists of this our happy but disputatious Union. It seizes upon the brain of a heated politician sometimes in one State, sometimes in another, and its natural offspring is the doctrine of nullification;—that is, the *sovereign* power of any one State of the confederacy to nullify any act of the whole twenty-four States, which the *sovereign* State shall please to consider as unconstitutional;—an error sustained by reasoners too respectable to be treated with derision, and, apart from that consideration, too absurd to be encountered with serious argument. Even under our present Federal Constitution, it has been directly asserted, or imprudently countenanced, at one time in Virginia and Kentucky, at another in Massachusetts and Connecticut, now in the temperate climate of Pennsylvania, and again in the warmer regions of the South. Fortunate has it been for our country, that the paroxysms of this fever have hitherto proved not extensively contagious! But we are admonished by one of the profoundest philosophers of modern ages,* not to measure the danger of discontentments in the body politic by this,— whether they be just or unjust; nor yet by this, whether the griefs whereupon they rise, be great or small—neither to be secure, because they have been often or long, without ensuing peril. Not every fume or vapor turns indeed to a storm, but from vapors and exhalations imperceptibly gathered, the tempest of desolation does come at last.

It was this hallucination of State sovereignty, identified with unlimited power, which blasted the Confederation from its birth. The delegates in Congress were representatives of the State Legislatures; for as such only they acted in the formation of the articles of confederation. The State Legislatures were representatives of the people of each separate State. Between these two representative bodies, primary and secondary, of the same parties, a Confederation was elaborated for the whole Union, memorable only for its impotence.

---

* Lord Bacon.

It was formed by many of the same pure and exalted patriots, who had pledged their lives, their fortunes, and their sacred honor, to the independence of their country. It was made with long, painful and anxious deliberation, animated with the most ardent love of liberty, purified with perfect disinterestedness, and digested with consummate ability. It was a bloodless corpse! Fire from Heaven alone could have given it life; and that fire, unduly sought, brought with it Pandora and her box. In the establishment of the Confederation the people of the whole Union had no part. It was an alliance of States, intent above all things to preserve their *sovereignty* entire; averse above all things to confer power, because power might be abused; and also because they perceived that every grant of power to the confederate body could be made only by the relinquishment of their own. These, however, were errors, not of intention, nor even of judgment so much as of inexperience. The Union was a novelty. Self-government was an innovation. The idea of recurring to the people of the Union for a constitution, does not appear to have presented itself then to any mind. Yet the Declaration of Independence had been issued in the name and by the authority of the whole people. The total inefficiency of the Confederation to fulfil any of the good offices for which it was intended, reinspired the idea of recurring to the first source of all political power, the people.

Thus rose to birth the Constitution of the United States under which we yet live. It was formed by a Convention of Delegates, appointed by the Legislatures of the respective States, upon a recommendation of Congress, under a profound conviction of its own incompetency to administer the affairs of the Union, either at home or abroad. The work of the Convention, when completed, was by their President, Washington, transmitted to Congress; and by them to the Legislatures of the several States. These, without undertaking to decide upon it themselves, referred it back to the people, by whom it was sanctioned through the medium of Conventions specially elected in every State, who, after long investigation, and severe scrutiny, accepted, adopted, and made it the supreme law of the land, anything in the constitution or laws of any State to the contrary notwithstanding.

In the formation of Constitutions for the several States, similar errors of inexperience were committed. The Constitutions were all republican, all popular—not monarchical—not military. An article amendatory to the Constitution of the United States, declares that the powers *not delegated* to the United States by the Constitution, nor prohibited by it to the States, are reserved to the States respectively, or to the people. There are powers, then, powers of government, reserved to the people, and which never have been delegated either to the United or to the separate States; nor do the United States, nor the separate States possess any powers, not delegated to them by the people—by the people of the whole Union to the United States—by the people of each separate State to that State. Hence it follows, too, that the people of each State were incompetent to delegate to the State, any power already delegated by the people of the whole Union to the United States. It was the people of the whole Union, who had declared the United Colonies free and independent States. But those States possessed no powers but such as had been delegated to the Colonies by their charters, or as, after their becoming States, were delegated to them by the people. There was no such thing in their constitutions as an absolute, irresistible, despotic power, lurking *somewhere* under the cabalistic denomination of *sovereignty.* In some of the States, the people thought it unnecessary to form new Constitutions. They abided by the forms of government established by their charters. In one, the ordinary Legislature of the State modified their government without consulting the people;—an usurpation sanctioned by the acquiescence of the people, until a very recent day, but now rectified. Of those which did form Constitutions during the revolutionary war, every one, New Jersey perhaps excepted, has within the first half century found a revisal of its own necessary. New powers have from time to time been delegated by the people of each State to their government; powers previously delegated have been annulled: but in vain would you search all the Constitutions past or present of the States, for a power to nullify any act of the United States in Congress assembled. The people of no State were competent to grant such a power. The pretence to grant it would itself have been null and void—a violation of the Constitution of the United States; a violation of the Declaration of Independence.

The most momentous error committed in the formation of several of the first State Constitutions, was the establishment of the legislative power in a single assembly of the representatives of the people. In the true theory of republican government, *all* the public functionaries are representatives of the people, proxies to perform the will, and give action to the power, of the community. To mere theorists in the construction of the social edifice, there is no idea so seducing as that of simplicity. Now the simplest of all forms of representative government would be, that all the officers of the State should at short intervals of time be chosen by majorities of the people; and that all the powers of government should be exercised by one elected body of men. This system was, however, never proposed by any one in the United States. The division of the offices of government into legislative, executive, and judicial, had been long established in the British Colonies, though not very effectively settled in their organization. At the time of the Declaration of Independence, Montesquieu was one of the most recent and esteemed writers upon government, and he had shown the division of powers to be essentially necessary to the preservation of liberty. Legislation, however, being merely the expression of the will of the community, is an operation so simple in its nature, that inexperienced reason cannot easily perceive the necessity of committing it to two bodies of men, each having a decisive check upon the action of the other. At the first formation of our State Constitutions it was made a question of transcendent importance, and divided the opinions of our most eminent men. All the arguments derived from the analogy between the movements of political bodies, and the operations of physical nature; all the impulses of political parsimony; all the prejudices against a second co-ordinate legislative assembly, stimulated by the exemplification of it in the British Parliament, were against a division of the legislative power. In several of the States the force of these arguments was found irresistible. Pennsylvania was told, that a legislature in two branches was a wagon drawn by a horse before and a horse behind, in opposite directions; and she invested a single assembly with her legislative authority. Other States were actuated by the same image or by others equally plausible; and a European philosophical statesman, once reputed profound, expressed, in his private and confidential correspondence with another, his dissatisfaction that most of the American States had confided their legislation to two concurrent bodies, instead of depositing all their authority in one centre, and that centre the nation.

The experience of a very few years brought back all the members of the confederacy who had tried the experiment of the wagon with a single horse, to the team tackled with a pair; and, as it was not found necessary to tackle them in front and rear of the carriage, they have seldom manifested a disposition to draw in opposite directions, and never so obstinately as to arrest the progress of the car. When the Constitution of the United States came to be formed, the problem was sufficiently solved to settle opinions on this continent; and not a solitary voice was heard to propose that the legislative power of the Union should be vested in a single assembly.

This Constitution, rising from the ashes of the first experimental and imbecile Confederacy, has now been in successful operation upwards of forty years. It has undergone, since its first establishment, very few, and, comparatively speaking, unimportant alterations. It has passed through the ordeal of six successive administrations; and is at this time in the hands of a seventh. It has stood the test of one formidable foreign war, and of two apparent changes of principle, effected by the conflict of parties, but resulting in no material change of the Constitution; and none in the administration itself, affecting in any perceptible degree the interest of the nation. It was originally the work of the party denominated Federal, in opposition to that party which adhered with the most tenacious inflexibility to the unlimited sovereignty of the separate States. The administration of the general government, however, has been alternately confided to individuals attached to the one and the other of those parties; and it is a circumstance which will not escape the observation of a philosophical historian, that the constructive powers of the national government have been stretched to their extremest tension by that party when in power, which has been most tenderly scrupulous of the State sovereignty, when uninvested with the authority of the Union themselves.

Of these inconsistencies our two great parties can have little to say in reproof of each other. The charge on either side can be much more easily retorted than repelled. Our collisions of principle have been little, very little more than conflicts for place; and in the mean time the nation has been advancing, with gigantic strides, in population, wealth and power. That this has been, under the blessing of Providence, the result of the *system*, no one can doubt who will compare the condition of the country under the Confederacy of State sovereignties, and under the Constitution ordained by the people of the United States. Yet no one of the administrations of the general government has ever given entire satisfaction to the whole people. Partial discontents have at different times been prevalent in different portions of the Union; and the degree of inflammation with which they have raged, has seldom been proportioned to the magnitude of their exciting causes. Washington's administration encountered an insurrection in arms. His immediate successor was upbraided for sparing the life of a convict for treason. Many attempts have been made to array separate, and even combined State sovereignties, against the government and laws of the Union; and even at this day, the people of twenty-three of our States might shudder at the imminent danger of a dissolution of the Union, but for the anticipation that the most ardent instigators to that catastrophe at this time, may, on recovery from the angry passions by which they are stimulated, erase from their own memories, and strive to expunge from those of others, the records of their delusion; wonder that they should ever have been suspected of disloyalty to the Union, for which even now they profess an affectionate regard; and, if their words and deeds should be too faithfully remembered by their country, recur to the acknowledgement of the poet, and exclaim,

"We angry lovers mean not half we say."

It is not to be expected that the present, or any future administration, will ever prove satisfactory at once to the whole people. A condition of relative comfort and happiness is all that the lot of mankind upon earth can attain; and if a denizen of the North American Union would form a candid estimate of the good and evil of his own destiny, let him compare it with that of any other inhabitant of the globe; or, contracting the comparison to that of the civilized and christian portion of the earth, let him look abroad among the nations of Europe, and of their descendants in our own hemisphere,—the portions of mankind whose opinions and feelings and fortunes have been most deeply agitated and extensively influenced by the principles proclaimed in our Declaration of Independence,—and draw an impartial parallel between their condition and our own.

The first of the European nations, which followed us in the revolutionary career, was France. Her government was an absolute monarchy. The uncontrolled, irresistible, despotic power, which, Blackstone and the jurists of the English school insist, must in every government reside *somewhere*, was in France vested in the person of the king. There was indeed an obsolete record of a constitution; an assembly of the States General in three orders, nobles, clergy and commons or third estate, which wore the semblance of a representation of the people.

The very same year when the present government of the United States was first organized, this uncontrolled monarch was compelled to call an assembly of the States General, a body which had not been permitted to meet before for nearly two hundred years. And this body did then no sooner assemble, than, under the influence of the principles promulgated by our Declaration of Independence, the third estate, or popular representation, assumed the supreme power to themselves, constrained the two other orders of nobles and clergy to unite with them in a self-constituted National Assembly, abolished the monarchy, and, under the name of a royal democracy, fabricated in the space of two years the first of a succession of constitutions, which now, at the end of forty years after that event, they are still making and mending with enthusiasm scarcely less ardent than when they first began. In the mean time they have been scourged with five and twenty years of civil and of foreign war; have inflicted on most of the other European nations, and suffered themselves, all the miseries and humiliations of conquest; have shed rivers of blood upon the scaffold; have ranged through all the extremes of popular anarchy and of military despotism; have beheaded, proscribed, recalled, reinstated, and expelled again the family of their ancient kings; and now acknowledge a collateral member of the same family as their hereditary sovereign. It is obvious that the career of revolution there is not yet closed. Throughout all these changes, the principles proclaimed in our Declaration of Independence, often overwhelmed by physical power, cowering under the sword of the soldier, withering under the imperial sceptre, laughed to scorn by the moral lectures of a foreign field marshal, and trampled in the dust by the heel of the Cossack, have never been effectively subdued. They have always re-emerged from the pressure to keep them down, as if destined, like the immortal soul of man, to survive the ruins of creation.

Fellow Citizens, I trespass upon the indulgence that I have invoked. Time fails me to pass in review the experiences of the other nations of the European continent, which, in the last half century, have been, and yet are, convulsed with the revolutionary spirit. In comparing their history during this period with our own, there is one point of difference between them, on which our attention cannot be too intensely rivetted. Our Declaration of Independence, our Confederation, the Constitution of the United States, and all our State Constitutions, without a single exception, have been voluntary compacts, deriving all their authority from the free consent of the parties to them. It may be doubted whether a single constitution has been formed in Europe or in Southern America, without some violence, some admixture of conflicting physical force in its confection. In the early and significant age of the ancient mythology, the god of boundaries was the only deity never to be propitiated by sacrifices of blood. He, too, was the only god who refused to yield his place, even to Jupiter. Here is the land-mark, bloodless and immoveable, more unerring than the magnet from the pole, firm as the everlasting hills, between freedom and force. It is not in the proclamation of principles. Declarations of the rights of man, as full, as copious, as formal as our own, have decorated the constitutions of Europe. Those constitutions, after a short and fitful existence, have passed into the memory of things beyond the flood; leaving the principles behind—blood-stained and defaced—monuments only of their own mutilation. We have proclaimed the principles, we have adhered to the practice; and our history has been a record of internal peace and general prosperity almost uninterrupted. Let the contemplation of the past, be the instructive lesson of the future. And in this connexion let us survey with calm, unblenching eye the newly revived doctrine of nullification; a word which contains within itself an absurdity, importing a pretended right of one State in this Union, by virtue of her *sovereignty,* to *make* that null and void, which it presupposes to be null and void before. The doctrine is not new, nor are those who now maintain it responsible for its introduction. It has been the vital disease of confederacies from the day when Philip of Macedon obtained a seat among the Amphyctions of Greece. It has never been, perhaps, involved in quite so much absurdity, as when appearing in its newest shape. It is now the claim for one State of this Union, by virtue of her sovereignty, not only to make, but to unmake the laws of the twenty-four, each equally sovereign with herself. This claim in its extent is most emphatically illustrated by its application to a revenue law. The Constitution of the United States declares that all duties, imposts, and excises shall be uniform throughout the United States. It forbids any preference to be given, by any regulation of commerce or revenue, to the ports of one State over those of another. The claim for the sovereign State is to nullify these provisions of the Constitution, indissolubly connected with all the acts of Congress for raising revenue. The Constitution of the United States, in express terms, supersedes all State Constitutions and laws conflicting with it. The sovereign State claims by her laws to supersede the Constitution of the United States, and the laws of all the other States in the Union. As a member of the Union, this advances a claim of appeal from the whole to a twenty-fourth part. As a sovereign State, a claim to make laws, not only for herself, but for others. Philosophically, politically, morally considered, it is an inversion of all human reasoning; it cannot be conceived without confusion of thought; it cannot be expressed without solecism of language, and terms of self-contradiction.

Its most hideous aspect is, not that its practical operation must issue in a severance of the Union, but that it substitutes physical force in the place of deliberate legislation. Stripped of the sophistical argumentation in which this doctrine has been habited, its naked nature is an effort to organize insurrection against the laws of the United States; to interpose the arm of State sovereignty between rebellion and the halter, and to rescue the traitor from the gibbet. The plan which it proposes, if pursued by merely individual association, would be levying war against the United States. It would not the less be levying war against the Union, if conducted under the auspices of State sovereignty; but as a State cannot be punished for treason, Nullification would case herself in the complete steel of sovereign power, as the heroes of ancient poetry were furnished with panoply from the armory of the gods.

You have seen, my fellow citizens, from the Declaration of Independence, that the States of this confederation were the offspring of the Union; that their sovereignty is not, and never was, a sovereignty as defined by Blackstone and the English lawyers, identical with unlimited power; that sovereignty, thus defined, is in direct contradiction to the Declaration of Independence, and incompatible with the nature of our institutions; that the States, united, and the States, separate, are both sovereign, but creatures of the people, and possess none but delegated powers; that the power of nullifying an act of Congress, never has been delegated to any one State, or to any partial combination of States, and that any, and every attempt at such nullification, by one or more States, less than the number required, and otherwise than in the forms prescribed for amendment of the Constitution, would, however colored, and however varnished, be neither more nor less than treason, skulking under the shelter of despotism.

Nullification is the provocative to that brutal and foul contest of force, which has hitherto baffled all the efforts of the European, and Southern American nations, to introduce among them constitutional governments of liberty and order. It strips us of that peculiar and unimitated characteristic of all our legislation—free debate. It makes the bayonet the arbiter of law; it has no argument but the thunderbolt. It were senseless to imagine that twenty-three States of the Union would suffer their laws to be trampled upon by the despotic mandate of one. The act of nullification would itself be null and void. Force must be called in to execute the law of the Union. Force must be applied by the nullifying State to resist its execution—

"Ate, hot from Hell,
Cries, Havoc! and lets slip the dogs of war."

The blood of brethren is shed by each other. The citizen of the nullifying State is a traitor to his country, by obedience to the law of his State; a traitor to his State, by obedience to the law of his country. The scaffold and the battle-field stream alternately with the blood of their victims. Let this agent but once intrude upon your deliberations, and Freedom will take her flight for heaven. The Declaration of Independence will become a philosophical dream, and uncontrolled, despotic sovereignties will trample with impunity, through a long career of after ages, at interminable or exterminating war with one another, upon the indefeasible and unalienable rights of man.

The event of a conflict in arms, between the Union and one of its members, whether terminating in victory or defeat, would be but an alternative of calamity to all. In the holy records of antiquity, we have two examples of a confederation ruptured by the severance of its members; one of which resulted, after three desperate battles, in the extermination of the seceding tribe. And the victorious people, instead of exulting in shouts of triumph, "came to the House of God, and abode there till even before God; and lifted up their voices, and wept sore, and said,—O Lord God of Israel, *why* is this come to pass in Israel, that there should be to-day one tribe lacking in Israel?" The other was a successful example of resistance against tyrannical taxation, and severed forever the confederacy, the fragments forming separate kingdoms; and from that day, their history presents an unbroken series of disastrous alliances, and exterminating wars—of assassinations, conspiracies, revolts, and rebellions, until both parts of the confederacy sunk in tributary servitude to the nations around them; till the countrymen of David and Solomon hung their harps upon the willows of Babylon, and were totally lost amidst the multitudes of the Chaldean and Assyrian monarchies, "the most despised portion of their slaves."*

In these mournful memorials of their fate, we may behold the sure, too sure prognostication of our own, from the hour when force shall be substituted for deliberation in the settlement of our Constitutional questions. This is the deplorable alternative— the extirpation of the seceding member, or the never ceasing

---

* Tacitus and Gibbon.

struggle of two rival confederacies, ultimately bending the neck of both under the yoke of foreign domination, or the despotic sovereignty of a conqueror at home. May Heaven avert the omen! The destinies, not only of our posterity, but of the human race, are at stake.

Let no such melancholy forebodings intrude upon the festivities of this anniversary. Serene skies and balmy breezes are not congenial to the climate of freedom. Progressive improvement in the condition of man is apparently the purpose of a superintending Providence. That purpose will not be disappointed. In no delusion of national vanity, but with a feeling of profound gratitude to the God of our Fathers, let us indulge the cheering hope and belief, that our country and her people have been selected as instruments for preparing and maturing much of the good yet in reserve for the welfare and happiness of the human race. Much good has already been effected by the solemn proclamation of our principles, much more by the illustration of our example. The tempest which threatens desolation, may be destined only to purify the atmosphere. It is not in tranquil ease and enjoyment that the active energies of mankind are displayed. Toils and dangers are the trials of the soul. Doomed to the first by his sentence at the fall, man, by submission, converts them into pleasures. The last are since the fall the condition of his existence. To see them in advance, to guard against them by all the suggestions of prudence, to meet them with the composure of unyielding resistance, and to abide with firm resignation the final dispensation of Him who rules the ball,—these are the dictates of philosophy—these are the precepts of religion—these are the principles and consolations of patriotism;—these remain when all is lost—and of these is composed the spirit of independence—the spirit embodied in that beautiful personification of the poet, which may each of you, my countrymen, to the last hour of his life, apply to himself.

> "Thy spirit, *Independence,* let me share,
>   Lord of the lion heart, and eagle eye!
>   Thy steps I follow, with my bosom bare,
>   Nor heed the storm that howls along the sky."*

*Smollett.

In the course of nature, the voice which now addresses you, must soon cease to be heard upon earth. Life and all which it inherits, lose of their value as it draws towards its close. But for most of you, my friends and neighbors, long and many years of futurity are yet in store. May they be years of freedom—years of prosperity—years of happiness, ripening for immortality! But, were the breath which now gives utterance to my feelings, the last vital air I should draw, my expiring words to you and your children should be, INDEPENDENCE AND UNION FOREVER!

"FALSIFIED LOGIC—FALSIFIED HISTORY—
FALSIFIED CONSTITUTIONAL LAW"

16. *Report of the Minority of the Committee on Manufactures, submitted to the House of Representatives of the United States, February 28, 1833* (Boston: John H. Eastburn, 1833).

No one had quite known what to make of him at first, this ex-president turned humble freshman congressman. Adams was sixty-four when the Twenty-second Congress commenced on December 5, 1831, the third oldest member and some twenty years older than most of his fellow representatives. His vast and exalted experience, distinguished lineage, even his austere manner—all singled him out as an oddity, and something of a wildcard. It might have been expected that, as the nation's most experienced diplomat, he would have been assigned to the Committee on Foreign Affairs, even to its chair, but that would have met with resistance from the Jacksonians. In the end Adams was named chairman of the Committee on Manufactures, a remit, as he confessed to his diary, "Far from the line of occupation in which all my life has been passed, and for which I feel myself not to be well qualified — I know not even enough of it to form an estimate of its difficulties." After a failed attempt to beg off the assignment, Adams did what he always did and hit the books to prepare.

Adams worked closely with the administration and its supporters on the committee to frame an agenda that contemplated the final extinction of the national debt, a compromise tariff to replace the Tariff of Abominations, and, in keeping with his own administration's priorities, a vigorous program of internal improvements. The first fruit of his work was the passage in July 1832 of a new tariff, soon known as the Adams Tariff in his honor, though he suggested in a letter to a friend that his "share in the accomplishment of the compromise ultimately effected was humble and secondary." Like any good compromise, the new tariff pleased no one entirely. While it made concessions to the South, particularly by reducing import duties on cheap woolens used to clothe the region's enslaved population, it gave no ground to the nullifiers on the principle that duties were well within Congress's constitutional mandate "to provide for the common Defence and general welfare."

South Carolinians only grew more intransigent, especially after local elections that year returned a solid majority of nullifiers to the state legislature, which promptly called for a special constitutional convention to deal with the tariff issue. On November 24, 1832, the convention, speaking in the name of the people of South Carolina, declared that all federal tariffs were null and void in the state. To enforce this ordinance, the convention mandated severe penalties on any state officers or citizens complying with the applicable federal laws and imposing test oaths to ensure obedience. Calhoun, now returned to the Senate having been dispatched by Jackson from the 1832 presidential ticket as vice president in favor of Van Buren, wrote another letter to the people of the United States (he listed the states individually, since he refused to recognize the people as a national polity) calling for a new convention of the states to deal with the "emergency."

The newly reelected Andrew Jackson stepped into this political maelstrom with his fourth annual message on December 4. Adams had little confidence that Jackson would meet South Carolina's defiance with the requisite spirit, and the president's message seemed to confirm his worst fears. "We should bear constantly in mind," the president advised, "the fact that the considerations which induced the framers of the Constitution to withhold from the General Government the power to regulate the great mass of the business and concerns of the people have been fully justified by experience, and that it can not now be doubted that the genius of all our institutions prescribes simplicity and economy." From the reduction of tariffs and imposts to his ongoing attack on the Bank of the United States to his proposal to transfer federal lands to the states to speed western settlement (reasoning that "the wealth and strength of a country are its population, and the best part of that population are cultivators of the soil"), Jackson advanced a program that seemed to reinforce the nullifiers' strict constructionism: "Relieved by its protecting shield from the fear of war and the apprehension of oppression, the free enterprise of our citizens, aided by the State sovereignties, will work out improvements and ameliorations which can not fail to demonstrate that the great truth that the people can govern themselves is not only realized in our example, but that it is done by a machinery in government so simple and economical as scarcely to be felt."

That same day, in his diary, Adams wrote that Jackson's message "recommends a total change in the Policy of the Union, with reference to the Bank, Manufactures, Internal Improvement and the Public Lands. It goes to dissolve the Union, into its original elements, and is in substance as complete surrender to the nullifiers of South-Carolina." Though Jackson soon thereafter issued his Proclamation Regarding Nullification, announcing his determination to enforce federal law and preserve the union, Adams still believed the structure of Jackson's message revealed a deeper capitulation. When the pro-administration majority of the Committee on Manufactures, mostly southerners, refused to issue any criticism of the president's antitariff agenda, Adams took to the press with this, one of the most famous minority reports in congressional history. Though the style appears to be entirely his own, he was joined in the report by fellow dissenter Lewis Condict of New Jersey, and they are referred to throughout as "the subscribers." The text itself is preceded in the original pamphlet by two enthusiastic advertisments, which are reproduced here.

REPORT

OF THE MINORITY OF THE

COMMITTEE ON MANUFACTURES,

SUBMITTED TO THE

HOUSE OF REPRESENTATIVES

OF THE UNITED STATES,

February 28, 1833.

**BY JOHN QUINCY ADAMS AND
LEWIS CONDICT.**

BOSTON:
JOHN H. EASTBURN.........PRINTER.........No. 18 STATE STREET

1833.

It will be recollected, that at the opening of the late session of Congress, so much of the President's message as related to manufactures, was in the House of Representatives referred in all due form to the Standing Committee on that subject. This Committee, however, had been so curiously constituted by the Speaker, as to present the spectacle of five out of its seven members opposed to the interest committed to their protection. The minority probably felt that this arrangement was intended not so much to promote, as to neutralise any influence which might possibly be exercised through this avenue upon the House; and this sentiment must have been strengthened upon perceiving that the Committee of Ways and Means was the selected channel through which a measure deeply affecting the manufacturing interest of the country, was to be presented to the attention of Congress.

The message of the President, this peculiar distribution of labor in the Committees; and the famous result of it, commonly called Mr. Verplanck's Submission Bill, manifested the force of the combinations formed to overthrow the manufactures of the country. The minority of the Committee, probably anxious to make some effort to counteract them, and aware that to have any hope of success, it must be directed to the people at large, sought to go back to foundations, and to give to the subject that scope, which in a national point of view properly belongs to it.

Under the guise of a Report, Mr. Adams enters into a full exposition of the domestic policy of the country, taken as *one connected system*, and he explains the principles which for forty years guided us in our unprecedented career. This system cannot be divided into parts, some of which may be taken and others rejected, because they all are founded upon one general basis, which is not divisible. The peculiar character of this paper is to be found in the solidity with which that basis is laid, and the complete issue it makes up with the President, and the whole race of what are called "strict construction" politicians, nullifiers, and all who would stop the prosperity of the nation on a cavil for a ninth part of a hair. It cannot be disguised that we are passing through a great crisis in regard to the strength of our Government. The late Congress, with the best opportunities has settled no principles. It yet depends upon the firmness of the people whether we shall be several, helpless, poor and distracted communities, or one vigorous, happy and united nation. It is for every citizen, more especially if he belongs to the free States, to reflect maturely upon the opposite lines of policy now distinctly presented to his attention, and *now to fix the principles of his political faith*, without any reference to the personal or party contention, which may be going on around him.

REPORT OF THE MINORITY | 1833

[*From Walsh's National Gazette of March* 13, 1833.]

Three pages of the National Intelligencer of yesterday morning are occupied by the Report of the Minority of the Committee on Manufactures, which Mr. Adams submitted on the 28 ult., to the House of Representatives, and which is the product of his athletic and capacious mind. It consists of the severest strictures on parts of the President's last annual message; of the ablest exposition of the dogmas and proceedings of the South Carolina nullifiers; and of a skilful and manifold plea for the manufacturing interest—with a strong and deep current of genuine political philosophy throughout the whole, in reference to our political system. The performance is altogether one of extraordinary strength and momentum; equal in masculine sense and argument, sustained impetus, intrepid candor, and importance of general maxims and conclusions, to any one of the antecedent state papers from the same pen. There is, perhaps, too much of amplification; but every sentence is valuable in itself for breadth of conception and vigor of phrase, or some ingredient salutary for the cause and the public.

Its length is as great as that of Mr. Calhoun's dissertation; but in every other respect it forms a contrast like that between true dialectics and the most artificial sophistry, wisdom and error, nutritive aliment and vitiating drug. Mr. Adams contends, with the utmost zeal and force for internal improvements by the agency of the general government; and, in asserting the real character, instrumentality and ends of our Union, he exhibits, with original traits, all the spuriousness and evil tendencies of the claim of nullification; all the enormity of the pretensions and measures of the nullifiers, and all the improvidence and weakness of any concessions to their arrogance and usurpation. We cannot convey by synopsis or extracts a sufficient idea of the multitude, variety and validity of the considerations which he offers to the judgment and patriotism of his countrymen. We shall republish the whole report, in divisions according to the distinction of topics. That part of it in which the relations between the slave-holding and non-slave-holding States, and the conduct and tone of the South towards the North, are treated, is particularly racy and impressive. In the art of *exploding* absurdities, Mr. Adams is, indeed, consummate.

Mr. Adams's Report on Manufactures

House of Representatives of the United States,
FEBRUARY 28, 1833.

Mr. ADAMS, by direction from the majority of the Committee on Manufactures, moved that the Committee be discharged from the further consideration of the matters referred to them by the House; and on the part of the minority of the same committee, he presented the following

REPORT

on so much of the President's annual message to Congress as relates to Domestic Manufactures and the protection necessary to be afforded the same; referred to the committee by resolution of the House, of 13th December, 1832.

The subscribers, members of the Committee on Manufactures, to which was referred so much of the message of the President of the United States to Congress, at the commencement of the present session, as relates to the protection necessary to domestic manufactures, dissenting from the report of the majority of the committee, present herewith respectfully to the House their own views upon the subject referred by the House to the committee to report thereon.

The parts of the message which relate to the protection necessary to domestic manufactures, may be considered separately or in connexion with other great national interests, forming the subject of the annual communication from the Chief of the Executive Department of the Government to the Legislature. In the message itself they are recommended to the consideration of Congress, in connexion with proposals for such further reduction in the revenue as may not be required for the objects of general welfare and public defence, which the Constitution authorizes, and for which reduction the occasion is stated by the President to result from the impending final discharge of the national debt; an event on the occurrence of which the subscribers most cordially sympathize with the sentiments expressed by the President. They consider the final and total discharge of the public debt as a subject of grateful acknowledgment to the wisdom, energy, and fidelity to their trust, of those who preceded us in the management of our national concerns; of mutual gratulation to ourselves, who enjoy the benefits of this alleviation of the burdens cheerfully borne by our fathers, and hitherto by us, for the sacred preservation of the public faith; and of anticipated felicity to our successors in the exemption from burdens which we and our fathers have borne without murmuring or complaint, to secure to them, our posterity, the blessings of freedom, independence, and union. Enjoying, in all the purity of patriotism, the comfort of this great alleviation of public burden, the subscribers deprecate, with equal earnestness and sincerity, the contingency of any event which should, at the very moment of fruition, dash from the lips of our prosperity the cup of joy, and substitute, in its place, the bitter portion of disunion, civil dissensions, and fraternal war.

Under these impressions, it was not without feelings of deep concern, and of painful sensibility, that the subscribers beheld, in the message of the President of the United States, the broad and unqualified assertion of principles, and the developement of an entire political system for the future government of the Union, as new and unheard of, as to them it appears incorrect, and incompatible with the foundations of our political existence.

The first of these principles, and that from which all the others appear to the subscribers to be derived—the basis of the message, and of the whole system of administration, for the futurity of this Union, is contained in the following position, which the subscribers submit to the consideration of the House in the very words of the message itself: "The wealth and strength of a country are its population, and the *best part* of that population are the cultivators of the soil. Independent farmers are, every where, the basis of society, and true friends of liberty."

That the President of the United States should in a public document, addressed to the Representatives of the whole people of this union, peremptorily declare one part of the population, by them represented, better than the rest, appears to the subscribers little compatible with that equality of rights upon which our whole social system is, by them, believed to be founded. If one part of the population, parties to the social compact, is the best, it necessarily follows that another part of the same population is the worst; that there are different degrees of merit in different portions of the same population, estimated not by their moral, but by their social condition; not by their individual qualifications of virtue and understanding, but by their respective occupations and possessions.

In examining this fundamental principle of politics and morals, thus put forth as the foundation for the system of policy to be hereafter erected for the government of this great and growing confederated nation, the subscribers have endeavored to ascertain to whom it is this proud preeminence of merit is assigned by the Chief Executive Magistrate of the Union. He asserts that the wealth and strength of a country are its population, and that the best part of that population are the cultivators of the soil. Now, the population of a country consists of the whole mass of human beings abiding within it; and, of the population of this country, a vast proportion of the cultivators of the soil, are in a state of servitude—possessing no rights, civil or political—and existing only as the property of another part of the same population. That these cultivators of the soil constitute a large portion of the wealth of this country, is undoubtedly true; that they constitute a considerable portion of its strength, is far more questionable; but the subscribers cannot believe it was to them that the intention of the President was to ascribe the transcendant honor of constituting the best part of our population; and, if not to them, neither was it to the class of freemen, in another part of the Union, also cultivators of the soil, laboring like them, by the sweat of their brow, for daily subsistance by daily labor, but in the full enjoyment of civil and political rights, and constituting in truth not a better, but as good, a part of the population as any other in the community. It was not, however, to them that the President intended to attribute the superiority of excellence as a component part of the population. His meaning is more fully disclosed in the subsequent clause of the sentence above cited, in the affirmation that "independent farmers are every where the basis of society, and true friends of liberty." Taking the whole sentence together, the subscribers believe that, in the understanding of the author of the message, the cultivators of the soil, in the first part of the sentence were identical with the independent farmers in the second; and that the sentiment, in the mind of the writer, and the aphorism of moral and of political economy laid down by the whole sentence, is that in all countries, generally, and especially in our own, the best part of the population—the basis of society—and the friends pre-eminently of freedom, are the *wealthy landholders.*

The principle is certainly not new in the history of the world, or of human government; it is the fundamental axiom of all landed aristocracies; it is the foundation of the feudal system, and, when carried out into practice, must inevitably resolve itself into it. The term aristocracy, by its derivation, is the government *of the best*; and where the property of the soil is distributed in portions so unequal, that its cultivators are divided into masters and slaves, or into landlords and tenants, power will naturally concentrate itself in the hands of the large holders of the lands, who will soon constitute themselves the basis of society—the independent farmers—the best part of the population—true friends of liberty, confined exclusively to themselves, but holding in oppressive servitude the real cultivators of the soil, and ruling, with a rod of iron, over all the other occupations and professions of men.

Such has been the developement of this fundamental principle of government, in the history of other ages and countries. So has it especially disclosed itself in the annals of France, of Spain, of Germany; of Poland, of Russia, and of England. The independent farmers, or wealthy landholders, of all those countries have constituted the ancient feudal barons, as they now constitute the modern nobles holding the laborious husbandmen of the same countries in servitude, or in abject poverty and the most degraded dependence.

The subscribers believe that the Declaration of Independence, and the Government of this Union, are founded upon a different and opposite principle—upon the principle that all men are born with equal rights; and that however in one portion of the Union, the independent farmers or planters, cultivating the soil by their slaves, may be considered, by one of themselves, as the basis of society, and the best part of the population, the assumption of such a principle, as a foundation of a system of national policy for the future government of these United States, is an occurrence of the most dangerous and alarming tendency; as threatening, at no remote period, not only the prosperity but the peace of the country, and as directly leading to the most fatal of catastrophes—the dissolution of the Union by a complicated, civil, and servile war.

Had it been possible for the subscribers to consider the principles thus authoritatively laid down in the message as a mere abstract speculative opinion, indicative only of a mind habitually occupied in meditation upon the first principles of Government, they might have deemed it their duty to pass it over in silence, regretting that an opinion so adverse to all the lessons of history, and to every rational theory of human rights, should ever have found its way into the mind of the Executive Chief of the Union; and still more into an official communication from him to the Legislative Assembly of the nation. But they find it pervading every part of the message relating to the administration of the internal affairs of the country—they trace it in the denunciation of uncompromising hostility to the Bank of the United States—they discern it in the general dissuasion of all future encouragement, or aid to be given to objects of internal improvement—they perceive it in the portentous recommendations to abandon all purpose of deriving a revenue for the general benefit from that invaluable fund of national wealth, the public lands; and in the astonishing proposal to give them all away to the states within which they are situated, or to adventurers who may be allured by promise of sharing in those spoils of the national domain, plundered from the whole people of the Union, to become members of this best part of the population, the independent farmers, cultivators of the soil, taken from all their fellow citizens to be gratuitously bestowed upon them. They see it, above all, in the destiny to which the message consigns the great manufacturing interest of the country, including the handicraftsmen and mechanics of all our populous cities and all our flourishing towns. These are not the basis of society—they are not the cultivators of the soil—they are not the best part of the population—their equal rights may be trampled upon—their highest interests may be sacrificed—their property may be wrested from their hands—themselves and their families may be driven by measures of national policy, by acts of the Government of the Union, to beggary and ruin, for the benefit of the independent farmers, the wealthy landholders—the best part of the population.

Such are the practical consequences which must flow from the reproduction by the head of this national Union, as a fundamental principle of Government of the old and long exploded doctrine, that the wealthy landholders of all countries constitute the best part of their population. Under this theory it can no longer be surprising to find in the message an entire system of propositions and of recommendations, which, if adopted and sanctioned by the Legislature, will accomplish a revolution in the Government of the United States, and, in the solemn and deliberate opinion of the subscribers, a total subversion of their Constitution.

In descending from the general axiom, that in all countries the independent farmers, or wealthy landholders, cultivators of the soil, constitute the best part of the population, to the measures of legislation recommended to Congress for carrying out this principle, in the administration of the Government, four features are discernible, as especially characteristic of the message. First, the abandonment for the future, of all appropriations of public moneys to purposes of internal improvement. Second, the practically total dereliction of all protection to domestic industry, whether agricultural, manufacturing, or mechanical. Third, the nullification of all future revenue from the public domains, by the bestowal of them in free donation to voluntary settlers upon them, from the privileged class of citizens, cultivators of the soil, to swell the numbers of the best part of the population, at the expense of all the rest, or to the favored States in which this common property happens to be situated. Fourth, the denunciation of the Bank of the United States, depreciating the value of the stock held in it by the nation; distressing the commercial community with suspicions of the solidity of its funds, and stimulating the profligacy of fraudulent gambling in its stock. In every one of these four particulars the recommendations of the message are in diametrical opposition to the well established, deliberately adopted, and long tried policy, by which the Union has hitherto been governed, under the present constitution of the United States—in diametrical opposition to the purposes for which it was formed—to the principles upon which it has been administered, and, with the most painful, but most undoubting conviction, the subscribers must add, to the solemn compacts and indefeasible obligations by which the nation is bound.

Although the plan of Government marked out and delineated in the message forms a whole system, sufficiently consistent with itself, and all derivable from the fundamental position that the wealthy landholders constitute the best part of the population, yet it is observable, that in every instance the subordinate principle advanced as the groundwork of each separate recommendation, is, by the terms of the message, so qualified in the theory, as scarcely, if at all, to differ from the views and opinions entertained by the friends of the interest which the recommendation itself is adopted to destroy. Thus, for example, in the recommendation to abandon all future appropriations of the public moneys for purposes of internal improvement, the only principle avowed is "that the Constitution does not warrant the application of the funds of the General Government to objects of internal improvement, *which are not national in their character.*" From this position, the most ardent and most liberal friend of internal improvement will not dissent. No appropriation ever has been asked—there is not the shadow of a danger that any appropriation of funds ever will be asked, but for objects alleged to be of a national character; and of their legitimate title to that character, the representatives of the whole people, and of all the State Legislatures in Congress assembled, under the control of a qualified negative by the Chief Magistrate of the Union, all acting under a constant responsibility to their constituents, are qualified and competent judges. That there will be, as there have been, diversities of opinion, whether any specified object of internal improvement is or is not of a national character, may be freely admitted; and that in all cases where it may be reasonably doubted, the wise and prudent policy of the constituted authorities will induce them rather to withhold than grant the appropriation, is a conclusion deducible not less from the experience of the past, than from the confidence due to the moral character of the delegated representatives of the nation. That in the great majority of applications for appropriations in aid of internal improvements, which have been made to Congress, the objects for which they were solicited have been of a national character could not be and was not doubted. Of the appropriations made, the subscribers confidently affirm, that none can be pointed out which are not unquestionably of that character. If there has been error in the administration of the Government, in the application or appropriations to these objects, it has been an error of parsimony and not of profusion; a refusal of the public money where it ought to have been granted, and not a bestowal where it ought to have been denied. In the sober and honest discretion of the Legislature, under the vigilant supervision of the Executive Chief, a guard amply sufficient for the protection of the public resources against wasteful or improvident expenditures, has been provided by the Constitution.

It is said in the message, that, "without some general and well defined principles, *ascertaining* those objects of internal improvement to which the means of the nation may be constitutionally applied, it is obvious that the exercise of the power can never be satisfactory." Suppose this position, in its fullest extent, to be admitted. The message does not deny that the power of granting appropriations for internal improvements of a national character is vested, completely and unequivocally vested in Congress by the Constitution; and the President himself, in the discharge of his official duties, has, in numerous instances, given his sanction to such appropriations. And in that grant of power, as in all others, is necessarily and unavoidably implied the power of ascertaining and defining the principles upon which, in the spirit of the Constitution, it shall be exercised. If, therefore, in the exercise of the power of making such appropriations hitherto, there has been a neglect or omission to ascertain and define the principles upon which they have been made, it is a duty yet to be performed by Congress itself, and which requires the interposition of no other power. It is obvious that to resort elsewhere than to Congress itself, to ascertain and define the objects upon which the power is unquestionably delegated to them of appropriating public moneys to internal improvements, is precisely equivalent to a denial of the right of Congress to exercise the power in all cases whatsoever.

With regard to the danger to which the message supposes Congress may be exposed, of making hasty appropriations to works of the character of which they may be frequently ignorant, the argument necessarily presupposes a habitual, gross, and criminal neglect of their duties, by a majority of both Houses of Congress, a reflection upon the honor and honesty of those bodies of which the subscribers deem it sufficient to say that it is equally unwarrantable and misplaced. So long as the members of both Houses of Congress shall entertain a just sense of their duties to their country, to their constituents, and to their own characters; so long as there is, and will be, no danger—none, whatever, of their being exposed to make hasty appropriations to works of the character of which they are ignorant, or to any other purpose. The members of both Houses of Congress, are accountable for the wisdom as well as for the purity of their official conduct not to the Executive Magistrate, himself accountable to them for his own, but to their constituents and to their country. Nor has that country committed to the Executive Magistrate the custody of its own purity, in the exercise of the elective franchise. If it be true that a prospect of making navigable a creek or river—or bringing commerce to the doors of the people—or of increasing the value of their property, may operate occasionally as inducements to individuals to favor by their suffrages the success of a candidate whom they may suppose to be better qualified than his opponent, to obtain for them those great and valuable improvements—is it justice or equity—is it a fair perception of the nature of things, to stigmatize this as a corrupting influence? No influence can be more just and pure. To benefit the people, by making navigable the river or creek in their neighborhood—by bringing commerce to their doors— and by increasing the value of their property, are among the most important and most valuable services that a representative *can* render to his constituents. To draw good from evil, is one of the high and holy attributes of Omnipotence.—To draw evil from good, is the peculiar attribute of the arch enemy of mankind; but singular, indeed, is the aspect of that political axiom, which imputes dishonesty to the representative in the zeal with which he promotes the interests of his constituents; and finds the evidence of corruption in the exercise of the highest beneficence. Suppose this calumniated influence to be successful; suppose a candidate to be elected to Congress by the confidence of his constituents in the superiority of his talent and capacity to obtain appropriations of public money to render their neighboring river navigable—to bring commerce to their doors, and to increase the value of their property—talent and capacity are qualities of which men seldom form erroneous estimates, in the choice of their representatives, when their judgments are enlightened by their interest. Talent and capacity, brought into the representative councils of the nation, by the selection of a member for one district, under the influence of a belief, that it will be exerted for the benefit of those by whom he is chosen, is talent and capacity available on the scene where it has been introduced, for all the great interests of the nation. It is there that the representative of every single district becomes a representative of the whole people.—As the representative of one district, he has, to promote the interests of his immediate constituents, but one of more than two hundred votes. But that one vote he has also upon all the questions within the competency of Congress, and affecting the interests of the whole nation, and of all its parts. The result then of every election which brings into this house, a member recommended to the favor of his constituents by the zeal and ability with which he may promote the internal improvement of his own neighborhood, is essentially advantageous to the whole nation, and has a direct tendency to establish a high standard of intellectual worth, as the measure of qualification for a seat in the House. It is congenial to that spirit of moral elevation and dignity which constitutes the only solid foundation of representative Government; and it is only by confounding the elements of good and evil, that it can be stigmatized as tainted with corruption.

As little can the subscribers yield their assent to the reasoning in the message, which effectively urges upon Congress to refrain from the exercise of all powers of which more than one-fourth, that is, seven States of this Union, would be unwilling now to make the grant, and which any still smaller portion of the people may, at any period since the existence of the Constitution, have opposed or resisted under the vague and indefinite denomination of doubtful powers. Fearful and hopeless, indeed, would be the condition of the people of these United States, if every grant of power delegated by them, for their own benefit and improvement, to their united national supreme legislature, should be annulled or struck with impotence by every scruple of doubt which the refinement of metaphysical subtlety, the transient ebullitions of popular excitement, or the factious instigations of electioneering artifice, have, from time to time, disseminated over different sections of the country. There is, perhaps, not a single grant of power to Congress in that great national compact of Government, the Constitution of the United States, which at some period of our history has not been assailed by numerous parties and their controversial wranglers, as doubtful powers; even at this hour we are, apparently, on the verge of a conflict in arms, on the very borders of a civil war with *one* of the States of the Union, for the exercise of powers, the want of which first gave rise to the Constitution itself, which have been quietly exercised from the organization of the Government now for nearly forty years without a dissenting voice; and which now, under the new lights of nullification, have been discovered to be such plain and palpable violations of the Constitution, as to warrant the State in which this discovery has been made, in resorting to her sovereign power, to declare them within her own borders null and void. There are seven States of this Union, the whole free population of which, by the returns of the last census, amounted only to seven hundred and seventy-one thousand two hundred and eighteen souls; a majority of these, sufficient to command the vote and decision of them all, would be less than four hundred thousand; and thus, upon the recommendations of the message, a nation, consisting of ten millions of freemen, must be crippled in the exercise of all their associated power, unmanned of all their energies applicable to the improvement of their own condition, by the doubts, scruples, or fanciful discontents of a portion among themselves, less in numbers than double the amount of population in the single city of New-York.

The subscribers assume as a principle, demonstrated beyond all possibility of doubt, that of the whole free population of the Union, a vast majority—they entertain, themselves, no question that it is a majority amounting to more than three-fourths of the whole—believe, without a scintillation of doubt, that the power of appropriating public moneys to objects of internal improvement of a national character, as understood by Congress itself, has been delegated to Congress by the whole people, in the Constitution of the United States. The message itself does not question this grant of power; and it is tacitly affirmed by the Chief Magistrate himself, in his sign manual affixed to every act of Congress making such appropriations which has received his signature. What reason or motive, then, can there be for Congress to interdict itself from the exercise of beneficent power, essential to the welfare and prosperity of the whole people, to gratify the dog-in-manger disposition of less than one-twentieth part of the community? Truly, very truly, does the message say that "there is nothing so worthy of the constant solicitude of this Government as the harmony and union of the people;" but is it imagined that harmony and union can be promoted by the perpetual sacrifice of the will, the interest, and the well-being of nineteen-twentieths of the whole people, to the contracted and envious passions or to the sordid parsimony of the remaining twentieth? The subscribers will neither express nor entertain a suspicion that the recommendation to apply to the States of this Union for grants of additional power to Congress, and in the mean time to abstain from the exercise of all powers, which the one-twentieth part of the people may be pleased or instigated to consider as *doubtful*, was not made in good faith and sincerity; but without questioning the motive which could lead to such a proposal, they cannot but regard it in effect as disclosing the purpose of disabling and abdicating all power of making appropriations for all and every great object of internal improvement hereafter and forever. As little hesitation have they in declaring it as their belief, that this purpose, and the whole system of which it forms a part, is in no wise calculated to promote the harmony and union of the people. It is a natural emanation from the fountain of a principle divided in itself, and the source of all fatal division; a principle which pronounces one class of the citizens of this Union, to the disparagement of all others, the best part of the population.

The subscribers disclaim all communion of sentiment with this opinion, to which they can assent as true in no sense whatever. They deny that there is any sense to which language can give utterance; and in which the *cultivators of the soil*, be they who they may, included under the denomination, can, with truth, be called the best part of the population. They believe, on the contrary, with the greatest orator, statesman, and patriot of ancient Rome, and with the sublimest genius of ancient Greece, with Cicero, and with Plato, that "whoever gives preference to one part of the citizens, and neglects another part, introduces into the community the elements of the most pernicious discord and sedition. It necessarily produces rival factions, some favoring the populace, and some favoring THE BEST, and leaving scarcely any favorers of ALL." This was the patriotism of Cicero; this was the philosophy of Plato, two thousand years and upwards before the Declaration of Independence. The doctrine is founded upon eternal truth. It is the only doctrine upon which Governments of equal rights can be founded; as that which divides the population into a best and a worst part is the never-failing source of tyranny and oppression, of civil strife, the shedding of brother's blood, and the total extinction of freedom.

The subscribers hope and trust, therefore, that Congress will not abdicate by nonuser, the power delegated to them by the Constitution of the United States, of making appropriations of public money to great national objects of internal improvements. They consider the exercise of the power as essential to the welfare and prosperity of the whole people; they believe it to have been delegated for the purpose of promoting that welfare; and that to refrain from the exercise of the power would be a dereliction of duty in Congress itself, and treachery to the trust committed to them by the people. They further believe that the people of the Union never will submit to a permanent abandonment of the principle, hitherto so successfully and so advantageously to them carried into practice, of making such appropriations: that however it may be suspended for a time, under a theory of partial preference to an imaginary *best part of the population*, it will never be extinguished but with the life-blood of the Union itself. For what is the final result of this doctrine of abdicating powers arbitrarily designated as doubtful? What but the degradation and impotence of the nation itself?—the degradation of chaining its own hands? of fettering its own feet? of disabling itself from bettering its own condition?—The impotence of inability to employ its own faculties for its own improvement? It is the principle upon which the roving Tartar denies himself a permanent habitation, because to him the wandering shepherd is the best part of the population; the principle upon which the savage of the American forest refuses to till the ground, because to him the hunter of the woods is the best part of the population. Imperfect civilization, in all states of human society, shackles itself with fanatical prejudices of exclusive favor to its own occupations, as the owner of a plantation with a hundred slaves, believes the summit of human virtue to be attained only by independent farmers, cultivators of the soil. Not by such opinions or such maxims of Government were the people of the United States animated and inspired, when, "in order to form a more perfect Union, establish justice, ensure domestic tranquility, provide for the common defence, promote the general welfare, and secure the blessings of liberty to themselves and their posterity, they did ordain and establish the Constitution of the United States of America." Their purpose, in this great and solemn *mutual covenant,* was their own improvement—the improvement of the condition of the whole. The Constitution itself is but one great organized engine of improvement—physical, moral, political. It directed the assemblage, from time to time, of chosen bodies of men; vested with limited powers, to consult, to deliberate, and to act upon all the great interests of peace and war, common to the people. It was no compact of separate and distinct bodies politic. The separate States were not competent to form any such compact, or to confer any such powers; the people of each State were competent to form, and did form, constitutions for themselves; but their sphere of action to ordain and establish was limited within their own boundaries. For where did the State, the creature of the sovereign people of Massachusetts, where did, or where could, that State acquire the right of bestowing upon the people of Pennsylvania a right of representation in this House? As well might the *State* of Massachusetts have undertaken to ordain and establish who should be represented in the Parliament of Great Britain, or in the Chamber of Deputies of

France. The whole people of the United States were alone competent to determine and to ordain how, and in what manner, they and their posterity should be represented in this assembly; and as well might it be contended that the state of Ohio, which had no existence, or the state of Louisiana, which was a Spanish colony, were parties to the Constitution of the United States at its formation, as that the parties to it were the thirteen States of which the old lifeless confederation had been composed. The Constitution was, as it is on its face declared to be, the act of the whole people, and it is the instrument by which they organized the means of effecting the improvements of their own condition, by the agency of their Government. In refraining from the exercise of the powers delegated to them for the good of the whole, the Government not only abdicate their power, but effectively disable that of the nation itself. The energy which slumbers in their hands, is no better than dead to the good of the people; it arrests the hand of Divine beneficence itself; degrades the nation to a level of inferiority among the families of mankind, and proclaims as the fundamental law of their association their inability to apply their own faculties to their own elevation in the scale of being.

It is, then, with sentiments of deep mortification and of unqualified dissent, that the subscribers have observed the earnest recommendations to Congress in the message, to abandon the whole system of appropriations for internal improvements, which has hitherto been pursued; which was in the full tide of successful experiment, and which, for a long series of years, has been contributing to increase the comforts, to multiply the enjoyments, and to consolidate the strength and happiness of the American people. To abandon them all, for in no other light can they consider the extraordinary though vague and indefinite commendations of *simplicity*, as the suitable characteristic for the government of a nation of swarming millions of human beings—the intensely urgent exhortations to Congress to refrain from the exercise of all beneficent powers, which one-twentieth part of the people may carp and cavil at as doubtful—the incomprehensible argument that harmony and union are to be promoted by stifling the firm and manly voice of nineteen-twentieths of our constituents, to satisfy the brainsick doubts, or appease the menacing clamors of less than one-twentieth—and finally the direct recommendation to Congress, to dispose of all stocks now held by the General Government in corporations, whether created by the General or State Governments, and to place the proceeds in the Treasury.

In these recommendations, and in the spirit with which they are pressed upon the consideration of Congress, the subscribers can discern nothing less than a proposed revolution of government in this Union—a *revolution*, the avowed purpose of which is, to *reduce* the General Government to a simple machine. A simple machine? The universe in which we daily revolve, and which seems to our vision daily to revolve round us, is a simple machine under the guidance of an omnipotent hand. The President of the United States, *one* of the functionaries provided by the Constitution for the ordinary management of the affairs of the Government, but not entrusted even with the power of *action*, upon any proposed alteration or amendment to the Constitution, undertakes to *reduce* the General Government to a simple machine—the simplicity of which shall consist of universal beneficence, in preserving peace, affording a uniform currency, maintaining the inviolability of contracts, diffusing intelligence, and discharging, *unfelt*, its other (nameless, unenumerated, and undefined) superintending functions. Truly, this *simplicity* may be aptly compared with that of the Government of the universe; needing only an omnipotent hand to guide and regulate its movements, and differing from it, as would seem, only in the self-denial of all power to improve the condition, or promote the general welfare of the community, by and for whom this simple machine was ordained. To the subscribers, it appears that of all the attributes of Government among men, simplicity is the last that deserves commendation. The simplest of all governments is an absolute despotism, and it may confidently be affirmed, that, in proportion as a Government approaches to simplicity, will always be its approaches to arbitrary power. It is by the complication of Government alone, that the freedom of mankind can be secured; simplicity is the essential characteristic in the condition of all slavery; and if the people of these United States enjoy a greater share of liberty than any other nation upon earth, it is because, of all the Governments upon earth, theirs is the most complicated. The simplicity to which the recommendations of the message would reduce the machine of Government, is a simplicity of impotence; an abdication of the power to do good; a divestment of all power in this confederated people to improve their own condition.

In the recommendations of the message, relating to the disposal of the public lands, the subscribers perceive the same speculative aversion to control, which seeks to reduce the Government to a simple machine, the same preference of one class of citizens—the independent farmers, cultivators of the soil—over all other members of the community. The recommendations of the message are, "that the public lands shall cease, as soon as practicable, to be a source of revenue—that they be sold to settlers, in limited parcels, at a price barely sufficient to reimburse to the United States the expenses of the present system, and the cost arising under our Indian compacts; and that, *in convenient time*, the machinery of accurate surveys and undoubted titles be withdrawn from the States, and the right of soil, and the future disposition of it, be surrendered to the States respectively in which it lies."

The proposition is to give away all the public lands—first, to enable individual adventurers to secure an independent freehold, because cultivators of the soil are the *best* part of the population; and finally to surrender all the remainder to the States in which the lands are situated, because "it cannot be expected that the new States will remain longer contented with the present policy, after the payment of the public debt."

The public lands are the property of the whole people of the United States; they are the national domain. To give them away to individual adventurers, is to take away the property of one portion of the citizens, and bestow it upon another; and, as if this outrage upon the right of property were not sufficient without the superaddition of insult, the plundered portion of the community are told that those on whom their lands are lavished, are the *best part of the population*. It is said in the message that "the proceeds arising from the sale of the lands are distributed chiefly among States which had not originally any claim to them."—Were this assertion true, what possible bearing can the places where the proceeds of the sale of property are distributed, have upon the right of the proprietor to the proceeds of the sale? The proceeds of the sales of public lands are not distributed in gratuities. What is meant by the assertion that they are distributed among States? They are not distributed among States at all. What is meant by "States which had not originally any claim to them?" What State had originally any claim to the public lands in Louisiana or Florida? What portion of the public lands is there to which the whole Union, and of course every State in the Union, had not originally *a claim*? From the very formation of the confederation, all the States, within which not an inch of public land existed, had a *claim* to their just proportion of the public lands situated within the boundaries of the other States—and that claim was just; in deference to the justice of that claim, all the cessions of public lands were made by the States in which they were situated; and without those cessions, the confederation never would have been formed. The right of the whole people, therefore, to all the public lands, is a perfect right, independent, totally independent, of all consideration of the localities where the proceeds of the sales of them may be distributed, and for the enjoyment of which, as a right founded in the first elements of human society, the States wherein the lands are situated have no more right to be discontented than the tenant of a dwelling house belonging to another has the right to be discontented that the fee of the possession is in his landlord and not in himself.

This right of property is, however, not wholly unqualified. The cessions of territory made to the United States by the States of New York, Virginia, Massachusetts, Connecticut, South Carolina and Georgia, were all conditional; and the common condition of all the grants was, that the lands by them respectively ceded should be held and disposed of for the use and benefit of all the United States, the ceding State included, and for no other use whatsoever. Upon this condition, all the cessions were accepted by the United States in Congress assembled, and the United States thereby contracted the solemn and positive *engagement* to hold and dispose of all the lands thus ceded conformably to that condition, and to no other use whatever.

The Constitution of the United States, in the third section of the fourth article, declares that "Congress shall have power to dispose of, and make all needful rules and regulations respecting the territory or other property belonging to the United States;"

with the express addition that "nothing in this Constitution shall be so construed as to prejudice any claims of the United States, or of any particular State." And in the sixth article, it provides "that all debts contracted and *engagements entered into*, before the adoption of this Constitution, shall be as valid against the United States under this Constitution as under the confederation."

It appears to the subscribers, that Congress could neither give away the public lands to individual settlers, to enable them to acquire independent freeholds, nor surrender them to the States in which they are situated, without a three-fold violation of the Constitution; first, by abdicating the power entrusted to them of disposing of the territory of the United States, conformably to the condition under which it is held, and of making all needful rules and regulations respecting it; secondly, by prejudicing the just and undoubted claims, both of the United States, and of every particular State within which there are no public lands; and, thirdly, by trampling under foot solemn engagements entered into before the adoption of the Constitution. In the list of powers to be exercised by Congress, when the government shall be reduced to the simple machine, avowed to be the purpose of the President by the recommendations of the message, this power of disposing of, and making needful rules and regulations for the territory and other property of the United States, is entirely overlooked; very consistently indeed; for if the whole property should be squandered away to make independent freeholders, or surrendered to the States wherein the common possession happens to be located, there will be no longer any territory belonging to the United States to dispose of, or needing rules and regulations to be prescribed by Congress. The Government will be made a much simpler machine; but it will be a simplicity purchased with all the wealth, all the rights, and all the good faith of the nation—purchased by prejudicing the claims of the United States, and of every State other than those in which the lands are situated—purchased by setting at naught the first principle of justice, the sacred rights of property, and the explicit engagements not only entered into before the adoption of the Constitution, but pledges of faith, without which the confederation itself never would have been sanctioned.

The same principles are applicable to the public lands situated within the States, formed from the territories included in the purchase of Louisiana, and in the Floridas.—These are lands not only belonging to the United States, but purchased with monies from their common treasury. Upon the principles recommended in the message, the whole mass of them may be given away to foreigners, to emigrants from every quarter of the globe, aliens, and perhaps enemies to this country, who may thus be converted into independent freeholders, and constitute, under this improved code of morals, the best part of the population. The subscribers deem it an excellent part of the policy of the Union, to welcome the industry of useful foreign freemen, seeking the enjoyment of liberty and equal rights, and honest subsistence, and the chances of affluence upon our shores; but they conceive it neither politic nor just to bestow upon them, or upon any adventurers, whether of foreign or of domestic birth, the acquisitions of the nation, made with the monies levied upon all the people in all the States.

Congress are told in the message that it cannot be expected that the new States will "remain longer contented with the present policy, after the payment of the public debt." By the present policy is here meant the policy of holding and disposing of the public lands as public property. The proposal is, therefore, to change the present policy, for that of giving away this public property, partly to individual adventurers, and the remainder to the "new States"—one of which is the State of Tennessee. And what are the arguments by which this change of policy, or, in other words, this surrender of property, is urged? It is said that "that adventurous and hardy population of the West, besides contributing their equal share of taxation under our impost system, have, in the progress of our Government, for the lands they occupy, paid into the treasury a large proportion of forty millions of dollars; and, of the revenue received therefrom, but a small part has been expended amongst them." Is this a reason for giving away to new adventurers, or to new States, the property belonging to the adventurous and hardy population of the West, in common with the adventurous and hardy population of all the rest of the Union? To the epithets of adventurous and hardy, applied to the population of the West, the subscribers take no exception, as descriptive of qualities truly belonging to that class of our fellow-citizens: that population went forth from the old and long settled States, from the thirteen confederates of the Revolution, and left behind them a population not less adventurous and hardy than themselves. If the population of the West have contributed their equal share of taxation under our impost system, so have the population of all the rest of the Union. If, in the progress of the Government, they have paid into the treasury a large portion of forty millions of dollars *for the lands they occupy*, they have received, in the *property* of those lands transferred to them by the nation, the value to them of many hundred millions of dollars as an equivalent. That a small part of revenue received from the proceeds of the public lands has been expended amongst them, if estimated in proportion to the relative amount of revenue collected amongst them, may be doubted; but the subscribers believe that justice and policy would alike dictate a larger expenditure of the revenue amongst the population in the West, than has yet been authorized. It is in the Western country that the greatest, the most useful, and the most expensive works of internal improvement have been undertaken, or are most urgently needed. To such works, unquestionably of a national character, the subscribers believe that a full and ample proportion of the public revenue, whether collected from the sales of public lands or from other sources, ought to be applied, and the monies so appropriated would be almost exclusively expended among the population of the West. It is in this manner that, without doing injustice to any other part of the Union, the proceeds of the sales of the public lands may be applied to the special improvement of the Western country; that they may be, beneficially to all, expended among the settlers on the public lands themselves, and, while contributing to the improvement of the whole Union, facilitate and encourage the progress of the new settlements, by furnishing, at once, occupation for industry, reward for labor, and the rapid appreciation of the lands upon which the settlers may fix their abode. Such, the subscribers believe, are the dictates of a policy, at once prudent and magnanimous: but this policy cannot be promoted by arresting the progress of works already commenced; by refusing appropriations for works demonstrated to be of a national character; or by giving away to single adventurers, or to the new States, the whole invaluable fund, inexhaustible if duly managed, for long centuries to come, of lands purchased by the blood of our Revolutionary fathers, and by their treasures or our own.

In this examination of the proposal to *give away* all the public lands of the Union, the subscribers have deemed it their indispensable duty, though a painful one it has been, to resort to the first principles of natural justice, to the sacred right of property, and to the positive injunctions of the Constitution, to prove that it is alike subversive of them all. The project itself is not new: the subscribers are unwilling either to trace its origin, or to scan the motives and purposes from which it proceeded.—But never before have they witnessed—never again, they will hope, may it be seen seriously recommended in a message from the President to the Congress of the United States. The public lands are the property of the Union; the possession, the use, and the disposal of them, for the benefit of the whole, are guarantied by the elementary principle at the foundation of civil society, by the immutable laws of justice, and by the express terms of the Constitution, which we have all sworn to support. The power to give them away has not only never been delegated to Congress, but it has been, by direct implication, prohibited. The attempt to give them away by an act of Congress, would be an act of transcendent usurpation, null and void in itself, and substituting arbitrary power in the place of constitutional right. The attempt to carry it into effect would be a dissolution of the Union—an inextinguishable brand of civil war. This the subscribers do with the profoundest conviction believe; this they cannot, without violating the trust reposed in them by their constituents, refrain from declaring. They solemnly deprecate the contingency that such a proposal should ever again be made.

Congenial with it, and apparently flowing from the same erroneous and partial fundamental principle of government, that the wealthy landholders are the best part of the population, the subscribers are constrained to consider all the recommendations of the message in relation to the manufacturing interest of the country. The spirit of the message looks steadily, though with occasional blenching, to that interest, as *a victim to be sacrificed*. The approaches to the altar are not always direct, but the instrument of death is never sheathed, and the grasp with which it is held is ever intent to strike the blow. As in the principle of limitation to the Congressional power of appropriating money for internal improvement, so, in the restriction of that which may be exercised for the protection of domestic industry, care is taken to commence with a general axiom, which the friends of the manufacturing interest themselves will readily admit. That the revenue of the National Government should be adapted to their expenditures, and that the expenditures should be strictly limited within the sphere of objects warranted by the Constitution, and regulated by a severe and vigilant economy, the most ardent friends of the manufacturers will cheerfully allow. Nor would they deny "that the protection afforded by existing laws to any branches of the national industry should *not exceed* what may be necessary to counteract the regulations of foreign nations, and to secure a supply of those articles of manufacture essential to the national independence and safety in time of war."—If the enunciation of the principle of legitimate protection in these terms discloses a mind in search of reasons for withdrawing the protection secured by existing laws, it is rather in the disposition thus evinced, than in the abstract proposition with which it is clothed, that the manufacturing interest may discern the determined hostility with which it is assailed.

The manufacturer asks for no protection beyond that which may be necessary to counteract the regulations of foreign nations, and to secure a supply of the articles essential to the national safety in time of war. But this protection has been extended to the manufacturing establishments by the existing laws. It has been extended to them, not as a favor to that separate interest, for no such favor has ever been indulged in the legislation of the Union, but for the purpose of counteracting the injury of foreign relations, and for the purpose of securing the supply of articles essential to the national safety in war. The manufacturers of the old and long settled States have been protected from the injurious regulations of foreign nations, as the planters of the South and the settlers of the West have been protected from the depredations and hostile incursions of Indian savages—Nearly the whole charge of the military peace establishment is borne by the nation for the protection of the South and of the West. Of the millions upon millions expended, ever since the existence of the Government, upon Indian wars and negotiations, the manufacturer of Pennsylvania, of New Jersey, and of Massachusetts, has paid and continues to pay, his full proportion. And what is Indian war or Indian negotiation to him? The whole naval establishment of the Union is maintained to *protect* the immediate interest of the commercial part of the community. The manufacturer, the farmer, the planter, have no direct interest in this; they all pay taxes to protect from foreign hostility the property of the merchant and the person of the navigator.—The war last waged with Great Britain, and which cost the nation upwards of a hundred millions of dollars, and perhaps fifty thousand lives, for what was it proclaimed but for wrongs to the merchant and the mariner, in which the manufacturer and the farmer, as distinct classes of society, had not one dollar of interest, yet for the maintenance of which they bore their equal portion of taxation, and devoted their equal portion of lives? The manufacturer of the interior has the same right to the protection of the whole Union against the regulations of foreign countries, as the merchant upon the coast, or the mariner upon the ocean. The manufacturer of the North has the same right to the protection of the nation against the competition of foreign rivals, armed with foreign laws, as the planter of the South, or the settler in the West, has to the same protection against the robberies and butcheries of Indian savages, instigated by the secret impulses and profuse subsidies of the same foreign rivals. The manufacturer asks no more. The principle in the message now under examination is in terms equally applicable to *all* branches of the national industry. The protection afforded by existing laws to the Southern planter and the Western settler, to the merchant and navigator, should *not exceed* what may be necessary to counteract foreign hostility, and secure the national independence and safety. If the separate and exclusive interest of the manufacturer or of the Northern farmer were consulted, the army might be disbanded; the wooden walls of the navy might be laid up in ordinary, and its gallant seamen be discharged from the service. Six or seven millions more of annual expenditure might be retrenched, and the Government be reduced to a machine of still more edifying simplicity—so simple, indeed, as to be left without occupation worthy of the cost of its own maintenance, and bound, in the pursuit of its own policy, to dissolve itself as a useless and cumbersome burden to the nation.

But the practical question of the message is not, what degree of protection ought to be *extended* to any branch of the national industry, but what degree of protection, by the existing laws, it ought *not to exceed*. And the principle is thus laid down by way of introduction, to a recommendation that the *protection* actually granted by the existing laws to a particular interest, namely, that of the manufactures, should be gradually diminished—if, upon investigation, it shall be found, *as it is believed it will be*, that the legislative protection granted to that interest is greater than is *indispensably* requisite for these objects, that is, for counteracting the regulations of foreign nations, and for securing a supply of those articles of manufacture essential to the national independence and safety in time of war.

To this inquiry and investigation the subscribers would interpose no objection whatever, provided that the same investigation shall be instituted to ascertain whether the protection granted by existing laws to other great though partial interests, namely, to the Southern planter and Western settler, to the merchant and the mariner, do not exceed what may be indispensably requisite for counteracting the regulations of foreign nations, and for securing the independence and safety of the nation. The investigation, to be just and impartial, must extend equally to all the interests *protected* by the expenditure of the national revenues; and, if the standard of inquiry shall be the smallest possible amount of *protection* indispensable to the manufacturers, let the same standard, the smallest possible amount indispensable to the planter and the settler, the merchant and the mariner, be applied to the estimates of expenditure to be hereafter bestowed upon them.

But the subscribers cannot forbear to call the attention of the House, and of the nation, to the formal abandonment in the message, of the very principle of just and lawful protection to the manufacturing interest laid down by itself. Scarcely has the circle of limitation been drawn round the unquestionable duty of the Government to protect the manufactures by its laws, when, by a most remarkable instance of self-contradiction, the message abandons its own principle, and substitutes another and a totally different one in its stead. "Those (it now says) who take an enlarged view of the condition of our country, must be satisfied that the policy of protection must be ultimately limited to those articles of domestic manufacture which are indispensable to our safety in time of war." The subscribers will not scrutinize, with logical acuteness, the further limitations, even of this measure, which may be detected in the subsequent qualifications of this diminished standard; nor inquire how the indefiniteness of a "reasonable scale and of a liberal support" can be applied to a list of articles *indispensable* to the safety of the nation. Articles indispensable to the safety of a nation would seem to admit of little latitude in the formation of their catalogue; nor can much commendation be due to the liberality which provides for its own indispensable necessities—but it is to the principle itself that the subscribers deem it their duty to take exception, as utterly inconsistent with that which had been just before laid down; as abandoning the future interests of domestic industry to the mercy of foreign legislation, leagued with foreign competition; and, finally, as consigning all the great manufacturing establishments of the country to speedy and inevitable destruction.

In this last proposition, as in the recommendation to give away all the public lands, the House and the country cannot fail to discern a projected revolution of Government. When the very first act of Congress, after the organization of the new government, that appears upon the statute book of the United States, declared the necessity that duties should be laid on goods, wares, and merchandises imported, the purposes to be accomplished by that act were declared to be the support of Government, the discharge of the debts of the United States, and *the encouragement and protection of manufactures.* Thus from the very foundation of this Government—from the day when George Washington was first inaugurated as President of the United States, the *protection*, aye, and the *encouragement*, of manufactures has formed one of the fundamental objects of the national policy. But here, in the compass of one short page of this message, we are told, first, that the *protection* afforded by *existing laws* to *any* branches of the national industry, should not exceed what may be necessary to counteract the regulations of foreign nations, and to secure a supply of those articles of manufacture essential to the national independence and safety in time of war. This, we are told, is, in justice, due in effecting the adjustment of the future revenue to the interests of the different States and even the preservation of the Union itself. And, in the next breath, we are told that the policy of protection must be ultimately limited to those articles of domestic manufacture which are indispensable to our safety in time of war. The principle of affording *encouragement* to manufactures, proclaimed in the first act of the first Congress, is discarded. The protection to be gradually diminished is the protection of existing laws. The revenue is to be reduced, not merely for adaptation to the necessities of the public expenditures, but with the express object and design of *discouragement* to manufactures, by diminishing the protection which they enjoy; nor is this discouragement to cease, till all the protection which now shields them from the deadly hostility of foreign competitors, dictating the death-warrants of foreign legislation, shall be withdrawn, and the niggardly boon of protection shall be denied to all but articles of indispensable necessity to safety in time of war.

It is, therefore, a revolution in the government which the message now proposes. It is the adoption for the future of a system of policy directly opposite to that with which the administration of Washington laid the foundations of the social existence of this great community—our National and Federal Union. Those foundations were, that *all* the great interests of the nation were *alike* entitled to defence and protection by the national arm, and from the national purse. And to the interest of manufactures was the first pledge of encouragement and protection self-imposed by the good faith of the nation. That pledge is now, by the recommendations of this message, to be withdrawn. The Government is to be reduced to a simple machine, and its operations of superintending beneficence are to be *unfelt*. The great body of the manufacturers, including the numerous classes of mechanics, handicraftsmen, and artificers, and with them great multitudes of cultivators of the soil, though not that best part of the population, the independent freeholders, all the hard working men, in short, the *laboring* part of the exclusively free population of the country, are to be turned out of the paternal mansion, cast off as worthless children of the common parent, and surrendered to the mercy of foreign laws, enacted for the express purpose of feeding foreign mouths with the bread denied by our simplified machine of Government to them.

Under that system of policy, thus now proposed to be abandoned and prescribed, the nation has risen from a depth of weakness, imbecility, and distress, to an eminence of prosperity unexampled in the annals of the world. It has flourished in despite of all foreign competition, and all foreign legislation, whether in peace or at war. It has flourished by the undeviating pursuit of that very policy, which we are now urged to abandon and to proscribe. It was by counter-legislation to the regulations of foreign nations, that the first operations of the Government of the United States were *felt* by their people; *felt*, in the activity given to their commerce—*felt*, in the encouragement and protection extended to their manufactures—felt, in the fulfilment of the public engagements to the creditors of the nation—felt, in the gradual, though the subscribers grieve to say yet imperfect, discharge of the debt of justice and of gratitude due to the warriors of the revolution—felt, in the rapid increase of our population, in the constantly and profitably occupied industry of the people, in the consideration and respect of foreign nations for our character,—in the comfort, and well-being, and happiness of the community—felt in every nerve and sinew, in every vein and artery of the body politic. That for this Government the proposition should now be earnestly pressed upon Congress to substitute another, the supreme excellence of which shall consist in its being *unfelt*, when we look to the source from which the exhortation proceeds, cannot but move our special wonder. The subscribers can have no partiality for a Government, founded upon the consideration that the benefit of its operations shall be *unfelt*.

From the great manufacturing interest of this country, then, and from all the interests, whether agricultural or commercial, indissolubly linked with it, the protection of the national laws now existing, is, so far as they are or may be affected by foreign regulations, by the recommendations of the message, to be gradually withdrawn; and protection is hereafter to be limited to one specific class of articles of manufactures, under the denomination of articles indispensable to the safety of the nation in time of war. The subscribers ask, what is the reason for this distinction; and what are the articles thus to be distinguished with pre-eminent and permanent favor? Why is protection, why is this specific mode of protection, by high and prohibitory duties, upon the article when imported from abroad, to be extended to articles indispensable to the national safety in time of war, when it is at the same time to be denied to all others? The protection of high duties is founded upon the principle of shielding the domestic manufacturer from the ruinous competition of foreigners, producers of the same article. This principle is founded, not upon the nature or uses of the article, but upon the right of the citizen to protection, pledged to him by the social compact, the correlative obligation of his country to him, for his duty and obligation of allegiance to her. Why is the planter of the South, and the new settler of the West, entitled to the protection of the nation, at the cost of many annual millions, to maintain an army to make that protection effective? Why, but because that planter and that settler are bound in allegiance to that country whose protection they are thereby entitled to claim? Why are the merchant, the mariner, the fisherman, entitled to protection, and why is a navy maintained at the cost of annual millions to make that protection effective? Because the merchant, the mariner, the fisherman, owe their allegiance to the country which protects them. This protection is due to them in peace as well as in war; else why do you maintain an army and a navy in time of peace? The manufacturer is entitled to the same protection from his country as the planter, as the new settler, as the merchant, as the mariner, as the fisherman, and for the same reason—because he owes to that country his allegiance. He bears his portion of the burden of expenditures, sustained by the nation to maintain an army and a navy for the protection of interests which are not his. He has a *right* to claim the same protection to his own. It is the *right of the citizen*, and not the necessities of the community, which constitutes the fundamental principle, upon which the obligation to protect the interest of the manufacturer, or of any other member of society, is incumbent upon the nation. The subscribers believe, therefore, that the distinction between articles of manufacture indispensable to the safety of the nation in time of war, and other articles, cannot in any manner affect the right of the manufacturer to protection, or the duty of the

Government to extend it. It is the interest of the citizen and not the wants of the country, which circumscribes the legitimate objects of protection. In the formation of the social compact, undoubtedly the safety and independence of the whole are the ultimate object of every engagement undertaken by the community to protect the interests of every one of its parts; but that safety and independence are to be secured as much by the protection of interests, contributing to her well-being in time of peace, as by that of securing to herself a supply of the instruments of death, necessary for a battle or a siege.

But were the distinction assumed in the message, of discriminating between articles of manufacture indispensable to the safety of the nation in time of war, and other articles, with reference to the respective rights of each of the classes to temporary or permanent protection, just, why is this specific mode of protection, high duties upon the imported article, recommended? If the object to be attained is to secure an abundant supply of the articles, the policy of the Government would seem to be, rather to admit them free of impost, and even to encourage the importation of them by bounties, than to burden them with onerous duties. The articles of most indispensable necessity in time of war, are articles of little or no use in time of peace. The policy of erecting and supporting manufactures of them in time of peace, that is, at a time when, from their very nature, and from the slender demand for them, they must be obtainable from abroad upon the cheapest terms, and when you have little or no demand or use for the articles which you thus deliberately make costly to you beyond all necessity or reason, seems to be exceedingly questionable. You saddle with burdensome taxation articles which you might obtain almost gratuitously from abroad; you tax yourselves to pay enormously dear for articles which you compel yourselves to buy, which you do not want, and for which you have no use, because the time may come when you will want them; and then you choose to have them made by your own citizen, and by no foreigner—when the very tax that you impose, would supply you from abroad with stores of the articles sufficient for a ten years' war, at less cost than you now lavish upon your manufacturer to furnish you the same supply. Again, it may very reasonably be questioned, whether in the present or any possible future condition of this country, and of the rest of the world, any article of domestic manufacture whatever can be essential to the independence or safety of the nation in the sense that it must necessarily be manufactured within the country, and not imported from abroad. Assume the broad principle that the independence and safety of a nation are highly promoted and rendered effective by her possessing within herself all the resources essential to the subsistence, the comfort and the enjoyments of her people in war and in peace, and the subscribers give to it their hearty assent—and from this principle they derive the firm belief that sound policy requires of the nation the constant, perpetual *protection* of the manufacturing interest generally, as the duties of the social compact impose the same protection upon her, as a duty to the citizen manufacturer. Narrow down your protective system to a mere list of contraband of war, and you not only load the nation with burdens utterly useless to herself when she bears them, inadequate to your purpose in the very contingency for which you would provide, but you put to the ban a vast multitude of the free laborers of the country, and involve yourselves in the inextricable absurdity of holding the nation bound to foster and encourage the arts of war, and to prostrate and sacrifice the arts of peace.

The subscribers are then convinced that the principle broadly laid down in the message, "that the policy of protection must be ultimately limited to those articles of domestic manufacture which are indispensable to our safety in time of war," is erroneous and unsound. They remark that this is the first time that such a policy has ever been suggested by any Chief of the Executive Government to Congress, from the establishment of the Constitution to this day, and that it is proposed avowedly to subvert the system of policy which has hitherto invariably prevailed. Alarmed at the violation of rights, and at the desolation of property which it portends in a special manner to the great mass of their constituents, they seek in the message itself the arguments by which this novel plan of government is attempted to be sustained. They are aware that it flows very naturally and directly from the fundamental maxim, that the wealthy landholders, cultivators of the soil, are the best part of the population. That it is entirely congenial to the determined purpose of abolishing the national bank. That it tallies exactly with the proposal to give away all the public lands, to multiply the best part of the population. That it is in perfect coincidence with the proposal to abandon *gradually* all appropriations for internal improvements, to sell all the stocks held by the Government in the funds of incorporated companies, and *then* to reduce the duties of impost to a simple, economical revenue standard.

"All are but parts of one stupendous whole."

And, in carrying out this system to its inevitable consequences, it is apparent that, when all this shall have been done, the same spirit of simplicity and reform will command that the army should be disbanded, because its only use is to protect one portion of the community at the expense of the rest; that the navy should be gradually diminished, and ultimately abolished; because the degree of protection which it extends to the commerce and navigation of the country, may exceed what shall be indispensably necessary to counteract the regulations of foreign powers; and, finally, that the Government of the Union, simplified into a machine of total uselessness and inability to protect any great interest of the nation, should dissolve into its original elements, and vanish—the baseless fabric of a vision.

The subscribers believe that to secure to the nation during war, a supply of *all* the articles necessary to the subsistence, comfort and well being of the people, is *one* of the objects which require and command the protection of manufactures generally, as one of the great duties of the nation to itself. But to limit the policy of protection to the *articles of domestic manufacture* indispensable to our safety in time of war, is tantamount to the denial of all protection to every article excepting those, the want of which, and the uses of which are applicable only to the state of war. Food and raiment are articles indispensable to the safety of a nation in war as well as in peace. If it were meant that all articles of domestic manufacture, serving for food or raiment, should be entitled to the permanent and ultimate protection of the National Government, the limitation itself presented by the message would be nugatory. With that understanding all the manufactures of woollen and of cotton, would have an equal claim to permanent protection with those of iron, lead or copper. The necessities of the nation in time of war, furnish an unanswerable argument for the protection of its manufactures—of all its manufactures in time of peace. This is the sound principle. The attempt to draw a line of distinction between articles indispensable to our safety in time of war, and all other articles, with a view to confer the exclusive privilege of permanent protection upon the former, and to withdraw all protection from the latter, must be utterly deceptive, and, if carried out into practice, could only terminate in gross injustice.

In the report of the Committee of Ways and Means, which accompanied their bill to reduce and otherwise alter the duties on imports, it is said that they have endeavored to arrange the duties with reference to the principle of raising twelve millions and a half of revenue upon from sixty-five to seventy millions of dutiable commodities, at rates from ten to twenty per cent. varying from them chiefly in those instances where national independence in time of war seemed to demand some sacrifice in peace, (as in the case of iron.) Thus iron is the only article specified by the Committee of Ways and Means as entitled to extraordinary and permanent protection, by heavy duties of impost, to defend the article of domestic production from the competition of importation from abroad—and the exemplification in their bill is, to shield the article of iron by duties five or six times heavier than the fragment of impost to which they abandon the articles of wool, woollens, and cotton fabrics. But this favoritism extended to articles of iron, is founded upon a misapplication of the principle upon which it professes to rely. The only reason which makes it an object of importance to the nation, to possess within itself a supply of articles of exclusive use and necessity in times and for purposes of war, is because the supply of those articles from abroad, in time of war, may be cut off or greatly obstructed by the power of the enemy. Of all other articles, the supply may be as abundant from abroad in time of war, by the conveyance of neutral flags, as in time of peace. The articles usually denominated contraband of war, may be intercepted by the enemy, and cannot be protected by the neutral flag. The list of these articles of contraband is usually regulated by treaties. The number of them, as recognized by the customary law of nations, independent of treaty stipulations, is very unsettled. Great Britain being almost always a belligerent nation, and possessed of preponderating power upon the ocean, has, in latter times, constantly struggled to enlarge the list, by including in it not merely the fabricated instruments of warlike destruction, such as cannon, muskets, swords, pikes, bombs, grenades, and the like, but provisions, and the materials especially for shipbuilding. All the other maritime nations, on their part, endeavor to contract the list of contraband, and confine it to articles actually wrought and manufactured, and used only and exclusively for war. We have had treaties both with France and Great Britain, each containing a list of articles to be understood between the parties as contraband of war. The treaties with France contain the most contracted, and the treaty of 19th November, 1794, with Great Britain, the largest list of contraband that has ever been claimed by modern belligerent nations; and it so happens that, in both these treaties, unwrought iron is expressly excluded from the list of contraband. No nation has ever pretended that it was or should be included in that list. The supply of it from abroad cannot, therefore, be intercepted by the enemy in time of war, and there is no reason whatever for protecting by high duties the domestic production of it against the foreign competitor, other than the reason common to all other articles or productions of domestic industry. It stands upon the same footing with all the rest, and has no claim whatever to superior protection, from its being merely the principal material from which the instruments of death are composed. It is, therefore, extreme injustice to all other articles of domestic growth or manufacture, to withdraw from them their just share of protection, to heap it upon the solitary article of iron.

The subscribers, therefore, believe that the principle itself advanced in the message, and illustrated by the recommendation gradually to withdraw from the manufactures of the country all the protection which they enjoy by the existing laws of the United States, with the single exception of the articles indispensably necessary for the national independence and safety in time of war, is incorrect, unjust, and unconstitutional. They believe that protection, permanent protection, to the interest of domestic industry, including agriculture, manufactures, and the mechanic arts, is a right secured to the citizens whose property and subsistence depend upon that protection, *by the Constitution itself, as well as by the laws*—that the withdrawal from them of that protection, would be the denial to them of a constitutional right, and equivalent to a sentence of banishment upon them. In saying this, the subscribers do not deny the right of the Government to modify this protection by an adjustment of the revenue to the necessary public expenditures. They object neither to the reduction of the revenue, nor to the reduction of duties of imposts; both these operations may be effected without impairing the protection enjoyed by domestic industry, and they are precisely the operations which it is at this time the duty of the Government of the United States to perform.

The recommendation of the message, gradually to withdraw from the manufactures the protection which they enjoy by existing laws, appears to the subscribers the more exceptionable, as it obviously countenances the principles asserted, as well as the attitude assumed of hostility to the manufacturing interest, and of defiance to the Government of the Union, under the shield of State sovereignty, by popular commotion in one of the members of the Union. Before the message was delivered, a convention, assuming to represent the people of South Carolina and to exercise, in their name, an absolute, unlimited, and, therefore, despotic power of sovereignty, had issued an ordinance, declaring and *ordaining* that all the several acts and parts of acts of the Congress of the United States, for imposing duties and imposts on the importation of foreign commodities, *and now having actual operation and effect within the United States*, were null, void, and no law, nor binding upon the State of South Carolina, its officers or citizens.

And the same convention, by the same ordinance had ordained that all promises, *contracts*, and obligations, made or entered into, or to be made or entered into, with purpose to secure the duties imposed by the said acts, and all judicial proceedings which should be thereafter had in affirmance thereof, were, and should be, held utterly null and void.

The same convention had further ordained that it should not be lawful for any of the constituted authorities whether of the State of South Carolina, or of the United States, to enforce the payment of duties imposed by the said acts of Congress within the limits of that State; that it should be the duty of the Legislature to adopt such measures, and pass such acts, as might be necessary to *prevent the enforcement and arrest the operation* of the said acts, and parts of acts, of the Congress of the United States, within the limits of that State, from and after the first day of February then next.

The same convention had further ordained that all the officers of the State, civil or military, except members of the Legislature, should take an oath to obey, execute, and enforce the said ordinance, and such act or acts of the Legislature as *might* be passed in pursuance thereof; that the offices of every individual who should omit or neglect to take this oath, should be, thereby, *ipso facto*, vacated; and that no juror should be empanelled in any of the courts of the State, in any cause in which should be in question the ordinance, or any act of the Legislature passed in pursuance thereof, unless he should, first, in addition to the usual oath, have taken an oath to obey, execute, and enforce the ordinance, and all acts of the Legislature to carry the same into operation and effect.

And the same convention, speaking as the people of South Carolina, further declared, that they would consider any act on the part of the Federal Government to enforce the laws thus nullified, *otherwise than through the civil tribunals of the country*, as inconsistent with the longer continuance of South Carolina in the Union; that they would thenceforth hold themselves absolved from all further obligation to maintain or preserve their political connexion with the people of the other States, and would forthwith proceed to organize a separate Government, and do all acts and things which sovereign and independent States might of right do.

This ordinance was issued bearing date the 24th day of November. Ten days after which, on the 4th of December, the message of the President, after noticing that, in one quarter of the United States, opposition to the revenue laws had risen to a height which threatened to thwart the execution, if not to endanger the integrity of the Union, observes, that whatever obstructions may be thrown in the way of the judicial authorities of the General Government, it was hoped they would be able, peaceably, to overcome them by the prudence of their own officers, and the patriotism of the people. But that, should this reasonable hope be disappointed, it was believed the laws themselves were fully adequate to the suppression of such attempts as might be immediately made; and that, should the exigency arise, rendering the execution of the existing laws impracticable, from any cause whatever, prompt notice of it would be given to Congress, with the suggestion of such views and measures as might be necessary to meet it.

The subscribers could not but observe with concern and surprise, that, in a message delivered at a time when the above mentioned ordinance of the South Carolina convention had been ten days issued, and when its contents had been several days fully known in this city, the condition of things, and the opposition to the execution of the laws of the United States, in the State of South Carolina, was described in terms so inadequate, as appeared to them, to the real magnitude of the crisis in the affairs of the Union. A document purporting to be the act of the sovereign people of South Carolina—an act of sovereignty so transcendent, as to speak in the language of command to the Legislature of the State, as to prescribe oaths to be taken by the existing officers, civil and military, of the State, on the penalty of forfeiting their offices—an act of an authority, spurning, as beneath it, the ties of morality, and assuming to annul, existing promises, contracts, and obligations—an act, first depriving the civil tribunals, both of the State and of the United States, of the power of performing their judicial functions, and then declaring that the first effort of the Federal Government to enforce the laws of the Union, otherwise than through the judicial tribunals, should be the signal to the State of South Carolina for dissolving her connexion with this Union, and forming a separate Government—this act, accompanied with addresses to the people of the State, and of the other twenty-three States, declaring that it was the fixed and unalterable determination of the people of South Carolina never more to submit to a protecting tariff, must have been in the possession of the President at the time when his message was communicated to the two Houses of Congress. Only six days after the delivery of this annual message, the proclamation, emanating from the same source, was published to the world, founded, as appears on its face, upon the ordinance alone, which had thus been in the President's possession before the message was sent to Congress. It would seem that the recommendations of the message were so nearly identical with the terms condescendingly proposed as a concession by the authors of the ordinance for the future revenue system of the Union, which South Carolina would graciously consent to prescribe, that an expectation was entertained that, on the receipt of the message in South Carolina, the nullifying ordinance would immediately be abrogated. And, indeed, upon an attentive comparison of the recommendations of the Chief Magistrate with the autocratic concessions of the South Carolina nullifying convention, there will be found between them a shade of difference so nearly imperceptible, that this expectation was not destitute of foundation. To the subscribers, this affords but a source of deeper mortification, upon perceiving that formal recommendation in the message of a gradual, and, ultimately, total withdrawal of all legislative protection from all the manufactures of the country, excepting only those articles indispensably necessary to the safety and independence of the nation in time of war; an exception so strangely expounded in the report and bill of the Committee of Ways and Means, to mean *unwrought iron*.

The proclamation did, indeed, take a direct and formal issue with the nullifying convention, upon both the articles of fundamental law, by virtue of which, that assemblage asserted their right to exercise sovereign despotic authority in the name of the people of South Carolina. The proclamation denied the right of the people of South Carolina to nullify the laws of the United States. It denied the right of the State of South Carolina to secede from that Union to which the people and State of South Carolina, by the pledge of their lives, their fortunes, and their sacred honor, in the Declaration of Independence, and by their own solemn accession to the Constitution of the United States, had bound themselves and their good faith, in the face of God and man. To both these principles of the proclamation, the subscribers assent and adhere; and the clear and indisputable consequence from them is, that the South Carolina convention was an unlawful and unconstitutional assembly, and their ordinance an unlawful and unconstitutional act—null and void in itself, and the enforcement of which, by physical power, would be levying war against the United States.

The duties incumbent upon the President of the United States in this emergency, and the deep responsibility by which he is bound to the performance of them, are fully and unequivocally set forth in the proclamation. The sense of those duties was profoundly impressed upon the mind of its author. The subscribers deem it altogether unnecessary, and irrelevant to the present state of this country, to inquire by whom or when, or for what purpose, the absurd doctrines of nullification and secession were first gotten up and promulgated. They well know that those doctrines never can be carried out in practice, but by a dissolution of the Union. The consummation of either of them must in itself, be a dissolution of the Union. If any organized power, under any circumstances whatever, in any one State, can nullify the laws of Congress, then has the Union no legislative, and consequently no judicial or executive power. The Government is *ipso facto* dissolved, and the Union must crumble to atoms with it. If any one State can at its pleasure secede from the Union, every other State must possess the same power; and the Constitution of the United States, instead of being a compact ordained and established by the people, to secure to them and *their posterity* the blessings of liberty, is but a partnership of corporate bodies without posterity, without soul, without faith, and ready to trample under foot, as is done by the ordinance of the South Carolina convention, its own promises, contracts, and obligations, as well as those of others, or the laws of the land. Resistance against certain laws of the United States, even under the authority of single State Governments, has more than once been attempted. The doctrines of nullification and secession have more than once been asserted or countenanced by resolutions of particular State Legislatures; but this is the first example since the establishment of the Constitution, when a formal organization of the power of the people of a State has been accomplished, not only for the avowed purpose of resisting the laws of Congress, but of annihilating the whole system of revenue laws, of dictating to the whole Union a new fiscal code, and of interdicting with a sentence of outlawry the *protection* secured by the Constitution and the laws to at least one-third part of the people.

The subscribers cannot but lament that the President of the United States, with this ordinance in his hand, with a full knowledge of its whole import, and with a thorough conviction of the duties which it devolved upon him, in defence of the Constitution and laws of the Union, should, by the whole tenor of his annual message, and especially by the recommendation gradually to withdraw from the manufacturing establishments the *protection* which they enjoy by the existing laws, have given so much countenance and encouragement to the most unjust claims and most groundless pretensions of the South Carolina convention.

There is an aspect in which this controversy must be considered, and in which the subscribers believe it was peculiarly incumbent on the President as the Chief Magistrate of the whole people, to withhold all countenance or shadow of support from those pretensions.

The foundation of the complaints alleged by the South Carolina convention as the justifying cause of their extraordinary proceedings, is a collision of *sectional* interests between the slave-holding and the exclusively free portions of the Union. The allegation is, that the protection extended to domestic industry, by the imposition of duties upon the productions of the like industry imported from abroad, necessarily operates to produce inequality in the burden of taxation upon the free and upon the slave-holding portions of the people, to the disadvantage and oppression of the latter: that whatever of taxation is levied by impost upon manufactures and free labor, is more than repaid by this *protection*; that it becomes thereby their interest to increase the protecting duties instead of reducing them; and that, as the labor of slaves cannot be applied to manufactures, and as the agricultural products of the South derive no benefit from this protection, the ultimate result of the impost system is to make it at once a tax upon the slave-holder of the South, and a bounty to the free laborer of the North.

This statement of the case presents two prominent points of consideration. The foundation of the argument is an irreconcilable opposition of *interests* between two of the great masses of population constituting the Union.

1. This opposition of interests is *geographical*, the division line being that between the States where the population is entirely free, and those where the population consists of masters and slaves; the divisions are of North and South.

2. It is an opposition of interests between *servile* and *free labor.*

The subscribers believe these positions to be very far from correct; but they deem it not necessary to discuss them here; they are the positions upon which the whole system of the proceedings of South Carolina is founded, and as such they must be considered.

It cannot be denied that in a community spreading over a large extent of territory, and politically founded upon the principles proclaimed in the Declaration of Independence, but differing so widely in the elements of their social condition, that the inhabitants of one half the territory are wholly free, and those of the other half divided into masters and slaves, deep, if not irreconcilable collisions of interest must abound. The question whether such a community can exist under one common Government, is a subject of profound, philosophical speculation in theory. Whether it can continue long to exist, is a question to be solved only by the experiment now making by the people of this Union, under that national compact, the Constitution of the United States.

At the formation of the Constitution itself, these collisions of interest presented themselves at the threshold. No sooner was the representation of the people in the popular branch of the Legislature to be adjusted, than it arose. It is one of the first principles of republican freedom, that the representation of the people should be proportioned to their *numbers*. It is another, that the taxation of the people should be proportioned to their numbers and their property. But here was a community, one half of whom held it for a principle that all popular representation should be proportioned to the numbers of the people, while the other half held a third part of their own numbers as the property of the other two thirds. They claimed, therefore, that in the popular branch of the Legislature, *they* should be privileged with a representation, not only of their numbers, but of their property—of their living machinery.

Here was a great, and, it would seem, an irreconcilable collision of interests between the aggregate parties to the compact under deliberation. How was it adjusted? By concession from the northern and wholly free States. They consented, that while in this hall, in the popular branch of the Legislature, they themselves should have a representation proportioned only to their numbers, the slave-holders of the South should, in addition to their proportional numbers, have a representation here for three fifths of their living property—of their machinery. What was the equivalent for this concession? A provision that *direct* taxation should be levied under this constitution, in the same compound proportion of numbers in the free, and of numbers and property in the slave-holding States.

The basis of this compromise between great conflicting interests was, that the proportion of representation in the popular branch of the Legislature, and the proportional burden of *direct* taxation, should be greater in the southern than in the northern, or, in other words, greater in the slave-holding than in the free States. Such was the compromise in principle; how has it operated in practice?

The representation of the slave population in this House has, from the establishment of the Constitution of the United States, amounted to rather more than one tenth of the whole number. In the present Congress, it is equivalent to twenty-two votes; in the next Congress, it will amount to twenty-five. This is a combined and concentrated power, always operating to the support and exclusive favor of the slave-holding interest, and against that northern free interest which is protected by the duties of impost. This privilege of representation for property has been always enjoyed by the slave-holding States, from the establishment of the Constitution to this day; and they will continue to enjoy it as long as the Constitution shall remain in force. But it was not enjoyed by them under the confederation, nor can they ever enjoy it under any confederation of States. But while their enjoyment of the privilege under the Constitution is constant and unremitting, the correlative and equivalent privilege of lighter direct taxation has been effective to the free States only twice, and for very short periods, in the forty-five years that the Constitution has existed. The history of the Union has afforded a continual proof that this representation of property, which they enjoy, as well in the election of President and Vice President of the United States, as upon the floor of the House of Representatives, has secured to the slave-holding States the entire control of the national policy, and, almost without exception, the possession of the highest executive office in the Union. Always united in the purpose of regulating the affairs of the whole Union by the standard of the slave-holding interest, their disproportionate numbers in the electoral colleges have enabled them, in ten out of twelve quadrennial elections, to confer the Chief Magistracy upon one of their own citizens. Their suffrages at every election, without exception, have been almost exclusively confined to a candidate of their own caste. Availing themselves of the divisions which, from the nature of man, always prevail in communities entirely free, they have sought and found auxiliaries in the other quarter of the Union, by associating the passions of parties, and the ambition of individuals, with their own purposes, to establish and maintain throughout the confederated nation the slave-holding policy. The office of Vice President, a station of high dignity, but of little other than contingent power, had been usually, by their indulgence, conceded to a citizen of the other section; but even this political courtesy was superseded at the election before the last, and both the offices of President and Vice President of the United States were, by the preponderancy of slave-holding votes, bestowed upon citizens of two adjoining and both slave-holding States. At this moment, the President of the United States, the President of the Senate, the Speaker of the House of Representatives, and the Chief Justice of the United States, are all citizens of that favored portion of the united republic. The last of these offices, being, under the Constitution, held by the tenure of good behavior, has been honored and dignified by the occupation of the present incumbent upwards of thirty years. An overruling sense of the high responsibilities under which it is held, has effectually guarded him from permitting the sectional slave-holding spirit to ascend the tribunal of justice; and it is not difficult to discern, in this inflexible impartiality, the source of the obloquy which that same spirit has not been inactive in attempting to excite against the Supreme Court of the United States itself, and of the insuperable aversion of the votaries of nullification to encounter or abide by the decision of that tribunal, the true and legitimate umpire of constitutional, controverted law.

The disproportionate numbers of the slave-holding representation in the House of Representatives have secured to it the absolute control of the general policy of the Government, and especially over the fiscal system, the revenues and expenditures of the nation. At the first establishment of the Government, it was the slave-holding interest which dictated the principle that the public revenues should be raised, not by direct taxes, but by impost. Had direct taxation been resorted to, the very letter of the Constitution prescribed that a heavier burden of it should fall upon them than upon the States where no slaves existed. The selection of impost, as the exclusive mode of taxation for raising revenue, was made and dictated by them, and for their special benefit. But they were then willing that, in raising the revenue, some protection should be extended to domestic industry. It had not occurred to them yet, that, by their disproportionate numbers in the popular branch of the Legislature, they could exclude all the free labor of the country entirely from the protection of the law.

Under that protection, the industry of freedom has thriven and flourished. Often checked and retarded by that preponderating system of policy which the slave-holding interest, by its disproportionate representation in the General Government, was always enabled to prescribe, and to which the labor of the free was compelled to submit, a right to *some* protection, under the compact of constitutional union, had never been denied to it. Sparingly, scantily, and grudgingly as it was dispensed, still the right to protection was conceded; and, in the raising of the revenue, actual protection was, to some degree, yielded. Free labor received its reward; but its prosperity never exceeded that of the slave-holder, nor was the protection which it enjoyed ever equal or comparable to that secured to the slave-holding interest, both by the Constitution and the laws.

In this condition of the common country, with the slave-holding interest in possession of all the highest offices of dignity and power, legislative, executive, and judicial, a discovery is suddenly made in South Carolina—the only State of the Union in which the slave population largely outnumbers the free, and where, consequently, six tenths of the people are the property of the other four tenths—there it is that the discovery bursts upon the nation, that duties of impost, levied for the *protection* of free labor, are unconstitutional; that domestic industry has no right to the *protection* of existing laws; and that *all* the revenue laws are palpable violations of the Constitution of the United States. Upon the heel of this discovery comes immediately the fixed and irrevocable determination, that free labor shall no longer and *never more* enjoy this protection of the law. And how is this determination carried into effect? A convention of the people—that is to say, of rather more than one half the four tenths of the owners of the rest—a convention, representing, at the utmost, one hundred and fifty thousand souls, and, of course, less in number than three fourths of the single city of New York, is assembled—itself unconstitutionally constituted, and assembled in defiance of the fundamental laws both of the Union and of the State. It assumes, in the broad face of day, the exercise of absolute, despotic, irresistible, uncontrollable power; nullifies the whole code of revenue laws of the United States; dissolves *contracts, promises, obligations*, sanctioned by solemn appeals to God; prescribes oaths, as abhorrent to the pure intelligence of the Being invoked to attest them, as to the souls of those upon whom they are imposed; declares the people of South Carolina absolved from all their ties of allegiance and fidelity to *their country;* annihilates the judicial tribunals of the Union within the State; and then declares that, if an attempt is made to execute the laws of the Union, otherwise than through those annihilated tribunals, South Carolina will secede from that Union to which her fathers pledged their lives, their fortunes, and their sacred honor: from that Union she will secede, and constitute herself a supreme, sovereign, feudal, dominion of despotic, irresistible, and uncontrollable power. Since the attempt of the Titans to scale the throne of Heaven, so bold an enterprise was never conceived. Since the project of the builders on the plain of Shinar to make themselves a name, lest they should be scattered abroad upon the whole earth, so gallant an exploit was never undertaken. And it was this moment, when rebellion was stalking forth under the worse than Gorgon shield of State sovereignty, that the President of the United States chose, for recommending to the insulted, vilified, and contemned legislative authority of the Union, tamely to yield, in substance, to this overbearing pretension, and gradually to withdraw from the manufacturing establishments, with some vague and indefinite exceptions, the whole protection of the existing *laws*.

It has been seen that by the Constitution of the United States, the right of representation in the popular branch of the

Legislature, and in the colleges of Electors to the offices of President and Vice President of the United States, is unequally divided between the Northern and Southern, or, in other words, the free and the slave-holding States; that while the free States are represented only according to their numbers, the slave-holders are represented also for their property; and that the equivalent for this privilege is, that they shall bear in like manner a heavier burden of all direct taxation. That by the ascendancy which their excess of representation gives them in the enactment of the laws, they have invariably, in times of peace, excluded all direct taxation, and thereby enjoyed their excess of representation, without any equivalent whatever. This is, in substance, an evasion of the bilateral provision in the Constitution. It is a privilege of the Southern and slave-holding sections of the Union, without any equivalent to the Northern and North-western freemen whatever.

It is not a little extraordinary that this new pretension of South Carolina, the State which above all others enjoys this unrequited privilege of excessive representation, released from all payment of the direct taxes, of which her proportion would be nearly double that of any non-slave-holding State, should proceed from that very complaint that she bears an unequal proportion of duties of imposts, which, by the Constitution of the United States, are required to be uniform throughout the Union. Vermont, with a free population of 280,000 souls, has five representatives in the popular House of Congress, and seven electors for President and Vice President. South Carolina, with a free population of less than 260,000 souls, sends nine members to the House of Representatives, and honors the Governor of Virginia with eleven votes for the office of President of the United States. If the rule of representation were the same for South Carolina and for Vermont, they would have the same number of Representatives in the House, and the same number of Electors for the choice of President and Vice President. She has nearly double the number of both. Were a direct tax now to be levied, to which South Carolina herself could not object as unconstitutional, her proportion of it must be just as nearly double that of Vermont, as is the number of her members in the House of Representatives. If, by the *protection* to her farmers, and mechanics, and manufacturers, against the competition of foreign labor, armed with foreign legislation, the men of the Green mountains find brisker markets for the productions of their toil, if their mountains themselves are clad in a fresher and more perennial verdure; if the very face of nature upon her soil gladdens with the hue of hope, and the smile of joy, at the beneficence of their government, acting in auxiliary subserviency to the beneficence of Heaven, while the slave-holder of South Carolina cannot derive so much benefit from the protection of man, because his industry is not his own, and all his profits must be earned by the sweat of another's brow, is this a reason to justify him for tearing to pieces the charter of national freedom by which he is bound to the freemen of Vermont? By the letter of that fundamental compact, his power in the enactment of the laws, to be binding upon both, is nearly twice that of the mountaineer. By the letter of that compact too, were the revenues of the whole community to be levied by *direct* taxation, his share of contribution must be nearly doubled. With what pretence of reason, therefore, can he complain of a slight inequality bearing upon him; not by the burden of the impost, which is every where the same, but by the primeval curse of Omnipotence upon slavery, denying to him the remote and contingent advantage which the free laborer of Vermont derives from the protection of the laws?

The subscribers believe, therefore, that the ground assumed by the South Carolina convention for usurping the sovereign and limitless power of the people of that State, to dictate the laws of the Union, and prostrate the legislative, executive, and judicial authority of the United States, is as destitute of foundation as the forms and substance of their proceedings are arrogant, overbearing, tyrannical, and oppressive: they believe that one particle of compromise with that usurped power, or of concession to its pretensions, would be a heavy calamity to the people of the whole Union, and to none more than to the people of South Carolina themselves. That such concession by Congress would be a dereliction of the highest duties to their country, and directly lead to the final and irretrievable dissolution of the Union.

That the President of the United States has a deep and just sense of the solemn duties devolving upon him in this great emergency, the subscribers have seen with great and most sincere satisfaction, by his proclamation, and by his message to

Congress communicating that document, and others issued from the Executive Department, together with those emanating from the disorganizing faction in South Carolina. It only remains for him to suit the action to the word. Bound by his official oath to take care that the laws shall be faithfully executed, those laws have armed him with ample power to discharge that duty so long as the execution of the laws shall meet with no resistance by force. Even that resistance also, he has not been left without means, lawful means, to overpower and subdue. If other means be necessary or expedient, it is the duty of the Legislature to invest him with them. But with the usurpations of the South Carolina convention there can be no possible compromise. They must conquer or they must fall.

The subscribers are the more deeply impressed with the conviction that no compromise can be authorised or permitted with the insurrectionary spirit of the documents from South Carolina, because they consider them utterly incompatible with the principles of Republican Government, and because they believe with equal confidence, that if met with open front and unyielding energy, there is nothing in this array of rebellion in the slightest degree dangerous, they will not say to the existence, but even to the peace and tranquillity of the Union. For a conflict of physical force, which may God in his mercy forbid, but should it unhappily ensue, the parties to it are one hundred and fifty thousand, at the utmost, strong on one side, and ten millions on the other. But the Ordinance of nullification itself, and all the other State papers of this new sovereignty in embryo, professedly disclaim all purpose or intention of resorting to physical force, unless in self defence. If, in the spirit of County Court litigation, they can by quibbles and quillets of the law, entangle the justice of the Union in a net of subtleties, by capiases, replevins, and withernams; if by imposing unhallowed and detested oaths upon their own citizens, in violation of their allegiance and obligations to their country—if by enjoining upon them under heavy penalties, fraud, perjury, the breach of their own promises, contracts, and obligations, and the forfeiture of all their civic duties as American freemen, if by all these ingenious and peaceable devices the collection of the revenues of the United States within the State of South Carolina, can be practically and permanently frustrated, the purpose of nullification is accomplished; she asks no more; she draws no sword; she faints at the very sight of blood; she thinks "the SOVEREIGN'ST thing on earth

> Is parmacity for an inward bruise,"

and as a *sovereign* State, she will administer nothing but parmacity to heal the inward bruises of the Constitution. From the principles announced by the President in his proclamation, and in his recent message, and from all the measures of the Government yet adopted in preparation for this exigency there is no reason to apprehend that force will, in the first instance, be used on the part of the United States. The determination not to yield, is a spirit passive in its nature until aggression provokes it to action. It endures until summoned to resistance in self defence. In the collision of exasperated passions, it is the temper of aggression that always strikes the first blow. Nullification, in assuming the attitude of self-defence, denies its own nature: it is essentially aggressive, and will assuredly find that it can never accomplish its purpose but by hostile action. So long as it stays its hand, however, the laws of the Union will have their execution. The executive minister of the law performs his duty until met by the resistance of physical force, and until then the thunder of the ordinance is but a *brutum fulmen*. Let the Government of the Union, in all its branches, manifest the pure, unaggressive, but firm and inflexible temper of self-defence, and nullification will vanish like a noxious exhalation before the morning sun.

By the Constitution of the United States, it is provided that the United States, shall guaranty to every State in this Union a Republican form of Government. The subscribers believe with one of the most eminent and virtuous citizens of South Carolina,* that Republican Government in that State, ceased, with the ordinance of Nullification. It ceased, as he says, "in spirit and in truth." It ceased even in form; Government is the enactment and administration of laws, or it is a dominion of arbitrary power—Republican Government is a Government of laws. The Government by Will, is not Republican Government.

* Thomas S. Grimke.

The Constitutions of several of the States, expressly declare the intent of their institution to be, to establish a Government of laws and not of men. In these United States, the people, although the true and legitimate source of all political power, have never exercised the powers of Government themselves. They delegate power by Constitutions of Government, all under strict limitations to secure the rights of the citizen from the oppression of arbitrary power. Under these constitutions the legislative, the executive, and the judicial powers are separated from each other, a separation without which, some of them expressly declare, and all tacitly recognize that there can be no enjoyment of liberty. They entrust the power of legislation to two co-ordinate assemblies of men, each operating as a check upon the other, and generally under the further check of a qualified negative in the Chief Executive Magistrate. Such is the Constitution of the United States. Such is the Constitution of the state of South Carolina. These Constitutions are the fundamental laws of the land, protective of the rights of every individual citizen. Under this protection, a convention is assembled, representing a part of the people of South Carolina, but assuming to represent them all—acknowledging no law; affecting the exercise of absolute, irresistible, uncontrollable power, and issues an Ordinance annulling the Constitution & Laws of the United States within the State of South Carolina, commanding the legislature of the State to enact laws in violation of the Constitution of the State; absolving the citizens of the State from the fulfilment of their promises, contracts, and obligations; and imposing upon them oaths, which they cannot take without giving the lie to their consciences in the face of God. The convention which issued this Ordinance has an existence authorized by the Legislature, for a whole year. After giving out this memorable Ordinance, it adjourns, to meet again at the convocation of the President. Upon the principles which it assumes as the rule of action for itself, it is invested with the whole *sovereign* power of the people of South Carolina, subject to no limitation but that of time, and that extending to a whole year. During all that period, its authority is paramount to that of the Legislature, to the Constitution of the State, to the Constitution of the United States. It possesses the whole power of the people, legislative, executive, judicial; it may constitute itself a tribunal for the trial of offenders against any ordinance which it may ordain; it may pass sentence of death upon any such offender; it may erect within its hall a guillotine or a gibbet, and execute its own sentences by the hand of its own President. It has passed a law, not only impairing, but nullifying in express terms, the obligation of contracts: it may, by the same sovereign power, pass bills of attainder, ex post facto laws: it may proscribe the freedom of the press, the freedom of speech, the freedom of conscience: it may establish a religion, and religious inquisition: it may grant titles of nobility: and lastly, it may invest all these powers in its President, to have, and to hold, and to exercise, to him and the heirs of his body forever. To say that they will not exercise these powers is only to say that they will not thus abuse the power which they claim to possess. It is pure unadulterated despotism: despotism in a single assembly, superseding the protection of the Constitution and the Laws, guaranteed by the United States to every State in the Union, and to all its citizens. During the existence of that convention, the Government of South Carolina is not republican. It has no Government. It is under the rule of an organized anarchy, with a nominal legislature subordinate to a lawless assemblage of tyrants, calling themselves the people of South Carolina.

It must especially not be forgotten that among the implied, necessarily implied powers, claimed by this Convention, is that of enacting laws for the United States—laws paramount even to the Constitution of the United States. To repeal a law is to enact a law—to nullify a law is an act of more transcendent authority. The power competent to repeal is competent to enact a law. To nullify a law is an act of superior and paramount authority. The Ordinance of South Carolina, nullifying in words only within the limits of that State, the whole code of revenue laws of the United States, assumes, in fact, the authority of repealing that whole code throughout the United States. It legislates for the whole Union. Submission to it for one instant would recognize an appellate power of legislation, co-extensive with the whole Union, in every one of its States. To call such a system Anarchy, would be to give it too mild a name. It is usurpation of the most odious character—usurpation of one State over the laws of twenty-three, and brands the State itself as well as the individuals by whom the absurd pretension is raised, with the indelible character of "close ambition varnished o'er with zeal."

From these pretensions the state of South Carolina must desist. The subscribers have no doubt that unless encouraged to persevere in them by some faltering or weakness of concession on the part of the government of the United States, she will desist from them, and thereby redeem herself from the obloquy of a desperate struggle to subdue the whole family of her sisters under the dominion of her own ungovernable will. She must resume her seat in the family circle, from which she has so unadvisedly started, and submit to the laws which she shared in establishing, until she can persuade her associated equals to concur with her in repealing them. Of this result the subscribers entertain not the slightest doubt, if the clear and indisputable rights of the whole Union shall be maintained with becoming perseverance and fortitude by the government of the United States.

But the subscribers have seen with deep regret that the Message upon which it has been their indispensable duty to animadvert, does in its whole purport relating to the administration of the internal affairs of the nation, and most especially in the recommendation to Congress gradually to withdraw from the manufacturing establishments of the country, with a vague and indefinite exception, the whole protection of the existing laws, give an alarming encouragement, not only to the unwarrantable proceedings of the South Carolina Convention, but to the most extravagant doctrines and outrages of nullification. Connected with the other effective recommendations to abandon all further purposes of national internal improvement, and all future revenues from the public lands, with the hand of Ruin raised against credit and currency, in the denunciations of the Bank of the United States, and, at the root of all, the proclamation of the principle that the wealthy landholders, or, in other words, the slaveholding planters of the South, constitute the *best part* of the national population, they can perceive nothing other than a complete system of future Government for this Union directly tending to its dissolution—a system totally adverse to that which has prevailed since the establishment of the Constitution, till the day of the delivery of the Message—a system altogether sectional in its character, wasteful of the property of the nation, destructive to its commerce, withering to its future improvement, blasting to the manufactures and agriculture of two thirds of the States, and looking in its ultimate results to sacrifice the labor of the free to pamper with bloated profits the owner of the slave.

The admission in the Message, that the laws for the raising of revenue by imposts have been in their operation unequal and oppressive upon the South, the subscribers believe to be utterly without foundation. They have proved that by the Constitution of the United States the principle is expressly recognized, that as an equivalent for the privilege of slave representation in the Legislature and the Electoral Colleges, the slaveholders should bear an additional and proportional burden of all *direct* taxation. It may be that under any possible system of taxation, the owner of slaves may feel the burdens of it more heavily than the free man, because he must pay the taxes of his slave as well as his own. All taxation is an assessment upon property—all just taxation bears some proportion to the property of the party taxed. If the rich pays a larger tax than the poor, it is not therefore a tax unequal and oppressive upon the rich. The unequal tax is that which exacts from the poor the same amount of contribution as from the rich. There are, to speak in round numbers, two millions of slaves in this Union. At the average value of three hundred dollars a head, they constitute a mass of six hundred millions of dollars of *property,* all owned in the slaveholding States, who possess, or may if they please possess, all other kinds of property which *can* be held in the States where slavery is exploded. The slaveholders, therefore, are, as respects the whole Union, the rich, and the freemen of the other States are the poor, of the community. The slaveholders own six hundred millions of dollars worth of wealth more than the inhabitants of the wholly free States. And this property is self-productive. It is no breed of barren metal, but a breed of living value—a breed of flesh and blood, of bone and sinew, of productive and profitable labor. Its owners hold it not only as individual property, but as collective political power. It yields them not only the increase of increasing population, equivalent in this country to a compound interest of three per cent. a year. It yields them not only the fruits of all the industry of two millions of human beings, but it yields them, collectively, twenty-five representatives in one branch of the common Legislature, and upwards of thirty votes of two hundred and eighty-eight Electors of President and Vice President of the United States. Upon what principle of natural justice or equity can the holders of this property pretend that they will not contribute to the revenues of the nation, more than the freeman who holds no such property, and enjoys no such representation?

It has been seen that with a free population of 280,000 souls, Vermont sends to the National House of Representatives only five members, while South Carolina, with a like population of less than 260,000, sends nine—New Hampshire, with a free population of 270,000, sends only five. In the year 1813, under the third census, Vermont and New Hampshire had each six members in the House of Representatives, and South Carolina the same number as at present, and as she will have under the new census; that is nine.

In the direct tax of the year 1813, the sum apportioned to the State of New Hampshire was ninety-six thousand seven hundred and ninety-three dollars and thirty-seven cents—that upon the State of Vermont was ninety-eight thousand three hundred and forty-three dollars and seventy-one cents—that upon the State of South Carolina was one hundred and fifty-one thousand nine hundred and five dollars and forty-eight cents.

If the fifteen millions of annual revenue, which are supposed by the Report of the Secretary of the Treasury to be necessary for the wants of the Government, and were proposed by the Report of the Committee of Ways and Means to be levied as a permanent revenue, should now be raised by a direct tax, the sum apportioned for its payment to the State of New Hampshire would fall a little short of four hundred thousand dollars—that to the State of Vermont would a little exceed the same amount. The sum apportioned to the State of South Carolina would be upwards of seven hundred and fifty-five thousand dollars, very little short of those of the two States of New Hampshire and Vermont together. Is there a human being who can imagine that the people of South Carolina will pay, of fifteen millions levied by impost, an amount approaching to that which will be paid by the people of Vermont and of New Hampshire united? In strict justice to the non-slaveholding States, all the revenues of the Union ought to be raised either by direct taxation, or by a system the operation of which would produce the same result. The slave representation is a permanent unintermitted privilege enjoyed by the owners of the slaves. The equivalent for it ought in justice to bear the same character. Duties of impost do so to a certain extent—but the substitution of them instead of direct taxation, is beyond all question favorable to the slave-holding States. Nine tenths, at least, of all the revenue raised by impost duties are levied upon the articles of cotton, wool, and woollens, silks, flax, and hemp, iron, spirits, and molasses, wines, coffee, tea, and sugar. Now, the consumption, by any part of the slave population, of any one of these articles, when imported, is exceedingly small; instead of being in the proportion of three to five in comparison with that of the free white population, it is certainly not in the proportion of one to ten. If we analyse the articles upon which the great mass of the revenue by impost is raised, we find it to be upon food and raiment; tea, coffee, sugar, wine, molasses, spirits, are of the first kind thus classified; wool, cotton, silk, flax, and leather, are of the second. Now, who does not know that the food and raiment of the slave are almost entirely of domestic growth and production? They are fed upon the fruits, and clad in the apparel produced by their own labor on the plantations to which they belong. It is probable that their owners consume more of the articles imported from abroad than an equal number of citizens in the States where all are free; but if so, it is either because they are more wealthy by the possession of slaves, or because they are not accustomed to habits of frugality so parsimonious and self-denying. The passions, the vices, and the virtues, of men are all modified by their condition in civil society. Among men who subsist only upon the fruits of their own labor, industry and frugality are constantly stimulated by the natural and perpetual impulse of bettering their own condition. Wherever one portion of the community lives in perpetual servitude to another, where master and slave both subsist upon the labor of the slave, industry and frugality not only lose much of their natural influence upon human conduct, but are apt even to lose the name and consideration of virtues. The slave feels neither the spur of industry nor the curb of frugality, for the fruits of his industry are not his own, and his scanty subsistence leaves him nothing to spare. The master's wants, supplied by another's toil, multiply with the means of gratification, and his natural tendencies will be to spend rather than to hoard. All labor to him will assume the hue and disrepute of servitude, and frugality to his eyes will lose her natural healthy bloom, and fade into the livid complexion of penurious avarice. Under these influences, South Carolina, with a free white population rather less than that of New Hampshire, may possibly, by the consumption of imported articles, contribute rather more to the public revenues of the Union; but the subscribers have no hesitation in declaring their belief that the difference of amount between them, if ascertained to a dollar, would be found too trifling and insignificant to warrant a whisper of complaint; and that it would bear no sort of comparison to the difference, disadvantageous to South Carolina, which would appear by the levy of an equal amount by direct taxation.

There is then neither injustice nor oppression upon South Carolina, nor upon the Southern portion of the Union generally, resulting from the collection of the National Revenues, by duties of impost—nor is it true that South Carolina has suffered impoverishment under this system of taxation, in comparison with New Hampshire, Vermont, or New England, generally. Of this the unanswerable demonstration is found in the same fact of relative representation in Congress, under the successive enumerations of the people. In 1813, under the third census, the representation of South Carolina in this House, consisted of nine members—that of Vermont was six, that of New Hampshire six. Under the last census, South Carolina retains for the next ten years the same number of nine members, New Hampshire has only five, Vermont only five—New Hampshire and Vermont have thus lost, each one member on the floor of the representative hall, while South Carolina has retained her number unimpaired. The relative increase of the population of South Carolina has therefore, for the last twenty years, been greater than that of Vermont or New Hampshire, and let it be remembered, that in South Carolina, this increase of population is at the same time in the most literal sense, an increase of wealth. There, population is property, and the increase of that part of the population which is the property of the remainder, has been in larger proportion. The slaves have multiplied more rapidly than their masters. Thus altogether, for the last twenty years, the population and the wealth of the people of South Carolina has increased more than those of Vermont or of New Hampshire, and this is the result of the system of impost, which the political economists of the new school would teach us to believe is grinding the South to dust for the benefit of the North, and fattening the New Hampshire farmer, and the shepherd of the Green Mountains, upon the spoils of the South Carolina planter.

In examining the part of the message specially referred by the House to the Committee of Manufactures, namely: that which relates to the *protection* necessary to domestic manufactures, the subscribers have necessarily been led not only to an examination of the principle laid down, as the basis of the recommendations, relating to its particular interest, but to a general survey of all the foundations of the new system of government for this Union, the outline of which is presented for the first time in this document. They have considered it as a whole of which all the parts are adapted to each other.—As a whole, which if carried into execution, would change the nature of the Government of the United States, and in their belief, at no distant day, effect its dissolution. The assumption of the principle, that with the exception of articles of indispensable necessity in time of war, all legislative protection must ultimately be withdrawn from domestic manufactures, the subscribers believe to be itself contrary to the vital spirit of the Constitution, and equivalent to a bill of attainder, not against one individual, but against a whole, respectable, and most important class of citizens—the denial to them of a right secured to them by the social compact of the Constitution itself. And this assumed principle appears to us the more exceptionable, in as much as it is the identical principle assumed by the nullifying faction of South Carolina, and had but too manifest a tendency to encourage them in the violent and unconstitutional measures by which they were, at the very moment when the message was delivered, arming the worse than Eastern despotism of State sovereignty, against that same right of the citizen to the protection of the laws. Had it stood by itself, the recommendation gradually to withdraw from the manufactures the protection of existing laws, would have appeared inconsiderate, and at the moment when made, most unseasonable. But coupled as it was, with recommendations totally to abandon all future purposes of internal national improvement, to give away without equivalent the immensely valuable property in the public lands, and to sacrifice with the National Bank, all the property of the nation, in corporate companies for roads and canals; and the whole system emanating from a speculative theory of political morality, pronouncing the wealthy land-holders of every country the best part of their population, the subscribers could neither disguise to themselves, nor could they, consistently with the sense of their duties to their country, withhold the exposure of their conviction that, taken all together, it presents a decomposition of all the elements which hold this Union together—an array of great interests *against* each other, instead of a combination, by mutual concession and mutual support of great interests, in union with each other. The planter of the South, the new settler of the West, the husbandman of the North and Centre, the merchant of the Atlantic shore, the navigator of the ocean, and the artisan of the workshop and the loom, have each, in his several sphere of action, a separate and distinct interest, but a common right, a common stake, a common pledge in that great social compact, the Constitution of the United States. All are equally entitled to its *protection,* and to that of its laws. To bind, to interweave, to rivet them in adhesion inseparable together, is the duty of the American patriot and statesman; to bring one of those great interests in hostile collision with all or any one of the others, is to loosen the bonds of the Union, and to kindle the fires of strife. A sound, uniform, and accredited currency; an inexhaustible and invaluable fund of common property in the public lands; an organized and effective application of the national energies and resources to great undertakings of internal improvement; and a firm efficient *protection* of commerce and navigation against the arm of foreign violence, and of manufactures and agriculture against the indirect aggressions of foreign legislation and competition:—these the subscribers believe are the cements, which can alone render this Union prosperous and lasting. To discompose and unsettle the currency, to cast away the treasure of the public lands, to abandon all enterprize of internal improvement, and systematically to deny all protection to the domestic manufactures, is to separate the great interests of the country, and to set them in opposition to each other. It is to untie the ligaments of the Union.

The subscribers with the most respectful consideration, but with the freedom which their sense of duty requires, cannot but indulge the hope that the author of the message will reconsider the principles upon which its recommendations are founded, and review them upon a scale of more enlarged political philosophy than that of favoritism for one part of the population to the disparagement of all the rest; or that of reducing the government of a nation, swelling from tens to hundreds of millions of governable population, to a simple machine. To solve civil society into its elements, is to send back man to the state of nature; it is to degrade the citizen to a savage.

The subscribers believe that this great confederated Union is an union of the people, an union of States, an union of great national interests; an union of all classes, conditions, and occupations of men; an union co-extensive with our territorial dominions; an union for successive ages, without limitation of time. They read in the preamble to the Constitution, that it was ordained and established by the people of the United States, among other great and noble purposes, to secure the blessings of liberty to themselves and their *posterity*. As sovereign States have no posterity, they are incompetent to enter into any such compact. The people of the United States in ordaining the Constitution, expressly bound to its observance their posterity, as well as themselves. Their posterity, that is the whole people of the United States, are the only power on earth competent to dissolve peaceably that compact. It cannot otherwise be dissolved but by force. But to make it perpetual, the first and transcendent duty of all, who at any time are called to participate in the councils of its government, is to harmonize and not to divide, to co-operate and not to conflict.

The most remarkable characteristic of the controversy, which now threatens the dissolution of the Union, is, that it originated in the discontent of one great *protected* interest, with the *protection* extended by the existing laws to another. The controversy is sectional in its nature. It is the superabundantly, the excessively protected interest of the South, which revolts at the feeble and scanty protection of the laws enjoyed by the

North, the Centre, and the West. To inflame these discontents, and to arm them with offensive weapons, sophisms which reason blushes to be called to confute, are wrought up into axioms of political economy; fiction usurps the place of fact, to invert the most authenticated story of our national independence. Construction nullifies the connection between words and their meaning to make the Constitution say what it denies, and deny what it says, and invention is beggared for tales of decay and desolation and poverty, and distress in the South, in the face of an increasing relative representation in this House, and a doubling amount at once of population and property. The Southern planter is told that duties of impost are paid, not by the consumer of the dutied articles, but by the producer of cotton, rice, and tobacco. What is the purpose of this absurdity? To stimulate his selfish and sordid passion of avarice, and his hatred of the Northern manufacturer. It is not true, but his anti-social passions believe it. He is told that this Union is a mere confederacy of States—of sovereign States, from which any one of them may break off at pleasure. This is grossly, palpably false, and to bolster it up the most notorious historical facts are falsified. He is told that each of the States of this Union separately declared itself sovereign and independent, and as bare untruth is not of itself sufficient to bear out this imposture, the county of Mecklenburg is metamorphosed into the sovereign and independent State of North Carolina, to stamp the legend of the sterling standard upon the base metal of nullification. The tale is utterly groundless, but the abused planter believes it. In the Constitution of the United States, the whole people of the Union; speaking in the first person, declare themselves parties to it; declare themselves to ordain and establish it for the most exalted purposes of human action, upon this side the grave—even to secure to themselves and to their *posterity* the blessings of liberty. The planter is told that these are idle, unmeaning, cabalistical words—that there is no people of the United States. That the paper called the Constitution of the United States, is a league of despotic corporations, which can have no posterity to whom the blessings of liberty may be secured—which having no soul, can have no dread hereafter of the penalties of violated vows, and can never be excommunicated—which having no conscience, can be bound by no ties of morality in the fulfilment of its promises, contracts and obligations—free from all restrictions, human or divine, independent of all laws of the land or of heaven—sovereign as the throne of Omnipotence, and competent to nullify not only the laws of the whole Union, but the unalienable rights of man and the decrees of eternal justice. He is substantially told all this, and he believes it.

He is then told that he is poor and miserable—that his plantation is going to ruin; that his slaves double their numbers in not less than twenty years—that they are not worth half so much as they were when cotton sold for thirty cents a pound. That in S. Carolina they cannot produce half so much as in Alabama, Mississippi, or Louisiana. But that it is all owing to the accursed tariff—all owing to the *protection* of Northern manufactures by the laws of the Union. He is told that the tariff takes money from his pocket and puts it into that of the Northern manufacturer. He is told that the Northern manufacturer is a thief and a robber, and that it is upon him the planter that his robberies are committed. He is told that a cruel, tyrannical, oppressive *majority* in both Houses of Congress are the representatives of this highwayman of the North; that they pervert the very principles of popular representation to the purposes of oppression and robbery—that they *dare not* open their hearts to the sentiments of justice and humanity. He is told all this and he believes it.

And behold the whole foundation of the superstructure of nullification. Falsified logic—falsified history—falsified constitutional law, falsified morality, falsified statistics, and falsified and slanderous imputations upon the majorities of both Houses of Congress for a long series of years. All—all is false and hollow. And for what is this enormous edifice of fraud and falsehood erected? To rob the free workingman of the North of the wages of his labor—to take money from his pocket and put it into that of the Southern owner of machinery. It has been said that there is no philosophic falsehood so absurd, but it has been maintained by some sublime philosopher. Surely there is no invention so senseless, no fiction so baseless or so base, but it has been maintained by some learned, intelligent, amiable and virtuous, but exasperated and bewildered statesman. Nor was there ever in the annals of mankind an example of a community fretted into madness and goaded into rebellion, by a concerted and persevering clamor of grievances so totally destitute of foundation, and pretences so preposterously fictitious, as that which has found its consummation in the nullifying ordinance of the South Carolina convention.

In the name of the people of South Carolina, that convention have declared, that they will never more submit to a protective tariff—and to place beyond all doubt what they mean by a protective tariff, they have nullified, that is, declared null and void, all the revenue laws of the United States. They have, to the extent of their power, extinguished all the revenues of the United States derived from duties of impost. To nullify the *protection* of the laws imparted to their fellow citizens, constituting more than half the population of the Union, they have abolished the revenues of the nation. They have in express terms declared that so long as the principles of protection shall be recognized by the laws of Congress, "NO MORE TAXES SHALL BE PAID HERE," that is to say in South Carolina.

South Carolina, then, by virtue of her sovereign power, has deprived the people of all the rest of the Union of the protection of the existing laws; and she has declared that she never more will pay her proportion of the taxes, not even of the taxes imposed for revenue alone, until the principle of protection, that is of protection by the imposition of duties, shall be renounced—renounced forever. In their theory, the South Carolina convention make an all-important distinction between duties imposed for revenue, and duties imposed for protection; but in their practice, they involve them all in one common ruin.

Now, the subscribers cannot suppress the mortification and alarm with which, at the very moment when the arm of one of the States of this Union was thus raised, proclaiming with a voice of thunder her inflexible purpose to strike a vital blow at the right, the first constitutional right of more than half the people of the Union, to protection—even to the protection of existing laws—that, at this peculiar moment, the Chief Magistrate of the United States should have addressed to the legislative councils a message, recommending not only a gradual withdrawal of *all* that protection, but a whole system of administration for the future government of the Union, adapted to that principle of withdrawn and nullified protection—a system revolutionary in its character, totally departing from all the paths of peace and prosperity trodden by Washington and all his successors, down even to him who now calls us to deviate from them; to explore new wastes of desolation, beyond which there is no promised land but all is one unbounded and interminable desert—a system impending with universal ruin, draining all the sources of fertility from the fountains of internal national improvement, shaking to its foundation all commercial confidence, by the determined annihilation of the Bank, and wresting forever from the people of the United States and from their posterity, for unnumbered ages, the inestimable inheritance of the public lands, bequeathed to them by their fathers, or acquired at the expense of their own toil and treasure, as a property common to them all, and already yielding them yearly millions of income, which may be, and ought to be, applied to the employment and compensation of the laborious poor, and at the same time to the permanent and growing improvement of the condition of the people.

Such, in the opinion of the subscribers, is the *protection* due to domestic manufactures—to the interest specially committed by the standing order of the House, to the charge of the Committee of which they are members. The protection necessary to domestic manufactures is the protection of the existing laws. It is the protection extended, though in other forms, to all the other great interests of which the community is composed—the protection enjoyed by the planter of the South, by the woodsman of the West, by the merchant of the populous cities, by the mariner of the seas—protection from foreign hostility—protection from foreign competition.

But the subscribers must not be misunderstood. This protection is in nowise incompatible with a reduction of the revenue, nor even with a reduction of the duties by impost. The taxation of the country may be reduced to the wants of the Government, at whatever scale the standard of these wants may be fixed by the wisdom of Congress, without at all impairing the principle of protection. The two principles have no necessary connexion with each other; and all this bitter controversy has arisen from the blending of them improperly together. That the taxation of the country ought now to be reduced, the subscribers do not believe, because at the present moment the treasury, so far from overflowing, is drained of more than its last dollar. Because the tariff act will not, in their opinion, bring any excess of revenue into the treasury, at least for the two succeeding years; and if even the prospect of such an unexampled evil should approach, the next Congress will be invested with ample powers to ward it off, and will certainly not be slow to exert them. Nothing can be more fallacious than the fancy that *we* can control the action of our successors upon subjects over which their jurisdiction will be the same as ours; with this exception, that theirs will be in full vigor, and ours forever extinct. It is not for the dead to give laws to the living. Prospective legislation upon the most uncertain of contingencies, if not absolute usurpation, is akin to it in the impotence of its claims. It is the broken column and mutilated inscription of ETERNAL ROME. If the time should come when even the prospect of a redundant treasury shall be imminent, taxation ought to be, and undoubtedly will be, reduced; and in reducing its amount, the obligations of Congress will be to accomplish that object without injuriously affecting any of the great interests of the country. That this cannot be done by one uniform ad valorem duty of any given per centage upon all imported articles, is certain; nor can it without great injustice be effected by discarding all discrimination, except that of articles charged with impost, and articles entirely free. Nothing can be more unequal and oppressive in taxation, than the assessment of the same rates of duty upon all dutied articles. Its first inequality is its bearing upon the rich and the poor; the same tax which is unfelt by the wealthy land-holder, may crush to the earth the day-laborer who tills his ground. Its next inequality is that produced by foreign legislation and foreign competition. An article of foreign manufacture comes into your market cheapened by a bounty upon its export, at the place whence it came; it comes in competition with a like article, the production of your own soil or of your own industry; tax it at the same rate of per centage upon its value, as you do an article upon the production of which none of your own citizens have staked their fortunes and subsistence, and you consume all your manufactures with fire. It may be taken as a rule of universal application, that with a uniform rate of ad valorem duties, without discrimination, there can be no domestic manufacturing establishments. This is the protection which they now enjoy by the Constitution and existing laws of the United States. This protection the subscribers believe to be indispensably necessary to their existence, and its withdrawal by the General Government, whether immediate or by gradual steps, leaves them only the melancholy alternative of sudden death, or slow and lingering extinction. In either event, it will be the sacrifice of all the free industry of the Union to that *best part of the population*, the wealthy land and slave-holder of the South. This is the policy recommended by the message of the President of the United States, and against which the subscribers, as members of the Committee of Manufactures, in submitting this their Report to the House, deem it their duty respectfully, but most earnestly to remonstrate.

> J. Q. ADAMS,
> LEWIS CONDICT.

"MR. CHAIRMAN, ARE YOU READY FOR ALL THESE WARS?"

17. *Speech of John Quincy Adams, on the Joint Resolution for Distributing Rations to the Distressed Fugitives from Indian Hostilities in the States of Alabama and Georgia. Delivered in the House of Representatives, Wednesday, May 25, 1836* (Washington, D.C.: National Intelligencer Office, 1836).

Less than a week after being sworn in as a congressman, Adams presented fifteen petitions from citizens of Pennsylvania calling for the abolition of slavery and the slave trade in the District of Columbia. Over the next few years he would bring forth hundreds more such appeals, and he would emerge as the nation's greatest advocate for the right of petition, particularly with respect to slavery. All this provoked the ire of Democrats, whose political coalition of southern planters and northern "plain republicans" depended on the preservation of the always delicate balance of sectional interests in Washington, and who therefore wanted to quash any discussion of slavery in Congress. They felt Adams was playing with fire. But "the madman from Massachusetts" was undeterred. One keen observer, Ralph Waldo Emerson, would later remark that "Mr. Adams chose wisely and according to his constitution, when, on leaving the Presidency, he went into Congress. He is no literary gentleman, but a bruiser, and loves the *melee*."

That pugnacious style is on full display here, Adams's after-the-fact reconstruction of a speech he gave on the floor of the House on May 25, 1836. For all their desire to keep slavery out of political debate, southern and western Jacksonians could not curb their constituents' desire for land, and that provided Adams with the opening he needed. As a new congressman, Adams had dedicated himself not only to exhaustive reviews of federal statute books but to a crash course in parliamentary procedures, and he would come to be a master of maneuvers, like the one he employs here, that enabled him to command the floor despite the often very vocal protests of his opponents. In this speech, ostensibly about a measure for the relief of white Americans affected by the so-called Second Seminole War, Adams unleashes a broadside against the whole superstructure of Jacksonian pro-slavery expansionism, from the Indian Removal Act of 1830 ("this violent and heartless operation"), to the agitation for the annexation of Texas and war with Mexico ("a war of conquest"), to the three recently adopted resolutions by South Carolina congressman Henry Laurens Pinckney. These measures denied to Congress any "constitutional authority to interfere, in any way, with the institution of slavery in any State," suggested that Congress "ought not" to interfere with slavery in the District of Columbia, where its authority to do so was unchallenged, and, "for the purpose of arresting agitation, and restoring tranquility to the public mind," stipulated that "all petitions, memorials, resolutions, propositions, or papers relating in any way to the subject of slavery, or the abolition of slavery, shall, without either being printed or referred, be laid upon the table; and that no further action whatever be had upon them."

This was the basis of the infamous Gag Rule, which Adams would dedicate himself to overturning. For now, riled up and "under the necessity," as he described it in a letter to his son, Charles Francis Adams, "of making some remarks offensive to the slaveholders and in no way pleasing to the northern men with southern principles," Adams zeroes in on what he saw as the slavocracy's point of maximum exposure: Congress's war powers. "From the instant that your slave-holding States become the theater of war, civil, servile, or foreign," he writes with striking prescience, "from that instant the war powers of Congress extend to the interference with the institution of slavery in every way by which it can be interfered with."

After Adams had his say, five of his most inveterate opponents rose to rebut him. With that, as he records in his diary, "the Resolution was carried through all its Stages, and passed and the House adjourned between 7 and 8 O'Clock, and I came home much exhausted, and soon sought my bed."

SPEECH

OF

JOHN QUINCY ADAMS,

ON

THE JOINT RESOLUTION FOR DISTRIBUTING RATIONS

TO THE

DISTRESSED FUGITIVES FROM INDIAN HOSTILITIES

IN THE

STATES OF ALABAMA AND GEORGIA.

DELIVERED

IN THE HOUSE OF REPRESENTATIVES,

WEDNESDAY, MAY 25, 1836.

———•———

WASHINGTON:

NATIONAL INTELLIGENCER OFFICE.

1836.

Speech on the Joint Resolution

THE joint resolution from the Senate authorizing the President of the United States to cause rations to be distributed to suffering fugitives from Indian hostilities in Alabama and Georgia, being under debate—

Mr. ADAMS asked that the resolution should be read; it was accordingly read, and was as follows:

> *Resolved by the Senate and House of Representatives of the United States of America in Congress assembled,* That the President of the United States be authorized to cause rations to be delivered from the public stores to the unfortunate sufferers, who are unable to provide for themselves, and who have been driven from their homes by Indian depredations, in Alabama and Georgia, until they can be re-established in their possessions, or so long as the President shall consider it necessary.

Mr. ADAMS, after observing that there was no appropriation annexed to the resolution, which, if there had been, the resolution must, by the Constitution of the United States, have been made to assume the form of a *bill*, proceeded to address the chairman of the Committee of the Whole on the State of the Union, in substance, as follows:

Mr. Chairman: There is no appropriation annexed to this resolution. We are called to vote upon it without knowing how deep it will dive into the public purse. We have no estimate from any Executive Department; no statement of the numbers of the distressed and unfortunate persons whom we are called upon to relieve, not with our own moneys, but with the moneys of our constituents. By an exception to the ordinary rules of the House, especially established to guard the public Treasury against the danger of rash and inconsiderate expenditures, we are to drive this resolution through all its stages in a single day. And it is, I believe, the first example of a system of gratuitous donations to our own countrymen, infinitely more formidable by its consequences as a precedent, than from any thing appearing upon its face. I shall, nevertheless, vote for it. But answerable to my constituents, as I am in this as in all other cases for voting away their money, I seek for a *principle* which may justify me, to their judgment and my own, in this *lavish* disposal of the public funds.

It is but one, sir, of a class of legislative enactments now upon the pages of our statute book, introduced first, I believe during the present session of Congress; but with which we are already becoming familiar, and which I greatly fear will, ere long, grow voluminous. I shall take the liberty to denominate them the *scalping knife and tomahawk laws.* They are all urged through by the terror of those instruments of death, under the most affecting and pathetic appeals from the constituents of the sufferers, to all the tender and benevolent sympathies of our nature. It is impossible for me to withhold from those appeals a responsive and yielding voice. I have voted for all those bills devoting million after million from the public chest, for the relief and defence of these the suffering fellow-citizens of my constituents. I will vote for this resolution. I will vote again and again for drafts from the Treasury for the same purpose, should they become necessary, till the Treasury itself shall be drained; but, for so doing, I must seek for a principle which may be satisfactory, first, to my own mind, and secondly, to my constituents.

And here, sir, the gentlemen who call upon us for these bountiful contributions from the public treasury, are compelled to resort to that *common defence and general welfare* declared by the Constitution of the United States to be among the purposes for which the Constitution itself was ordained by the People. I admit their claim. There are, indeed, two grounds upon which some of them think their claim sustainable. One of them produces precedent for this exercise of power, and yet disclaims the authority of the precedent itself. You have already, by a resolution in the same words with those of the resolution now before this committee, extended this same relief to the inhabitants of Florida. But Florida is one of your Territories, and you are under obligations of protection more comprehensive to its inhabitants than those which bind you to the People of the States. These receive and are entitled to the protection of their State Government, and you are bound to extend that species of protection to the inhabitants of the

Territories, besides the protection which the inhabitants of the several States are entitled to, as members of the great confederation. The precedent, therefore, of the resolution of relief to the inhabitants of Florida, does not cover the case. We are reminded, however, that some twenty years or more ago, the people of Caraccas were visited at once with a tremendous earthquake, with famine, and with the still more heavy misfortune of a civil war. The convulsions of nature by earthquakes, the ravages of famine, and the raging passions of man in the desolations of civil war, are as destructive to human life, and as calamitous to multitudes whom they do not absolutely destroy as the tomahawk and the scalping knife. But whatever may have been the motives or the justifying authority of Congress, more than twenty years ago, for appropriating any portion of the public moneys to the relief of the inhabitants of Caraccas, it could not establish the principle that Congress have the constitutional power to appropriate money for the relief of all human suffering, whether by earthquake, famine, civil war, or Indian ferocity. And the gentleman from Alabama himself, who so ardently urges the adoption of this resolution, tells you that he should have voted against that measure of relief to the wretched sufferers in Caraccas. Mere commiseration, though one of the most amiable impulses of our nature, gives us no power to drain the Treasury of the People for the relief of the suffering object. You *must*, therefore, seek another, an additional source of power, for authority to pass this resolution; and where will you, where can you, find it but in the *war power*, and its *limitation*, not its enlargement, in that very declaration of the transcendent purposes for which the People of the United States ordained their Constitution—the *common defence and general welfare*. Step one hair's breadth out of the circle bounding the true intent and meaning of these words, and you have no more authority to pass this resolution, than you have, by an act of Congress, to saddle the People of the United States with the insupportable burden of the whole system of the poor laws of England.

Sir, in the authority given to Congress by the Constitution of the United States to *declare war*, all the powers incidental to war are, by necessary implication, conferred upon the *Government* of the United States. Now, the powers incidental to *war*, are derived, not from the internal municipal sources, but from the laws and usages of nations. In your relations with the Indian tribes, you never declare war, though you do make and break treaties with them, whenever either to make or to break treaties with them, happens to suit the purposes of the President and a majority of both Houses of Congress. For, in this matter, you have set aside the judiciary department of the Government as effectually as if there were none such in the Constitution.

There are, then, Mr. Chairman, in the authority of Congress and of the Executive two classes of powers, altogether different in their nature, and often incompatible with each other—the war power and the peace power. The peace power is limited by regulations, and restricted by provisions, prescribed within the Constitution itself. The war power is limited only by the laws and usages of nations. The power is tremendous: it is strictly constitutional, but it breaks down every barrier so anxiously erected for the protection of liberty, of property, and of life. This, sir, is the power which authorizes you to pass the resolution now before you, and, in my opinion, there is no other.

And this, sir, is the reason which I was not permitted to give this morning for voting with only eight associates against the first resolution reported by the committee on the abolition petitions; not one word of discussion had been permitted on either of those resolutions. When called to vote upon the first of them, I asked only five minutes of the time of the House to prove that it was utterly unfounded. It was not the pleasure of the House to grant me those five minutes. Sir, I must say that, in all the proceedings of the House upon that report, from the previous question, moved and inflexibly persisted in by a member of the committee itself which reported the resolutions, (Mr. OWENS, of Georgia,) to the refusal of the Speaker, sustained by the majority of the House, to permit the other gentleman from Georgia, (Mr. GLASCOCK,) to record upon the journal his reasons for asking to be excused from voting on that same resolution, the freedom of debate has been stifled in this House to a degree far beyond any thing that ever has happened since the existence of the Constitution of the United States; nor is it a consolatory reflection to me how intensely we have been made to feel, in the process of that operation, that

SPEECH ON JOINT RESOLUTION | 1836   407

the Speaker of this House is a slaveholder. And, sir, as I was not then permitted to assign my reasons for voting against that resolution before I gave the vote, I rejoice that the reason for which I shall vote for the resolution now before the committee is identically the same with that for which I voted against that.

[Mr. ADAMS at this, and at many other passages of this speech, was interrupted by calls to order. The chairman of the committee, (Mr. A. H. SHEPPERD, of North Carolina,) in every instance decided that he was not out of order, but at this passage intimated that he was approaching very close upon its borders; upon which Mr. ADAMS said, Then I am to understand, sir, that I am yet within the bounds of order, but that I may transcend them hereafter.

Mr. Chairman, I claim the privilege of speech accorded to every other member of this House. I will not advert to the latitude in which that privilege has been, throughout this session, enjoyed in Committee of the Whole by every member of the House who has chosen to exercise it. I will appeal only to what happened no longer ago than the sitting of yesterday and of this morning, when, at the hour of one, the Speaker adjourned the House, not in the usual form of ten o'clock to-morrow morning, but to ten o'clock of Wednesday morning, that is, of this day. Is it not within the recollection of every one who hears me, that two gentlemen, both distinguished members of the House, from the State of Maryland, from the hour of seven to that of ten, or little short of that time, last evening, entertained and instructed the Committee of the Whole House with a controversial disquisition upon the Constitution of the State of Maryland, and upon the very important question whether the voice of the Legislature of that State was or was not an exponent of the popular will? Is it not remembered that this disquisition was held in the form of a dialogue so animated, that the retort courteous, the quip modest, the counter-check quarrelsome, and almost the lie circumstantial, passed between those gentlemen, without interruption from the chairman, and without call to order, till at last an honorable member from Tennessee proposed that the difference between the two members should be settled by *arbitration*? And what was the question before the committee, sir, upon which this spirited and eloquent conference was held? Was it upon an appropriation of seven hundred thousand dollars for arming the fortifications of the United States? or upon an *amendment* to that proposal, by a reduction of the salaries of all your principal executive officers, and of the compensation of members of Congress? Sir, it was upon one of these two propositions, so exceedingly relevant to each other, that the colloquy between the two gentlemen from Maryland, upon the Constitution, Legislature, and People of that highly respectable State, was held, for hours, without interruption or call to order. And now, sir, am I to be disconcerted and silenced, or admonished by the Chair that I am approaching to irrelevant matter, which may warrant him to arrest me in my argument, because I say that the reason for which I shall vote for the resolution now before the committee, levying a heavy contribution upon the property of my constituents, is identically the same with the reason for which I voted against the resolution reported by the slavery committee, that Congress has no authority to interfere, *in any way*, with slavery in any of the States of this Union? Sir, I was not allowed to give my reasons for that vote, and a majority of my constituents, perhaps proportionably as large as that of this House, in favor of that resolution, may, and probably will, disapprove of my vote against it, unless my reasons for so voting should be explained to them. I asked but five minutes of the House to give those reasons, and was refused. I shall, therefore, take the liberty to give them now, as they are strictly applicable to the measure now before the committee, and are my only justification for voting in favor of this resolution.]

I return, then, to my first position, that there are two classes of powers vested by the Constitution of the United States in their Congress and Executive Government: the powers to be exercised in time of peace, and the powers incidental to *war*. That the powers of peace are limited by provisions within the body of the Constitution itself; but that the powers of war are limited and regulated only by the laws and usages of nations. There are, indeed, powers of peace conferred upon Congress which also come within the scope and jurisdiction of the laws of nations, such as the negotiation of treaties of amity and commerce, the interchange of public ministers and consuls, and all the personal and social intercourse between the individual inhabitants of the United States and foreign nations, and the

Indian tribes, which require the interposition of any law. But the powers of war are *all* regulated by the laws of nations, and are subject to no other limitation. It is by this power that I am justified in voting the money of my constituents for the immediate relief of their fellow-citizens suffering with extreme necessity even for subsistence, by the direct consequence of an Indian war. Upon the same principle, your consuls in foreign ports are authorized to provide for the subsistence of seamen in distress, and even for their passage to their own country.

And it was upon that same principle that I voted *against* the resolution reported by the slavery committee, "that Congress possess no constitutional authority to interfere, *in any way*, with the institution of slavery in any of the States of this Confederacy," to which resolution most of those with whom I usually concur, and even my own colleagues in this House, gave their assent. I do not admit that there is, even among the peace powers of Congress, such authority; but in *war* there are many ways by which Congress not only have the authority, but are bound to interfere with the institution of slavery in the States. The existing law prohibiting the importation of slaves into the United States from foreign countries, is itself an interference with the institution of slavery in the States. It was so considered by the founders of the Constitution of the United States, in which it was stipulated that Congress should not interfere, *in that way*, with the institution, prior to the year 1808.

During the late war with Great Britain, the military and naval commanders of that nation issued proclamations inviting the slaves to repair to their standards, with promises of freedom and of settlement in some of the British colonial establishments. This, surely, was an interference with the institution of slavery in the States. By the treaty of peace, Great Britain stipulated to evacuate all the forts and places in the United States, without carrying away any slaves. If the Government of the United States had no authority to interfere, *in any way*, with the institution of slavery in the States, they would not have had the authority to require this stipulation. It is well known that this engagement was not fulfilled by the British naval and military commanders; that, on the contrary, they did carry away all the slaves whom they had induced to join them, and that the British Government inflexibly refused to restore any of them to their masters; that a claim of indemnity was consequently instituted in behalf of the owners of the slaves, and was successfully maintained. All that series of transactions was an interference by Congress with the institution of slavery in the States in one way—in the way of protection and support. It was by the institution of slavery alone that the restitution of slaves enticed by proclamations into the British service could be claimed as *property*. But for the institution of slavery, the British commanders could neither have allured them to their standard, nor restored them otherwise than as liberated prisoners of war. But for the institution of slavery, there could have been no stipulation that they should not be carried away as property, nor any claim of indemnity for the violation of that engagement.

But the war power of Congress over the institution of slavery in the States is yet far more extensive. Suppose the case of a servile war, complicated, as to some extent it is even now with an Indian war; suppose Congress were called to raise armies, to supply money from the whole Union to suppress a servile insurrection: would they have no authority to interfere with the institution of slavery? The issue of a servile war *may* be disastrous. By war the slave may emancipate himself; it may become necessary for the master to recognise his emancipation by a treaty of peace; can it for an instant be pretended that Congress, in such a contingency, would have no authority to interfere with the institution of slavery, *in any way*, in the States? Why, it would be equivalent to saying that Congress have no constitutional authority to make peace.

I suppose a more portentous case, certainly within the bounds of possibility—I would to God I could say not within the bounds of probability. You have been, if you are not now, at the very point of a war with Mexico—a war, I am sorry to say, so far as public rumor may be credited, stimulated by provocations on our part from the very commencement of this Administration down to the recent authority given to General Gaines to invade the Mexican territory. It is said that one of the earliest acts of this Administration was a proposal, made at a time when there was already much ill-humor in Mexico against the United States, that she should cede to the United States a very large portion of her territory—large enough to constitute nine States equal in extent to Kentucky. It must be confessed that a device better calculated to produce jealousy, suspicion, ill-will, and hatred, could not have been contrived. It is further affirmed that this overture, offensive in itself, was made precisely at the time when a swarm of colonists from these United States were covering the Mexican border with land-jobbing, and with slaves, introduced in defiance of the Mexican laws, by which slavery had been abolished throughout that Republic. The war now raging in Texas is a Mexican civil war, and a war for the re-establishment of slavery where it was abolished. It is not a servile war, but a war between slavery and emancipation, and every possible effort has been made to drive us into the war, on the side of slavery.

It is, indeed, a circumstance eminently fortunate for us that this monster, Santa Ana, has been defeated and taken, though I cannot participate in that exquisite joy with which we have been told that every one having Anglo-Saxon blood in his veins must have been delighted on hearing that this ruffian has been shot, in cold blood, when a prisoner of war, by the Anglo-Saxon leader of the victorious Texian army. Sir, I hope there is no member of this House, of other than Anglo-Saxon origin, who will deem it uncourteous that I, being myself in part Anglo-Saxon, must, of course, hold that for the best blood that ever circulated in human veins. Oh! yes, sir! far be it from me to depreciate the glories of the Anglo-Saxon race; although there have been times when they bowed their necks and submitted to the law of conquest, beneath the ascendency of the Norman race. But, sir, it has struck me as no inconsiderable evidence of the spirit which is spurring us into this war of aggression, of conquest, and of slave-making, that all the fires of ancient, hereditary national hatred are to be kindled, to familiarize us with the ferocious spirit of rejoicing at the massacre of prisoners in cold blood. Sir, is there not yet hatred enough between the races which compose your Southern population and the population of Mexico, their next neighbor, but you must go back eight hundred or a thousand years, and to another hemisphere, for the fountains of bitterness between you and them? What is the temper of feeling between the component parts of your own Southern population, between your Anglo-Saxon, Norman French, and Moorish Spanish inhabitants of Louisiana, Mississippi, Arkansas, and Missouri? between them all and the

Indian savage, the original possessor of the land from which you are scourging him already back to the foot of the Rocky Mountains? What between them all and the native American negro, of African origin, whom they are holding in cruel bondage? Are these elements of harmony, concord, and patriotism between the component parts of a nation starting upon a crusade of conquest? And what are the feelings of all this motley compound of your Southern population towards the compound equally heterogeneous of the Mexican population? Do not you, an Anglo-Saxon, slave-holding exterminator of Indians, from the bottom of your soul, hate the Mexican-Spaniard-Indian, emancipator of slaves and abolisher of slavery? And do you think that your hatred is not with equal cordiality returned? Go to the city of Mexico, ask any of your fellow-citizens who have been there for the last three or four years, whether they scarcely dare show their faces, as Anglo-Americans, in the streets. Be assured, sir, that, however heartily you detest the Mexican, his bosom burns with an equally deep-seated detestation of you.

And this is the nation with which, at the instigation of your Executive Government, you are now rushing into war—into a war of conquest; commenced by aggression on your part, and for the re-establishment of slavery, where it has been abolished, throughout the Mexican Republic. For your war will be with Mexico—with a Republic of twenty-four States, and a population of eight or nine millions of souls. It seems to be considered that this victory over twelve hundred men, with the capture of their commander, the President of the Mexican Republic, has already achieved the conquest of the whole Republic. That it may have achieved the independence of Texas, is not impossible. But Texas is to the Mexican Republic not more nor so much as the State of Michigan is to yours. That State of Michigan, the People of which are in vain claiming of you the performance of that sacred promise you made them, of admitting her as a State into the Union; that State of Michigan, which has greater grievances and heavier wrongs to allege against you for a declaration of her independence, if she were disposed to declare it, than the People of Texas have for breaking off their union with the Republic of Mexico. Texas is an extreme boundary portion of the Republic of Mexico; a wilderness inhabited only by Indians till after the Revolution which separated Mexico from Spain; not sufficiently populous at the organization of the Mexican Confederacy to form a State by itself, and therefore united with Coahuila, where the greatest part of the indigenous part of the population reside. Sir, the history of all the emancipated Spanish American colonies has been, ever since their separation from Spain, a history of convulsionary wars; of revolutions, accomplished by single, and often very insignificant battles; of chieftains, whose title to power has been the murder of their immediate predecessors. They have all partaken of the character of the first conquest of Mexico by Cortez, and of Peru by Pizarro; and this, sir, makes me shudder at the thought of connecting our destinies indissolubly with theirs. It may be that a new revolution in Mexico will follow upon this captivity or death of their President and commanding general; we have rumors, indeed, that such a revolution had happened even before his defeat; but I cannot yet see my way clear to the conclusion that either the independence of Texas, or the capture and military execution of Santa Ana, will save you from war with Mexico. Santa Ana was but one of a breed of which Spanish America for the last twenty-five years has been a teeming mother—soldiers of fortune, who, by the sword or the musket ball, have risen to supreme power, and by the sword or the musket ball have fallen from it. That breed is not extinct; the very last intelligence from Peru tells of one who has fallen there as Yturbide, and Mina, and Guerrero, and Santa Ana have fallen in Mexico. The same soil which produced them is yet fertile to produce others. They reproduce themselves, with nothing but a change of the name and of the man. Your war, sir, is to be a war of races—the Anglo-Saxon American pitted against the Moorish-Spanish-Mexican American; a war between the Northern and Southern halves of North America; from Passamaquoddy to Panama. Are you prepared for such a war?

And again I ask, what will be your *cause* in such a war? Aggression, conquest, and the re-establishment of slavery where it has been abolished. In that war, sir, the banners of *freedom* will be the banners of Mexico; and your banners, I blush to speak the word, will be the banners of slavery.

Sir, in considering these United States and the United Mexican States as mere masses of power coming to collision against each other, I cannot doubt that Mexico will be the greatest sufferer by the shock. The conquest of all Mexico would seem to be no improbable result of the conflict, especially if the war should extend no farther than to the two mighty combatants. But will it be so confined? Mexico is clearly the weakest of the two Powers; but she is not the least prepared for action. She has the more recent experience of war. She has the greatest number of veteran warriors; and although her highest chief has just suffered a fatal and ignominious defeat, yet that has happened often before to leaders of armies too confident of success and contemptuous of their enemy. Even now, Mexico is better prepared for a war of invasion upon you, than you are for a war of invasion upon her. There may be found a successor to Santa Ana, inflamed with the desire, not only of avenging his disaster, but what he and his nation will consider your perfidious hostility. The national spirit may go with him. He may not only turn the tables upon the Texian conquerors, but drive them for refuge within your borders, and pursue them into the heart of your own territories. Are you in a condition to resist him? Is the success of your whole army, and all your veteran generals, and all your militia-calls, and all your mutinous volunteers against a miserable band of five or six hundred invisible Seminole Indians, in your late campaign, an earnest of the energy and vigor with which you are ready to carry on that far otherwise formidable and complicated war?—complicated, did I say? And how complicated? Your Seminole war is already spreading to the Creeks, and, in their march of desolation, they sweep along with them your negro slaves, and put arms into their hands to make common cause with them against you; and how far will it spread, sir, should a Mexican invader, with the torch of liberty in his hand, and the standard of freedom floating over his head, proclaiming emancipation to the slave and revenge to the native Indian, as he goes, invade your soil? What will be the condition of your States of Louisiana, of Mississippi, of Alabama, of Arkansas, of Missouri, and of Georgia? Where will be your negroes? Where will be that combined and concentrated mass of Indian tribes, whom, by an inconceivable policy, you have expelled from their widely distant habitations, to embody them within a small compass on the very borders of Mexico, as if on purpose to give that country a nation of natural allies in their hostilities against you? Sir, you have a Mexican, an Indian, and a negro war upon your hands, and you are plunging yourself into it blindfold; you are talking about acknowledging the independence of the Republic of Texas, and you are thirsting to annex Texas, ay, and Coahuila, and Tamaulipas, and Santa Fe, from the source to the mouth of the Rio Bravo, to your already over-distended dominions. Five hundred thousand square miles of the territory of Mexico would not even now quench your burning thirst for aggrandizement.

But will your foreign war for this be with Mexico alone? No, sir. As the weaker party, Mexico, when the contest shall have once begun, will look abroad, as well as among your negroes and your Indians, for assistance. Neither Great Britain nor France will suffer you to make such a conquest from Mexico; no, nor even to annex the independent State of Texas to your Confederation, without their interposition. You will have an Anglo-Saxon intertwined with a Mexican war to wage. Great Britain may have no serious objection to the independence of Texas, and may be willing enough to take her under her protection, as a barrier both against Mexico and against you. But, as aggrandizement to you, she will not readily suffer it; and, above all, she will not suffer you to acquire it by conquest and the re-establishment of slavery. Urged on by the irresistible, overwhelming torrent of public opinion, Great Britain has recently, at a cost of one hundred millions of dollars, which her People have joyfully paid, abolished slavery throughout all her colonies in the West Indies. After setting such an example, she will not—it is impossible that she should—stand by and witness a war for the re-establishment of slavery where it had been for years abolished, and situated thus in the immediate neighborhood of her islands. She will tell you, that if you must have Texas as a member of your Confederacy, it must be without the taint or the trammels of slavery; and if you will wage a war to handcuff and fetter your fellow-man, she will wage the war against you to break his chains. Sir, what a figure, in the eyes of mankind, would you make, in deadly conflict with Great Britain: she fighting the battles of emancipation, and you the battles of slavery; she the benefactress, and you the oppressor, of human kind! In such a war, the enthusiasm of emancipation, too, would unite vast numbers of her People in aid of the national rivalry, and all her natural jealousy against our aggrandizement. No war was ever so popular in England as that war would be against slavery, the slave-trade, and the Anglo-Saxon descendant from her own loins.

As to the annexation of Texas to your Confederation, for what do you want it? Are you not large and unwieldy enough already? Do not two millions of square miles cover surface enough for the insatiate rapacity of your land jobbers? I hope there are none of them within the sound of my voice. Have you not Indians enough to expel from the land of their fathers' sepulchres, and to exterminate? What, in a prudential and military point of view, would be the addition of Texas to your domain? It would be weakness, and not power. Is your southern and southwestern frontier not sufficiently extensive? not sufficiently feeble? not sufficiently defenceless? Why are you adding regiment after regiment of dragoons to your standing army? Why are you struggling, by direction and by indirection, to raise *per saltum* that army from less than six to more than twenty thousand men? Your commanding General, now returning from his excursion to Florida, openly recommends the increase of your Army to that number. Sir, the extension of your seacoast frontier from the Sabine to the Rio Bravo would add to your weakness tenfold; for it is now only weakness with reference to Mexico. It would then be weakness with reference to Great Britain, to France, even perhaps to Russia, to every naval European Power, which might make a quarrel with us for the sake of settling a colony; but, above all, to Great Britain. She, by her naval power, and by her American colonies, holds the keys of the gulf of Mexico. What would be the condition of your frontier from the mouth of the Mississippi to that of the Rio del Norte, in the event of a war with Great Britain? Sir, the reasons of Mr. Monroe for accepting the Sabine as the boundary were three. First, he had no confidence in the strength of our claim as far as the Rio Bravo; secondly, he thought it would make our union so heavy that it would break into fragments by its own weight; thirdly, he thought it would protrude a long line of sea coast, which, in our first war with Great Britain, she might take into her own possession, and which we should be able neither to defend nor to recover. At that time there was no question of slavery or of abolition involved in the controversy.

The country belonged to Spain; it was a wilderness, and slavery was the established law of the land. There was then no project for carving out nine slave States, to hold eighteen seats in the other wing of this capitol, in the triangle between the mouths and the sources of the Mississippi and Bravo rivers. But what was our claim? Why it was that La Salle, having discovered the mouth of the Mississippi, and France having made a settlement at New Orleans, France had a right to one-half the sea coast from the mouth of the Mississippi to the next Spanish settlement, which was Vera Cruz. The mouth of the Rio Bravo was about half way from the Balize to Vera Cruz; and so as grantees, from France, of Louisiana, we claimed to the Rio del Norte, though the Spanish settlement of Santa Fe was at the head of that river. France, from whom we had received Louisiana, utterly disclaimed ever having even raised such a pretension. Still we made the best of the claim that we could, and finally yielded it for the Floridas, and for the line of the 42d degree of latitude from the source of the Arkansas river to the South sea. Such was our claim; and you may judge how much confidence Mr. Monroe could have in its validity. The great object and desire of the country then was to obtain the Floridas. It was Gen. Jackson's desire; and in that conference with me to which I have heretofore alluded, and which it is said he does not recollect, he said to me that so long as the Florida rivers were not in our possession, there could be no safety for our whole Southern country.

But, sir, suppose you should annex Texas to these United States; another year would not pass before you would have to engage in a war for the conquest of the Island of Cuba. What is now the condition of that island? Still under the nominal protection of Spain. And what is the condition of Spain herself? Consuming her own vitals in a civil war for the succession to the crown. Do you expect, that whatever may be the issue of that war, she can retain even the nominal possession of Cuba? After having lost *all* her continental colonies in North and South America, Cuba will stand in need of more efficient protection; and above all, the protection of a naval power. Suppose that naval power should be Great Britain. There is Cuba at your very door; and if you spread yourself along a naked coast, from the Sabine to the Rio Bravo, what will be your relative position towards Great Britain, with not only Jamaica, but Cuba, and Porto Rico in her hands, and abolition for the motto to her union cross of St. George and Saint Andrew? Mr. Chairman, do you think I am treading on fantastic grounds? Let me tell you a piece of history, not far remote. Sir, many years have not passed away since an internal revolution in Spain subjected that country and her king for a short time to the momentary government of the Cortes. That revolution was followed by another, by which, under the auspices of a French army with the Duke d'Angouleme at their head, Ferdinand the Seventh was restored to a despotic throne; Cuba had followed the fortunes of the Cortes when they were crowned with victory; and when the counter revolution came, the inhabitants of the island, uncertain what was to be their destination, were for some time in great perplexity what to do for themselves. Two considerable parties arose in the island, one of which was for placing it under the protection of Great Britain, and another was for annexing it to the confederation of these United States. By one of these parties I have reason to believe that overtures were made to the Government of Great Britain. By the other *I know* that overtures were made to the Government of the United States. And I further know that secret, though irresponsible assurances were communicated to the then President of the United States, as coming from the French Government, that *they* were secretly informed that the British Government had determined to take possession of Cuba. Whether similar overtures were made to France herself, I do not undertake to say; but that Mr. George Canning, then the British Secretary of State for Foreign Affairs, was under no inconsiderable alarm, lest under the pupilage of the Duke d'Angouleme, Ferdinand the Seventh might commit to the commander of a French naval squadron the custody of the Moro Castle, is a circumstance also well known to me. It happened that just about that time a French squadron of considerable force was fitted out and received sailing orders for the West Indies, without formal communication of the fact to the British Government; and that as soon as it was made known to him, he gave orders to the British Ambassador at Paris to demand, in the most peremptory tone, what was the destination of that squadron, and a special and positive disclaimer that it was intended even to visit the Havana; and this was made the occasion of mutual explanations, by which Great Britain, France, and the United States, not by the formal solemnity of a treaty, but by the implied engagement of mutual assurances of intention, gave pledges of honor to each other, that neither of them should in the then condition of the island take it, or the Moro Castle, as its citadel, from the possession of Spain. This engagement was on all sides faithfully performed; but, without it, who doubts that from that day to this either of the three Powers might have taken the island and held it in undisputed possession?

At this time circumstances have changed—popular revolutions both in France and Great Britain have perhaps curbed the spirit of conquest in Great Britain, and France may have enough to do to govern her kingdom of Algiers. But Spain is again convulsed with a civil war for the succession to her crown; she has irretrievably lost all her colonies on both continents of America. It is impossible that she should hold much longer a shadow of dominion over the islands of Cuba and Porto Rico; nor can those islands, in their present condition, form independent nations, capable of protecting themselves. They must for ages remain at the mercy of Great Britain or of these United States, or of both; Great Britain is even now about to interfere in this war for the Spanish succession. If by the utter imbecility of the Mexican confederacy this revolt of Texas should lead immediately to its separation from that Republic, and its annexation to the United States, I believe it impossible that Great Britain should look on while this operation is performing with indifference. She will see that it must shake her own whole colonial power on this continent, in the Gulf of Mexico, and in the Caribbean Seas, like an earthquake; she will see, too, that it endangers her own abolition of slavery in her own colonies. A war for the restoration of slavery where it has been abolished, if successful in Texas, must extend over all Mexico; and the example will threaten her with imminent danger of a war of colors in her own islands. She will take possession of Cuba and of Porto Rico, by cession from Spain or by the batteries from her wooden walls; and if you ask her by what authority she has done it, she will ask you, in return, by what authority you have extended your sea coast from the Sabine to the Rio Bravo. She will ask you a question more perplexing, namely—by what authority you, with freedom, independence, and democracy upon your lips, are waging a war of extermination to forge new manacles and fetters, instead of those which are falling from the hands and feet of man. She will carry emancipation and abolition with her in every fold of her flag; while your stars, as they increase in numbers, will be overcast with the murky vapors of oppression, and the only portion of your banners visible to the eye will be the blood-stained stripes of the task master.

Mr. Chairman, are you ready for all these wars? A Mexican war? a war with Great Britain, if not with France? a general Indian war? a servile war? and, as an inevitable consequence of them all, a civil war? For it must ultimately terminate in a war of colors as well as of races. And do you imagine that while with your eyes open you are wilfully kindling, and then closing your eyes and blindly rushing into them; do you imagine that while, in the very nature of things, your own Southern and Southwestern States must be the Flanders of these complicated wars, the battle field upon which the last great conflict must be fought between slavery and emancipation; do you imagine that your Congress will have no constitutional authority to interfere with the institution of slavery *in any way* in the States of this confederacy? Sir, they must and will interfere with it—perhaps to sustain it by war; perhaps to abolish it by treaties of peace; and they will not only possess the constitutional power so to interfere, but they will be bound in duty to do it by the express provisions of the Constitution itself. From the instant that your slaveholding States become the theatre of war, civil, servile, or foreign, from that instant the war powers of Congress extend to interference with the institution of slavery in every way by which it can be interfered with, from a claim of indemnity for slaves taken or destroyed, to the cession of the State burdened with slavery to a foreign power.

Sir, it is by virtue of this same war power, as now brought into exercise by this Indian war in Florida, Alabama, and Georgia, that I vote for the resolution before the committee. By virtue of this, I have already voted in the course of this session to increase your standing army by a second regiment of dragoons, to authorize your President to accept the services of ten thousand volunteers, and to appropriate millions of the public money to suppress these Indian hostilities—all for the common defence, all for the general welfare. And if, on this occasion, I have been compelled to avail myself of the opportunity to assign my reasons for voting against the first resolution reported by the slavery committee, it is because it was the pleasure of the majority of the House this morning to refuse me the permission to assign my reasons for my vote, when the question was put upon those resolutions themselves.

Sir, it is a melancholy contemplation to me, and raises fearful forebodings in my mind when I consider the manner in which that Report and those Resolutions have been disposed of by the House. I have twice asked permission of this House to offer two resolutions calling for information from the President upon subjects of infinite importance to this question of slavery, to our relations with Mexico, and to the peace of the country. When I last made the attempt, a majority of the House voted by yeas and nays to suspend the rules to enable me to offer *one* of the two resolutions—but the majority not amounting to two-thirds, my resolution has not yet obtained from the House the favor of being considered. Had it been the pleasure of the House to indulge the call, or to allow me the privilege of assigning my reasons for my vote on the resolution this morning, the remarks that I have now made might have been deemed more appropriate to those topics of discussion, than to the question more immediately now before the committee. They are reflections, however, which I deem it not less indispensable to make than they are painful to be made—extorted from me by a condition of public affairs unexampled in the history of this country. Heretofore, calls upon the Executive Department for information, such as that which I have proposed to make, were considered as among the rights of the members of this House, which it was scarcely deemed decent to resist. A previous question, smothering all discussion upon resolutions reported by a committee, affecting the vital principles of the Constitution, moved by one of the members who reported the resolutions, and sustained by the members of that committee itself, is an occurrence which never before happened in the annals of this Government. The adoption of those resolutions of the House had not even been moved. Upon the mere question whether an extra number of the report of the committee should be printed, a member moves the recommitment of the report, with instructions to report a new resolution. On this motion the previous question is moved, and the Speaker declares that the main question is not on the motion to recommit, not on the motion to print an extra number of copies of the report, but upon the adoption of three resolutions, reported, but never even moved in the House. If this is to be the sample of our future legislation, it is time to awake from the delusion that freedom of speech is among the rights of the members of the minority of this House.

To return, Mr. Chairman, to the resolution before the committee. I shall vote for this application of moneys, levied by taxation upon my constituents, to feed the suffering and starving fugitives from Indian desperation and revenge. How deeply searching in the coffers of your Treasury this operation will ultimately be, no man can at this time foretell. The expenditure authorized by this resolution may be not in itself very considerable; but in its progress it has already stretched from Alabama to Georgia—how much further it may extend, will be seen hereafter. I turn my eyes away from the prospect of it now; but am prepared to meet the emergency, if it should come, with all the resources of the Treasury.

But, sir, I shall not vote for this relief to the suffering inhabitants of Alabama, and of Georgia, upon the ground on which the gentleman from Alabama, (Mr. LEWIS) and the gentleman from South Carolina, (Mr. THOMPSON) have been disposed to place it. Little reason have the inhabitants of Georgia and of Alabama to complain that the Government of the United States has been remiss or neglectful in protecting them from Indian hostilities: the fact is directly the reverse. The People of Alabama and Georgia are now suffering the recoil of their own unlawful weapons. Georgia, sir, Georgia, by trampling upon the faith of our national treaties with the Indian tribes and by subjecting them to her State laws, first set the example of that policy which is now in the process of consummation by this Indian war. In setting this example, she bade defiance to the authority of the Government of the nation; she nullified your laws: she set at naught your Executive and judicial guardians of the common Constitution of the land. To what extent she carried this policy, the dungeons of her prisons and the records of the Supreme Judicial Court of the United States can tell. To those prisons she committed inoffensive, innocent, pious ministers of the Gospel of Truth, for carrying the light, the comforts, and the consolations of that Gospel to the hearts and minds of these unhappy Indians. A solemn decision of the Supreme Court of the United States pronounced that act a violation of your treaties and of your laws. Georgia defied that decision: your Executive Government never carried it into execution: the imprisoned missionaries of the Gospel were compelled to purchase their ransom from perpetual captivity by sacrificing their rights as freemen to the meekness of their principles as Christians; and you have sanctioned all these outrages upon justice, law, and humanity, by succumbing to the power and the policy of Georgia, by accommodating your legislation to her arbitrary will; by tearing to tatters your old treaties with the Indians, and by constraining them, under *peine forte et dure*, to the mockery of signing other treaties with you, which, at the first moment when it shall suit your purpose, you will again tear to tatters and scatter to the four winds of Heaven, till the Indian race shall be extinct upon this continent, and it shall become a problem beyond the solution of antiquaries and historical societies *what* the red man of the forest was.

This, sir, is the remote and primitive cause of the present Indian war: your own injustice, sanctioning and sustaining that of Georgia and Alabama. This system of policy was first introduced by the present Administration of your National Government. It is directly the reverse of that system which had been pursued by all the preceding Administrations of this Government under the present Constitution. That system consisted in the most anxious and persevering efforts to civilize the Indians; to attach them to the soil upon which they lived; to enlighten their minds; to soften and humanize their hearts; to fix in permanency their habitations; and to turn them from the wandering and precarious pursuits of the hunter, to the tillage of the ground; to the cultivation of corn and cotton; to the comforts of the fire-side; to the delights of *home*. This was the system of Washington and of Jefferson, steadily pursued by all their successors, and to which all your treaties and all your laws of intercourse with the Indian tribes were accommodated. The whole system is now broken up; and instead of it you have adopted that of expelling by force or by compact, all the Indian tribes from their own territories and dwellings, to a region beyond the Mississippi, beyond the Missouri, beyond the Arkansas, bordering upon Mexico; and *there* you have deluded them with the hope that they will find a permanent abode—a final resting-place from your never-ending rapacity and persecution. *There* you have undertaken to lead the willing and to drive the reluctant, by fraud or by force; by treaty, or by the sword and the rifle; all the remnants of the Seminoles, of the Creeks, of the Cherokees, of the Choctaws, and of how many other tribes I cannot now stop to enumerate. In the process of this violent and heartless operation, you have met with all the resistance which men in so helpless a condition as that of the Indian tribes could make. Of the *immediate* causes of the war we are not yet fully informed; but I fear you will find them, like the remoter causes, all attributable to yourselves. It is in the last agonies of a people, forcibly torn and driven from the soil which they had inherited from their fathers, and which your own example, and exhortations, and instructions, and treaties, had rivetted more closely to their hearts; it is in the last convulsive struggles of their despair, that this war has originated; and if it brings with it some portion of the retributive justice of Heaven upon our own People, it is our melancholy duty to mitigate, as far as the public resources of the National Treasury will permit, the distresses of the innocent of our own kindred and blood, suffering under the necessary consequences of our own wrong. I shall vote for the resolution.

[NOTE.—This Speech was delivered without premeditation or notes. No report of it was made by any of the usual reporters for the newspapers. Mr. ADAMS has written it out, himself, from recollection, at the request of several of his friends, for publication. It is, of course, not in the precise language used by him in the House. There is some amplification of the arguments which he used, and, perhaps, some omissions which have escaped his recollection. The substance of the Speech is the same.]

"I AM NOT TO BE FRIGHTENED FROM THE DISCHARGE OF A DUTY"

18. *Letters from John Quincy Adams to his Constituents of the Twelfth Congressional District in Massachusetts. To which is Added his Speech in Congress, Delivered February 9, 1837* (Boston: Isaac Knapp, 1837).

Adams would serve uninterrupted from the opening of the Twenty-second Congress in 1831 until his death in 1848, in the Capitol, midway through the Thirtieth Congress. As his tenure progressed, his status as an elder statesman only grew. By his last Congress, he was fully twenty-five years older than the next most senior member, and thirty-seven years older than the mean. He struck many of his colleagues as a living link to another age, the age of the founders. And in some ways, as for instance in his ideas about electioneering, Adams could fairly have been called old-fashioned, adhering to certain habits of mind that had become outmoded by the 1830s. But in at least one respect—what we might call constituent communications—Congressman Adams was on the cutting edge of American politics, as the following piece illustrates. With frequent recourse to the press, and liberal use of his franking privileges, "Old Man Eloquent," as he came to be called, was nimble on his feet when it came to getting his message out, particularly when as in this case he could not rely on the official congressional record to capture the debate fully or fairly.

"Am I gagged, or am I not?" Adams had famously demanded to know after the passage of the Pinckney resolutions limiting debate on slavery in the House in May 1836. Because that original gag came in the form of a resolution, rather than as a standing House rule, it had to be actively reaffirmed each session, affording Adams with regular opportunities to challenge support for it. Perhaps the most dramatic of his many attempts to whittle away at the rule—to expose it as both a folly and as a cancer on the Constitution—is the one he records in this pamphlet gathering four letters to his constituents along with a reconstruction of his February 9, 1837, speech on the House floor. Introduced by the abolitionist poet John Greenleaf Whittier, this collection is a dramatization of Adams's crusade on behalf of freedom of speech and the right of petition and a masterpiece of public relations. It is politics presented as high drama, with Adams performing simultaneously as lead actor and stage manager. (At one point he even likens his many opponents to "actors of all work," those nondescript, lesser-rank thespians who assume multiple roles within a production.)

The original provocation for the events recorded here was a letter that Adams had received "purporting to come from slaves." With mock innocence, Adams inquires of the House Speaker, future president James K. Polk, whether the letter falls under "the resolution of the 18th of January," that is, the most recent iteration of the Gag Rule, which had passed the House the month before. At which point, as Adams describes in vivid detail, the House erupts, with a rapid-fire succession of motions to censure him. The debate that ensues, culminating in one of the most passionate speeches of Adams's career, reveals almost in real time the evolution of his thinking about slavery, and about race and citizenship in America. At one point, after the motion of censure has been modified to read "any member who shall hereafter present any such petition to the House, ought to be considered as regardless of the feelings of the House, the rights of the South, and an enemy to the Union," Adams asks defiantly, "What are the rights of the South?" He goes one step further: "What is the *South*?" exposing the true nature of the slave power in Congress, the "mastery" as he calls it, with a new and discomfiting clarity. Even as the centrifugal energies unleashed by his resistance to the Gag Rule brought him closer and closer to abolitionists like Whittier, Adams, always a passionate advocate for union, was not immune to a certain discomfiture himself. Two months after these events, on April 2, 1837, Adams confessed to his diary that "the subject of Slavery, to my great sorrow and mortification is absorbing all my faculties."

LETTERS

FROM

JOHN QUINCY ADAMS

TO

HIS CONSTITUENTS

OF THE

TWELFTH CONGRESSIONAL DISTRICT
IN MASSACHUSETTS.

TO WHICH IS ADDED

HIS SPEECH IN CONGRESS,

DELIVERED

FEBRUARY 9, 1837.

BOSTON:

PUBLISHED BY ISAAC KNAPP,

No. 25 Cornhill.

1837.

INTRODUCTORY REMARKS

THE following letters have been published, within a few weeks, in the Quincy (Mass.) Patriot. Notwithstanding the great importance of the subjects which they discuss, the intense interest which they are calculated to awaken throughout this commonwealth and the whole country, and the exalted reputation of their author as a profound statesman and powerful writer,—they are as yet hardly known beyond the limits of the constituency to whom they are particularly addressed. The reason of this is sufficiently obvious. John Quincy Adams belongs to neither of the prominent political parties, fights no partisan battles, and cannot be prevailed upon to sacrifice truth and principle upon the altar of party expediency and interest. Hence neither party is interested in defending his course, or in giving him an opportunity to defend himself. But, however systematic may be the efforts of mere partisan presses to suppress, and hold back from the public eye, the powerful and triumphant vindication of the Right of Petition, the graphic delineation of the Slavery spirit in Congress, and the humbling disclosure of northern cowardice and treachery, contained in these letters, they are destined to exert a powerful influence upon the public mind. They will constitute one of the most striking pages in the history of our times. They will be read with avidity in the North and in the South, and throughout Europe. Apart from the interest excited by the subjects under discussion, and viewed only as literary productions, they may be ranked among the highest intellectual efforts of their author. Their sarcasm is Junius-like—cold, keen, unsparing. In boldness, directness, and eloquent appeal, they will bear comparison with O'Connell's celebrated letters to the Reformers of Great Britain. They are the offspring of an intellect unshorn of its primal strength, and combining the ardor of youth with the experience of age.

The disclosure made in these letters, of the Slavery influence exerted in Congress over the representatives of the free states,—of the manner in which the rights of freemen have been bartered for southern votes, or basely yielded to the threats of men educated in despotism, and stamped by the free indulgence of unrestrained tyranny with the "odious peculiarities" of Slavery,—is painful and humiliating in the extreme. It will be seen, that, in the great struggle for and against the Right of Petition, an account of which is given in the following pages, their author stood, in a great measure, alone, and unsupported by his northern colleagues. On his "gray, discrowned head" the entire fury of slaveholding arrogance and wrath was expended. He stood alone—beating back, with his aged and single arm, the tide which would have borne down and overwhelmed a less sturdy and determined spirit.

We need not solicit for these letters, and the speech which accompanies them, a thorough perusal. They deserve, and we trust will receive, a circulation throughout the entire country. They will meet a cordial welcome from every lover of human liberty, from every friend of justice and the rights of man, irrespective of color or condition. The principles which they defend, the sentiments which they express, are those of Massachusetts, as recently asserted, almost unanimously, by her legislature. In both branches of that body, during the discussion of the subject of slavery and the right of petition, the course of the ex-President was warmly and eloquently commended. Massachusetts will sustain her tried and faithful representative; and the time is not far distant, when the best and worthiest citizens of the entire North will proffer him their thanks for his noble defence of *their* rights as *freemen*, and of the rights of the slave as a MAN.

J. G. W.

Boston, May 16, 1837.

Letters

HOUSE OF REPRESENTATIVES U.S. }
WASHINGTON, 3d March, 1837. }

To the Inhabitants of the Twelfth Congressional District of Massachusetts.

FELLOW-CITIZENS:—The proceedings of the House of Representatives, on the presentation of abolition and antislavery petitions, on the 23d of January, were so incorrectly reported in the National Intelligencer of the 25th, that I addressed a letter to the editors of that paper, pointing out some of its errors and omissions, which was published in their paper of the 30th.

On that day, I presented twenty-one petitions, all of which were laid on the table without being read, though, in every instance, I moved for the reading, which the Speaker refused to permit. From his decision I took, in every case, an appeal, and the appeal was in every case *laid on the table*, by a vote of the House, at the motion of a member from New Hampshire, Mr. Cushman. This gentleman, having been reported, in the Globe, as having voted against *receiving* the abolition petitions, addressed to the editors of that paper a letter correcting that error, and stating that he had voted for receiving them, and then for laying them on the table, where they might be taken up and acted upon whenever the House should think fit. Here, you will observe, was the line of separation between the northern anti-abolitionists and the southern slaveholders in the House. The practical result to the petitioner was the same. His right of petition was in both cases suppressed. The freedom of speech in the House was equally denied to the members presenting the petition, to support, by argument, its prayer. But the slaveholder denied the right of Congress to *receive* the petition. His northern auxiliary receives the petition, and lays it on the table, to be taken up when time shall serve, but in the meantime refuses to hear it read. The slaveholder would strip Congress of the power. The northerner holds it in reserve. This distinction may hereafter prove to be a difference. Its present issue is the same.

I considered, as I stated in my address of the 31st of January, the system of action of the House upon the abolition petitions as settled for the remainder of the session. But between that and the next day for receiving petitions, Monday, the 6th of February, I received thirty petitions, among which were two which came to me by the mail, postmarked Fredericksburg, Virginia; one of them signed by nine names of women, in various hand-writing; some of them good, none of illiterate appearance. It prayed not for the abolition of slavery, but that Congress would put a stop to the slave-trade in the District of Columbia. It was accompanied by a letter signed by one of the names subscribed to the petition, requesting me to present it. The other purported to be from twenty-two *slaves*, subscribed so as to have every appearance of being genuine; the first name being in a hand-writing not absolutely bad, and subscribed also alone to a letter requesting me to present the petition. I believed the petition signed by female names to be genuine, and did not believe them to be names of free negroes or mulattoes; but had I known them to be such, that would not have deterred me from presenting it; the object of it being not only proper in itself, but laudable, and eminently fit for subscription by virtuous women of any color or complexion. I had suspicions that the other, purporting to be from slaves, came really from the hand of a master, who had prevailed on his slaves to sign it, that they might have the appearance of imploring the members from the North to cease offering petitions for their emancipation, which could have no other tendency than to aggravate their servitude, and of being so impatient under the operation of petitions in their favor, as to pray that the northern members who should persist in presenting them should be *expelled*. Intimations of the same desire had already been manifested in quarters very remote from servitude, and not even professors of servility. They had been seen in a newspaper of this city, professedly devoted to the pure coinage of democracy from the mint of Van Buren and Rives, against the counterfeit currency of Benton and Amos Kendall. The Albany Argus itself, a paper known to be under the same influences, had lamented that the Massachusetts madman should *be permitted,* week after week,—to do what? to persist in presenting abolition petitions! This was the head and front of my offending; and for this alone, the petition from *slaves*, for my expulsion from the House, was but the echo of the distinct and explicit *call* from the Albany Argus and the Van Buren and Rives's Washingtonian.

But the petition, avowedly coming from slaves, though praying for my expulsion from the House if I should persevere in presenting abolition petitions, opened to my examination and inquiry a new question; or at least a question which had never occurred to me before, and which I never should have thought of starting upon speculation, namely: whether the right to petition Congress could in *any* case be exercised by slaves? And after giving to the subject all the reflection of which I was capable, I came to the conclusion, that however doubtful it might be whether slaves could petition Congress for anything incompatible with their condition as slaves, and with their subjection to servitude, yet that, for all other wants, distresses, and grievances, incident to their nature as men, and to their relation as members,—degraded members as they may be,—of this community, they do enjoy the right of petition; and that, if they enjoy the right in any case whatever, there could be none in which they were more certainly entitled to it than that of deprecating the attempts of deluded friends to release them from bondage—a case in which they alone could, in the nature of things, speak for themselves, and their masters could not possibly speak for them. The next question which I considered was, whether this paper was embraced by the resolution of the 18th of January; and of that, no man, understanding the English language, could entertain a moment's doubt.

But after settling these two questions to the satisfaction of my own mind, there remained another, with what temper they would be received in a House, the large majority of which consisted of slaveholders, and of their political northern associates, whose mouth-pieces had already put forth their feelers to familiarize the freemen of the North with the sight of a representative expelled from his seat for the single offence of persisting to present abolition petitions. I foresaw that the very conception of a petition from slaves would dismount all the slaveholding philosophy of the House, and expected it would produce an explosion, which would spend itself in wind. Without therefore presenting, or offering to present, the petition, I stated to the Speaker that I had such a paper in my possession, which

I had been requested to present, and inquired whether it came within the resolution of the 18th of January. Now, the Speaker had decided that, under that order, no such paper should be read; yet his first impulse was to get possession of that paper; but I declined presenting it, till it should be decided whether it was embraced by the resolution of the 18th of January, or not. The Speaker, conscious as he was that it came so clearly within the *letter* of the resolution that it was *impossible* for him to decide that it did not, yet horrified at the idea of receiving and laying on the table a petition from slaves, said that, in a case so novel and extraordinary, he felt himself incompetent to decide, and must take the advice and direction of the House. One of the gross absurdities of the resolution, as administered by the Speaker, was, that every *paper* relating to slavery, or the abolition of slavery, should, *without being read,* be laid on the table. I had repeatedly remonstrated both against the resolution and against his construction of it—in vain; and one of my purposes in putting this question to him was to expose the absurdity in its uncoverable nakedness. The resolution of the 18th of January presupposed by its own terms that every PAPER, relating to slavery or the abolition of slavery, should be *received*, without examination or inquiry whence it came, or what were its contents. There was neither exception nor qualification in the resolution, and the Speaker had decided that no such paper should be *read*. If I had stated that I had a petition from sundry persons in Fredericksburg, *relating to slavery*, without saying that the petitioners were, by their own avowal, *slaves*, the paper must have gone upon the table; but the discovery would soon have been made that it came from slaves, and then the tempest of indignation would have burst upon me with tenfold fury, and I should have been charged with having fraudulently introduced a petition from slaves, without letting the House know the condition of the petitioners.

To avoid the responsibility of such a charge, I put the question to the Speaker, giving him notice that the petition purported to come from slaves, and that I had suspicions that it came from another and a very different source. The Speaker, after failing in the attempt to obtain possession of the paper, referred my question to the House for decision; and then ensued a scene of which I propose to give you an account in a subsequent address, entreating you only to remember, if what I have said, or may say to you hereafter, on this subject, should tax your patience, that the stake in question is your right of petition, your freedom of thought and of action, and the freedom of speech in Congress of your representative.

JOHN QUINCY ADAMS.

WASHINGTON, 8th March, 1837.
To the Inhabitants of the Twelfth Congressional District of Massachusetts.

FELLOW-CITIZENS:—When, on the 6th of February last, the Speaker of the House of Representatives of the United States transferred to *the House* the responsibility of answering the question which I had addressed to him, whether a petition, which I held in my hand, purporting to come from *slaves,* was or was not embraced by the resolution of the preceding 18th of January, prescribing that all such papers should be laid on the table, without being printed or referred, and without any further action of the House upon them whatever; the most remarkable characteristic of the debate which followed, was the struggle of the slave representation to escape from answering the question. They never did answer it. There are in the House one hundred representatives of slaves, about eighty of whom were present. There was not a man among them who did not know, or who dared to deny, that it was included in that resolution; and the first of them who rose, Mr. Haynes, of Georgia, after expressing his astonishment and surprise at my audacity, not only then, but on former days, in presenting abolition petitions, fairly acknowledged that he did not know how to answer my question, and thought it might be giving too much importance to the petition to object to its being received. He then proceeded in a strain of invective upon me, till I called him to order; upon which he proceeded to announce his intention to move that the petition should be rejected, subject to the alternative of a permission, that it should be withdrawn. But I had not presented the petition. It was not in the possession of the House, and therefore could neither be rejected, nor by the order of the House withdrawn. Besides, the impulse of the slave representation was not to answer the question, but to punish, or at least to frighten the inquirer. Mr. Haynes was immediately admonished that no slaveholder must offer such a motion, and immediately withdrew that which he had proposed to make. The torrid zone was in commotion. Half-subdued calls of *Expel him, expel him*, were heard from various parts of the Hall, and the boldest spirits, without yet venturing upon any specific charge, were instigating each other to some deed of noble daring, and of instant execution, to vindicate the insulted honor of the South. At this moment, Mr. John M. Patton, of Virginia, the representative of the District of which Fredericksburg forms a part, one of the ablest, most independent, and most rational of the slaveholding members, seeing into what absurdities they were about to rush, attempted to divert the torrent of their wrath into another channel. He said he was for going to the fountain-head at once, and asked leave to offer a resolution, not concerning the petition from slaves, but that the petition from nine *women*, of Fredericksburg, which had been received and laid on the table, under the order of the 18th of January, should be taken off the table and returned to the member from Massachusetts who had offered it. The rules of the House were forthwith suspended, to enable him to offer it; and he did offer it. The reason that he alleged for his resolution was, that the petition came from free negroes, and colored persons of bad character. This was ingeniously devised, but did not suit the fiery temper of the moment. One member was of opinion, that if the gentleman from Massachusetts was to receive any countenance from the House, it was time for the members from the South to go home. Another thought that if any man should disgrace the government under which he lived, by presenting a petition from slaves praying for emancipation, the petition should, by order of the House, be committed to the flames, to which combustion another member opined, that the man who should present the petition should also be consigned. The furnace was now sufficiently heated, and Mr. Thompson, of South Carolina, a gentleman of great politeness and courtesy, offered as an amendment to the proposition the following resolution:

> "*Resolved*, That the Honorable John Quincy Adams, by the attempt just made by him to introduce a petition, purporting

on its face to be from slaves, has been guilty of a gross disrespect to the House, and that he be *instantly* brought to the bar, to receive the severe censure of the Speaker."

This was the first of a series of resolutions, which absorbed three days of the time of the House, but upon which I shall not now waste yours. I invite your attention to it now, only to request you to mark its characteristic *tone*. Mr. Jefferson has observed that the intercourse between master and slave is a perpetual succession of boisterous and degrading passions; and it is in the order of nature that the habitual indulgence of this temper of overbearing domination insensibly pervades the general character of the master, and urges him to assume a tone of superiority over his equals, and to hold this lofty bearing just so far as he finds it tolerated without rebuke. On the floor of the House of Representatives, the members, whether representing slaves or mere freemen, are upon a footing of perfect equality with each other. Can you believe that your representative, on that common floor, for asking of the Speaker the simple question, whether a petition from slaves came within the resolution of the House, which it unquestionably did, became, from that instant, in the eyes of these master-members, a criminal to be punished, and that the only question between them was, whether he should be *instantly* dragged to the bar, and severely censured by a master-speaker, or expelled from the House, or burnt with his petition at the stake?

The whole transaction, from beginning to end, was in the highest degree disorderly. The resolution offered by Mr. Waddy Thompson was itself wholly out of order as an amendment to Mr. Patton's resolution, which related to a subject altogether different. The Speaker's duty was to reject at once Mr. Thompson's resolution as out of order; but the Speaker was a master, and he received it. Mr. Thompson's resolution was tinkered between him and Mr. Haynes, and Mr. Lewis, of Alabama, till it assumed the following shape:—

"*Resolved*, That John Quincy Adams, a member from the State of Massachusetts, by his attempts to introduce into this House a petition from slaves, for the abolition of slavery in the District of Columbia, committed an outrage on the rights and feelings of a large portion of the people of this Union; a flagrant contempt of the dignity of this House; and, by extending to slaves a privilege only belonging to freemen, directly invites the slave population to insurrection; and that the said member be forthwith called to the bar of the House, to be censured by the Speaker."

My constituents! reflect upon the purport of this resolution, which was immediately accepted by Mr. Thompson, as a modification of his own, and as unhesitatingly received by the Speaker. He well knew that I had made no attempt to introduce in the House a petition from slaves, and if I had, he knew that I should have done no more than exercise my right as a member of the House, and that the utmost extent of the power of the House, would have been to refuse to receive the petition. The Speaker's duty was to reject instantaneously this resolution, and to tell Mr. Lewis and Mr. Thompson, that the first of his obligations was, to protect the rights of speech of members of that House, which I had not in the slightest degree infringed. But the Speaker was a *master*.

Observe, too, that, in this resolution, the notable discovery was first made, that I had directly invited the slaves to insurrection, of which bright thought Mr. Thompson afterwards availed himself, to threaten me with the grand jury of the District and the penitentiary, as an incendiary and a felon. I pray you to remember this, not on my account, or from the suspicion that I could, or shall ever, be moved from my purpose by such menaces, but to give you the *measure* of slaveholding freedom—of speech, of the press, of action, of thought! If such a question as I asked of the Speaker is a direct invitation of the slaves to insurrection, forfeiting all my rights as a representative of the people, subjecting me to indictment by a grand jury, to conviction by a petit jury, and to an infamous penitentiary cell—I ask you not what freedom of speech is left to your representative in Congress, but what freedom of speech, of the press, and of thought, is left TO YOU?

A slaveholding President of the United States has urgently recommended to Congress the enactment of a law to prohibit, *under severe penalties*, "the circulation in the Southern States, through the mail, of incendiary publications, intended to instigate the slaves to insurrection." That law the Congress of the United States have hitherto had too much self-respect to pass. But if it had, this resolution, the fruit of the combined wisdom of slave representation from South Carolina and Alabama, furnishes for your use an ample commentary to expound what *they* understand and mean by incendiary publications intended to instigate the slaves to insurrection; and what they of course would have excluded by severe penalties from circulation by the mail.

Mr. Patton, whose seat was next to mine, and at the same table, had got a hint, perhaps from me, or from hearing my answer to some inquirer at my seat, that the petition was *not* for the abolition of slavery, and he knew that I had not attempted to offer it; he therefore cautioned the movers of the resolutions, that their proceedings were rather harsh, and somewhat over-hasty in their assumption of facts. This gave me the first opportunity of interposing a word of self-defence—for which I refer you to my next address.

JOHN QUINCY ADAMS.

WASHINGTON, 13th March, 1837.
To the Inhabitants of the Twelfth Congressional District of Massachusetts.

FELLOW-CITIZENS:—When the cooling potion administered, by Mr. Patton, to the burning thirst for my punishment, of the members from Alabama and South Carolina, began to take effect, I rose and inquired of the Speaker how it happened that a direct resolution calling for instantaneous censure upon me, had been substituted for the resolution offered by Mr. Patton, and which he had obtained, by a vote of two thirds of the House, the suspension of the rules to enable him to offer—which resolution was that the petition from the *nine women* of Fredericksburg, which had been laid on the table under the order of the 18th of January, should be taken and returned to me. The Speaker said that it was by the well-known parliamentary rule that a *question of privilege* supersedes all other subjects of debate, and takes precedence of all others. I told him I was satisfied, for I knew it would be in vain to remonstrate. But the Speaker well knew there was no ground for a question of privilege, and it was his duty to arrest the resolution of censure at its first presentation. But if there had been such ground, the resolution of censure could not be offered as an amendment to a resolution which involved no question of privilege. Mr. Patton's resolution respecting the petition of the nine women, was no question of privilege. When Mr. Thompson offered, as an amendment to it, the resolution of direct censure upon me, the Speaker's duty was to reject it as not in order, and he would have saved three days of very useless debate. The Speaker, whether from incompetency or unwillingness to discriminate between the questions of privilege and the unprivileged questions in this case, continued to confound them together throughout the whole of these discussions, and contributed thereby to render the whole debate as ridiculous as it was disorderly. The whole proceeding hitherto had been such a scene of blind precipitancy and fury, that I had not had a moment of time to interpose and stay the whirlwind. I had compassion upon Messrs. Thompson and Lewis, and told them, that, if they intended to bring me to the bar, to receive the censure of the Speaker, they must amend their resolution, and then intimated to them, that their specification of my crime must be, that I had in my possession a petition from slaves, praying for that which they themselves most ardently desired—namely, my expulsion from the House, if I should persist in presenting abolition petitions. The fact was so—but the ludicrous position into which they had floundered was that of calling down censure upon a member of the House for they knew not what—for phantoms of their own imagination—for the contents of a petition which they had not suffered to be read, and which no one but myself knew.

You will readily conceive that this explanation was not altogether satisfactory to those whose passions had so far outstripped their reason. Mr. Mann, a somewhat distinguished member from the state of New York, supplied them with cold comfort, by a long discourse against abolition and *fanatics*—entreating *the gentlemen from the South* not to make themselves uneasy about their slaves, nor to take too much to heart my exceedingly improper conduct in presenting, week after week, these abolition petitions; but to consider that I was a venerable, superannuated person, who in my better days would not have done so; and that now some mischievous persons had been trifling with me, and I had been trifling with the House.

But the *gentlemen from the South* were not to be so appeased. They very justly thought that this was no joking matter. Mr. Thompson, of South Carolina, now thought my conduct worse than he had thought before—and instead of one resolution, he was now prepared to offer three.

> "1. That the Hon. John Quincy Adams, by an effort to present a petition from slaves, has committed a great contempt of this House.
> 2. That the member from Massachusetts above named, by creating the impression, and leaving the House under that impression, that the said petition was for the abolition of slavery, when he knew that it was not, has trifled with the House.
> 3. That the Hon. John Quincy Adams receive the censure of the House for his conduct referred to in the preceding resolutions."

Here you see, instead of one crime, I had committed two—first, by *an effort* to present a petition from slaves, which was a great contempt of the House; secondly, by creating an impression, and leaving the House under it, that the petition was for the abolition of slavery, when I knew it was not—this was trifling with the House, and for these crimes I was to be censured. An *effort to present a petition*, a great contempt of the House! Creating an impression, and leaving the House under that impression, trifling with the House! In the annals of parliamentary deliberation, were such offences ever heard of before? Where, but in an assemblage of slave drivers and slaves, would you have believed that such resolutions could be offered, and entertained, and discussed, hour after hour? Yet there they stand, recorded on the Journals of the House of Representatives of the United States. They consumed all the remnant of the day. The gentlemen from the South had all the argument to themselves, and went on creating impressions and leaving the House under them, till, as evening twilight came on, Mr. Cambreleng told them that he was himself a native of a Southern State, and held the abolitionists in proper abomination; that he did at first intend to vote with them for censuring me, till he discovered that the petition was not for the abolition of slavery, but the reverse. It was evidently *a hoax*, played upon me *by a southern man*; and there might be members in the House who knew something about it. That I, to be sure, had been very troublesome by presenting so many abolition petitions; but I had *made atonement* for that by declaring my opinion against the abolition of slavery in the District of Columbia, and more than five years since he had heard me say that the remedy was worse than the disease. The gentlemen from the South were exasperated by these cool and cutting sarcasms, gravely delivered by the Chairman of the Committee of Ways and Means, till he was called upon for personal explanations. Some of them were for transferring the resolutions of censure for trifling with the House, from me to him; and some for joining him with me as an accomplice in the offence. In this temper the House adjourned; not a word having been said by me, or by any one in my behalf, since the new batch of censorial resolutions had been brought forth. Towards the close of the day, Mr. Haynes, the gentleman who at first did not know whether it would not be giving too much importance to a petition from slaves to object to receiving it, moved as an amendment to the three resolutions of Mr. Thompson, the following:—

> "*Resolved*, That John Quincy Adams, a representative from the state of Massachusetts, has rendered himself justly liable to the severest censure of this House, and is censured accordingly, for having attempted to present to the House the petition of slaves."

And this resolution came on the next morning, immediately after the reading of the Journal, and its correction, which was amended at my motion.

The question before the House was thus much simplified, and my crime now consisted only in *attempting* to present to the House a petition from slaves. But Mr. Jenifer, a very spirited slaveholding gentleman from Maryland, who had taken the floor at the close of the session of the day before, now announced that he wanted more specific information, before he should vote upon this resolution, and, in something of an overseer's tone, called upon me explicitly to declare whether a statement in the Globe of that morning, of what I had said the day before, was or was not correct—or whether I had attempted to present a petition from slaves. I answered his inquiry without delay; by stating that I had made no such attempt; that the report in the Globe was correct; that I had merely told the Speaker that I had a paper purporting to be a petition from slaves, which I was requested to present; that I had inquired of the Speaker whether it came within the resolution of the 18th of January, to which question I was yet waiting for an answer, and, if that answer should be that it did, I should present the petition. For the gentleman from Maryland must understand, that if slaves were laboring under grievances and afflictions not incident to their condition as slaves, but to their nature as human beings, born to trouble, as the sparks fly upward, and it were within the power and competency of the House to afford them relief, and they should petition for it—if the House would permit me, I most assuredly would present their petition, and if that avowal deserved the censure of the House, I was ready to receive it—for petition was prayer—it was the cry of the suffering for relief; of the oppressed for mercy. It was what God did not disdain to receive from man, whom he had created; and to listen to prayer—to hearken to the groan of wretchedness—was not merely a duty; it was a privilege; it was enjoyment; it was the exercise of a godlike attribute, indulged to the kindly sympathies of man. I would therefore not deny the right of petition to slaves—I would not deny it to a horse or a dog, if they could articulate their sufferings, and I could relieve them. If slaves should petition for any thing improper, unreasonable, or which ought not to be granted, I might pause, or refuse to present their petition; but if the object prayed for was just and reasonable in itself, and I had the power to grant it, I would—unless forbidden by the House—I would present it;

> "For earthly power doth then show likest God's,
>   When mercy seasons justice."

From this time, Mr. Jenifer was ready to pass any censure upon me without hesitation. He was sure I was the only man in the House who believed that slaves could, in any case whatever, have the right to petition, and he gave me up as a reprobate spirit, worthy of any punishment that could be inflicted upon me— only regretting that I had not presented the petition, that he might have the opportunity to vote for my expulsion from the House.

Still, it was obvious, on the state of facts, that I had not *attempted* to present to the House a petition from slaves. The resolution of Mr. Haynes, therefore, could not be made to suit the *master* appetite of revenge, till at last Mr. Dromgoole, of Virginia, bethought himself of suggesting to Mr. Waddy Thompson, as a substitute for his three resolutions, the following:—

> "*Resolved*, That the Hon. John Quincy Adams, a member of the House, by stating in his place that he had in his possession a paper, purporting to be a petition from slaves, and inquiring if it was within the meaning of a resolution heretofore adopted, (as preliminary to its presentation,) has *given color to the idea* that slaves have the right to petition, and of his readiness to be their organ; and that, for the same, he deserves the censure of this House.
>
> *Resolved*, That the aforesaid John Quincy Adams receive a censure from the Speaker, in the presence of the House of Representatives."

Here I must do Mr. Dromgoole the justice to admit, that the facts were for the first time stated with correctness and precision. I had given color to the idea, that the right of petition is confined to no color, and of my readiness to be the organ of slaves petitioning for redress of grievances which they only could suffer, and of which no voice but their own could complain. This was my offence, and this I had the more readily avowed, at the requisition of Mr. Jenifer, because, in the peremptory bluster of his manner, I had perceived the disposition to alarm me out of the admission, as, in the taunting confidence of his reply, that I was the *only* man in the House who entertained that opinion, I saw at once the exultation of his reliance upon numbers to put me down, and the disappointment of his failure in the attempt to intimidate me into a recantation or apology. And so satisfactory to the master-spirit of the South were the resolutions of Mr. Dromgoole, that Mr. Waddy Thompson accepted them as a modification of his own; and Mr. Haynes, with a view to speedy action, withdrew his proposed amendment, and left them in the possession of the field.

And thus my crime of *giving color to an idea*, was bandied about among *the gentlemen from the South*, till two of the slave representation themselves, men of intelligent minds and of intrepid spirits, fairly revolting at the senseless injustice of all these resolutions of censure upon me, dared to come out and declare their resistance to any resolution of censure upon me, for what I had done.—The first of these was Mr. Robertson, of Virginia, who thought, indeed, my course in persisting to present abolition petitions very offensive; and my avowal that I did believe slaves to possess in *any* case a right to petition, an aggravation of all my preceding offences—but who could not consent to join in trampling under foot the freedom of speech of the members of the House. Mr. Robertson was also the first who assigned a reason for denying to slaves the right of petition, which was, that Congress, having no right to interfere in the law of slavery at all, could not grant the prayer of any petition from slaves. This was begging the question; but it was argument, and not frenzy. From this time, all hope of carrying a vote of direct censure upon me was forlorn. Mr. Thompson complained of the instability of his brother slaveholders in the House, but yesterday so fiercely bent upon punishment, that they had spurred him on, and thought his resolutions not severe enough, now dropping off one by one, and flinching even from a vote of disapprobation against me. He, however, was not to be found so pliable. He would adhere inflexibly to his resolutions, though he should be left to vote for them alone, and would comfort himself with the reflection that the smaller the number who should support him, the greater the honor.

This was the last flickering of the flame which had burnt so intensely for nearly two days. Mr. Robertson's speech had broken the spell of slaveholding unanimity into which they had been constantly spiriting and lashing one another against me, and against the abolitionists, and against the North. To cover their retreat, Mr. Bynum, of North Carolina, one of the warmest champions of the South, after a long and bitter speech, moved, as a substitute for Mr. Waddy Thompson's third modification of his resolutions, the following:—

"*Resolved*, That any attempt to present any petition or memorial, from any slave or slaves, negro or free negroes, from any part of the Union, is a contempt of the House, calculated to embroil it in strife and confusion, incompatible with the dignity of the body; and any member guilty of the same justly subjects himself to the censure of the House.

Resolved, further, That a committee be appointed to inquire into the fact whether any such attempt has been made by any member of the House, and report the same as soon as practicable."

The whole doctrine of *contempts*, as borrowed from the practice of the British Parliament, is a law of tyranny, in which the House is at once accuser, party, judge, and executioner. Mr. Bynum's resolutions improve upon this system, by adding to these complicated attributes of the House, that of a retrospective legislator. Mr. Bynum dropped all mention of direct censure upon me, but he proposed, ex post facto, to declare to be a contempt of the House, that which no one before had even dreampt to be such. To *attempt* to present a petition not only from any slave, but from any free negro in any part of the Union, was, by Mr. Bynum's resolutions, not made a contempt for the future, but declared to be so already; and his second resolution proposed the appointment of a committee to inquire and report to the House whether such an *attempt* had been made by any member of the House.

Now, the Journals of the House bear record of repeated instances of petitions from free negroes and people of color, received, referred to committees, and reported upon, like others, without question of the right of the petitioners. The Constitution of the United States prohibits Congress from passing any *law* abridging the right of petition; and here, Mr. Bynum proposes, without law, by a mere resolution of the House, to abridge the right of petition, by declaring it a contempt of the House to attempt to present one—and then he institutes a court of inquiry, with himself at its head, and associates appointed by the master-Speaker, to ascertain and report whether such an attempt had been made by any member.

By the propositions of Mr. Bynum, the House, by resolution, would have made a law constituting a crime ex post facto; and then raised a Committee to ascertain and report whether any member had broken the law before it was made.

At this new turn of the debate, Mr. Graves, of Kentucky, following the example of Mr. Robertson, declared himself explicitly opposed to any resolution of censure upon me. He went further, and avowed the opinion that Congress have *power* to abolish slavery in the District of Columbia, though well aware that by this avowal he hazarded the displeasure of a great part of the slave representation in the House, and of many of his own constituents. Mr. Graves, like Mr. Robertson, was severe in his animadversions upon my course as a presenter of abolition petitions; and I should have felt with deep mortification the reproof of men so intelligent, fair-minded, and honorable, as I know them to be, had I not acted throughout the whole of these transactions under an impulse of a higher duty than it is in the competency of human approbation to command or to reward. They hazarded much in the land of slavery, even in showing by their deeds and words that they know what freedom is. I honor them for their spirit; I thank them for their defence of the freedom of speech in the House of which they were members—a defence the more creditable to them, inasmuch as it was the defence of their adversary against their allies; and I regret that, refusing to join in a vote of formal censure upon me by the House, they should have thought it necessary to express their individual censure upon my exercise of a right which they could not deny, and would not refuse.

Immediately preceding the offer of Mr. Bynum's resolutions, Governor Lincoln spoke the first word in my defence which had been uttered in the House. His speech has been well reported, published in several newspapers, and in a pamphlet, and has, I presume, been generally read by you. On the manner in which he spoke of me, it would not become me to remark. Of that in which he vindicated your character and honor, his hearers will long retain the memory; nor will it ever be forgotten by me.

Mr. Phillips represented to the Speaker that Mr. Bynum's resolutions, not being within the question of privilege, could not be moved as an amendment to the resolutions of censure; but the Speaker decided that they were in order, and Mr. Phillips had no alternative but to submit.

Mr. Patton tried his hand again. He moved as an amendment to Mr. Bynum's amendment of Mr. Waddy Thompson's third set of censorial resolutions, all moved as amendments to Mr. Patton's resolution that the petition from nine women of Fredericksburg should be taken up from the table and returned to me, and all decided by the Speaker to be perfectly in order. Mr. Patton now moved the following:—

> "*Resolved*, That the right of petition does not belong to the slaves of this Union, and that no petition from them can be presented to this House, without derogating from the rights of the slaveholding states, and endangering the integrity of the Union.
> *Resolved*, That any member who shall hereafter present any such petition to the House, ought to be considered as regardless of the feelings of the House, the rights of the South, and an enemy to the Union.
> *Resolved*, That the Hon. John Quincy Adams having solemnly disclaimed all design of doing any thing disrespectful to the House, in the inquiry he made of the Speaker, as to the petition purporting to be from slaves, and having avowed his intention not to offer to present the petition, if the House was of opinion that it ought not to be presented: therefore all further proceedings in regard to his conduct now cease."

These resolutions of Mr. Patton were one step further backward behind those of Mr. Bynum. The first of them declares that the right of petition does not belong to the slaves of this Union, and thus far it approached my question to the Speaker, but did not answer it; and to the negation of the right of the slave, it added a new offence to the criminal code, which, taken in connection with the second resolution, amounted to nothing less than constructive treason.

The second resolution endeavors, indeed, to elude the prohibition, by the constitution, of the enactment of *ex post facto* laws, by confining to future time the declaratory law of treason. Nor does it provide a punishment for this atrocious crime. It only says that any member who shall *hereafter* present any such petition to the House *ought to be considered* as regardless of the feelings of the House, the rights of the South, and an *enemy to the Union*.

Now, the Constitution of the United States declares that treason against the United States shall consist *only* in levying war against them, or in adhering to their *enemies*, giving them aid and comfort: but here is a resolution declaring that a member of the House ought to be considered as an *enemy to the Union*—FOR PRESENTING A PETITION.

The Constitution of the United States gives to each House of Congress the power to determine the rules of its proceedings, to punish its members for disorderly behavior, and, with the concurrence of two thirds, to expel a member. The power of punishment by the House is limited to the offence of disorderly behavior. If this resolution had been adopted, and any member should hereafter have presented a petition from slaves, what could they have done with him? There is not a word or syllable in the Constitution or laws of the United States, which prohibits slaves from petitioning, or a member of either House of Congress from presenting their petitions. There is an express provision of the Constitution that Congress shall pass no *law abridging* the right of petition; and here is a resolution, declaring that a member ought to be considered as regardless of the feelings of the House, the rights of the South, and an enemy to the Union, *for presenting a petition*.

Regardless of the feelings of the House! What have the feelings of the House to do with the free agency of a member in the discharge of his duty? One of the most sacred duties of a member is to present the petitions committed to his charge—a duty which he cannot refuse or neglect to perform, without violating his oath to support the Constitution of the United States. He is not, indeed, bound to present all petitions. If the language of the petition be disrespectful to the House, or to any of its members—if the prayer of the petition be unjust, immoral, or unlawful—if it be accompanied by any manifestation of intended violence or disorder on the part of the petitioners, the duty of the member to present it ceases; not from respect for the feelings of the House, but because these things themselves strike at the freedom of speech and action, as well of the House as of its members. Neither of these can be in the slightest degree affected by the mere circumstance of the condition of the petitioner, nor is there a shadow of reason why the feelings of the House should be outraged, by the presentation of a petition from slaves, any more than by petitions from soldiers in the army, from seamen in the navy, or from the working-women of a manufactory.

Regardless of the rights of the South! What are the rights of the South? What is the *South*? As a component portion of this Union, the population of the South consists of masters, of slaves, and of free persons, white and colored, without slaves. Of which of these classes would the *rights* be disregarded by the presentation of a petition from slaves? Surely not those of the slaves themselves; the suffering, the laborious, the *producing* class. Oh, no! there would be no disregard of *their* rights in the presentation of a petition from them. The very essence of the crime consists in an alleged *undue* regard for their rights; in not denying them the rights of human nature; in not classing them with horses, and dogs, and cats. Neither could the rights of the free people, without slaves, whether white, black, or colored, be disregarded by the presentation of a petition from slaves. Their rights could not be affected by it at all. The rights of the South, then, here mean the rights of the masters of slaves, which, to describe them by an inoffensive word, I will call the rights of *mastery*. These, by the Constitution of the United States, are recognized, not directly, but by implication; and protection is stipulated for them, by that instrument, to a certain extent. But they are rights incompatible with the inalienable rights of all mankind, as set forth in the Declaration of Independence; incompatible with the fundamental principles of the constitutions of all the free states of the Union, and therefore, when provided for in the Constitution of the United States, are indicated by expressions which must receive the narrowest and most restricted construction, and never be enlarged by implication. There is, I repeat, not one word, not one syllable in the Constitution of the United States, which interdicts to Congress the reception of petitions from slaves; and as there is express interdiction to Congress to abridge, by law, the right of petition, that right, upon every principle of fair construction, is as much the right of the South as of the North, as much the right of the slave as of the master; and the presentation of a petition from slaves, for a legitimate object, respectful in its language, and in its tone and character submissive to the decision which the House may pass upon it, far from disregarding the rights of the South, is a mark of signal homage to those rights.

An enemy to the Union! for presenting a petition! an enemy to the Union! I have shown that the presentation of petitions is among the most imperious duties of a member of Congress. I trust I have shown that the right to petition, guarantied to the people of the United States, without exception of slaves, express or implied, cannot be *abridged* by any act of both Houses, with the approbation of the President of the United States; but this resolution, by the act of one branch of the legislature, would effect an enormous abridgment of the right of petition, not only by denying it to one full sixth part of the whole people, but by declaring an enemy to the Union any member of the House who should present such a petition.

The third resolution, as if repenting of the concession that the presentation of petitions from slaves was not yet the heinous crime, which, according to the second, it was to be considered hereafter, graciously tendered to me a cessation of prosecution, for what was no offence, in consideration of my disclaimer of any intention to trifle with the House, and my promise not to present the petition if the House should refuse to receive it.

Yet these were the resolutions of a gentleman, who, upon every question disconnected with the color of the skin, is just, and fair, and intelligent, and inflexibly devoted to the principles of freedom.

These resolutions did not answer my question, but the first of them distinctly affirmed that the right of petition does not belong to the slaves of this Union. Mr. Patton assigned no reason for this averment, nor is there any thing in the Constitution or laws to sustain it. In the debate which ensued, and which consumed the remainder of the day, Mr. Cushing, in a very eloquent speech, proved it to be utterly untenable, and that the right of petition was a primitive, inalienable right, recognized by the Constitution of the United States as preëxisting to itself, and guarded from *abridgment,* in express terms, by one of its articles.

At this stage of the proceedings of the House, the day for opening and counting the votes, and declaring the result of the presidential election for the term of four years, then about to commence, intervened. The question for that day was suspended, and resumed on Thursday, the 9th of February, by an elaborate speech from Mr. French, of Kentucky. This gentleman is a judge, and made the only argument against the right of slaves to petition, which was delivered in the whole of this three days' debate. And what think you was the main stay of his argument? It was, that if slavery should be abolished in the slaveholding states, they would lose a part of their representation in Congress.

Mr. Milligan, the member from Delaware, moved to lay the whole subject on the table, but, upon my earnest remonstrance against this course, withdrew the motion.

Mr. Evans, of Maine, took the floor, and after reviewing and covering with ridicule the whole series of resolutions of censure upon me, was proceeding to a full defence and vindication of the abolition petitions, and of the character of the petitioners, when he was arrested by calls to order. The slave representation in the House could not endure, and would not tolerate, the discussion of the question whether slavery is a blessing to be perpetuated, or an evil to be removed. Mr. Evans was not permitted to proceed but upon restrictions and conditions to which he would not submit, and he yielded the floor to the *mastery* impartiality of the Speaker.

Mr. Patton presented a new modification of his resolutions, omitting the first, and reducing the second to the following terms:—

> "*Resolved*, That any member who shall hereafter present to the House any petition from the slaves of this Union, ought to be considered as regardless of the feelings of the House, the right of the Southern States, and unfriendly to the Union."

The third resolution was left as it had been offered on Tuesday.

This was the ultimatum, after three days of debate, nine tenths of which, at least, were occupied by the slave representation in adjusting the form in which they were to settle the principles of this controversy; this was the ultimatum of the law which they were now to dictate, and of the new offence by which they were to circumscribe the freedom of speech of the members of the House from the free portion of this Union, with reference to petitions from slaves.

The averment that the right of petition does not belong to the slaves of this Union was withdrawn, and the resolution, denouncing as a crime the presentation hereafter of any petition from the slaves of this Union was so far mitigated as to make it not quite treason. The member who should dare to present such a petition, was still to be considered as regardless of the feelings of the House—not indeed of the rights of the South, but of the right of the Southern States—and although not absolutely an enemy, yet *unfriendly* to the Union.

This, I say, was the ultimatum of the slave representation. Mr. Waddy Thompson accepted Mr. Patton's two resolutions, now presented, as a modification of all his preceding modifications. Mr. Bynum withdrew his proposed amendment, and Mr. Vanderpool, of New York, called for the *previous question.*

I had not yet been heard in my own defence. I claimed that privilege, and entreated Mr. Vanderpool to withdraw his motion, which he declined. The House, however, by a vote of 100 to 79, refused to second him, and I had permission to speak.

The substance of what I said has been published in the National Intelligencer, and more fully in the Boston Daily Advocate. It has also been republished in one of the newspapers within your district.

The previous question was then renewed, and after some explanations from Mr. Thompson, of South Carolina, separate questions were taken, by yeas and nays, upon each of Mr. Patton's resolutions; the first of which was rejected by a vote of 105 to 92; the second by a vote of 137 to 21; thirty-nine members, who had voted upon the first resolution, not voting at all upon the second.

The first was the only question of any importance with regard to the settlement of principles. Had it passed, it would have put an end to all freedom of speech and action in the House, for its object was not to declare that slaves have not the right of petition, but to make it an offence against the House, the Southern States, and the Union, to *present a petition.* The resolution applied, not to the right of the slave to petition, but to the right of the member to present the petition of slaves.

The vote upon this resolution drew the line of demarcation between the free and the slave representation more closely than perhaps any other vote ever taken in the House. Of the ninety-two members, who voted for the resolution, thirteen only were from the non-slaveholding states; and in the following proportions—six from New York, two from Maine, one from New Hampshire, one from Connecticut, two from Ohio, and one from Indiana, all politically devoted to the President elect. Of the slaveholding states, four members only voted against the resolution—the member from Delaware, almost a free state, two from Kentucky, and one from Missouri.

Fellow citizens:—Had the transactions of which I have given you this tedious detail, been merely conflicts of personal concernment to me—had they been merely desperate assaults upon my good name and character, for the purpose of destroying or undermining your confidence in me as your representative—I should have felt myself justified in asking your patient indulgence to the narrative, in justification of myself and of my conduct in your service. But higher motives have impelled me to this appeal to yourselves.

Since the existence of the Constitution of the United States, there has never before been an example of an attempt in the House of Representatives to punish one of its members for words spoken by him in the performance of his duty. The utmost constitutional power of the House would be to regard such words as disorderly, and to reprove the speaker of them by declaring them such. It is expressly provided by the Constitution, that for any speech or debate in either House of Congress, no senator or representative shall be questioned in any other place; but in this case, your representative was seriously, deliberately, and persistingly threatened with a prosecution, by a slaveholding grand jury, and a sentence to the penitentiary as an incendiary, for asking a question of the Speaker of the House. I will not recur to the history of the country from which we derive our descent, and especially our principles of freedom of speech and action in legislative assemblies, for examples, in which motions for total revolutions in the government, for subversion of the established religion, for setting aside and altering the succession to the crown, have been invariably held to be within the general freedom of speech and action to which every member of parliament is entitled. If I had offered in the House a resolution proposing an amendment to the Constitution of the United States, emancipating all the slaves in the Union, and declaring slavery, within its borders, forever abolished, I should have done nothing beyond the exercise of my rights; but let it once be settled and admitted that the House can, by resolution, put a member to the bar for offering to present a petition from slaves, and what is there to prevent the extension of the same interdict to any other subject than slavery? Mr. Bynum's resolutions actually proposed to extend it to petitions from free negroes. Had Mr. Patton's resolutions been adopted—had the House once assumed a censorial power over its members for acts performed in the discharge of their duty—I have no doubts that at the very next session of Congress, the same proscriptive censure would have been applied to all petitions for the abolition of slavery in the District of Columbia, and from thence to every other petition, the prayer of which would be displeasing to a party majority in the House, till the right of petition itself, the rod of Aaron in the Ark of your Constitution, would wither into a mere instrument of oppression and revenge, wielded by the hand of faction.

The decision of the House upon the two resolutions last offered by Mr. Patton, proved that a majority of the House were not yet prepared to assume this censorial power over its members; but the proceedings of the House on the subject of this petition, and *all* petitions relating to slavery, did not terminate here. I must ask your further attention and patience for the conclusion of my story, which may conduct you to the close of the session, and possibly to the inaugural address of the new President of the United States.

JOHN QUINCY ADAMS.

WASHINGTON, 20th March, 1837.
*To the Inhabitants of the Twelfth Congressional
District of Massachusetts.*

FELLOW-CITIZENS:—In my preceding addresses, I have spread before you the fifteen successive resolutions, the result of the whole combined slave statesmanship of the House of Representatives of the United States, all having one and the same purpose of passing a vote of censure upon me, for asking, in the discharge of my duty as a member, a question of the Speaker.

The two resolutions upon which they had finally forced a vote of the House, by yeas and nays, were rejected, but my question was not answered, and they were aware that it could not be answered, negatively. It had not been, whether the House would receive a petition from slaves, but whether a petition from slaves came within the resolution of the 18th of January. When the resolution declaring that I had trifled with the House was under consideration, one of the most prominent allegations laid to my charge was, that, by asking the question, I had intended indirectly to cast ridicule upon that resolution, and upon the House for adopting it. Nor was this entirely without foundation. I did not intend to cast ridicule upon the House, but to expose the absurdity of that resolution, against which I had protested as unconstitutional and unjust. But the characteristic peculiarity of this charge against me was, that while some of the gentlemen of the South were urging the House to pass a vote of censure upon me, for a distant and conjectural inference of my intention to deride that resolution, others of them, in the same debate, and on the same day, were showering upon the same resolution direct expressions of unqualified contempt, without even being called to order. Like the saints in Hudibras—

> "The saints may do the same thing by
> The Spirit in sincerity,
> Which other men are prompted to,
> And at the devil's instance do;
> And yet the actions be contrary,
> Just as the saints and wicked vary."

So it was with the gentlemen of the South. While Mr. Pickens could openly call the resolution of the 18th of January a miserable and contemptible resolution; while Mr. Thompson could say it was fit only to be burnt by the hands of the hangman, without rebuke or reproof,—I was to be censured by the House for casting ridicule upon them, by asking the question whether the resolution included petitions from slaves.

They were dissatisfied with the result of their crusade against me, in the vindictive pursuit of which they had not only forgotten to answer my question, but even to obtain from the House a declaration denying the right of slaves to petition. On Friday morning, several of them were absent from their seats in the House, and mysterious givings out were circulated that a caucus meeting of the South had been held, in which grave proposals had been made that they should secede in a body and go home. This was an old expedient tried before, some years since, and not without some effect upon the simple good nature of the North. Whether it was really brought forward at this time, I cannot absolutely say; but the rumors were, that a first and second meeting were held, at which the opinions expressed were found so discordant, that it was finally concluded to be the wisest course to return to their seats in the House, and negotiate with the free representation for a *reconsideration* of one of the rejected resolutions. The interposition of the President elect of the United States was also said to have been solicited and obtained; and there is authority from his southern adherents for the assurance that it was exercised in a manner altogether satisfactory to them. The sympathies of the whig members from the free states were likewise invoked, by their opposition associates of the nullification creed, and the Pennsylvania delegation, who, to a man, had been found inaccessible to the censorial resolutions, were now many of them coaxed into a compromise with the dark spirit of slavery, so indignantly and justly characterized by the governor of that commonwealth.

The gentlemen from the South had rung all the changes of their censorial resolutions exclusively among themselves. The peace-offering to their wounded sensibilities was to come entirely from representatives of freemen. The motion for reconsideration of the first rejected resolution of Mr. Patton, was made on Friday evening by Mr. Lane, of Indiana, and carried the next morning by the immediate application of the previous question. Even before this vote of reconsideration, Mr. Taylor, of New York, and Mr. Ingersoll, of Philadelphia, had asked leave of the House to offer resolutions propitiatory to the anxieties and resentments of the gentlemen of the South. The resolution presented by Mr. Taylor deserves special attention, as it may be considered as indicative of the opinions and councils of the present President of the United States; that of Mr. Ingersoll as expressive of the anti-abolition sentiments prevailing at this time in the city of Philadelphia, and less intensely throughout the northern part of the Union. The first of these resolutions was offered by Mr. Taylor, and the second by Mr. Ingersoll, probably in concert with Mr. Thompson, of South Carolina, the mover of the first resolution of censure upon me, and who finally accepted Mr. Ingersoll's resolution as a substitute for his own.

Both the resolutions underwent sundry modifications before they were adopted by the House. That of Mr. Ingersoll was, in its last mutation, reduced to this shape:—

> "An inquiry having been made by an honorable gentleman from Massachusetts, whether a paper which he held in his hand, purporting to be a petition from certain slaves, and declaring themselves to be slaves, came within the order of the House of the 18th of January, and the said paper not having been received by the Speaker, he stated that, in a case so extraordinary and novel, he would take the advice and counsel of the House.
> *Resolved*, That this House cannot receive said petition without disregarding its own dignity, the rights of a large class of the citizens of the South and West, and the Constitution of the United States."

You will remark, that while the preamble recites my inquiry of the Speaker, as the reasons for the resolutions, yet the resolution itself evades answering my inquiry. My question was, whether the petition came within the order of the 18th of January. The answer is, that the House cannot *receive* said petition, &c. It is no answer at all. The Speaker had already decided that two petitions presented by me, and not *received*, were included within the order of the 18th of January; and therefore the fact that the petition from slaves had not been received, afforded no reason for excluding it from the operation of the order of the 18th of January. I moved as an amendment to Mr. Ingersoll's resolution, that the order of the 18th of January should be inserted in it word for word, followed by a declaration that the petition from slaves was not within the order of the House, and I asked him to accept this as a modification of his resolution, which he declined. He said he would give his reasons for declining, if I desired; but he gave none. His resolution was carried by the previous question; but if you will read his resolution, as it would have read with the insertion of the order, you will not need to inquire what his reason was.

The resolution contains the averment of three distinct propositions, declaring that the House could not receive the petition, without disregarding,

1. Its own dignity.
2. The rights of a large class of the citizens of the South and West, and,
3. The Constitution of the United States.

How the House could disregard its dignity by receiving a petition, is beyond my comprehension. The only reason assigned for it, is the condition of the petitioners, because they are slaves. The sentiment, in the bosom of any free American, that one sixth part of his countrymen are, by the accident of their birth, deprived even of the natural right of prayer, is degrading enough to human nature; but that because, in one portion of this Union, the native American becomes, by descent from African ancestry, an outcast of human nature, classed with the brute creation, within the boundaries of the state in which he was born, therefore, it is beneath the dignity of the General Legislative Assembly of a nation, founding its existence upon the natural and inalienable rights of man, to listen to his prayer, or even to receive his petition, is an opinion to which I trust your judgments will never assent, and a sentiment which your hearts will reject with disgust.

"The *rights* of a large class of the citizens of the South and West," for the prayer of the petition, was not for, but against the abolition of slavery in the District of Columbia. It was the voice of slaves hugging their chains, and praying that they might not be broken. It was impossible that *any* action of the House upon that petition, whether of compliance or of refusal, could in any manner impair any rights of any citizen of the South or of the West.

Nor was Mr. Ingersoll more fortunate in his third averment, that the House could not *receive* the petition without disregarding the Constitution of the United States. The truth is directly the reverse. It was his resolution that disregarded and trampled under foot the Constitution of the United States, which expressly forbids Congress from abridging, even by *law*, the right of petition, and which, not by the remotest implication, limits that right to freemen. This, fellow-citizens, is a point upon which every one of you can judge for himself. Let him who is not familiarly acquainted with that instrument, read it—let him read and search it, for the article, section, or paragraph, from which so much as a plausible *inference* can be drawn, forbidding either House of Congress from *receiving* a petition from slaves. He will find abundant evidence that the authors of the Constitution considered slavery as one of those vessels of dishonor, which, albeit impairing the purity of our political institutions, could not even be *named* with decency in a compact formed for securing to the people of the Union the blessing of liberty. He will find that, in every instance where slaves are alluded to, it is always as *persons*, and not as property; that the words *slave* or *slavery* are not found in the whole document; that they are recognized as members of the community, possessing rights even in the provisions depriving them of their exercise and enjoyment; that their right to be represented in Congress is admitted, even in the provision which curtails it by two fifths, and transfers the remainder to their masters; that their right to the protection of the laws, and to the enjoyment of freedom in the free states, is admitted even in the provisions that when *escaping* from the states where they are held to service or labor, they shall be delivered up to their masters. But you will not find one word which expressly, no, not one word which, by rational construction, liberal or strict, deprives them of the right of petition.

This resolution, therefore, far better suited to the meridian of Charleston than to that of Philadelphia, is a worthy companion of the three reported by Mr. H. L. Pinckney, at the first session of the last Congress, and the second of which was repeated by the order of the 18th of January last. Of that order, many of you have manifested your high disapprobation, by petitioning the House to rescind it. But the resolution of Mr. Ingersoll bows the knee yet nearer to prostration before the spirit of slavery. It surrenders the post at which the tottering freedom of the North and Centre had erected a breastwork of defence to the right of petition. The gentlemen of the South had been desperately struggling through two sessions of Congress, for a positive refusal of the House to *receive* any petition for the abolition of slavery in the District of Columbia, or in any manner relating to slavery. This refusal to *receive*, they had not been able to carry, till a representative from the city of William

Penn, came forward as their volunteer auxiliary. His resolution has set the example of refusing to *receive* petitions, on no better ground than the condition of the petitioners. At the next step in the progress of servility, the same argument will be applied with more plausibility to *the object of the petition*, and the House will be called to resolve a formal exclusion and refusal to receive any petition relating to slavery or the abolition of slavery—and with the right of petition on this subject, the freedom of speech in the House will be in like manner abridged. That the freedom of the press in this city will share the same fate, you have premonitory symptoms in the pledge already extorted from the National Intelligencer, immediately after the publication of Mr. Slade's letter, containing the argument which he intended to address to the House on the right of slaves to petition, but which was cut off by the previous question.

If this refusal to receive petitions, and to hear deliberative argument upon any question relating to slavery, could be confined to that subject alone, I might have spared myself the reluctant labor, and you the weary perusal of these addresses—but if coming events cast their shadows before them, we shall soon be hurried into the midst of a revolution more formidable than any collision between the coordinate departments of the government for patronage, any transitory tampering with the currency, any scramble between rival usurers and stock-jobbers for deposits of the public money, any swindling Indian treaties, or more swindling Indian wars, or any deep dissension between the cotton-gin of the planter and the spinning-jenny of the factory. All these may be compromised—all these may be occasionally used as ladders to power, and ascended or overleaped, according to the shrewdness or the impetuosity of the aspirants, to reach the summit of ambition. On all these lines of separation and opposition between the different portions of the Union, the counteracting impulses of popular leaders may balance each other, and the result is nothing worse than fluctuations of public policy, and perhaps shortened presidential terms. But the conflict of interests, and of principles involved in the jarring elements of freedom and slavery implanted in the physical, moral, intellectual nature of our institutions, must sooner or later come to an issue, and must control the destinies not merely of this nation, but of this hemisphere, and of man upon this planet. The abolition of slavery in the District of Columbia is but a drop of water to the ocean—but a mite in the mountain laboring with the freedom of man. The convulsive spasm produced in the House of Representatives of the United States, by the mere question whether they would in *any* case receive a petition from slaves, was not occasioned by any galvanism in the question itself—it was the flash of light over the closed eyes of the slaveholder, exhibiting to him his slave petitioning for his freedom. It is said that in the turbulent diets of Poland, before her subjugation, every member of the body possessed the veto power over every act of their legislation. The assemblies were held in open air. The nobles attended them, mounted on coursers fleet as the winds. The right to pronounce the veto was strictly constitutional; but woe to him who pronounced; for from the moment that it issued from his lips, his only safety was in flight. His life was on the speed of his horse. If he did not start as he spoke, his noble associates of the diet rushed upon him instantly, and cut him to pieces. If he fled, they gallopped in pursuit, and whoever overtook him, by a stroke of his partisan, severed his head from his body as he flew. This was the remedy for the exercise of a constitutional right in the republican monarchy of Poland. The tiger turn of the gentlemen from the South, upon the member who asked the obnoxious question, was indicative of the same spirit habitually prevalent among the nobles of the Polish diet. Mr. Ingersoll's resolutions partook of the same infusion—no longer vindictive, but still minatory.

Mr. Taylor's resolution was in far more measured, and less questionable terms. It was in these words:—

> "*Resolved*, That slaves do not possess the right of petition, secured to the citizens of the United States by the Constitution."

This resolution was probably prepared by, or after consultation, with the President elect of the United States. It was amply sufficient, so long as a majority of the House of Representatives shall concur in that opinion, to exclude the reception of any petition from slaves; but it was not satisfactory to the gentlemen from the South. Their purpose was to stigmatize the presentation, or, by one of Speaker Polk's distinctions, the offer to present such petition. The resolution of Mr. Ingersoll *gave color to their idea*, and furnished them with a precedent for the future refusal of *any* petition relating to the abolition of slavery.

Both the resolutions are mere opinions of a majority of the House, reversible at any day when the majority of the House shall entertain a contrary opinion. It is not competent for the House of Representatives to adjudicate what are or are not the rights secured to the citizens of the United States by the Constitution; but if Mr. Taylor's resolution is true, a citizen of the United States, enslaved at Algiers, Tunis, or Tripoli, would possess no right to petition Congress for his redemption, or for any measures to effect it.

The question whether slaves possess the right of petition, is of no practical importance, except as the denial of the right is an abridgment of the right itself. Their masters will take care to keep the redressing of all their grievances in their own hands, and will redress them in their own way. But the resolution that the House cannot *receive* a petition from them, is an abridgment not only of their right of petition, but of the constitutional power of the House; and the precedent of that abridgment of power in one case yields a principle that may be applied in numberless others, till the whole right of petition shall, like the attainment of office, be numbered among the *spoils of victory*—the exclusive possession of the dominant party of the day.

Both the resolutions were adopted by yeas and nays—that of Mr. Ingersoll, by a vote of 160 to 35; that of Mr. Taylor, by 162 to 18.

The vote of the House, on both the resolutions, indicates, with much precision, the *temper of the House* upon the subject of the abolition of slavery. I believe further, that the comparative numbers on both sides fairly represented the numbers, as well as the opinions of the constituent body, the people of the United States. I have no reason to think there was one member of the House who would have voted for the immediate abolition of slavery in the District of Columbia. The majority were very averse to receiving any petitions for that object;

nor was there opportunity afforded me of presenting any more, of the multitudes which I received and was requested to present. On Monday, the 13th of February, the order of receiving petitions was reversed; commencing with the territories, and proceeding from South to North; and upon the state of Massachusetts being called, the House adjourned at the motion of Mr. Cave Johnson, a Van Buren member, from Tennessee. On the 20th and 27th of February, days when, by the rules of the House, petitions should have been received, the rules were suspended to give preference to other business. In the mean time, an average of eight or ten petitions every day, were coming to me, with requests that I would present them. On the last day of the session, I had two hundred of them in my hands, from the states of Massachusetts, Maine, New Hampshire, Vermont, New York, Pennsylvania, Ohio, Indiana, and North Carolina. It had been customary to allow members having petitions, which they had not had the opportunity to present, to leave them, at the close of the session, with the clerk, and they were entered upon the journals. This the Speaker now declined to allow, without a special order of the House. Mr. Lawrence, who had also a number of petitions to present, moved for such an order; but objection was made to the reception of his resolution, and the presentation of several hundreds of petitions was suppressed; and, among the rest, several relating to subjects in no wise connected with slavery or its abolition. Sons of the Plymouth Pilgrims! I have given you a statement, faithful and accurate, of the condition of your right of petition, in the House of Representatives of the United States, at the close of the twenty-fourth Congress. In the Senate, the same right was equally prostrated, though with less resistance, and by the means of other forms.

Since then, the inauguration of Mr. Van Buren has placed a new chief magistrate at the head of this Union. To those of you who have petitioned for the abolition of slavery in the District of Columbia, it cannot be indifferent to learn that the only specific point of policy upon which he has thought proper to pledge the conduct of his administration in advance, is the denial of that very measure. He declares that, even if a bill for abolishing slavery in the District of Columbia should obtain the sanction of a majority in both Houses of Congress, he would oppose to its enactment his constitutional negative. If this declaration means no more than it imports, there is little prospect that its sincerity or the firmness of his adhesion to its principle will ever be put to the test. There is not the remotest prospect, that, within the term of his administration, a majority of either, much less of both Houses of Congress, will be found prepared to vote for that measure; and if so great a change in the public mind should be effected, as would produce majorities of both Houses in favor of abolition, it will not be within the efficacy of his veto to resist the course of the torrent. But if, as there is reason to apprehend, this premise is intended as a pledge, that the whole influence, official and personal, of the President of the United States shall be applied to sustain and perpetuate the institution of domestic slavery, it is a melancholy prognostic of a new system of administration, of which the dearest interests of New England will be the first victims, and of which the ultimate result can be no other than the dissolution of the Union.

Slavery has already had too deep and too baleful an influence upon the affairs and upon the history of this Union. It can never operate but as a slow poison to the *morals* of any community infected with it. Ours is infected with it to the vitals. We are told that the national government has no right to interfere with the institution of domestic slavery in the states, *in any manner*. What right, then, has domestic slavery to interfere in any manner with the national government? What right has slavery to interfere in the free states with the dearest institutions of their freedom? with the right of habeas corpus? with the right of trial by jury? with the freedom of the press? with the freedom of speech? with the sacred privacy of correspondence by the mail? What right has slavery to interfere with the laws of other nations productive of freedom? What right to interfere with the laws of Bermuda? of the Bahama Islands? of Great Britain? What right has she to cast her living chattels upon a soil which has banished her forever, and then come whining to the national government that the touch of the soil of liberty has quickened her chattels into freemen; and requiring of the national government to claim indemnity for her emancipated chattels. Nay, more and worse—what right has slavery to chide the national government for not demanding her indemnity in a tone sufficiently peremptory? for not threatening Great

Britain with WAR, if she lingers longer to pay the price of sinews bought and sold?

If the national government has no right to interfere with the institution of domestic slavery in the states, *in any manner*, what right has domestic slavery to issue from her consecrated boundaries, and call on the national government for protection, for defence, for vindication of her pretended and polluted rights? What right has she to show her face upon the ocean, where the laws of the nation have pronounced her detested traffic PIRACY? The independence of sovereign states, from all foreign interference with their municipal institutions, is reciprocal, or it is nothing. If you have no right to interfere with the slavery of South Carolina, the slavery of South Carolina has no right to interfere with your freedom.

If the national government has no right to interfere with the institution of domestic slavery in any of the states, what right has that same government to hang on your neck the millstone of Texian slavery?—reinstituted slavery, in a land where once that curse of God had been extinguished?—slavery restored by fraud and treachery, and the imposture of a painted harlot, usurping the name of freedom? Is the annexation of Texas, with her execrable load of *eternal* slavery, to the Union—is that one of the engagements implied in Mr. Van Buren's pledge never to sign a bill for the abolition of slavery in the District of Columbia? If the pledge of the inaugural address means any thing more than soothing sound, it means that the maintenance and perpetuation of slavery in this Union, shall be the cardinal point, the polar star, of Mr. Van Buren's administration. And with that pledge, can you doubt that the manacles of Texian slavery will be fastened upon your hands, and the fetters of Texian slavery upon your feet?—Children of Carver, and Bradford, and Winslow, and Alden!—the pen drops from my hand!

JOHN QUINCY ADAMS.

SPEECH OF JOHN QUINCY ADAMS,

OF MASSACHUSETTS,

IN THE U. S. HOUSE OF REPRESENTATIVES,

February 9, 1837,

On the Resolutions to censure him for inquiring of the Speaker, whether a paper purporting to be from Slaves, came within the order of the House, which laid on the table all petitions relating to Slavery.

[Reported by the Editor of the Boston Daily Advocate.]

———

Mr. Speaker:—I shall endeavor to occupy as little of the time of this House as possible, in what I am about to say; and shall forbear to introduce into my remarks a great deal I had intended to say, should I be permitted to speak in my defence. I wish to bring back the House to the only question really before it; and that is, the question I propounded to the Speaker, and which he put to the House last Monday, whether a paper, which I held in my hand, purporting to come from slaves, was within the resolution of this House, laying on the table all petitions, resolutions and papers relating to the subject of slavery. On that inquiry, no question has been taken by the House. I am anxious that question should be taken by yeas and nays, whether this House, under any circumstances, will receive a petition from slaves.

When I made that inquiry, a member from Georgia (Mr. Haynes) said he could not tell in what manner to meet a proposition of this kind. It might be giving it more importance than it deserved, to notice it at all. Well, sir, if it was deserving of no attention, why did not the House vote directly on the proposition of the Speaker, yea or nay, whether that paper came within the resolution of the House? Instead of that, the House has been occupied four days, by the attempts of gentlemen to censure me for doing what I did not attempt to do.—Now, sir, I did not present that paper to the House. I knew it was a question that demanded deliberation. I knew it would receive deep attention from this House, from this nation, and from the civilized world. I was prepared to submit to any decision the House might take upon it, but I was desirous that the House should take a direct vote upon it, and that the vote should remain a record for all time. But I was aware that it opened the whole question of the condition of slavery in this country, and the whole extent of the rights and privileges of members of this House, in the exercise of the liberty of speech. That freedom of speech is, I trust, to one portion of the House, still dear. Of another portion, I cannot say, from what I have seen and heard within these four days, that I entertain that hope. I say I was aware that the answer to my question opened the whole subject of the condition of slaves, and the right of speech of members of this House. Well, sir, *has this question been considered?* Of all the gentlemen who, for three days, have consumed the time of this House upon the succession of resolutions of censure upon me for asking that question, one gentleman only, (Mr. French, of Kentucky,) who has filled a judicial station, gave us what he thought a sound constitutional argument, to show that this House ought not to receive petitions from slaves under any circumstances. The argument of that gentleman was able; but if the rejection of the petition depends on that argument, those who vote with him must recur to other arguments to sustain their course. What was his argument? It was, that, if you abolish slavery in the states of this Union, by taking away a portion of the representation in slave states, you violate the Constitution. Now, I ask for the chain or connection between the premises and the conclusion. Is that the gentleman's logic, that, if you abolish slavery, you take away a portion of the right of representation, secured by the Constitution, and *therefore* the slave has no right to petition?

[Mr. FRENCH rose and explained, not materially varying the proposition.]

Mr. ADAMS. Has the gentleman connected his premises and conclusion any better than before? Suppose, for a moment, that slavery were abolished; how would it follow that the slave states would lose any portion of their representation? Would not the consequence be directly the reverse, and increase, instead of diminishing, their representation? If slavery were abolished in the states, those who are now represented as slaves, would form a part of the whole number of free persons, and would be represented as such. But suppose, for argument sake, that the abolition of slavery *should* reduce the proportional representation of the slave states. What has my question to do with the abolition of slavery in the states? My question was, whether a petition from slaves came within the order of the 18th of January, that *all* memorials, resolutions, petitions, *and papers*, relating, in any manner, to slavery or the slave trade, should, without being printed or referred, be laid on the table, and no further action of the House should be had thereon. The order made no discrimination of persons, from whom the petitions or papers should come. It included *all* petitions—*all* papers. The paper that I held was a petition—it was a *paper*. It came rigidly within the letter of the order—and what was there to exclude it from its spirit? It was to be laid on the table without reading, without printing, without being referred, without further action upon it by the House. Why should it not come under that order? It came from slaves? There was nothing in that order excluding petitions from slaves. There is not a word in the Constitution of the United States excluding petitions from slaves. Suppose the abolition of slavery *should* reduce the representation of the slave states; does that prove that, without the abolition of slavery, the slave shall not be permitted to cry for mercy? to plead for pardon? to utter the shriek of perishing nature for relief? The gentleman argued upon a question entirely different from that put by the Speaker to the House, and which I yet hope the House will answer, whether, under *any* circumstances, they will receive a petition from slaves?

I beg leave to explain my views of the argument on the right of petition. One of my colleagues (Mr. Cushing) has justly said, that the right of petition is not a right derived from the Constitution, but a preëxisting right of man, secured by a direct prohibition in the Constitution to Congress to pass any law to impair or abridge it. Sir, the framers of the Constitution would have repudiated the idea that they were giving to the people the right of petition. No, sir. That right God gave to the whole human race, when he made them *men*,—the right of prayer, by asking a favor of another. My doctrine is, that this right belongs to humanity,—that the right of petition is the right of prayer, not depending on the condition of the petitioner; and I say, if you attempt to fix any limit to it, you lay the foundation for restriction to any extent that the madness of party spirit may carry it. This is my belief, and if the House decide that the paper I have described comes within the resolution, I will present it, and, in so doing, shall feel that I am performing a solemn duty.

What, sir! place the right of petition on the character and condition of the petitioner, or base it upon a mere political privilege! Such a decision would present this country to all the civilized world as more despotic than the worst of barbarian nations. The sultan of Turkey cannot walk the streets of Constantinople and refuse to receive a petition from the vilest slave, who stands to meet him as he passes by. The right of petition contests no power; it admits the power. It is supplication; it is prayer; it is the cry of distress, asking for relief; and, sir, sad will be the day when it is entered on the Journals of this House, that we will, under no circumstances, receive the petition of slaves. When you begin to limit the right, where shall it stop? The gentleman on my left (Mr. Patton, of Virginia) objected to another petition, which I did present, from women of Fredericksburg, because it came from free colored people. That was giving *color to an idea* with a vengeance!* But the gentleman went further, and made the objection that I had presented a petition from women of infamous character—prostitutes, I think he called them.

[Mr. PATTON rose to explain. It was not so. When the gentleman presented that petition, which I knew came from mulattoes in a slave state, I meant to confine my objection to petitions of mulattoes or free negroes in the Southern States. I meant to rescue the ladies of Fredericksburg from the stigma of having signed such a petition. Sir, no lady in Fredericksburg would sign such a petition.]

Mr. ADAMS. With respect to the question what female is entitled to the character of a lady, and what not, I should be sorry to enter into a discussion here. I have never made it a

---

* One of the resolutions proposed to censure Mr. Adams for having attempted to give *color to the idea* that slaves had a right to petition!

condition of my presenting a petition here, from females, that they should all be ladies, though, sir, I have presented petitions for the abolition of slavery in this District, from ladies as eminently entitled to be called such, as the highest aristocrats in the land. When I have presented these petitions, I have usually said they were from *women,* and that, to my heart, is a dearer appellation than *ladies.*

But, sir, I recur to my first position—that when you establish the doctrine that a slave shall not petition because he is a slave, that he shall not be permitted to raise the cry for mercy, you let in a principle subversive of every foundation of liberty, and you cannot tell where it will stop. The next step will be that the character, and not the claims, of petitioners will be the matter to be discussed on this floor; and whenever, as in the case of the gentleman from Virginia, (Mr. Patton,) any member finds a name on a petition which belongs to a person whom he says he knows to be of bad character, a motion will be made not to receive the petition, or to return it to the member who offered it. The gentleman from Virginia (Mr. Patton) says he knows these women, and that they are infamous. *How* does the gentleman know it? [A laugh.]

[Mr. PATTON. I did not say that I knew the women, personally. I knew from others that the character of one of them was notoriously bad.]

Mr. ADAMS. I am glad the gentleman now says he does not know these women, for if he had not disclaimed that knowledge, I might have asked *who* it was that made these women infamous,—whether it was those of their own color or their masters. I have understood that there are those among the colored population of slaveholding states, who bear the image of their masters. [Great sensation.]

Mr. GLASCOCK, of Georgia, here went across the hall to the seat of Mr. Adams, and, amidst cries of "Order," held up to him the petition of the women of Fredericksburg, and said, "Is not that your hand-writing, endorsed 'From ladies of Fredericksburg'?"

Mr. ADAMS. Mr. Speaker, I did not designate them as ladies when I presented the petition. That is my hand-writing; but when I endorsed it, and sent it to the table, I did not know or suspect that the petitioners were colored people.

Here, then, is another limitation to the right of petition. First, it is denied to slaves, then to free persons of color, and then to persons of notoriously bad character. Now, sir, if you begin by limiting this right as to slaves, you next limit it as to all persons of color, and then you go into inquiries as to the character of petitioners before you will receive petitions. There is but one step more, and that is to inquire into the political faith of petitioners. Each side will represent their opponents as being infamous; and what becomes of the right of petition? Where and how will the right of petition exist at all, if you put it on these grounds?

A gentleman from Virginia, (Mr. Robertson,) to whose candor and generosity on this occasion I offer my tribute of thanks, as it contrasts with the treatment I experience from others,—though disapproving, in the strongest terms, the pertinacity of zeal which I have so often manifested in behalf of this right of petition,—is unwilling to pass a vote of formal censure upon me, because he sees how manifestly incompatible that would be with *any* freedom of speech in this House. He says—and he is a distinguished lawyer—that there can be no right to petition, where there is no power to grant the prayer. This is ingenious and plausible; but that gentleman, even whose disapprobation is more painful to me than would be the formal censure of others, might excuse me, if I cannot assent to the correctness of his argument. The want of power to grant the prayer of a petition is a very sufficient reason for rejecting that prayer, but it cannot impair the right of the petitioner to pray.

The question of power applies to the authority to grant the petition, but not to the right of the petitioner to present his petition. The power to grant it is often one of the most mooted questions in the world. In relation to this very matter of slavery, the power to grant the prayer of those who ask for its abolition in the District of Columbia, is the question that divides this House. Ask the gentlemen from slaveholding states, in this House, whether Congress has that power. Not one of them will say they have.

[Mr. GRAVES, of Kentucky, who was sitting near Mr. Adams, and who had declared, in this debate, that he held Congress had that power, reminded him of the fact.]

Mr. ADAMS.   Yes, one gentleman from Kentucky has affirmed that Congress has the power to abolish slavery in this District, but very few from slaveholding states will say so; and I do not know what it may cost that gentleman for having uttered such an opinion on this floor. Ask two of the representatives from Maine, ask the members from Vermont, from Massachusetts, from Rhode Island, from Connecticut, from—no, I will not go to New Hampshire nor New York, until I see how they vote on the question before the House. Ask the representatives of none but freemen on this floor, and their answer will be that Congress has the power.

The ground of the gentleman from Virginia, who denies the right of petition without the power to grant, is perfectly consistent with his doctrine that Congress has no power to abolish slavery in the District of Columbia; but, sir, that is not the opinion of this House, and this House is anti-abolition, by an overwhelming majority. I am so myself; but, upon the single question of the power of Congress to abolish slavery within the District, there is a great majority of this House in favor of the power.

The gentleman from Virginia (Mr. Robertson) believes that Congress has no such power, and here he denies the right of petition for the exercise of a power which Congress does not possess. Well, sir, for the sake of the argument, I might grant him his premises, and then deny his conclusion. It would reduce the right of petition to nothing more than the right of the predominant party, for the time being, to petition. It would exclude all petitions from those who held with a minority in Congress, as to the right to exercise any given power; and the right of petition would be hedged in, until it would be reduced to a mere nullity as to its essential characteristic—a supplication from one man in distress to another, who, he believes, has the power to relieve him. I wish it was in my power to illustrate this principle further, without taking up more of the time of the House than I intend to do; but I forbear. This, sir, is the ground of my doctrine—that the right of petition cannot be limited, by any act of this House, so as to deny the right to supplicate to the slave.

In the course of the argument on the right of petition, I should say *debate*, sir, during three days, the real question before the House has been changed to an almost countless series of resolutions, bearing down upon me, all intended, directly or indirectly, to censure me for asking a question of the Speaker, which he referred to the House, and which the House has not yet answered. I will not go through a detail of all these resolutions, with which gentlemen from the South pounced down upon me like so many eagles upon a dove. I make no account of the cries heard all around, when I asked that question, "Expel him, expel him!" They are not in the resolutions. The first resolution to censure me came from the gentleman from Georgia, (Mr. Haynes.) That was not strong enough, and was followed by one more bitter, from the gentleman from South Carolina, (Mr. Waddy Thompson.) Even that was thought too mild for my offence, and was followed by a *modification* from the gentleman from Alabama, (Mr. Lewis,) which the gentleman from South Carolina accepted. I will not enumerate the rest, as they were showered upon me in quick succession, all reminding me of the exclamation of Dame Quickly,

"O! day and night, but these are bitter words!"

But, in the midst of the exultation of the gentlemen,—for they seemed sure of two thirds of the House to carry any thing they chose to propose,—I was under the necessity of rising, as soon as I could get the floor, and asking the gentlemen, before they brought me as a culprit to the bar to be censured, to amend their resolution, and make it conform to the facts, about which they had not thought it worth while, in their very great zeal to put me down, to inquire at all. Well, instead of admitting their error into which they had run, without a word from me to justify it, the gentlemen took advantage of my explanation of the nature of the paper purporting to come from slaves, and pounced upon me with another resolution, charging me with the high crime and misdemeanor of their own false construction of the contents of the paper, which they assumed to be a petition from slaves for abolition, and that I had *permitted* the House to believe it was true! So I was to be gravely censured for gentlemen believing what they had no right to believe, nor even to infer, and what I had never said one word to justify them in believing! But it was soon found that this would not do, and another proposition came from the gentleman from Georgia, which answered the purpose no better, and which he was obliged to withdraw. There came another resolution, from the honorable gentleman from Virginia, (Mr. Dromgoole,) charging a new crime of most alarming import, and that was, that I had "*given color to an idea!*" [Laugh.] I will not say a word upon that charge in the indictment against me. The gentleman from Maine (Mr. Evans) has so keenly exposed it to the ridicule it deserves, that those who introduced it cannot desire to hear any thing more said upon that subject.

Sir, there was, for once in this House, a remarkable unanimity between gentlemen found in opposition to each other on all other questions. A gentleman, whose speeches on this floor have not caused him to be regarded as the most devoted friend of this administration, (Mr. Waddy Thompson, of South Carolina,) proposed his resolution of censure. A devoted friend of the administration (Mr. Dromgoole, of Virginia) proposed an amendment which the gentleman from South Carolina accepted at once, and that was to censure me for giving color to an idea! Sir, it was in vain that I rose, and gave the gentlemen the sober advice to attend a little more to their facts. The moment I attempted to explain, and set aside all their assumed facts, whisk! there came another resolution of censure, charging me with trifling with the House. It was not what I did, but what I did *not* do.

I did not get up soon enough, it seems, to show these gentlemen the best way to censure me, and enable them to correct their resolutions, which they had brought forward with such zeal and in such rapid succession, but in which, unfortunately for them, there was not one word of truth.

When I say there was not one word of truth in the resolutions of the gentlemen from South Carolina and Alabama, I do not call in question their veracity. There are no men in whose veracity I would sooner trust my whole life; but I tell them that, when they undertake to charge a member of this House, who never gave them the slightest cause of offence, with crimes that should draw down upon him the censure of this body, without first ascertaining the facts, they have stepped beyond the bounds of discretion and propriety; and I will give them one word of advice,—that, when they draw up resolutions to censure me, they should first be careful to pay a little attention to facts.

[This allusion brought Mr. Lewis and Mr. Thompson both on their feet. Mr. LEWIS, of Alabama, said that he came into the House in the midst of the excitement, and, on inquiry, was told that the gentleman from Massachusetts, Mr. Adams, had attempted to present a petition from slaves. He took it for granted it was a petition for abolition, and it was full two hours before he understood that it was of a different character. Had he known the object of the petition, he should not have offered the resolution.]

Mr. ADAMS. Sir, I very readily admit the explanation of the gentleman. He took for granted what happened not to be true. But I do not intend the slightest disrespect to the gentlemen. I only take the occasion to give them a little advice, the advice of an old man to ardent young men, to govern their future conduct in this House when they undertake to censure their colleagues. But I want another explanation from the gentleman from South Carolina, (Mr. Waddy Thompson,) and I want to know if the language I find here reported in the Intelligencer as his, is really the expression of his deliberate opinion. [Mr. Thompson rose to explain.]

Mr. ADAMS. I shall want an explanation of another matter from the gentleman, and he may explain both when I have stated it fully. I read from the report of that gentleman's remarks in the National Intelligencer:—

"Does the gentleman, even in the latitude which he gives to the right of petition, think that it includes slaves? If he does not, he has wilfully violated the rules of the House, and the feelings of its members."

[Mr. Thompson was on his legs again to explain.— Mr. ADAMS. I have not done yet. There is more of it to come.—He then continued reading—]

"Does that gentleman know, that there are laws in all the slave states, and here, for the punishment of those who excite insurrection? I can tell him that there are such things as *Grand*

Juries; and if, sir, the juries of this District have, as I doubt not they have, proper intelligence and spirit, he may yet be made amenable to *another tribunal*, and we may yet see, an incendiary brought to condign punishment."*

[Mr. WADDY THOMPSON was now permitted to explain. He stated he had thought there was not a human being who believed that slaves had a right to petition, until he heard, with astonishment, that gentleman avow that he held that slaves had a right to petition. As to the other portion of what the gentleman had read, at the time the remark was made, he (Mr. T.) understood that the paper the gentleman called the attention of the House to, was a petition from slaves for the abolition of slavery. I did characterize it as an incendiary act, the presenting of such a petition; and any person, in my judgment as a lawyer, is amenable to the laws, who will present a petition from slaves for the abolition of slavery. Had I known the character of the petition, I certainly should not have made those remarks. I take the responsibility, personally and direct, of every one of those epithets, so far as they apply to a petition from slaves for the abolition of slavery. I do not now apply it to the gentleman from Massachusetts.]

Mr. ADAMS. The House may take the explanation of the gentleman as they please. There, sir, stands the sentiment—there is the printed language, in which the gentleman threatened me with indictment by a grand jury of the District, as a felon and an incendiary, *for words spoken in this House*! The gentleman has again avowed it, and declares that, if the petition had been for abolition, and I had presented it, he would not only have brought me to the bar to be censured by this House, or have voted to expel me, but he would have invoked upon my head the vengeance of the grand jury of this District! Yes, sir, he would make a member of this House, for words spoken in this

---

* The above report is known to have been written by Mr. Thompson himself, but the last clause of the quotation is not correctly reported. The precise language of Mr. Thompson was—"It is a violation of the criminal law of this District. What is the difference between presenting the petitions of slaves to be emancipated, and aiding them to escape? My life on it, if the gentleman has the courage to carry it thus far, and will present that petition—my life on it, we shall yet see him within the walls of a penitentiary!"—*Reporter.*

House, amenable to the grand and petit juries of the District of Columbia! Sir, the only answer I make to such a threat from that gentleman, is to invite him, when he returns home to his constituents, to *study a little the first principles of civil liberty*! That gentleman appears here the representative of slaveholders; and I should like to be informed, how many there are of such representatives on this floor, who endorse that sentiment. ["I do not," exclaimed Mr. UNDERWOOD, of Kentucky. "I do not," was heard from several other voices.] Is it to be tolerated, that, for any thing a member says on this floor, though it were blasphemy or treason, he is to be held accountable and punished by a grand and petit jury of the District, and not by this House? If that is the doctrine of the slaveholding representatives on this floor, let it, in God's name, go forth, and let us see what the people of this nation think of such a sentiment, and of those who make such an avowal.

Mr. WISE, of Virginia, rose.—Does any man say he will endorse that sentiment for the South?

Mr. ADAMS. I only say, let those of the South who will endorse it, avow it. I want the country should know who they are.

Mr. WISE. I will *not* endorse it. If I believed that the members of this House were amenable in any way, as such, to the juries of this District, I would not hold a seat here for one moment. Sir, this petty tribunal of the District, to which, it is suggested, the people of the United States, in the persons of their representatives, are to be held amenable, is notoriously under the dictation of the President, and is selected by an officer of his appointment. Have we not seen the Executive dictating to the Senate and to this House, and calling upon members to purge themselves of contempt?

[Mr. WADDY THOMPSON was brought up again. He referred, he said, to the laws of South Carolina, and, by those laws, if any member of the Legislature should present a petition from slaves, he would be liable to indictment by a grand jury.]

Mr. ADAMS. That may do for a Southern Legislature, to help out the gentleman; and if it is the law of South Carolina, that the members of her Legislature are held amenable to petit and grand juries, for words spoken in debate, God Almighty receive my thanks that I am not a citizen of South Carolina!

[Great sensation. Mr. Pickens, of South Carolina, rose, apparently to explain this subject.]

Mr. ADAMS, (waving his hand.) I cannot yield the floor to that gentleman. Sir, in Great Britain, which we call a monarchy, the legislative body corresponding to this House—the Commons—cannot elect their Speaker without the approbation of the King. Suppose, sir, a member of this House should propose to send a message to the President for his approval of our choice of a Speaker. What would be the opinion of that act, by the slaveholding representatives themselves? Then would be the time, if ever, to send the member who should make such a proposition, to the grand jury.

Well, sir, the first act of the Speaker chosen by the British Commons, subject to the approval of the King, is to demand of the King freedom of speech for the Commons, and the King never sends them to the grand juries of Westminster to settle it.

I will not take up the time of the House on this point, but I cannot express the amazement with which such a doctrine, such a threat, will be regarded when it shall go forth in this debate to all the non-slaveholding states—amazement that, the moment it was uttered, it was not instantly rebuked by the Speaker from the Chair. Sir, if I ever could bring my mind to censure a member of this House for any language uttered here, I can conceive of nothing more deserving it, than such a real, gross contempt of the House as this. What, sir! the members of this House, the representatives of this whole nation, answerable to a grand jury of this District for words spoken in this House! The members from New England, from New York, New Jersey, Pennsylvania, Ohio, and the free Western States, amenable to grand juries of the District of Columbia for their acts as representatives! liable to be tried as felons, and punished as incendiaries, for presenting, or "*giving color to the idea*" that they may present, petitions not exactly agreeable to certain gentlemen from the South! Sir, if that is the condition upon which we hold our seats here, and exercise our functions as the representatives of our constituents, the gentleman from Virginia (Mr. Wise) has anticipated me in what I had to say; and that is, that, if grand juries, constituted as they will be here, if they are to be made the avengers of whatever may be said or done in this House, how long will it be before the gentleman from South Carolina himself (Mr. Waddy Thompson) will have to answer before a grand and petit jury of the District, as an incendiary, for words spoken here against the Executive! And I ask him with what firmness or freedom he could resist executive power, if, for every word he utters, he is to be held amenable to a grand jury selected by the marshal, an officer appointed by the President? Let that gentleman, let every member of this House, ask his own heart, with what confidence, with what boldness, with what freedom, with what firmness, he would give utterance to his opinions on this floor, if, for every word, for a mere question asked of the Speaker, involving a question belonging to human freedom, to the rights of man, he was liable to be tried as a felon or an incendiary, and sent to the penitentiary! And this jury, selected by an officer of the President, are to be the supreme judges of the sovereign American people, in the persons of their representatives? Such is the avowed doctrine of the gentleman from South Carolina; such are his notions of freedom of speech and of civil liberty!

I have dwelt long on this topic, and will abridge what I had to say of other matters brought into this debate. I might, perhaps, have been willing to have had the yeas and nays taken on this resolution to censure me, without saying one word; but it was impossible for me to remain silent without calling on the House to mark and repel this sentiment avowed by the gentleman from South Carolina. I could not pass over such a sentiment uttered on this floor, and not, as it ought to have been, at once put down by the Speaker.

Sir, I do not know how far the southern gentlemen will endorse that sentiment. Probably I never shall know. What I have said, and more than I have time to say, has been called for by an imperative sense of duty, as I regard it, when such a threat as this has been uttered, though by but a single member of this House.

Did the gentleman think he could frighten me from my purpose by his threat of a grand jury? If that was his object, let me tell him, *he mistook his man*. I am not to be frightened from the discharge of a duty by the indignation of the gentleman from South Carolina, nor by all the grand juries in the universe. The right by which the national representative holds his seat here, is of vital importance, and, that it may be understood, I hope that this debate will go forth and be read by the whole people, and that, among other remarkable things, they will *mark* this *threat* of the gentleman from South Carolina.

Sir, we have heard much of the great superiority of Anglo-Saxon blood. Is there a man living, with a drop of that blood in his veins, who will subscribe to this doctrine of the member from South Carolina? Are these the principles of freedom by which to regulate the deliberations of a legislative assembly? I ask any member of this House what he thinks would be the issue, if a member of the British House of Commons should rise in his place, and tell another member that, for words spoken there, he should be held amenable to a grand jury of Westminster. Sir, it would be considered too ridiculous for indignation: it would be received with one universal shout of laughter, and from thenceforth subject the author of such a measure to be held up

> "*Sacred* to ridicule his whole life long,
> And the *sad* burden of some *merry* song."*

[Laughter.] Arraigned, as I have been, Mr. Speaker, on such a variety of charges, changing their ground in such rapid succession, it has been impossible to make my defence with any system or order. All that I say is unavoidably desultory. Whenever my accusers presented *the color of an idea*, before I could fix it, it was gone, and other ideas of other colors presented in its stead. The gentlemen have performed their parts here like those persons known in theatrical companies by the name of actors of all work, who assume many characters in the same play, and change their dresses so often, that you never know it is the same actor that comes in, in so many different parts, all so unlike. So has it been in the rapid changes of the gentlemen, who, in a variety of characters, have arraigned me as a criminal to be brought to the bar, on the charge of gross contempt, for "*giving color to an idea!*" How can I reply to such a charge, or how defend myself against the allegation of such a crime? Such are the attempts made to bring down upon my head the

---

* Mr. Thompson is a violent opposition member, and vehement in his denunciations of the President.—*Reporter.*

indignation and censure of this House; a calamity, sir, which I should regard as the heaviest misfortune of a long life, checkered as it has been by many and severe vicissitudes. Yes, sir, I avow, that, if a vote of censure should pass upon my name, for any act of mine in this House, it would be the heaviest of all calamities that have ever befallen me.

Sir, am I guilty, have I ever been guilty, of contempt to this House? Have I not guarded the honor of this House as a cherished sentiment of my heart? Have I not respected this House as the representatives of the whole people of the whole Union? Have I ever been regardless of the great representative principle of the people, here exhibited? Have I ever been wanting, as a member of this body, in a proper *esprit du corps*? Have I not defended the honor of this House on more than one occasion? Was I not the first, on a former occasion, to vindicate members of this House from the charge of being susceptible to bribery and corruption—a charge coming from one to whom the majority were most devoted? Have I not defended this House from charges from another quarter, to which I wish no further to allude?* And am I now to be censured for doing what I have not done, or for not doing what I did not do, under pretence of a contempt of this House, in an act which was done from motives of the highest possible respect to this House? for never, in any act of my life, did I more consult the respect due to this House, than in proposing the question I put to the Speaker, touching that paper from slaves.

Sir, if he be an enemy who shall succeed in bringing down upon me, directly or indirectly, the censure of this House—I say, if he be an enemy who votes for this, let him know he has his revenge, his triumph; for a heavier calamity could never fall upon me on earth!

And this brings me to the resolutions before the House.† I object to the first resolution (offered by Mr. Patton, of Virginia)

---

* Referring, it is presumed, to the able defence Mr. A. made, the last session, against the attacks of Mr. Webster on the majority of the House for voting the three millions appropriation, on the French question.—*Reporter*.

† The resolutions were as follows:—

"*Resolved*, That the right of petition does not belong to slaves of this Union; that no petition from them can be presented to this House, without because it does not meet and answer my question. Let the question be put by yeas and nays, and I am willing to record my *yea* that it is the duty of the House to receive petitions from slaves; and I shall regard it as of high import to free institutions, if, on full deliberation, the House *refuse* to say that they will receive petitions from slaves. The resolution does not say whether they will or not. That question, and the only question really before the House, is not met. We do not know whether it is proper or not to present such petitions. But suppose it is *not* proper. Can there be any offence, before the House have settled or considered that question, for a member respectfully to ask whether it be proper? Now, sir, this question is not met, and that is my objection to the first resolution.

The second resolution touches neither my question nor me, but pounces on an ideal man. It says, "Every member who shall *hereafter* present such petition ought to be considered an enemy to the Union," &c. What is that, sir, but the same threat, indirectly made, which the member from South Carolina (Mr. Waddy Thompson) directly made, of sending the man who should present such a petition, to the grand jury of the District of Columbia? This resolution declares that the member who shall hereafter make an attempt to present any such petition, shall be held *infamous.* Is this another maxim of the slaveholding representatives, touching the freedom of speech in this House? Sir, if that resolution passes, I will submit to it so far as not to present any petitions of slaves, but I shall consider it as a resolution most disgraceful and dishonorable to this House. What, sir! is any member of this House to be

---

derogating from the rights of the slaveholding states, and endangering the integrity of the Union.

Resolved, That every member, who shall hereafter present any such petitions to this House, ought to be considered as regardless of the feelings of this House, the rights of the South, and an enemy to the Union.

Resolved, That, the Hon. John Quincy Adams having solemnly disclaimed a design of doing any thing disrespectful to the House, in the inquiry he made of the Speaker, as to the right of petition purporting to be from slaves, and having avowed his intention not to offer to present the petition, if the House was of opinion that it ought not to be presented,—therefore all further proceedings as to his conduct now cease."

pronounced infamous for offering to aid human misery so far as to present its cry for mercy and relief to this House?

But, sir, not only would such a resolution dishonor this body in the eyes of the whole civilized world, it would also limit the rights and the liberties of members of this House, so as, in fact, to surrender them all. If, sir, you can get a vote to pronounce a member infamous who shall hereafter present a petition from slaves, you have but one step further to take, and that will be easy in the rage of the spirit of party; you will declare that every man shall be held infamous if he proposes any thing displeasing to the majority.

As to the third resolution, I ask of the justice of the House not to go for it. It indirectly does what the other resolutions of censure did directly. It says that no further proceedings shall be had against me, because I have disclaimed disrespect, and disavowed an intention which no one had the shadow of a right to impute to me. What is this but saying that, if I had not disclaimed and disavowed, I should have been censured and punished by an ex post facto law? but that, having done so, having in fact pleaded guilty, therefore, out of pure kindness, they will forgive me! Forgive me, sir, for what? For violating the rules of this House, for contempt of this House? No, sir. Had I done so, the Speaker should have called me to order, and rebuked me on the instant. And suppose, sir, for a moment, it was a violation of any rule for me to put the question I did to the Speaker, concerning that paper, and this is the offence for which I am to be forgiven,—how stands the case of the Speaker himself, who put that very question to the House? I don't see but that, if I am to be indicted by a grand jury, the Speaker must be indicted with me, for aiding and abetting. I did but ask the question of the Speaker; he asked it of the House; and if there was contempt or crime in either case, which was the greater?

Sir, I am content that this whole debate should go forth as it has been begun in the National Intelligencer. I am willing that my constituents, the people of this nation, the world, and all after times, should judge of me and my action on this great moral question. And here I say, that I have not done one single thing I would not do again, under like circumstances; not one thing have I done that I have not done under the highest and most solemn sense of duty.

But it is said that I have trifled with the House. That I deny. I have disclaimed, I again disclaim, any such intention. No, sir, I had a higher purpose than trifling with this House; and, having disclaimed such intention, no man has a right to charge me with it. Sir, I never acted under a more solemn sense of duty; I never was more serious in any moment of my life. I take it, therefore, that the last resolution, excusing and forgiving me, will not pass. It is founded on a supposition of disclaimer and retraction on my part. Sir, I renounce all favor from this House on the ground of disclaimer or retraction. I have disclaimed nothing I have done or said. I have retracted nothing: I have done my duty; and I should do it again, under the same circumstances, if it were to be done to-morrow!

Members of this House have accused me of consuming the time of the House, by presenting abolition petitions. Is it I, or they, who have done this? If, sir, gentlemen who are opposed to these petitions had permitted them to pass to the table under the rule, no time would have been consumed. If the Speaker had promptly answered my question, no time would have been consumed in this debate. I should never have occupied half an hour on a Monday, in presenting these petitions, which I have felt it due to the petitioners generally, to present singly, had not gentlemen risen to thwart me in the discharge of my duty. Sir, I protest against the consummation of the time, taken up by debates growing out of objections made by other members, being charged to me. I appeal to the House, I appeal to the nation, that it is not I, but those who object to my doings in the discharge of my duty, who are answerable for this consumption of time.

And now, sir, I have done. I have only to add that I had hoped that the gentleman from Virginia, (Mr. Patton,) seeing that the House could not be brought to a direct censure of me, would have had the magnanimity to withdraw his resolution to effect that object indirectly. He insists upon having the question taken, and the House must decide.

[The effect of this speech on the House has been rarely if ever exceeded by the influence of any speech on any assembly. It was delivered after the opponents of Mr. A. had inflamed themselves, to the highest exacerbation, by most vehement harangues for four days. The speaker had to address a majority strongly prejudiced against him, and eager to seize any tolerable ground of censure for his previous course in presenting abolition petitions. And yet the result of this speech, under all these disadvantages, was, that but 22 members could be found to vote even indirectly and remotely to censure. All the resolutions were rejected.]

"A SELF-CONSTITUTED COUNTRY"

19. *The Jubilee of the Constitution. A Discourse delivered at the request of the New York Historical Society, in the City of New York, on Tuesday, the 30th of April, 1839; being the fiftieth anniversary of the Inauguration of George Washington as President of the United States on Thursday, the 30th of April, 1789* (**New York: Samuel Colman, 1839**).

As he entered his eighth decade, and as his exploits in the House made him something of a folk hero in the North, Adams was inundated with invitations from local governments and civic organizations to speak on ceremonial occasions. Notwithstanding the anxiety these talks induced in him, he frequently found himself saying yes, unable to forgo the opportunity to address his "fellow-citizens" about "the great questions which agitate the country," as he once referred to them. This speech, which became one of his best known and most reprinted, is a case in point. In his diary entry for March 23, 1839, Adams writes that "I have determined to accept the invitation of the New-York Historical Society, to deliver, if I possibly can, an address before them on the 30th of next Month, the 50th Anniversary of the inauguration of George Washington, as first President of the United States. I have brought myself to this conclusion with extreme repugnance. . . . My reputation, my age, my decaying faculties have all warned me to decline the task — Yet I cannot resist. . . . The day was a real epocha in our history; but to seize and present in bold relief all its peculiar characters would require a younger hand, and brighter mind."

Rising to the task despite these reservations, and a nagging cough that made it virtually impossible for him to sleep, Adams was within a week writing three pages a day, though still sometimes overwhelmed by the scale of the assignment. "I have come to the review of Washington's administration of the foreign Affairs, and the subject opens upon me so that I know not when to stop — Britain, France, Spain, Portugal, Algiers, the French Revolution, and the Indians, how is it possible to touch upon these topics, without falling into garrulity?" By April 12, he had completed a draft, "Carelessly and hastily composed, requiring much pruning, and yet so knit together that I know not where to abridge." While revising the text, Adams was again struck by the contrast between the Founders' era and his own: "The Revolutionary age and the Constituent age were the times for great men — The administrative age is an age of small men, and small things."

The finished speech, a portion of which he delivered before a capacity crowd in the Middle Dutch Reformed Church at the corner of Nassau and Cedar Streets in lower Manhattan, is the fullest expression of Adams's constitutionalism he ever made. It posits the Constitution as the fulfillment of the Declaration of Independence, the realization of its annunciation of the American people as a "self-created sovereign." And it once again forcefully rejects "the irresponsible despotism of state sovereignty," as expressed in the recurring specter of nullification and secession. The reception in the church was enthusiastic, and afterward Adams and his son Charles were given a tour of Columbia College and made guests of honor at a dinner for three hundred at the City Hotel. Adams had arranged with the Historical Society for the publication of his address, and within weeks it had sold more than eight thousand copies. Adams himself was tireless in sending out presentation copies to congressional colleagues, state and local officials, even nieces and nephews. Among the many recipients was an old friend and sometimes nemesis: "I had sent a copy of my Jubilee of the Constitution to Mr Harrison Gray Otis, and received this day an acknowledgment from him with remarks in that style of hyperbolical praise which he is accustomed to use, and in which he is not conscious of insincerity but which it is incumbent upon me to consider not as deliberate opinion, but as gentlemanly courtesy." He further reflected that "the reception of that Discourse by the public is one of the multitude of events, even in this dark and declining stage of my existence, for which I can never be sufficiently grateful to God."

THE

JUBILEE OF THE CONSTITUTION.

A DISCOURSE

DELIVERED AT THE REQUEST OF

THE NEW YORK HISTORICAL SOCIETY,

IN THE CITY OF NEW YORK,

ON TUESDAY, THE 30th OF APRL 1839;

BEING THE FIFTIETH ANNIVERSARY

OF THE

INAUGURATION OF GEORGE WASHINGTON

AS

PRESIDENT OF THE UNITED STATES,

ON THURSDAY, THE 30th OF APRIL, 1789.

Serit arbores, quae alteri seculo prosint— * * quid spectans, nisi etiam postera secula ad se pertinere ? Ergo arbores seret diligens agricola, quarum adspiciet baccam ipse nunquam ; vir magnus leges, instituta, rempublicam non seret ?
CICERO. TUSC. QUAEST. 1.

BY JOHN QUINCY ADAMS.

NEW YORK:
PUBLISHED BY SAMUEL COLMAN,
VIII ASTOR HOUSE.
M DCCC XXXIX.

Entered according to Act of Congress, in the year 1839,
By JOSEPH BLUNT,
For the New York Historical Society,
In the District Court of the Southern District of New York.

The Jubilee of the Constitution

A DISCOURSE

WHEN in the epic fable of the first of Roman Poets, the Goddess mother of Æneas delivers to him the celestial armour, with which he is to triumph over his enemy, and to lay the foundations of Imperial Rome, he is represented as gazing with intense but confused delight on the crested helm that vomits golden fires—

> "His hands the fatal sword and corslet hold,
>   One keen with temper'd steel—one stiff with gold.
>   He shakes the pointed spear, and longs to try
>   The plated cuishes on his manly thigh;
>   But most admires the *shield's* mysterious mould,
>   And Roman triumphs rising on the gold"—

For on that shield the heavenly smith had wrought the anticipated history of Roman glory, from the days of Æneas down to the reign of Augustus Cæsar, cotemporaneous with the Poet himself.

FELLOW-CITIZENS AND BRETHREN, ASSOCIATES OF THE NEW YORK HISTORICAL SOCIETY:—

Would it be an unlicensed trespass of the imagination to conceive, that on the night preceding the day of which you now commemorate the fiftieth anniversary—on the night preceding that thirtieth of April, one thousand seven hundred and eighty-nine, when from the balcony of your city-hall, the chancellor of the state of New York, administered to George Washington the solemn oath, faithfully to execute the office of President of the United States, and to the best of his ability, to preserve, protect and defend the Constitution of the United States—that in the visions of the night, the guardian angel of the Father of our country had appeared before him, in the venerated form of his mother, and, to cheer and encourage him in the performance of the momentous and solemn duties that he was about to assume, had delivered to him a suit of celestial armour—a helmet, consisting of the principles of piety, of justice, of honour, of benevolence, with which from his earliest infancy he had hitherto walked through life, in the presence of all his brethren—a spear, studded with the self-evident truths of the Declaration of Independence—a sword, the same with which he had led the armies of his country through the war of freedom, to the summit of the triumphal arch of independence—a corslet and cuishes of long experience and habitual intercourse in peace and war with the world of mankind, his cotemporaries of the human race, in all their stages of civilization—and last of all, the Constitution of the United States, a SHIELD embossed by heavenly hands, with the future history of his country.

Yes, gentlemen! on that shield, the CONSTITUTION OF THE UNITED STATES was sculptured, (by forms unseen, and in characters then invisible to mortal eye,) the predestined and prophetic history of the one confederated people of the North American Union.

They had been the settlers of thirteen separate and distinct English colonies, along the margin of the shore of the North American continent: contiguously situated, but chartered by adventurers of characters variously diversified, including sectarians, religious and political, of all the classes which for the two preceding centuries had agitated and divided the people of the British islands—and with them were intermingled the descendants of Hollanders, Swedes, Germans, and French fugitives from the persecution of the revoker of the Edict of Nantes.

In the bosoms of this people, thus heterogeneously composed, there was burning, kindled at different furnaces, but all furnaces of affliction, one clear, steady flame of LIBERTY. Bold and daring enterprise, stubborn endurance of privation, unflinching intrepidity in facing danger, and inflexible adherence to conscientious principle, had steeled to energetic and unyielding hardihood the characters of the primitive settlers of all these Colonies. Since that time two or three generations of men had passed away—but they had increased and multiplied with unexampled rapidity; and the land itself had been the recent theatre of a ferocious and bloody seven years' war between the two most powerful and most civilized nations of Europe, contending for the possession of this continent.

Of that strife the victorious combatant had been Britain. She had conquered the provinces of France. She had expelled her rival totally from the continent over which, bounding herself by the Mississippi, she was thenceforth to hold divided empire only with Spain. She had acquired undisputed control over the Indian tribes, still tenanting the forests unexplored by the European man. She had established an uncontested monopoly of the commerce of all her colonies. But forgetting all the warnings of preceding ages—forgetting the lessons written in the blood of her own children, through centuries of departed time, she undertook to tax the people of the colonies *without their consent.*

Resistance, instantaneous, unconcerted, sympathetic, inflexible resistance like an electric shock startled and roused the people of all the English colonies on this continent.

This was the first signal of the North American Union. The struggle was for chartered rights—for English liberties—for the cause of Algernon Sidney and John Hambden—for trial by jury—the Habeas Corpus and Magna Charta.

But the English lawyers had decided that Parliament was omnipotent—and Parliament in their omnipotence, instead of trial by jury and the Habeas Corpus, enacted admiralty courts in England to try Americans for offences charged against them as committed in America—instead of the privileges of Magna Charta, nullified the charter itself of Massachusetts Bay; shut up the port of Boston; sent armies and navies to keep the peace, and teach the colonies that John Hambden was a rebel, and Algernon Sidney a traitor.

English liberties had failed them. From the omnipotence of Parliament the colonists appealed to the rights of man and the omnipotence of the God of battles. *Union! Union!* was the instinctive and simultaneous cry throughout the land. Their Congress, assembled at Philadelphia, once—twice had petitioned the king; had remonstrated to Parliament; had addressed the people of Britain, for the rights of Englishmen— in vain. Fleets and armies, the blood of Lexington, and the fires of Charlestown and Falmouth, had been the answer to petition, remonstrance and address.

Independence was declared. The colonies were transformed into States. Their inhabitants were proclaimed to be *one people*, renouncing all allegiance to the British crown; all co-patriotism with the British nation; all claims to chartered rights as Englishmen. Thenceforth their charter was the Declaration of Independence. Their rights, the natural rights of mankind. Their government, such as should be instituted by themselves, *under the solemn mutual pledges of perpetual union*, founded on the self-evident truths proclaimed in the Declaration.

The Declaration of Independence was issued, in the excruciating agonies of a civil war, and by that war independence was to be maintained. Six long years it raged with unabated fury, and the Union was yet no more than a mutual pledge of faith, and a mutual participation of common sufferings and common dangers.

The omnipotence of the British Parliament was vanquished. The independence of the United States of America, was not granted, but recognised. The nation had "assumed among the powers of the earth, the separate and equal station, to which the laws of nature, and of nature's God, entitled it"—but the one, united people, had yet NO GOVERNMENT.

In the enthusiasm of their first spontaneous, unstipulated, unpremeditated union, they had flattered themselves that no general government would be required. As separate states they were all agreed that they should constitute and govern themselves. The revolution under which they were gasping for life, the war which was carrying desolation into all their dwellings, and mourning into every family, had been kindled by the abuse of power—the power of government. An invincible repugnance to the delegation of power, had thus been generated, by the very course of events which had rendered it necessary; and the more indispensable it became, the more awakened was the jealousy and the more intense was the distrust by which it was to be circumscribed.

They relaxed their union into a league of friendship between sovereign and independent states. They constituted a Congress, with powers co-extensive with the nation, but so hedged and hemmed in with restrictions, that the limitation seemed to be the general rule, and the grant the occasional exception. The articles of confederation, subjected to philosophical analysis, seem to be little more than an enumeration of the functions of a national government which the congress constituted by the instrument was *not* authorized to perform. There was avowedly no executive power.

The nation fell into an atrophy. The Union languished to the point of death. A torpid numbness seized upon all its faculties. A chilling cold indifference crept from its extremities to the centre. The system was about to dissolve in its own imbecility—impotence in negotiation abroad—domestic insurrection at home, were on the point of bearing to a dishonourable grave the proclamation of a government founded on the rights of man, when a convention of delegates from eleven of the thirteen states, with George Washington at their head, sent forth to the people, an act to be made their own, speaking in their name and in the first person, thus: "We the people of the United States, in order to form a more perfect union, establish justice, ensure domestic tranquility, provide for the common defence, promote the general welfare, and secure the blessings of liberty, to ourselves and our posterity, do ordain and establish this Constitution for the United States of America."

This act was the complement to the Declaration of Independence; founded upon the same principles, carrying them out into practical execution, and forming with it, one entire system of national government. The Declaration was a manifesto to the world of mankind, to justify the one confederated people, for the violent and voluntary severance of the ties of their allegiance, for the renunciation of their country, and for assuming a station themselves, among the potentates of the world—a self-constituted sovereign—a self-constituted country.

In the history of the human race this had never been done before. Monarchs had been dethroned for tyranny—kingdoms converted into republics, and revolted provinces had assumed the attributes of sovereign power. In the history of England itself, within one century and a half before the day of the Declaration of Independence, one lawful king had been brought to the block, and another expelled, with all his posterity, from his own kingdom, and a collateral dynasty had ascended his throne. But the former of these revolutions had by the deliberate and final sentence of the nation itself, been pronounced a *rebellion*, and the rightful heir of the executed king had been restored to the crown. In the latter, at the first onset, the royal recreant had fled—he was held to have *abdicated* the crown, and it was placed upon the heads of his daughter and of her husband, the prime leader of the conspiracy against him. In these events there had been much controversy upon the platform of *English* liberties—upon the customs of the ancient Britons; the laws of Alfred, the Witenagamote of the Anglo-Saxons, and the Great Charter of Runnymede with all its numberless confirmations. But the actors of those times had never ascended to the first foundation of civil society among men, nor had any revolutionary system of government been rested upon them.

The motive for the *Declaration* of Independence was on its face avowed to be "a decent respect for the opinions of mankind." Its *purpose* to declare the *causes* which impelled the people of the English colonies on the continent of North America, to separate themselves from the political community of the British nation. They declare *only* the *causes* of their separation, but they announce at the same time their assumption of the separate and equal station to which the laws of nature and of nature's God entitle them, among the powers of the earth.

Thus their first movement is to recognise and appeal to the laws of nature and to nature's *God*, for their *right* to assume the attributes of sovereign power as an independent nation.

The causes of their *necessary* separation, for they begin and end by declaring it necessary, alleged in the Declaration, are all founded on the same laws of nature and of nature's God— and hence as preliminary to the enumeration of the causes of separation, they set forth as self-evident truths, the rights of individual man, by the laws of nature and of nature's God, to life, to liberty, to the pursuit of happiness. That all men are created *equal*. That to *secure* the rights of life, liberty and the pursuits of happiness, governments are instituted among men, deriving their *just* powers from the *consent* of the governed. All this, is by the laws of nature and of nature's God, and of course presupposes the existence of a God, the moral ruler of the universe, and a rule of right and wrong, of just and unjust, binding upon man, preceding all institutions of human society and of government. It avers, also, that governments are instituted to *secure* these rights of nature and of nature's God, and that *whenever* any form of government becomes destructive of those ends, it is the right of THE PEOPLE to alter, or to abolish it, and to institute a new government—to throw off a government degenerating into despotism, and to provide new guards for their future security. They proceed then to say that such was then the situation of the Colonies, and such the necessity which constrained them to alter their former systems of government.

Then follows the enumeration of the acts of tyranny by which the king, parliament, and people of Great Britain, had perverted the powers to the destruction of the ends of government, over the Colonies, and the consequent necessity constraining the Colonies to the separation.

In conclusion, the Representatives of the United States of America, in general Congress assembled, appealing to the Supreme judge of the world for the rectitude of their intentions, do, *in the name and by the authority of the good people of these Colonies*, solemnly publish and declare that these *United* Colonies, are, and of right ought to be, free and independent States; that they are absolved from all allegiance to the British crown; and that all political connexion between them and the state of Great Britain, is, and ought to be totally dissolved; and that as free and independent States, they have full power to levy war, conclude peace, contract alliances, establish commerce, and to do all other acts and things which independent States may of *right* do. The appeal to the Supreme Judge of the world, and the rule of right and wrong as paramount events to the power of independent States, are here again repeated in the very act of constituting a new sovereign community.

It is not immaterial to remark, that the Signers of the Declaration, though qualifying themselves as the Representatives of the United States of America, in general Congress assembled, yet issue the Declaration, *in the name and by the authority of the good people of the Colonies*—and that they declare, *not* each of the separate Colonies, but *the United Colonies*, free and independent States. The whole people declared the Colonies *in their united condition*, of RIGHT, free and independent States.

The dissolution of allegiance to the British crown, the severance of the Colonies from the British empire, and their actual existence as Independent States, thus declared of *right,* were definitively established *in fact,* by war and peace. The independence of each separate State had never been declared of *right.* It never existed *in fact.* Upon the principles of the Declaration of Independence, the dissolution of the ties of allegiance, the assumption of sovereign power, and the institution of civil government, are all acts of transcendant authority, which the people *alone* are competent to perform— and accordingly, it is in the name and by the authority of the people, that two of these acts—the dissolution of allegiance, with the severance from the British empire, and the declaration of the United Colonies, as free and independent States, were performed by that instrument.

But there still remained the last and crowning act, which *the People* of the Union alone were competent to perform—the institution of civil government, for that compound nation, the United States of America.

At this day it cannot but strike us as extraordinary, that it does not appear to have occurred to any one member of that assembly, which had laid down in terms so clear, so explicit, so unequivocal, the foundation of all just government, in the imprescriptible rights of man, and the transcendant sovereignty of the people, and who in those principles, had set forth their only personal vindication from the charges of rebellion against their king, and of treason to their country, that their last crowning act was still to be performed upon the same principles. That is, the institution, by the *people* of the United States, of a civil government, to guard and protect and defend them all. On the contrary, that same assembly which issued the Declaration of Independence, instead of continuing to act in the name, and by the authority of the good people of the United States, had immediately after the appointment of the committee to prepare the Declaration, appointed another committee, of one member from each Colony, to prepare and digest the form of *confederation,* to be entered into between the Colonies.

That committee reported on the 12th of July, eight days after the Declaration of Independence had been issued, a draught of articles of confederation between the *Colonies.*

This draught was prepared by John Dickinson, then a delegate from Pennsylvania, who voted against the Declaration of Independence, and never signed it—having been superseded by a new election of delegates from that State, eight days after his draught was reported.

There was thus no congeniality of principle between the Declaration of Independence and the Articles of Confederation. The foundation of the former were a superintending Providence—the rights of man, and the constituent revolutionary power of the people. That of the latter was the sovereignty of organized power, and the independence of the separate or dis-united States. The fabric of the Declaration and that of the Confederation, were each consistent with its own foundation, but they could not form one consistent symmetrical edifice. They were the productions of different minds and of adverse passions—one, ascending for the foundation of human government to the laws of nature and of God, written upon the heart of man—the other, resting upon the basis of human institutions, and prescriptive law and colonial charters. The corner stone of the one was *right*—that of the other was *power*.

The work of the founders of our Independence was thus but half done. Absorbed in that more than Herculean task of maintaining that independence and its principles, by one of the most cruel wars that ever glutted the furies with human wo, they marched undaunted and steadfast through that fiery ordeal, and consistent in their principles to the end, concluded, as an acknowledged sovereignty of the United States, proclaimed by their people in 1776, a peace with that same monarch, whose sovereignty over them they had abjured in obedience to the laws of nature and of nature's God.

But for these United States, they had formed no *Constitution*. Instead of resorting to the source of all constituted power, they had wasted their time, their talents, and their persevering, untiring toils, in erecting and roofing and buttressing a frail and temporary shed to shelter the nation from the storm, or rather a mere baseless scaffolding on which to stand, when they should raise the marble palace of the people, to stand the test of time.

Five years were consumed by Congress and the State Legislatures, in debating and altercating and adjusting these Articles of Confederation. The first of which was:—

"Each State *retains* its sovereignty, freedom and independence, and every power, jurisdiction, and right, which is not by this confederation expressly delegated to the United States in Congress assembled."

Observe the departure from the language, and the consequent contrast of principles, with those of the Declaration of Independence.

Each state RETAINS its sovereignty, &c.—where did each State get the sovereignty which it *retains*? In the Declaration of Independence, the delegates of the Colonies in Congress assembled, *in the name and by the authority of the good people of the Colonies*, declare, not each Colony, but the *United* Colonies, in fact, and of right, not *sovereign*, but free and independent States. And why did they make this declaration in the name and by the authority of the one people of all the Colonies? Because by the principles before laid down in the Declaration, the people, and the people alone, as the rightful source of all legitimate government, were competent to dissolve the bands of subjection of all the Colonies to the nation of Great Britain, and to constitute them free and independent States. Now the people of the Colonies, speaking by their delegates in Congress, had not declared *each* Colony a sovereign, free and independent State—nor had the people of each Colony so declared the Colony itself, nor could they so declare it, because each was already bound in union with all the rest; a union formed de facto, by the spontaneous revolutionary movement of the whole people, and organized by the meeting of the first Congress, in 1774, a year and ten months before the Declaration of Independence.

Where, then, did *each* State get the sovereignty, freedom and independence, which the articles of confederation declare it *retains*?—not from the whole people of the whole union—not from the Declaration of Independence—not from the people of the state itself. It was assumed by agreement between the legislatures of the several States, and their delegates in Congress, without authority from or consultation of the people at all.

In the Declaration of Independence, the enacting and constituent party dispensing and delegating sovereign power, is the whole *people* of the United Colonies. The recipient party, invested with power, is the United Colonies, declared United States.

In the articles of confederation, this order of agency is inverted. Each state is the constituent and enacting party, and the United States in Congress assembled, the recipient of delegated power—and that power, delegated with such a penurious and carking hand, that it had more the aspect of a revocation of the Declaration of Independence than an instrument to carry it into effect.

It well deserves the judicious inquiry of an American statesman, at this time, how this involuntary and unconscious *usurpation* upon the rights of the people of the United States, originated and was pursued to its consummation.

In July, 1775, soon after the meeting of the second revolutionary Congress, and a year before the Declaration of Independence, Dr. Franklin had submitted to their consideration, a sketch of articles of confederation between the colonies, to continue until their reconciliation with Great Britain, and in failure of that event, to be perpetual.

The third article of that project provided "that each colony shall enjoy and retain as much as it may think fit, of its own present laws, customs, rights, privileges, and peculiar jurisdictions *within its own limits*; and may amend its own constitution, as shall seem best to its own assembly or convention." Here was and could be no assertion of sovereignty.

This plan appears to have been never discussed in Congress. But when, on the 7th of June, 1776, the resolution of independence was offered and postponed, another resolution was submitted and carried for the appointment of a committee of one member from each colony, to prepare and digest a form of a confederation.

The third article of the draught reported by that committee, was in these words:—

"Each colony shall retain as much of its *present* laws, rights, and customs, as it may think fit, and reserve to itself the sole and exclusive regulation and government of its *internal police*, in all matters *that shall not interfere with the articles of this confederation*."

The first article had declared the name of the confederacy to be the United States of America.

By the second, the colonies "unite themselves, so as never to be divided by any act whatever," and entered into a firm league of friendship with each other.

From the 12th of July to the 20th of August, 1776, the report of the committee was debated almost daily, in a committee of the whole house, and they reported to Congress a new draught, the first article of which retained the name of the confederacy.

The second left out the warm-hearted *Union,* so as never to be divided by any act whatever, and only *severally* entered into a firm league of friendship for special purposes. By the third, "Each state reserves to itself the sole and exclusive regulations and government of its *internal police in all matters that shall not interfere with the Articles of this Confederation.*"

The gradual relaxation of the fervid spirit of union which had quickened every sentence of the Declaration of Independence, is apparent in these changes of phraseology and omission.

The articles reported by the committee of the whole were laid aside on the 20th of August, 1776, and were not resumed till the 7th of April, 1777.

They were then taken up, and pertinaciously and acrimoniously debated two or three times a week till the 15th of November, 1777, when they were adopted by Congress in a new and revised draught.

And here the reversal of the fundamental principles of the Declaration of Independence was complete, and the symptoms of disunion proportionally aggravated. The first article instead of the *name* declared the *style* of the confederacy to be the United States of America. Even in this change of a single word, there was the spirit of disunion; a *name* being appropriately applied to the unity, and a *style* to the plurality of the aggregate body.

An alteration still more significant was the inversion in the order of the second and third articles. In all the former draughts, in the sketch presented by Dr. Franklin in 1775, in the draught reported by the select committee in July, 1776, and in that reported after full debate by the committee of the whole house to Congress, on the 20th of August, 1776, the union had been constituted in the second article, and the reservation of separate rights *not interfering with the articles of the confederation*, had been made in the third.

But now the reservation of separate rights came first in order, appeared as the second article, and instead of being confined to internal police, and all matters that shall *not interfere* with the articles of this confederation, was transformed into a direct assertion of *sovereignty*, not in the people of each state, but in each state. And thus it was that each state had acquired that sovereignty, which the third article, now made the second, declared it *retained*. It was a power usurped upon the people, by the joint agency of the state legislatures and of their delegates in Congress, without any authority from the people whatever. And with this assertion of sovereignty, each state retained also every power, jurisdiction and right, not by the confederation *expressly delegated to the United States in Congress assembled*. And then came limping on in the third article, degraded from its place as the second, the firm league of friendship of these several states with each other, for their common defence, the security of their liberties, and their mutual and general welfare.

In the debates upon these articles of confederation, between the 7th of October, and the 17th of November, the conflict of interests and of principles between the people of the whole Union, and each of the states, was strongly marked. The first question was upon the mode of voting in Congress.

It was moved that in determining questions, each state should have one vote for every fifty thousand white inhabitants.

That each state should have a right to send one delegate to Congress for every thirty thousand of its inhabitants—each delegate to have one vote.

That the quantum of representation of each state should be computed by numbers proportioned to its contribution of money or tax laid and paid into the public treasury.

These propositions, all looking to a representation proportional to numbers or to taxation, that is, to persons or property, were all rejected, and it was resolved that in determining questions *each state* should have one vote.

Then came the question of the common charges and expenses. The first proposition was that they should be proportioned to the number of inhabitants of each state. Then to the value of all property, excepting household goods and wearing apparel, both of which were rejected, and the proposition was fixed according to the *quantity of land granted and surveyed*, with the estimated improvements thereon.

But the great and insurmountable difficulty, left altogether unadjusted by these articles of confederation, was to ascertain the boundaries of each of these sovereign states. It was proposed that these boundaries should be ascertained by them; for which purpose the state Legislatures should lay before Congress a description of the territorial lands of each of their respective states, and a summary of the grants, treaties, and proofs, upon which they were claimed or established.

It was moved that the United States, in Congress assembled, should have the sole and exclusive right and power to ascertain and fix the western boundary of such states as claimed to the South sea; and to dispose of all land beyond the boundary so ascertained, for the benefit of the United States.

And that the United States in Congress assembled, should have the sole and exclusive right and power to ascertain and fix the western boundary of such states, as claimed to the Mississippi or South sea, and to lay out the land beyond the boundary so ascertained, into separate and independent states, from time to time, as the numbers and circumstances of the people might require.

All these propositions were rejected, and the articles of confederation were sent forth to the sovereign, free and independent states for ratification, without defining or ascertaining the limits of any one of them; while some of them claimed to the South sea, and others were cramped up within a surface of less than fifteen hundred square miles.

It is further remarkable that in the progress of these debates, the institution of an executive council, which in all the previous draughts had been proposed, was struck out, and instead of it was substituted a helpless and imbecile committee of the states, never but once attempted to be carried into execution, and then speedily dissolved in its own weakness.

Such was the system, elaborated with great, persevering, and anxious deliberation; animated with the most ardent patriotism; put together with eminent ability and untiring industry, but vitiated by a defect in the general principle—in the departure from the self-evident truths of the Declaration of Independence; the natural rights of man, and the exclusive, sovereign, constituent right of the people.

The result corresponded with this elementary error. The plan of confederacy was sent forth to the state Legislatures with an eloquent and pathetic letter, pointing out the difficulties and delays which had attended its formation, urging them candidly to review the difficulty of combining in one general system the various sentiments and interests of a continent divided into so many *sovereign and independent communities*. Assuring them that the plan proposed was the best which could be adapted to the circumstances of all, and that alone which afforded any tolerable prospect of general ratification; and urging its *immediate* adoption in the following deeply affecting and impressive admonition:—

"We have reason to regret the time which has elapsed in preparing this plan for consideration. With additional solicitude we look forward to that which must be necessarily spent before it can be ratified. Every motive loudly calls upon us to hasten its conclusion.

More than any other consideration, it will confound our foreign enemies, defeat the flagitious practices of the disaffected, strengthen and confirm our friends, support our public credit, restore the value of our money, enable us to maintain our fleets and armies, and add weight and respect to our councils at home, and to our treaties abroad.

In short, this salutary measure can no longer be deferred. It seems essential to our very existence as a free people; and without it we may soon be constrained to bid adieu to independence, to liberty and safety—blessings which from the justice of our cause, and the favour of our Almighty Creator, visibly manifested in our protection, we have reason to expect, if in an humble dependence on his divine providence, we strenuously exert the means which are placed in our power."

In this solemn, urgent, and emphatic manner, and with these flattering and sanguine anticipations of the blessings to be showered upon their country by this cumbrous and complicated confederacy of sovereign and independent states, was this instrument transmitted to the state Legislatures; and so anxious were the framers of it for the sanction of the states at the earliest possible moment, that it was recommended to the executive of each of the states to whom it was addressed, if the Legislature was not assembled at the time of its reception, to convene them without delay.

Not such however was the disposition of the several state Legislatures. Each of them was governed as it naturally and necessarily must be by the interests and opinions predominating within the state itself. Not one of them was satisfied with the articles as they had been prepared in Congress. Every state Legislature found something objectionable in them. They combined the enormous inconsistency of an equal representation in Congress of states most unequal in extent and population, and an imposition of all charges, and expenses of the whole, proportioned to the extent and value of the settled and cultivated lands in each. A still more vital defect of the instrument was that it left the questions of the limits of the several states and in whom was the property of the unsettled crownlands, not only unadjusted, but wholly unnoticed.

The form of ratification proposed by Congress, was that each of the state Legislatures should authorize their delegates in Congress to subscribe the Articles; and in their impatience for a speedy conclusion, two motions were made to recommend that the states should enjoin upon their delegates invested with this authority, to attend Congress for that purpose, on or before the then ensuing first of May or tenth of March.

These however did not prevail. This extreme anxiety for the prompt and decisive action of the states, upon this organization of the confederacy, was the result of that same ardent and confiding patriotism so unforeseeing, and yet so sincere, which could flatter itself with the belief that this nerveless and rickety league of friendship between sovereign, independent, disunited states, could confound the foreign enemies of the Union, defeat the practices of the disaffected, support the credit of the country, restore the value of their depreciating money, enable them to maintain fleets and armies, and add weight and respect to their counsels at home, and to their treaties abroad.

This fervid patriotism, and all these glowing anticipations were doomed to total disappointment. Seven months passed away, and on the 22d of June, 1778, Congress proceeded to consider the *objections* of the states to the articles of confederation. Those of Maryland were first discussed and rejected. Those of Massachusetts, Rhode Island, Connecticut, New York, New Jersey, Pennsylvania, and South Carolina, followed, and all shared the same fate. No objections were presented by New Hampshire or Virginia. Delaware and North Carolina had no representation then present, and Georgia only one member in attendance.

On the 9th of July, 1778, the Articles were signed by the delegates of New Hampshire, Massachusetts Bay, Rhode Island, Connecticut, New York, Pennsylvania, Virginia and South Carolina.

The delegates from New Jersey, Delaware and Maryland, informed Congress that they had not *yet* received powers to ratify and sign. North Carolina and Georgia were not represented—and the ratification of New York was conditional that all the other states should ratify.

The delegates from North Carolina signed the Articles on the 21st of July, 1778. Those of Georgia on the 24th of the same month. Those of New Jersey on the 26th of November, 1778. Those of Delaware on the 22d of February, and 5th of May, 1779—but Maryland held out to the last, and positively refused the ratification, until the question of the conflicting claims of the Union, and of the separate states to the property of the crown-lands should be adjusted. This was finally accomplished by cessions from the claiming states to the United States, of the unsettled lands, for the benefit of the whole Union.

Is it not strange again that it appears not to have been perceived by any one at that time that the whole of this controversy arose out of a departure from the principles of the Declaration of Independence, and the substitution of state sovereignty instead of the constituent sovereignty of the people, as the foundation of the Revolution and of the Union. The war from the beginning had been, and yet was, a revolutionary popular war. The colonial governments never had possessed or pretended to claim sovereign power. Many of them had not even yet constituted themselves as independent States. The Declaration of Independence proclaims the natural rights of man, and the constituent power of the people to be the *only* sources of legitimate government. State sovereignty is a mere argument of power, without regard to right—a mere reproduction of the omnipotence of the British parliament in another form, and therefore not only inconsistent with, but directly in opposition to, the principles of the Declaration of Independence.

The cessions of the claiming states of the crown lands to the Union, originated the territorial system, and eventuated in the ordinance for the government of the North Western Territory. It also removed the insuperable objection of the State of Maryland to the articles of confederation, and her delegates signed them on the 1st of March, 1781, four years and four months after they had been submitted by Congress to the sovereign states, with a solemn averment that they could no longer be deferred; that they seemed essential to the very existence of the Union *as a free people*; and that without them they might be constrained to bid adieu to independence, to liberty, and safety.

But the dispute relating to the jurisdiction and property of the crown lands, was only one of a multitude of stumbling blocks which were perpetually crossing the path of the new nation, in the collisions between the principles of the Declaration of Independence and the sovereignty of the separate states. In the adjustment of that, both the systems were substantially set aside. For the claiming states, by the cessions themselves, abandoned their pretensions, so far as that interest was concerned, to the rights of independent state sovereignty, and the Congress of the confederation by an enactment of the ordinance for the government of the North Western Territory, assumed an authority which had not been delegated to them, either by the constituent sovereign people, or by the separate sovereign states.

The articles of confederation had withheld from Congress, the power of regulating the commerce of the Union, and of levying money by taxation upon the people; yet they were authorized to make war and conclude peace—to contract debts and bind the nation by treaties of commerce. The war was raging in its most inveterate fury, and to defray its indispensable charges and expenses, the only power of Congress was to issue *requisitions* to the states, which their sovereign power complied with, or disregarded, or rejected, according to their sovereign will and pleasure.

So seldom had this been to furnish the required supplies, that even before the first ratification of the articles of confederation, on the 3d of February, 1781, it had been resolved that it be recommended to the several states, as *indispensably necessary*, that they vest a power in Congress, to levy for the use of the United States, a duty of five per cent. ad valorem, at the time and place of importation, upon all foreign goods, wares, and merchandise of foreign growth and manufactures, imported after the 1st of May, 1781; also a like duty upon all prize-goods, to be appropriated to the discharge of the principal and interest of the debts contracted on the faith of the United States, for the support of the war.

Indispensably necessary! But according to the principles of the Declaration of Independence, the state legislatures themselves had no authority to confer this power upon Congress. It was *taxation*—one of the powers which the people alone are competent to bestow, and which their servants, the state legislatures, if they possessed it themselves, had no right to delegate to any other body.

Upon the principles of state sovereignty—power without right, this authority might have been conferred upon Congress by the state legislatures, and several of them did enact laws for bestowing it. But by the articles of confederation, no alteration of them could be effected without the consent of all the states, and Rhode Island, the smallest state in the Union, inflexibly held out in the refusal to grant the indispensably necessary power. Virginia granted and soon repealed it. Congress issued bills of credit as long as they had any credit; but all the states did the same till their bottomless paper depreciated to a thousand for one, and then vanished by a universal refusal to receive it. Congress issued four successive requisitions upon the states, for their respective quotas to pay the debts and current expenses of the Union. Not one of the states paid one half the amount of its contribution. Congress borrowed money in France, in Spain, in Holland, and obtained it there when they could not raise a dollar at home, and they were compelled to resort to new loans to pay the interest upon those that had preceded.

Under the pressure of all these distresses, the cause of independence was triumphant. Peace came. The United States of America were recognised as free and independent, and as *one People* took the station to which the laws of nature and of nature's God entitled them among the powers of the earth.

But their confederacy of sovereign states was as incompetent to govern them in peace as it had been to conduct them in war. The first popular impulse to union had carried them through the war. As that popular impulse died away, the confederation had supplied its place with hope and promise, the total disappointment of which, though discovered before the peace, was providentially not permitted to prevent its conclusion.

Peace came. The heroic leader of the revolutionary armies surrendered his commission. The armies were disbanded, but they were not paid. Mutiny was suppressed; but not until Congress had been surrounded by armed men, demanding justice, and appealed in vain for protection to the sovereign state within whose jurisdiction they were sitting. A single frigate, the remnant of a gallant navy, which had richly shared the glories, and deeply suffered the calamities of the war, was dismantled and sold. The expenses of the nation were reduced to the minimum of a peace establishment, and yet the nation was not relieved. The nation wanted a government founded on the principles of the Declaration of Independence—a government constituted by the people.

The commerce, navigation, and fisheries of the nation, had been annihilated by the war. But as a civilized nation cannot exist without commerce, an illicit trade with the enemy had sprung up towards the close of the war, highly injurious to the common cause, but which Congress had not the power to suppress. The same causes had given rise to another practice not less pernicious and immoral, by which privateersmen *ransomed* the prizes captured from the enemy at sea—that is, by releasing the captured vessel for a contribution taken in bills upon the owner of the prize, which were punctually paid, thereby converting the trade of the privateer into a species of gambling piracy.

These practices ceased with the peace. But the commerce of the United States, for want of a regulating power, was left at the mercy of foreign and rival traders. Britain immediately took advantage of this weakness, declined entering into any commercial treaty with us, which Congress had proposed, and brought to bear upon the American trade all the weight of her navigation laws. Massachusetts and Virginia made the experiment of counteracting laws, the only effect of which was to exclude a little remnant of their trade from their own ports, and to transfer it to the ports of neighbouring states.

On the 18th of April, 1783, Congress renewed the demand upon the states, for authority to levy an impost duty, specific on sundry articles of importation, and five per cent. ad valorem on others, to raise not quite one million of dollars, or about two fifths of the annual interest accruing upon the public debt; and that the states should themselves establish some system for supplying the public treasury with funds, for the punctual payment of the other three fifths of the annual interest; and also, for an alteration in the articles of confederation, changing the proportional rule of contribution of the states, from the surface of settled land to the numbers of population.

And on the 30th of April, 1784, Congress recommended to the state legislatures to vest the United States in Congress assembled, for the term of fifteen years, with powers to prohibit importations of merchandise in foreign vessels of nations with whom the United States had no treaties of commerce, and to prohibit foreigners, unless authorized by treaty, from importing into the United States, merchandise, other than the produce or manufacture of their own country. In other words, to enact a navigation law.

None of these indispensably necessary powers were ever conferred by the state legislatures upon the Congress of the confederation; and well was it that they never were. The system itself was radically defective. Its incurable disease was an apostacy from the principles of the Declaration of Independence. A substitution of separate state sovereignties, in the place of the constituent sovereignty of the people, as the basis of the confederate Union.

But in this Congress of the confederation, the master minds of James Madison and Alexander Hamilton, were constantly engaged through the closing years of the Revolutionary War, and those of peace which immediately succeeded. That of John Jay was associated with them shortly after the peace, in the capacity of Secretary to the Congress for Foreign Affairs. The incompetency of the articles of confederation for the management of the affairs of the Union at home and abroad, was demonstrated to them by the painful and mortifying experience of every day. Washington, though in retirement, was brooding over the cruel injustice suffered by his associates in arms, the warriors of the Revolution; over the prostration of the public credit and the faith of the nation, in the neglect to provide for the payment even of the interest upon the public debt; over the disappointed hopes of the friends of freedom; in the language of the address from Congress to the States of the 18th of April, 1783—"the pride and boast of America, that the rights for which she contended were the rights of human nature."

At his residence of Mount Vernon, in March, 1785, the first idea was started of a revisal of the articles of confederation, by an organization of means differing from that of a compact between the state Legislatures and their own delegates in Congress. A convention of delegates from the state Legislatures, independent of the Congress itself, was the expedient which presented itself for effecting the purpose, and an augmentation of the powers of Congress for the regulation of commerce, as the object for which this assembly was to be convened. In January, 1786, the proposal was made and adopted in the Legislature of Virginia, and communicated to the other state Legislatures.

The Convention was held at Annapolis, in September of that year. It was attended by delegates from only five of the central states, who on comparing their restricted powers, with the glaring and universally acknowledged defects of the confederation, reported only a recommendation for the assemblage of another convention of delegates to meet at Philadelphia, in May, 1787, from all the states and with enlarged powers.

The Constitution of the United States was the work of this Convention. But in its construction the Convention immediately perceived that they must retrace their steps, and fall back from a league of friendship between sovereign states, to the constituent sovereignty of *the people*; from *power* to *right*—from the irresponsible despotism of state sovereignty, to the self-evident truths of the Declaration of Independence. In that instrument, the right to institute and to alter governments among men was ascribed exclusively to *the people*—the ends of government were declared to be to *secure* the natural rights of man; and that *when* the government degenerates from the promotion to the destruction of that end, the right and the duty accrues to the people, to dissolve this degenerate government and to institute another. The Signers of the Declaration further averred, that the one people of the *United Colonies* were then precisely in that situation—with a government degenerated into tyranny, and called upon by the laws of nature and of nature's God, to dissolve that government and to institute another. Then in the name and by the authority of the good people of the Colonies, they pronounced the dissolution of their allegiance to the king, and their eternal separation from the nation of Great Britain— and declared the United Colonies independent States. And here as the representatives of the one people they had stopped. They did not require the confirmation of this Act, for the power to make the Declaration had already been conferred upon them by the people; delegating the power, indeed, separately in the separate colonies, not by colonial authority, but by the spontaneous revolutionary movement of the people in them all.

From the day of that Declaration, the constituent power of the people had never been called into action. A confederacy had been substituted in the place of a government; and state sovereignty had usurped the constituent sovereignty of the people.

The Convention assembled at Philadelphia had themselves no direct authority from the people. Their authority was all derived from the state legislatures. But they had the articles of confederation before them, and they saw and felt the wretched condition into which they had brought the whole people, and that the Union itself was in the agonies of death. They soon perceived that the indispensably needed powers were such as no state government; no combination of them was by the principles of the Declaration of Independence competent to bestow. They could emanate only from the people. A highly respectable portion of the assembly, still clinging to the confederacy of states, proposed as a substitute for the Constitution, a mere revival of the articles of confederation, with a grant of additional powers to the Congress. Their plan was respectfully and thoroughly discussed, but the want of a government and of the sanction of the people to the delegation of powers, happily prevailed. A Constitution for the people, and the distribution of legislative, executive, and judicial powers, was prepared. It announced itself as the work of the people themselves; and as this was unquestionably a power assumed by the Convention, not delegated to them by the people, they religiously confined it to a simple power to propose, and carefully provided that it should be no more than a proposal until sanctioned by the confederation Congress, by the state Legislatures, and by the people of the several states, in conventions specially assembled, by authority of their Legislatures, for the single purpose of examining and passing upon it.

And thus was consummated the work, commenced by the Declaration of Independence. A work in which the people of the North American Union, acting under the deepest sense of responsibility to the Supreme Ruler of the universe, had achieved the most transcendent act of power, that social man in his mortal condition can perform. Even that of dissolving the ties of allegiance which he is bound to his country—of renouncing that country itself—of demolishing its government, of instituting another government, and of making for himself another country in its stead.

And on that day, of which you now commemorate the fiftieth anniversary—on that 30th day of April, one thousand seven hundred and eighty-nine, was this mighty revolution, not only in the affairs of our own country, but in the principles of government over civilized man, accomplished.

The revolution itself was a work of thirteen years—and had never been completed until that day. The Declaration of Independence and the Constitution of the United States, are parts of one consistent whole, founded upon one and the same theory of government, then new, not as a theory, for it had been working itself into the mind of man for many ages, and been especially expounded in the writings of Locke, but had never before been adopted by a great nation in practice.

There are yet, even at this day, many speculative objections to this theory. Even in our own country, there are still philosophers who deny the principles asserted in the Declaration, as self-evident truths—who deny the natural equality and inalienable rights of man—who deny that the people are the only legitimate source of power—who deny that all just powers of government are derived from the *consent* of the governed. Neither your time, nor perhaps the cheerful nature of this occasion, permit me here to enter upon the examination of this anti-revolutionary theory, which arrays state sovereignty against the constituent sovereignty of the people, and distorts the Constitution of the United States into a league of friendship between confederate corporations. I speak to matters of fact. There is the Declaration of Independence, and there is the Constitution of the United States—let them speak for themselves. The grossly immoral and dishonest doctrine of despotic state sovereignty, the exclusive judge of its own obligations, and responsible to no power on earth or in heaven, for the violation of them, is not there. The Declaration says it is not in me. The Constitution says it is not in me.

The confederacy of sovereign states has made itself known by its fruits; but there is one observation so creditable to our revolutionary fathers, that it ought never to be overlooked. The defects of the confederacy were vices of the institution, and not of the men by whom it was administered. The jealousy of delegated power pervaded every part of the articles of confederacy, and indeed, almost all the separate constitutions. The prevailing principle of every provision made under the influence of this distrusting maxim, was that the same power should not long be intrusted to the same hands—but it never extended to the exclusion of any person from office, after a designate term of service in another. One of the articles of confederation had interdicted every person from holding the office of a member of Congress more than three years in six. But any member excluded by the expiration of his limited term of service in Congress, was eligible to any other station in the legislative, executive, or judicial departments of his state, or to any office, civil or military, within the general jurisdiction of Congress.

In point of fact, the great measures by which the revolution was commenced, conducted, and concluded, were devised and prosecuted by a very few leading minds, animated by one pervading, predominating spirit. The object of the Revolution was the transformation of thirteen dependant and oppressed English colonies, into one nation of thirteen confederated states. It was as the late Mr. Madison remarked to Miss Martineau, an undertaking to do that which had always before been believed impossible. In the progress to its accomplishment, obstacles almost numberless, and difficulties apparently insurmountable, obstructed every step of the way. That in the dissolution and re-institution of the social compact, by men marching over an untrodden path to the very fountains of human government, great and dangerous errors should have been committed, is but an acknowledgment that the builders of the new edifice were fallible men. But at the head of the convention that formed the Constitution, was George Washington, the leader of the armies of the Revolution—among its prominent members were Benjamin Franklin and Roger Sherman, two of the members of that memorable committee who had reported the Declaration of Independence—and its other members without exception, were statesmen who had served in the councils of the Union, throughout the Revolutionary struggle, or warriors who had contended with the enemy upon the field.

The Signers of the Declaration of Independence themselves, were the persons who had first fallen into the error of believing that a confederacy of independent states would serve as a substitute for the repudiated government of Great Britain. Experience had demonstrated their mistake, and the condition of the country was a shriek of terror at its awful magnitude. They did retrace their steps—not to extinguish the federative feature in which their union had been formed: nothing could be wider from their intention—but to restore the order of things conformably to the principles of the Declaration of Independence, and as they had been arranged in the first plans for a confederation. To make the people of the Union the constituent body, and the reservation of the rights of the states subordinate to the Constitution. Hence the delegation of power was not from each state retaining its sovereignty, and all rights not expressly delegated by the states, but from the people of each and of all the states, to the United States in Congress assembled, representing at once the whole people and all the states of the Union.

They retained the federative feature pre-eminently in the constitution of the Senate, and in the complication of its great powers, legislative, executive, and judicial—making that body a participant in all the great departments of constituted power. They preserved the federative principle and combined it with the constituent power of the people in the mode of electing the President of the United States, whether by the electoral colleges, or by the House of Representatives voting by states. They preserved it even in the constitution of the House, the popular branch of the Legislature, by giving separate delegations to the people of each state. But they expressly made the Constitution and constitutional laws of the United States paramount not only to the laws, but to the constitutions of the separate states inconsistent with them.

I have traced step by step, in minute and tedious detail, the departure from the principles of the Declaration of Independence, in the process of organizing the confederation—the disastrous and lamentable consequences of that departure, and the admirable temper and spirit, with which the Convention at Philadelphia returned to those principles in the preparation and composition of the Constitution of the United States. That this work was still imperfect, candour will compel us all to admit, though in specifying its imperfections, the purest minds and the most patriotic hearts differ widely from each other in their conclusions. Distrustful as it becomes me to be of my own judgment, but authorized by the experience of a full half century, during which I have been variously and almost uninterruptedly engaged in both branches of the Legislature, and in the executive departments of this government, and released, by my own rapid approach to the closing scene of life, from all possible influence of personal interest or ambition, I may perhaps be permitted to remark, that the omission of a clear and explicit Declaration of Rights, was a great defect in the Constitution as presented by the Convention to the people, and that it has been imperfectly remedied by the ten Articles of amendment proposed by the first Congress under the Constitution, and now incorporated with it. A Declaration of Rights would have marked in a more emphatic manner the return from the derivative sovereignty of the states, to the constituent sovereignty of the people for the basis of the federal Union, than was done by the words, "We the people of the United States," in the preamble to the Constitution. A Declaration of Rights, also, systematically drawn up, as a part of the Constitution, and adapted to it with the consummate skill displayed in the consistent adjustment of its mighty powers, would have made it more complete in its unity, and in its symmetry, than it now appears, an elegant edifice, but encumbered with superadditions, not always in keeping with the general character of the building itself.

A Declaration of Rights, reserved by the constituent body, the people, might and probably would have prevented many delicate and dangerous questions of conflicting jurisdictions which have arisen, and may yet arise between the general and the separate state governments. The rights reserved by the people would have been exclusively their own rights, and they would have been protected from the encroachments not only of the general government, but of the disunited states.

And this is the day of your commemoration. The day when the Revolution of Independence being completed, and the new confederated Republic announced to the world, as the United States of America, *constituted* and organized under a government founded on the principles of the Declaration of Independence, was to hold her course along the lapse of time among the civilized potentates of the earth.

From this point of departure we have looked back to the origin of the Union; to the conflict of war by which the severance from the mother-country, and the release from the thraldom of a trans-Atlantic monarch, were effected, and to the more arduous and gradual progression by which the new government had been constructed to take the place of that which had been cast off and demolished.

The first object of the people, declared by the Constitution as their motive for its establishment, *to form a more perfect Union*, had been attained by the establishment of the Constitution itself; but this was yet to be demonstrated by its practical operation in the establishment of justice, in the ensurance of domestic tranquility, in the provision for the common defence, in the promotion of the general welfare, and in securing the blessings of liberty to the people themselves, the authors of the Constitution, and to their posterity.

These are the great and transcendental objects of all legitimate government. The primary purposes of all human association. For these purposes the confederation had been instituted, and had signally failed for their attainment. How far have they been attained under this new national organization?

It has abided the trial of time. This day fifty years have passed away since the first impulse was given to the wheels of this political machine. The generation by which it was constructed, has passed away. Not one member of the Convention who gave this Constitution to their country, survives. They have enjoyed its blessings so far as they were secured by their labours. They have been gathered to their fathers. That posterity for whom they toiled, not less anxiously than for themselves, has arisen to occupy their places, and is rapidly passing away in its turn. A third generation, unborn upon the day which you commemorate, forms a vast majority of the assembly who now honour me with their attention. Your city which then numbered scarcely thirty thousand inhabitants, now counts its numbers by hundreds of thousands. Your state, then numbering less than double the population of your city at this day, now tells its children by millions. The thirteen primitive states of the revolution, painfully rallied by this constitution to the fold from which the impotence and dis-uniting character of the confederacy, was already leading them astray, now reinforced by an equal number of younger sisters, and all swarming with an active, industrious, and hardy population, have penetrated from the Atlantic to the Rocky Mountains, and opened a paradise upon the wilds watered by the father of the floods. The Union, which at the first census, ordained by this Constitution, returned a people of less than four millions of souls; at the next census, already commanded by law, the semi-centural enumeration since that day, is about to exhibit a return of seventeen millions. Never since the first assemblage of men in social union, has there been such a scene of continued prosperity recorded upon the annals of time.

How much of this prosperity is justly attributable to the Constitution, then first put upon its trial, may perhaps be differently estimated by speculative minds. Never was a form of government so obstinately, so pertinaciously contested before its establishment—and never was human foresight and sagacity more disconcerted and refuted by the event, than those of the opposers of the Constitution. On the other hand its results have surpassed the most sanguine anticipations of its friends. Neither Washington, nor Madison, nor Hamilton, dared to hope that this new experiment of government would so triumphantly accomplish the purposes which the confederation had so utterly failed to effect. Washington—far from anticipating the palm of glory which his administration of this government was to entwine around his brow, transcending the laurel of his then unrivalled military renown, in the interval between the 4th of March, when the meeting of the first Congress had been summoned, and the 14th of April, when he received from them the notification of his election as President of the United States, thus unbosomed to his friend Knox the forebodings of his anxious and agitated mind. "I feel," wrote he, "for those members of the new Congress, who hitherto have given an unavailing attendance at the theatre of action. For myself, the delay may be compared to a reprieve; for in confidence I tell *you*, (with the world it would obtain little credit,) that my movements to the chair of government will be accompanied by feelings not unlike those of a culprit who is going to the place of his execution. So unwilling am I, in the evening of life, nearly consumed in public cares, to quit a peaceful abode for an ocean of difficulties, without that competency of political skill, abilities, and inclination, which are necessary to manage the helm. I am sensible that I am embarking the voice of the people and a good name of my own, on this voyage, but what returns can be made of them, Heaven alone can foretell. Integrity and firmness are all I can promise: these, be the voyage long or short, shall never forsake me, although I may be deserted by all men: for of the consolations which are to be derived from them, under any circumstances, the world cannot deprive me."

One of the most indubitable tests of the merit of human institutions for the government of men, is the length of time which they endure; but so fluctuating is the character of nations and of ages, as well as of individuals, that in the history of mankind before our own age, this durability of human governments has been exclusively confined to those founded upon conquests and hereditary power. In summing up the character of William the Conqueror, the Scottish historian, Hume, remarks, that "though he rendered himself infinitely odious to his English subjects, he transmitted his power to his posterity, and the throne is still filled by his descendants; a proof," says the historian, "that the foundations which he laid, were firm and solid, and that amidst all his violence, while he seemed only to gratify the present passion, he had still an eye towards futurity."

The descendant from William the Conqueror, who filled the throne of Britain when the Scottish historian made this remark, was the person whom his American subjects, to whom he had rendered himself odious, unseated from that portion of his throne which ruled over them; and in discarding him they had demolished the throne itself for ever. They had resolved for themselves and their posterity, never again to be ruled by thrones. The Declaration of Independence had promulgated principles of government, subversive of all unlimited sovereignty and all hereditary power. Principles, in consistency with which no conqueror could establish by violence a throne to be trodden by himself and by his posterity, for a space of eight hundred years. The foundations of government laid by those who had burnt by fire and scattered to the winds of Heaven, the ashes of this conqueror's throne, were human rights, responsibility to God, and the consent of the people. Upon these principles, the Constitution of the United States had been formed, was now organized, and about to be carried into execution, to abide the test of time. The first element of its longevity was undoubtedly to be found in itself—but we may, without superstition or fanaticism, believe that a superintending Providence had adapted to the character and principles of this institution, those of the man by whom it was to be first administered. To fill a throne was neither his ambition nor his vocation. He had no descendants to whom a throne could have been transmitted, had it existed. He was placed by the unanimous voice of his country, at the head of that government which they had substituted for a throne, and his eye looking to futurity, was intent upon securing to after ages, not a throne for a seat to his own descendants, but an immoveable seat upon which the descendants of his country might sit in peace, and freedom, and happiness, if so it please Heaven, to the end of time.

That to the accomplishment of this task he looked forward with a searching eye, and even an over-anxious heart, will not be surprising to any who understands his character, or is capable of comprehending the magnitude and difficulty of the task itself.

There are incidental to the character of man two qualities, both developed by his intercourse with his fellow-creatures, and both belonging to the immortal part of his nature; of elements apparently so opposed and inconsistent with each other, as to be irreconcilable together; but yet indispensable in their union to constitute the highest excellence of the human character. They are the spirit of command, and the spirit of meekness.

They have been exemplified in the purity of ideal perfection, only once in the history of mankind, and that was in the mortal life of the Saviour of the world. It would seem to have been exhibited on earth by his supernatural character, as a model to teach mortal man, to what sublime elevation his nature is capable of ascending. They had been displayed, though not in the same perfection by the preceding legislator of the children of Israel;—

> "That Shepherd, who first taught the chosen seed
> In the beginning, how the heavens and earth
> Rose out of Chaos;"

but so little were they known, or conceived of in the antiquity of profane history, that in the poems of Homer, that unrivalled delineator of human character in the heroic ages, there is no attempt to introduce them in the person of any one of his performers, human or divine. In the poem of his Roman imitator and rival, a feeble exemplification of them is shadowed forth in the inconsistent composition of the pious Æneas; but history, ancient or modern, had never exhibited in the real life of man, an example in which those two properties were so happily blended together, as they were in the person of George Washington. These properties belong rather to the moral than the intellectual nature of man. They are not unfrequently found in minds little cultivated by science, but they require for the exercise of that mutual control which guards them from degenerating into arrogance or weakness, the guidance of a sound judgment, and the regulation of a profound sense of responsibility to a higher Power. It was this adaptation of the character of Washington to that of the institution over the composition of which he had presided, as he was now called to preside over its administration, which constituted one of the most favorable omens of its eventful stability and success.

But this institution was republican, and even democratic. And here not to be misunderstood, I mean by democratic, a government, the administration of which must always be rendered comfortable to that predominating public opinion, which even in the ages of heathen antiquity, was denominated the queen of the world: and by republican I mean a government reposing, not upon the virtues or the powers of any one man—not upon that *honour*, which Montesquieu lays down as the fundamental principle of monarchy—far less upon that *fear* which he pronounces the basis of despotism; but upon that *virtue* which he, a noble of aristocratic peerage, and the subject of an absolute monarch, boldly proclaims as a fundamental principle of republican government. The Constitution of the United States was republican and democratic—but the experience of all former ages had shown that of all human governments, democracy was the most unstable, fluctuating and short-lived; and it was obvious that if virtue—the virtue of the people, was the foundation of republican government, the stability and duration of the government must depend upon the stability and duration of the virtue by which it is sustained.

Now the *virtue* which had been infused into the Constitution of the United States, and was to give to its vital existence the stability and duration to which it was destined, was no other than the concretion of those abstract principles which had been first proclaimed in the Declaration of Independence—namely, the self-evident truths of the natural and unalienable rights of man, of the indefeasible constituent and dissolvent sovereignty of the people, always subordinate to a rule of right and wrong, and always responsible to the Supreme Ruler of the universe for the *rightful* exercise of that sovereign, constituent, and dissolvent power.

This was the platform upon which the Constitution of the United States had been erected. Its VIRTUES, its republican character, consisted in its conformity to the principles proclaimed in the Declaration of Independence, and as its administration must necessarily be always pliable to the fluctuating varieties of public opinion; its stability and duration by a like overruling and irresistible necessity, was to depend upon the stability and duration in the hearts and minds of the people of that *virtue*, or in other words, of those principles, proclaimed in the Declaration of Independence, and embodied in the Constitution of the United States.

With these considerations, we shall be better able to comprehend the feelings of repugnance, of pain, of anguish, of fearful forebodings, with which Washington had consented to be placed at the head of this new and untried experiment to consolidate the people of the thirteen then disunited states into one confederated and permanent happy Union. For his own integrity and firmness he could answer; and these were sufficient to redeem his own personal responsibility—but he was embarking on this ocean of difficulty a good name already achieved by toils, and dangers, and services unparalleled in human history—surpassing in actual value the richest diadem upon earth, and more precious in his estimation than the throne of the universal globe, had it been offered as an alternative to his choice.

He knew the result would not depend upon him. His reliance was upon the good providence of Heaven. He foresaw that he might be deserted by all mankind. The Constitution itself had been extorted from the grinding necessity of a reluctant nation. The people only of eleven of the thirteen primitive states had sanctioned it by their adoption. A stubborn, unyielding resistance against its adoption had manifested itself in some of the most powerful states in the Union, and when overpowered by small majorities in their conventions, had struggled in some instances successfully, to recover their ascendancy by electing to both Houses of Congress members who had signalized themselves in opposition to the adoption of the Constitution. A sullen, embittered, exasperated spirit was boiling in the bosoms of the defeated, then styled anti-Federal party, whose rallying cry was state rights—state sovereignty—state independence. To this standard no small number even of the ardent and distinguished patriots of the Revolution had attached themselves with partial affection. State sovereignty—unlimited state sovereignty, amenable not to the authority of the Union, but only to the people of the disunited state itself, had, with the left-handed wisdom characteristic of faction, assumed the mask of liberty, pranked herself out in the garb of patriotism, and courted the popular favour in each state by appeals to their separate independence—affecting to style themselves exclusively *Republicans*, and stigmatizing the Federalists, and even Washington himself their head, as monarchists and tories.

On the other hand, no small number of the Federalists, sickened by the wretched and ignominious failure of the Articles of Confederation to fulfil the promise of the Revolution; provoked at once and discouraged by the violence and rancour of the opposition against their strenuous and toilsome endeavours to raise their country from her state of prostration; chafed and goaded by the misrepresentations of their motives, and the reproaches of their adversaries, and imputing to them in turn, deliberate and settled purposes to dissolve the Union, and resort to anarchy for the repair of ruined fortunes—distrusted even the efficacy of the Constitution itself, and with a weakened confidence in the virtue of the people, were inclining to the opinion, that the only practicable substitute for it would be a government of greater energy than that presented by the Convention. There were among them numerous warm and sincere admirers of the British Constitution; disposed to confide rather to the inherent strength of the government than to the self-evident truths of the Declaration of Independence, for the preservation of the rights of property and perhaps of persons—and with these discordant feelings and antagonizing opinions, were intermingled on both sides individual interests and ambitions, counteracting each other as in the conduct and management of human affairs they always have and always will—not without a silent and secret mixture of collateral motives and impulses, from the domestic intercourse of society, for which the legislator is not competent to provide, and the effect of which not intuition itself can foresee.

The same calm, but anxious and even distrusting contemplation of the prospect before him, and of the difficulties and dangers which he was destined to encounter in his new career, followed him after he received the annunciation of his election, and the summons to repair to his post. The moment of his departure from the residence of his retirement, was thus recorded in his diary: "About ten o'clock I bade adieu to Mount Vernon, to private life, and to domestic felicity; and with a mind *oppressed with more anxious and painful sensations, than I have words to express*, set out for New York—with the best disposition to render service to my country in obedience to its call, but with less hope of answering its expectations."

His progress from Mount Vernon to New York, was one triumphal procession. At Alexandria, at Georgetown, at Philadelphia, at Trenton, at Brunswick, at the borders of the state of New Jersey, at Elizabethtown Point, he was surrounded, addressed, escorted, by crowds of his grateful, confiding, hoping, affectionate fellow-citizens, of all classes, of both sexes, of every age and condition, showering upon him in every variety of form demonstrations of the most enthusiastic attachment. Corporations of magistrates addressed him in strains of pious, patriotic, and fervid eloquence. The soldiers of their country, in the prime of life, in the pride and pomp of war, but in the circumstance of honourable peace, preceded him as a guard of ornament and of glory. At his passage over the Schuylkill bridge, a crown of unfading laurel was unconsciously to himself, dropped by a blooming boy from a thickly laurelled arch upon his head. At Trenton, he was welcomed by a band of aged matrons commemorating his noble defence of them, thirteen years before on that spot, at the turning tide of the War of Independence—while their virgin daughters strewed the path before him with flowers, and chanting a song like that of Miriam, hailed him as *their* protector, who had been the defender of their mothers. A committee of Congress met him on his approach to the Point, where a richly ornamented barge of thirteen oars, manned by thirteen branch pilots of your own harbour, prepared by your forefathers, then the inhabitants of your bright-starred city, was in waiting to receive him. In this barge he embarked. But the bosom of the waters around her, as she swept along, was as populous as had been the shores. The garish streamers floated upon the gale—songs of enchantment resounded from boat to boat, intermingled with the clashing of cymbals, with the echoing of horns, with the warbling of the flute, and the mellowing tones of the clarionet, weakened, but softened as if into distance, by the murmur of the breeze and the measured dashing of the waters from the oars, till on reaching your city! . . . . . but let his own diary record the emotions of his soul: "The display of boats,"—I quote from his biographer, the lamented late Chief Justice Marshall,—"which attended and joined on this occasion, some with vocal, and others with instrumental music on board, the decorations of the ships, the roar of cannon, and the loud acclamations of the people, which rent the sky as I passed along the wharves, filled my mind with sensations as PAINFUL (contemplating the reverse of this scene, which may be the case after all my labours to do good) as they were pleasing."

How delightful is it, my beloved countrymen, on this festive day of jubilee, commemorating that day so pregnant with *your* weal or wo, and with that of your children's children, how delightful is it at the distance of fifty years from that day of promised blessings and of anticipated disappointments, to reflect that all the fairest visions of hope were to be more than realized, and all the apprehensions of wary prudence and self-distrusting wisdom more than dissipated and dispelled.

Yes, my countrymen, we have survived to this day of jubilee, and the only regret which shades the sober certainty of waking bliss, with which he who now addresses you, turns back the retrospective eye upon the long career between that time and the present, is the imperfection of his power to delineate with a pencil of phosphorus, the contrast between the national condition of your forefathers at that day, as it had been allotted to them by the articles of confederation, and your present state of associated existence, as it has been shaped and modified by the Constitution of the United States, administered by twenty-five biennial Congresses, and eight Presidents of the United States.

By the adoption and organization of the Constitution of the United States, these principles had been settled:—

1. That the affairs of the people of the United States were thenceforth to be administered, not by a confederacy, or mere league of friendship between the sovereign states, but by a *government*, distributed into the three great departments—legislative, judicial, and executive.

2. That the powers of government should be limited to concerns interesting to the whole people, leaving the internal administration of each state, *in peace*, to its own constitution and laws, provided that they should be *republican*, and interfering with them as little as should be necessary in *war*.

3. That the legislative power of this government should be divided between two assemblies, one representing directly the people of the *separate* states; and the other their *legislatures*.

4. That *the executive power* of this government should be vested in one person chosen for four years, with certain qualifications of age and nativity, re-eligible without limitation, and invested with a qualified negative upon the enactment of the laws.

5. That the judicial power should consist of tribunals inferior and supreme, to be instituted and organized by Congress, but

to be composed of persons holding their offices during good behaviour, that is, removable only by impeachment.

The organization and constitution of the subordinate executive departments, were also left to the discretionary power of Congress.

But the exact limits of legislative, judicial, and executive power, have never been defined, and the distinction between them is so little understood without reference to certain theories of government, or to specific institutions, that a very intelligent, well-informed and learned foreigner, with whom I once conversed, upon my using the words executive power, said to me, "I suppose by the executive power, you mean the power that MAKES the laws." . . . . Nor is this mistake altogether unexampled, even among ourselves; examples might be adduced in our history, national and confederate, in which the incumbents both of judicial and executive offices have mistaken themselves for the power that *makes* the laws—as on the other hand examples yet more frequent might be cited of legislators, and even legislatures, who have mistaken themselves to be judges, or executives supreme.

The legislative, judicial, and executive powers, like the prismatic colours of the rainbow, are entirely separate and distinct; but they melt so imperceptibly into each other that no human eye can discern the exact boundary line between them. The broad features of distinction between them are perceptible to all; but perhaps neither of them can be practically exercised without occasional encroachment upon the borders of its neighbour. The Constitution of the United States has not pretended to confine either of the great departments of its government exclusively within its own limits. Both the senate and the house of representatives possess, and occasionally exercise, both judicial and executive powers, and the president has at all times a qualified negative upon legislation, and a judicial power of remission.

To complete the organization of the government by the institution of the chief executive departments and the establishment of judicial courts, was among the first duties of Congress. The constitution had provided that all the public functionaries of the Union, not only of the general but of all the state governments, should be under oath or affirmation for its support.

The homage of religious faith was thus superadded to all the obligations of temporal law, to give it strength; and this confirmation of an appeal to the responsibilities of a future omnipotent judge, was in exact conformity with the whole tenor of the Declaration of Independence—guarded against abusive extension by a further provision, that no religious test should ever be required as a qualification to any office or public trust under the United States. The first act of the Congress, therefore, was to regulate and administer the oaths thus required by the Constitution.

The Constitution had already "*formed a more perfect union*" of the people of the United States; but it was not yet consummated or completed. The people of Rhode Island had taken no part in the formation of the Constitution, and refused their sanction to it. They had virtually seceded from the Union. North Carolina had been represented in the Convention at Philadelphia, but her people had refused to ratify their constitutional act.

Recent events in our history, to which I wish to make no unnecessary allusion, but to which the rising generation of our country cannot and ought not to close their eyes, have brought again into discussion questions, which, at the period to which we are now reverting, were of the deepest and most vital interest to the continued existence of the Union itself. The question whether any one state of the Union had the right to secede from the confederacy at her pleasure, was then practically solved. The question of the right of the people of any one state, to nullify within her borders any legislative act of the general government, was involved in that of the right of secession, without, however, that most obnoxious feature of the modern doctrine of nullification and secession—the violation of the plighted faith of the nullifying or seceding state.

Rhode Island had not only neglected to comply with the requisitions of the confederation-Congress to supply the funds necessary to fulfil the public engagements; but she alone had refused to invest the Congress with powers indispensable for raising such supplies. She had refused to join in the united effort to revivify the suspended animation of the confederacy, and she still defied the warning of her sister states, that if she persevered in this exercise of her sovereignty and independence, they would leave her alone in her glory, and take up their march in united column without her. North Carolina, not more remiss than her sister states in the fulfilment of her obligations, after joining them in the attempt to draw the bonds of union closer together by a new compact, still refused to ratify it, though recommended by the signature of her own delegates and under a similar admonition. Rhode Island and North Carolina still held back. The Union and Washington marched without them. Their right to secede was not contested. No unfriendly step to injure was taken; no irritating measure to provoke them was proposed. The door was left open for them to return, whenever the proud and wayward spirit of state sovereignty should give way to the attractions of clearer-sighted self-interest and kindred sympathies. In the first acts of Congress they were treated as foreigners, but with reservations to them of the power to resume the national privileges with the national character, and when within two years they did return, without invitation or repulsion, they were received with open arms.

The questions of secession, or of resistance under state authority, against the execution of the laws of the Union within any state, can never again be presented under circumstances so favourable to the pretensions of the separate state, as they were at the organization of the Constitution of the United States. At that time Rhode Island and North Carolina might justly have pleaded, that their sister states were bound to them by a compact into which they had voluntarily entered, with stipulations that it should undergo no alteration but by unanimous consent. That the Constitution was a confederate Union founded upon principles totally different, and to which not only they were at liberty to refuse their assent, but which all the other states combined, could not without a breach of their own faith establish among themselves, without the free consent of *all* the partners to the prior contract. That the confederation could not otherwise be dissolved, and that by adhering to it, they were only performing their own engagements with good faith, and claiming their own unquestionable rights.

The justification of the people of the eleven states, which had adopted the Constitution of the United States, and of that provision of the Constitution itself, which had prescribed that the ratification of nine states should suffice to absolve them from the bonds of the old confederation, and to establish the new Government as between themselves, was found in the *principles* of the Declaration of Independence. The confederation had failed to answer the purposes for which governments are instituted among men. Its powers or its impotence operated to the destruction of those ends, which it is the object of government to promote. The people, therefore—who had made it their own only by their acquiescence—acting under their responsibility to the Supreme Ruler of the universe, absolved themselves from the bonds of the old confederation, and bound themselves by the new and closer ties of the Constitution. In performing that act, they had felt the duty of obtaining the co-operation to it, of a majority of the whole people, by requiring the concurrence of majorities in nine out of the thirteen states, and they had neither prepared nor proposed any measure of compulsion, to draw the people of any of the possibly dissenting states into the new partnership, against their will. They passed upon the old confederation the same sentence, which they had pronounced in dissolving their connexion with the British nation, and they pledged their faith to each other anew, to a far closer and more intimate connexion.

It is admitted, it was admitted then, that the people of Rhode Island, and of North Carolina, were free to reject the new Constitution; but not that they could justly claim the continuance of the old Confederation. The law of political necessity, expounded by the judgment of the sovereign constituent people, responsible only to God, had abolished that. The people of Rhode Island, and of North Carolina, might dissent from the more perfect union, but they must acquiesce in the necessity of the separation.

Of that separation they soon felt the inconvenience to themselves, and rejoined the company from which they had strayed. The number of the primitive States has since doubled, by voluntary and earnest applications for admission. It has often been granted as a privilege and a favour. Sometimes delayed beyond the time when it was justly due—and never declined to any one State entitled to demand it.

Yet the boundary line between the constitutional authority of the General Government, and that of the separate States, was not drawn in colours so distinct and clear, as to have escaped diversities of opinion, and grave and protracted controversy. While the people of distant lands, of foreign races, and of other tongues, have solicited admittance to the North American Union, and have been denied, more than once have serious and alarming collisions of conflicting jurisdiction arisen between the General Government, and those of the separate States, threatening the dissolution of the Union itself. The right of a single state, or of several of the states in combination together, to secede from the Union, the right of a single state, without seceding from the Union, to declare an act of the General Congress, a law of the United States, null and void, within the borders of that state, have both been at various times, and in different sections of the Union, directly asserted, fervently controverted, and attempted to be carried into execution. It once accomplished a change of the administration of the General Government, and then was laid aside. It has occasionally wasted itself in abortive projects of new confederacies, and has recently proceeded to the extremity of assembling a Convention of the people of one state in the Union, to declare a law of the United States unconstitutional, null, and void. But the law was nevertheless executed; and in this, as in other instances, a temporary turbulent resistance against the lawful powers of Congress, under the banners of State sovereignty, and State rights, is now terminating in a more devoted adherence and willing subserviency to the authority of the Union.

This has been the result of the working of the Institution, and although now, as heretofore, it has been effected by means and in a manner so unforeseen and unexpected, as to baffle all human penetration, and to take reflection itself by surprise; yet the uniformity of the result often repeated by the experience of half a century, has demonstrated the vast superiority of the Constitution of the United States over the Confederation, as a system of Government to control the temporary passions of the people, by the permanent curb of their own interest.

In the calm hours of self-possession, the right of a *State* to nullify an act of Congress, is too absurd for argument, and too odious for discussion. The right of a state to secede from the Union, is equally disowned by the principles of the Declaration of Independence. Nations acknowledge no judge between them upon earth, and their Governments from necessity, must in their intercourse with each other decide when the failure of one party to a contract to perform its obligations, absolves the other from the reciprocal fulfilment of his own. But this last of earthly powers is not necessary to the freedom or independence of states, connected together by the immediate action of the *people*, of whom they consist. To the people alone is there reserved, as well the dissolving, as the constituent power, and that power can be exercised by them only under the tie of conscience, binding them to the retributive justice of Heaven.

With these qualifications, we may admit the same right as vested in the *people* of every state in the Union, with reference to the General Government, which was exercised by the people of the United Colonies, with reference to the Supreme head of the British empire, of which they formed a part—and under these limitations, have the people of each state in the Union a right to secede from the confederated Union itself.

Thus stands the RIGHT. But the indissoluble link of union between the people of the several states of this confederated nation, is after all, not in the *right*, but in the *heart*. If the day should ever come, (may Heaven avert it,) when the affections of the people of these states shall be alienated from each other; when the fraternal spirit shall give away to cold indifference, or collisions of interest shall fester into hatred, the bands of political association will not long hold together parties no longer attracted by the magnetism of conciliated interests and kindly sympathies; and far better will it be for the people of the disunited states, to part in friendship from each other, than to be held together by constraint. Then will be the time for reverting to the precedents which occurred at the formation and adoption of the Constitution, to form again a more perfect union, by dissolving that which could no longer bind, and to leave the separated parts to be reunited by the law of political gravitation to the centre.

While the Constitution was thus accomplishing the first object declared by the people as their motive for ordaining it, by forming a more perfect union, it became the joint and co-ordinate duty of the legislative and executive departments, to provide for the second of those objects, which involved within itself all the rest, and indeed all the purposes of government. For justice, defined by the Institutes of Justinian, as the constant and perpetual will of securing to every one his *right*, includes the whole duty of man in the social institutions of society, toward his neighbour.

To the establishment of this JUSTICE, the joint and harmonious co-operation of the legislative and executive departments was required, and it was one of the providential incidents of the time, that this zealous and hearty co-operation had been secured, by that over-ruling and universal popularity with which the Chief Magistrate was inducted into his most arduous and responsible office.

It has perhaps never been duly remarked, that under the Constitution of the United States the powers of the executive department explicitly and emphatically concentrated in one person, are vastly more extensive and complicated than those of the legislative. The language of the instrument, in conferring legislative authority is, "*All* legislative powers herein granted, shall be vested in a Congress of the United States, which shall consist of a Senate and House of Representatives." But the executive trust it committed in unrestricted terms: "THE executive power shall be vested in a President of the United States of America." The legislative powers of Congress are, therefore, limited to specific grants contained in the Constitution itself, all restricted on one side by the power of internal legislation within the separate States, and on the other, by the laws of nations, otherwise and more properly called the rights of war and peace, consisting of all the rules of intercourse between independent nations. These are not subject to the legislative authority of any one nation, and they are, therefore, not included within the powers of Congress. But *the* executive power vested in the President of the United States, confers upon him the power, and enjoins upon him the duty, of fulfilling all the duties and of exacting all the rights of the nation in her intercourse with all the other nations of the earth. The powers of *declaring* war, of *regulating* commerce, of *defining* and *punishing* piracies and felonies committed on the high seas, and *offences* AGAINST THE LAW OF NATIONS, are among the special grants to Congress, but over that law itself, thus expressly recognised, and all-comprehensive as it is, Congress has no alterative power. While *the* power of executing it, is conferred in unlimited terms upon the President of the United States.

The *exercise* of this more than dictatorial power is indeed controlled, first, by the participation of the Senate in the conclusion of treaties and appointments to office. Secondly, by the reservation of the discretionary power of the House of Representatives, to refuse the supplies necessary for the executive action. And thirdly, by the power reserved to the house to impeach the President for mal-administration, and to the senate to try that impeachment, and sentence him to removal and to disqualification for official station for ever. These are great and salutary checks upon the abusive application of the granted power. But the power is not the less granted.

And herein was the greatest and most pernicious deficiency of the articles of confederation, most effectively supplied. The Congress of the confederation had no *executive* power. They could contract, but they could not perform. Hence it was impossible for them to establish justice in the intercourse of the nation with foreign states. They could neither exact the justice due to the country, nor fulfil the duties of justice to others, and this was the reason assigned by the British government for declining to regulate the commerce between the two countries by treaty.

The establishment of *justice* in the intercourse between the nation and foreign powers, was thus pre-eminently committed to the custody of one man, but that man was George Washington.

How far the establishment of justice, by the administration of the affairs of the nation, abroad and at home, was accomplished by the Constitution of the United States, can be estimated only by a review of the history of fifty years. For this, neither the time nor the limits within which this discourse must be circumscribed, will permit more than a rapid and imperfect summary.

The relations of the United States with the other powers of the world, were then slight and of trifling importance, in comparison with what they were destined to become. In their colonial state their commercial intercourse had been restricted almost exclusively to the mother-country. Their political relations were only those of a subordinate dependance of a great empire.

The Declaration of Independence recognised the European law of nations, as practised among Christian nations, to be that by which they considered themselves bound, and of which they claimed the rights. This system is founded upon the principle, that the state of nature between men and between nations, is a state of peace. But there was a Mahometan law of nations, which considered the state of nature as a state of war—an Asiatic law of nations, which excluded all foreigners from admission within the territories of the state—a colonial law of nations, which excluded all foreigners from admission within the colonies—and a savage Indian law of nations, by which the Indian tribes within the bounds of the United States, were *under their protection*, though in a condition of undefined dependance upon the governments of the separate states. With all these different communities, the relations of the United States were from the time when they had become an independent nation, variously modified according to the operation of those various laws. It was the purpose of the Constitution of the United States to *establish justice* over them all.

The commercial and political relations of the Union with the Christian European nations, were principally with Great Britain, France, and Spain, and considerably with the Netherlands and Portugal. With all these there was peace; but with Britain and Spain, controversies involving the deepest interests and the very existence of the nation, were fermenting, and negociations of the most humiliating character were pending, from which the helpless imbecility of the confederation afforded no prospect of relief. With the other European states there was scarcely any intercourse. The Baltic was an unknown sea to our navigators, and all the rich and classical regions of the Mediterranean were interdicted to the commercial enterprise of our merchants, and the dauntless skill of our mariners, by the Mahometan merciless warfare of the Barbary powers. Scarcely had the peace of our independence been concluded, when three of our merchant-vessels had been captured by the corsairs of Algiers, and their crews, citizens of the Union, had been pining for years in slavery, appealing to their country for redemption, in vain. Nor was this all. By the operation of this state of things, all the

JUBILEE OF THE CONSTITUTION | 1839

shores of the Black sea, of the whole Mediterranean, of the islands on the African coast, of the southern ports of France, of all Spain and of Portugal, were closed against our commerce, as if they had been hermetically sealed; while Britain, everywhere our rival and competitor was counteracting by every stimulant within her power every attempt on our part to compound by tribute with the Barbarian for peace.

Great Britain had also excluded us from all commerce in our own vessels with her colonies, and France, notwithstanding her alliance with us during the war, had after the conclusion of the peace adopted the same policy. She was jealous of our aggrandizement, fearful of our principles, linked with Spain in the project of debarring us from the navigation of the Mississippi, and settled in the determination to shackle us in the development of the gigantic powers which, with insidious sagacity, she foresaw might be abused.

Notwithstanding all these discouragements, the inextinguishable spirit of freedom, which had carried your forefathers through the exterminating war of the Revolution, was yet unsuppressed. At the very time when the nerveless confederacy could neither protect nor redeem their sailors from Algerine captivity, the floating city of the Taho beheld the stripes and stars of the Union, opening to the breeze from a schooner of thirty tons, and inquired where was the ship of which that frail fabric was doubtless the tender. The Southern ocean was still vexed with the harpoons of their whalemen; but Britain excluded their oil, by prohibitory duties and the navigation act, from her markets, and the more indulgent liberality of France would consent to the illumination of her cities by the quakers of Nantucket, only upon condition that they should forsake their native island, and become the naturalized denizens of Dunkirk.

In the same year, when the Convention at Philadelphia was occupied in preparing the Constitution of the United States for the consideration of the people, two vessels, called the Columbia and the Washington, fitted out by a company of merchants at Boston, sailed upon a voyage combining the circumnavigation of the globe, discovery upon the shores of the Pacific ocean, and the trade with the savages of the Sandwich Islands, and with the celestial empire of China, all in one undertaking. The result of this voyage was the discovery of the Columbia river, so named from the ship which first entered within her capes, since unjustly confounded with the fabulous Oregon or river of the West, but really securing to the United States the right of prior discovery, and laying the foundation of the right of extension of our territory from the Atlantic to the Pacific ocean.

All this however was but the development of national character in the form of private enterprise. The foreign affairs of the Union when President Washington assumed the administration of *the* executive power, were in a state of chaos, out of which an orderly and harmonious world was to be educed.

In conferring *the* executive power upon the President of the United States, the Constitution had left its subordinate organization partly to the discretion of Congress. It had spoken of *heads* and chief officers of the executive departments, but without defining their offices, or prescribing their functions. Under the Revolutionary Congress, the executive power, such as it was, had been exercised by committees of their own body. Under the confederation Congress, by Secretaries of Foreign Affairs and of War, and successively by a single financier, and by a board of Commissioners of the Treasury.

The first Constitutional Congress, in the true spirit of the Constitution itself, instituted three executive departments, each with a single head, under the denomination of Secretaries of Foreign Affairs, of the Treasury, and of War. There was no Home Department, a deficiency which has not yet been supplied—but on reconsideration, the first Congress at their first session, combined the duties of the Home Department with those of Foreign Affairs, by substituting a Department and Secretary of State in the place of a Department and Secretary of Foreign Affairs. There was no navy—not so much as a barge—and of course no Navy Department, or Secretary of the Navy. That was to be created, and the Department was instituted in the second year of the succeeding administration.

In the interval, until the organization of the new departments, the Secretaries of Foreign Affairs and of War, of the confederation Congress, continued by order of President Washington to execute the duties of their respective offices.

During the first Congress also, the Judiciary Department was organized by the establishment of a Supreme, Circuit, and District Courts. The Ordinance for the government of the

Northwestern Territory was adapted to the newly constituted Government, as was the establishment of the Post Office.

In the erection of the Executive Departments a question arose, and was debated with great earnestness and pertinacity, in both houses of Congress, the decision upon which, in perfect conformity with the spirit of the Constitution, settled the character of that instrument as it has continued to this day. The Constitution had prescribed that the President should *nominate*, and by and with the advice and consent of the Senate, should *appoint*, all the officers of the United States, with the exception that Congress might by law vest the appointment of such inferior officers as they should think proper in the President alone, in the courts of law, or in the heads of departments. The Constitution had also provided, that the President should commission *all* the officers of the United States—and that the judges both of the supreme and inferior courts should hold their offices during good behaviour. But it had prescribed no term of duration to executive offices, civil or military, nor how, nor by whom, nor for what, they should be removable from office. The institution of the first Executive Department gave rise to that question. After a long and able discussion, it was ultimately settled, that by the investment of the executive power in the President, and the duty imposed upon him to take care that the laws should be faithfully executed, the discretionary power of removing all subordinate executive offices must necessarily be vested in him; and the law was accordingly so expressed. It must be admitted that this, like all other discretionary powers, is susceptible of great abuse—but while exercised as it always must be, under the powerful influence of public opinion, its abuse cannot be so pernicious to the welfare of the community, as would be a tenure of ministerial office, independent of the superior, responsible for its faithful execution.

Another, and perhaps a still more important *character* was given by President Washington to the government of the United States, in all their relations with foreign powers, by the principle which he assumed, and the example which he set to his successors, of referring the ministers from foreign powers, to the head of the Department of State, for all direct negotiations with which they might be charged by their governments.

The Count de Moustier happened at that time to be the Minister of France to the United States. He had been appointed by the unfortunate Louis XVI., in the last days of his absolute power. A spark, emitted from the self-evident truths of the Declaration of Independence, had fallen into the powder-magazine of monarchy, and inexpressibly terrible was the explosion about to ensue. Among the last evidences of the anti-republican spirit of the Bourbon dynasty, was an effort of this plenipotentiary minister to degrade the Chief Magistrate of the newly constituted Republic to an official level with himself, a minister of the second rank, commissioned by an European king. Immediately after the inauguration of President Washington, the Count de Moustier addressed a note directly to him, requesting a personal interview. On receiving for answer that the Secretary for Foreign Affairs was the officer with whom his official communications should still be held, he persisted in his application for a personal conference with the President, who uniting firmness of purpose with undeviating courtesy of forms, indulgently granted his request. He received the Count in a private interview, and listened for an hour to an argument, fortified by a *confidential* private letter which the royal envoy had the assurance to deliver to him, in which, under the base pretension of a supposed unfriendly disposition of the Secretary of Foreign Affairs towards France, he urged the adoption of a practice of direct inter-communication between the President of the United States and himself, in all his diplomatic negotiations, without the intervention of any third person whomsoever.

With a perfect preservation of patience and of good humour, the President answered his reasoning and referred him again for his future official transactions to the Secretary of Foreign Affairs, who, he assured him, entertained no feelings towards France but such as would render entire justice to her rights and her representative. The Count de Moustier fell back into his proper station, and very soon after was recalled by his master, and had his place supplied by the representative of another shade in the transition of France from an arbitrary monarchy to a portentious and short-lived nominal democracy.

The pretension that the President of the United States was to be considered by the ministers of foreign nations, not as the chief magistrate of the country, but as ranking as a minister of state, subordinate to the sovereign in European governments, was not confined to the Count de Moustier. It was afterward reproduced in still more offensive form, by the first minister from France in her republican transformation. It was then again repelled and finally withdrawn. Since then the President of the United States, in their intercourse with foreign nations represents them as their chief, and the ministers of foreign powers negotiate with the Secretary of State under his direction, and instructions.

At the same time, President Washington fully understood that by the investment of *the* executive power, he was authorized to enter directly into negociation with foreign nations, formally or informally, through the department of State, or by agents privately accredited by himself at his discretion. The state of the public relations of Great Britain was then such as rendered it proper for him to resume the political intercourse with her government, in the direct, personal, and informal, rather than the regular official manner. Shortly after the conclusion of the peace of independence, the confederation-Congress had appointed a minister plenipotentiary to Great Britain, and had authorized a treaty of commerce on the most liberal terms, to be negotiated with her. The minister had been graciously received; but mutual reproaches, too well founded on both sides, of a failure to fulfil the stipulations of the treaty of peace, had left a rankling of animosity on both sides. The British government had declined to conclude a commercial treaty, while the engagements of the treaty of peace remained unfulfilled; and the impotence of the confederation-Congress disabled them from the fulfilment of the stipulations on our part—particularly with regard to debts, the payment of which had been suspended by the Revolutionary war. After a fruitless mission of three years, the minister of the United States had returned home, and no minister from Great Britain had been accredited to the Congress in return. Immediately after the close of the first session of the first constitutional Congress, during which the judicial department of the government had been organized, and John Jay, the Secretary of Foreign Affairs to the preceding Congress, appointed Chief Justice of the United States, and before Thomas Jefferson, appointed Secretary of State in his absence, had repaired to his post, President Washington, on the 13th of October, 1789, wrote two letters to Gouverneur Morris, then in France, but recently before, a member of the Philadelphia Convention which had formed the Constitution, and at an earlier date, a member of the confederation-Congress. One of these letters was to serve him as a credential to hold conferences with the cabinet ministry of Great Britain, and the other a letter of instructions upon the topics to be discussed with them.

The glance of a moment at the relative position of the two countries at that time, will disclose to an attentive observer the peculiar propriety of the mode adopted by President Washington, and of the selection of the agent for entering upon this negotiation. It will serve also to illustrate the wisdom of the extensive grant of *the* executive power in the Constitution of the United States, to a single hand. The self-respect of the nation would have been humiliated in the eyes of the world, by the public and formal appointment of a second minister, after the return home of the first, without the reciprocation of courtesy by the appointment of a minister from Great Britain to the United States. There was no diplomatic intercourse between the two countries; yet there were great interests involving the peace between them, and urgently calling for adjustment. The commercial intercourse between them was very considerable; but for want of a countervailing power of regulation on our part, it was left at the mercy of the orders of the British king in council, the predominating spirit of which influenced by the loyalist refugees of the Revolution, was envious, acrimonious, and vindictive. The forts on the Canadian lakes, the keys to our western territories, and the stimulants to savage warfare, were withheld, in violation of the treaty of peace; while by the institution of the judicial courts of the Union, the door was open for the recovery of British debts, and the pretext for the detention of the posts was removed. It was necessary to advise the British government of the change which had been effected in our national institutions, and of the duty of the new government to exact justice from foreign nations, while ready to dispense it on the part of the nation to them. Yet, as peace was of all external blessings, that of which our country at that juncture most needed the continuance, it was a dictate of prudence to take no hasty public step which might commit the honour of the country and complicate the entanglement from which she was to be extricated.

Mr. Morris was a distinguished citizen of the United States, already in Europe—well known in England, where he had relatives in the royal service. He had been an active member of the Convention which had formed the Constitution—a secret mission committed to him would attract no premature public notice by any personal movement on his part, and whatever the result of it might be, the government of the United States itself would be uncommitted in the eyes of the world, and free to pursue such further course, as justice might require, and policy might recommend.

Mr. Morris executed his trust with faithfulness and ability. In personal conference with the Duke of Leeds, then the British Secretary of State for Foreign Affairs, and with William Pitt, first Lord of the Treasury and Chancellor of the Exchequer, and by correspondence with the former, he made known to the British government the feelings, purposes, and expectations of the newly organized government of the United States with regard to Great Britain—and he ascertained the dispositions, the doubts and the reluctances of the British cabinet toward the United States. They still declined the negotiation of a treaty of commerce. They parried, by counter-complaint of the non-execution of the treaty of peace, the demand for the surrender of the western posts—but they promised, with no small hesitation, some supercilious courtesy and awkward apologies for delay, the appointment of a Minister to the United States.

This negotiation occupied more than one year of time—and in February, 1791, just before the expiration of the first Constitutional Congress, President Washington communicated to the Senate in secret session the fact of its existence, and the correspondence by which it had been conducted. In the Message transmitting these documents to the Senate, he said: "I have *thought it proper* to give you this information, as it might *at some time* have influence on matters under your consideration."

While the negotiation was in progress, a controversy respecting the northeastern boundary of the United States bordering upon the British provinces, then confined to the question of what river had been intended in the treaty of peace, by the name of the St. Croix, was kindling a border war, and complicating the difficulties to be adjusted by negotiation.

In the summer of 1791, the promised Minister Plenipotentiary from Great Britain to the United States, was sent in the person of Mr. George Hammond, who had been the secretary to David Hartley, in the negotiation of the definitive treaty of peace in 1783. Mr. Hammond however had only powers to negotiate, but not to conclude—to complain, but not to adjust—to receive propositions, but not to accept them. With him a full discussion was had of all the causes of complaint subsisting between the parties. In the meantime a change had come over the whole political system of Europe. The principles proclaimed in the Declaration of Independence, as at the foundation of all lawful government, had been sapping the foundations of all the governments founded on the unlimited sovereignty of force—the absolute monarchy of France was crumbling into ruin; a wild and ferocious anarchy, under the banners of unbridled Democracy was taking its place, and between the furies of this frantic multitude, and the agonies of immemorial despotism, a war of desolation and destruction was sweeping over the whole continent of Europe. In this war all the sympathies of the American people were on the side of France and of freedom, but the freedom of France was not of the genuine breed. A phantom of more than gigantic form had assumed the mask and the garb of freedom, and substituted for the principles of the Declaration of Independence, anarchy within and conquest without. The revolution of the whole world was her war-cry, and the overthow of all established governments her avowed purpose.

Under the impulses of this fiend, France had plunged into war with all Europe, and murdered her king, his queen, his sister, and numberless of his subjects and partisans, with or without the forms of law, by the butchery of mock tribunals, or the daggers of a blood-thirsty rabble. In this death-struggle between inveterate abuse and hurly-burly innovation, it is perhaps impossible even now to say which party had been the first aggressor; but France had been first invaded by the combined forces of Austria and Prussia, and under banners of Liberty, Equality, Fraternity, had become an armed nation to expel them from her borders. The partialities of the American people still sympathized with France. They saw that her cause was the cause of national independence. They believed her professions of liberty, equality, and fraternity; and when the same Convention which had declared France a republic, and deposed and put to death her king, declared war against the kings of Great Britain and Spain, shocked as they were at the merciless extermination of their ancient great and good ally, they still favoured at heart the cause of France, especially when in conflict under the three-coloured banners of liberty, equality, fraternity, with their ancient common enemy of the Revolutionary war, the British king, and with their more recent, but scarcely less obnoxious foe, the king of Spain.

At the breaking out of this war, Washington and his administration, and with them, the Constitution, and peace and existence of the Union, were brought into a new, critical, and most perilous position. From the very day of his inauguration, notwithstanding his unparalleled personal popularity, a great, active, and powerful opposition to his administration had arisen, consisting at first almost universally of the party which had opposed the adoption of the Constitution itself—then known by the name of anti-federalists. The most plausible and the most popular of all the objections to the Constitution, had been the accumulation of power in the office of the President. His exercise of those powers was watched with a jealous and suspicious eye—trifles lighter than air in his personal deportment and his domestic establishment, were treasured up, and doled out in whispers and surmises, that he was affecting the state, and adopting the forms of a monarchy, and when this war between the new-born republic of France, and our old tyrant, George the Third, blazed out, the party opposed to Washington's administration, seized upon it, to embarrass and counteract his policy, by arraying the passions of the people, their ardent love of liberty, the generous feeling of their national gratitude, their still rankling resentments against the beldame step-mother Britain, and their soreness under the prevaricating chicanery of Spain, at once in favour of France and against Washington.

The treaty of alliance with France, of 6th February, 1778, had stipulated, on the part of the United States, a guarantee to *the king of France* of the possessions of *the crown of France* in America—and one of the first incidents of the war of republican France with Britain, was a British expedition against the French colonies in the West Indies.

By the laws of nations, the duty of the United States in this war was *neutrality*—and their rights were those of neutrality. Their unquestionable policy and their vital interest was also neutrality. But the maintenance of the rights, depended upon the strict performance of the *duties* of neutrality.

A grave question immediately presented itself, whether the guarantee of the French possessions in America to the king and crown of France in 1778, was so binding upon the United States, as to require them to make good that guarantee to the French republic by joining her in the war against Great Britain.

The neutrality of the United States was in the most imminent danger. The war between France and Britain, and Spain and the Netherlands, was a maritime war. In the spasms of the Revolutionary convulsion, the new republic had sent to the United States an incendiary minister, with a formal declaration, that they *did not* claim the execution of the guarantee in the treaty of 1778, but stocked with commissions for a military expedition against the Spanish territories on our western borders, and for privateers to be fitted out in our ports, and to cruize against all the nations with which France was at war.

All the daring enterprise, the unscrupulous ambition, the rapacious avarice floating in the atmosphere of this Union, were gathering to a head, and enlisting in this cause of republican France. The commissions for the military expedition against Louisiana, were distributed with so little secresy, that the whole conspiracy was soon detected, exposed, and defeated. But the privateering commissions were accepted in many of our seaports, and citizens of the United States sallied forth from their harbours, under the shelter of neutrality, in vessels, built, armed, equipped, and owned there, against the defenceless commerce of friendly nations, and returned in three days, laden with their spoils, under the uniform of the French republic, her three-coloured cockade, and her watchwords of liberty, equality, and fraternity—transformed into French citizens, by the plenipotentiary diploma, and disposing of their plunder under the usurped jurisdiction of a French republican consul.

At this crisis Washington submitted to his confidential advisers, the heads of the Executive Departments, a series of questions, involving the permanent system of policy, to be pursued for the preservation of the peace, and the fulfilment of the duties of the nation in this new and difficult position. The measure immediately contemplated by him as urgently required, was the issuing a proclamation declaring the *neutrality* of the United States in the war, just kindled in Europe; but the obligation of the treaties with France, and particularly that of the guarantee, were specially involved in the propriety and the particular purport of the proclamation. On this occasion, a radical difference of opinion equally dividing the four members of the administration, not upon the expediency of the proclamation, but upon the contingent obligation of the guarantee, aggravated intensely the embarrassments and difficulties which the temperance, the fortitude, and the good fortune of Washington were destined to encounter and to surmount.

The conduct of Great Britain, the leading party to the war with republican France, served only to multiply and to sharpen the obstructions with which his path was beset, and the perplexities of his situation. In the origin of the war, the first fountains of human society had been disturbed and poisoned. The French Convention had issued a decree, stimulating the people of all the countries around her to rebellion against their own governments, with a promise of the support of France. They had threatened an invasion of England, in the name of liberty, equality, and fraternity, to fraternize with the people of the British Islands in a revolt against their king; and strange and incredible as it may sound in your ears, there were elements within the bosoms of the British islands, of no inconsiderable magnitude, prepared to join and assist the threatened invader in this unhallowed purpose. A decree of the National Convention had forbidden their armies to make any prisoners in battle with their foes, or in other words to give quarters to the vanquished in arms. The mass of the British nation was exasperated to madness; and their government deliberately determined, that such an enemy was not entitled to the ordinary mitigations of war: that France had put herself out of the pale of civilized nations, and that no commerce of neutral nations with her was to be tolerated. Besides and yet more unjustifiable than this, from the very commencement of the war, the British government had indulged their naval officers in the outrageous and atrocious practice of impressing *men* from the vessels of the

United States upon the high seas—claiming it against the principles of her own Constitution no less than against the principles of the Declaration of Independence, as a *right* with regard to her own subjects, and leaving the question of *fact*, whether the impressed seaman was or was not a British subject, to the irresponsible discretion or caprice of every midshipman in her navy. The practice was not less provoking, than the pretension was insolent and unjust. The capture by a naval armament from Great Britain, of several French islands in the West Indies, gave occasion to another conflict of belligerent pretensions and neutral rights. During the peace that followed the war of the American Revolution, France under the usual maxims of European Colonial policy, had confined the commerce of her American possessions to herself. When the war came, her own merchant-vessels were excluded by the British maritime supremacy from the navigation of the ocean. The French islands were then opened to the neutral commerce, and hence it was that the French Executive Council forbore to claim the guarantee stipulated by the treaty of 1778—aware that the neutral commerce of the United States would be more useful to the islands, than any assistance that we could give for their defence against Great Britain by war. Upon the opening of the islands, numerous vessels of the United States crowded into their ports, for the enjoyment not only of a profitable direct trade, but to be freighted for the direct commerce between the Colonies and France herself. The commanders of the British maritime expedition broke up this trade, and captured every vessel engaged in it upon which they could lay their hands, whether in ports which surrendered to their arms, or upon the high seas.

The temperature of the public mind in calm and quiet times, is like the climate of the lofty table-lands of the equator, a perpetual spring. Such are the times in which we live, and were it not for the distant vision of a Chimborazo with eternal sunshine over its head, and eternal frost upon its brow, or of a neighbouring Ætna or Vesuvius bursting from time to time with subterranean fires, and pouring down from their summits floods of liquid lava, to spread ruin and destruction over the vales below, elementary snows and boiling water-courses would be objects scarcely within the limits of human conception. At such times, imagination in her wildest vagaries can scarcely conceive the transformations of temper, the obliquities of intellect, the perversions of moral principle effected by junctures of high and general excitement. Many of you, gentlemen, have known the Republican plenipotentiary of whom I have here spoken, settled down into a plain Republican farmer of your own state, of placid humour, of peaceable demeanour, addicted to profound contemplation, passing a long life in philosophical retirement, devising ingenious mechanical inventions, far from all the successive convulsions of his native land, and closing a useful career as a citizen of this his adopted country. Who of you could imagine, that this was the same man, who at the period which I am recalling to your memory, was a Phaeton, grasping at the reins of the chariot of the Sun to set the world on fire. Who could imagine, that coming with words of liberty, equality, fraternity, of generous friendship and disinterested benevolence upon his lips, he had brought with him like Albaroni, a torch to set fire to all the mines. His correspondence with the government of Washington, is recorded upon the annals of our country. Our time will admit but of a transient allusion to it. You remember the frank and dignified candour with which he was received by Washington himself; the warm-hearted enthusiasm with which, as the representative of the new sister Republic, he was welcomed by the people; and the wanton, lascivious courtship of the faction opposed to Washington—congenial spirits to the cannibals, then in the name of Democracy ruling in France—blistering him up into open defiance, and an appeal against Washington himself, TO THE PEOPLE.

His recall was at length demanded. His violence was turning the current of popular opinion here against his country. The party which had despatched him from France was annihilated. The heads of his patrons had passed under the edge of the guillotine. Their successors disavowed his conduct and recalled him. In self-vindication he published his instructions, disclosing the secrets both of monarchical and republican France, dampers to the affectionate gratitude of the American people, and he renounced his country for ever.

The party opposed to the administration of Washington, saw nothing in France but the republic of liberty, equality, and fraternity. Like the mass of the French people themselves, they followed with obsequious approbation every resolution by which an armed detachment of Democracy from the Fauxbourg Saint Antoine, swept away one set of rulers after another, and smothered them in their own blood. The Brissotine, the Dantonian, the Robespierrian factions crowded each other to the guillotine with the fury of uncaged tigers, and the accession of a popular chieftain to the summit of power was the signal of his proscription and murder by that national razor. At every exhibition of this horrid scene, the Parisian rabble shouted applause, and clapped their hands for joy—and every shout and every clapping of hands was re-echoed from these western shores of the Atlantic, by the opposition to the administration of Washington. With this wilfully blind devotion to France, was necessarily associated, a bitter and malignant hatred of Britain; inflamed by the wrongs which she was inflicting upon our commerce and seamen, and ulcerated by the tone of her negotiator here in the discussion of the long standing mutual complaints, which he had yet not been authorized by his government to compromise or to settle.

In the spring of the year 1794, the sixth year of Washington's administration, this congregating mass of evil humours was drawing to a head. The national feeling against Britain was irritated to the highest pitch of excitement. Resolutions looking and tending directly to war, were introduced and pending in the House of Representatives of the United States, and that war in all human probability would have been fatal to the fame of Washington, and to the independence of the Union and the freedom of his country. At that moment he fixed his eyes, with calm and considerate firmness at once upon James Monroe, as a messenger of peace, of conciliation, and of friendship to the Republic of France; and upon John Jay, as an envoy extraordinary, bearer of the same disposition, and interpreter of the same spirit to Great Britain. They were despatched at the same time with instructions concerted in one system, and diversified to meet the exigencies of the two respective missions.

Mr. Monroe was at that time a member of the Senate of the United States, from Virginia—a soldier of the Revolution, in the service of which he had passed from youth to manhood with distinguished honour. Personally attached to Washington, he had been a moderate opponent to the adoption of the

Constitution, and although adverse to some of the leading measures of the administration, and partially favourable to the cause of France, the confidence of Washington in his abilities and in his personal integrity made his political propensities rather a recommendation, than an objection to his appointment.

Mr. Jay was then Chief Justice of the United States. And how shall I dare to speak to YOU of a native of your own state, and one of the brightest ornaments not only of your state, but of his country, and of human nature. At the dawn of manhood he had been one of the delegates from the *people* of New York, at the first continental Congress of 1774. In the course of the Revolutionary War, he had been successively President of Congress, one of their ministers in Europe—one of the negotiators of the preliminary and definitive treaties of peace, and Secretary of Foreign Affairs to the Confederation Congress, till the transition to the constitutional government, and at the organization of the judicial tribunals of the Union, was placed with the unanimous sanction of the public voice, at their head. With this thickening crowd of honours gathering around him as he trod the path of life, he possessed with a perfectly self-controlled ambition, a fervently pious, meek and quiet, but firm and determined spirit. As one of the authors of the Federalist, and by official and personal influence as Secretary of Foreign Affairs, and as a most respected citizen of New York, he had contributed essentially to the adoption of the Constitution: and his administration of the highly responsible office of chief justice, had given universal satisfaction to the friends of Washington's administration, and to all who desired the practical operation of the Constitution conformably to the spirit in which it had been ordained by the people. He had no European partialities, and least of all for England; but he was for dispensing equal justice to all mankind, and he felt the necessity of peace for the stability of the Constitution, and the preservation of the Union.

His negotiation terminated in a treaty, the ratification of which brought on the severest trial, which the character of Washington and the fortunes of our nation have ever passed through. No period of the war of independence, no other emergency of our history since its close, not even the ordeal of establishing the Constitution of the United States itself, has convulsed to its inmost fibres, the political association of the North American people, with such excruciating agonies as the consummation and fulfilment of this great national composition of the conflicting rights, interests and pretensions of our country and of Great Britain. The party strife in which it originated and to which it gave birth is not yet appeased. From this trial, Washington himself, his fame, the peace, union and prosperity of his country, have issued triumphant and secure. But it prepared the way for the reversal of some of the principles of his administration, and for the introduction of another and widely different system six years after, in the person of Thomas Jefferson.

The treaty concluded by Mr. Jay, with the exception of one article, which the British government readily consented to relinquish, was ratified. The peace, the union, the prosperity, the freedom of the nation, were secured; but revolutionary France, and the opposition to Washington's administration, were defeated, disconcerted, disabled, but not subdued. The rabble government of the fauxbourg St. Antoine was passing away. The atheism of the strumpet goddess of reason, had already yielded to a solemn decree of the national Convention, proposed by Robespierre himself, in the name of the people of France, acknowledging—the existence of a God! a worm of the dust, recognising as a co-ordinate power—the Creator of all worlds. The counter-revolution had advanced a step further. A constitutional republic, with a legislature in two branches, and a plural executive, had succeeded to the despotism of a single assembly, with a jacobin club executive. France had now a five-headed executive Directory, and a new union of church and state, with a new theo-philanthropic religion, halfway between simple Deism and Christianity. And republican France had now another element in her composition. A youthful soldier by the name of Napoleon Bonaparte, who by the election of the whole people of France, with the help of his holiness the Pope, and the iron crown of Lombardy, was destined at no distant day to restore the Christian calendar and Sabbath for the godless decimal division of time of Fabre d'Eglantine, and to ascend a double carpeted throne of emperor and king. Through all these varying phases of the French Revolution, the party opposed to Washington's administration still clung in affection and in policy to France, and when by the election of Mr. Jefferson as President of the United States, that party came into power, it was precisely the moment when Napoleon at the head of his brave grenadiers had expelled the two legislative councils from their halls, had turned out the theo-philanthropic Directory from their palace; and under the very republican name of first of three consuls, was marching with fixed eye and steady step to the consulate for life, to the hereditary imperial throne, and to the kingdom of the iron crown. To all those transmutations the pure republicanism of Jefferson was to accommodate itself without blench and without discarding his partiality for France. Nor was it to fail of its reward, in the acquisition of Louisiana—a measure, not embraced or foreseen by the administration of Washington, accomplished by a flagrant violation of the Constitution, but sanctioned by the acquiescence of the people, and if not eventually leading to the dissolution of the Union, shaped by the healing and beneficent hand of Providence from a portentous evil into a national blessing.

The consequences of *that* revolution in our Union (for it was nothing less) are not yet fully developed—far otherwise. But whether for weal or wo—for the permanent aggrandizement, or the final ruin of our confederated nation, it belongs to the memory of Jefferson, and not to that of Washington or his administration. Hitherto it has exhibited its fairest side. It has enlarged our borders and given us the whole valley of the Mississippi. The pernicious and corrupting example of an undissembled admitted prostration of the Constitution—the more concealed, but not less real displacement of the internal sectional balance of power—have not yet borne their fruits. Upon the opening of Pandora's box, Hope was left behind. Hitherto no seed of deadly aconite has generated into pestilential poison. Let us rejoice at the past and hope for the future. But in leaving to the judgment of aftertime, the ultimate decision of that which we see as yet but in part, and through a glass darkly, let us look back to the principles of Washington and his administration, and to the unbroken faith of the Constitution, for the source of that prosperity which no variation of seasons can wither, and that happiness which no reverse of fortune can turn into bitter disappointment.

The ratification of Mr. Jay's treaty was the establishment of *justice* in our national intercourse with Great Britain. But it was deeply resented by all the parties which successively wielded the power of France. Victorious in the midst of all their internal convulsions over all the continent of Europe, they were unable to cope with the naval power of Britain upon the sea. Although Mr. Jay's treaty had expressly reserved all the obligations of the United States in previously existing treaties with other nations; France complained, that it had conceded the long-contested principle of protecting the cargo of an enemy with the flag of the friend—that it had enlarged the list of articles of contraband; and even while claiming the exemption of provisions from that list, had by stipulating the payment for them when taken, admitted by implication the right of taking them. A long and irritating discussion of these complaints ensued between the American Secretary of State, and the successive Plenipotentiaries of France, and between the French Ministers of Foreign Affairs, and Mr. Monroe. The opposition to Washington's administration, strengthened by the unpopularity of Mr. Jay's treaty, had acquired an ascendancy in the House of Representatives; countenanced and justified every reproach of France; and made a persevering and desperate effort to refuse the means and the supplies for carrying the treaty into execution, even after it had been ratified.

After a long and doubtful struggle, in the course of which the documents of the negotiation, called for by the House of Representatives, were refused by Washington, the House by a bare majority voted the supplies. The treaty was carried faithfully into execution, and *justice* was established in the relations between the United States and Great Britain.

The last act of the confederation Congress had been to refer over to the new government the negotiations with Spain, especially for the free navigation of the Mississippi. These were immediately taken up, and transferred from the seat of government of the United States to Spain. Two commissioners were appointed to negotiate with the Spanish government at Madrid, who prepared the way for the treaty of San Lorenzo, concluded on the 27th of October, 1795, by Thomas Pinckney, Minister Plenipotentiary from the United States, and the Prince of the Peace, then the Minister of Spain for Foreign Affairs. This treaty secured to the people of the United States, the free navigation of the Mississippi, and a port of deposite at New

Orleans—and politically considered as a part of the comprehensive system of Washington's policy, was at once a sequel to the treaty of 19th November, with Great Britain, and a precursor to the treaty for the acquisition of Louisiana with France.

In the accomplishment of these objects, the principal agent of the nation had been *the* Executive power, vested in Washington as President of the United States. But the justice for the establishment of which the Constitution of the United States had been ordained, was required at home as well as abroad, and for this it was the peculiar province of the Legislature to provide.

The first attention due from that body was to the public creditors of the country, and the first measure to be adopted was the raising of a revenue to satisfy their righteous claims. On the 8th of April, immediately after the organization of the two Houses, and before the President of the United States had been notified of his election, Mr. Madison introduced into the committee of the whole House of Representatives a proposition for levying duties of impost. The remarks with which he submitted this proposal, so explicitly indicative of this purpose of establishing justice, that I cannot forbear to repeat the first sentences of them in his own words:—

"I take the liberty, Mr. Chairman," said he, "at this early stage of the business, to introduce to the committee a subject which appears to me to be of the greatest magnitude; a subject, Sir, that requires our first attention, and our united exertions.

No gentleman here can be unacquainted with the numerous *claims upon our justice*; nor with the impotency which prevented the late Congress of the United States, from carrying into effect the dictates of gratitude and policy.

The Union by the establishment of a more effective government, having recovered from the state of imbecility that heretofore prevented a performance of its duty, ought in its first act to revive those principles of honour and honesty, that have too long lain dormant.

The deficiency in our treasury has been too notorious to make it necessary for me to animadvert upon that subject. Let us content ourselves with endeavouring to remedy the evil. To do this, a national revenue must be obtained; but the system must be such a one, that, while it secures the object of revenue, it shall not be oppressive to our constituents. Happy it is for us that such a system is within our power; for I apprehend, that both these objects may be obtained from an impost on articles imported into the United States."

And thus was laid the foundation of the revenues of the Union; and with them the means of paying their debts and of providing for their common defence and general welfare. The act of Congress framed upon this proposal, received the sanction of Washington on the 4th of July, in the first year of his administration. It stands the second on the statute book of the United States, immediately after that which binds all the officers of the Union to the support of the Constitution, by the solemnities of an appeal to God, and declares in a brief preamble, the necessity of its enactment, "for the support of government, for the discharge of the debts of the United States, and the encouragement and protection of manufactures."

With the act for laying duties of impost, there was associated another, imposing duties of tonnage on ships, in which to encourage the shipping and ship-building interest, a double discrimination was made between ships built in the United States and belonging to their citizens, ships built in the United States, belonging to foreigners, and ships foreign built and owned. The duty upon the first of these classes being six, on the second thirty, and on the third fifty cents a ton. The same discriminating principle favourable to the navigation of the United States, was observed in every part of the Act for levying duties of impost.

An Act for regulating the *collection* of these duties, with the establishment of ports of entry and delivery, and for the appointment of officers of the customs throughout the United States: an Act for the establishment and support of light-houses, beacons, buoys, and public piers; and an Act for regulating the coasting-trade, completed the system for raising a revenue.

Thus the organization of the government, conformably to the new constitution, and to give it practical operation, was effected at the first session of the first Constitutional Congress, between the 4th of March, and the 29th of September, 1789. A comprehensive and efficient system of revenue—a graduation of judicial tribunals, inferior and supreme—the Departments of State, of the Treasury, and of War—a temporary establishment of the Post Office, provisions for the negotiation of treaties with the Indian tribes; for the adaptation to the new order of things, of the ordinance for the government of the northwestern Territory, and of the shadow of a military establishment then existing; for fixing the compensation of the President and Vice President, the members of Congress, and of all the officers of the United States, judicial and executive—and for the payment of invalid pensions, were all effected within that time. Twelve Amendments to the Constitution, to serve as a substitute for the omission of a Declaration of Rights, were agreed to by a majority of two thirds of the members present of both Houses, and transmitted to the Legislatures of the several states—ten of those Amendments were adopted by three fourths of the state Legislatures, and became parts of the Constitution—only two other Amendments have since obtained the same sanction. An Act of appropriation for the service of the year 1789, amounting to six hundred and thirty-nine thousand dollars, with twenty thousand more for negotiating Indian treaties, defrayed all the expenses of the year; and if compared with the thirty-six millions and upward, appropriated at the session of Congress recently expired, for the service of the year 1839, may give a pregnant exemplification in the science of political economy, of the contrast between the day of small things, and the present: an inversion of the microscope might present a comparison between the *results* of the former and the latter appropriations, not so much to the advantage of the present day.

But at the close of the first session, there was yet much to be done for the establishment of justice at home and abroad. On the 29th of September, 1789, Congress adjourned, to meet again on the 4th of January, 1790. That second session continued until the 12th of August of that year. The institution of the Departments of State and of the Treasury, were among the latest acts of the first session, and on the 11th of September, Alexander Hamilton had been appointed Secretary of the Treasury; and on the 26th of the same month, Thomas Jefferson was appointed Secretary of State. Henry Knox, the Secretary of War to the confederation Congress when it expired, was reappointed to the same office, adapted to the new Constitution.

The Secretaries of State and of the Treasury, both possessing minds of the highest order of intellect; both animated with a lofty spirit of patriotism, both distinguished for pre-eminent services in the Revolution—Jefferson, the author of the Declaration of Independence—Hamilton, almost entitled to be called jointly with Madison, the author of the Constitution itself, both spurred to the rowels by rival and antagonist ambition, were the representatives and leading champions of two widely different theories of government. The Constitution itself was not altogether satisfactory to either of those theories. Jefferson, bred from childhood to the search and contemplation of abstract rights, dwelling with a sort of parental partiality upon the self-evident truths of the Declaration of Independence, and heated by recent communion with the popular leaders and doctrines of revolutionary France, in the convulsive struggles to demolish her monarchy, had disapproved the Constitution for its supposed tendency to monarchy, and for its omission of a Declaration of Rights, and finally acquiesced in its adoption upon a promise of amendments. Hamilton, prompted by a natural temper aspiring to military renown—nurtured to a spirit of subordination by distinguished military service in the Revolutionary War, and disgusted with the dishonest imbecility of the confederacy of sovereign states, of which he had suffered the mortifying experience, had inclined to a government higher toned than that of the Constitution, to which he had however cheerfully acceded—and which he had most ably advocated as the principal author of the Federalist, and in the state Convention of New York. But the whole drift and scope of his papers in the Federalist was directed to sustain the position, that a government *at least as energetic* as that provided by the Constitution, was indispensable to the salvation of the Union—the inference is clearly deducible from this form of expression, and from the tenor of all his argument, that he believed a still stronger government necessary. His opinions thus inclined to the doctrine of implied powers; and to a liberal construction of all the grants of power in the Constitution. These prepossessions, so discordant in themselves, and fortified on both sides with so much genius and talent, soon manifested themselves in the cabinet councils, with so much vehemence and pertinacity, as made it impossible for Washington, as he designed, to hold an even balance between them.

On the 21st of September, 1789, upon the report of a committee on a memorial and petition of certain of the public creditors in the state of Pennsylvania, two Resolutions were adopted by the House of Representatives, without debate or opposition.

> 1. That this house consider an adequate provision for the support of public credit, as a matter of high importance to the national honour and prosperity.
> 2. That the Secretary of the Treasury be directed to prepare a plan for that purpose, and to report the same to the House at its next meeting.

Accordingly on the 14th of January, 1790, a plan for the support of public credit was reported by Mr. Hamilton to the House, and was followed by others proposing the establishment of a national bank and a mint; and upon manufactures, with a review of the operation of the revenue, and collection and navigation Acts of the preceding session—all reports of consummate ability, and proposing measures for the restoration of the public credit, the funding of the public debt, and the management of the revenue, which were adopted by Congress almost without alteration, and constituted altogether a system for the fulfilment of the nation's obligations, and the final discharge of the debt of the Revolution, which has been carried into complete execution, and immortalized the name of Hamilton, as a statesman of high and permanent reputation, and among the first financiers of his age.

But in the consummation of these plans, questions of great difficulty, not only in politics but in morals, and questions not less controvertible of constitutional power, were necessarily involved. It is deeply to be lamented that the complete success of Mr. Hamilton's plans; the restoration through them of the honour of the country, and the discharge to the last dollar of her debt, have not to this day definitively settled all these questions. In the long-protracted controversies which grew out of Mr. Hamilton's funding system, the efforts to discriminate between the public creditors of different classes, the violent opposition to the assumption of the state debts, and the strain of strict construction, denying the power of Congress to establish a national bank, by the same party which afterward by Acts of Congress, purchased a foreign realm, with its people, governed them for years with the rod of Spanish colonial despotism, parcelled the land out in states, and admitted them all to the Union, were all as I believed morally and politically wrong. The discrimination between the public creditors, and the assumption of the state debts, were questions which once settled could not again recur; but the power of Congress to establish a bank as a regulation of commerce, and appendage to the power of borrowing money and regulating its value, an instrument for the management of the reverses and for effecting the receipts and expenditures of the nation, has unfortunately become a foot-ball of contention between parties, and mingling itself with the baneful spirit of unlimited separate state sovereignty, even now hangs as a dark cloud over the future destiny of the Union. That cloud will pass away. The advice of empirics, administering the bane for the antidote, will give way to the surgery of sober reason; and exemption from debt, and superfluity of revenue, shall no longer by the financiering economy of the executive head, be felt as a public calamity.

The establishment of the funding system of Mr. Hamilton, and especially the incorporation of the bank, operated like enchantment for the restoration of the public credit; repaired the ruined fortunes of the public creditors, and was equivalent to the creation of many millions of capital, available for the encouragement of industry and the active exertions of enterprise. His reputation rose proportionably in the public estimation. But his principles thus developed brought him in the cabinet of Washington, immediately into conflict with those of the Secretary of State, and in the house of representatives, with those of Mr. Madison, his late friend and associate in the composition of the Federalist, and in framing and erecting the admirable fabric of the Constitution. Mr. Madison was the intimate, confidential, and devoted friend of Mr. Jefferson, and the mutual influence of these two mighty minds upon each other, is a phenomenon, like the invisible and mysterious movements of the magnet in the physical world, and in which the sagacity of the future historian may discover the solution of much of our national history not otherwise easily accountable.

The system of strict construction of state rights, and of federative preponderance in the councils of the nation, become thus substitutes for the opposition to the Constitution itself, and elements of vehement opposition to the administration of Washington, of which the funding system thenceforward formed a vital part. At the head of this opposition Mr. Jefferson was in the cabinet, and Mr. Madison in the house of representatives.

This opposition soon assumed the shape of a rival system of administration, preparing for the advancement of Mr. Jefferson to the succession of the Presidency, and thoroughly organized to the accomplishment of that purpose. It was conducted with more address, with more constant watchfulness of the fluctuations of public opinion, and more pliable self-accommodation to them than the administration itself. It began with a studious and cautious preservation of deference to the character and reputation of Washington *himself*, never wholly abandoned by Mr. Jefferson, always retained by Mr. Madison, but soon exchanged by some of their partisans in Congress for hostility ill-disguised, and by many of the public journals and popular meetings, for the most furious assaults upon his reputation, and the most violent denunciations, not only of his policy, but of his personal character.

Mr. Jefferson was in the meantime fortifying his own reputation, and raising himself in the estimation of his countrymen, by a series of reports to the President, and to both houses of Congress, upon weights and measures, upon the fisheries, upon the commerce of the Mediterranean sea, upon the commercial intercourse with the European nations, and afterward by a correspondence with the ministers of Britain, and of France and of Spain, with an exhibition of genius, of learning, and of transcendant talent, certainly not inferior, perhaps surpassing that of Hamilton himself. The two systems, however, were so radically incompatible with each other, that Washington was, after many painful efforts to reconcile them together, compelled reluctantly to choose between them. He decided in the main for that of Hamilton, and soon after the unanimous re-election of Washington to the Presidency, Mr. Jefferson retired from the administration, to Monticello, and ostensibly to private life.

Within a year afterward, Hamilton also retired, as did Washington himself at the close of his presidential term. He declined a second re-election. The opposition to his administration, under the auspices of Mr. Jefferson, had acquired a head, which in the course of four years more, might have broken it down, as it was broken down in the hands of his successor.

When Solon, by the appointment of the people of Athens, had formed, and prevailed upon them to adopt a code of fundamental laws, the best that they would bear, he went into voluntary banishment for ten years, to save his *system* from the batteries of rival statesmen working upon popular passions and prejudices excited against his person. In eight years of a turbulent and tempestuous administration, Washington had settled upon firm foundations the practical execution of the Constitution of the United States. In the midst of the most appalling obstacles, through the bitterest internal dissensions, and the most formidable combinations of foreign antipathies and cabals, he had subdued all opposition to the Constitution itself; had averted all dangers of European war; had redeemed the captive children of his country from Algiers; had reduced by chastisement and conciliated by kindness, the most hostile of the Indian tribes; had restored the credit of the nation, and redeemed their reputation of fidelity to the performance of their obligations; had provided for the total extinguishment of the public debt; had settled the Union upon the immovable foundation of principle, and had drawn around his head for the admiration and emulation of after times, a brighter blaze of glory than had ever encircled the brows of hero or statesman, patriot or sage.

The administration of Washington fixed the character of the Constitution of the United States, as a practical system of government, which it retains to this day. Upon his retirement, its great antagonist, Mr. Jefferson, came into the government again, as Vice President of the United States, and four years after, succeeded to the Presidency itself. But the funding system and the bank were established. The peace with both the great belligerent powers of Europe was secured. The disuniting doctrines of unlimited separate state sovereignty were laid aside. Louisiana, by a stretch of power in Congress, far beyond the highest tone of Hamilton, was annexed to the Union—and although dry-docks, and gun-boats, and embargoes, and commercial restrictions, still refused the protection of the national arm to commerce, and although an overweening love of peace, and a reliance upon reason as a weapon of defence against foreign aggression, eventuated in a disastrous though glorious war with the gigantic power of Britain, the Constitution as construed by Washington, still proved an effective government for the country.

And such it has still proved, through every successive change of administration it has undergone. Of these, it becomes not me to speak in detail. Nor were it possible, without too great a trespass upon your time. The example of Washington, of retiring from the Presidency after a double term of four years, was followed by Mr. Jefferson, against the urgent solicitations of several state Legislatures. This second example of voluntary self-chastened ambition, by the decided approbation of public opinion, has been held obligatory upon their successors, and has become a tacit subsidiary Constitutional law. If not entirely satisfactory to the nation, it is rather by its admitting one re-election, than by its interdicting a second. Every change of a President of the United States, has exhibited some variety of policy from that of his predecessor. In more than one case, the change has extended to political and even to moral principle; but the policy of the country has been fashioned far more by the influences of public opinion, and the prevailing humours in the two Houses of Congress, than by the judgment, the will, or the principles of the President of the United States. The President himself is no more than a representative of public opinion at the time of his election; and as public opinion is subject to great and frequent fluctuations, he *must* accommodate his policy to them; or the people will speedily give him a successor; or either House of Congress will effectually control his power. It is thus, and in no other sense that the Constitution of the United States is democratic—for the government of our country, instead of a Democracy the most simple, is the most complicated government on the face of the globe. From the immense extent of our territory, the difference of manners, habits, opinions, and above all, the clashing interests of the North, South, East, and West, public opinion formed by the combination of numerous aggregates, becomes itself a problem of compound arithmetic, which nothing but the result of the popular elections can solve.

It has been my purpose, Fellow-Citizens, in this discourse to show:—

1. That this Union was formed by a spontaneous movement of *the people* of thirteen English Colonies; all subjects of the

King of Great Britain—bound to him in allegiance, and to the British empire as their country. That the first object of this Union, was united resistance against oppression, and to obtain from the government of their country redress of their wrongs.

2. That failing in this object, their petitions having been spurned, and the oppressions of which they complained, aggravated beyond endurance, their Delegates in Congress, *in their name and by their authority*, issued the Declaration of Independence—proclaiming them to the world as *one people*, absolving them from their ties and oaths of allegiance to their king and country—renouncing that country; declaring the UNITED Colonies, Independent States, and announcing that this ONE PEOPLE of thirteen united independent states, by that act, assumed among the powers of the earth, that separate and equal station to which the laws of nature and of nature's God entitled them.

3. That in justification of themselves for this act of transcendent power, they proclaimed the principles upon which they held all lawful government upon earth to be founded—which principles were, the natural, unalienable, imprescriptible rights of man, specifying among them, life, liberty and the pursuit of happiness—that the institution of government is to *secure* to men in society the possession of those rights: that the institution, dissolution, and reinstitution of government, belong exclusively to THE PEOPLE under a moral responsibility to the Supreme Ruler of the universe; and that all the *just* powers of government are derived from the *consent* of the governed.

4. That under this proclamation of principles, the dissolution of allegiance to the British king, and the compatriot connection with the people of the British empire, were accomplished; and the *one people* of the United States of America, became one separate sovereign independent power, assuming an equal station among the nations of the earth.

5. That this one people did not immediately institute a government for themselves. But instead of it, their delegates in Congress, by authority from their separate state legislatures, without voice or consultation of the people, instituted a mere confederacy.

6. That this confederacy totally departed from the principles of the Declaration of Independence, and substituted instead of the constituent power of the people, an assumed sovereignty of each separate state, as the source of all its authority.

7. That as a primitive source of power, this separate state sovereignty, was not only a departure from the principles of the Declaration of Independence, but directly contrary to, and utterly incompatible with them.

8. That the tree was made known by its fruits. That after five years wasted in its preparation, the confederacy dragged out a miserable existence of eight years more, and expired like a candle in the socket, having brought the union itself to the verge of dissolution.

9. That the Constitution of the United States was a *return* to the principles of the Declaration of Independence, and the exclusive constituent power of the people. That it was the work of the ONE PEOPLE of the United States; and that those United States, though doubled in numbers, still constitute as a nation, but ONE PEOPLE.

10. That this Constitution, making due allowance for the imperfections and errors incident to all human affairs, has under all the vicissitudes and changes of war and peace, been administered upon those same principles, during a career of fifty years.

11. That its fruits have been, still making allowance for human imperfection, a more perfect union, established justice, domestic tranquility, provision for the common defence, promotion of the general welfare, and the enjoyment of the blessings of liberty by the constituent *people*, and their posterity to the present day.

And now the future is all before us, and Providence our guide.

When the children of Israel, after forty years of wanderings in the wilderness, were about to enter upon the promised land, their leader, Moses, who was not permitted to cross the Jordan with them, just before his removal from among them, commanded that when the Lord their God should have brought them into the land, they should put the curse upon Mount Ebal, and the blessing upon Mount Gerizim. This injunction was faithfully fulfilled by his successor Joshua. Immediately after they had taken possession of the land, Joshua built an altar to the Lord, of whole stones, upon Mount Ebal. And there he wrote upon the stones a copy of the law of Moses, which he had written in the presence of the children of Israel: and all Israel, and their elders and officers, and their judges, stood on the two sides of the ark of the covenant, borne by the priests and Levites, six tribes over against Mount Gerizim, and six over against Mount Ebal. And he read all the words of the law, the blessings and cursings, according to all that was written in the book of the law.

Fellow-citizens, the ark of *your* covenant is the Declaration of Independence. Your Mount Ebal, is the confederacy of separate state sovereignties, and your Mount Gerizim is the Constitution of the United States. In that scene of tremendous and awful solemnity, narrated in the Holy Scriptures, there is not a curse pronounced against the people, upon Mount Ebal, not a blessing promised them upon Mount Gerizim, which your posterity may not suffer or enjoy, from your and their adherence to, or departure from, the principles of the Declaration of Independence, practically interwoven in the Constitution of the United States. Lay up these principles, then, in your hearts, and in your souls—bind them for signs upon your hands, that they may be as frontlets between your eyes—teach them to your children, speaking of them when sitting in your houses, when walking by the way, when lying down and when rising up—write them upon the doorplates of your houses, and upon your gates—cling to them as to the issues of life—adhere to them as to the cords of your eternal salvation. So may your children's children at the next return of this day of jubilee, after a full century of experience under your national Constitution, celebrate it again in the full enjoyment of all the blessings recognised by you in the commemoration of this day, and of all the blessings promised to the children of Israel upon Mount Gerizim, as the reward of obedience to the law of God.

"HERE THE CAT IS LET OUT OF THE BAG"

20. *Mr. Adams' Speech, on War with Great Britain and Mexico; with the Speeches of Messrs. Wise and Ingersoll, to which it is in reply* (Boston: Emancipator Office, 1842).

On April 23, 1841, Adams noted in his diary that he had received "two days since a Letter from a Stranger advising me now to retire from the world." Whether this was one of the many menacing threats that Adams received over the years of his public crusade against slavery in Congress, or a more friendly solicitation from a concerned constituent, he does not make clear. But his response to the suggestion, made privately to his diary, is unmistakable: "More than sixty years of incessant active intercourse with the world has made political movement to me as much a necessary of life as atmospheric air. This is the weakness of my nature, which I have intellect enough to perceive, but not energy to control. And thus, while a remnant of physical power is left to me to write and speak, the world will retire from me before I shall retire from the world."

Events over the previous winter had served to reinvigorate him. In the election of 1840, the Whig Party—a recently formed coalition of National Republicans, members of the short-lived Anti-Masonic Party, and disaffected Democrats—had ridden to victory behind the ticket of "Tippecanoe and Tyler Too": William Henry Harrison of Ohio, hero of the 1811 Battle of Tippecanoe, and former Democrat John Tyler of Virginia. Whigs gained control of both the House and the Senate for the first time, and Adams, though never a rigid party man, enjoyed the rare sensation of being aligned with the majority in the national legislature. The new president had promptly moved to convene Congress in special session, eager to get under way with the new governing agenda. And just the month before, in March, Adams had successfully argued the *Amistad* case before the United States Supreme Court, bringing him immense personal satisfaction and further burnishing his reputation as a leader of the political antislavery movement in America.

But any spring exuberance would prove short-lived. On April 4, Harrison had died suddenly—victim, it is now thought, of a septic fever, complicated by the deleterious effects of nineteenth-century emergency medical care—and the vice president, for the first time in the nation's history, took the oath of office. Adams recorded the sad events of the day in his diary, denouncing "the acting president," as he would insist on calling Tyler, as "a political sectarian of the Slave-driving, Virginian Jeffersonian school — Principled against all improvement." And indeed, the dream of a revived American System would die with Harrison, as Tyler vetoed one measure after another in the Whig program. The party's coalition in Congress soon began to show signs of breaking under the weight of its disappointment. In December, as the regular second session of the Twenty-seventh Congress got under way, Adams was finally elevated to the chairmanship of the Committee on Foreign Affairs, replacing fellow Whig Caleb Cushing, who had remained loyal to Tyler.

In his new capacity, Adams confronted a daunting mix of issues, most involving, inevitably, Great Britain: the still-unresolved matter of the northeastern boundary between the United States and Canada, now compounded with the controversy surrounding Alexander McLeod, a Canadian official who had been arrested and detained in New York in September for his alleged involvement in the sinking of the American ship *Caroline*, which had been supplying arms to antigovernment rebels in Ontario in 1837; fallout from the refusal of officials in the Bahamas to extradite 135 enslaved people who in October 1841 had seized control of the American brig *Creole*, which had been plying the coastal slave trade from Virginia to Louisiana, and redirected it to the British islands; and the disputed right of "visitation" claimed by British ships policing the ban on the international slave trade in the Atlantic, especially with respect to vessels seeking to evade inspection by illegally flying the American flag. (This last issue had been aggravated by actions of Lewis Cass, the Anglophobic U.S. minister to France, who was alleged to have lobbied French officials to withhold ratification of the Quintuple Treaty, an agreement signed on December 20, 1841, by Austria, France, Prussia, Russia, and Great Britain declaring the slave trade to be piracy and granting mutual right of search.)

By the end of 1841, it was clear that Tyler was a president without a party. Seeking rapprochement with Democrats in advance of the 1844 elections, Tyler and his supporters began to agitate for the annexation of Texas, reviving an issue that had been dormant since 1838. (In the interim, Texans had mounted a failed expedition against Santa Fe that included a small number of U.S. citizens. Taken into custody by Mexican authorities, the so-called Santa Fe prisoners became a cause célèbre in pro-annexationist circles.) On December 18, Adams's diary records a visit from New York congressman Seth Gates and abolitionist Joshua Leavitt, editor of *The Emancipator*, who had been instrumental in organizing the legal defense of the *Amistad* captives. "They are alarmed at numerous indications of a design to revive the project of annexing Texas to the United States . . . and they asked if any thing could now be done to counteract this movement. — I know of nothing, but to make it as soon and as extensively known as possible." He concluded that the "developments of this project are not yet sufficiently clear and explicit to know how to meet and counteract it."

Things became much clearer on April 14, 1842, when two Tyler men, Henry A. Wise of Virginia and Charles J. Ingersoll of Pennsylvania, took to the House floor during debate over a seemingly anodyne bill for the restructuring of U.S. diplomatic missions abroad to launch a bellicose one-two punch in favor of war for Texas. For good measure, they used the occasion to cast aspersions on the chairman of the foreign affairs committee. Adams once again rose from his desk to meet the challenge, delivering one of the greatest floor speeches of his congressional career. It was quickly published, complete with Wise and Ingersoll's speeches and intermittent colloquies, in the following pamphlet issued by Leavitt.

Mr. Adams' Speech, on War with Great Britain and Mexico:

WITH THE SPEECHES OF MESSRS. WISE AND INGERSOLL,
TO WHICH IT IS IN REPLY,

HOUSE OF REPRESENTATIVES.
Thursday, April 14.

[The House being in committee of the whole on the state of the Union, on the bill making appropriations for the civil and diplomatic expenses of government for the year 1842, and having under consideration the following item, viz.,

"No. 218. For salaries of the ministers of the United States to Great Britain, France, Russia, Prussia, Austria, Spain, Mexico, and Brazil, seventy-two thousand dollars."

Mr. Linn, of New York, moved to strike out so much of the said item as related to the mission to Mexico.]

Mr. Wise said he had not expected to be called to enter into this discussion; the motion which gave rise to it was wholly unexpected by him; but as the question had been opened, he felt it a duty to his constituents and the country to take a part in it. He should, in a manner perfectly calm and dispassionate, address a few words to that class to which the gentlemen from New York (Mr. Linn,) and Vermont (Mr. Slade) belonged.

The gentleman from New York had moved to strike from this bill this item for the salary of a minister to Mexico, and this just at the moment when the New Orleans papers had announced to the world his immediate departure as minister to a government toward which we stood in the most delicate and important relations—relations to be settled by the negotiations he was to conduct. Yes, and whilst, for all Mr. W. knew, there might be ten or a dozen of our own native citizens in the mines of Mexico, wearing the chains of a degrading bondage, although at the very first hint from the British minister a British citizen, taken in company, side by side with the very men of ours whom they had manacled and set to clean the streets, was promptly released. Yet the gentleman from New York would have our fellow citizens still wear their fetters, and still endure their public degradation; and why? Because, forsooth, it had been the ulterior object of the President and of a certain party in this country to annex Texas to the Union. Our citizens had claims on that government to the amount of twelve or thirteen millions, and yet we must not send a minister to demand the property or protect the freedom of our citizens in Mexico.

The tyrant of Mexico was now at war with Texas, and had threatened that he would invade her territory, and "never stop until he had driven slavery beyond the Sabine," and the gentleman would let him let loose his servile horde on the citizens of Louisiana, yet send no minister to remonstrate or to threaten him.

[Mr. Slade here explained. He had not been opposed to our having a minister at the court of Mexico, but only to the individual selected to occupy that post.]

Mr. Wise said he could forgive the gentleman, because he knew not the consequences that might flow from the doctrines he was accustomed to advance. These gentlemen would not send a minister to prevent the invasion even of the United States itself, lest by any possibility it might lead to the annexation of Texas.

[Mr. Linn explained, insisting that he had not opposed the mission, but had conceded that there might be sufficient grounds for it. He had moved to withhold the salary at present, because he believed that the whole movement had originated in a desire to annex Texas to the Union. Being, however, well satisfied that the committee would not consent to strike out the appropriation, he was willing to withdraw his motion.]

(Loud cries of, "No, no.")

Mr. Wise.   No, the gentleman shall not withdraw it now.

Mr. Steenrod said he had listened attentively to the gentleman from New York, and his entire argument, from beginning to end, had been directed against the mission, and not the individual who now filled it.

Mr. Wise resumed, and repeated what he had before said as to the possibility that the Mexican arms might drive back the slaves of Texas beyond the Sabine upon Louisiana and Arkansas. The English papers openly advocated the doctrine that it was the aim and policy of Great Britain to make what she was pleased to denominate the insolvent nations pay their debts to her by the cession of territory. Thus Spain must surrender Cuba, and Mexico must surrender Texas and California.

Let her obtain Cuba, and she will command the Gulf of Mexico and the mouth of the Mississippi, and nothing will prevent her from making that sea a *Mare Clausum* to the people of the West. Let her obtain California, and establish a naval station there, and she at once controls the whole trade of the Pacific ocean. From this we can understand her policy towards Spain, and it is a part of the same policy, that she should keep increasing the debt of Mexico, by affording to her the means of invading Texas and the United States, and thus ultimately force her to give up California. The gentleman had stated that it was the design of the President to accomplish the annexation of Texas, if possible. Mr. W. demanded on what proof he made that assertion?

Mr. Linn.   Does the gentleman deny it?

Mr. Wise.   I have no authority to deny it or to admit it.

Mr. Linn.   Do you make the issue, and I will give you the proof, &c.

Mr. Wise said that, although he did not know anything of the matter he might for the argument's sake, deny it, and if he should do so, could the gentleman produce any proof of it? What was the authority on which the House was asked to believe it? The gentleman's mere *ipse dixit*. What did he know of the opinions or purposes of the President of the United States? His assertion must go for nothing. But suppose the President should be desirous of such an issue, what then? Mr. W. knew no more of the fact than the gentleman, but he earnestly hoped and trusted that the President was as desirous as he was represented to be. But Mr. W. was prepared to show, and from the highest authority, not what was the opinion of a slaveholder, but of an individual now on that floor, but who occupied the Presidential chair at the time the gentleman from Vermont, (Mr. Slade) was a clerk in the Department of State. He would show that when that individual was President, his Secretary of State in 1825, and again in 1827, had offered a million of dollars for the addition of that territory to the United States. Here Mr. W. quoted the following letter from Mr. Clay, then Secretary of State, to Mr. Poinsett, then our minister at Mexico, dated March 16, 1825. Speaking of the boundary between us and Texas, the letter said:

> "Some difficulties may possibly hereafter arise between the two countries from the line thus agreed on, against which it would be difficult to guard, if practicable; and, as the government of Mexico may not be supposed to have any disinclination to the fixation of a new line which would prevent those difficulties, the President wishes you to sound it on that subject, and to avail yourself of a favorable disposition, if you should find it, to effect that object. The line of the Sabine approaches our great Western mart nearer than could be wished. Perhaps the Mexican government may not be unwilling to establish that of the Rio Brassos de Dios, or the Rio Colorado, or the Snow Mountains, or the Rio del Norte, in lieu of it. By the agreed line, portions of both the Red River and branches of the Arkansas are thrown on the Mexican side, and the navigation of both those rivers, as well as that of the Sabine, is made common to the respective inhabitants of the two countries," &c.

Here the object is avowed, under the pretext of establishing a new line of boundary. In a subsequent letter, dated March 15, 1827, the same officer opened the subject more fully to our minister in Mexico, as follows:

> "The great extent and facility which appears to have attended the procurement of grants from the government of the United Mexican States, for large tracts of country to citizens of the United States, in the province of Texas, authorize the belief that but little value is placed upon the possession of the province by that government. These grants seem to have been made without any sort of an equivalent, judging according to our opinions of the value of land. They have been made to, and apparently in contemplation of being settled by, citizens from the United States. These emigrants will carry with them our principles of law, liberty, and religion; and however much it may be hoped that they might be disposed to amalgamate with the ancient inhabitants of Mexico, so far as political freedom is concerned, it would be almost too much to expect that all collisions would

be avoided on other subjects. Already some of these collisions have manifested themselves, and others, in the progress of time, may be anticipated with confidence. These collisions may insensibly enlist the sympathies and feelings of the two republics, and lead to misunderstandings.

The fixation of a line of boundary of the United States on the side of Mexico, should be such as to secure not merely certainty and apparent safety in the respective limits of the two countries, but the consciousness of freedom from all danger of attack on either side, and the removal of all motives for such attack. That of the Sabine brings Mexico nearer our great Western commercial capital than is desirable; and although we are now and for a long time may remain, perfectly satisfied with the justice and moderation of our neighbor, still, it would be better for both parties that neither should feel that he is in any condition of exposure on the remote contingency of an alteration in existing friendly sentiments.

Impressed with these views, the President has thought the present might be an auspicious period for urging a negotiation, at Mexico, to settle the boundary between the territories of the two republics. The success of the negotiation will probably be promoted by throwing into it other motives than those which strictly belong to the subject itself. If we could obtain such a boundary as we desire, the government of the United States might be disposed to pay a reasonable pecuniary consideration. The boundary which we prefer is that which, beginning at the mouth of the Rio del Norte in the sea, shall ascend that river to the mouth of the Rio Puerco, thence ascending this river to its source, and from its source, by a line due North, to strike the Arkansas, thence following the course of the Southern bank to its source, in latitude 42 degrees North, and thence by that parallel of latitude to the South sea. The boundary thus described would, according to the United States Tanner's map, published in the United States, leave Santa Fe within the limits of Mexico, and the whole of Red River or Rio Roxo, and the Arkansas, as far up as it is probably navigable, within the limits assigned to the United States."

Here is a proposition to procure twice as large a territory as is now included in Texas, and the *then* President of the United States was not only willing to have it annexed, but was willing to pay for it. The letter proceeds:

"If that boundary be unattainable, we would, as the next most desirable, agree to that of the Colorado, beginning at its mouth, in the Bay of Bernardo, and ascending the river to its source, thence by a line due North to the Arkansas, and thence, as above traced, to the South Sea. This latter boundary would probably also give us the whole of the Red River, would throw us somewhat further from Santa Fe, but it would strike the Arkansas possibly at a navigable point. To obtain the first described boundary, the President authorizes you to offer to the government of Mexico a sum not exceeding one million of dollars. If you find it impracticable to procure that line, then you are authorized to offer for the above line of the Colorado, the sum of five hundred thousand dollars. If either of the above offers should be accepted, you may stipulate for the payment of the sum of money, as you may happen to agree, within any period not less than three months after the exchange at the city of Washington of the ratifications of the treaty.

Should you be able to conclude a treaty, it will be necessary that it should contain a stipulation for the mutual right of navigation of the Rio del Norte or the Colorado, as the one or the other may be agreed on, and for the exercise of common jurisdiction over the river itself. The treaty may also provide for the confirmation of all grants for lands made prior to *its date*, with the conditions of which there shall have been a compliance; and it may contain a provision similar to that in the Louisiana and Florida treaties, for the incorporation of the inhabitants into the Union, as soon as it can be done consistently with the principles of the Federal Constitution, and for the enjoyment of their liberty, property, and religion.

There should also be a provision made for the delivery of the country to the United States simultaneously, or as nearly so as practicable, with the payment of the consideration. We should be satisfied with the surrender of possession at that time, as far as the river line extends, (the Del Norte or the Colorado,) and to receive the residue as soon as the line to the Arkansas can be traced, which the treaty ought to provide should be done without unnecessary delay, and, at all events, before a future day to be specified."

Thus this former president was not only desirous of procuring all this territory, but of admitting its inhabitants into the Union. This is not hearsay, it is authentic information, information on which the gentleman might rely with much more certainty than on any vague report about the existing Chief Magistrate. This was a line of policy which Mr. W. had approved and applauded at the time, and which he still applauded and approved, if, as was said, it was the policy of Mr. Tyler. There was now no money to be paid for the territory, and it was occupied by a sovereign power which had authority to transfer it. If the annexation had been wise and peaceable, and practicable and desirable in 1827, it was not less so in 1842. It was fair to presume that the same motives still continued to operate on those who sought the same thing. We may well suppose the present Executive to be in favor of it, as every wise statesman must be, who is not governed by fanaticism or local sectional prejudice. And why should not Texas be united to this Union? What would the effect of such an event be? To extend slavery? Not at all. Slavery existed in Texas to just the same extent now as it would were Texas a part of the United States. The only difference would be to bring it under our own jurisdiction, which now it is not. Philanthropy itself, even the philanthropy of the class to which the gentleman belongs, according to their own views of it, would be promoted by the annexation of Texas. It increases no more bondage, it makes no more slaves, but it will bring that wide territory within your reach, according to your own ideas. What power have you now over slavery in Texas? None at all. It is a foreign State, where you can exert no influence over slavery, either to mitigate its severity or restrain its abuse. But let it be annexed to the Union, and it is then within the jurisdiction which you claim over slavery in our own country. I ask, is it in the spirit of philanthropy that gentlemen oppose it? Is it in the spirit of Christian missionaries? Mr. W. thought it was held among them that to benefit the heathen, they must be reached, you must be among them. Christianity must be brought to bear upon their minds; and so, if these philanthropic gentlemen wanted to mitigate those evils of slavery over which they made such doleful lamentations, let them bring it within our reach and jurisdiction.

Could they multiply their petitions ten thousand fold, would they reach slavery in a foreign State? If the spirit of emancipation was to go forth, like a delivering angel, from the

North toward the South, striking off manacles and drying up tears, (Mr. W. now spoke as one of themselves,) why not bring the slavery of Texas also within its range? Why leave that one dark spot untouched? Did they not perceive that, as long as Texas remained in a separate State, it would be an asylum for slavery? Drive it South, as they might, here the slaveholder could set them at defiance; for, once beyond the Texian boundary line, their jurisdiction was at an end. Yet they were banded together as one man to oppose the annexation. I ask them if they are acting wisely? Could any thing more strikingly show the blindness of fanaticism?

But possibly they would evade the force of this argument by looking to England to emancipate the slaves of Texas: if so, they utterly mistook the motives and the means of England. She had in the Republic of Texas a rival to the United States in the production of cotton, and as long as she wished to retain her as such, she would keep up the slave labor in Texas against the slave labor in the United States. Mr. W. scouted the idea of England being sincerely engaged in the work of emancipation, referred to the late detection of a conspiracy between British cruisers on the coast of Africa and the slave dealers, and also to her undeviating course of oppression in India, as proofs to the contrary. If gentlemen wished to keep Texas as a foreign State in juxtaposition with our Southwestern border, that she might be a mart for contraband dealers in cotton for the benefit of England, and to the injury of the Southern States—if that was their plan—then it was the surest way that could be taken to rivet upon her the chains of slavery for ever. No: if they were really sincere in their professed desires to see slavery abolished, their true and only course was to annex Texas to the United States. [A laugh in certain portions of the House.]

Mr. W. now took a different view of the subject. There was an anomaly connected with Texas, which, when first stated, appeared to be a paradox, but, when duly considered, was quite intelligible and undoubtedly true. While she was, as a State, weak and almost powerless in resisting invasion, she was herself irresistible as an invading and a conquering Power. She had but a sparse population, and neither men nor money of her own to raise and equip an army for her own defence; but let her once raise the flag of foreign conquest—let her once proclaim

SPEECH ON WAR WITH MEXICO | 1842

a crusade against the rich States to the south of her, and in a moment volunteers would flock to her standard in crowds from all the States in the great valley of the Mississippi—men of enterprise and hardy valor before whom no Mexican troops could stand for an hour. They would leave their own towns, arm themselves, and travel on their own cost, and would come up in thousands to plant the lone star of the Texian banner on the Mexican capital. They would drive Santa Anna to the South, and the boundless wealth of captured towns, and rifled churches, and a lazy, vicious, and luxurious priesthood, would soon enable Texas to pay her soldiery and redeem her State debt, and push her victorious arms to the very shores of the Pacific. And would not all this extend the bounds of slavery? Yes, the result would be that before another quarter of a century the extension of slavery would not stop short of the Western Ocean. We had but two alternatives before us; either to receive Texas into our fraternity of States, and thus make her our own; or to leave her to conquer Mexico, and become our most dangerous and formidable rival.

To talk of restraining the people of the great Valley from emigrating to join her armies was all in vain; and it was equally vain to calculate on their defeat by any Mexican forces, aided by England or not. They had gone once already; it was they that conquered Santa Anna at San Jacinto; and three fourths of them, after winning that glorious field, had peaceably returned to their homes. But once set before them the conquest of the rich Mexican provinces, and you might as well attempt to stop the wind. This Government might send its troops to the frontier, to turn them back, and they would run over them like a herd of buffalo. Or did the gentleman intend to put forth the odious, exploded, detestable doctrine of "no expatriation?" The Western people would mock at such a barrier; they would come armed to the frontier, and who should stop them from going where they pleased? Let the work once begin, and Mr. W. did not know that the House would hold *him* very long.

Give me, said Mr. W., five millions of dollars, and I would undertake to do it myself. Although I do not know how to set a single squadron in the field, I could find men to do it, and with five millions of dollars to begin with, I would undertake to pay every American claimant the full amount of his demand, with interest, yes, four-fold. I would fix our boundary, not where

Mr. Adams tried to fix it, at the Rio del Norte, but far, far beyond. I would place California where all the power of Great Britain should never be able to reach it. Slavery should pour itself abroad without restraint, and find no limit but the Southern ocean. The Camanches should no longer hold the richest mines of Mexico; but every golden image which had received the profanation of a false worship should soon be melted down, not into Spanish milled dollars, indeed, but into good American eagles. [Laughter, mixed with some exclamations.] Yes; there should more hard money flow into the United States than any exchequer or sub-treasury could ever circulate; I would cause as much gold to cross the Rio del Norte as the mules of Mexico could carry; ay, and make a better use of it, too, than any lazy, bigotted priesthood under heaven. [A general laugh.]

I am not quarrelling with the particular religion of these priests, but I say that any priesthood that has accumulated and sequestered and hoarded such immense stores of wealth, ought to disgorge, and it is a benefit to mankind to scatter their wealth abroad, where it can do good. He knew that gentlemen might hold all this as chimerical; but he told them it was already begun, and it would go on. He here referred to the story of Captain Boyle, an enterprising commander of a small craft in the Revolution, who proclaimed a blockade of all the coast of England, and actually had his proclamation printed and circulated in the streets of London. Yes; the peaceable cockneys had gone quietly to sleep in all security, and waked up in the morning and found London blockaded!—[Loud laughter.] And this adventurous Capt. Boyle had threaded all the dangers of the British channel, escaped all their cruisers, and returned in safety to this country, having performed the feat of blockading Great Britain. So Texas had proclaimed a blockade against all the coast of Mexico, and though she had no fleet to enforce it, she would be able to make it good by hewing her way to the Mexican capital. Nor could all the vaunted power of England stop the chivalry of the West till they had planted the Texian star on the walls of the city of Montezuma. Nothing could keep these booted loafers from rushing on till they kicked the Spanish priests out of the temples they profaned. Gentlemen might be horror-stricken at this.

SPEECH ON WAR WITH MEXICO | 1842

[A voice: "Oh no, sir, not at all; we are quite calm."]

Mr. W. went into a calculation to show that it would be impossible for Mexico to resist the force of Texas when recruited from the Western States: referred, in illustration, to the heroic resistance by 600 American troops under Fanning of a Mexican army 3,000 strong, causing even their cavalry to recede before men who had not a bayonet among them; and inquired with what hope of success they could withstand a regiment of flying artillery, a couple of regiments of riflemen, and a body of light infantry?

He wanted no war with Mexico: he went for sending a minister to preserve peace; but, unless she treated our citizens on an equal footing with those of England, he was for war, and cared not how soon.

It was said that this would marry us to a war with England. This had been too well answered by his friend (Mr. Cushing) already; but for his own part, if he was to choose a war with any Power, the prospect of a war with England was the very thing he should desire. If he were to pick out a war to suit his taste, it would be a war with England. Here was a "foeman worthy of our steel." He would leave Mexico to Texas and the people of the Valley: they could soon dispose of her. Let a war come; with France, the United States, and Texas, on the one side, and England and Mexico on the other; he would ask nothing better.

Mr. W. proceeded to insist that a majority of the people of the United States were in favor of the annexation: at all events, he would risk it with the democracy of the North. He would ask the men of Maine and New Hampshire, and the whalers of Nantucket, whether they were willing that England should get possession of California? He would risk all the blue lights. Our policy was peace, but our people were warlike: and to threaten them with the growl of the British lion was the very way to rouse the American eagle from her eyrie, cause her to plume her wings, and take her soaring flight to the ramparts of Mexico, and there demand a compliance with all our just demands.

Sir, said Mr. W., it is not only the duty of this Government to demand the liquidation of our claims and the liberation of our citizens, but to go further and demand the non-invasion of Texas. Shall we sit still while the standard of insurrection is raised on our borders, and let a horde of slaves and Indians and Mexicans roll up to the boundary line of Arkansas and Louisiana? No. It is our duty at once to say to Mexico, "if you strike Texas, you strike us:" and if England, standing by, should dare to intermeddle, and ask, "Do you take part with Texas?" his prompt answer should be, "Yes, and against you."

Such, he would let gentlemen know, was the spirit of the whole people of the great valley of the West.

One of the best effects of this state of things would be to cause the abolition party, to which these gentlemen belonged, to hide their diminished heads. Yes; it would very quickly subject them to the law of tar and feathers. Let them utter such sentiments as they now poured forth so freely when the country was once in an actual state of war, and they would meet the fate which their friends met in the last war.

Mr. W. then referred to the situation of politicians with respect to war. Sir, said he, they dare not oppose a war again. They remember the fate of those who opposed the last war, and who suffered political death in consequence of it. No politician will again risk his prospects and reputation in opposing a war. It is in the power of a resolute minority to push the majority into war at any time, simply because the politicians are afraid to oppose it. They are burnt children, and they never would venture to oppose another war; if they do, they are doomed men.

Mr. W. then touched on the intimation which had been thrown out that the President sought to involve the country in war to promote his own ambitious purposes. Did he believe John Tyler to be such a man, he would denounce him from the Capitol to Accomac. But, on the other hand, he would denounce him as loudly if he suffered a tittle of the national honor to be sacrificed. He adverted to the growth of the worship of mammon throughout our country in these piping times of peace, and said that, if the crystal waters of peace proved insufficient to cleanse us from the accumulated corruption, he would let the bloody streams of war perform the work. It would sweep off drones and loafers, and men of broken fortunes and broken reputation, many of whom would hail the first blast of the trumpet as the renovating note of their emancipation. War was a curse, but it had its blessings too, as the destroying lightning of heaven purified the atmosphere. He would vote for this mission as the means of peace; but if it must lead to war, then he would vote it the more willingly.

MR. INGERSOLL'S SPEECH.

Mr. C. J. Ingersoll moved to amend the amendment by reducing the sums of appropriation for the missions to Austria and Prussia one-half.

He desired to add in connection with this subject a very few words on what he conceived to be one of the most misunderstood interests in the country. There had come among us lately an envoy extraordinary from Great Britain; a gentleman whom he had the honor to know personally a great many years ago, and who, it gave him great pleasure to say, as far as his personal inclinations and personal temper were concerned, he was sure came to us in a peaceable spirit, because he was sure that was his nature; and he took great pleasure in saying it, as this gentleman had been the subject of some animadversion in the newspapers, that he never would be convicted of any dishonorable charge, and that in all his intercourse with Americans, at all times, throughout a long life, he had been a candid, deliberate and generous man. What instructions this minister had, he knew nothing about; but in his (Mr. I.'s) apprehension, he could win his way at least without any difficulty by taking one course, and that he would take the liberty publicly to suggest.

It was a remarkable fact, not often adverted to, that on the five great points of controversy between the United States and Great Britain, she was in every one of them an egregious aggressor. On the Maine question, she took our soil; on the Caroline question, our property; on the Oregon, our property; on the Creole case, what we believed to be our property; and, on the question of restitution, she came across the great ocean, from the old world to the new, demanding that we should submit not only our vast commerce in all the seas of the ocean, but our coasting trade, to visitation and search of those who say that all they desire is to be constables of the ocean.

He was a man of peace, and he hoped we should have no war. He was not insensible to the evils of war; but he wished the

British minister here to understand that he might depend on it, (and he said it with the voice of friendship,) that war would not do us so much harm as his country. In the first place, if we chose to apply the principles of war, it paid all the States' debts at once—$200,000,000 debts would be settled—[laughter]— or, at all events, it suspended the interest on the capital during the war. In the next place, when they talked of preparation, he had hardly patience to sit still and hear it. We were prepared beyond the preparation for either of the former wars; in the first place, in having a sufficient population, in the capacity of clothing that population, and in having all the materials of war greatly superior to the materials of any other nation in the world. There was nothing in any navy of the world to be compared with the two vessels now arrived almost within the sound of his voice. There were none in the British or the French navy at all comparable with these vessels; so he was informed by an officer in the navy, and that these ships were superior to any thing in the world. All our lakes and rivers were covered with transporting steamboats, which he was informed could readily be made efficient for harbor defence.

On this subject of preparation, it appeared to him that we were under a lamentable delusion. He should be sorry if we were better prepared, because we must always compromise, if we live in a republican country, our republicanism by the existence of an armed nation; and he would rather take this nation as it is than the most completely armed nation of the world. Give him, if we were to go to war, that moral nation in whom the principles of liberty, independence, and defiance exist, in preference to all the armed power on earth. It was a monstrous humbug to talk of the British going into New York and burning it. He had been told by the first officer in the American navy that it was just as easy to burn London as New York, and that he would answer for it, if they burned New York, give him a little opportunity and he would burn London too. [Laughter.]

They talked of a servile insurrection, of setting the slaves of the South on us, and dismembering the North. Were they to be talking in this way when they knew that Ireland, India, and Canada hung by a thread? and instead of dismembering us, we had only to let loose what their own brilliant Canning called the spirit of freedom, and they would fall to pieces like the banking system of the United States? [A laugh.] He did not wish to see Great Britain otherwise than Great Britain, except when she made aggressions on our own country. He wished to tell her, (he was understood to say,) when they talked of dismembering us, that we were in a state of perfect union, and he hoped this mission now pending here would terminate by this Administration taking its position and saying, "We are for peace; we do not want to fight. Do not make it for our interest; we are not going to yield any of our positions; we are not going to make war; but as to this and other things we cannot yield them. We cannot make war; the Senate and House of Representatives will prevent us; we are very unpopular, &c." We had the sympathies of all France, Prussia, Russia, Sweden, Denmark, every maritime nation in the world, and Texas too. [Laughter.]

He had said these things in a spirit of peace; he had no hostile temper or disposition. He trusted that it might be heard, and be not altogether without some use. He saw no difficulty at all in settling the Maine boundary question; nothing insuperable in the Caroline case, or the Creole case, or the question of the Oregon country. He saw no difficulty in settling all these questions, excepting one, and that could be settled in one day if Lord Ashburton were to say as to this question of search and visitation, "I find the President and Congress so much against me, the country so much against me, I must, as a matter of necessity, give it up."

He challenged opposition to the opinion he asserted, that there was no right of search in time of war; much less, and it was monstrous for Great Britain to come to us and talk of our yielding it, in time of peace. It was merely an exercise of brute force. He believed, in the thirty treaties he had examined within the last two hundred years, [general and prolonged laughter, in which Mr. I. participated,]—he acknowledged that he was an old man, but he had intended to say that he had examined the treaties made for two hundred years, which, as well as the law of nature, vindicated that there was no right of search, and that this demand was a monstrosity.

The greatest question in the world, which now agitated all Christendom nearly, was this mixed question of the slave trade and this right of visitation and search; and if they were left alone, it appeared by the correspondence of Mr. Stevenson and the pamphlet of Mr. Cass, that it would be for the United States to stand up in a peaceable attitude and say, We do not mean to go to war unless you coerce us; we do not mean to strike unless you strike first; but that we will vindicate these principles, which are the true American principles. He trusted the British Minister would be successful in his mission, and he believed he would be. It seemed to him that it was easy for him to succeed in his mission, provided he took the proper course; and if he should, before they adjourned to go to their homes, he conceived that almost every difficulty would be settled. There was no difficulty in their settlement by the application of a little good sense.

―

MR. ADAMS'S SPEECH.

Mr. Adams rose to reply to the gentleman from Pennsylvania. My only difficulty, said he, is, to reply to the gentleman's speech, so that my remarks shall have any bearing upon the gentleman's motion. [A laugh.] The gentleman talked with great eloquence and great ingenuity in favor of pushing this country into a war, under the mask of a very great solicitude for peace. He has drained the whole world of argument to prove to this House that, in the event of a war, we can burn London, and to establish the principle that there exists no such thing as the right of search in time of war. Now, the two parts of the gentleman's argument do not seem to me to agree together. If we do go to war—in favor of which the gentleman has brought forward the attractive arguments that a war will pay all our State debts to England, and enable us to burn the city of London, and establish the doctrine that there exists no right of search in time of war—it seems to me that the thing most essential to us, of all others, is the right of search. To take away from us the right of search in time of war, is to take away our principal means of defence. How does the gentleman expect we are to burn London, without the right of searching neutral vessels at sea? I ask him, and I ask this House, if this very right will not be the most powerful of all the means we can employ against Great Britain? And whether, though it may not enable us to succeed in burning London, it will not enable us to avail ourselves of the bravery of our noble tars to meet upon the ocean and to capture that property of our enemy which they will otherwise protect, by using the flag of every neutral vessel under heaven? To take away this right would at once throw a shield over the entire mass of British commerce, which would all continue to be carried on in perfect safety from any injury by us.

What bearing the arguments of the learned gentleman could possibly have on the question of our retaining a full minister at the courts of Austria and Prussia, I am totally at a loss to conjecture. But I do see that, under color of this motion, he has undertaken to instruct the new British Minister how he may, with the greatest possible facility, settle all the questions between us and Great Britain, and gain for himself an earldom. And, how, pray, is he to do it? Why, by simply yielding every thing on every point in dispute. This, I confess, seems to me to be at least a very unusual basis of negotiation.

[Mr. Ingersoll—I did not say any thing like that.]

If the gentleman did not in substance say that, I must very greatly have misunderstood him.

[Mr. Ingersoll—I said no such thing.]

The gentleman assumes that there are five points in controversy, and he says that on every one of them Great Britain is the aggressor, and that the only way to settle them is for her to agree to submit to every thing we demand. He included even the case of the Creole.

[Mr. Ingersoll—What I said was, that the main questions in dispute are not difficult of settlement; that I thought there could be no difficulty in settling the question of the Creole; and on that point I should rather have supposed that I was entitled to some little forbearance from the gentleman for my forbearance. I said further, that the Caroline case would be settled without much difficulty; and, after what the gentleman said last summer on that case, I think I am still more entitled to the credit of forbearance. I said, too, that I did not know much about the Oregon question, but believed, from what I did know, that the question could be adjusted without difficulty. And I said, lastly, that the demand for the exercise of the right of search must be abandoned.]

Mr. Adams—Well, sir, the gentleman has again had his say; he now takes back what I understood him to advance, which was, that on all the five points in dispute Great Britain was the aggressor, and that it was our duty to yield nothing. I appeal not to the gentleman, but to the conscience of every member of this committee, and to their common sense, to decide whether that was not what the gentleman did say. If he chooses now to recant it all, let him do it.

[Mr. Ingersoll—I do not choose to recant any thing. Although, as usual, the gentleman chooses to indulge his passion, and play the termagant whenever any thing is said which does not happen to suit his own senile notions.]

Mr. Adams resumed. For a rebuker of a little transient intemperance of feeling, I think the gentleman himself seems a little excited. [A laugh.] The gentleman is mistaken if he thinks I was actuated in what I said by any feeling unfriendly to him. That what I said, and that what I shall yet say, is "senile," I admit; for I am much older than the honorable gentleman, and am very conscious of the infirmities which that advanced age has brought upon me. I refer it to the gentleman's conscience to decide whether such allusions are made in a moderate and a kind temper, or are very likely to restore good feeling if it has for a moment been lost. I say again, and I appeal not to the gentleman, but to the conscience of all who hear me if it is so, that the gentleman said that on every one of the five points in controversy Great Britain was the aggressor; and whether his advice to the British negotiator, in order to gain an earldom, was to yield up every point; and that we ought not to concede one tittle on any one of the points. And now the gentleman says he does not choose to recant. There was perhaps one slight qualification in the Creole case. Then I think the gentleman added, in his usual mode, [here Mr. Adams imitated very closely the tones of Mr. Ingersoll's voice, and his peculiar manner while quoting his language. In the laugh produced by this, the closing words were lost to the reporter save this—"as *we* say."] Thus far I am willing to admit his explanation. I was happy to hear that the gentleman, in the midst of his supererogatory display of valor, did seem to feel that this was rather a tender place, and that it would be best for him to get over it as soon as he could. He certainly did add, in a lower and a somewhat subdued tone, "as *we* say."

The gentleman has gone through such a range of the laws of nations, and of the condition of the world, and has altogether made us a discourse quite equal to "the admirable Crichton," who made speeches off hand on all sorts of subjects that were proposed to him, that really I feel myself unprepared to meet him on a great many of the points he made; and therefore I shall confine myself to a few of them only; for indeed I can find not a point in all his speech which bears at all upon his own motion. What has the question about burning London or burning New York to do with our sending a full minister to the courts of Vienna or Berlin? But I do say that the whole course of his argument seemed to me, under a profession of giving to us and to the British envoy a perfect solution of all the disputed questions between this country and England, to be aimed, throughout, at driving us into a war, and preventing the present administration from settling our controversy with Great Britain. What was the tenor of his argument?

He began by saying that he was for peace—for universal peace. Then followed a most learned dissertation to prove that it was an entire mistake to suppose that we are not now prepared for war, and to demonstrate that a nation which goes into a war unprepared will infallibly conquer; that it must be so; that every unarmed and unprepared nation always had conquered its armed opposers. No; we are not unprepared for war; not at all, because we have in sight of the windows of this Capitol two armed steamers; one of them, as I am informed, nearly disabled, so that she will need in a great measure, to be rebuilt. So that, in case of immediate hostilities, we have one entire steamer, and with that we are to burn London; and though the gentleman readily admitted that it was possible, nay, very probable, that New York would be burnt too, yet as London was four or five times as large, we should have a great balance of burning on our side. Yes; we were to conquer Great Britain and burn London, and that it would be a very cheap price for all this to have the city of New York burnt in turn, or burnt first. And this was an argument *for peace*!

What else did the gentleman say? (What else did he not say?) He made a great argument, and a valorous display of zeal, in relation to the right of search. O, that—that was a point never to be conceded—no, never. He maintained that there is no such thing as a right of search,—no such right in time of war,—none in time of peace. Well, I do agree with the gentleman partially, on that one point, so far as to believe that there is no need of our coming to an issue with Great Britain on that point—and we have not as yet. After reading, as I have done, and carefully examining the papers put forth on both sides, I asked myself, what is the question between us? and I have heard men of the first intelligence say that they found themselves in the very same situation. The gentleman has made a total misrepresentation of the demand of Great Britain in the matter. She has never claimed the right to search American vessels—no such thing; on the contrary, she has explicitly disclaimed any such pretension, and that to the whole extent we can possibly demand. What is it we do demand? Not that Great Britain should disclaim the right to search American vessels, but we deny to her the right to board pirates who hoist the American flag; yes, and to search British vessels, too, that have been declared to be pirates by the laws of nations—pirates by the laws of Great Britain—pirates by the laws of the United States. That is the demand of our late minister to London, whose letters are so much admired by the gentleman from Pennsylvania. Now, it happens that behind all this exceeding great zeal against the right of search, is a question which the gentleman took care not to bring into view—and that is, the support and perpetuation of the African slave trade. That is the real question between the ministers of America and Great Britain; whether slave traders, pirates, by merely hoisting the American flag, shall be saved from capture.

I say there is no such thing as an exemption from the right of search by the laws of nations, and I challenge and defy the gentleman to produce the proof. The right of search, in time of war, we have never pretended to deny. Nay, we have ourselves exercised that right during the last war. And the Supreme Court of the United States, in their decisions of prize cases brought before them, sustained us in doing so, and said it was lawful according to the laws of nations. And, indeed, we should have had a very poor chance indeed in a war with Great Britain without it.

But what is the right of search in time of peace? And how has Congress felt, and how has the American government acted on this point? I have some knowledge on this subject. In the year 1817, when I was about to return from England to the United States, Mr. Wilberforce, then a member of the

British Parliament, very celebrated for his long and persevering exertions to suppress the African slave trade, wrote me a note requesting an interview. I acceded promptly to his request; and in conversation he stated to me that the British government had found that, without a mutual right of search between this country and that, upon the coast of Africa, it would be impossible to carry through the system she had formed in connection with the United States for the suppression of that infamous traffic. I had then just signed with my own hand a treaty declaring "the traffic in slaves (not the African slave trade, but THE TRAFFIC IN SLAVES) unjust and inhuman," and in which both nations engaged to do all in their power to suppress it. Mr. Wilberforce inquired of me whether I thought that a proposal for a mutual, restricted, qualified right of search would be acceptable to the American government?

I had at that moment a feeling to the full as strong against the right of search, as it had then been exercised by British cruisers, as ever the gentleman from Pennsylvania (Mr. Ingersoll) had in all his life. I had been myself somewhat involved in the question as a public man. It constituted one of the grounds of my unfortunate difference from those with whom I had long been politically associated; and it was for the exertions I had made against the admission of that right, that I forfeited my place in the other end of the Capitol; and, which was infinitely more painful to me, for this I had differed with men long dear to me, and to whom I had also been dear, insomuch that for a time it interrupted all friendly relations between us. The first thing I said, in reply to Mr. Wilberforce, was, "No; you may as well save yourselves the trouble of making any proposals on that subject; my countrymen, I am very sure, never will assent to any such arrangement." He then entered into an argument, the full force of which I felt, when I said to him, "You may, if you think proper, make the proposal; but I think some other mode of getting over the difficulty must be resorted to; for the prejudices of my country are so immoveably strong on that point, that I do not believe they ever will assent."

I returned home, and under the administration of Mr. Monroe, I filled the office of Secretary of State; and in that capacity, I was the medium through which the proposal of the British Government was afterwards made to the United States, to arrange a special right of search for the suppression of the slave trade. This proposition I resisted and opposed in the Cabinet, with all my power. And I will say, that, although I was not myself a slaveholder, I had to resist all the slaveholding members of the Cabinet and the President also. Mr. Monroe himself was always strongly inclined in favor of the proposition, and I maintained the opposite ground against him and the whole body of his official advisers, as long as I could.

At that time, there was in Congress, and especially in the House, a spirit of concession which I could not resist. From the year 1818 to the year 1823, not a session passed without some movement on this point, and some proposition made to request the President to negotiate for the mutual concession of this right of search. I resisted it to the utmost, and so earnest did the matter become, that, on one occasion, at an evening party in the President's house, in a conversation between myself and a distinguished gentleman of Virginia, a principal leader of this movement, now living but not now a member of this House, words became so warm, that what I said was afterwards alluded to by another gentleman of Virginia, in an address to his constituents, against my election as President of the United States. It was made an objection against me, that I was an enemy to the suppression of the slave trade. That address, and my reply to it, are in existence, and the latter in the hands of a gentleman of Virginia, now in this house, and who can correct me if I do not state the matter correctly. The address was written, and would have been published with an allusion to what I had said in the conversation, (which the writer heard, although it was not addressed to him,) but the gentleman with whom I was conversing went to him and told him that if he did refer in print to that private conversation, he would never speak to him, and so it was suppressed. I state these facts, sir, that I may set myself right on this question of the right of search.

At that time, a gentleman who was the leader of one of the parties in this House had endeavored, from year to year, to prevail with the House to require of the President a concession of the right asked: I name him to honor him; for he was one of the most talented, laborious, eloquent, and useful men upon this floor.—I allude to Charles Fenton Mercer, of Virginia. Session after session he brought forward his resolution; and he continued to press it until, finally, in 1823, he brought the House, by yeas and nays, to vote their assent to it; and, strange to say, there were but nine votes against it. The same thing took place in the other House; the joint resolution went to the President, and he, accordingly, entered into the negotiation. It was utterly against my judgment and wishes; but I was obliged to submit, and I prepared the requisite despatches to Mr. Rush, then our Minister at the Court of London. When he made his proposal to Mr. Canning, Mr. Canning's reply was, "Draw up your convention, and I will sign it." Mr. Rush did so; and Mr. Canning without the slightest alteration whatever, without varying the dot of an *i*, or the crossing of a *t*, did affix to it his signature; thus assenting to our own terms, in our own language. The convention came back here for ratification; but, in the meanwhile, another spirit came over the feelings of this House as well as of the Senate; a party had been formed against the administration of Mr. Monroe; the course of the Administration was no longer favored, and the House came out in opposition to a convention drawn in conformity to its own previous views. In the Senate, however, all that could be got was the modification of one article. The Senate ratified the treaty, giving the right of search, in the fullest manner, to Great Britain, with the exception, I think, of one article, which extended the right to the coast of the United States; that was rejected.

[Mr. Ingersoll. There were three articles negatived; the second article was rejected, and some words altered in the third.]

I cannot say as to a word or two, and I am willing to take the gentleman's statement as correct. Of one thing I am sure; no exception was taken to the right of search; that was conceded fully. In consequence of these alterations, further negotiation became necessary; and, finally, the treaty was not ratified. But, as to the right of search, in the bitterness of my soul, I say it was conceded by all the authorities of this nation. I say this, because I am not now for conceding it. I hope the negotiations now about to take place may be carried on without any such concession. There has been blustering and bullying far more than in my opinion was necessary on the subject; but no issue has yet been come to, and far less have we come to war about it.

In this very pamphlet, of which the gentleman from Pennsylvania has spoken with so much honor, (and I shall treat it with honor, too, as having proceeded from a public minister of the United States at one of the most important courts of Europe,) there is a proposition made which I do not say we ought to concede. As a political question, involving the peace of two great countries, and the suppression of the African slave trade (for which I could bring myself to almost any concession,) it might have strong claims to consideration; but, as a politician, a statesman, as a negotiator, I doubt if this expedient of General Cass be not even more objectionable than the right of search itself.

The proposal is that the cruising vessels of either nation should have on board a naval officer (a lieutenant I suppose) belonging to the other, and that he shall make the requisite search in person. This is held forth by way of compromise between the two parties, and as a mode of avoiding the difficulties which embarrass the question. I will not say that if the negotiation shall concentrate on this, as the only practicable expedient, it should be rejected; but I will say this: If the gentleman from Pennsylvania, or the Senate, or this House shall be so pressed as to concede that, very little ground will be left them for refusing the right of search as heretofore proposed.

But as to this question itself of the right of search, when before was the question made a matter of such infinite importance? When, in the history of this nation, was the pretension raised that no such right existed on the high seas? I will ask the Clerk to read the 54th section, I think it is, of the collection law of the United States, passed, I believe, in 1798 or '99.

[While the Clerk was searching for the act referred to—

Mr. Ingersoll stated that although there was a majority in the Senate for the ratification of the treaty which Mr. A. had referred to, there had been a large minority opposed to it throughout.

The Clerk then read, from the Act of 1799, Sect. 54, that, "it shall be lawful for all collectors, naval officers, inspectors, and the officers of revenue cutters, to go on board of ships or vessels in any port of the United States, *or within four leagues of the coast thereof*, if bound to the U. S. whether in or out of their respective districts, for the purpose of demanding the manifests aforesaid, and of *examining or searching* the said ship or vessel; and the said officers, respectively, shall have free access to the cabin, and every other part of the said ships or vessels; and if any box, trunk, chest, cask, or other package, shall be found in the cabin, steerage, or forecastle of such ship or vessel, or in any other place, separate from the residue of the cargo, it shall be the duty of such officer to take an account of the same, and if necessary to put his seal thereon," &c.]

The point, said Mr. A. for which I have cited this act is, that it is here assumed that upon the *high seas*, at four leagues distance from the coast of the United States, you possess and may freely exercise the right of search. This is assumed in your revenue law; and, either by your revenue cutters or your vessels of war, you may *search* any vessel of any nation approaching within four leagues of your coast. Look to your laws for the suppression of the slave trade,* and you find the same thing. You exercise that right now. If a British vessel freighted with slaves should come to-morrow within four leagues of any point of the coast, your vessels may search her, and bring her in for adjudication; and all the slaves on board of her would, on their coming on shore, at once be free. Now, if this be so, what becomes of the doctrine that upon the high seas the right of search does not exist at all? If, indeed, the question should be whether the right should not

---

* The following is the clause referred to by Mr. Adams, but not read, in the "Act to prohibit the importation of slaves," approved March 2, 1807.

SECT. 7. That if any ship or vessel shall be found in any river or bay, or on the high seas, within the jurisdictional limits of the U.S., or hovering on the coast thereof, having on board any negroes, for the purpose of selling as slaves, or with intent to land the same, contrary to this act, the ship or vessel shall be forfeited, &c. and the President of the United States is authorized to cause any of the armed vessels of the U.S. to cruise on any part of the coast of the United States, where he may judge attempts will be made to violate the provisions of this act, and to instruct the commanders to *seize, take and bring into any port of the U.S. all such ships or vessels.*

In addition to the section of the Revenue Collection Act, of 1799, quoted above, the following extracts are from the same Act.

SECT. 98. The said revenue cutters shall, whenever the President of the U. S. shall so direct, co-operate with the navy of the U.S., during which time they shall be under the direction of the Secretary of the Navy.

SECT. 99. The officers of the said revenue cutters are hereby required and directed to go on board all ships or vessels which shall arrive within the U.S. or *within four leagues* of the coast thereof, if bound for the U.S., and *to search and examine the same, and every part thereof*, and to certify the manifests required to be on board, &c.

be refused to be extended beyond the distance of four leagues, and such an article should be inserted in the convention, it would be effective, and no objection whatever could be made to it. Give Great Britain this right of search within four leagues of the coast of Africa, and what would become of the question about the "rights of nations?" The position is false. No such right exists between nations, that they shall be exempted from all right of search in time of peace. The only authority for such a position is a declaration of Sir William Scott, in the case of a French vessel called the *Louis*; but even that solitary declaration was made hypothetically, and extrajudicially; it was a mere *dictum* of that distinguished man, and not delivered in a case which he was called to decide: while, at the same time, there is another declaration of Sir William Grant, an authority fully equal to that of Sir William Scott, directly to the contrary. And this is the gentleman's authority from the law of nations.

I will take this occasion to say, in reference to the decisions of Sir William Scott, that in cases where the West India slave trade was concerned his decisions in regard to the right of search are very different from those which he was in the habit of making at the period of the French Revolution. He was then a perfect scourge to our merchants. He extended his construction of the law even to vessels under convoy, as in the case of the Swedish convoy. But as soon as the peace took place, and the West India planters' interest was concerned, his decisions were very greatly changed. I say this with no purpose of reflection on the memory of that able and upright Judge; a man with whom I formerly had the happiness to be personally acquainted. He was a highly amiable man in private life, and in conversation one of the most charming of companions. Yet, truth demands from me the declaration, that, while all the supporters of neutral rights were revolted by his decisions on the bench during the war, I have myself been quite as much so by those made since the war in cases of West India slaves. In some cases, he has gone even beyond the severity of the laws of our own Southern States; for in one case he decided that a slave who had once become free by having landed in England, if he returned to the residence of his former master returned at the same time to his bondage as a slave—which is directly contrary, as I understand, to the decisions of the courts in the slaveholding States of this Union.

I mention this to show what was the bias of Sir William Scott's mind. All such decisions, however, have since been annulled—annihilated—nullified—(I do not like that word, but here it is appropriate,) by the Universal Emancipation proclaimed by Great Britain in all her West India colonies. This opinion is now of no earthly authority. And there is nothing else extant. There is no other authority in existence for the gentleman's doctrine about the Laws of Nations. In all the discussions that have taken place on this subject, as, for instance, in the case of the schooner *Amistad*, through all the courts, the District Court, the Circuit Court, and the Supreme Court of the United States, this opinion in the case of the *Louis* was the sole authority. And in all the newspaper discussions, the decision, as it is called, of Sir William Scott, sustaining the African Slave Trade, is the eternal burden of the song; and no notice is taken of the contrary decision of Sir William Grant, a judicial authority of at least as much weight.

What have I brought this question before the committee for in this form? And why have I quoted the revenue law? To show that there is no ground whatever for this attempt to blow up a flame about the right of search; for declaring that this is a question never, never to be given up, and to make it the burden of *a pacific war speech.* [A laugh.]

I do apprehend that the noble negotiator, to whose character and merits the gentleman from Pennsylvania has paid a just and very honorable tribute, and who to me is an acquaintance of nearly half a century's standing, whom I formerly knew as a young man of distinguished ability then scarcely of age, as I had known his father with whom I was on the most friendly footing—I apprehend, I say, that this British minister will not take his instructions from the honorable gentleman from Pennsylvania. If the mode pointed out by that gentleman is the only mode of settling the delicate and difficult questions subsisting between the two Governments, I think he will not take it. If, indeed, I could believe that the only alternative was between taking this advice to acknowledge at once that his country has been the aggressor on every one of the disputed points, and yield every thing that is demanded on every one of these questions, and a desolating bloody war, however light such a war may appear in the gentleman's eyes, (which he protests it does not, but which all his arguments show that it does,) why then should I despair of my own times, for good, and go home and die, if I could. For the gentleman may make as light of it as he pleases, this is no light question with me. Should the resort eventually be to war, I certainly have as little personal interest in it as any human being, for my career, at all events, must soon close; whatever calamities may grow out of it either to this country or to other countries, (and I have learned to feel that all my sympathies ought not to be absorbed in one, however dear,) I can have no interest in them, looking to myself alone. To be sure, as to that amiable little process of the burning of London and New York, what interest other gentlemen may feel in it I cannot pretend to say—and there is many a man in this House who has a far deeper interest in it than I have or can have; but this I will say, if there is a man in this House who could hear the gentleman from Pennsylvania, with that cold indifference which animated his entire speech, (if indifference can be said to animate any thing,) put the case of the burning of the city of London as a revenge for the previous burning of the city of New York, without feeling a thrill of horror, I should wish to have little further intercourse with that man. The burning of London! and the hope of that is to be a motive for our assuming such an attitude and pursuing such a course as must infallibly bring us into a war! Would it much comfort the three hundred thousand men, women, and children who would be turned homeless in the world by the burning of New York to know that London, with a population four times as great, was to burn too? A fiend could hardly bring his mind to contemplate such a thought without horror.—Would it be nothing to the People of the United States, nothing to the civilized world, nothing to the human race, that two such cities were swept from the face of the earth? Yet the gentleman very coolly spoke of such a consummation as by no means impossible or improbable—he admitted that, in the event of a war, this might be one of the results.

[Mr. Ingersoll. What I said was, that a distinguished naval officer had assured me that it would be just as easy for us to burn London as for the British to burn New York.]

Well: and that was stated as an argument why we ought to take such a stand with Great Britain as would bring us into war with her. I suppose the naval officer who said this was himself eager for the distinction of such a deed—and distinguished he assuredly would be.

[Mr. Ingersoll. Yes, he was; and he declared that he would do it.]

Mr. A. resumed. I remember that one of our most celebrated naval officers once gave this toast, "Our country: may she be always right; but, whether right or wrong, may she be always successful." This might be a very good toast for an officer of the navy. Military men, I admit, are not bound to enter into the moral questions which may arise between nations; by their commissions they are bound to take it for granted that their country is in the right, when those departments of their government to whom the right of judging is consigned have so determined. The question of right and wrong in war is a question for such an assembly as this, not for the deck of a man-of-war. I do not therefore, disapprove of the toast as one to be taken by a naval officer; but, as a moral question, to be decided by a vote in this House within two months' time from this day, I never would adopt the sentiment. I would rather say, "Our country: may she always be successful; but, whether successful or not, may she always be in the right." That is the sentiment which I think every man should bring home to his heart on questions so weighty and so delicate as those involved in our present relations with Great Britain. If war we must have, O let us have it for the right: and let us not expect the God of battles to give us success when we are in the wrong.

I hope that the idea of our defenceless state, of which the gentleman seemed to make so light, as being of little consequence, and as presenting no obstacle to our going to war, because, if the British burn New York, we can burn London, will be very differently viewed by this House, and that arguments of such a description will have no weight here.

Still less ought another argument which that gentleman presented to our consideration to prevail. He said that in reference to the threats by Great Britain to raise the flag of emancipation in our Southern States, that, too, was a thing to be made light of, because Great Britain herself was in a condition so precarious that her own people were as like to overturn her government as it was to injure us at the South.

I will not meet the gentleman on that question. I believe that Great Britain, like all the other powers of Europe, and more especially France, (to whom we are advised to look as our chief reliance,) is in a most precarious situation. I believe that they are all in danger of a tremendous revolution, and none so much as that very France. I must say here (and I do not know whether it will be very acceptable to this House) that if it be true, as the gentleman from Pennsylvania intimates, that the interference of our minister in France, by the publication of the pamphlet on which he bestowed so high praise, was the occasion of the refusal by France to ratify the quintuple treaty, I do not hold that proceeding in as much admiration as the gentleman does; it comes too near success in doing wrong. Her minister had signed that treaty, and the refusal to ratify it was not based in the refusal by France of the right of search, for that right she had already granted by other and independent treaties now in force. She is bound already on that subject by a special treaty. And I say that, for the sake of the moral principles which govern the intercourse and conduct of nations, France owes an explanation to the world of her refusal to ratify that treaty. If it be true that General Cass has effected this result, I, for one, do not thank him for it. Not only because he has persuaded France to break her faith and put herself in the wrong in the future controversies which may arise between her and the other parties to that treaty, but also because it looks like an intermeddling with the political affairs of Europe; it has the aspect of engaging us in entangling alliances with foreign nations, the very evil against which the venerable Washington and the venerable Jefferson both so emphatically warned their countrymen.

In Washington's Farewell Address (a paper which had lately been read in that hall, and which ought always to be read and heard with the deepest reverence) there is a paragraph expressly devoted to that subject. And Mr. Jefferson made it a sort of political motto, to have "peace, friendship, and commercial relations with all nations, but entangling alliances with none." Such has been the policy of the United States from that time to this. And I must say that the pamphlet which was put forth by our minister (of which he did me the honor to send me a copy, and which I have read with the most profound attention) has suggested to me the question as to the prudence and expediency of thus making us in any sort parties to the wars which are ahead. And I here ask this House and the country to believe that if the refusal of France to ratify the quintuple treaty shall be persevered in, (which I can scarcely believe possible,) that the right of search has not any part in the wars which may follow, and in which we are in some danger of becoming entangled. That, I say, will form no part in such wars. It is no question between France and the four powers. France has conceded it. It is her bad faith in refusing the ratification that is more likely than any thing else to embroil her with those powers, just as it happened in what was called the Syrian question. She was then on the very verge of a war, when she found, before she was aware of it, that the fleets and armies of Great Britain had settled the question for her: and she then, for the first time, gave back and signed the league.

And what will be our condition if, in consequence of the intrigues of our minister, we are involved in a European war, on the hollow pretence of this right of search? There is in the French House of Deputies, which the gentleman from Pennsylvania says was influenced by General Cass in its refusal to ratify, an interest whose constant aim is to overthrow the dynasty of Louis Phillippe, and destroy every remnant of it; a party who are much more bitterly opposed to him than any portion of either House of Congress is opposed either to Martin Van Buren or to John Tyler. They would annihilate his family, root and branch, and for ever abolish the monarchical power he holds. I will not enter upon the question by what authority Louis Phillippe holds his throne; it is not a question for this place or for this time; but I will say that France and her representative body have that question clutched between the parties which there prevail; and that, in this coming war, which it seems this pamphlet of Mr. Cass is to kindle up, I would not give a picayune for his crown. And this is the state of things in which we are invited to go to war with France for our ally!

[Mr. Ingersoll—The vote in the Chamber was nearly unanimous.]

Very well; that makes no difference. I am showing that what the party which refuses the ratification are after is not the right of search. They may throw dust in Mr. Cass's eyes, and make him believe that it is; but that is not the question, I repeat, between France and the allies; nor was it the question in the Chamber of Deputies. The gentleman says the vote was nearly unanimous; but we know what that often means, viz., that nobody votes against a thing.—But there was no a*ppel nominal*, (as they call it,) no polling of the Chamber.—M. Guizot saw the flame that was spreading, and he did not think it politic to oppose it. Whatever may have been the vote, be assured that France never will go to war on the question of the right of search. And suppose we have her assistance, pray of what avail will it be to us in a naval war with Great Britain, when France herself will be torn to pieces with the armies of Russia and Prussia marching on Paris? When she refused the other league, she found herself in such circumstances of danger that she thought it necessary to expend I do not know how many millions of francs in throwing a wall around Paris. And now, if she does not ratify this quintuple treaty, she may find herself in the like case—they may have to put Paris within walls again, (just as if that could save them.) What good could she do with her (fifty) steamers, I believe, and our one, against the hundred owned by Great Britain? One against a hundred—or say two. Well, that is two per cent.—rather worse than even the stock of the Bank of the United States. [A laugh.]

The gentleman has made a speech to incite us to war with England, because we may count upon the aid of France! And what good can France do us with such a burning mountain in the midst of her own territory? Threatened as she is every hour with a renewal of the scenes of her revolution, when the *Chouans*, as they were called, went roaming and ranging through the country, burning and slaying—rifling churches and breaking open nunneries, and tying the nuns and friars together to drown them, calling it "republican marriages;" butchering prisoners in cold blood, and keeping the guillotine in play till the kennels literally ran down with the blood of those whom they called aristocrats—their nobles and men of property. The sort of liberty there enjoyed was a jail delivery of prisoners to a mob who surrounded the prison doors, and as the victims were set free, clove them down in the street with their *Bowie knives*. That is history; and it will be history again if the very danger which the gentleman from Pennsylvania sees should be realized. And what sort of an ally is this for the United States in a war against England?

What I say is of necessity desultory. It must be so; I was taken entirely by surprise. The gentleman's motion and his speech were alike unexpected by me. I had other topics which I intended to touch, but I have had no time to methodize.

[Here some gentleman proposed that the Committee should rise. Others said, O, no. Others cried, Go on, go on. Mr. A. proceeded.]

The gentleman from Pennsylvania talks of a war between the United States and Great Britain as a very light thing, and then gives us all his good advice in order to prevent its occurrence. And next, for the instruction of the noble negotiator who has visited our shores, he tells him how certain it is that she must be beaten because we are unarmed—such must be the consequence: it always has been. Unarmed nations always have beaten those that were armed. It is natural they should. Really, this is a discovery—not in natural history, but in the history of war—not to be found in the books.

If we are to have a war, I hope that the negotiator will not take the gentleman's advice so far as to become alarmed, and give the advice to his government which the belief of such positions might lead to. I hope he will not give that importance to the remarks of the gentleman from Pennsylvania—to whose remarks I always attach great importance—and hope that the nation will weigh them well, and make up their minds as to the necessity of preparation. I hope he will think that the honorable gentleman has been indulging his fine imagination a little; that he has been displaying his ingenuity; that he has been speaking for the admiration of this House; or, if you please, has been making a speech for Buncombe, which means, in his case, I believe, the third district of the city of Philadelphia. [A laugh.] I hope he will conclude to give it this turn; that he will take it for granted all this is intended for the gentleman's constituents; that he is not really serious in this thing; and that, on the whole, he will conclude to go on with the negotiation just as if the speech had never been made. [Roars of laughter.]

But, suppose it should be otherwise,—suppose the British negotiator, on seeing this speech of the gentleman from Pennsylvania in the papers, and very possibly in pamphlets, and becoming aware of its deep impression on this House and this country, should conclude that war is probably to take place, and should write home to his government, giving them an account of the gentleman's speech, [renewed laughter,] and commending it to their meditations. We have had one experiment of the effect such a document may produce in England. There was, I believe, a certain report from a member of the Committee on Foreign Relations quite as warlike as the gentleman's speech, and made, too, under the same profession of a great desire for peace. Well, sir, that report, through the agency, I suppose, of the British minister here, went home to his government, and when it got to London it produced a sort of combustion of London—not that it actually burnt the city down, as the gentleman's warlike friend is to do, but it set the city in a flame. And what was the effect of it? Why, sir, our minister wrote forthwith to the valiant commander of our squadron in the Mediterranean to lose no time in getting nearer home. [Loud laughter.] Take my word for it, if the speech of the honorable gentleman, or any thing else, shall get us into a war with Great Britain, the constituents of the honorable gentleman and of other gentlemen who represent our great commercial capitalists on this floor will wish they could call to the two hundred millions worth of their floating commercial marine to get nearer home, too; but it will be then too late.

There is one consideration which ought to operate on this House, especially on those who here represent the commercial and navigating interests of this country; and that is, the difference between the Constitutions of England and this country in relation to the declaration of a war. If we go to war with Great Britain, we must do it by act of Congress. Though our ministers and our Executive officers may utter threatening words, yet, thanks be to God, they have not the power to put the country into a state of war at their pleasure, whether it will or no. Should the President and his Cabinet think with the gentleman from Pennsylvania, (Mr. Ingersoll,) or with the gentleman from Virginia, who spoke so bravely yesterday, (Mr. Wise,) still the people have reason to bless themselves that the power is not lodged with that department of the government. Meantime, we cannot commit any act of hostility until war has been regularly declared.

But how is it with Great Britain? This very envoy has only to write home a letter of five lines, saying, "I perceive that the spirit of this people is for war," and another order, secretly issued by the British privy council, expressed in five lines more, directing all naval commanders to take every American vessel they find afloat, and straightway our ships will be carried, without further delay or ceremony, into British ports, there to be, not condemned, but kept under sequestration; not confiscated, but just kept snug to abide the result of this negotiation.

[Mr. Snyder, of Pennsylvania—I hope he will write such a letter.]

And then, if we do (as the gentleman holds out to our hopes) confiscate the two hundred millions of dollars of our State debt, the British will have something to compensate them for the loss.

Am I drawing a fanciful picture? The gentleman well knows that it is a practical and sober account of just what has heretofore taken place. That is the way in which Great Britain always begins a war. Let any one look to the past history of her proceedings, to the war of 1763, for instance. What was the complaint of France against her at that day? That her fleets swept the ocean before she had made any declaration of war. War is not there proclaimed by act of Parliament. No; an order in council to her commanders, naval or military, is all that is requisite. Are the gentleman's constituents prepared for this?

[Mr. Snyder. "Yes, yes."]

Is this one of the advantages we shall enjoy in the desired war with England, that the first notice we shall have of it is the capture of our commerce in every sea?

I am well aware that it is a very easy thing for one to get up here, and cry in loud and boastful tones, "Perish commerce, perish credit," perish every thing, but keep the nation's honor untarnished! "yield nothing, make no concession!" And if the minister of Great Britain is then to yield every thing, why that is the way to get an earldom! An earldom! an earldom for giving up the demands of his own country! Is that the spirit of John Bull? No, sir; that is not the way that earldoms are won in England. Rodney never got beyond the dignity of a viscount for doing much more than that. Nelson, it is true, did get to be an earl, and Wellington was created a duke, but it was not by surrendering any thing to any body. It is not the practice of

John Bull to ennoble "sots or cowards;" the titles he bestows may possibly be fancies of the brain, unworthy the notice of a philosopher; but such as they are, they are not to be won by surrendering. There is one name in British history connected with surrendering, and it is that of Byng; and I think myself that the chance of sharing the fate of Byng is much more likely to be the fate of him who surrenders all his country demands than the possession of an earldom.

[Here Mr. A. yielded to a motion for the committee's rising, which motion prevailing, the committee rose accordingly.]

FRIDAY, April 15.

Mr. Adams, who was entitled to the floor from Thursday, rose and addressed the committee nearly as follows:

When the committee rose yesterday I was endeavoring, as much as lay in my power, to make a reply to the very extraordinary, and, to me, most unexpected and sudden introduction into this House of no less a question, in substance, than that of peace and war between this country and Great Britain, and that on so slender a peg as a motion to reduce the full Ministers to the Courts of Vienna and Berlin to the rank of Chargés. The preceding day had been occupied, in a manner equally sudden, with the consideration of the like question of peace and war, not with Great Britain only, but also with the empire of Mexico. These were topics solemn and painful to me, to a most extreme degree. As Chairman of the Committee on Foreign Affairs I had hoped that the only duty I should be called to discharge in relation to these diplomatic appropriations was to sustain the estimates received from the Department of State, and to answer the resolution of this House inquiring whether the expenses of our diplomatic relations might not be lessened by the reduction of our missions to Europe and to South America? But in that expectation I have been very painfully and unexpectedly disappointed.

Now, I must premise by saying that the Committee of Foreign Relations is to be discharged from all responsibility for any remarks I may make in regard to all the topics on which I am now to speak. They had not taken into their consideration any part of those subjects. The House is well acquainted with the present composition of that committee, and with certain circumstances relating to the history of that matter. I refer to them only to say that, since the present composition of that body, no committee of this or of the other House, at any Congress since the formation of the Government, could have proceeded in the discharge of its duties with more perfect harmony. No question has agitated its deliberations so as to divide its opinion on any important point; and having been charged by them with the duty of supporting the necessity of the expenditures estimated for by the Department—because, after full consideration, the committee all saw that there was no occasion to alter the existing number or grade of our missions abroad—I did hope that having done that, my whole duty would have been discharged. I say this, because, appearing as I do in some sort officially, as far as these appropriations are concerned, and having been suddenly called, both yesterday and now, to enter on the discussion of topics totally different, and topics which have not occupied the attention of the committee, I wish it to be understood that what I said yesterday, and what I may have occasion to say to-day, is not spoken by virtue of any instructions from the committee, but solely in my individual capacity as the Representative of one of the Congressional districts of the People of the United States. I speak on my own personal responsibility, and without the concurrence, so far as I know, of any other member of the Committee on Foreign Affairs.

And here I must be permitted to notify the House that, if I should manifest want of due preparation for the discussion of these great and all-important topics before this committee; if I shall exhibit a deficiency of means and of power to do justice to the cause I support, by which I mean, the cause of the peace of the country and of the world—I can only express my hope that other members of this committee, better informed and better qualified to meet, as they will have to meet, in the discussion, some of the ablest members of this body, will take the duty upon them and discharge it in a more worthy manner. My remarks must, of necessity, be very desultory, and in a great degree destitute of order and arrangement, from the entire want of time for suitable preparation.

But it is, I say, a question of peace and war which has suddenly been sprung upon this House, from two distinct and totally different quarters of the House, apparently, but which are united by ties which, perhaps, it will require considerable time to solve and unfold in the face of the world. I must take them as I find them, united in one great object, which is to involve us in a war both with Great Britain and Mexico, with the ultimate purpose of preserving and perpetuating the institution of slavery and the slave trade. This is the object of war with Mexico, as recommended to us by the gentleman from Virginia, (Mr. Wise.) This is the object of war with Great Britain as recommended to us by the gentleman from Pennsylvania, (Mr. Ingersoll.) In this they are perfectly united; and there is danger to the country of an immediate war at once, with these two Powers, which must probably involve in it a war of the whole civilized portion of the human race. This is the object which they have united with all their forces to recommend.

Now, I must say that, all unexpected as it has been to me, and unprepared as I am to discuss the subject in the manner it deserves, I am not sorry, I do not regret in the slightest degree, that this subject has been brought before the House. If I have any regret upon the subject, it is that it was not brought here before; that the House has heretofore suppressed all debate on the general subject, or at least on a great part of it, when it might have been discussed under circumstances so much more favorable, at a moment when there was no negotiation pending on any subject between Great Britain and the United States within hearing of my voice. I should have been much more delighted to have gone into the discussion before any of those delicate complexities were in the way to restrain the course of argument, which I dare not now enter upon and which yet belong essentially to the subject.

It is a question of peace and war, immediate and present; the danger of war is at the doors; and here, if any man dares to raise his voice against going to war, he is immediately charged with being a *British* partisan—an *English* orator. This is not a moment in which imputations of that kind are likely to be received with indifference, more especially when negotiations are in actual progress. I should have been much more gratified to have discussed the subject at the commencement of the session, or even before that. But I must take it as it comes; and, speaking as I do as the Representative of a single district, I must say what is necessary to be said, though it should be imputed to English feeling or any other, in quarters from which I may be sure there never will come the imputation of a good purpose to any thing I can say.

When the committee rose last evening, I was endeavoring to answer some of the arguments for war made amidst professions of the most pacific spirit by the gentlemen (the more recent of the two) who have recommended to us a war with Great Britain. And what were the points of his argument? 1. That a war would extinguish two hundred millions of our debt to England. 2. That it would enable us to burn London. And, 3. That because we were totally unprepared, therefore, this was the proper moment for beginning it. In the course of that argument he brought into view, I think, five points of controversy with England. Now, if I recollect right, there is in the city of New York a somewhat distinguished place called "the Five Points," [laughter] and really, if I were to judge of the character of the gentleman's speech from its own intrinsic merits, I should have thought that precisely the place it must have come from. [Great laughter.] The gentleman, I believe, represents a district in which there are some places somewhat like the celebrated Five Points in the city of New York.

[Mr. Ingersoll here asked leave to explain.

The Chair.   Does the gentleman from Massachusetts yield the floor?

Mr. Adams.   Oh yes; the gentleman may explain as much as he pleases.

Mr. Ingersoll here spoke earnestly for some minutes, but in a spot and in a position which brought his back to the reporter, and rendered it impossible to hear much of what he said. He was understood to say that the gentleman from Massachusetts had thought proper to make the most indecent allusions to his person by connecting it with the number of places which, for aught he knew, the gentleman might be in the habit of frequenting himself; but he knew that in this hall, dressed in a black gown and mounted on a cushion, the gentleman had the indecency to speak of the English nation in terms which deserved to fix upon him universal execration. Mr. I. also alluded to a letter written by Mr. A. while a public minister of peace at Ghent, in which he had spoken of his own country in terms like these: "With three frigates for a navy, and five regiments for an army, what can we expect but defeat and disgrace?" These were his expressions while his country's accredited minister to conclude peace with Great Britain.]

Mr. Adams continued. It is undoubtedly extremely apposite to the question whether our ministers to Austria and Prussia shall be exchanged for Chargés. Well, sir; the gentleman, in the great mildness and calmness of his temper, which is never to be ruffled by any thing, thought proper to allude to certain circumstances in my past life. I shall not reply to his remarks, because I hope to have a better use for my time. I meant no unkindness to the honorable gentleman when I spoke of his speech and observed that it might have proceeded from a place in the city of New York as moral and peaceable in its habits, and as respectable in its inhabitants, as the district which the gentleman himself represents—a district to which I made no unfriendly or disrespectful allusion, and in which I have no doubt there reside as many warm-hearted patriots, as many virtuous and upright citizens, as are to be found about the Five Points in New York. [Loud laughter.] I said that the speech was such a one as might have proceeded either from the Five Points, or from the honorable gentleman's district. If he chooses to receive this as a reflection either upon the Five Points or his own district, that is his affair; *qui capit ille facit*. The gentleman, at any rate, I consider as representing a portion of that democracy which, in a letter from Governor Clement C. Clay, of Alabama, is said to be the natural ally of the "peculiar institutions" of the South. Of that democracy I have no doubt a very large portion is to be found both at the Five Points and in the gentleman's district. And the gentleman is the representative, not of that party which, in the war of our revolution, would have made the gentleman a combatant on the side of Great Britain; not of that portion of the community which he would have represented at the time Heaven and earth were moved to prevent his confirmation as District Attorney in the other House of Congress, (by whom he was nominated to that office he knows;) not of those by whom the strongest tariff paper was sent here that ever I saw in my life; not of those he represented when he was a candidate for the appointment of Director of the Bank of the United States;—

[Mr. Ingersoll here calling on Mr. Adams for an explanation, Mr. A. replied, "I will tell the gentleman in private whenever he pleases."]

Not of that portion of them whom he represented when Gen. Jackson turned him neck and heels out of the same office of District Attorney, and which act he generously rewarded by declaring that Gen. Jackson was "every inch a President." No, sir; many changes have come over the dream of that honorable gentleman.

[Here Mr. Ingersoll asked for the floor to explain.]

Mr. Adams. I am tired of yielding him the floor. I take this House to witness that I did not begin this examination into past history; and if it does not meet the feelings of the gentleman, he has to thank himself for it.

[Mr. Ingersoll. It suits me perfectly.]

Now he is the representative of the war party in this country— the pure democracy of the third Congressional district of the city of Philadelphia.

But, to turn from this subject to what, perhaps, more properly belongs to the discussion, and adverting to the powerful argument made by the gentleman yesterday, in which he made such an exulting, such a triumphant use of a pamphlet put forth by our minister to France, and pronounced such lofty encomiums on the correspondence of our late minister to the Court of St. James, which was let off like a Parthian shaft, when he was just about to fly—a shaft which he let off just after he had given his admonition to our commander that it was time to get nearer home; the courage and spirit of which the gentleman so warmly admired, though darted at the British minister at the very moment he who sent it was on the point of departure to get out of harm's way himself. In commenting on the pamphlet of Gen. Cass, (of whom I shall always speak with due respect and honor,) I said that the very fact for which the gentleman so much admired it excited any thing but admiration in me; because I considered it as an interference with the internal affairs of France, under color of sounding the tocsin of alarm against a concession of the right of search. I said it was, in fact, a tocsin against the crown of Louis Phillippe, and that, if its effect should be to produce a war between France and the other four powers who had signed the quintuple treaty, under the false pretence of objecting to the right of search, we should find ourselves totally deceived; for that the right of search was not at all involved in the refusal of the Chamber of Deputies to assent to the ratification of that treaty.

It has so happened that this very morning I have seen a letter directly from France, containing an account of that very debate, from which I will now read, in order to show the correctness of the positions I took, that the right of search was not the ground of the decision, that being not a question between France and the four powers, but that it was a movement hostile to the reigning dynasty of France. The letter begins thus:

PARIS, January 30, 1842.
"Louis Phillippe continues his unrelenting hostility to the press. It made him what he is. Royal gratitude shows itself by persecuting it. Charles the Tenth wanted to gag the press, and lost his throne; let us see if Louis Phillippe will be more fortunate in the long run."

Does not this passage expressly show what is the present condition of that dynasty, at the head of which stands Louis Phillippe?—the danger by which he is surrounded—the immense mass of prejudice and passion which is accumulated against him? Does it not show what confidence is to be reposed in laws and treaties proceeding from such a source? and what sort of an inducement it is for us to go to war with England that we shall have a power like this for our ally? The letter then proceeds to relate the fact that a certain officer in the National Guards had been dismissed for certain reflections on the government published by him in a newspaper, and of his re-election by his own company in defiance of this act of government, and presents this fact in proof of the great unpopularity of Louis Phillippe. The letter goes on to say that "Thiers, in the debate on the address, has been speaking all manner of hard things against England." This Thiers is the democrat whose great object is the overthrow of the throne of Louis Phillippe to open the way to the introduction of a democratic form of government. This was the man who was for going to war with the four powers on the

Syrian question, in consequence of which he lost his place. This man, it seems, had been speaking all manner of harsh things against England. Had the two gentlemen from Pennsylvania and Virginia been studying in the same school? This seems a pretty good account of one of these speeches. And here I will take occasion to say, that speaking all manner of hard things against any foreign nation is no very good instrument of negotiation for peace. If we doubt this, let us only for a moment bring the case to ourselves. Should we, if a British minister should come to this country and openly say all manner of hard things against us, consider that as a proper mode to aid him in a successful negotiation with this government? It may be said that we have given no occasion for hard things to be spoken of us, and I hope it is true that we have given as little occasion as others. But if we are to take our own opinion of each other, as a just standard of judgment, if we are to be guided, for instance, by what one-half of this House says of the other half, (and in this I have no reference to particular parties,) we cannot complain should very hard things indeed be said of us. In this present debate, frequent mention has been made of the head of the Mexican government; and he has been called on this floor little else than a merciless tyrant, an upstart, a usurper, and the like. This may be a very good means to adopt, if the object is to go to war with Mexico; but I should scarcely consider it a likely mode of preserving amicable relations with that power.

And here I beg that I may not be misunderstood nor represented as making a Santa Anna speech, which I have no doubt I shall be, and I do not know but that it may also be said that General Santa Anna knows the proper means to propitiate members of this House. General Hamilton, at least, thought that there were certain means of propitiating him, which, when tried, did not prove quite as effective as he had anticipated. I profess no special regard for General Santa Anna. He may, for aught I know, be a merciless tyrant. I certainly do not much approve of some of his exploits in war, and still less his negotiations here at the White House some four or five years ago. I wish I could know more of what passed in that negotiation, and I should be very glad if this House would call for the correspondence which took place between a late President of the United States and General Santa Anna when he was here.

That there was a negotiation of some kind has not only been acknowledged by Santa Anna himself, but a letter of President Houston to him has caused me still more to wish to know what its nature was. Nor do I believe that the true relations of this country either with Texas or with Mexico can be rightly understood without this; and yet if I were to offer a resolution calling for that information, some gentleman from Mississippi or Alabama would instantly start up and object, when it must lie over under the rule, and would descend to the tomb of the Capulets. Could I have an assurance that no such result would follow, I promise you I would offer such a resolution at once.

But to return. This Monsieur Thiers said all manner of hard things against England, and, if he can get France into a war, he is himself to be the Minister of Louis Phillippe. Then what will happen to France no man knows, and sorry am I to say that what will probably happen to this country, if she shall be allied to France, I cannot look upon with satisfaction as a "member of the Peace party."

The letter then goes on to say of the discourse of M. Thiers: "His harangue excited great interest, not from its eloquence or wisdom, but because it is believed that it spoke the sentiments of the war party, *which is headed by the Duke of Orleans.*"

This opens up to us a view of the real source of the present parties in France. This Duke of Orleans, as the eldest son of the King, is the presumptive heir of the Crown. He is head of the war party in the nation, as Mons. Thiers is in the House of Deputies. He wants war, and what he wants it for I stated yesterday. There are intestine divisions in that country. Here we see the heir of the Crown conspiring against his father, probably thinking, as his grandfather did before him, that, instead of conducting him to the guillotine, it will bring him to the Crown. In war he anticipates the opportunity of displaying his talents as a military commander, of fighting battles and winning fields, and by military renown securing his passage to the throne:

> "The quintuple slave trade treaty was attacked by Thiers, and then an amendment was moved. The Royal speech contained this paragraph: 'I am endeavoring, at the same time, by negotiations prudently conducted, to extend our commercial

relations, and to open new markets for the productions of our soil and of our arts.'

The address echoed this sentence, and M. Billault proposed, as an amendment, the following: 'The prudence of the Government is a guaranty that in the arrangements relative to the repression of a culpable traffic, our Government will carefully protect the legitimate interests of our maritime commerce and *the complete independence of our flag against all foreign attempts.*'"

That is the amendment in which is couched the effect of Gov. Cass's pamphlet. Is there any thing there about the right of search? Not a word. How could there be? France is already committed. She is bound to Great Britain to admit the right—bound by express treaty stipulations, and has been for ten years past. The amendment could not even glance at what was its real object, viz., to induce France to break her faith. No; but this was the mask which was held up there and is held up here for going to war.

The letter writer proceeds:

"It was finally arranged that the amendment should run thus: 'The Chamber hoped that the Government, in still concurring in measures for the suppression of the slave trade, would still know how to preserve from injury the interests of French commerce *and the independence of our flag*'."

This is still more guarded, still more remote from the question of the right of search.

"Remember," says the writer, "to understand the *animus* of this amendment, that the new European treaty for the suppression of the slave trade mutually grants the right of search at sea."

The *animus* of the amendment, its true intent, is so little apparent that it must be pointed out.

"Thiers argued that the English cruisers on the Guinea coast are kept there chiefly for the sake of disturbing the French trade, that the *prevention* of the slave trade was inhuman"—

Yes, that the prevention of the slave trade was inhuman. There is Thiers's argument, openly advanced in the face of the world. Here is the *animus*, indeed! Here the cat is let out of the bag. The object of the resolution, its true intent, is to preserve and perpetuate the slave trade; and now, let this committee, let this House, let this country reflect what are the principles really involved in all this blustering about the right of search. The object at the bottom of it all is the *restoration and preservation of the* AFRICAN SLAVE TRADE. He gives his reasons:

> "—as it sometimes led to whole cargoes of slaves being cast into the sea to prevent capture, and that the treaty of 1833 (made when himself was Minister of Commerce!) was illegal, as it confiscated all vessels which were proved to carry slaves."

There is the argument of M. Thiers.

> "M. BILLAULT strongly denounced the English claim to 'the right of search.' They have claimed it, as an attribute of the sovereignty of the seas, for more than a century. In war it was natural they should push it; in peace, he contended, England had claimed it under the pretext of philanthropy. In 1830 this same 'right of search' had been conceded by France, and insisted on ever since by England. However, America did not concede the point, and England was using the anti-slave trade treaty as a cloak to carry this point. The freedom of the seas was involved in this question. France might concede it, but he anticipated that before long the United States would dispute the sovereignty of the seas with England in every quarter of the globe."

If claiming the right of search under the pretext of philanthropy is a proof of hypocrisy, we were ourselves the first to give it, for we were once zealous in the prevention of the slave trade; but now we have done away with all that. As the French anatomist says, in one of Moliere's plays, "The heart used to be on the left side, but now we have changed all that, and the heart is on the right side." Yes, I hope we shall ever maintain the freedom of the seas. I adhere to that, as I ever did. It is a part of the freedom of the land; it is a part of the great question of human liberty. I admit that the claim of England to the sovereignty of the seas is an evil to be resisted by all the other nations of the earth. Our contest is for the freedom of the seas, not for the sovereignty of the seas.

> "M. GUIZOT made an important reply. M. Jacques Lefebvre's amendment (the *second* one above) was a censure on the slave trade treaty of 1841, and was meant to oppose any extension of the treaties of 1831 and 1833. The Minister defended *all* the treaties, and said what those of 1831 and 1833 'had done was to consider human flesh as contraband of war.'"

The gentleman from Pennsylvania said that the determination of the Chamber was nearly unanimous, on which I yesterday remarked that this unanimity is often only apparent, and a vote is sometimes recorded as unanimous when there is perhaps not even a majority in its favor. But what says M. Guizot?

> "They did nothing more and nothing less; they assimilated the crime of the slave trade to that of contraband of war. The sea remained free as before; there was only one more crime added to the code of nations, and there were nations which in common wished to repress this crime. And on the day in which *all* nations shall have taken this engagement, the crime of slave trade will disappear; on that day the men who have pursued that noble aim through political storms and party battles, will be honored in the world; and I hope that my name will appear among those."

[The word I have italicised was taken to reflect on the United States.]

The word italicised is the word "all"—"when *all* nations shall have taken this engagement, the crime of the slave trade will disappear." This was considered as glancing at the United States, as the only civilized nation that now resisted the right of search for the suppression of the slave trade. He hints that we stand alone among the community of nations; but says that when we, with the rest, shall concur in granting the right, then slavery will disappear.

Now, I entreat the members of this committee to remember that I am not for conceding the right of search. I repeat it. I cannot consent to it even for the suppression of the slave trade; because I believe that other expedients can be formed to accomplish that object without this resort; and because, in the correspondence of the British Minister with Mr. Stevenson, I see no demand for such concession. On the contrary, the right to search our ships is expressly disclaimed by Great Britain. We may, indeed, be called upon to aid her in the suppression of the slave trade by the services of a part of our naval force, but this we can do without conceding the right of search.

> "What he also said will be read with great interest in America. Here we have M. Guizot decidedly vindicating England and condemning the United States by implication. I give the very words. M. Guizot said: 'I wish it were in my power to induce the United States to become a party to the convention, for my success would do honor to my country, *and render a great service to humanity*; but God forbid that the slightest constraint should be used in order to compel any nation to become a party to the treaty. The United States are free, and will remain free. *On the day when they shall have acceded to the conventions, they will have performed a noble work*, for they will then have accomplished the abolition of the trade in the whole world; but do not let it be imagined for a moment that the freedom of the seas will be involved in this question. That will remain as it was. The slave trade has no connexion with the question of the freedom of the seas; for, like piracy, this traffic is excluded from all common right. It has been assimilated also to the recognised right which exists in the case of the contraband of war. Are you willing that the traffic in human flesh should be treated with the rigor which, in the case of the contraband trade of war, is admitted by all the world? And does this exception to the great principle of the freedom of the seas affect that principle? No, gentlemen; on the contrary, the principle is rendered more sacred by the exception.
>
> The implication is, that America must be charged with inhumanity *until* you accede to the Anti-Slave Trade Convention.
>
> The amendment was carried: Ministers choosing to adopt it, rather than run the risk of defeat on the original motion."

There: there is the explanation of that unanimity, or approach to unanimity, of which the gentleman from Pennsylvania made, or attempted to make, so much yesterday.

But now, as I do not wish to intrude on the attention of this committee a single moment longer than is necessary, I will pass over the rest of what I might say on this subject, and recur in a few observations to the other war trumpet which we have heard within the last two days.

They unite in one purpose, though they seem to be pursuing it by different means. The gentleman from Virginia, (Mr. Wise,) confining his observations to our relations with Mexico, also urges us to war with the same professions of a disposition for peace as were so often repeated by the gentleman from Pennsylvania in regard to Great Britain. He does not immediately connect the questions of war with Mexico and war with Great Britain, but apparently knows and feels that they are in substance and in fact but one and the same question; and that, so surely as we rush into a war with Mexico, we shall shortly find ourselves in a war with England. The gentleman appeared entirely conscious of that, and I hope that no member of this committee will come to the conclusion that it is possible for us to have a war with Mexico, without, at the same time, going to war with Great Britain. On that subject I will venture to say that the Minister from England has no instructions. That is not one of the five points on which the gentleman from Pennsylvania tells us our controversy with England rests, and the surrendering of which is to open to that Minister so easy a road to an earldom. The war with Mexico is to be produced by different means and for different purposes. I think the gentleman from Virginia in his speech rested the question of the war with Mexico on three grounds: 1st. That our citizens had claims against the Mexican Government to the amount of ten or twelve millions; 2d. That some ten or twelve of our citizens had been treated with great severity and suffered disgrace and abuse from the Mexican Government, having been made slaves and compelled to work at cleansing the streets; that these citizens were detained in servitude, while one British subject had been promptly released on the first demand of the British Minister there; and 3d, That a war with Mexico would accomplish the annexation of Texas to the Union. The gentleman was in favor of war, not merely for the abstract purpose of annexing Texas to the Union, but he was for war by peremptorily prohibiting Santa Anna from invading Texas. I will take up these reasons in order.

And first, as to going to war for the obtaining of these ten or twelve millions of dollars, being the claims of our own citizens on Mexico. This seems a very extraordinary reason, when, according to the doctrine of the gentleman from Pennsylvania, a state of war at once extinguishes all national debts. If we go to war with Mexico, her debts to our citizens will be spunged at once, if the doctrine of the gentleman from Pennsylvania be true. He did, to be sure, qualify the position by saying that war would at least suspend the payment of interest. If so, then it would equally suspend interest in the case of Mexico. The arguments of the two war gentlemen happened to cross each other, though they are directed to the same end. One of them will have us to go to war with Mexico to recover twelve millions of dollars; the other would have us to go to war with England to wipe out a debt of two hundred millions. I will not compare the arguments of the two gentlemen together, but I will say in regard to the doctrine of the gentleman from Pennsylvania that it has quite too much of repudiation in it for my creed. I do not think that a war with England would extinguish these two hundred millions, but that, on the contrary, Great Britain would be likely to say to us, we will go to war to recover the money you owe us. That is one of the questions which we must settle if we go to war, but which we might otherwise, at least for a time, stave off. But, if we go to war, what must be the effect of the peace that follows? We must pay our two hundred millions, with the interest. As to our debt from Mexico, I believe the way to recover it is not to go to war for it; for war, besides failing to recover the money, will occasion us the loss of ten times the amount in other ways.

As to war producing a suspension of interest on a national debt, let the gentleman look back a little to the wars of France. In 1793 France was at war with almost all the countries of Europe, and she immediately confiscated all her debts to them. But what happened thirty years after, when the re-action came? The Allies took Paris, and in the settlement which then took place they compelled France to pay all her debts, with full interest on the whole period during which payment had been suspended. That was the consequence to France of going to war to extinguish debts. And if we go to war with Great Britain tomorrow, she will make us, as one of the conditions of peace, pay our whole debt of 200 millions, with interest. And what shall we gain? Spend millions upon millions every year as long as the war continues: and unless it is greatly successful, have to pay our debt at last, principal and interest. This would depend on the chances of war, or the issue of battle. And as our contests would be chiefly on the ocean, we must first obtain a superiority on the seas before we can put her down and vanquish her; and this to save ourselves from the payment of 200 millions justly due from our citizens to hers!

I have seen a letter from the Governor of Mississippi in defence of the repudiation of debts by the Legislature of that State: an operation, the justice of which one of her Representatives here (Mr. Thompson) *endeavored* to explain to the satisfaction of this House and the country. The letter of the Governor gives an account of the motives of the people of Mississippi for repudiating: and the Governor in that letter says that he expects the subject will be made a matter of negotiation between Great Britain and the United States, and thinks it will present a very delicate question.

[Mr. Thompson here was desirous of obtaining the floor for an explanation, but what he said could not be distinctly heard.

Mr. Adams.   I say that it is true: I have myself seen the letter, and read it.

Mr. Thompson.   There must be some mistake; because no part of the debts (and I have examined and traced them all) is due to the people of England.

Mr. Adams.   I speak of a letter which has been published in all the papers of the country; it is signed with the name of Governor McNutt, and never has been contradicted so far as I know. He says that he expects the matter will be a subject of negotiation; and adds that a great majority of the people of Mississippi would sooner go to war than yield to the payment of the debt. I cannot take the assertion of the gentleman that there is a mistake as sufficient evidence against a document which I have seen in various papers, uncontradicted.*

---

* The National Intelligencer, of Dec. 2, 1841, contains a letter of Gov. M'Nutt to the editor of the Richmond Enquirer, dated Jackson, Miss., Nov. 10, 1841, of which the following is an extract:

"Our Senator, ROBERT J. WALKER, and our Representatives, GWINN and THOMPSON, sustain me in the position I have taken. A demand will probably be made on the Government of the United States for the payment of the bonds referred to. This will raise an exciting and perplexing question. This State has

Mr. Thompson here repeated his explanation. The Governor could not have expected that debts would be made the subject of negotiation with England, not one dollar of which was owing to any British subject.]

Mr. Adams.   Well; it is possible the letter does not name the foreign Power with whom the negotiation is to be held. He says that he expects it to become a subject of negotiation. I will not undertake to say that he actually names Great Britain, nor is it material; the principle is there; the People would rather go to war than consent to pay their debts. I shall not enter on the subject of the propriety or expediency of the Legislature of Mississippi repudiating their State debt; but the gentleman from Pennsylvania and the gentleman from Virginia both made this a question, in their arguments for war. The gentleman from Virginia says we must go to war with Mexico to recover the ten or twelve millions due by her, and the gentleman from Pennsylvania tells us that if we will only go to war with England we shall at one dash sponge our whole debt of two hundred millions. Now, in reference to moral principles, I must say that I prefer the doctrine of the gentleman from Virginia. I had rather, if I must go to war, do it to recover a just debt, than to sponge a debt justly due. I make a deep distinction between the moral principle of the gentleman from Virginia and the moral principle (if moral it can be called) of the gentleman from Pennsylvania. I speak of it as a matter of fact. Both gentlemen make motives for war out of the debts due to us or from us. But I am now replying more particularly to the argument of the gentleman from Virginia. I am not willing to go to war for the recovery of the ten or the twelve millions of dollars due us by Mexico. I think it not justifiable to do so; and, if I am in favor of retaining a full minister at that court, it is precisely for the reason that I am for conducting a pacific negotiation for that debt, and not for going to war to recover it. I am therefore for a pacific mission to Mexico. I am for staving off as long as possible the final right of the Government of the United States to assume a threatening tone in order to recover this debt. That time, I think, has not arrived. When it shall arrive, there will

---

defined her position, and will maintain it. *I firmly believe that four-fifths of the people of this State* PREFER GOING TO WAR TO PAYING THE BONDS."

be no occasion for a special mission, but for raising money, a thousand fold more than the whole amount of the debt, in order to obtain right and justice. Going to war with Mexico, even though it should present to us the tempting advantage of robbing churches and priests, would not be my mode for recovering our debt. I do not think it the proper remedy, and that is one of the reasons why I am for retaining the full mission.

There is a second reason given by the gentleman from Virginia in favor of war. He reminds us, with great warmth, that there are some ten or twelve citizens of the United States now prisoners in the city of Mexico, and dragging chains about the streets of that city; that a British subject taken with them has been liberated while they are kept in bondage. Now, if I am correctly informed, one American citizen, a son of General Combs, has been liberated on the application of the Minister of the United States, who was as fairly a subject of imprisonment as the British subject of whom the gentleman speaks. I certainly have no objections to our Minister's making such representations as he can in favor of the release of citizens of the United States, although taken in actual war against Mexico in association with Texian forces; but I am not prepared to go to war to obtain their liberation. I must first be permitted to ask, how is it that these men happen to be in the streets of Mexico? Is it not because they formed part of an expedition, got up in Texas against the Mexican city of Santa Fe? Were they not taken *flagrante bello*, actually engaged in a war which they had nothing to do with, to which the United States were no party? In all this great pity and sympathy for American citizens, made to travel hundreds of miles barefoot and in chains, the question "how came they there?" seems never to be asked. And yet, so far as the interposition of this nation for their recovery is concerned, that is the very first question to be asked. It was a regular warlike expedition, got up by the President of the republic of Texas for conquest within the Mexican territory, the object being, no doubt, to secure to Texas the possession of the sources of the Rio del Norte, for Santa Fe is situated at the source of that river. The State of Texas has never explicitly declared her boundaries, so that they are not exactly known; but, whatever they are, they are no bounds to them, for President Houston has declared that he means to transcend them, and to push on into Mexico; and the gentleman from Virginia tells us that if Houston does not do it, he himself is ready to go and plant his standard on the lofty summit of that city. [A laugh.]

Well, sir, this same President of Texas has done another thing. I do not know whether it is likely to bring us into difficulty with him, for really the symptoms among us are such that it seems he will be allowed to do any thing. He has proclaimed a blockade of the ports of Mexico. Now, a blockade must have the effect of cutting off our trade with those ports. Not a vessel of the United States can approach the port of Vera Cruz, but she will be stopped and turned back, to the total derangement of her voyage and the probable ruin of her owner, and that under this paper blockade. The two States are at war; and the most recent act of hostility is this expedition against Sante Fe with a view to conquer and attach it to the territory of Texas. From our own valley of the Mississippi, on whose valiant and enterprising sons the gentleman from Virginia pronounced so high a panegyric, and whose high-souled patriotism is so strongly stimulated by the prospect of robbing priests and pillaging churches, [a laugh,] ten or twelve persons, in the ardor of their disinterested zeal for liberty, joined this Texian expedition against a part of the dominions of Mexico; but fortune did not smile upon the enterprise. I have heard of no very valiant exploits achieved by their arms; but, on the contrary, the moment they came in actual contact with the Mexican authorities, weak as they are, they laid down their arms and became prisoners of war at discretion. They were treated as Mexico treats her prisoners of war. I do not undertake to justify that course of treatment; but I will say, that if our Minister to Mexico has received instructions imperatively to demand their release, and, if that shall be refused, to come immediately home, what will be the consequences? I hope the consequences will be to save to the Treasury a little of his salary as minister: any other consequence than this I earnestly deprecate. If, however, he does come back, I confess I shall not regret it; for, even after the high eulogium bestowed upon his character and qualifications by the gentleman from Virginia, if my opinion were asked, I should still say that I prefer that some other individual should occupy the post. I say nothing in opposition to the eloquent panegyric pronounced upon the individual: my reasons are, that, upon the questions in

SPEECH ON WAR WITH MEXICO | 1842 625

controversy between Mexico and this country, I know that his views are such as will not be very likely to perpetuate a state of peace between the two countries, or very advantageous to the union of these States as now constituted. On a subject collateral to, if not identical with, that union, I have had some experience of the sentiments entertained by him, by the gentleman from Virginia, and by another gentleman, from Maryland, who I do not now see in his place, (supposed to be Mr. W. C. Johnson,) who fastened upon this House that execrable 21st rule, which is fast driving this Union to its dissolution. I say this without hesitation. A rule which has created more dissension and more ill blood than all other measures adopted in this House, and which is leading a large portion of the People of this country to approximate towards the opinion that even an open dissolution of the Union would be better than the state of things in which we now live. As to the talents of the gentleman in debate, I, too, have known him on this floor; and, perhaps, the gentleman from Virginia may say of me, as he said of my excellent friend from Vermont, that I, also, have great reason to appreciate the gallant valor of his friend from South Carolina. Sir, his friend threatened me with the penitentiary once—[roars of laughter;] that is the greatest exploit of his valor that I am acquainted with.—I have met him in this House, and from what I have witnessed here I should give it as my opinion that my friend from Vermont is more than a match for him; and I would say so to his face if he were here. Whether or not I have felt the power of his lance I leave posterity and the world to say. At the same time, I disclaim all feelings of unkindness toward the gentleman in question. I must say that in the private and individual relations of society there is not a man in this House with whom I have had more friendly intercourse during the whole time of his continuance here, even within three days after he had threatened me with the penitentiary. [A laugh.]

I beg the gentleman from Virginia distinctly to understand that if he means to apply the remarks he made as to his friend, our present Minister to Mexico, being so very terrific a champion in this House, I have never felt the dread which the gentleman thinks he was calculated to inspire. I met him on his station here. I never was afraid to meet him. I appreciated and respected his talents, and I have sometimes lamented the influence he exerted in the House.—I have often differed from him, but he never assumed the airs of that superiority which here seems to be claimed for him by his friend from Virginia; and I hold it scandalous for any gentleman in this House to assume to speak of any other as dreading a fellow member upon the floor. I know nothing of such dread. I speak of the Minister to Mexico, as I would speak of him if he were here, and as I am in the habit of speaking on all occasions. It does not befit my spirit, and I hope it never will befit the spirit of any of those representing that part of the country from which I come, to meet any man here under a spirit of slavish inferiority. I hold in disgust every thing like the assumption of superiority, or the exaction of personal deference in a body like this. I meet gentlemen here in open debate, and I speak my mind, sometimes perhaps too strongly, instigated it may be by a momentary feeling of irritation which soon passes over, and which I am afterwards the first to regret; but the gentleman from Virginia has never seen me flinch from meeting him on a footing of perfect equality, or any other member of this House, past or present.

But there is one observation which I feel called upon to make at this time, and which I make most unwillingly; and that is, that heretofore, when our present Minister to Mexico was a member of this House, and also very recently, within but four days past, it has happened that members from two sections of this Union are not permitted to stand on the same footing whenever what are called the rights of the South are involved. I refer more particularly to the case of my friend from Vermont, (Mr. Slade,) who rose here and proceeded to speak most perfectly in order, if any such thing as order does exist, but was arrested for touching upon what are called the peculiar institutions of the Southern States, and was compelled, by a decision of the Chair, to take his seat.

At witnessing that decision I was greatly afflicted, for I had been so much entertained and so much instructed too by the remarks of my friend, that I felt persuaded, had he been permitted to proceed, he would have continued to enlighten us by remarks strictly to the purpose. Yet within half an hour afterwards the gentleman from Virginia (Mr. Wise) rose and almost immediately broached the same subject of slavery, and was permitted, without let or interruption, to pursue the whole range of argument he chose to adopt in regard to it. (And for saying this I do not know but I may be arrested and ordered to take my seat, and not to touch upon the subject of slavery.) I, for one, am not disposed to submit to that inequality any longer. I have witnessed it too long, and in a great variety of forms; but I have always resisted it, and I hope that a sufficient number will here be found resolved to submit to it no longer, but determined to maintain their rights upon this floor; and that, if put down here by the force of numbers, they will make their appeal to the justice of the nation.

I must ask pardon of the House for the desultory character of these remarks. It was said by one of the principal speakers of ancient times, as an apology for having detained a public assembly by a long speech, that he "had not had time to make it shorter." I may say the same thing now. If I had had the requisite time for preparation, I should have endeavored to condense and methodize what I say; but as such is not the fact, I must be permitted to hope that the House will bear with me.

The second reason in favor of war, put forth by the gentleman from Virginia, I say, is no reason at all. I am willing that our Minister should present a modest sober solicitation to the Government of Mexico, for the release of such of our citizens as were taken in the act of marching to invade the Mexican territory under the standard of Texas. But I would not make it a ground of war with Mexico, if her Government should reply, "Your citizens thought proper to join themselves with the forces of Texas, and have exposed themselves to even worse treatment than they have received." And, if they did say so, they might refer to the case of two British subjects by the names of Arbuthnot and Ambrister, who once interfered in a certain war between the United States and Seminole Indians, carried on, not in our own territory but on a foreign territory. In that case these men, Arbuthnot and Ambrister, were not brought to this city of Washington, to traverse our streets in chains; they were not exposed to the severity of travelling barefoot for hundreds of miles. No; a course much more summary was observed in their case; they were tried by a court martial, and one of them being a young man, scarcely of age, the court were disposed to let the prisoners off with a punishment comparatively mild, and the court so found; but what did General Jackson do? He struck his pen across that line in the finding of the court, and they were both hung up. I never complained of that decision of General Jackson, though there were many others who did. I did not, indeed, specifically defend or support the act, in itself considered, but as a national question between us and Spain, and between us and Great Britain, whose subjects they were. The ground I took by the order of my Government, not so much to justify the act as to put off the ground of claim by Great Britain, was, that these individuals had intermeddled in a war they had nothing to do with; in a war not between us and Great Britain, but between us and certain Indian tribes, and that if they choose thus to expose themselves they must abide the consequences.—It was a question of the same character as that on which we are now asked to go to war. I did sustain, as a question of national law, the right of Gen. Jackson to treat them as he did: and the Minister of Great Britain at that time, Lord Castlereagh, told our Minister, Mr. Rush, that they had concluded to pass it over, after many anxious consultations held by the British Privy Council. But, he said, If I had but lifted my finger, you would have had to answer that act of Gen. Jackson by war. In that case there was quite as much to be said for Great Britain, had she taken up the quarrel for the hanging of these two British subjects, as for us if we should go to war for the ten or twelve citizens of the United States taken in the expedition to Santa Fe. I say again, if the Government has ordered our Minister to Mexico peremptorily to demand the release of the American citizens now held as prisoners of war, and in case of refusal to come home, as a signal of the purpose of this country to pursue the demand by a resort to war, they have gone beyond what is right, and, as I believe, have gone beyond their power.

I say, further, that, in my judgment, we have adopted too menacing a tone in our negotiations with that Power. I speak not, of course, with certainty, for I do not positively know; but I do say, if our Minister has been ordered to return on the condition I have stated, the Government have transcended their power; I say, further, that the Executive department is not authorized to threaten any foreign nation with war, because they have no power to proclaim war and because that power is among the most precious powers held by this and the other House of Congress, who, under the Constitution, are made trustees of the war power of the nation—the most solemn trust that can be committed to human hands. It becomes this House to vindicate its own authority, and to let the Executive department know that it is not for them to threaten foreign Governments with war. If a war is coming, and especially if there is immediate danger of its occurrence, and if the Executive is apprized of the fact, it is his duty to inform Congress, and especially this House, of such a state of things, and refer to them the terrific question of authorizing war—a question involving, whenever it comes, the lives, the fortunes, and the happiness of millions. If instructions of the kind I have mentioned have been given, I shall much regret it, though I shall not be displeased that the present Minister shall return.

I come now to the third ground for war urged by the gentleman from Virginia. And I hope I do not misrepresent him when I say that I understood him to affirm that if he had the power he would prohibit the invasion of Texas by Mexico, and if Mexico would not submit to such a requirement, and should persist in her invasion, he would go to war. The gentleman stated, as a ground for war, that Santa Anna had avowed his determination "to drive slavery beyond the Sabine." That was what the gentleman from Virginia most apprehended—that slavery would be abolished in Texas—that we should have neighbors at our door not contaminated by that accursed plague spot. He would have war with Mexico sooner than slavery should be driven back to the United States, whence it came! If that is to be the avowed opinion of this committee, in God's name let my constituents know it—the sooner it is proclaimed upon the housetops the better. The House is to go to war with Mexico for the purpose of annexing Texas to this Union. Yes; and the gentleman produced, as a triumphant authority (not indeed in his eyes, for he has not been in the habit of regarding the source of it with much respect, but still as good authority,) a document from a former Administration, intended by him to justify the existing Executive in proclaiming that he was resolved to do all in his power for the annexation of Texas. Yes, a predecessor of the present incumbent, even myself, for want of better authority, was referred to, and alleged to have entertained the same feeling, the same disposition for the acquisition of this territory.

The gentleman was so good as to send me two letters written by a distinguished gentleman now in my eye, then Secretary of State, to our Minister at the Court of Mexico; I have not had time to read them over. [A voice: "The extracts are given in the Intelligencer."] From those letters the gentleman caused certain extracts to be read, with a view to prove that in 1825 and again in 1827 instructions had been given to propose to the Mexican Government a cession of the territory of Texas to the Rio del Norte, and a sum of money was to be offered in consideration. I thank him for citing this paper; it is a correct document. I had myself, in the negotiation of our treaty with Spain, labored to get the Rio del Norte as our boundary, and I adhered to the demand till Mr. Monroe and all his Cabinet directed me to forego it, and to assent to take the Sabine.

And now I repeat what I have said before, that before the treaty was signed it was carried by me, at the command of Mr. Monroe, to Gen. Jackson, who, after examining it with the map in his hand, approved of the Sabine as the boundary. That fact was contested, with the usual candor of the organ of the administration, and it was declared that a member of the House went to General Jackson, in person, and he recollected nothing of the matter. I then sent for the document in which the fact was put down in writing at the time, and though it was not published in the papers, it was sent to Mr. Van Buren for his inspection, and after looking at it he became satisfied that it was true.—Perhaps this is not a material fact; I used it as an answer to the gentleman from Virginia to show that I did not originally negotiate the treaty with the present boundary of the Sabine. I maintained my demand for the Rio del Norte till Mr. Monroe and his Cabinet overruled me and assented to the Sabine. But at that time Texas was a wilderness with no population, or at least no American population. I do not believe there were 5,000 people in the whole territory, and they were Spanish subjects. In the course of negotiation, and after the terms of the treaty had been concluded, the first American project for the settlement of the country was brought into being. I received a very long letter from Moses Austin, I think his name was Moses, (father of Stephen Austin,) stating that his object was to make a settlement in the wilderness. He was a sort of a Boon; and he proposed to collect in the midst of New England as large a colony as he could, and with them to go into Texas and settle the country. That was the state of things under which I was in favor of annexation.

When my proposition was made to the Mexican Government in 1825, slavery had been abolished in that territory. There was not a slave there, nor was there the least reason to expect there ever would be. There existed therefore no reason why I should be averse to the annexation of this new region to the territory of the Union. Had it been annexed, it would have been settled by freemen. I should certainly have had no objection to that, nor do I know that I should object now, if it were brought within the scope of possibility. I should not indeed desire it, because I think we have quite enough territory already. We have certainly as much as we can manage. But even as territory, it is not desirable. I should not wish it to form a part of the Union, even if it were settled with freemen, and were a free State, as I would have wished it in 1825 or 1827. Slavery was then abolished, and if Texas had come into the Union, there would have been no power in the United States to restore it. Does the gentleman from Virginia think that because, under such circumstances, I wished to see the annexation at that time, that this is an argument either to show the expediency of its annexation now, or any inconsistency in me because I am now utterly opposed to it.

[Mr. Wise here asked liberty to explain, and Mr. Adams having yielded the floor, Mr. Wise said, I rise to ask the gentleman a question.

Mr. Adams.   No, sir: no questions. Explain, if you please.

Mr. Wise.   I wish to ask him if he did not instruct our Minister to protest against the abolition of slavery in Mexico.

Mr. Adams.   (With vehemence.) No, sir! never!

Mr. Wise.   Not while the gentleman was President?

Mr. Adams.   No, sir! never!

Mr. Wise.   It is so charged.]

Mr. Adams.   As to charges, I hope the gentleman does not expect me to answer them. I never could have protested against the abolition of slavery in Mexico or any where else. I have said that I was not prepared at this time to vote for abolishing slavery in the District of Columbia, and I have offended numbers of my constituents by repeating that declaration; but that is a different thing. But even if I could have protested against the abolition of slavery after it had been instituted, still if my voice could be heard either here or in Texas, or in any other part of the civilized or the savage world, I would have protested from the bottom of my soul against its restoration, and that is the insurmountable reason why I never will consent to the annexation of Texas to the United States. I would not take the territory if it were ten thousand times more valuable than it is, sullied as it is with the crime of slavery restored. The people of Texas have not the apology which, with whatever force, is pleaded by many of those in our Southern States, that the slavery which now infects them was a vice, a crime, a misfortune, a disease, inflicted upon them by the parent State, and that is the reason why they must support it now. I must say, that in my heart, if not in my mind, that is the strongest article they ever have adduced in support of it: but Texas has no such defence to set up; slavery was not bequeathed to them from a selfish and cruel stepmother, as almost all the liberal men of Virginia used to say of it in their Commonwealth not many years ago, and as some among them still say. If there can be an apology for this plague spot, I say again that the people of Texas have none to plead, and that is the reason why Texas never shall, with my consent, or, as I hope, with the consent of my constituents, or of any portion of the free people of the United States, become an integral part of the Union.

There is another reason—a reason I admit vastly inferior to the other, but still it is a reason. Texas has acceded to the right of search: she is bound by treaty to that effect. If you take her as a part of ourselves, you take her with her treaties, and then we shall be bound to cede the right of search to Great Britain. I say that this is a reason of infinitely less importance; yet so like am I to a drowning man, who clings even to straws, that I will not consent to the annexation on that account. And now the gentleman may go to the organ here of I know not what party, and insert an article accusing me of having made an "English argument." Let him go as soon as he pleases, I know it will be said I have made a British speech.

Most joyfully indeed would I compound with the gentlemen from the Southern portion of the Union, if by our joint efforts we could prevail on Texas to abolish slavery again, of which indeed, there seems some faint gleam of hope in the published correspondence between General Hamilton, the Texian envoy, and Lord Palmerston. I would compound never to take Texas, or, if they will agree that slavery shall be abolished there, I will agree to take her. But no, never, while breath is in my body, will I consent to the annexation of any foreign State which is burdened with the curse of slavery.

What I am now to say, I say with great reluctance and with great pain. I am well aware that it is touching upon a sore place, and I would gladly get over it if I could. It has been my effort, as far as was in my power, to avoid any allusion whatever to that question which the gentleman from Virginia tells us that the most lamblike disposition in the South never can approach without anger and indignation. Sir, that is my sorrow. I admit that the fact is so. We cannot touch that subject without raising throughout the whole South a mass of violence and passion, with which one might as well reason as with a hurricane. That I know is the fact in the South, and that is the fact in this House. And it is the reason why members coming from a free State are silenced as soon as they rise on this floor; why they are pronounced out of order; made to sit down; and, if they proceed, are censured and expelled. But, in behalf of the South and of Southern institutions, a man may get up in this House and expatiate for weeks together. On this point I do complain, and I must say, I have been rather disappointed that I have not been put down already as speaking out of order. What I say is involuntary, because the subject has been brought into the House from another quarter, as the gentleman himself admits. I would leave that institution to the exclusive consideration and management of the States more peculiarly interested in it, just as long as they can keep within their own bounds. So far I admit that Congress has no power to meddle with it. As long as they do not step out of their own bounds, and do not put the question to the People of the United States, whose peace, welfare, and happiness are all at stake, so long I will agree to leave them to themselves. But when a member from a free State brings forward certain resolutions, for which, instead of reasoning to disprove his positions, you vote a censure upon him, and that without hearing, it is quite another affair. At the time this was done I said that, as far as I could understand the resolutions proposed by the gentleman from Ohio, (Mr. Giddings,) there were some of them for which I was ready to vote, and some which I must vote against; and I will now tell this House, my constituents, and the world of mankind, that the resolution against which I would have voted was that in which he declares that what are called the slave States have the exclusive right of consultation on the subject of slavery. For that resolution I never would vote, because I believe that it is not just, and does not contain constitutional doctrine. I believe that so long as the slave States are able to sustain their institutions without going abroad or calling upon other parts of the Union to aid them or act on the subject, so long I will consent never to interfere. I have said this, and I repeat it; but if they come to the free States and say to them you must help us to keep down our slaves, you must aid us in an insurrection and a civil war, then I say that with that call comes a full and plenary power to this House and to the Senate over the whole subject. It is a war power. I say it is a war power, and when your country is actually in war, whether it be a war of invasion or a war of insurrection, Congress has power to carry on the war, and must carry it on according to the laws of war; and by the laws of war an invaded country has all its laws and municipal institutions swept by the board, and martial law takes the place of them. This power in Congress has, perhaps, never been called into exercise under the present Constitution of the United States. But when the laws of war are in force, what, I ask, is one of those laws? It is this: that when a country is invaded, and two hostile armies are set in martial array, the commanders of both armies have power to emancipate all the slaves in the invaded territory. Nor is this a mere theoretic statement. The history of South America shows that the doctrine has been carried into practical execution within the last thirty years. Slavery was abolished in Colombia, first, by the Spanish General Morillo, and, secondly, by the American General Bolivar. It was abolished by virtue of a military command given at the head of the army, and its abolition continues to be law to this day. It was abolished by the laws of war, and not by municipal enactments; the power was exercised by military commanders, under instructions, of course, from their respective Governments. And here I recur again to the example of Gen. Jackson. What are you now about in Congress? You are about passing a grant to refund to Gen. Jackson the amount of a certain fine imposed upon him by a Judge under the laws of the State of Louisiana. You are going to refund him the money, with interest; and this you are going to do because the imposition of the fine was unjust. And why was it unjust? Because Gen. Jackson was acting under the laws of war, and because the moment you place a military commander in a district which is the theatre of war, the laws of war apply to that district. I have a correspondence between Gen. Jackson and the Governor of Georgia during the Seminole campaign, in which Gen. Jackson, addressing Governor Rabun, asserted the principle that he, as Governor of a State within his (Gen. J.'s) military division, had no right to give a military order while he (Gen. Jackson) was in the field. The then Governor of Georgia (and I do not know but what it killed the poor man, for he died soon after) did contest the power of Gen. Jackson. He said all he could for State rights, [a laugh,] but Andrew Jackson had given an order, and that order was carried into effect, while the order of the Governor was suppressed.

[Mr. Warren, of Georgia, here asked leave to make a statement in explanation, and the floor having been yielded to him for that purpose by Mr. Adams, he proceeded to give a history of the facts of the case to which Mr. A. had just alluded, but owing to his position at a distance from the Reporter, he was imperfectly heard. The conclusion of what he said was, however, that the Governor of Georgia never yielded the ground he had taken, nor did he die in consequence of the difficulty. See Appendix.]

Mr. Adams resumed. I am glad to hear the explanation, and am entirely willing to concede whatever of merit is due to the Governor of Georgia for resisting what he conceived to be military tyranny. But I am afraid, nevertheless, whatever may have been the success of Governor Rabun in this contest, General Jackson had the right of the question. I might furnish a thousand proofs to show that the pretensions of gentlemen to the sanctity of their municipal institutions under a state of actual invasion and of actual war, whether servile, civil, or foreign, is wholly unfounded, and that the laws of war do, in all such cases, take the precedence. I lay this down as the law of nations. I say that the military authority takes for the time the place of all municipal institutions, and slavery among the rest; and that, under that state of things, so far from its being true that the States where slavery exists have the exclusive management of the subject, not only the President of the United States but the commander of the army has power to order the universal emancipation of the slaves. I have given here more in detail a principle which I have asserted on this floor before now, and of which I have no more doubt, than that you, sir, occupy that chair. I give it in its development, in order that any gentleman from any part of the Union may, if he thinks proper, deny the truth of the position, and may maintain his denial; not by indignation, not by passion and fury, but by sound and sober reasoning from the laws of nations and the laws of war. And if my position can be answered and refuted, I shall receive the refutation with pleasure; I shall be glad to listen to reason, aside, as I say, from indignation and passion. And if, by the force of reasoning, my understanding can be convinced, I here pledge myself to recant what I have asserted.

Let my position be answered; let me be told, let my constituents be told, the people of my State be told—a State whose soil tolerates not the foot of a slave—that they are bound by the Constitution to a long and toilsome march under burning summer suns and a deadly Southern clime for the suppression of a servile war; that they are bound to leave their bodies to rot upon the sands of Carolina, to leave their wives and their children orphans; that those who cannot march are bound to pour out their treasures while their sons or brothers are pouring out their blood to suppress a servile, combined with a civil or a foreign war, and yet that there exists no power beyond the limits of the slave State where such war is raging to emancipate the slaves. I say, let this be proved—I am open to conviction, but till that conviction comes I put it forth not as dictate of feeling, but as a settled maxim of the laws of nations, that in such a case the military supersedes the civil power; and on this account I should have been obliged to vote, as I have said, against one of the resolutions of my excellent friend from Ohio, (Mr. Giddings,) or should at least have required that it be amended in conformity with the Constitution of the United States.

In the mean time, this is a reason with me for not desiring the annexation of Texas to this Union, because, if we go to war for that annexation, I entertain serious apprehensions that this will become a practical question. If we shall go to war with Mexico, and, which necessarily follows, go to war with Great Britain, to annex Texas to this Union, the day is not remote, when, in one of the slave States, an invading army from abroad may be combined with an insurrection of the slaves and with a civil war, and the danger still further heightened by an irruption of that whole body of Indians whom you have accumulated and compressed together as if for the very purpose of organizing them for a hostile movement upon our frontier. I put this possibility to the Representatives of the Southern States as presenting a most serious and painful consideration to my mind. The gentleman from Virginia makes very light of this. He talks to us about the star of Texas, which he calls the "lone star of Liberty." Liberty of Texas! The star illumined by the radiance of slavery restored! Yes, that is the star which is to lead us on to victory. So, I suppose, if war shall come, we shall not only acquire this solitary brilliant star of Texas, but we shall have all Mexico added to the United States. Sir, the Isthmus of Panama will hardly stop our victorious arms, and I really wonder the gentleman did not carry us on to Cape Horn. [A laugh.] The gentleman in his dreams, (shall I call them?) told us that President Houston was to plant this same lonely star of Texas on the walls of the city of Mexico, and that if President Houston did not do it, the gentleman himself would. [Loud laughter.] And he means, in this heroic enterprise, to lead on the brave spirits of thousands from the great valley of the Mississippi, inspirited by the hope of robbing churches and priests!

So it is to be a religious as well as a civil expedition—a sort of crusade, in which the gentleman from Virginia is likely far to transcend the exploits of Tamerlane and Ghengis Khan. The gentleman is soon to plant the lone star of Texas and slavery on the walls of Mexico; and then what is to become of the liberties of these United States? [A laugh.] Is it conformable to the history of the world that the leader of such an army after conquests not reaching to one-tenth the extent of those which the gentleman will achieve, should remain content with the station of an humble, private citizen? No. No. The experience of all mankind has given us warning that if that is to be the course of our public affairs, and such are to be the brilliant fortunes of the gentleman from Virginia, our liberties will stand as little chance in after times as those of the nine millions of the people of Mexico after he shall have conquered them.

But I am inclined to consider all this rather as approaching to what is sometimes called rhodomontade, than a thing in the serious contemplation of the gentleman from Virginia; and I look forward to the time when, in the records of history, the gentleman's name shall be placed side by side, not with the names of Ghengis Khan or Tamerlane, but with that of a still more glorious conqueror by the name of TOM THUMB. [Roars of laughter, long and loud.]

But it is growing late; and as the time has been fixed when this debate is to close, and as the time I have already occupied bears upon my conscience, I will close by repeating my request that the House will pardon the imperfect and desultory manner in which I have endeavored to furnish some reply to the war trumpets of the gentlemen from Virginia and Pennsylvania. I will now yield the floor to some other member who may desire to occupy it.

APPENDIX.

Mr. Warren, of Georgia, desires the publication of the following statement, explanatory of the transaction between Gen. Jackson and Gov. Rabun, referred to by Mr. Adams. It will be seen that the actual result does not at all determine the question which was right. Mr. A. adduced the case as an illustration, not as a proof.

> I said in substance that, having been connected with the military expedition ordered by Gov. Rabun, which occasioned the correspondence to which the gentleman from Massachusetts had referred, and although a mere youth, commissioned in that expedition, I could not willingly remain silent, hearing the version of that correspondence given by the gentleman from Massachusetts. No order of Gov. Rabun was ever suppressed by Gen. Jackson; but, on the contrary, the order of Gen. Jackson arresting the commanding officer of that expedition (Capt. Obed Wright) was suppressed by the Judiciary of Georgia.
>
> Sir, after General Jackson, with his army, had arrived in Florida, Indian incursions on the frontier of Georgia and the massacre and plunder of our citizens were common, and the depredators were followed in a direction to Oponee and Pheleme towns, west of Flint river. Governor Rabun ordered a military expedition, giving the command to Capt. Wright, directing the destruction of these towns. And, in April, 1818, a pilot employed by Capt. Wright took him to the Chehaw town. It was destroyed. The troops were disbanded, and Capt. Wright, on his way home, and making some stay in the village of my residence, was overtaken by Gen. Jackson's arresting officer, Major John M. Davis, of the U. S. army. Major Davis called upon me, and in great confidence disclosed his business, and inquired for Capt. Wright, to whom in a few minutes I introduced him, and who submitted to the order for arrest, and went with Major Davis, in the execution of the order, until a writ of habeas corpus was issued by the inferior court of Baldwin county against Major Davis, and Capt. Wright discharged from his custody. Gov. Rabun then ordered Capt. Wright to be arrested for breach of orders, in not destroying the two towns ordered, and for destroying a town not ordered. Capt. Wright was allowed his liberty on parole of honor, and afterwards left the country.

No order given by General Jackson in relation to the matter was ever carried into effect, nor was any order given by Gov. Rabun ever suppressed. Gov. Rabun, so far from yielding any right assumed, maintained and executed every order given, and died not of this correspondence, but of disease incident to the climate in which he lived.

I have, gentlemen, prepared this statement, made by me in substance, for your paper, because I am unwilling that any impression should exist any where that any Governor of Georgia, and especially Gov. Rabun, had allowed an order given by him to be suppressed by the dictation of any military commander. I have to say that no instance can be found in the history of Georgia and the Federal Government where Georgia has allowed any officer of the Federal Government, either judicial, executive, or military, either with or without force, to suppress an order made by her Governor; and I trust I may not live to see such suppression effected.

No blame can attach to your Reporters for not hearing my remarks, but I nevertheless desire they should appear in your paper.

I am yours, &c. LOTT WARREN.

"HAVE WE EMANCIPATED OUR SLAVES?"

21. *Letter from Hon. John Quincy Adams, read at the recent celebration of West India Emancipation in Bangor, (Me.)* (Quincy, MA: [Office of the *Patriot*, August 1843]).

Adams's association with Leavitt and other abolitionists in the 1840s signaled one of the last and most surprising developments of his long career as a public figure. Though he is perhaps best known today as an antislavery tribune—as "the acutest, the astutest, the archest enemy of Southern slavery that ever existed," in the words of Virginia congressman Henry Wise—his road to outspoken opposition to slavery was a tortured one. Adams was not by nature or temperament a radical and he had long considered single-issue advocacy groups, like the abolitionists, to be "fanatical associations." Whatever his private principles and sentiments, multiple reinforcing factors had combined to encourage a studied silence about slavery. First, and maybe foremost, was his political ambition. Always conscious of his status as a northerner, Adams understood that the advancement of his career would depend on his ability to be perceived as more than just a sectional figure. His commitment to a nation united by internal improvements and dedicated to moral improvement grew naturally, one might say unconsciously, out of his desire to assume himself a unifying national role. Finally, the very nature of the posts and positions he had—diplomat, U.S. senator, peace envoy, secretary of state, and president—had conditioned him to think and speak on behalf of the United States as a whole, and to be jealous of its sovereign rights, even when those involved slavery.

We can look to Adams's diary to measure the gap between his private and public selves and trace his cautious evolution. On January 15, 1807, Adams notes that the U.S. Senate has taken up the bill to suppress the slave trade—with the period of constitutional prohibition on such a measure due to elapse the next year—and makes his first observations about an individual who will figure prominently in his future. The bill "occasioned a long debate," he recalls. "Mr. Clay, the new member from Kentucky made an ardent Speech upon one of the Sections — He is quite a young man — an Orator — and a Republican of the first fire." But as for himself, "I took, and intend to take no part in the debates on this subject." This would continue to be his policy even through the stormy, two-year controversy over whether to admit Missouri as a slave state, which forced the nation to confront the issue as never before. On January 10, 1820, he admits that "the Missouri Question has taken such hold of my feelings and imagination, that finding my ideas connected with it very numerous but confused for want of arrangement, I have within these few days begun to commit them to paper, loosely as they arise in my mind." Concluding that the controversy is a harbinger of worse to come—"a mere preamble; a title page to a great tragic volume"—he writes that "I have hitherto reserved my opinions upon it, as it has been obviously proper for me to do. The time may, and I think will come, when it will be my duty equally clear to give my opinion." A month later, on February 11, he laments the lack of first-rate, courageous orators on the "free side of the question": "Oh! if but one man could arise with a Genius capable of comprehending, a heart capable of supporting and an utterance capable of communicating those eternal truths that belong to this question, to lay bare in all its nakedness that outrage upon the goodness of God, human Slavery, now is the time, and this is the occasion upon which such a man would perform the duties of an Angel upon Earth." Adams was not such a man, at least not yet.

It would be as a congressman, free from the ambition for higher office, that Adams began to find the strength to publicly avow his beliefs. In this new role he was no longer speaking for the nation but charged with the responsibility of representing the particular views of his constituents in southeastern Massachusetts. And he was confronted daily by an increasingly and expressly *pro*-slavery faction among his colleagues. His diary entry for December 24, 1833, records a conversation with representatives James Findlay of Ohio and Michael Hoffman of New York, both Democrats, in which he tells them that "the real question now convulsing this Union, was whether a population spread over an immense territory, consisting of one great division, all Freemen, and another of Masters and Slaves, could exist permanently together as members of one Community or not — That to go a step further back, the question at issue was Slavery." Even still, he had misgivings, as evident in this remarkable confessional entry from April 19, 1837:

> I answered a Letter from John G. Whittier inviting me on the part of the managers of the Massachusetts Anti-Slavery Society, to attend the meeting of the New-England Anti-Slavery Convention at Boston, to be held on the last Tuesday of May. I have not absolutely declined to attend, but have assigned reasons for not attending which will probably be decisive to my own mind. Upon this subject of Anti-Slavery, my principles and my position make it necessary for me to be more circumspect in my

conduct than belongs to my Nature — I have therefore already committed indiscretions of which all the political parties avail themselves to proscribe me in the public opinion — The most insignificant error of conduct in me at this time would be my irredeemable ruin in this world, and both the ruling political parties are watching with intense anxiety for some overt act by me, to set the whole pack of their hireling Presses upon me. It is also to be considered that at this time the most dangerous of all the subjects for public contention is the Slavery question — In the South it is a perpetual agony of conscious guilt and terror, attempting to disguise itself under sophistical argumentation and braggart menaces. In the North, the People favour the whites and fear the blacks of the South — The Politicians court the South because they want their votes — The abolitionists are gathering themselves into Societies increasing their numbers and thriving upon persecution — But in proportion as they increase in numbers and in zeal they kindle the opposition against themselves into a flame; and the Passions of the Populace, are all engaged against them — The exposure through which I passed at the late Session of Congress was greater than I could have imagined possible: and having escaped from that fiery furnace, it behooves me well to consider my ways before I put myself in the way of being cast into it again — On the other hand may God preserve me from the craven Spirit of shrinking from danger in the discharge of my duty — Between these two errors let me pursue the path of rectitude unmov'd, and put my trust in God.

Read against this backdrop, the following letter to an antislavery group in Bangor, Maine—the most forthright and most passionate public statement on the subject Adams ever made—represents the inspiring culmination of a long and often painful personal journey and a capstone to a political career unlike any other in our nation's history.

Letter from Hon. John Quincy Adams

READ AT THE RECENT CELEBRATION OF
WEST INDIA EMANCIPATION IN
BANGOR, (ME.)

―――――――――

ASA WALKER, C. A. STACKPOLE, and F. M. SABINE, Esqrs.—Committee Correspondence of a meeting of the citizens of Bangor and its vicinity, holden on the 27th of May, 1843.

Quincy, 4th *July*, 1843.

FELLOW CITIZENS:

I have received your letter of the 9th ult., and perhaps, in answering it, my safest and most prudent course would be to express my regret, that the precarious state of my health, and particularly of my voice, would not warrant me in undertaking an engagement to deliver a public address upon any subject whatever, on the first day of next August. This answer I have been most reluctantly constrained to give to several other kind invitations to address the people on various subjects, in the course of the ensuing summer and autumn. But the occasion of which you propose to celebrate the anniversary, is viewed in lights so entirely different and opposite to each other that it cannot be denied to have assumed both a religious and a political aspect, and this must be my apology, while returning my thanks for your friendly invitation, for frankly unfolding to you other reasons which would have dictated to me the same conclusion, even if the state of my health admitted of my compliance with it.

The extinction of SLAVERY from the face of the earth, is a problem, moral, political, religious, which at this moment rocks the foundations of human society throughout the regions of civilized man. It is, indeed, nothing more nor less than the consummation of the Christian religion. It is only as *immortal* beings that all mankind can in any sense be said to be born equal—and when the Declaration of Independence affirms as a self-evident truth, that all *men* are born equal, it is precisely the same as if the affirmation had been that all men are born with immortal souls. For take away from man his soul, the immortal spirit that is within him, and he would be a mere tameable beast of the field, and like others of his kind, would become the property of his tamer. Hence it is, too, that by the law of nature and of God, man can never be made the property of man. And herein consists the fallacy with which the holders of slaves often delude themselves, by assuming that the test of property is human law. The soul of one man cannot by human law be made the property of another. The owner of a slave is the owner of a living corpse; but he is not the owner of a man.

The natural equality of mankind, affirmed by the signers of the Declaration of Independence to be *held by them* as self-evident truth, was not so held by their enemies. It was not so held by the King and Parliament of Great Britain. They held the reverse. They held that sovereign power was unlimitable. That the tie of allegiance bound the subject to implicit obedience, and, therefore, that the natural equality of mankind was a fable. This was THE question of the American Revolutionary War. In the progress of that war, France, Spain, the United Netherlands became involved in it. The Governments of France and Spain, absolute monarchies, had no sympathies with the American cause—the rights of human nature. Vergennes had plotted with Gustavus of Sweden, the revolution in Sweden, from liberty to despotism. Turgot, very shortly before the surrender of Burgoyne, but after our Declaration of Independence, had formally advised Louis the Sixteenth, that it was for the *interest* of France and Spain that the insurrection in the Anglo-American colonies should be *suppressed*. France and Spain had been *warned* of the remote consequences to them *as owners of colonies*, of the success of the Anglo-Americans. But neither Turgot nor Vergennes, nor any one European or American statesman of that age, foresaw or imagined what would be the consequence, by no means remote, upon their own Governments at home, of the dismemberment of the British Empire, and the triumphant establishment, by a seven years' war on the continent of North America, of an Anglo-Saxon confederate nation, on the foundation of the natural equality of mankind, and the inalienable rights of man.

After Louis the Sixteenth lost his crown, he remembered, and bitterly repented the part he had taken on the side of the natural equality of mankind, and the rights of human nature in the American revolutionary war. For the revolution in France, by which he lost his throne and his life, was another fruit of the same self-evident truth, that all men are born equal, and have a RIGHT to life, liberty and the pursuit of happiness, *without infringing* upon the same right of all other men.

Until the day of the Declaration of Independence, the condition of slavery was recognized as lawful in *all* the English colonies. The Constitution of the Commonwealth of Massachusetts, established three years after the Declaration of Independence, adopted its self-evident truths, and the Judges of the Supreme Court of the Commonwealth, under that Constitution, judicially decided that slavery within the Commonwealth was thereby *ipso facto* abolished. Since that day, there has not been a slave within the State.

The author of the Declaration of Independence was a slaveholder. His self-evident truths taught him that slave-holding was an outrage upon the natural rights of mankind, at least as great as Parliamentary taxation without representation. He held that opinion to his dying day. He introduced it into his draught of the Declaration of Independence itself, imputing the existence of slavery in Virginia, to George the Third, as one of the crimes which proved him to be a tyrant unfit to rule over a free people.

Among the signers of the Declaration of Independence, there were at least twenty slave-holders—or probably, thirty. They could not stomach the application of self-evident truths to themselves, and they lopped it off as an unsightly excrescence upon the tree of Liberty. But his grandson and executor has carefully preserved it in the double form of print and fac simile, in the edition which he has published of his writings, and there it stands, an unanswerable testimony to posterity, that in the roll of American Abolitionists, first and foremost after the name of George Washington, is that of *Thomas Jefferson*.

The result of the North American Revolutionary War had prepared the minds of the people of the British Islands, to contemplate with calm composure the new principle engrafted upon the association of the civilized race of man, the self-evident truth, the natural equality of mankind, and the rights of man.

They had waged against it a cruel and disastrous war of seven years. Hundreds of thousands of valiant Britons had fallen victims, hundreds of millions of British treasure had been squandered to sustain the principle of illimitable sovereignty against the principle of illimitable human rights. The prize of the conflict was the liberty and the immortal soul of man. The contest was over between Britain and her children. The Lord of Hosts had decided the wager of battle. Human liberty was triumphant, and a new confederation entered upon the field of human affairs, with the Urim and Thummim of the Law from Sinai, "Light and Right," inscribed upon her bosom, and upon the diadem around her brow, "Holiness to the Lord."

But while this contest had been in progress, both of intellectual conflict and of mortal combat, the same question of human right against lawless power had been started in the land of both the combatant parties to this controversy. The question of the American Revolution had been of political government in the relations of sovereign and subject. Anthony Benezet, a native of France, settled in Pennsylvania, a member of the Society of Friends, and Granville Sharp, an English philanthropist, at London, were at the same time blowing the bugle horn of human liberty and the natural equality of mankind, against the institution of slavery practiced from time immemorial by all nations, ancient and modern. There were two modes of slavery which had crept in upon the relations of mankind to one another, first as the results of war, by the right of conquest, and secondly, by the voluntary servitude of the feudal system. They had both become odious by the silent progress of Christianity. The practice of enslaving enemies taken in war had already ceased between Christian nations. The traffic in slaves had been denounced by the popular writers both of France and England—by Locke, Addison, and Sterne, as well as by Raynal, Rousseau, Montesquieu, and Voltaire. It was every where odious, but every where practiced, till just after the close of the American Revolutionary War arose the cry for the abolition of the African slave trade. The first assault of the Reformers was upon the trade which was prosecuted with such atrocious cruelty that the mere narrative of its ordinary details excited disgust and horror.

"Sweet are the uses of adversity" saith Shakespeare, and "in the day of adversity *consider*," saith yet higher authority. In the summer of 1783, when the results of the Revolutionary War presented themselves to the people of the British Islands, in the darkest form of adversity, they had, and they improved the opportunity, of considering the principle for which, and the principle against which they had so obstinately and fiercely contended. Their warfare had been against the self-evident truth of human rights. Thomas Clarkson, with two or three other Englishmen, associated themselves together with the purpose of arraying the *power* of the British Empire, for the total abolition of slavery throughout the earth; and the commission with which they went forth to regenerate the race of man, by leading captivity captive, was the same identical, self-evident truth against which Britain had just closed her relentless war, in humiliation and defeat. She was now to make the identical principle the inscription upon her banners—to war against *slavery* for the natural rights of mankind, and to proclaim the jubilee shout of *liberty* throughout the land—throughout the globe.

Of that undertaking, Clarkson himself has written the history. He has shown in what small beginnings it commenced, by what slow and almost imperceptible progress it advanced—by what interests, prejudices and passions, it was perpetually obstructed. How many years it was before it could obtain admission to the hall of legislation in the British House of Commons. How, in the meantime, it had been silently making its way to the hearts of the British people. How many struggles of argument and of eloquence it had to encounter, before it could lay prostrate all opposition at its feet—and how this emanation of the Christian faith, after waiting eighteen hundred years for its development, came down at last like a mighty flood, and is even now under the red cross of St. George, overflowing from the white cliffs of Albion, and sweeping the slave trade and slavery from the face of the terraqueous globe.

People of that renowned Island! children of the land of our forefathers, proceed, proceed in this glorious career, till the whole earth shall be redeemed from the greatest curse that ever has afflicted the human race—proceed, until millions upon millions of your brethren of the human race are restored to the rights with which they were endowed by your and their Creator, but of which they have been robbed by ruffians of their own race, shall send their choral shouts of redemption to the skies in blessings upon your names. Oh! with what pungent mortification and shame must I confess, that in the transcendant glories of that day, our names will not be associated with yours! May Heaven, in mercy grant that we may be spared the deeper damnation of seeing our names recorded, not among the liberators, but with the oppressors of mankind.

Fellow citizens! the first impulse of the regeneration of humanity came from us—the Fourth of July is our anniversary day. Then was the principle proclaimed to the world as that which was to be the vital spark of our existence as a community among the nations of the earth. This is the brightness of our glory, and of this we cannot be bereaved. But how can we presume to share in the festivities and unite in the songs of triumph of the first of August? Have we emancipated our slaves? Have we mulcted ourselves in a hundred millions of dollars, to persuade and prevail upon the man-stealer to relinquish his grasp upon his prey? Have we encompassed sea and land, and sounded the clarion of freedom to the four ends of Heaven, to break the chain of slavery in the four quarters of the earth? Has the unction of our eloquence moved the bowels of compassion of the holy pontiff of the Roman Catholic Church, to give his commands to his Christian flock against slavery and the slave trade? Have we softened the heart of the fiery Mussulman of Tunis, the follower of the war-denouncing prophet of Mecca, to proclaim liberty throughout his land? Are *we* carrying into Hindostan the inexpressible blessings of emancipation? Are *we* bursting open the everlasting gates, and overleaping the walls of China, to introduce into that benighted empire in one concentrated sunbeam, the light of civil and of Christian liberty? Oh no, my countrymen! No! nothing of all this! Instead of all this, are *we* not suffering our own hands to be manacled, and our own feet to be fettered with the chains of slavery? Is it not enough to be told that by a fraudulent perversion of language in the Constitution of the United States, we have falsified the Constitution itself, by admitting into both the Legislative and Executive departments of the Government, an overwhelming representation of one species of *property* to the exclusion of all others, and that the odious property in slaves?

Is it not enough, that by this exclusive privilege of property representation confined to one section of the country, an irresistible ascendency in the action of the General Government has been secured, not indeed to that section, but to an oligarchy of slaveholders in that section—to the cruel oppression of the poor in that same section itself? Is it not enough that by the operation of this radical iniquity in the organization of the Government, an immense disproportion of all offices, from the highest to the lowest, civil, military, naval, Executive and judicial, are held by slave-holders? Have we not seen the sacred right of petition totally suppressed for the people of the free States during a succession of years, and is it not yet inexorably suppressed? Have we not seen for the last twenty years, the Constitution and solemn treaties with foreign nations, trampled on by cruel oppression and lawless imprisonment of colored mariners in the Southern States? In cold-blooded defiance of a solemn adjudication by a Southern judge in the Circuit Court of the Union? And is this not enough? Have not the people of the free States been required to renounce for their citizens the right of habeas corpus and trial by jury, and to coerce that base surrender of the only practical security to all personal rights? Have not the slave-breeders, by State legislation, subjected to fine and imprisonment, the colored citizens of the free States, for merely coming within their jurisdiction? Have we not tamely submitted, for years, to the daily violation of the freedom of the post office and of the press, by a committee of seal-breakers: and have we not seen a sworn Post-Master General, formally avow, that though he could not license this cut-purse protection of the peculiar institutions, the perpetrators of this highway robbery must justify themselves by the plea of necessity? And has the pillory or the penitentiary been the reward of that Post-Master General? Have we not seen printing presses destroyed—halls erected for the promotion of human freedom levelled with the dust, and consumed by fire, and wanton, unprovoked murder perpetrated with impunity, by slave-mongers? Have we not seen human beings, made in the likeness of God, and endowed with immortal souls, burnt at the stake, not for their offences but for their color? Are not the journals of our Senate disgraced by resolutions calling for *war*, to indemnify the slave-pirates of the Enterprise and the Creole, for the self-emancipation of their slaves, and to inflict vengeance, by a death of torture, upon the heroic self-deliverance of Madison Washington? Have we not been fifteen years plotting rebellion against our neighbor Republic of Mexico, for abolishing slavery throughout all her provinces? Have we not aided and abetted one of her provinces in insurrection against her for that cause? And have we not invaded openly, and sword in hand, another of her provinces, and all to effect her dismemberment and to add ten more slave States to our confederacy? Has the cry of war for the conquest of Mexico, for the expansion of re-instituted slavery, for the robbery of priests, and the plunder of religious establishments, yet subsided? Have the pettifogging, hair-splitting, nonsensical, and yet inflammatory bickerings about the right of search, pandering to the thirst for revenge in France, panting for war, to prostrate the disputed title of her king, has the sound of this war-trumpet yet faded away upon our ears? Has the supreme and unparalleled absurdity of stipulating by treaty to keep a squadron of eighty guns for five years, without intermission, upon the coast of Africa, to suppress the African slave trade, and at the same time denying at the point of the bayonet, the right of that squadron to board or examine any slaver all but sinking under a cargo of victims, if she but hoist a foreign flag—has this diplomatic bone been yet picked clean? Or is our *indirect* participation in the African slave trade to be protected at whatever expense of blood and treasure? Is the Supreme Executive Chief of this Commonwealth yet to speak not for himself, but for her whole people, and pledge *them* to shoulder their muskets, and to endorse their knapsacks against the fanatical, non-resistant abolitionists, whenever the overseers may please to raise the bloody flag, with the swindling watchword of the UNION? Oh! my friends! I have not the heart to join in the festivity of the first of August, the British anniversary of disenthralled humanity, while all this, and infinitely more than I could tell— but that I would spare the blushes of my country—weigh down my spirits, with the uncertainty, sinking into my grave as I am, whether she is doomed to be numbered among the first liberators or the last oppressors of the race of immortal man.

Let the long trodden-down African, restored by the cheering voice and Christian hand of Britain, to his primitive right and condition of manhood, clap his hands and shout for joy on the anniversary of the first of August. Let the lordly Briton strip off much of his pride on other days of the year, and reserve it all for the pride of conscious beneficence on that day. What lover of classical learning can read the account in Livy or in Plutarch, of the restoration to the freedom of the Grecian cities by the Roman Consul Flaminius, without feeling his bosom heave and his blood flow cheerily in his veins? The heart leaps with sympathy when we read, that on the first proclamation by the herald, the immense assembled multitude in the tumult of astonishment and joy, could scarcely believe their own ears— that they called back the herald and made him repeat the proclamation, and then—"*Tum ab certo jam gaudio tantus cum clamore plausus est ortus, totiesque repetitus, ut facile appareret, nihil omnium bonorum multitudini gratius quam libertatem esse.* Then rang the welkin with long and redoubled shouts of exultation, clearly proving that of all the enjoyments accessible to the hearts of men, nothing is so delightful to them as Liberty." Upwards of two thousand years have revolved since that day, and the first of August is to the Briton of this age, what the day of the proclamation of Flaminius was to the ancient Roman. Yes—let them celebrate the first of August as the day to them of deliverance and of glory—and leave to us the pleasant employment of commenting upon their motives, of devising means to shelter the African slaver from their search, and of squandering millions to support on a pestilential coast a squadron of the stripes and stars, with instructions sooner to scuttle their ships than to molest the private slaver who shall make his flag-staff the herald of a lie.

Apologizing to you, gentlemen, for the length of this letter, I will close it with an ejaculation to Heaven, that *you* may live to substitute for the first of August, the day when *slavery* shall be proclaimed a word without a meaning in all the languages of the earth, and when the power of emancipation shall be extinguished in Universal Freedom. To share in the jubilant chorus of that day, if my voice could burst from the cerements of the tomb, it should be to shout Hallelujah! for the Lord God Omnipotent reigneth! let the earth rejoice and be glad!

John Quincy Adams.

CHRONOLOGY

NOTE ON THE TEXTS

NOTES

INDEX

Chronology

1767 Born July 11 in Braintree, Massachusetts, the second child of John Adams, a lawyer and rising patriot leader, and Abigail Smith Adams. (Father, born 1735, Harvard 1755, is the great-great-grandson of Henry Adams, who immigrated to Massachusetts from Somerset, England, in 1638. Mother, born 1744, is the daughter of the Reverend William Smith of Weymouth, and the granddaughter of Colonel John Quincy, a former Speaker of the Massachusetts House of Representatives. Parents married October 25, 1764. Sister Abigail "Nabby" born July 14, 1765.) Baptized July 12 and named for his ailing great-grandfather, who dies the next day.

1768 Father declines reelection as a Braintree selectman and moves family to a rented house on Brattle Street in Boston to accommodate increased legal practice and political activities. The first of five British regiments lands at Boston on October 1 to quell unrest arising from newly imposed imperial taxes and trade regulations. Sister Susanna born December 28.

1770 Sister Susanna dies on February 4. British soldiers under the command of Captain Thomas Preston fire on an aggressive crowd on March 5, killing five civilians in what becomes known as the Boston Massacre. Father agrees to defend Preston and eight soldiers after they are indicted for murder. Brother Charles born May 29. After trials in the autumn, Preston and six of the soldiers are acquitted, while the other two are convicted of manslaughter.

1772 Brother Thomas Boylston born September 15.

1773 In Boston, the ongoing imperial crisis escalates when on December 16 a large crowd boards East India Company ships carrying taxed tea—"that bainfull weed," as mother refers to it—and tosses 342 chests worth an estimated £10,000 into the harbor.

1774 In February father purchases his father's homestead (now known as the John Adams Birthplace) and the family again returns to Braintree. In response to the Boston Tea Party, the British Parliament passes Coercive Acts abrogating the Massachusetts colonial charter and closing the port of Boston effective June 1. Massachusetts House of Representatives calls on June 20 for a "Meeting of Committees from the several Colonies on this Continent" to address the crisis and elects father and four others as delegates. First Continental Congress opens in Philadelphia on September 5. In October, father is elected to Second Continental Congress, to meet in May 1775. John Quincy, who is principally educated by his parents, also begins to be tutored by his father's law clerks, John Thaxter, a cousin of his mother, and Nathan Rice. During his long absences from home, John Adams writes exhortatory letters to Abigail Adams about the education of "our lovely Babes": "Let us teach them not only to do virtuously but to excell. To excell they must be taught to be steady, active, and industrious."

1775 Parliament declares Massachusetts to be in a state of rebellion on February 9. Hostilities begin with skirmishes at Lexington and Concord on April 19. Second Continental Congress convenes on May 10. Father nominates George Washington as commander-in-chief of Continental Army, June 14–15. With mother at Penn's Hill in Braintree, John Quincy observes fires in Charlestown and hears the report of cannons at the battle of Bunker Hill on June 17, and is later grieved to learn of the death that day of the family's friend and "beloved Physician," Dr. James Warren, who has recently saved his badly fractured forefinger from amputation. Father signs Olive Branch Petition to George III, adopted by Congress on July 5.

1776 Father supports resolution introduced on June 7 stating that all political bonds with Great Britain ought to be dissolved and is appointed to committee to draft a declaration. Congress approves independence on July 2 and the Declaration of Independence is adopted on July 4. George III proclaims the thirteen colonies in rebellion on August 23. On July 12 John Quincy travels to Boston with mother and siblings, family servants, and several relatives to receive inoculation against smallpox, returning to Braintree in September. Father obtains leave from Congress, and reaches home in early November.

1777 Father leaves to rejoin Congress in January. On July 11, John Quincy's tenth birthday, mother gives birth to a sister, Elizabeth, who is stillborn. American forces achieve their first major victory of the Revolutionary War at Saratoga, New York, on October 17, bolstering American appeals for financial support from the French. Father again obtains leave from

CHRONOLOGY 659

Congress, and in November returns to Braintree intending to resume his law practice; instead he is nominated by Congress to replace Silas Deane as commissioner to France, joining fellow envoys Benjamin Franklin and Arthur Lee.

1778 France and the United States sign treaties of alliance and commerce in Paris on February 6. John Quincy sails for France with father on February 15; they land at Bordeaux on April 1 and join Franklin at Passy on April 9. He attends Monsieur Le Coeur's boarding school along with Benjamin Franklin Bache, Franklin's grandson, studying French (in which he will become fluent), Latin, dancing, drawing, music, and fencing. War begins between Great Britain and France on June 14. Congress abolishes the three-member diplomatic commission and appoints Benjamin Franklin sole minister plenipotentiary to France on September 14.

1779 Father learns of the termination of his mission on February 12 and leaves Passy with John Quincy on March 8, traveling to Nantes and Lorient in search of passage to America. In Nantes, they make the acquaintance of American merchant Joshua Johnson and his family before finally sailing for Massachusetts on June 17 aboard the French frigate *La Sensible*, arriving in Boston on August 3. Father is promptly named by Congress minister plenipotentiary to negotiate treaties of peace, amity and commerce with Great Britain. On November 12, John Quincy begins first diary as he prepares once more to accompany his father to Europe, sailing again on *La Sensible*, this time also with brother Charles, his father's private secretary John Thaxter, and legation secretary Francis Dana. Leaks force the ship to land at El Ferrol, on the northeast coast of Spain, on December 8, and the party travels overland to Paris.

1780 Arrives in Paris on February 8. Father is stymied in his diplomatic efforts by the French court and resolves to leave Paris on July 27 and travel with John Quincy and Charles to the Netherlands in search of support for the American cause. The boys are enrolled at Amsterdam's Latin School on September 30, then withdrawn in December to attend public lectures at the University of Leyden under the supervision of tutors Thaxter and Benjamin Waterhouse, an American medical student at the university. Congress appoints father to negotiate a treaty of amity and commerce with the Dutch Republic, December 29.

1781 Formally admitted as a scholar to the University of Leyden, January 10. On July 7, departs Holland with Francis Dana, who has been commissioned envoy to the court of the Russian empress Catherine the Great at St. Petersburg. Having passed through Berlin and Riga, arrives at St. Petersburg on August 29 and serves as Dana's private secretary and interpreter, French being the official language of the Russian court. (Catherine withholds recognition of the United States.) Brother Charles, desperately homesick, is sent back to the United States on August 12. French and American forces achieve a decisive victory over the British at Yorktown, Virginia, on October 19.

1782 Departs St. Petersburg for The Hague on October 3, traveling through Stockholm, Copenhagen, and Hamburg. On October 8, father signs Treaty of Amity and Commerce with the Dutch Republic, which had earlier recognized American independence, on April 19.

1783 Arrives at The Hague on April 21 and reunites with father there on July 22. Proceeds with him to Paris, where on September 3 John Adams signs definitive treaty of peace between Great Britain and the United States of America along with Benjamin Franklin, John Jay, and British negotiator David Hartley. Travels with father to England in October where they pass two months in and around London before visiting Bath in December.

1784 Accompanies father to The Hague, arriving on January 12. Mother and sister depart Boston, June 20, and arrive in London July 21. John Quincy is reunited with them there on July 30, carrying a letter from his father to his mother that reads, "I Send you a son who is the greatest Traveller, of his Age, and without Partiality, I think as promising and manly a youth as is in the World." Father arrives in London on August 7, and the family travels to Paris and settles in Auteuil, where John Quincy becomes acquainted with Thomas Jefferson, who like his father has been commissioned by Congress to negotiate commercial treaties with states in Europe and North Africa. (John Adams will recall this period in an 1825 letter to Jefferson in which he refers to John Quincy as "our John": "I call him our John, because when you was at Cul de sac at Paris, he appeared to me to be almost as much your boy as mine.")

1785 On January 1, begins new diary ("Ephemeris. Volume 1.") in which he inscribes Voltaire's maxim *"La mollesse est douce et sa suite est cruelle*" ("Indolence is sweet, its consequences bitter"). Departs from Lorient for the United States aboard *Courier de l'Amérique*, May 21; arrives at New York on July 17 and at Boston on August 25. Meets with Harvard College president Joseph Willard on August 31, who grants admission but advises him to wait until the spring to begin classes. Resides with mother's sister Elizabeth and her husband, the Reverend John Shaw of Haverhill, Massachusetts, who have been caring for younger brothers Charles and Thomas.

1786 Matriculates on March 15 as a junior at Harvard, which waives tuition fees for him and his brother Charles, a freshman, in recognition of their father's public service. In London, where father is the first U.S. minister to the Court of St. James's, sister Nabby marries Colonel William Stephens Smith, secretary to the American legation, on June 12. Adams is alarmed in the autumn by reports of the wave of agrarian protests in the western part of Massachusetts that becomes known as Shays's Rebellion.

1787 Graduates from Harvard on July 16 as a member of Phi Beta Kappa. Delivers senior oration "Upon the importance and necessity of public faith, to the well-being of a Community." Dr. Jeremy Belknap arranges for publication of the oration in the *Columbian Magazine* in September. Begins clerkship in the law offices of Theophilus Parsons in Newburyport, Massachusetts, in September. Expresses skepticism regarding the proposed U.S. Constitution in October. Parents arrange for the purchase of the Vassall-Borland house in the North Precinct of Braintree, known as the "Old House," in preparation for their return from Europe. (North Precinct reincorporated as Quincy in 1792, in honor of maternal great-grandfather.)

1788 Massachusetts ratifies the U.S. Constitution, February 6. Parents arrive in Boston on June 17, and John Quincy joins them at their new estate in Braintree in October.

1789 On February 4, George Washington is elected president of the United States, receiving the votes of all sixty-nine electors, and John Adams is elected vice president with thirty-four electoral votes; they are sworn in at New York City, the temporary federal capital, on April 21.

1790 Becomes increasingly enamored with sixteen-year-old Mary Frazier of Newburyport. Admitted to the bar on July 15 and opens law office at 23 Court Street in Boston on August 9.

1791 The first American edition of Thomas Paine's *Rights of Man* is published in May with a prefatory letter by Thomas Jefferson referring to "political heresies which have sprung up among us," an obvious allusion to "Discourses on Davila," a series of newspaper essays (April 1790–April 1791) in Philadelphia's *Gazette of the United States* highly critical of the French Revolution and unbalanced democracy; though anonymous, the Discourses are widely understood to be the work of Vice President Adams. John Quincy responds by publishing under the pseudonym "Publicola" eleven letters critical of Jefferson and Paine in Boston's *Columbia Centinel*, June 8–July 27; these are soon reprinted throughout the country.

1792 On December 5, George Washington is reelected as president, again unanimously, with 132 electoral votes, and John Adams is reelected as vice president with 77 votes. John Quincy publishes three essays as "Menander" in defense of theatrical performances, then prohibited in Massachusetts, in the *Columbia Centinel*, December 19–22. He writes, "no obedience is due to an unconstitutional act of the legislature."

1793 Revolutionary France declares war on Great Britain and the Netherlands on February 1; President Washington issues proclamation of neutrality on April 22. John Quincy writes three essays as "Marcellus" in defense of American neutrality published in the *Columbia Centinel*, April 24–May 11. Delivers annual Fourth of July oration in Boston, which is published as a pamphlet. Publishes five more essays as "Columbus" in the *Columbia Centinel*, November 30–December 18, denouncing "the intrusion of a foreign influence into the administration" of American affairs. Like his December "Barneveld" essays, in which he defends the president's right to "receive and dismiss foreign ministers and consuls," these essays are written in response to the controversial mission of Edmond-Charles Genêt, the first minister sent to the United States from the new French Republic; their authorship is widely known, and they bring John Quincy to the president's attention.

1794 Nominated minister resident to the Netherlands by President Washington on May 29 and unanimously confirmed by the Senate the following day. Departs Boston for Philadelphia, June 30. Receives commission from Secretary of State Edmund Randolph on July 11, at Philadelphia. Sails with brother and secretary Thomas Boylston aboard *Alfred* from Boston to England en route to The Hague, September 15. In

London in October, meets with and delivers papers to Chief Justice John Jay, who has been dispatched by the president to negotiate a treaty with Great Britain amid rising tensions over neutral rights and other unresolved issues between the two countries. Arrives at The Hague on October 31. Presents credentials to Stadtholder Prince William V, November 15. Jay's Treaty signed November 19.

1795 William V flees to England on January 18 in the face of a French-supported uprising that results in the proclamation of the Batavian Republic the following day. Brother Charles marries Sarah Smith, sister of William Stephens Smith, in New York, August 29. John Quincy departs for London October 22 to ratify Jay's Treaty in the absence of the U.S. minister to Great Britain, Thomas Pinckney. Regularly visits the family of Joshua Johnson, now American consul at London, and becomes acquainted with his daughters.

1796 Attends audience with George III, January 9. Sits for portrait by John Singleton Copley, begun February 11, which he will regard as one of the few successful likenesses taken of him. Courts and becomes engaged to Louisa Catherine Johnson, born February 12, 1775, daughter of Maryland native Joshua Johnson and Englishwoman Catherine Nuth, but declines to set a wedding date. Departs London on May 28 and arrives at The Hague on May 31. Nominated by President Washington to be minister plenipotentiary to Portugal, May 30. On December 7, John Adams receives seventy-one electoral votes and is elected president of the United States; Thomas Jefferson, leader of the opposition party, receives sixty-eight electoral votes and becomes vice president.

1797 Father is inaugurated as president on March 4. Receives final orders to depart for Portugal. On July 26, marries Louisa Catherine Johnson at the parish church of All Hallows Barking, London. Though many of his belongings have already been dispatched to Lisbon, is nominated by his father to serve instead as minister plenipotentiary to Prussia and is confirmed by the Senate 19–9. Former schoolmate Benjamin Franklin Bache accuses the Adamses of nepotism in the Philadelphia *Aurora*. Johnson family leaves for the United States; Joshua Johnson's bankruptcy is revealed as creditors dun his new son-in-law, who does not receive promised marriage settlement. John Quincy, Louisa Catherine, and Thomas Boylston arrive at Berlin on November 7, just nine days before the king of

Prussia, Friedrich Wilhelm II, dies. On November 30, Louisa Catherine suffers the first of many miscarriages. John Quincy is elected to the American Academy of Arts and Sciences.

1798 Louisa Catherine loses pregnancies in the spring and summer. Amid ongoing violations of American neutral rights by the warring European powers, the revelation of the "XYZ" Affair stirs American public opinion against France. Congress authorizes the navy and armed merchant vessels to capture armed French ships, July 9. John Quincy devotes much time to the study of German. Louisa Catherine succeeds charmingly at the Prussian court, while John Quincy and his mother Abigail worry that she will be "allured by the splendor."

1799 Signs renewed Treaty of Amity and Commerce with Prussia on July 11 before embarking with Louisa Catherine on four-month tour of Bohemia and Saxony. Begins work on a translation of *Oberon*, German epic poem by Christopher Martin Wieland; it will be completed the following spring, but remain unpublished until 1940. George Washington dies on December 14.

1800 Louisa Catherine endures another miscarriage in January. President Adams persists in his determination to avert open war with France by dispatching a peace mission to Paris, provoking the anger of Federalists, especially those in the cabinet. Ensuing protests result in the president demanding the resignations of Secretary of State Timothy Pickering and Secretary of War James McHenry. In June, Alexander Hamilton meets with New England Federalists to persuade them to support Charles Cotesworth Pinckney for president rather than Adams. From July 23 to September 24, John Quincy and Louisa Catherine tour Silesia. Hamilton publishes pamphlet on October 24 calling John Adams "unfit for the office of chief magistrate." Brother Charles dies of complications from alcoholism in New York on November 30. Presidential electors meet December 3. Aaron Burr and Thomas Jefferson each receive seventy-three electoral votes, defeating John Adams who receives sixty-five votes. John Quincy publishes translation from the German of Friedrich von Gentz, *The Origin and Principles of the American Revolution*, which argues that the American and French Revolutions had nothing important in common.

1801 "Letters from Silesia" and a translation of "The Thirteenth Satire of Juvenal" are published in the inaugural issue of *The*

Port Folio, January 3, 1801; the former will be reprinted as a book in 1804. Jefferson is elected president by the House of Representatives after thirty-six ballots and Aaron Burr becomes vice president. Recalled by father from Prussia. Jefferson is inaugurated March 4; John Adams does not attend. In Berlin, on April 12, the Adamses' first child is born, and named for George Washington: "I know not whether upon rigorous philosophical principles it be wise to give a great and venerable name to such a lottery-ticket as a new-born infant." The family departs Berlin June 17 and sails from Hamburg to Philadelphia aboard *America*. While Louisa Catherine and George proceed to her family in Washington, John Quincy continues on to Quincy, where on September 21 he is reunited with his parents for the first time in seven years. In October dines at Executive Mansion with President Jefferson and visits Martha Washington and family at Mount Vernon, October 27–28. Moves to Boston to reestablish law practice in November. Louisa Catherine travels to Boston later, and meets the Adams family for the first time on November 25.

1802 Joins Society for the Study of Natural Philosophy and attends his first meeting on January 7. Elected to the Massachusetts state senate as a Federalist in April. Writing in the guise of Thomas Paine, publishes in the October 30 edition of *The Port Folio* a mock-Horatian ode ridiculing Thomas Jefferson's relationship with Sally Hemings. Publishes *An Address, to the Members of the Massachusetts Charitable Fire Society* and *An Oration, Delivered at Plymouth, December 22, 1802. At the Anniversary Commemoration of the First Landing of Our Ancestors, at that Place.* Loses election to U.S. House of Representatives for the Boston district by fifty-nine votes in November.

1803 Appointed United States senator by the Massachusetts senate on February 3 to fill an unexpired term lasting until 1809, and is soon joined by fellow senator Timothy Pickering in the Massachusetts delegation. Son John Adams II born July 4. After his parents lose $13,000 in the failure of a London bank, Adams works tirelessly to compensate against these losses, selling various family properties in installments. Great Britain declares war on Napoleonic France on May 18, once again bringing the issue of American neutral rights to the fore. Senator and Mrs. Adams arrive at Washington, October 20, and board with Louisa Catherine's sister Ann and her husband, Walter Hellen. Supports House bill funding the necessary bonds to purchase Louisiana in November, breaking with Pickering and other Federalists.

1804 Sides with Federalists against Republican efforts to impeach federal judges. Spends the summer in Quincy reviewing the record of U.S. laws enacted since 1789, while Louisa Catherine and children remain in Washington near her Johnson and Hellen relations. Writing as "Publius Valerius," publishes "Serious Reflections, Addressed to the Citizens of Massachusetts," a series of articles in the Boston weekly *The Repertory*, October 26–November 16, critical of the three-fifths clause of the Constitution and the resulting disproportionate power of southern slaveholders in the federal union.

1805 Family moves with Louisa Catherine's sister Eliza to Quincy when the Senate goes into recess. Brother Thomas Boylston marries Ann Harrod of Haverhill, May 16. Adams becomes first Boylston Professor of Rhetoric and Oratory at Harvard, June 26.

1806 Sons George and John remain in Quincy with grandparents. Member of committee that presents, on February 5, three resolutions to the Senate protesting British captures and condemnations of American vessels, calling on President Jefferson to demand restoration and indemnity and recommending nonimportation of British goods. Supports Non-Importation Act of April 15. Begins lectures at Harvard during the long congressional summer recess (May to October). Louisa Catherine, pregnant, remains in Washington; on June 22 she delivers a son, stillborn. Adams receives honorary Doctor of Laws degree from the College of New Jersey (Princeton).

1807 Proposes resolution for a national plan of internal improvements in February. Again as "Publius Valerius," publishes a series of articles in *The Repertory* concerning the *Chesapeake-Leopard* affair of June 22, when the USS *Chesapeake*, in international waters having just departed from Norfolk, Virginia, was fired upon and four of its crew were seized by HMS *Leopard*; he is the sole Federalist to participate in a meeting at the Massachusetts State House that resolves to support the Jefferson administration in response to the affair, which, he will later recall, marks the beginning of "the really important period of my life." Son Charles Francis born, August 18, named for his deceased uncle, and for Francis Dana. Departs, with Louisa

Catherine and infant Charles for Washington in October. Professing to place the country's welfare over partisan or sectional interests, Adams is the sole Federalist to vote for the administration's Embargo Act, December 18.

1808 Attends the Republican Party caucus in Boston, January 23. Discusses foreign affairs with President Jefferson, March 15. On June 3, six months ahead of schedule, the Federalist-controlled Massachusetts state legislature elects James Lloyd to replace Adams at the end of his term, and forwards positive instructions to vote to repeal the Embargo; faced with this clear repudiation, Adams resigns from the Senate, June 8. Publishes *A Letter to the Hon. Mr. Harrison Gray Otis . . . on the Present State of our National Affairs*, explaining his support of the Jefferson administration. Continues lectures at Harvard.

1809 Leaves for Washington to represent clients before U.S. Supreme Court. In March, serves as one of three chief lawyers for the appellee in *Fletcher v. Peck*, a dispute over the validity of the Georgia law abrogating the Yazoo Land Act of 1795, by which the state legislature had previously granted some 54,000 square miles in present-day Alabama and Mississippi. The case results in a landmark decision in which the Court strikes down a state law for the first time. Attends the inauguration of James Madison on March 4; meets with the new president two days later and learns he will be nominated as minister to Russia. Publishes *American Principles. A Review of the Works of Fisher Ames* in the *Boston Patriot* in April and as a pamphlet in June; its vigorous critique of Federalism, as embodied in the career and writings of the deceased Massachusetts senator, marks his final break with the party that had elevated him into national politics. Appointment as the nation's first minister plenipotentiary to Russia confirmed by Senate, June 27. Departs for Russia aboard *Horace* on August 5, accompanied by his wife, youngest son Charles, sister-in-law Catherine "Kitty" Johnson, and nephew and secretary William Steuben Smith; his two oldest sons, George and John, remain in Massachusetts in the care of relatives. The party arrives at St. Petersburg, October 23. Begins cordial diplomatic relationship with Russian chancellor Count Nikolai Petrovich Rumiantzov. Has first audience with Czar Alexander I on November 5.

1810 As Adams settles into the diplomatic routine in Russia, a two-volume edition of his *Lectures on Rhetoric and Oratory,*

Delivered to the Classes of Senior and Junior Sophisters in Harvard University is published in Cambridge. (John Adams will send a set to Thomas Jefferson as a kind of peace offering on January 1, 1812, renewing their correspondence after years of estrangement.)

1811   At mother's behest, Adams is appointed by President Madison an associate justice of the Supreme Court on February 22, and confirmed by Senate. But he declines the appointment when he learns of it, preferring to remain at his post in St. Petersburg. Daughter Louisa Catherine Adams born August 12.

1812   Over united Federalist opposition, the Republican majority in Congress votes to declare war on Great Britain, June 17, citing impressment of American sailors under the British orders-in-council as the principal grievance, and President Madison signs the act the following day. Napoleon invades Russia, June 24. An American army invades Upper Canada, July 12, but is repelled by British forces and their Indian allies, who in turn take possession of Detroit and other key posts in the Old Northwest. Undersupplied French forces occupy Moscow on September 14, and shortly after are forced to begin a disastrous retreat. Daughter Louisa Catherine dies, September 15. Last French troops depart Russia, December 14.

1813   In March, the Madison administration embraces a Russian offer of mediation with Great Britain and dispatches Secretary of the Treasury Albert Gallatin and Federalist senator James A. Bayard of Delaware to St. Petersburg to join Adams for negotiations; the pair are en route before news arrives that British cabinet has declined the mediation. Sister Nabby dies of cancer at the Old House on August 15. In the autumn another major American offensive into Canada, this time aiming for Montreal, ends in failure.

1814   When Britain signals its willingness to enter into direct talks, Adams is appointed in January as chief negotiator of a five-member commission comprising Gallatin, Bayard, Henry Clay of Kentucky, and Jonathan Russell of Massachusetts. Travels alone from St. Petersburg to Ghent, April 18–June 24. Negotiations begin on August 8, and the British plenipotentiaries lay down aggressive terms reflecting their stronger military hand. On August 24 and 25, British forces occupy Washington and burn the capital's public buildings. A similar assault on Baltimore is repulsed by American defenders, September 13–14. That same month, British naval and land forces take control of more than a hundred miles of the Maine coast, from Eastport to Castine, but a large British invasion of northern New York is turned back at Plattsburg. By early December, pressed by bad news from North America and by demands for tax relief at home, the British government resolves to extricate itself from the American war. The Treaty of Peace and Amity between His Britannic Majesty and the United States of America, signed on December 24, does not address the issue of impressment and restores the status quo between the two nations prior to the war. Federalists convene in Hartford, Connecticut, December 15–January 5, to protest the war and a decade of Republican policies, and dispatch a delegation to Washington to present their grievances.

1815 On January 8, American forces led by General Andrew Jackson overwhelmingly defeat a British invasion force at New Orleans in the last major action of the War of 1812. Word of Jackson's victory and of the signing of the peace treaty at Ghent reaches Washington in the second week of February, at the same time as the delegation from Hartford arrives, a coincidence that serves to greatly discredit Federalist opposition to the war. Adams is appointed minister plenipotentiary to the Court of St. James's in February. He is reunited with Louisa Catherine and Charles Francis, who have made a hazardous overland winter journey from Russia, in Paris, March 23, and witnesses Napoleon's brief return to power (the Hundred Days). On May 7, receives word of his new commission. The family departs Le Havre for London, May 23; two days later they are reunited with sons George and John, just arrived from America, who have not seen their parents in almost six years. Presents credentials to Prince Regent, June 8. With fellow commissioners Clay and Gallatin, concludes commercial convention with Great Britain, July 3, the first accord between the two nations signed on the principle of diplomatic equality. Settles family at Little Ealing, a village outside London. Suffers a near-fatal injury while instructing George and John how to handle a pistol in October. In December, nephew John Adams Smith arrives in London to serve as private secretary.

1816 Begins negotiations with British foreign secretary Lord Castlereagh on northern borders and armaments, January 25. Brother-in-law William Stephens Smith dies June 10.

1817 Named secretary of state by new president James Monroe, March 6. Nomination confirmed by the Senate with only one dissenting vote. Receives notification of his appointment in a letter from the president, April 16. The Rush-Bagot agreement, limiting naval armaments on the Great Lakes, signed in Washington on April 29. Sails from Cowes on the Island of Wight aboard *Washington* on June 15 and arrives at Sandy Hook Lighthouse on August 6. Louisa Catherine suffers final miscarriage while at sea. Passes a month in Quincy before setting forth for Washington on September 9. Son George enters Harvard in August. Arrives at Washington on September 20 and swears oath of office two days later. Begins service in President Monroe's cabinet along with Secretary of the Treasury William H. Crawford, Secretary of War John C. Calhoun, Secretary of the Navy Benjamin Crowninshield, and Attorney General William Wirt. In December, Monroe orders General Andrew Jackson to subdue Seminole and Creek Indians in Georgia. American forces occupy Amelia Island, on southern border of Georgia, December 23.

1818 The new secretary of state and his wife become embroiled in a "visiting controversy" when members of Congress and their wives insist upon being called on at home before accepting invitations to parties at the Adamses' residence. Eventually, Louisa Catherine will become a leading hostess and serve effectively as her husband's "campaign manager" in Washington. Begins negotiations with Luis de Onís y González-Vara, Spain's envoy to the United States, to settle status of Florida and boundaries in the West. Andrew Jackson pursues his Indian targets into Florida, occupying Pensacola, St. Augustine, and St. Marks, and executes two British subjects, Robert Ambrister and Alexander Arbuthnot, believed complicit in fomenting Seminole attacks on American interests. In a July 15 cabinet meeting, Adams is alone in his defense of Jackson's actions. Instructs Richard Rush and Albert Gallatin in negotiations with Great Britain resulting in the Anglo-American Convention of 1818, which settles disputes relating to the status of enslaved people who escaped to the British during the War of 1812, American access to Canadian fisheries, and transatlantic commerce, and which establishes free and open access to the Oregon Country for both nations for ten years. Mother dies of typhoid fever on October 28. In November, sends and publishes letter of instruction to U.S. envoy George W. Erving in Spain, justifying Jackson's actions in Florida and demanding that Spain police Florida or sell it to the United States. In his diary, Adams begins to record emerging intrigues in the cabinet surrounding which of the officers will be put forward to succeed Monroe.

1819 Signs Transcontinental Treaty with Spain, alternatively known as the Adams-Onís Treaty, February 22, acquiring Florida for the United States and defining the boundary between the Spanish Viceroyalty of New Spain and the United States. Treaty is ratified unanimously by the Senate, but Spain's King Ferdinand VII withholds ratification to pressure the United States not to recognize the revolutionary states of South America. Son John enters Harvard in August. Controversy over admission of Missouri with slavery erupts in Congress. In cabinet, Adams declares the restriction of slavery in the territory to be constitutional, but avoids the issue in public. The young nation experiences its first major financial crisis, now known as the Panic of 1819, when, as foreign demand for American agricultural goods wanes with a return to normalcy in Europe, the postwar land boom collapses, and the country's overleveraged banking system follows suit. The poorly managed Second Bank of the United States has contributed to the situation first through inflationary lending and then by initiating a severe credit contraction in the summer of 1818.

1820 January to February, debates in Congress over admission of Missouri continue. Missouri Compromise admitting the district of Maine as a free state, the state of Missouri with slavery, and banning slavery north of 36°30' passes March 2. Purchases house on F Street in Washington in April. King Ferdinand VII ratifies Transcontinental Treaty on October 24. James Monroe, who is effectively unopposed, is reelected with 228 of 229 electoral votes. The sole dissenting vote, cast by New Hampshire elector William Plumer, is for Adams.

1821 On February 19, the Senate ratifies Adams-Onís Treaty for a second time, this time after rejecting a proposal by Henry Clay demanding that Spain cede Texas. Treaty proclaimed on February 22. Submits his exhaustive "Report Upon Weights and Measures" to the Senate on the same day, and it is later published. Asserts the justness of colonial revolutions for independence in a Fourth of July oration delivered in the House, later published as *An Address, Delivered at the Request of a Committee of the Citizens of Washington . . . on the Fourth of July, 1821*, while warning of British designs and defending policy of neutrality against calls by Clay and others for the United States to involve itself in liberal movements in South America and Europe. Son George graduates from Harvard in August. On September 16, Czar Alexander issues a ukase restricting to Russian subjects whaling, fishing, and all other industry in Russian territory on the northwest coast of America, and prohibiting the approach of foreign vessels within one hundred Italian miles of Russian claims, at a degree of latitude farther south than the United States or Great Britain has ever conceded.

1822 On March 8, President Monroe signals to Congress his desire to recognize the independence of South American states. Congress appropriates funds for missions therewith, May 4. Treaty of commerce signed with France, June 24. Through spring and summer Adams engages in a newspaper controversy with fellow Ghent commissioner Jonathan Russell, a political ally of presidential aspirant Henry Clay; the exchange culminates in September with his publication of *The Duplicate Letters, the Fisheries, and the Mississippi*, which reveals that Russell has faked a letter purporting to show that Adams had sold out the interests of the West in favor of New England during the Ghent negotiations.

1823 On February 23, House of Representatives passes resolution calling upon President Monroe to negotiate with maritime powers for the abolition of the African slave trade. Congress also passes resolution calling for American ships to be granted equal standing in British colonial ports, after the British impose a discriminatory tax on U.S. tonnage. Adams sends a proposal to London for convention to discuss freedom of the seas, July 29, which the British government rejects. Attempting to make provision for a return to private life after the coming presidential elections, purchases Columbian Mills, a grist and flour mill in the District of Columbia, from wife's cousin George Johnson. At the request of President Monroe, Adams draws up general instructions for American ministers to South America directing them to uphold republicanism against monarchy, to support their separation from Europe, to be open to discussing a Pan-American congress, and to offer them favored-nation status in commercial treaties, April 30. Son John is expelled from Harvard for participating in a student rebellion. In August, Thomas Jefferson expresses his preference for William H. Crawford in the next presidential election. Crawford suffers a debilitating stroke in September. Adams receives on November 17 a note from the Russian government announcing its resolution, shared by other members of the Holy Alliance (Austria and Prussia), to strive against republican movements worldwide. In a series of cabinet meetings in November he outlines the principle that European powers must abstain from interfering in the independent states of the Americas, which the president incorporates into his December 2 addresses to Congress and which becomes known as the Monroe Doctrine.

1824 The Adamses host a ball in honor of General Andrew Jackson on the anniversary of the battle of New Orleans. Anglo-American Convention on the African slave trade concludes on March 13 with both parties agreeing to punish slave traders as pirates, to allow a reciprocal right of visit and search of merchant ships, to render captured ships to their home country, to leave individuals belonging to crews on accused vessels, and to hold ships' officers responsible for the prevention of resistance to the right of search and visit. William Crawford leads opposition to the convention, successfully attaching an amendment stipulating that ships on the American coast be exempt from search. Great Britain is unwilling to accept this amendment and the convention fails. Russo-American Convention signed on April 17. Russia agrees to abandon its claims in the Pacific Northwest south of 54°40'N and the United States agrees to prohibit sale of alcohol and firearms to native peoples in the region, a point first raised by Count Rumiantzov during Adams's residency at St. Petersburg. Negotiates new commercial treaty with France, June 24. In the November presidential election Andrew Jackson receives ninety-nine electoral votes, Adams eighty-four, Crawford forty-one, and Clay, now Speaker of the House, thirty-seven. No candidate receiving a majority, the election is sent to the House of Representatives, where members will vote by state for one of the top three candidates. John C. Calhoun is elected vice president.

1825 Clay, whose support as Speaker is widely seen as decisive in the forthcoming presidential election in the House, calls on Adams in Washington, January 9. Representative George Kramer anonymously accuses Adams and Clay of having struck a bargain in the January 28 edition of Philadelphia's *Columbia Observer*, and the *National Intelligencer* quickly picks up the story. Adams is elected president of the United States on February 9, receiving the votes of thirteen of twenty-four state delegations in the House of Representatives. Illinois, Maryland, and Louisiana defect from Jackson and Clay brings the votes of Kentucky, Ohio, and Missouri to Adams. On March 3, Senate consents to Treaty of Indian Springs, signed by two United States commissioners and a rump group of Creek leaders; it stipulates the exchange of all Creek lands in Georgia for equal acreage west of the Mississippi, plus a bonus of $400,000 and annuities. Adams is inaugurated on March 4 and appeals for national unity and the final extirpation of the "baneful weed of party strife." Cabinet consists of Secretary of State Henry Clay, Secretary of the Treasury Richard Rush, Secretary of War James Barbour, Attorney General William Wirt, Postmaster General John McLean, and Secretary of the Navy Samuel L. Southard. Son John serves as private secretary. Ratifies the Treaty of Indian Springs despite charges by Creek leaders that it is unjust and fraudulent. Sends orders to Major General Edmund P. Gaines, already in Georgia to investigate, to impose a moratorium on the survey of Indian lands. Georgia governor George Troup demands the recall of Gaines. After meeting with a delegation of Creek leaders, Adams determines that a new treaty must be negotiated to supplant the previous one. Almost drowns while taking morning swim in Potomac River, June 13. First of several acts passed by Parliament nearly shuts down U.S. trade in the British Caribbean, June 27. Spends part of the summer with father in Quincy. Charles Francis graduates from Harvard in August. Sends message on State of the Union to Congress, December 5. "Liberty is power," he tells Congress, recommending, among other measures, the establishment of a Department of the Interior, the founding of a national naval academy and a national university, a uniform national bankruptcy law, more effective patent laws, and a vigorous system of internal improvements. Nominates a mission to attend the Congress of Panama, December 26. Congressional opposition delays confirmation of appointments; in the end, one U.S. delegate arrives after the conclusion of discussions, while the other dies en route.

1826 Creek leaders sign Treaty of Washington on January 24. This second treaty cedes all Creek lands east of the Chattahoochee River and guarantees to the Creeks lands not ceded. Resolution introduced by Senator Martin Van Buren condemns Adams for accepting invitation to Panama Congress without consulting Senate, February 15. Nominates Robert Trimble of Kentucky to the Supreme Court, April 11. Son George, who struggles with alcoholism and depression, is elected to the Massachusetts House of Representatives, and serves only one year. Both John Adams and Thomas Jefferson die on July 4, the fiftieth anniversary of independence. Adams spends part of summer and early fall vacation arranging father's estate in Quincy. Governor Troup ignores the Treaty of Washington and sends surveyors to Creek lands immediately after September 1, the date prescribed in the Treaty of Indian Springs. In a cabinet meeting, Adams is advised to order troops to Georgia, but demurs in the face of Troup's pledge to resist. William Morgan, a disgruntled Mason from Batavia, New York, is abducted and likely murdered by a band of Masons on September 18. The Masonic Order fails to condemn the act and an anti-Masonic movement begins in western New York. Adams becomes a communicating member of the Congregational Church of Quincy, October 1. Convention signed with Great Britain to pay for enslaved people "carried off" during War of 1812, November 13.

1827 On February 5, Adams sends a message to Congress explaining his desire to avoid violent conflict in Georgia and calling upon Congress to enact expedient legislation. Congressional committee proposes to purchase title to all Indian lands in Georgia and to maintain the Treaty of Washington in the interim. Governor Troup declares Georgia will fight federal troops if sent to Georgia. Controversy over the administration's tariff bill, which increases the schedules in place since 1816, ends with a tie-breaking vote by Vice President Calhoun in the Senate against the tariff, March 1. On May 5, Andrew Stevenson of Virginia is elected Speaker of the House, cementing the loss of pro-administration majorities in both houses of Congress.

1828 On February 25, son John marries his cousin Mary Catherine Hellen, who had previously been engaged to older brother George. On April 8, delivering documents to Congress in his capacity as his father's secretary, John has his nose pulled by journalist Russell Jarvis, an assault that nearly precipitates a duel. Signs into law on May 19 a protective tariff initiated by Van Buren and anti-tariff Democrats, called the "tariff of abominations" because its schedule was designed to be so prohibitive as to ensure its defeat. Breaks ground for Chesapeake and Ohio Canal, July 4. Presidential election is held from October 31 to November 5. Andrew Jackson receives 178 electoral votes, while Adams receives 83. Granddaughter Mary Louisa, first child of John and Mary Catherine, born December 2. Engages in public controversy with Virginia senator William Branch Giles over his actions as a senator during Jefferson's administration. Letters between Adams and his antagonists in New England are published by Federalists as *Correspondence Between John Quincy Adams, Esquire . . . and Several Citizens of Massachusetts* early the next year. Writes but withholds from the press a lengthy review of the actions of Massachusetts Federalists before and during the War of 1812; it is eventually published with the correspondence by grandson Henry Adams as *Documents Relating to New England Federalism, 1808–1815* (1877).

1829 Charles Francis is admitted to the Massachusetts bar in January. The Adamses move from the Executive Mansion to a residence on Meriden Hill, a mile to the north. Drafts the beginning of history of political parties in the United States and commences work on a biography of John Adams, both left incomplete. Traveling from Boston to Washington to join the family, son George disappears from a steamship in Long Island Sound on April 30, an apparent suicide. His body is discovered on City Island, New York, on June 10. Adams returns to Quincy. Charles Francis marries Abigail Brooks, daughter of wealthy Massachusetts merchant Peter Chardon Brooks, September 3. Returns to Washington, joining Louisa Catherine, John, Mary Catherine, and Mary Louisa, December 5.

1830 Elected to Board of Overseers of Harvard University. Writes lengthy essays on the Russo-Turkish War and on Greece for *The American Annual Register.* Returns to Quincy with Louisa Catherine in May. Granddaughter Georgiana Frances, John and Mary Catherine's second child, born September 10. Nominated as a candidate for the House of Representatives at a National Republican convention in Halifax, in Plymouth County, Massachusetts, October 12. Election is held on November 1. Adams receives three fourths of all votes cast and is elected to represent Massachusetts's Eleventh District in the Twenty-Second Congress.

1831 Publishes epic poem *Dermot Mac Morrogh, or The Conquest of Ireland; An Historical Tale of the Twelfth Century. In Four Cantos* in April. Attends an Anti-Masonic Convention at Faneuil Hall in May. Responding to the national crisis that has arisen from South Carolina's stated intention to nullify the Tariff of 1828 as unconstitutional, delivers Fourth of July address at Quincy in which he refutes the doctrine of state nullification. Arguing that the Union began with the Declaration of Independence, which codified a previously existing Union and never granted sovereignty to the separate states, he declares "Independence and Union Forever!" From August through September, writes a series of letters to various correspondents confirming his anti-Masonic leanings. Louisa Catherine, first child of Charles Francis and Abigail Brooks, is born August 13. Delivers a eulogy to James Monroe at Boston, August 25, subsequently published, in which he further defines his nationalist interpretation of the Constitution. Has an interview in September with William H. Seward in which he expresses his willingness to accept the Anti-Masonic nomination for president, though he later declines the nascent party's nomination for governor of Massachusetts. Meets twice in October with Alexis de Tocqueville and Gustave de Beaumont on their investigative tour of America. In November, Adams sells his shares in the Bank of the United States to divest himself "of all personal interest in it" before entering Congress, where he will argue for the renewal of its charter. Twenty-Second Congress begins December 5. Reluctantly accepts appointment as chair of the Committee on Manufactures and uses position to advance a balanced solution to the emerging sectional crisis over the tariff dispute. Presents fifteen petitions from citizens of Pennsylvania calling for the abolition of the slave trade and slavery in the District of Columbia, December 12.

1832 Brother Thomas Boylston dies, March 13, the second sibling to succumb to the effects of alcoholism. Serves on special committee to investigate the Bank of the United States. Writes supplement to committee's minority report defending the Bank against charges of usury and other violations of its charter. President Jackson signs compromise tariff bill on July 14; drafted by Adams, it becomes known as the Adams Tariff. On December 10, Jackson issues proclamation denouncing the doctrine of nullification and declaring acts of disunion treasonous.

1833 Speaking on February 4 against efforts to revise the 1832 tariff, Adams decries the "protection" of southern interests inherent in the Constitution's three-fifths and fugitive slave clauses and in the safeguards provided by the federal army against servile insurrection and hostile Indians. "My constituents possess as much right to say to the people of the South, 'We will not submit to the protection of your interests,' as the people of the South have the right to address such language to them." Writes minority report on the president's annual message, later published as the *Report of the Minority of the Committee on Manufactures, Submitted to the House of Representatives of the United States, February 28, 1833*, in which he examines the philosophical underpinnings of the tariff debates and those on other controversial issues, including internal improvements, the management of federal lands, and the national bank. He warns that continued acquiescence to southern control over the federal government threatens "not only the prosperity but the peace of the country" and will lead to "the most fatal of catastrophes—the dissolution of the Union by a complicated, civil, and servile war." At the urging of President Jackson, Congress, with Adams voting in the affirmative, passes the Force Bill on March 1, empowering the president to compel South Carolina to comply with federal law; South Carolina repeals its Nullification Ordinance on March 15, defusing the constitutional crisis ffor the moment. Adams is reelected to Congress on April 1, now from Massachusetts's Twelfth District, which he will represent in the Twenty-Third through Twenty-Seventh Congresses, increasingly aligning himself with the Whig caucus. John Quincy II, second child of Charles Francis and Abigail Brooks, is born on September 22. Adams survives derailment on the Camden and Amboy Railroad without injury, November 8. Stands as Anti-Masonic nominee for governor of Massachusetts. After no candidate receives a majority of votes, Adams withdraws to support the National Republican candidate, John Davis.

1834 Publishes a speech critical of President Jackson's intention to withdraw public deposits from the Bank of the United States in the *Daily National Intelligencer*, April 12. By the summer, John Adams II's descent into alcoholism has become painfully evident to the family. Under his mismanagement the Columbian Mills is an increasing drain on his father's finances. When John dies, October 23, Adams becomes guardian of his two daughters. Delivers an address to Congress on December 31 in honor of the recently deceased Marquis de Lafayette.

| | CHRONOLOGY | 679 |

1835 Grandson Charles Francis Adams Jr. is born on May 27. In December, Adams is appointed chairman of a special House committee established to make provision for the $500,000 bequest of Englishman James Smithson to the United States government "to found at Washington, under the name of the Smithsonian Institution, an Establishment for the increase and diffusion of knowledge among men." For several years following Adams will play a leading role in ensuring that the United States applies the legacy to Smithson's desired end.

1836 On January 22, in a three-hour speech on the House floor, defends Andrew Jackson's policy toward France regarding reparations for spoliations that occurred during the Napoleonic Wars and criticizes Daniel Webster and the Senate for their unpatriotic opposition. This speech earns Adams the sobriquet "Old Man Eloquent." On March 2, Texas declares independence from Mexico. On May 25, in remarks later published as *Speech of John Quincy Adams on the Joint Resolution For Distributing Rations to the Distressed Fugitives from Indian Hostilities*, again raises the possibility of wartime slave emancipation and denounces the Second Seminole War and the threat of a war with Mexico in defense of Texas as manifestations of a larger proslavery agenda. Also in May, Henry Laurens Pinckney of South Carolina proposes three resolutions denying the constitutional power of Congress to interfere with slavery in the states, suggesting Congress ought not interfere with slavery in the District of Columbia, where its power to do so is acknowledged, and advocating that all petitions, memorials, and resolutions relating to slavery be peremptorily tabled and not acted upon. Denied an opportunity to speak against these proposals, Adams demands, "Am I gagged or am I not?" During a roll call vote on the third resolution Adams protests, "I hold the resolution to be a direct violation of the Constitution of the United States, of the Rules of the House, and of the rights of my constituents." For each of the next four Congresses, despite his efforts and over his protests, the House will successfully reintroduce what becomes known as the gag rule. Delivers at Boston, September 27, and later publishes a much longer version of *A Eulogy on the Life and Character of James Madison*. In the presidential elections, Vice President Martin Van Buren, a Democrat, easily defeats Whig candidates William Henry Harrison and Hugh L. White.

1837 On February 6, Adams presents an abolitionist petition from nine ladies of Fredericksburg, Virginia, and asks Speaker James K. Polk to consider another petition "purporting to come from slaves" before presenting it; outraged southern members seek a motion of censure. When Representative John Mercer Patton of Virginia claims that the Fredericksburg petitioners were free blacks or mulattoes of "infamous character," Adams, observing "great resemblances between the progeny of the colored people and the white men who claim possession of them," levels the charge of infamy "on those who made it, as originating from themselves." On March 3, in the last act of the Jackson presidency, the United States recognizes the Republic of Texas. Gives *An Oration Delivered before the Inhabitants of the Town of Newburyport* on July 4, expanding on his interpretation of the Declaration of Independence and the Constitution. Writes and publishes a series of letters to his constituents defending his introduction of antislavery petitions. On August 4, Texas presents the Van Buren administration with a formal offer to annex itself to the United States. With the nation once again in the throes of a financial crisis, Congress convenes in special session on September 4 to consider a measure, known as the Sub-Treasury bill, to remove government funds from state banks, which were widely seen as contributing to the ongoing economic panic, and assign control of these monies to designated federal agents. In the autumn, involves himself in the controversial slave auction of Dorcas Allen and her children, and eventually contributes fifty dollars toward the purchase of their freedom; for Adams the episode exposes with new clarity the byzantine cruelty of slavery. Delivers an anti-Texas annexation speech in the House on December 13, describing the Texas revolution as in reality a revolt against Mexico's abolition of slavery in 1829, and prods the president to accept arbitration with Mexico.

1838 Grandson Henry Brooks, fourth child of Charles Francis and Abigail Brooks, is born on February 16. Overcoming long-held suspicions of the movement, Adams grows closer to abolitionists; Louisa Catherine corresponds with abolitionist Sarah Grimké. By parliamentary strategy, Adams seizes control of the House floor during the morning hour for committee business for three weeks from June into July, delivering a speech in which he describes a plot to annex Texas, upholds the propriety of women petitioning Congress, and declares slavery to be a sin.

1839 Introduces and sponsors an anti-dueling law for the District of Columbia originated in the Senate by Samuel Prentiss of Vermont. The Prentiss-Adams law is enacted on February 20. On February 25, asks leave of Speaker Polk to present resolutions for three constitutional amendments outlining his preferred program of emancipation: (1) to end hereditary slavery and for every child born after July 4, 1842, to be born free, (2) with the exception of the Territory of Florida, to henceforth never admit a slave state, and (3) to prohibit the slave trade in the District of Columbia after July 4, 1845. Writes and presents *The Jubilee of the Constitution. A Discourse Delivered at the Request of the New-York Historical Society* on April 30. In May and June, publishes letters explaining why he presents petitions on behalf of the abolition of slavery in the District of Columbia but will not support legislation for its immediate effect, citing the dictates of "justice, the Constitution, and prudence." On August 26, Thomas R. Gedney, commander of the USS *Washington*, boards and captures *La Amistad*, a Spanish schooner under the control of Mende captives (forty-nine adults and four children) recently transported from Africa, who have seized the ship and killed the captain and crew, sparing only José Ruiz and Pedro Montes so they could navigate the ship back to Africa. The ship is interned in New Haven, Connecticut, and the Mende captives are placed under court jurisdiction. Louisa Catherine and Mary Hellen continue to read, record, and file the large number of petitions directed to Adams. Elected to the American Antiquarian Society on October 23. Granddaughter Georgiana Frances dies November 20. In December, serves as Speaker of the House for ten days during a controversy over the organization of the House for the session.

1840 District court trial of the *Amistad* case is heard in New Haven and results in a January 23 ruling that the majority of the captured Africans be freed. Decision is appealed to the Supreme Court of the United States, scheduled to convene in January 1841. Suffers fall in the House chamber on May 18, dislocating his shoulder and badly wounding his head. In October, Adams agrees to help argue the *Amistad* case before the Supreme Court. In November, Charles Francis is elected to the Massachusetts House of Representatives. In the presidential election, the Whig candidate William Henry Harrison easily defeats the incumbent Martin Van Buren. The

Whigs also gain control of the House of Representatives and the Senate for the first time.

1841 *United States v. The Amistad* begins on February 22. Adams closes for the defense on February 24 by focusing on the underlying issue of whether the Africans were slaves under Spanish law. Adams is set to conclude his argument the following day but Justice Philip Barbour dies that night. The Court reconvenes on March 1 and Adams concludes by arguing that rendering the Africans to Spanish authorities would "disable forever the effective power of *habeas corpus.*" On March 9, Supreme Court rules in favor of the captured Mende and frees them. Just a month after his inauguration, President Harrison dies of pneumonia on April 4 and for the first time in the nation's history the vice president assumes the presidency. After the euphoria of Harrison's election, the unexpected advent of John Tyler of Virginia to the presidency and his subsequent repudiation of Whig principles leave the Whig Party in disarray. Grandson Arthur Adams, fifth child of Charles Francis and Abigail Brooks, is born on July 23. On September 4, Adams defends the British position in the extradition case of Alexander McLeod, a Canadian who participated in the sinking of the *Caroline*, an American vessel, during a cross-border action related to the 1837 rebellion against British rule in Upper Canada (Ontario). When the House rejects the British demand for McLeod's repatriation, Adams warns his colleagues not to allow a point upon which the United States is wrong to be entangled with one upon which it is right, the northeast boundary. Publishes poem, *The Wants of Man*.

1842 Speaks, January 4–6, against the bellicose rhetoric aimed at Mexico and Great Britain regarding the Texas question and again warns that slave emancipation could come by martial law. Presents a petition, January 25, from forty-six citizens of Haverhill, Massachusetts, requesting that Congress adopt "measures peaceably to dissolve the Union of these States" so that they might no longer be complicit in the perpetuation of slavery. An attempt is once again made to reprimand Adams, who vigorously defends the right of petition over several days of intense debate. Finally, on February 9, the motion of censure is tabled. This most recent effort to silence Adams draws national attention to the gag rule and to the right of petition as a matter of constitutional principle. Debates possibility of congressional emancipation during wartime with Henry Wise and Charles Jared Ingersoll, April 14. Elected to the Twenty-Eighth Congress as a Whig nominee in November, now representing Massachusetts's Eighth Congressional District; in the House as a whole, the Whigs lose their majority in dramatic fashion, with the Democrats gaining forty-nine seats. Publishes *The Social Compact, Exemplified in the Constitution of the Commonwealth of Massachusetts*, laying out his beliefs about democracy and his opposition to women's suffrage.

1843 Delivers address to the Massachusetts Historical Society on the seventeenth-century confederation of New England colonies on May 29. Tours western New York and Ohio in July to September on trip to lay cornerstone at the new observatory of the Cincinnati Astronomical Society; celebrated by crowds at many towns en route and also on return trip through Kentucky and Pennsylvania, October to November.

1844 In February, Adams proposes, as he had in 1838, resolution denying the power of the government to annex a foreign state or people, and to declare any attempt by "act of Congress or treaty" to annex Texas unconstitutional. On March 3, Adams and twelve other antislavery congressmen sign a public circular of protest, written by Adams, against Texas annexation. World Antislavery Convention of June 1843 in London adopts a resolution in his honor, citing "the moral heroism with which he has thrown himself into the breach." On October 7, Adams delivers an antislavery and anti-Texas address at a Whig rally at Tremont Temple in Boston and refutes the long-standing charge that he gave away Texas in the 1819 treaty with Spain. Adams's speech is reprinted around the North on the eve of the national election. Charles Francis is elected to the Massachusetts state senate. In the presidential election, Democratic candidate James K. Polk defeats the Whig Henry Clay. On December 3, Adams introduces a resolution to rescind the 25th Standing Rule (the gag rule), which the House adopts by a vote of 105 to 80. Writes in his diary that night, "blessed ever blessed be the name of God!"

1845 Granddaughter Mary Gardner, sixth child of Charles Francis and Abigail Brooks, is born February 19.

1846 Grandson Arthur Adams dies from diphtheria on February 9. On February 19, Texas is formally annexed to the United States. Adams votes for the Wilmot Proviso, August 8, an attempt to ban slavery from any territory gained in the war with Mexico, which has begun in April. On August 27, he presides over a civic meeting protesting the rendition of a fugitive slave at Faneuil Hall. Is reelected to Congress in November. Suffers a stroke on November 20 that leaves him partially paralyzed.

1847 Speaks in the House against proposal to provide indemnity to the owners of the *Amistad* in March and the proposal is defeated 94–28. On May 11, Adams is one of only fourteen congressmen to vote against a bill authorizing President Polk to pursue war with Mexico. Presents two petitions for peace with Mexico on December 20.

1848 Suffers a cerebral hemorrhage and collapses in the House of Representatives on February 21. He is carried to the Speaker's chamber where he dies on February 23. His last words are variously reported as "This is the last of earth. I am content." and "This is the end of earth, but I am composed." His remains are interred temporarily in a vault in the Congressional Cemetery in Washington before being removed in March to Quincy, to be buried next to his parents. Brooks Adams, seventh child of Charles Francis and Abigail Brooks, born June 24. In November, Charles Francis runs as vice presidential candidate of the Free-Soil Party, an alliance of antislavery Whigs and Democrats.

Note on the Texts

John Quincy Adams was a varied and prolific writer, the author of more than a hundred published works on a wide range of topics, as well as a diary that runs to more than fifteen thousand closely written pages, extensive personal, diplomatic, and political correspondence, and many unpublished works in various stages of completion, including a biography of his father and a history of political parties in the early republic. Adams's published writings reflect his broad literary, religious, and scientific interests, and they include travel writings, works of translation, academic lectures, literary criticism, and even epic poetry. This volume collects the texts of twenty-one works selected to trace Adams's core political concerns over his half-century in the public eye. All the works were published contemporaneously in newspapers or pamphlets, or in some cases both. Two of the earlier works, serial essays ("letters") in a Boston newspaper, were published under pseudonyms. Except where otherwise noted and explained, the texts of the selections in this volume are taken from their first publications. By focusing on his published works, this selection reveals that whatever Adams's other limitations as a practical politician in an increasingly democratic society, he understood well the power of the printed word to establish and sustain his public profile and to convey his vision for the nation to whose service he dedicated his long life.

What follows is a brief account of the publication history of each of the works collected here, along with some details about its composition, dissemination, and reception. For a full listing of Adams's works, and suggestions for further reading, see *John Quincy Adams: A Bibliography*, compiled by Lynn H. Parsons (Greenwood Press: Westport, CT, 1993).

1: HARVARD ORATION | 1787

Few of the men who were until recently conventionally called the Founding Fathers themselves had sons of an age and in a position to possibly play a public role in the new nation. John Adams, with three college-age sons in 1787, was an exception. It is perhaps not surprising then that his eldest son's Harvard graduation oration should have attracted attention. Harvard's annual commencement was always a key event in the civic calendar of the Commonwealth of Massachusetts, with public officials, often including the governor, in attendance. Such was the case on July 18, 1787, when a twenty-year-old

John Quincy Adams delivered this oration. Also present was the Reverend Jeremy Belknap, Harvard Class of 1762, newly installed as the pastor at Boston's Long Lane (Federal Street) Church. A liberal Unitarian—a sect then just emerging—Belknap was also a highly regarded historian and man of letters, a member of both the American Philosophical Society (elected 1784) and the American Academy of Arts and Sciences (1785). (He would go on to cofound the Massachusetts Historical Society in 1791.) Impressed by Adams's oration, Belknap proposed that it be published in the *Columbian Magazine*, a Philadelphia monthly edited and printed by Charles Cist, Thomas Seddon, William Spotswood, and James Trenchard, to which Belknap was a contributor. "Highly honored" by the proposal, Adams sent Belknap a copy of the oration on July 30, though he requested that it be published anonymously and in conjunction with a classmate's poem, lest it "be considered a mark of presumption in me to assume a distinction, which others, much more meritorious, had declined through modesty." Belknap, replying on August 3, urged Adams to consent to publication without the poem (a copy of which he had trouble locating) and under his name, arguing that "the friends of Liberty and Virtue will have the farther Satisfaction to see the features of the Parent in the Son," and that the "Country will have a pledge of a succession of abilities in the same Family still to aid her Cause and espouse her Interest." Adams relented in a letter to Belknap three days later, and in his diary wrote that "I have ventured upon a step, which perhaps some persons may censure; but as the circumstances are I know not what else to do, and if I am justified in the minds of men, possessed of candid and liberal sentiments, I feel very indifferent to whatever may be said by people of another description." [John Quincy Adams Digital Diary, August 6, 1787. Hereafter, JQADD. All JQADD quotations are made by courtesy of the Massachusetts Historical Society.] Adams's oration was published in the September 1787 issue of the magazine (his name is misspelled in the table of contents as "Mr. John Quincey Adams"). The text of Adams's oration in the current volume is drawn from this published version, which differs in small ways from the manuscript version Adams included in his diary, reflecting changes he may have made before delivery or afterward in response to Belknap's solicitation. (The textual changes, which have been enumerated by the Adams Papers editors at the Massachusetts Historical Society, may be found at https://founders.archives.gov/documents/Adams/03-02-02-0002-0007.) The copy of the oration that Adams sent to Belknap was returned to him on October 7, 1822, in a letter from George M. Dallas, whose father Alexander, a cabinet secretary under James Madison, had earlier been an editor for the *Columbian Magazine*. In his diary that day Adams wrote:

Received a Letter from George M. Dallas of Philadelphia, enclosing a copy of the Oration, which I delivered, on the 17th of July 1787 at Commencement, upon taking my degree of bachelor of Arts. He says he found it among some of his late father's papers, but does not know how it came there—Nor do I: but it is the copy which at the request of the late Dr. Belknap, I furnished him, for publication, in a Monthly Magazine, then published at Philadelphia; and it was printed in the number for the Month of September 1787. I little thought of ever seeing the manuscript again—but the delivery of that Oration was one of the most memorable Events of my life—The incidents attending it were of a nature to make and leave a deep impression upon my mind. The appointment to deliver it was itself a high distinction—Yet it was but the second honour of the Class; and he who took the first, the preferred rival, sunk at the age of 35, to be forgotten—I reperused this production now with humiliation; to think how proud of it I was then, and how much I must blush for it now. [David Waldstreicher, ed., *John Quincy Adams: Diaries 1821–1848* (New York: Library of America, 2017), 31–32. Hereafter *JQAD2*.]

2: LETTERS OF PUBLICOLA | 1791

These essays were written in response to the first American edition of the first part of Thomas Paine's *Rights of Man*, which was published in Philadelphia by Samuel Harrison Smith in late April 1791. Smith's edition carried a commendatory note by Secretary of State Thomas Jefferson, who had read the first London edition of Paine's work. Jefferson's note, which he later said was included without his knowledge or consent, praised Paine's new book as an answer to "political heresies" that had sprung up in the new republic. Most astute readers took this to be an allusion to Vice President John Adams, whose recently published "Discourses on Davila" were critical of the French Revolution and of democratic systems of government unbalanced by some kind of aristocratic influence. (In a May 8, 1791, letter to President Washington, Jefferson referred to John Adams's "apostacy to hereditary monarchy and nobility.") Assuming the name Publicola, "friend of the people," the younger Adams took the pages of the Boston *Centinel*, a pro-administration newspaper published by Benjamin Russell, to mount a defense of his father. The series was published in eleven installments: I (June 8), II (June 11), III (June 15), IV (June 18), V (June 22), VI (June 29), VII (July 2), VIII (July 9), IX (July 13), X (July 20), and XI (July 27). The text in the current volume is drawn from this serial publication. Believed to be the work of the vice president himself, the "Letters of Publicola" were soon reprinted in newspapers throughout the country, most prominently in Philadelphia in John Fenno's *Gazette of the United States* from June 18 to

August 6. These publications fueled the emerging partisan divide between governing Federalists and opposition Republicans. Even as the series was still unfolding, Russell remarked in a preface to the July 2 installment that Publicola's "*animadverters*, not answerers, . . . swarm like *Bees*; and, like *Drone-Bees*, they only *buz*." The letters quickly made their way across the Atlantic where they were collected as a pamphlet and issued in multiple editions in London, Dublin, Glasgow, and Edinburgh. A Dutch translation was published in Dordrecht. The Edinburgh edition includes this note: "The following Letters were originally published (Summer 1791) in a Boston Newspaper, called the COLUMBIA SENTINEL, afterwards in New York and other American papers. In America, they are generally ascribed to JOHN ADAMS, the present Vice-President of the American States. They are now published here, and recommended to the serious attention of those who, with Mr PAINE and others, think Revolutions in Government so easily effected." As late as 1793, editions in Great Britain were still published under John Adams's name, though the February 1793 issue of *The European Magazine and London Review* included an anonymous attestation that John Adams was not the author. According to Charles Francis Adams, John Quincy Adams's son and the author/editor of his *Memoirs*, these various European editions were of dubious quality, "each differing materially from the other," a fact that had largely escaped John Quincy Adams's notice, and which Charles Francis discovered only when he came across various copies during his tenure as U.S. minister to Great Britain in the 1860s. As John Quincy Adams himself would write in his diary more than a half century after the fact, in a listing of his lifetime of publications: "The papers signed Publicola, in the Boston Centinel 1791. were republished in a pamphlet in England, but I was never able to procure a copy of it." [JQADD, September 4, 1845.]

3: LETTERS OF MARCELLUS | 1793

After the outbreak of a war in Europe that pitted France against an array of foreign powers, including Great Britain, President Washington issued a proclamation of neutrality on April 22, 1793. This action stirred considerable protest in the United States, particularly among Republicans sympathetic to the French cause and among New England seamen eager to engage in privateering. Adams, here writing as "Marcellus," had already submitted the first of these three essays before learning of Washington's proclamation, with which he was clearly sympathetic. Like the Publicola letters, the Marcellus essays were published in Benjamin Russell's *Columbian Centinel*. I (April 24), II (May 4), III (May 11). The third installment was also published in the

May 25 edition of the *Gazette of the United States*. This volume takes the serial publication in the *Columbian Centinel* as its text.

4: FOURTH OF JULY ORATION | 1793

On April 30, 1793, just days after the first of the Marcellus letters appeared in print—its authorship little in doubt—Adams was approached by a delegation of Boston's selectmen with the news that he had been appointed to deliver the town's official annual Fourth of July oration, a significant honor. Adams immediately set to work. On June 23, he reported in his diary that he was drafting a new "exordium," or introductory passage, for the address. Four days later, he wrote: "The day spent as usual—coming to the close of my oration, but obliged to write it over the third time." [JQADD, June 27, 1793.] On July 1, he rehearsed his delivery in front of two close friends. On the day itself, he presented his oration before a large audience assembled in Boston's Old South Meeting House. Its favorable reception relieved him. That afternoon, after the ceremony, he was guest of honor at a celebratory dinner (turtle soup was on the menu) and that evening he met Boston printer Benjamin Edes, "who was very solicitous to print." [David Waldstreicher, ed., *John Quincy Adams: Diaries 1779–1821* (New York: Library of America, 2017), 41. Hereafter *JQAD1*.] *An Oration, Pronounced July 4th, 1793, at the Request of the Inhabitants of the Town of Boston, in Commemoration of the Anniversary of American Independence* was published by Edes on July 13. A second edition followed that same year. This volume publishes the complete text of the first Edes edition.

5: PLYMOUTH ORATION | 1802

Adams recorded in his diary on August 3, 1802, that he accepted an invitation he had received from "the Committee of the town of Plymouth, to deliver their next Anniversary address, on the landing of our fore-fathers." Like the 1793 Fourth of July oration in Boston, this was a major honor. He delivered his address in Plymouth's meetinghouse a little after noon on December 22, speaking for an hour and ten minutes. As indicated on the title page, it was published by the printers John Russell and James Cutler at their office on Congress Street in Boston at the request of the same Plymouth town fathers who had invited Adams: James Thacher, William Jackson, and Joshua Thomas, a probate court judge who hosted Adams for breakfast on the morning of the commemoration. Adams likely delivered a manuscript copy of his address to Russell and Cutler soon after he returned to Boston on December 23. *The Boston Magazine* reported on January 1, 1803, that the oration was at press and due to be issued on January 3. The published pamphlet, *An Oration, Delivered at Plymouth, December 22, 1802. At the Commemoration of the First Landing of our Ancestors, at that Place*, carries an 1802 publication date. A subsequent edition was published in Plymouth in 1820 (the same year that Daniel Webster delivered his own famous Plymouth oration). Esteemed as a model both of historical inquiry and of oratory, Adams's address was excerpted at some length in Jedidiah Morse and Elijah Parish's *Compendious History of New England, Designed for Schools and Private Families* (Charlestown [MA]: 1804), 378–81, and republished in full in the fifth and final volume of E. B. Williston's *Eloquence in America* (Middletown, CT: 1827), V: 173–90. The present volume publishes the complete text of the Russell and Cutler first edition.

6: LETTERS OF PUBLIUS VALERIUS | 1806

After the close of the first session of the Eighth Congress in March 1804, the Massachusetts legislature (the General Court) instructed Adams, now a U.S. senator, together with the state's other senator, the arch-Federalist Timothy Pickering, to be prepared in the next session to introduce an amendment striking out the three-fifths clause in the U.S. Constitution. The General Court believed that in the absence of equitable direct taxation, which had been key to the compromise on representation struck at the Constitutional Convention, but which had failed to materialize in practice, the clause had resulted in an unjustified and disproportionate southern influence in the federal government. Adams drafted a speech in support of the amendment but never delivered it, perhaps because of a lingering anxiety about taking part in debate on the Senate floor as a relatively new member who felt inadequate as a public speaker. Instead, he took to his writing desk, crafting these "Serious Reflections, Addressed to the Citizens of Massachusetts," which were published serially in *The Repertory*, a Boston newspaper owned by the Federalist publisher and educator John Park. They appeared in the weeks before the state and national elections in November and December 1804. Written under the pseudonym "Publius Valerius," a call back to his earlier "Publicola" letters (both allude to the Roman leader Publius Valerius Publicola), the five-part series was issued as follows: I (October 26), II and III (October 30), IV (November 2), and V (November 6). The final installment conveys the substance of Adams's undelivered Senate speech. This volume presents the complete text of this serial publication. Twenty years later, visiting his father at his home in Quincy, Adams noted in passing in his diary that "General W[illiam]. H[yslop]. Sumner came and invited me to dine with him at Dorchester. He gave me the manuscripts of several papers written by me in the year 1804 and then published in the Repertory." [JQADD, September 10, 1824.] Manuscripts for three of the five installments are included in the Adams Papers collection at the Massachusetts Historical Society.

7: BOYLSTON ORATION | 1806

On June 26, 1805, Senator Adams learned that he had been named Harvard's first professor of rhetoric and oratory, an appointment confirmed by a visit from a committee of the college's board of overseers on August 1. "I mentioned to them the impossibility, I should be under of performing all the duties assigned to the professor in the Rules and Statutes; and that I could neither bind myself to residence, at Cambridge, or to attendance more than a part of the year. They supposed that the Statutes might be so modified, as to accommodate me in these particulars; and requested me to state my own wishes in this respect to the chairman of the Committee in a letter, to which I agreed." [*JQADI*, 124–25.] Even as negotiations continued, Adams began reading in earnest (burnishing his rusty Greek) to prepare for his lectures. By the time Adams returned to Washington in November, terms had been largely agreed upon. Adams completed a draft of this inaugural lecture on May 17, 1806, and at a ceremony at Harvard formally installing him on June 12 "I delivered the discourse I had prepared for the Occasion; it was well received; but the company present was very small—The business was concluded by a hymn sung." [*JQADI*, 133.] Five days later, Harvard student William Smith Jr., a relative on Adams's mother's side, "brought me an application from the Students at the University, for a copy of my last Week's discourse to be printed; which I agreed to furnish them." [JQADD, June 17, 1806.] The oration was published on July 1 by the Boston firm of Edmund Munroe and David Francis, which issued it simultaneously as a pamphlet and as a feature in the June issue of *The Monthly Anthology and Boston Review* (3: 288–95). This volume prints the complete text of the first edition of the Munroe and Francis pamphlet. Adams ultimately prepared thirty-six lectures for his course, which he taught until his appointment as U.S. minister to Russia in 1809 forced him to tender his resignation. Before departing for St. Petersburg, Adams arranged to have the lecture series published, with the inaugural oration appended as a preface. *Lectures on Rhetoric and Oratory, Delivered to the Classes of Senior and Junior Sophisters in Harvard University* was published in two volumes by the Cambridge printers William Hilliard and Eliab Wight Metcalf in 1810. (On January 1, 1812, John Adams sent a set to Thomas Jefferson, from whom he had been estranged for many years, thereby reigniting their correspondence: "As you are a Friend to American Manufactures under proper restrictions, especially Manufactures of the domestic kind, I take the Liberty of Sending you by the Post a Packett containing two Pieces of Homespun lately produced in this quarter by One who was honoured in his youth with Some of your Attention and much of your kindness." The books did not arrive with Adams covering letter, leaving the Sage of Monticello temporarily confused by Adams's wordplay.) The *Lectures* were reissued in a facsimile edition in 1962, edited by Jeffrey Auer and Jerald L. Banninga. In his introduction Auer posits that "the lectures represent the first attempt by an American to reunite rhetorical theory with classical doctrines."

8: LETTER TO HARRISON GRAY OTIS | 1808

Enacted by Congress in December 1807, President Jefferson's Embargo Act deeply divided both the nation and the Massachusetts congressional delegation. The Commonwealth's junior senator, Timothy Pickering, was adamantly opposed to the measure, and he took his case to the press in a public letter, dated February 16, 1808, which the Boston firm of Greenough and Stebbins issued in pamphlet form as *A Letter from the Hon. Timothy Pickering, a Senator of the United States from the State of Massachusetts, Exhibiting to his Constituents a View of the Imminent Danger of an Unnecessary and Ruinous War. Addressed to His Excellency James Sullivan Governor of the Said State*. Though the pamphlet's nominal addressee, the state's Republican governor, paid it little heed, Pickering's pamphlet was widely circulated, going through several editions. It is to this pamphlet that Adams responds here. He completed his response on March 31, 1808, and gave it to his cousin, William Smith Shaw, "with a request that he would get it printed immediately." [JQADD.] *A Letter to Mr. Harrison Gray Otis on the Present State of Our National Affairs; With Remarks upon Mr. Pickering's Letter to the Governor of the Commonwealth* was promptly published by the firm of David Everett and Isaac Munroe, editors of the *Boston Patriot*. The current volume takes this first edition as its text. More than twenty editions followed, along with numerous published responses, including the very hostile *Letter to the Hon. John Quincy Adams, Occasioned by His Letter to Mr. Otis* ([New York]: 1808), written by "Alfred," and *Remarks and Criticism on the Hon. John Quincy Adams's Letter to the Hon. Harrison Gray Otis* (Boston: Joshua Cushing, 1808) by Hamilton protégé William Colman. Adams's *Letter* was reissued sixteen years later in Baltimore with the following preface from the office of the *Baltimore Patriot*, dated July 28, 1824: "Since the publication of Col. PICKERING's Review of the Cunningham correspondence, in which Mr. ADAMS' letter on the Embargo, and Mr. ADAMS himself are animadverted upon, we have received many calls for the letter in question. It being almost entirely out of print, we determined to reprint it, and some time since, announced our intention to do so. Soon after this annunciation, we received in manuscript from Mr. ADAMS an APPENDIX, with permission to add it to our intended publication, which will be found at the close of this pamphlet." Adams's appendix, dated July 27, 1824, was one of the very few (frustratingly so from the perspective of his political supporters) public statements Adams issued in the months before the presidential election of 1824, and as such is worthy of notice. It reads as follows:

> On the 18th of December, 1807, Mr. Jefferson sent a *confidential* message to both houses of congress, recommending an immediate *embargo*; and enclosing two documents, one of which was a recent proclamation of the king of Great Britain, authorizing and commanding the impressment by his naval officers, of British seamen, from neutral merchant vessels, and the other a correspondence between General Armstrong, then our minister in France, and the French minister of foreign affairs, Champagny, shewing that the emperor Napoleon had finally determined to carry into full execution, without regard to the treaty between the United States and France, his Berlin decree of 21st November, 1806, which had for some months after it was issued, been suspended with regard to vessels of the United States.
>
> The attack by a British squadron upon our frigate Chesapeake, had very recently occurred, in consequence of which all British armed vessels had been interdicted from entering the ports of the United States. The British Orders in Council of 11th November, 1807, professedly retaliatory upon the French decree of Berlin, had issued, and were already announced in the newspapers of the United States, though not yet officially authenticated. The general state of our commercial affairs was momentous and full of alarm. The British government had disavowed the attack upon the Chesapeake, but instead of giving immediate satisfaction for it, had appointed Mr. Rose to come out upon a mission of subterfuge and prevarication concerning it, and *at the same moment* had issued without notification either to the government of the United States, or to their minister in London, the orders in council, which but for the embargo would, while Mr. Rose was amusing us with the fragrance of his diplomacy, have swept three-fourths of the tonnage of the United States into the ports of Great Britain for confiscation.
>
> It was in this state of things that the message recommending the embargo was received and discussion, *in secret session*, by the senate. The *only* motive for debating it with closed doors was the necessity, if the measure recommended was deemed proper, of adopting it

Immediately. Every hour of debate tended to defeat the object of the message. For the instant it should be known in the commercial cities that an embargo was impending, the spirit of desperate adventure would have rushed to sea, with every plank that could have been made to float; and the delay of a week in deliberation, instead of sheltering the property of our merchants from depredation, would only have cast it forth upon the waters to be intercepted by the cruizers of both the combating nations.

The message was referred, in senate, to a committee of five, of which general Samuel Smith, himself an eminent merchant, brother to the secretary of the navy, and in the full confidence of Mr. Jefferson, was chairman, and of which I was a member. The chairman proposed to the committee, to report a bill in compliance with the recommendation of the message. I objected that the two documents with the message were not sufficient to justify so strong and severe a measure as an embargo; and enquired, whether besides the general notoriety of the dangers, mentioned in the message, the executive had other reasons for the measure, which it might not be convenient to assign. The chairman said, it was expected, and hoped that the act would have a favourable effect, to aid the executive in the negociation with Mr. Rose; and also that it was intended as a substitution for the non-importation act, which had passed on the 18th of April, 1806, but pending the negotiations had been suspended until the 14th of December, 1807, only four days before the message. This act was itself nearly equivalent to a total commercial non-intercourse with Great Britain; and to have repealed, or longer suspended it at *that* time, would have been a surrender at discretion, upon *all* subjects of controversy, then in so high a state of aggravation, with that power. To these reasons I yielded, and the bill for laying the embargo was reported to the Senate with the *unanimous* assent of the committee.

The bill was opposed in the Senate very feebly upon its merits, and exclusively by the federal members, then only four in number. The principle [sic] effort made by them was to obtain *delay*, which would, as has been shown, have defeated in a great measure the object of the bill. They obtained against the bill only the vote of Mr. Maclay of Pennsylvania, and of Mr. Crawford, then a new member, but who afterwards constantly supported the adherence of the administration to the act, as long as it was continued.

In assigning to the Senate very briefly my reasons for assenting to the bill, and for the belief that it ought to pass without delay, I admitted that the two documents transmitted with the message, would not have been of themselves, to my mind, sufficient to warrant the measure recommended in it; but referring to the existing state of things, of public notoriety, and denominated in the message "*the present crisis*," I observed that the executive, having recommended the measure upon his responsibility, had doubtless other reasons for it which I was persuaded were satisfactory; that with this view, convinced of the expediency of the bill, I was also impressed with the necessity of its immediate adoption; that it was a time, not for deliberation but for action; and that I wished the bill, instead of lingering through the dilatory process of ordinary legislation, might pass through all the stages of its enactment in a single day. With these views a decided majority of the Senate concurred. The rule which required that bills should be read three times on three different days, was suspended; all motions of postponement were discarded, and the bill was passed in the Senate by a vote of 22 to 6.

My allusion to the recommendation of the executive upon his responsibility and to my confidence in it, was purposely made in general terms; but it had reference to the reasons which had been assigned to me in the committee, by the chairman. I deemed it less necessary to specify them, because as I have observed, the opposition to the bill upon its merits was exceedingly feeble; scarcely calling for an answer.

About two months after the embargo had been enacted, and while it was bearing with severe pressure upon the commercial, navigating and fishing interests of the north, Mr. Pickering wrote a letter to the governor of Massachusetts, for communication to the legislature, denouncing the executive and congress of the United States, for passing the embargo; and calling for the *interposition* of the commercial states to save the country from ruin. The governor sent it back to him, with a letter of rebuke for expecting him to make such a communication to the legislature. Mr. Pickering, apprehensive, as he says, that he should not obtain his object through the governor, sent a copy to his excellent friend, George Cabot, (SINCE PRESIDENT OF THE HARTFORD CONVENTION,) who after waiting a few days, finding that the original was not communicated to the legislature, *sent a copy to the printer.*

The governor of Massachusetts, in his answer to Mr. Pickering, had stated that my opinion had been and still was in favor of the embargo. Mr. Pickering replied, and in terms supported by his feelings at the time, charged me with having in the debate on the embargo, expressed a sentiment which resolved the whole business of legislation into the will of the executive. To support the charge, he quoted several words, which he said I used in the debate, and which detached from this context, and from the explanation I have now given them, might deserve all the severity of his commentary.

In the same letter Mr. Pickering explicitly admitted that I had never given him the slightest cause of offence, and that in five years of service together as Senators from the same state, "though often opposed in opinion on national measures, there had never existed for a moment any personal difference between us." I notice now this admission, merely to mark the period and manner in which this mutual respect and forbearance between us ceased, and to whom it was justly imputable.

On my part it did not cease even then. It was impossible to have framed a charge more destitute of foundation; more easily refuted; or more open to the chastisement of severe retaliation. Yet I took no public notice of it; nor shall I now go further beyond the simple declaration that *I never expressed or felt the sentiment* imputed to me by Mr. Pickering, than to observe, that if I had uttered it, and had been understood in the sense which he has given my words, it was his duty, and the duty of every Senator present, who so understood me, not only to have had my words taken down at the time, but instantly to have called me to order for using them. The words as Mr. Pickering professes to have understood them, were undoubtedly in the highest degree disorderly—and a decisive proof that they were not generally so understood is found in the circumstance, that no exception was taken to them at the time. It is a rule of the Senate and of all equitable deliberative assemblies, that exceptionable words shall not only be taken down at the time when spoken, but that he who speaks them shall immediately be called to account for, to retract, or to explain them. Had this rule been observed by Mr. Pickering, when called upon to explain what I meant by recommendation of the executive, upon his responsibility, and to the *other reasons*, which he might have, and which I had no doubt were satisfactory, I should have had the opportunity of giving the explanation herein contained, and of shewing that my words imported no sentiment even of improper deference for the opinions or wishes of the executive. But it is also a breach of order, to refer by way of censure, at one time, to words spoken at another; and a rule equally just that no member shall be called to account in any other place, for words spoken in the Senate. These rules are founded upon principles which every man of a fair and honorable mind feels himself bound to observe; and they apply with peculiar force to a debate with closed doors, which is in its nature secret and confidential.

The error of Mr. Pickering's charge consists in his connecting my expression of confidence in the recommendation of the executive, which I assigned as one of my reasons for agreeing to the act, with my argument for the necessity of despatch, which was founded in the nature of the act itself, and the portentous crisis of the times.

The reference to the recommendation of the executive was made in answer to the objection that the documents sent with the message did not justify the measure recommended in it. Knowing that there were other reasons, and referring to them for the justification of my own vote, both in committee and in the Senate, in favour of the bill, nothing could have been farther from my thoughts, as nothing would have been more in conflict with the whole tenour of my conduct through five years of active service as a member of the Senate, than the utterance of a sentiment of subserviency to the *will*, or even to the *wishes* of the executive.

The confidence in the executive which I avowed, was applicable to the particular circumstances of the time, and to the particular subject in discussion. Nor was that confidence misplaced. In the house of representatives the embargo message was debated three days on the merits—but after the three days the house came to the same conclusion at which the senate had arrived in four hours. It was a wise, a provident, and above all, a purely patriotic measure. The share that I had in it, and the part that I took in promoting it, remains among the transactions of my public life to which my memory recurs with the most gratifying recollections. Many other events have been less trying to the fortitude of adversity, and more favoured by the vicissitudes of fortune: but on no occasion has the consciousness of upright intentions, and a spirit independent alike of obsequiousness to executive will, and of factious opposition borne me with more firm and even step through the temporary furnace of affliction, and sustained me under the abandonment of friends, the alienation of popular favour at home, and all the obloquy that Mr. Pickering and his co-adjutors have from that day to this been able to conjure upon my head.

Between the *system of policy*, of which the embargo was a prominent measure, and that of which Mr. Pickering and his friend the president of the Hartford convention were the "pillars of state," the final and irrevocable sentence of time has now passed—I shall not dwell upon it.

If there be a lesson of political wisdom, which the people of this union have had cause to learn from their own experience, as well as from the uniform tenour of human history, it is that of carrying a temper of mutual forbearance, through all their divisions; of making the party feeling, which never can include more than a portion of the republic subordinate to the civic spirit which embraces the whole. In the collisions of political systems, it is the duty of the citizen to take his stand upon deliberate conviction, and to pursue his principles, regardless of consequences to himself. But when the conflict is past, and the contest of *principle* is at an end, both parties, and above all, the prevailing party, should remember, and practice upon the maxim of the Roman republic, that in civil dissensions, success was but a lesser evil than defeat, and that no honours of triumph could ever be awarded to victory.

JOHN QUINCY ADAMS

9: DEFENCE OF GENERAL JACKSON | 1818

Andrew Jackson's actions in Florida in the spring of 1818 (see page 181) provoked a series of four diplomatic notes from Spanish foreign minister José García Pizarro, which arrived in Washington in late autumn. These notes conveyed the Spanish government's formal protest and were the impetus for Adams's November 28 letter to George W.

Erving, the U.S. minister in Madrid, the most famous and most consequential state paper of his diplomatic career. As he recorded in his diary, he began work on it on November 8: "After finishing the Journal [diary entry] of yesterday, which employed a great part of the morning I began the draft of a despatch to G. W. Erving, in which I propose to give a succinct account of the late Seminole War, from its origin, and to trace the connections between Arbuthnot, Ambrister, Woodbine, Nicholls and M'Gregor with that War, in such a manner as to justify completely the measures of this Government relating to it, and as far as possible the proceedings of General Jackson—The task is of the highest order; may I not be found inferior to it! I made some progress in the draft but it must be the work of several days." [*JQADI*, 458.] He had completed this work by November 14, when, as he wrote in his diary, "I left with the President my draft of a Letter to Mr Erving—And at the Office was preparing the search of documents to be communicated next week with the Message." [JQADD.] Adams refers here to relevant documentation from Jackson and others communicated to or located by the State Department as part of its fact-finding efforts, with which Adams intended to bolster his claims. Monroe returned the draft to Adams two days later: "There were two or three words which he thought it would be best to omit, and which I accordingly struck out; but there was a passage which I thought it highly important to retain and to which he objected from the apprehension of its giving Offence to the British Government; by referring too directly to their policy in relation to our Indian Affairs—It was precisely in the kernel of the vindication of Jackson's execution of Arbuthnot and Ambrister, and if left out would very much weaken the case made. I defended the passage so strenuously, that the President finally directed me to shew it to Mr. Crawford [Secretary of the Treasury William Crawford] and Mr. Calhoun [Secretary of War John C. Calhoun], and if they should agree with me in opinion to retain it." [*JQADI*, 459.] In the end he softened it in response to notes from Calhoun and Crawford. The finished letter is clearly written for a public, indeed an international, audience, very much including Congress, which was then in the throes of debate over the government's policy in Florida, with the Speaker, Henry Clay, and others seeking to use Jackson's incursion to embarrass the administration. Adams bundled up the letter and supporting materials and sent them on their way to Erving on November 28. On December 16, Congress issued a formal call for the communiqué, and Adams was still preparing and reviewing copies to comply with the request on December 23. Four days later, he reported in his diary, "On my return home, I found that Mr D. Brent [State Department clerk Daniel Brent] had been here with the copies of my two Letters to G. W. Erving, prepared for publication in the National Intelligencer, by the President's desire—I revised the copies; and have read over these letters till they are disgusting to me." [JQADD, December 27, 1818.] The letter (dispatch "No. 7") was published with an excerpt from a second note to Erving ("No. 9") in the December 31 edition of the *National Intelligencer.* The *Intelligencer* was Washington's oldest newspaper, and its publishers, Joseph Gales and William Winston Seaton, were also the official printers of Congress. Reported under the two-line heading "OUR RELATIONS WITH SPAIN / DOCUMENTS TRANSMITTED TO CONGRESS," the letters take up the bulk of two five-column news sheets and include bracketed numerical callouts to the supporting material that Adams had assembled. These callouts are explained with a note at the end of the second letter: "The numeral letters and figures in the margin of the above letters, refer to documents contained in the Appendix thereto, which will be published so soon as we can obtain copies of them." This volume presents the complete text of Dispatch No. 7, the most substantial and ultimately most important of Adams's communiqués on the subject, from the *National Intelligencer.* The effect of this letter in Congress was electric, as he noted in his diary on January 5 after a conversation with a group of members: "Some of them gave me notice, that a formidable and concerted attack upon my Letter to Erving is to be brought forward in the House of Representatives next week. Clay has already commenced his attack, upon it, in convivial companies out of doors—Last Winter Clay's principal attack was levelled against the President himself, but finding that this only injured himself he has this winter confined his hostilities to me. My Letter to Erving has been so well received in Congress and by the public that it has redoubled his rancour against me and among all the knots of intriguers in Congress, by the partizans of half a dozen Candidates for the next Presidency (including Genl. Jackson) there is one common object, of decrying me." [JQADD.] The House promptly ordered the printing of Adams's November 28 letter and supporting materials in pamphlet form, a copy of which reached Adams on January 26. Reflecting considerable public demand, Adams's letter was published in at least two pamphlet editions, neither of which is identified by printer or publication date: *Letter of John Quincy Adams, In Explanation and Vindication of Gen. Jackson's Invasion and Occupation of Florida and the Execution of Arbuthnot and Ambrister* and *Mr. Adams' Defence of General Jackson's Conduct in the Seminole War.* Adams's letter silenced opposition to the administration's policy in Florida both at home and abroad, especially in Spain and Great Britain. As Adams's nephew, John Adams Smith, reported from the U.S.

legation in London, "there has been scarcely a pistol flashed since the great gun from Washington to Madrid." [Quoted in Samuel Flagg Bemis, *John Quincy Adams and the Foundations of American Foreign Policy* (New York: Alfred A. Knopf, 1956), 328.] As Adams foresaw, his defense of Jackson would have presidential reverberations; it was republished during the election of 1824 in a Jacksonian campaign piece, *Memoirs of General Andrew Jackson, together with the Letter of Mr. Secretary Adams, in Vindication of the Execution of Arbuthnot and Ambrister, and the Other Public Acts of Gen. Jackson in Florida.*

10: FOURTH OF JULY ADDRESS | 1821

As indicated on page 208, arrangements were made for the publication of this oration by the same group of District of Columbia dignitaries that had invited Adams to deliver it. *An Address Delivered at the Request of a Committee of the Citizens of Washington; on the occasion of reading the Declaration of Independence, on the Fourth of July, 1821* was soon published by the Washington firm of William A. Davis and Peter Force, publishers of the *National Journal*. The address was issued in a "second edition" shortly after in Cambridge, Massachusetts, "at the Univ. Press," by the firm of Hilliard and Metcalf under the title *An Address, Delivered at the Request of the Committee of Arrangements for Celebrating the Anniversary of Independence, at the City of Washington on the Fourth of July 1821, upon the occasion of reading the Declaration of Independence.* Back home in Boston in September, Secretary of State Adams got a sense of this edition's impact when he was waylaid by the French actor and man of letters Joseph Linna Artiguenave, then on an extended stay in the city: "His main object was to tell me that H[arrison]. G[ray]. Otis was the instigator of all the clamour in this town against my fourth of July address, and he expressed his astonishment at the excessive partiality prevailing among many people here for England. He said that he himself had been so much pleased with the Address, that he had made a translation of it into French, and sent it to Marshal [Emmanuel de] Grouchy, now in France." [JQADD, September 7, 1821.] The present volume publishes the complete text of the Davis and Force first edition.

11: INAUGURAL ADDRESS | 1825

Adams completed a draft of his inaugural address at least by February 23, 1825, when, as he noted in his diary, he read it to his diplomatic protégé Alexander H. Everett and received notes from Daniel Brent, his longtime clerk at the State Department. Two days later he read the draft to President Monroe, who remarked that he had done the same thing with his predecessor, James Madison. On March 2, Joseph Gales, publisher of the *National Intelligencer*, called on Adams to request a copy of the address for a special extra edition of his paper. Presented as a four-column broadside, this special printing appeared on March 4, the day of the inauguration, and is the source of the text presented here. Peter Force of the *National Journal* also requested a copy on March 3, and, though it is not mentioned in Adams's diary, a copy must have also found its way into the hands of Alexandria printer W. H. Thornton, publisher, with Samuel Snowden, of the recently established *Phenix Gazette*, serving the community that was then still part of the District of Columbia. All three papers issued the address as an extra on March 4.

12: FIRST ANNUAL MESSAGE | 1825

President Adams began work on his first annual message to Congress on October 31, 1825, collecting reports from the various departments of the federal government and framing from them a governing vision for the nation. A little more than two weeks later he was still at it, as he recorded in his diary: "I employed the little leisure of the day in reading papers for the preparation of the Message—Evening employed upon it; and labouring with it; not for matter, but for brevity." [JQADD, November 15, 1825.] He was finally ready to present the message to his cabinet on November 23, reading it to them for over an hour and a half. (The nature of the cabinet's response is characterized on page 244.) Ten days later Adams's diary records his wry comment on the many sometimes contradictory revisions proposed by the cabinet: "[Secretary of State Henry] Clay good humouredly remarked this alternate stripping off from my draft; and I told them I was like the man with his two wives—one plucking out his black hairs and the other the white till none were left." [*JQAD2*, 115.] Peter Force, of the *National Journal*, came by Adams's house early on the morning of December 2 to pick up a copy of the message, which Adams gave him with the caveat that he not publish it "before its time," that is, before it was formally transmitted to Congress on December 6. Force reported that "he had been applied to, from Cincinnati, and also from Alexandria, to print several hundred copies, to be forwarded the moment it is delivered—I mentioned to Force Mr Walsh's [Philadelphia *National Gazette* editor Robert Walsh] request to have a copy mailed the morning of the day when it will be delivered, and assented to it." [JQADD, December 2, 1825.] The next day, W. H. Thornton, of the *Phenix Gazette*, came by to request a copy, and Adams referred him to Force. On December 6, the day appointed for the message, Adams recorded the following in his diary: "It was half past eleven when the Committee from the two Houses came, and General S. Smith [Maryland senator Samuel Smith] speaking for them said they had been appointed to inform me, that they had assembled, and were ready to receive any communication I should be pleased to make to them—I answered that I would thank them to inform the two houses of Congress, that I proposed to make them a Communication in writing this day at 12 O'Clock, upon which they immediately departed—At 12 O'Clock I sent accordingly my Son John [the president's official secretary] with the Message." [JQADD, December 6, 1825.] This volume uses the December 8 publication of the message in the *National Journal* as its source text.

13: MESSAGE ON PANAMA CONGRESS | 1826

When Adams alluded in his annual message to his determination to accept an invitation to participate in a congress of the newly independent states of South and Central America to be held in Panama, he ignited a firestorm of controversy in the Congress. By the middle of February, debate over funding for the mission was consuming the House, while the Senate deliberated on the nominations for the American commission, each body making repeated requests for documents from the administration. Adams decided to issue this formal message to explain his decision, and it was communicated to the House on Wednesday, March 15, in response to the House's March 5 document request. It was promptly published in a special supplement to Gales and Seaton's *National Intelligencer* on the following Saturday. This is the source of the text presented here. Gales and Seaton also published the message on behalf of the House as "Doc. No. 129." Entitled *Message from the President of the United States, Transmitting the information required by a resolution of the House of Representatives, of 5th ult. in relation to the Proposed Congress to be held at Panama, etc. etc.* Dated March 17, this eighty-nine-page pamphlet supplemented the message with a report from Secretary of State Clay and copies of relevant treaties between and among the American states, a listing of which had been supplied at the end of the *National Intelligencer* article. Adams's Panama message was also printed by Peter Force's *National Journal* as an oversized extra, a three-column broadside printed on silk and measuring 25½ by 10¼ inches.

14: C&O CANAL DEDICATION | 1828

On July 3, 1828, the day before he delivered this address, Adams made the following note in his diary:

Mr Mercer called this Evening, and mentioned to me the definitive arrangements for the ceremony—The company to assemble between 7 and 8 to-morrow Morning at Tilley's Union Hotel, in Georgetown. To walk in procession to the Steam-boats—then ascend the river to the first bridge and thence in Canal Boats to the spot where the work is to commence—Where he will present to me a spade; addressing me with a few sentences, occupying not more than five minutes—I told him that as at this time, I must expect that whatever I might say would be severely criticised, and misrepresented, I had thought proper to write what I should say, so that at least I might be responsible for nothing else—That deeming the work to be commenced of great importance to the Country and to future ages I thought it suitable to the occasion to give to the ceremony somewhat of a religious character; and I read to him the address as I proposed to deliver it—He approved of it altogether, though he thought the last paragraph, expressing good wishes for the success of the Baltimore Rail-road which is also to be commenced to-morrow, would not meet with sympathy from my hearers, as they believed that to be a rival project: but it was nevertheless entirely proper for me to speak thus and the religious cast of my address was conformable to his own Sentiments. He would adapt the few words that he should say on presenting me the Spade to the purport of my own discourse. [*JQAD2*, 183.]

The ceremonies at the dig site were covered by Force's *National Journal* in the July 8 edition, in a front-page feature that included a full transcription of President Adams's remarks. This volume presents the full text of Adams's speech as recorded there. The speech was also reproduced in Gales and Seaton's *National Intelligencer*, in a feature article picked up a week later in *Niles' Weekly Register*, a newspaper of national significance published in Baltimore by Hezekiah Niles, and in part or in full by other newspapers around the country, making it the most publicized public appearance of Adams's presidency. Adams's diary entry for the day after his speech records a coda of sorts: "As I was going out of the yard I met a young man who told me his name was Towner—That he belonged to Shepardstown, 70 miles distant from this place, in Virginia: that he had come all that distance to witness the ceremony of yesterday and had seen it; and being now about to return home he had felt a curiosity to see me; and having succeeded was entirely satisfied." [JQADD, July 5, 1828.]

15: FOURTH OF JULY ORATION | 1831

Adams began working on this address, the third formal Fourth of July oration of his career (after #4 and #10 above), in early June. "To avoid repetitions of what I have said before upon the same Subject, is one of the difficulties of my present task," he wrote in his diary on June 7. "As I proceed, I perceive the effect of age upon the Style of composition." [*JQAD2*, 264.] By July 3 he was focused on the oration's conclusion: "I was occupied much of the day in writing a closing paragraph for my Discourse—At this late hour I absolutely sickened at that which I had written—It was gloomy, inauspicious, and affectedly rather than affectingly full of myself—The new paragraph, totally changed its character: gave to the future an aspect of hope and gladness instead of despondency—urged to generous and energetic action, and to calm reliance on a superintending Providence—leaving a slight allusion to my own age and proximity to my end, at the close; but merely to give additional Solemnity to the dying Sentiment of my father, and linking the perpetuity of Union with that of Independence pointing all at the same time to the future Prospects of my Auditory—As it is, my judgment pronounces the Peroration good—As it was till this very day, it was execrably bad, and I was utterly unaware of it—My self-criticism, was disarmed by the pathos of a close, in the last words of my father, and I had not remarked the awkwardness of manner in which I had brought it forth—How severe a Censor, it behooves me to be upon myself." [*JQAD2*, 267.] Adams delivered his address the next day in Quincy's new stone meetinghouse, which had been completed in 1828, constructed with granite quarried from land deeded to the town by John Adams in 1822. He was preceded by prayers, a reading of the Declaration of Independence, and a choral performance of Adams's own versification of the 149th Psalm. His oration lasted for an hour and twenty-five minutes and was punctuated with sustained applause. In the end, Adams omitted roughly a third of what he had written. In the audience was his son, Charles Francis Adams, who wrote in his diary that "the *matter* was very good but I fear for him lest in his age it should bring upon him the War of words to which through all his life he has been accustomed. It is the character of my Father vehemently to attack. He does it through all his writings more or less, and attack in every community creates defence; Controversy rises, from which issue anger, and ill blood. All this is not to my taste and therefore I presume I must be set down as preferring insignificance and inglorious ease." [Marc Friedlaender and L. H. Butterfield, eds., *Diary of Charles Francis Adams*, Volume 4: March 1931–December 1832 (Cambridge, MA: Harvard University Press, 1968), 82.] As indicated on page 298, Adams delivered the manuscript of his oration to William

Seaver, Quincy's schoolmaster, et al., on July 13 for publication by the Boston firm of Eleazer Richardson, Melvin Lord, and John Holbrook (he also included his version of the 149th Psalm): "Thus goes into the world my third Independence day Rhapsody, to be like the second lacerated, and cut to pieces by the Critics, after having been received with the warmest approbation by the auditory." [*JQAD2*, 270.] It was soon published as a forty-four-page pamphlet entitled *An Oration Addressed to the Citizens of the Town of Quincy, on the Fourth of July, 1831, the Fifty-fifth Anniversary of the Independence of the United States of America*, the source of the text presented here. The original edition includes this note on the final page:

The following version of the 149th Psalm was sung by the Choir, immediately before the delivery of the Oration.

1.

Sing to the Lord a song of praise;
    Assemble, ye who love his name;
Let congregated millions raise
    Triumphant Glory's loud acclaim.
From earth's remotest regions come;
    Come greet your Maker and your King;
With harp, with timbrel, and with drum,
    His praise let hill and valley sing.

2.

Your praise the Lord will not disdain,
    The humble soul is his delight;
Saints, on your couches swell the strain,
    Break the dull stillness of the night.
Rejoice in glory! Bid the storm,
    Bid thunder's voice his praise expand;
And while your lips the chorus form,
    Grasp for the fight his vengeful brand.

3.

Go forth in arms! Jehovah reigns;
    Their graves let foul oppressors find;
Bind all their sceptred kings in chains;
    Their peers with iron fetters bind.
Then to the Lord shall praise ascend;
    Then all mankind, with one accord,
And Freedom's voice, till time shall end,
    In pealing anthems—Praise the Lord.

As was his custom, Adams sent inscribed copies of the published oration to many friends and associates, including Chief Justice John Marshall, who in response agreed with Adams that the doctrine of sovereignty is "the root from which many of the extravagancies of the day, including nullification, unquestionably spring," and Associate Justice Joseph Story, who replied that "I have gathered many useful hints for my own lectures upon constitutional law." Former Maryland governor Joseph Kent (with whom as president Adams had partnered in advancing the C&O Canal project) responded, "Your views upon the doctrine of nullification were not only very strong, but somewhat original, to me at least, and places that subject, odious as it has become, in a point of view too preposterous to be tolerated." [All three reactions quoted in Samuel Flagg Bemis, *John Quincy Adams and the Union* (New York: Alfred A. Knopf, 1956), 236.] Somewhat more belatedly, on September 9, Adams sent a copy of the address (along with his recently published eulogy of James Monroe) to John C. Calhoun, confessing in his cover letter: "Its more than simple dissonance from sentiments which you was understood and are now known to entertain, restrained me from asking your acceptance of it before—lest it might have been liable to the surmise of motives other than of kindness and respect. Disclaiming at this time all others, I present it with the single assurance of my regret that upon topics of transcendent importance, our opinions should be so much at variance with each other." Calhoun replied in a similar spirit: "It is on my part as well as yours, a subject of pain that we should differ so widely on a point so fundamental in our political system. . . . Whatever may be the final disposition of the people, I hope the Union will be safe." [Ibid., 237.]

16: REPORT OF THE MINORITY | 1833

The origins of Adams's minority report are briefly described on page 330. He conceived the idea for it on December 29, 1832, as he reported to Lewis Condict, his colleague on the Committee on Manufactures, two days later: "I then paid a morning visit to Dr Condict, and had conversation with him upon the course to be pursued by us as members of the Committee of Manufactures—The Recommendations of the President's Message look to the annihilation of our Manufactures, and to the depression of all free domestic Industry. I told the Doctor, I thought it would be my duty as chairman of the Committee to prepare a Report examining the Doctrines of the Message in their full extent; and demonstrating their pernicious nature; especially with reference to the Protection necessary for the domestic manufactures—It was very certain that

five members of the Committee would dissent from this Report—
They would not permit that it should be made to the House at all,
and would doubtless prepare a Report of a different and opposite
character—Probably the House itself, would refuse to receive such
a Report as I should prepare; but I could not endure the idea of
suffering the ruinous principles and recommendations of the Message to pass, as if they were uncontroverted—The Doctor agreed
with me, and I promised to prepare a Report, and communicate it
to him, for his examination and emendations, before presenting it to
the Committee." [JQADD, December 31, 1832.] By February 20, he
could report that it was nearing completion and on February 25, in a
series of telegraphic notes to himself in his diary, he wrote: "Right to
complain—Not a Report—a written Speech—Respectful manner."
[Ibid.] Adams unveiled the report to the committee the next day and
was met with opposition from the majority. He later moved to have
the report tabled and printed by the full House, which after some
debate was agreed to on March 1. On March 6, he recorded in his
diary: "The Minority Report of the Committee of Manufactures not
being published, I wrote a Note to Duff Green the Public Printer,
enquiring if he had put it to the Press—He promised me last Friday
that he would print it immediately; and that he would also publish
it in his Extra Telegraph—I received this Evening an answer from
his foreman W. W. Moore, to my note, informing me that it has not
been put to the Press." [Ibid.] And the next day, "Finding Mr Duff
Green, the Printer for Congress, in no hurry to print the Report
of the Minority of the Committee of Manufactures, I wrote him
a Note asking for the Manuscript for a few days, and he sent it to
me—I took it to the Office of the National Intelligencer, and left it
with Mr Gales, who promised me that it should be published entire
in the Intelligencer of next Tuesday." [Ibid.] Just two days later, on
March 9, he received proof sheets from Gales, which he set about
reviewing, returning them to the printer on the following day. On
March 12, he "Went to the Office of the National Intelligencer, and
received from Mr Gales, the Manuscript of the Report—He sent me
forty copies of the Newspaper containing it, part of which I distributed to some of my friends, by despatching them by this Evening's
Mail—This document is an Appeal to the People, I fear a vain and
fruitless one, against the system of Government promulg[at]ed in the
last Annual Presidential Message—leading to the dissolution of the
Union." [Ibid.] The publication was noticed in the following day's
edition of the *National Gazette*, in a review excerpted in the final
pamphlet publication of the report (see page 331). Adams spent much
of March 14 revising the *National Intelligencer* printing of his report,

which he then forwarded, with the manuscript, back to Duff Green, who had replaced Gales as the official printer to Congress with the election of Andrew Jackson. He received press proofs from Green on March 22, which he returned the next day. This would result in its eventual publication in the appendix to the *Register of Debates of the Twenty-second Congress*. On March 24 he noted that the *Intelligencer*'s publication of the report had been reprinted by the *National Gazette* and the *New-York American*. The next day, after receiving a letter from Charles in Boston, Adams noted: "The Advocate is the only Paper in Boston which publishes the whole Report—The rest give extracts." Adams added: "It is also republished in the Advocate of New-York—The Southern Papers do not notice its existence." [Ibid.] Many more newspaper publications followed, some presenting the report in full, sometimes in serial form, others in part. As the newspaper publications were circulating, Adams's son Charles arranged for the report to be published as a pamphlet by the Boston printer John Eastburn. With subvention for "gratuitous circulation" from a trio of wealthy Bostonians (Isaac P. Davis, a trustee of the Boston Athenaeum; Abbot Lawrence, the pioneering industrialist; and the merchant Thomas Handasyd Perkins), Eastburn struck off five thousand copies of the forty-page pamphlet, entitled *Report of the Minority of the Committee on Manufacturers, submitted to the House of Representatives of the United States, February 28, 1833*, which includes the unattributed preface and the excerpt from the *National Gazette* review. This is the source of the text presented here. (The setting, which grows progressively more compressed throughout, suggests that paper supply may have been an issue.) Adams received two copies of this edition on March 31, and many more the following week, and promptly began sending them out, including to every member of the Massachusetts legislature. He also received a letter from the Philadelphia printer Robert Walsh, publisher of the *National Gazette*, informing him that he intended to circulate "many thousand copies" of the *Gazette*'s special supplement reprinting the report. Another edition of the report soon appeared in Boston from the firm of Beals, Homer & Co. under the title *Tariff Report of Mr. John Quincy Adams, in the House of Representatives, at Washington, February 28*. Altogether, these multiple imprints make this one of the most circulated publications of Adams's career, and fittingly so, since he regarded it as something like a testament of his core political vision.

17: SPEECH ON JOINT RESOLUTION | 1836

On Thursday, May 26, 1836, the day after he delivered this speech, Adams reported in his diary that Joseph Gales "gave me a note requesting me to write out my Speech of yesterday to be reported in the National Intelligencer." [JQADD, May 26, 1836.] The following Sunday Adams spent "all the leisure of the day and evening in writing out for publication my Speech made last Wednesday in the House of Representatives, one of the most hazardous that I ever made, and the reception of which even by the People of my own district and State is altogether uncertain." [*JQAD2*, 384–85.] This was no easy task, as Adams was forced to re-create the speech, which he had delivered extemporaneously, from memory. Adams completed his draft on June 1, and it was published in the *National Intelligencer* the next day, as Adams described in his diary: "My Speech on the distribution of rations to the fugitives from Indian hostilities in Alabama and Georgia was published in the National Intelligencer of this morning, and a subscription paper was circulated in the House for printing it in a pamphlet, for which Gales told me there were 2500 copies ordered—Several members of the House of both parties spoke of it to me; some with strong dissent." [Ibid., 285.] This volume uses that pamphlet, entitled *Speech of John Quincy Adams, on the Joint Resolution for Distributing Rations to the Distressed Fugitives from Indian Hostilities in the States of Alabama and Georgia. Delivered in the House of Representatives, Wednesday, May 25, 1836*, as its source text; it includes a note at the end of the text describing the process of its transcription (see page 424). With its publication the mixed reception in the House was soon replicated nationwide, as Adams observed in his diary entry for June 19: "My Speech on the rations, comes back with echoes of thundering vituperation from the South and West, and with one universal shout of applause from the North and East—This is a cause upon which I am entering at the last Stage of Life, and with the certainty that I cannot advance in it far—My Career must close leaving the cause at the threshold—To open the way for others, is all that I can do. The cause is good and great." [Ibid.]

18: LETTERS TO HIS CONSTITUENTS | 1837

For Adams the late winter of 1837, when he emerged, sometimes against his better judgment, as a vocal antislavery figure in the House, was one of the most trying periods of his life, so much so that "for [the] first time for more than forty years I have suffered a total breach in my Diary for several weeks." By way of expiation for this lapse, he wrote, "The Journals of the House of Representatives of the United States, my Letter Book, and my Addresses to my Constituents the Inhabitants of the 12th. Congressional District of Massachusetts must supply the vacancy," referring in the last instance to the letters that make up the first part of this text. [JQADD, March 30, 1837.] In his diary entry summarizing the month of March, Adams noted that "I have written four long Addresses to my Constituents the Inhabitants of the 12th Congressional District of Massachusetts to be published in the Quincy Patriot, and all this has contribute[d] to divert my mind from sorrows and troubles which otherwise would have rendered me wretched without relief." [JQADD.] It was during this tense period that Adams began corresponding with the abolitionist poet John Greenleaf Whittier, who had written to Adams to express his admiration for his principled stand in support of the right of petition in Congress and urging him to more forthrightly embrace antislavery principles. Adams responded with a letter, composed over two days and dated January 26, 1837, affirming his shared belief in the evil of slavery but urging the abolitionist to temper his zeal with realism about what Adams could do given the state of politics and public opinion. Writing again to Whittier on April 19, Adams continued in the same vein: "Under these circumstances, you will perceive that great prudence and caution become indispensably necessary to me, with regard to any manifestation on my part giving countenance to the movements of Antislavery Societies." [Quoted in Bemis, *John Quincy Adams and the Union*, 350.] Whittier's admiration for Adams and his desire to envelop the elder statesman in the antislavery cause were on full display in his introduction (dated May 16) to this pamphlet, *Letters from John Quincy Adams to his Constituents of the Twelfth Congressional District in Massachusetts. To which is Added his Speech in Congress, Delivered February 9, 1837*, issued by Boston publisher Isaac Knapp, which as billed brings together Adams's four letters originally published in the *Quincy Patriot* and his speech of February 9 on the House floor, which had been recorded by Benjamin F. Hallett, editor of the Boston *Daily Advocate*. This volume presents the full text of that pamphlet, excepting three poems by Whittier and an advertisement for a forthcoming collection of his work that was appended at the end of Adams's speech. On June 2, Adams, now in Quincy for the summer recess, reported in his diary that abolitionists "Mr [James G.] Birney, and Mr Francis Jackson were here—Having been in attendance upon a State Anti-Slavery convention this week in Boston—Mr Birney gave me a pamphlet copy of my Letters to my Constituents the Inhabitants of the 12th. Congressional District of Massachusetts of the 3d. 8th. 13th. and 20th. of March, and of my Speech of the 9th. of February—He said it was proposed to publish another edition of the same pamphlet." [JQADD.]

19: JUBILEE OF THE CONSTITUTION | 1839

Adams sent the manuscript of this address (the solicitation and composition of which are described on page 487) to New York lawyer Joseph

Blunt on May 8, a little over a week after he delivered a significant portion of it before a large audience in New York City. Blunt, a member of the New-York Historical Society, which had invited Adams to speak at the celebration of the fiftieth anniversary of George Washington's inauguration as president, arranged for its publication by the New York printer Samuel Colman. The resulting 136-page pamphlet is the source of the text presented here. It included a single-plate frontispiece featuring an engraving of Chancellor Livingston's administration of the oath of office to Washington on the balcony of New York's Old City Hall on April 30, 1789. Adams received his first 50 copies of the finished book on June 10 and began sending them out. He picked up a second shipment in Boston later that month, and at one point was sending thirty to forty packages a day to the post office in Quincy. All told, he signed and sent at least 296 copies that month. (Numerous signed copies are available today from rare book dealers and auction houses.) All this effort prompted Adams to take stock of his personal inventory of his published writings, which he had come to feel were his single greatest legacy. In his diary he wrote that "I took to the book binder Caleb Gill junrs. shop a collection of printed pamphlets of my writing to be bound up in a volume, to give to my Granddaughter Mary Louisa—I have the materials for a second Volume, and the collection will yet be very imperfect—Of several of my earliest published pamphlets I have only one copy left—Of some—particularly of the Report on the case of John Smith of Ohio, I have no copy at-all—But of pamphlets in number sufficient to make two thick Octavo Volumes, I have copies enough to make up a set for each of my six grand children—and as the three girls being the eldest have asked me for copies of my Oration at Newbury-Port and for the Jubilee of the Constitution, I have put together with them copies of all the supernumeraries, to be bound up to give them as tokens of memory, when I shall be forgotten by the rest of the world—I am making a more complete collection, of the same pamphlets, with others of which I have only one copy, to leave to my Son." [JQADD, June 29, 1839.] On August 6, Adams received a letter from Blunt informing him "that the demand for the Jubilee of the Constitution in New-York's neighbourhood is unprecedented and still continues—and that they have already sold 8000 copies." [Ibid.] Adams was still distributing copies of *Jubilee of the Constitution* as late as 1845. A second edition was issued in 1848, as part of the nationwide mourning and commemoration after Adams's death.

20: SPEECH ON WAR WITH MEXICO | 1842

On April 14–15, 1842, Adams engaged in a dramatic two-day exchange of speeches on the House floor with Henry A. Wise of Virginia and

Charles J. Ingersoll of Pennsylvania. In his diary entry for April 15 Adams sets the scene: "Charles J. Ingersoll's speech yesterday in Committee of the whole on the state of the Union, upon a motion to strike out and reduce the appropriation for Ministers to Vienna and Berlin by razeeing them down to the rank of Chargé d'Affaires, was a Congreve rocket thrown into the house to kindle a blazing War spirit and push a stumbling block in the way of the negotiation with Great Britain—Profligate as were his leading principles, and glaring with absurdity as were his leading arguments and perverted and distorted as were his leading facts, such was the impression of his speech upon the house, that when he sat down, every eye in the house was fastened on me, as if in a voice of thunder to call upon me to meet him. I was almost prostrated by the *loudness* and suddenness of the *silent* call—I paused for a moment to give every other member the chance for the floor—no one rose—I did, under a sense of depression from which I could not wholly recover. My discourse was rambling and desultory—The result of my speech was apparently satisfactory to my friends; but by no means to myself." [JQADD, April 15, 1842.] Two days later, catching up in his diary with the events of the day before, Adams wrote that "I had called yesterday at the National Intelligencer Office, and asked Mr Gales to send me the slips of my speech of yesterday to be published to morrow, for my revisal—He sent them this evening—seven columns of small print, reported by Stansbury [reporter Arthur Stansbury].—I employed two hours in revising them, and found very few and slight corrections to make.—This speech was made under deep and solemn conviction of duty—Its issues are with the father of Spirits—I must abide by its consequences—May they be auspicious to the Peace of my Country, and to human freedom." [Ibid., April 17, 1842.] The speech appeared in the *National Intelligencer* on April 18. It was Joshua Leavitt, editor of the antislavery weekly *The Emancipator*, who would ensure that it reached an even wider audience. Adams had been corresponding with Leavitt since July 1839, when the New York–based abolitionist invited him to attend an antislavery convention in Albany (Adams declined). As a member of the so-called Amistad Committee, Leavitt was instrumental in securing Adams's involvement in that celebrated case in 1840. By November 1841, the two men had become associates, friends even, and Adams visited him in New York while en route from Quincy back to Washington: "I called at the Emancipator Office and saw there Mr Leavitt, who is going on, in two or three days to Washington to report the proceedings of Congress at the approaching Session." [Ibid., November 30, 1841.] In his diary entry for April 19, 1842, Adams reports that "Mr Leavitt, who lodges at Spriggs had given me this morning, his notes of my speech of last Thursday to be published in the Emancipator—It is the report in the National Intelligencer partially revised—I revised them myself this afternoon, and returned them to him when he called for them this Evening and he engaged to have the whole speech on both days, published in a pamphlet from the columns of the Emancipator." [Ibid., April 19, 1842.] The resulting thirty-six-page pamphlet, entitled *Mr. Adams' Speech, on War with Great Britain and Mexico; with the Speeches of Messrs. Wise and Ingersoll, to which it is in reply*, is the source of the text presented here.

21: LETTER ON ABOLITION | 1843

This public letter arose out of another invitation to attend an antislavery gathering, this time in Bangor, Maine: "I received this morning a Letter from Asa Walker and two others a Committee of Correspondence for a public meeting of the citizens of Bangor and vicinity, holden on the 27th. of last month, and at which a Resolution was adopted to observe the first of next August as the Anniversary of West India emancipation, by a public address and other suitable exercises—and the committee appointed to carry the resolution into execution, invite me to deliver the address—The temptation is almost irresistible, but must be resisted—My time is not yet come—How shall I answer this Letter?" [JQADD, June 13, 1843.] Almost two weeks later, Adams was still laboring over his response: "I continued without finishing my answer to the invitation from Bangor to deliver there an Oration on the first of August in celebration of the emancipation of Slaves in the British West Indies—This answer will be instead of the oration itself; but it is already too long and must be much longer to be worthy of the theme. I shall probably not send it after all, but I feel an irremissible duty to bear my testimony once more, before I go hence against Slavery. To select the time, the place and the manner is a subject of great consideration and must be neither precipitated nor too long delayed—My ideas are yet crude indigested and confused. I will begin to collect and assort them in this Letter, with the firm resolve to persevere in the pursuit." [Ibid., June 26, 1843.] He finally finished his response on July 3. On August 10 he received in the mail a copy of the *Bangor Courier*, containing the letter: "It is announced as a Letter from John Quincy Adams on Slavery—with a statement that it was read at the Meeting on the 1st. of August and without one word of comment upon it—I have expected the publication of this Letter, and expect to be held to severe responsibility for writing it—Before my lamp is burnt out, I am desirous that my opinions concerning the great movement throughout the civilized world for the abolition of Slavery should be explicitly avowed and declared—God grant that they may contribute to the final consummation of that event—There are sundry errors of the press, and of the manuscript to be rectified, and to which I must attend." [Ibid.] Two days later, "The Boston Courier of this morning republishes from the Bangor Courier my Letter of 4 July last to the Bangor Committee for celebrating the anniversary of the emancipation of Slaves in the British West India Islands; with all the errors of the Bangor, and several more. Not a word of comment upon the Letter is in either of the papers—I expected the publication of that Letter; and wrote it for the purpose of exhibiting in as brief a compass as possible my principles, feelings and opinions, relating to the abolition of Slavery and the Slave-trade throughout the world—I meant it as a note of defiance to all the Slave-holders, Slave traders and Slave breeders upon earth. As the experiment of Summons to the whole Freedom of this Union in its own defence, I sent it forth alone, to try its Fortune in the world, and made it purposely bold and startling, to rouse if possible both friend and foe—The two publications without comment, give no promise of a rally for the support of Freedom. As yet there is no hostile notice of it abroad—It may remain altogether unnoticed, which is the worst fate that can befall it—for if I can but raise a controversy by it—that is; an adversary worthy of being answered, it shall be if my life and health will admit, a text book for future enlargement and illustrative for the whole remnant of my toilsome days." [Ibid.] On August 18 Adams visited the office of *Emancipator* in Boston and learned that they were finalizing a reprint of the letter, and he requested proofs to review. He made a similar trip to the *Quincy Patriot* the next day, where he ordered one hundred copies of the corrected letter. This *Quincy Patriot* edition appeared on August 26, and Adams was pleased with the corrected text, which is the source for the present volume. The Quincy edition, which Adams mailed far and wide, was then picked up by newspapers and antislavery periodicals throughout the North, including in the December issue of *The Liberty Tree*, a new antislavery monthly published in Chicago by Zebina Eastman. Eastman devoted a portion of that issue to a celebration of Adams, including the full text of the Bangor letter and the following supplemental material inspired by Adams's tour through western New York and Ohio in the autumn of 1843. This material included an encomium extracted from a recent publication by William Henry Channing, worth recording as a measure of the stature Adams had achieved as a national icon, largely through the reach of his published writings:

NOTE ON THE TEXTS 715

MR. ADAMS' TRIUMPH.

In the Present, a new monthly publication, edited by W. H. Channing, we find the following extract, under the head of "Mr. Adams' Triumph," referring to the celebration of the completion of the Bunker Hill Monument, and the triumphal processions which have greeted the "Patriarch Statesman."

Grander than the vast assemblage at Bunker Hill were the triumphal processions which greeted our Patriarch statesman. Who does not feel that John Quincy Adams is a nobler memorial to the last generation than that towering obelisk? Truly, there has been a fresh enthusiasm, a romantic love, a reverent affection poured out as sacred oil upon the head of this High Priest of Freedom, which are rarely seen in modern times. The power wielded by this faithful servant of his country is true sovereignty. Official dignity would rather lessen the purity of honors with which a nation by unbought impulse crowns him. He has glorified humbler stations. That plain chair in the Hall of Representatives is a prouder seat than the throne of a king. But words of panegyric impair the simple grandeur of Mr. Adams' position and character. The most indifferent heart has joined to swell by its sympathies his unsought, well deserved and splendid triumph. Verily, verily, this hearty greeting given by old and young, and rich and poor of all parties to the man who above all our statesmen has been true to the professed principles of our country, proves that the Nation is sound at heart. Let us treasure in our memories his words.

This volume presents the texts of the newspaper articles or pamphlets chosen for inclusion here without change, except in the following respects. Typographical errors have been corrected, and inverted letters, a common error in typesetting during this period, have been silently rectified. The use of quotation marks to begin every line of a quoted passage, a convention of the time, has been dispensed with, though the inclusion of the identification of the speaker within the quotation marks, also conventional, has been retained. In those instances where a sentence clearly ends, but without terminal punctuation, a period has been added. Spelling, punctuation, capitalization, and italicization are often expressive features, and they have not been altered, unless otherwise indicated. Each pamphlet reflects the style of its publisher, and no effort has been made to standardize its use of italics for proper names and large and small capitals for emphasis. With the exception of facsimile title pages, this edition does not attempt to reproduce nontextual features of typographical design or such features of period typography as the long "s." The following is a list of typographical errors corrected in this edition, cited by page and line number: 17.5, destinction; 18.16, effect; 18.24, unalineable; 22.37, contitutional; 34.10, compararison; 35.15, feeely; 35.38, has has; 37.38, constituant; 38.26, absurdity; 38.40, poper; 40.3, limitted; 44.23, probly; 47.20, mnst; 48.26, ROSSEAU; 49.27, in in; 55.32, *Unnited*; 75.25, separaration; 86.29, honoraable; 93.21, principle; 103.6, Represensatives; 104.8, suppported; 104.26, herelf; 105.12, New England; 106.34, Governours; 108.15, dismisson; 111.24–25, principle; 111.30, dirict; 112.4, futher; 112.22, Louiana; 114.7, the the; 114.24, a year a year; 114.25, *Mediterraneum*; 117.9, to to; 117.10, Masschusetts; 117.17, turued; 119.26, imginary; 120.35, principle; 129.11, Masschusetts; 144.34, elasped; 159.39, decrees of; 159.40, acquiessed; 160.3, Napolean; 160.18, maintainance; 160.27, comittee; 163.35, king England; 169.2, *agricultral*; 174.10, of of; 177.13, exsercised; 177.17, is to; 178.13, Holland I; 178.25, sat; 184.13, goverment that; 188.20, to the Creek Nation by; 191.16, con-compliance; 193.23, Negro, Indian; 197.29, document; 199.8–9, Hila Hildjo; 203.34, Armbrister; 210.35–36, knowlege; 214.34, visto; 214.39, sufficent; 225.11, Goliah; 236.15, Jubile; 237.22, liberty,—; 238.17, benificence; 283.13, their; 302.33, downfall; 313.19, has been; 319.20, fo; 333.23, messsage; 335.34, righls; 336.15, inevitable; 341.15, whatevever; 352.26, Tenessee; 354.33, fundemental; 354.36, manufactdring; 355.7, adopted; 368.14, empannelled; 368.30, Sstates; 371.9, cecession; 380.5, be be; 389.15, tis; 394.24, forever,; 396.30, competion; 415.23–24, irrisistible; 416.34, far the; 470.28, FULTON; 485.15, petitions Is; 501.6, delgated; 507.8, bay; 516.25, it; 518.26, provison; 518.30, transcendantal; 522.36, comfortable; 531.37, declined by any; 535.40, mother-country.s; 576.8, strike Arkansas; 578.28, ever No:; 579.15, Ocean We; 588.19, it it; 592.19, become; 593.4, in the the; 600.40, atttention; 610.31, to found; 611.13, floor I; 617.26, "all"—when; 617.28, diappear; 622.39, THE BONDS.; 629.32, go war; 629.33, gentlemen; 648.16, combatants; 649.38 race restored; 651.21, rights, have.

Notes

In the notes below, the reference numbers denote page and line of this volume (the line count includes headings, but not rule lines). No note is made for material included in the Merriam-Webster's Collegiate Dictionary, except for certain cases where common words and terms have specific historical meanings or inflections. Biblical quotations and allusions are keyed to the King James Version; references to Shakespeare to *The Riverside Shakespeare*, ed. G. Blackmore Evans (Boston: Houghton Mifflin, 1974). For further historical and biographical background and references to other studies, see *John Quincy Adams: Diaries 1779–1821* and *John Quincy Adams: Diaries 1821–1848*, David Waldstreicher, ed. (New York: Library of America, 2017); Waldstreicher and Matthew Mason, *John Quincy Adams and the Politics of Slavery: Selections from the Diary* (New York: Oxford University Press, 2016); Waldstreicher, ed., *A Companion to John Adams and John Quincy Adams* (Malden, MA: Wiley-Blackwell, 2013); Samuel Flagg Bemis, *John Quincy Adams and the Foundations of American Foreign Policy* (New York: Alfred A. Knopf, 1949); Bemis, *John Quincy Adams and the Union* (New York: Alfred A. Knopf, 1956); Leonard L. Richards, *The Life and Times of Congressman John Quincy Adams* (New York: Oxford University Press, 1986); Lynn Hudson Parsons, *John Quincy Adams* (Madison, WI: Madison House, 1998); Fred Kaplan, *John Quincy Adams: American Visionary* (New York: Harper, 2014); James Traub, *John Quincy Adams: Militant Spirit* (Basic Books, 2016); Randall Woods, *John Quincy Adams: A Man for the Whole People* (New York: Dutton, 2024); Gordon S. Wood, *Empire of Liberty: A History of the Early Republic, 1789–1815* (New York: Oxford University Press, 2009); and Daniel Walker Howe, *What Hath God Wrought: The Transformation of America, 1815–1848* (New York: Oxford University Press, 2007).

1: HARVARD ORATION | 1787

3:11–15 "I am good for nothing . . . really get into the world?"] David Waldstreicher, ed., *John Quincy Adams: Diaries 1779–1821* (New York: Library of America, 2017), 31. [Hereafter *JQAD1*.]

4.25–28 "I was present at the Commencement . . . on public credit."] David Humphries to Henry Knox, July 27, 1787. Gilder Lehrman Collection GLC02437.03624. Humphries had first met Adams in France two years earlier.

4.29–33 "The public expectations . . . with great energy."] *Massachusetts Centinel*, July 21, 1787. This assessment may have been written by the paper's publisher, Benjamin Russell (1761–1845).

6.8 "when then the souls of men were tried,"] An allusion to the famous opening line of Thomas Paine's pamphlet *The American Crisis*, written in December 1776.

6.23 the distinguished patriot] John Hancock (1737–1793), who had been the first governor of Massachusetts under its new constitution, serving from 1780 to 1785, became its third when elected again on May 30, 1787, just six weeks before the Harvard commencement; he was in attendance, along with the governor's council.

8.4–5 the disastrous fate of Alba, and of Carthage] According to Livy, the ancient city of Alba Longa in Latium was a precursor and rival to Rome until it was destroyed by the Romans in the seventh century BCE. The Carthaginians, who were conquered by Rome in the Third Punic War in the second century BCE, were characterized by their victorious rivals as a proverbially dishonorable people.

8.8–9 Britain attacked . . . the united power of four mighty nations] Over the course of the War of American Independence (1775–1783), France, Spain, and the Dutch Republic joined the fight against Great Britain.

9.27 Our eagle] The bald eagle was a late addition to the Great Seal of the United States, which was officially adopted by the Confederation Congress on June 20, 1782.

2: LETTERS OF PUBLICOLA | 1791

11.16 Thomas Paine's *Rights of Man*] See Eric Foner, ed., *Thomas Paine: Collected Writings* (New York: Library of America, 1995), 431–661.

12.21–23 "There is more of method . . . writings."] James Madison to Thomas Jefferson, July 13, 1791. In Julian P. Boyd, ed., *The Papers of Thomas Jefferson*, vol. 20, 1 April–4 August 1791 (Princeton: Princeton University Press, 1982), 299.

13.3 MR. RUSSELL] Benjamin Russell assumed sole ownership of Boston's leading newspaper in 1790, renaming it the *Columbian Centinel*.

14.18–19 "There is but one Goddess . . . her prophet."] A flippant paraphrase of the Shahada, one of the five pillars of Islam: "There is no God but God, and Muhammad is the Prophet of God."

14.27 "*Nullius in . . . magistri*"] The full phrase, from Horace's first epistle, is *Nullius addictus jurare in verba magistri*. In Philip Francis's oft-reprinted eighteenth-century edition of Horace's works, it is translated as "You ask, perhaps, what Sect, what Chief I own; / I'm of all Sects, but blindly sworn to none."

17.29–30 Doctor *Price* had asserted] Burke's pamphlet was prompted, in part, by Richard Price's *Discourse on the Love of Our Country*, which the radical dissenting minister and moral philosopher had delivered in November 1789 to celebrate the centennial of the Glorious Revolution and published in 1790, and from which Adams quotes here. Price (1723–1791) and John Adams had become friends during the latter's residence in London as the first U.S. minister to the Court of St. James's.

20.10–11 when the glorious Congress of 1774 declared] Adams quotes from the Declaration and Resolves of the First Continental Congress, issued on October 14, 1774.

21.37–38 the principle . . . *Rousseau* founds the social compact] In Book II, chapter xv of the *Social Contract*—first published in 1762 as *Du contrat social; ou, Principes du droit politique*—Jean-Jacques Rousseau writes that "the sovereignty, however, cannot be represented, and that for the same reason that it cannot be alienated. It consists essentially of the general will, and the will cannot be represented: it is either identically the same, or some other; there can be no mean term in the case. The deputies of the people, therefore, neither are nor can be their representatives; they are only mere commissioners, and can conclude definitively on nothing. Every law that is not confirmed by the people in person is null and void; it is not in fact a law. The English imagine they are a free people; they are however mistaken they are such only during the election of members of parliament. When these are chosen, they become slaves again; and indeed they make so bad a use of the few transitory moments of liberty, that they richly deserve to lose it." (From the first English edition.)

24.10 appeal to Heaven] This phrase evokes John Locke's *Second Treatise on Government* (1689): "And where the body of the people, or any single man, is deprived of their right, or is under the exercise of a power without right, and have no appeal on earth, then they have a liberty to appeal to heaven, whenever they judge the cause of sufficient moment."

24.25–27 "acquiesce in the necessity . . . of their intentions."] Quoting from the Declaration of Independence, which was principally drafted by Thomas Jefferson.

28.10–11 under the direction of Lord GEORGE GORDON] On June 2, 1780, Gordon (1751–1793), head of the Protestant Association of London, led a crowd of about fifty thousand people to the Houses of Parliament, where he presented a petition calling for repeal of the Catholic Relief Act of 1778, which granted limited civil rights to Catholics who swore allegiance to the king. Although the crowd dispersed peacefully, rioting broke out in London later that night and continued for a week as mobs destroyed Catholic chapels, ransacked Catholic neighborhoods, burned Newgate and several other prisons, and attacked the Inns of Court, the Bank of England, and the homes of prominent persons, including magistrate Sir John Fielding and Lord Chief Justice William Murray, Earl of Mansfield. At least 285 and perhaps as many as 850 people were killed during the riots, and twenty-one persons were later hanged.

32.12 "*ex nihilo, nihil fit*,"] Latin: from nothing, nothing comes.

33.6 says Judge *Blackstone*] In the first volume of *Commentaries on the Laws of England* (1765–69). This seminal four-volume work by British jurist William Blackstone was essential reading for young lawyers like Adams.

36.19 This article] Adams refers to Article V of the U.S. Constitution, which provides for amendments.

37.8–9 we must wait our appointed time] The Massachusetts constitution, which was principally drafted by John Adams and adopted by a state convention in 1780, included a fifteen-year moratorium on any amendments (Chap. VI, art. X).

37.18 the Spanish Monarch, of ridiculous memory] Charles II of Navarre, whose death by immolation in Pamplona in 1387 became a sort of cautionary tale. Charles the Bad, as he was also known, was confined to his bed with illness, "a mass of disease, from the viciousness of his habits," as one moralist put it, when his physicians wrapped him in linen soaked in highly flammable aqua vitae, which caught fire from a candle.

38.29–30 The very act . . . in *England*] The Septennial Act of 1715, which changed the required minimum frequency of parliamentary elections from three to seven years. The measure helped to consolidate Whig dominance in Parliament and to establish more firmly the Hanoverian succession to the British Crown in response to threats from a renewed Jacobite rebellion.

39.24 according to *Rousseau* . . . a republick of Gods] In the *Social Contract*, Book III, chapter iv: "Did there exist a nation of Gods, their government would doubtless be democratical; it is too perfect a form, however, for mankind."

44.7 *Loaves* and *Fishes*."] That is, the cynical distribution of political spoils, recast by analogy to Jesus's miraculous feeding of the multitude (Matthew 14:13–21 and 15:32–39).

47.11 "the sinews of war,"] A phrase coined by Cicero in the *Fifth Philippic*.

48.28–34 "The act of declaring war . . . shall be ascertained."] See *Social Contract*, Book II, chapter ii. Rousseau died in 1778.

50.18 a torrent of abuse] As described in the Philadelphia *Federal Gazette*, from July 1791: "It would seem as if Mr. Fenno [John Fenno, publisher of the Philadelphia *Gazette of the United States*, which republished Publicola's letters] and Mr. Russell had entered into a league to insert the detestable heresies of Publicola, without publishing a single essay to counteract their pernicious tendency. But it is to be hoped that the ex parte perusal which Publicola obtains in this way will not procure many proselytes either to monarchy or aristocracy. Publicola seems to have some talents, but perverted as they are, they are worse than thrown away. Like Burke he has attempted to raise a structure upon a rotten foundation; and his tottering edifice, like that of Burke, would soon have fallen into ruins of itself. Its fate, however, has been accelerated by the numerous assailants it has had to encounter. It is a circumstance highly honorable to the political character of our country, that an host of enlightened writers have arisen, in every part of the United States, to oppose the abominable heresies of Publicola."

52.29 the Salic Law of descents] Referring to an ancient Frankish civil code (the *lex Salica*), which included a provision barring from royal succession individuals descended from a previous sovereign only through a woman, a concept Paine, as an ardent Republican, would have little interest in or sympathy for.

3: LETTERS OF MARCELLUS | 1793

57.14–15 "to add a perfume to the violet."] Cf. *King John*, IV.ii.12.

57.35–36 "War is murder,"] From "Elegy, Written on the Plain of Fontenoy," 1785 poem by English poet Robert Merry.

58.10 "NON NOSTRUM, TANTAS COMPONERE LITES."] "'Tis not for us, the contest to decide." From a 1783 translation of Virgil, *Eclogues*, III.108.

58.31–32 says the new Declaration of Rights] Adams quotes from Article II of a plan for a new French constitution and declaration of rights, drafted in late 1792.

58.33 says the Saviour of mankind] See Matthew 7:12.

59.9–10 "*damus petimusque vicissim:*"] Latin: we give and ask in return. From the *Ars Poetica* of Horace.

59.27–28 still refuse . . . the treaty of peace] Only after the signing of Jay's Treaty on November 19, 1794, would the British finally relinquish control of forts in the northwestern territory of the United States as stipulated in the 1783 Treaty of Paris.

61.23 "OMNIUM PRIMUM RATUS TUERI PUBLICAM FIDEM."] "[Scipio] judged it absolutely necessary, to cause the public faith to be observed." From a 1763 translation of Livy, *The History of Rome*, Book XXIX, chapter 1.

62.30 opening the *Scheldt*] On November 16, 1792, as French troops pressed their advantage by pursuing retreating Imperial (Austrian) troops into the Low Countries, the French Convention declared the navigation of the Scheldt River open to all nations, upending a long-standing treaty arrangement by which the river had served as a natural barrier protecting the Netherlands from French encroachment. Great Britain, which had regarded the "closure" of the Scheldt as essential to maintaining the balance of power on the continent, immediately began preparing for war.

63.38–39 to keep almost all their islands in . . . rebellion and civil War] Of all the colonial ramifications of France's revolution, the one that most concerned Americans, especially southerners, was the uprising of the enslaved population of Saint-Domingue (Haiti), which began in August 1791.

64.8–10 a formal deputation . . . of the British government] After France declared war on Great Britain in April 1792, the most prominent white planters on Saint-Domingue (*les grands blancs*), unhappy with the French National Assembly's granting of civil rights to free men of color in the colonies a month earlier, appealed to Great Britain to take control of the island and restore slavery and racial restrictions. This the British endeavored to do for the next five years, unsuccessfully in the end, at tremendous cost in men, matériel, and moral standing.

64.22 the Lion to lie down with the Lamb] An idiomatic paraphrase of Isaiah 11:6–9, which offers a messianic vision of peace and harmony.

4: FOURTH OF JULY ORATION | 1793

68.4–5 "well received . . . as I ought."] *JQADi*, 41.

68.7–9 "with a warmth . . . my memory ever since."] John Quincy Adams to Charles Francis Adams, July 9, 1828. Quoted in Kaplan, *John Quincy Adams: American Visionary*, 116.

68.13–14 "Writings have given him . . . than he is aware of."] John Adams to Abigail Adams, May 19, 1794. In Margaret A. Hogan et al., eds., *Adams Family Correspondence*, vol. 10, January 1794–June 1795 (Cambridge, MA: Harvard University Press, 2011), 183–84.

69.14 O NOMEN DULCE LIBERTATIS!] "O liberty, thou dear and much-loved name!" From a 1787 translation of *The Orations of Marcus Tullius Cicero against Caius Cornelius Verres*.

69.15–18 *YE shades of ancient heroes* . . . *The wonder done!*] From "Winter," 1726 poem by Scottish poet James Thomson.

72.29–30 the oppressive glory of a successful war] In 1763 Great Britain emerged from the Seven Years' War—or the French and Indian War as the American colonists called it—with the world's largest empire, including unrivaled control over much of the North American continent.

73.22–23 by the stripes . . . their wounds would be healed.] Cf. Isaiah 53.5.

74.10–11 the American Samson . . . while asleep] Cf. Judges 16:19–21.

74.32 "all the varieties of untried being,"] Cf. Joseph Addison, *Cato, A Tragedy* (1713), V.i.10.

75.14–17 like the stripling of Israel . . . British power.] Adams likens the Americans to David, in his contest with Philistine champion Goliath, depicted in 1 Samuel 17:1–58.

77.5–9 the two first offices of this Commonwealth . . . a British proscription.] Adams refers to Massachusetts governor John Hancock (then fifty-six and ill, with just a few more months to live) and Lieutenant Governor Samuel Adams, then seventy. In April 1775, Massachusetts's royal governor, the British general Thomas Gage, received instructions from Lord Dartmouth, the British secretary of state for the colonies, to arrest Hancock and Adams as "the principal actors and abettors in the Provincial Congress whose proceedings appear in every light to be acts of treason and rebellion." Their capture was one of the aims of the British expeditionary force that Gage fatefully dispatched to Lexington and Concord on April 18.

78.22–23 let slip the dogs of war] *Julius Caesar*, III.i.273.

5: PLYMOUTH ORATION | 1802

82.10–11 "which was afterwards . . . I still think unanswerable."] Worthington C. Ford, ed., *Writings of John Quincy Adams* (New York: The Macmillan Company, 1914), III.11.

83.16–20 Ad illa mihi pro . . . quod imitere, capias.] Adams combines two passages from the proem to the first book of Livy's *History of Rome*, which read as follows in a 1783 translation: "I shall only request the reader's serious attention to what respects the lives and manners of this people, the men and measures, in the cabinet and in the field, by which their empire was founded and extended—There you have example of every kind set before you, in a conspicuous point of view; whence you may set up models for your imitation, as an individual, or a state."

84.3–7 the narratives in Purchas . . . Dr. Belknap's American Biography] Adams's sources include Samuel Purchas, *Purchas his pilgrimage. Or Relations of the world and the religions observed in all ages and places discovered, from the creation unto this present*, 4th ed. (London, 1626); Thomas Prince, *A Chronological History of New England, in the form of Annals* (Boston, 1736); Thomas Hutchinson, *The History of the Province of Massachusets-Bay, from the charter of King William and Mary, in 1691, until the year 1750* (Boston, 1767); and Jeremy Belknap, *American Biography*, 2 vols. (Boston, 1798). Belknap, publisher of Adams's maiden speech, and the leading American historian of his generation, died in 1798, at the age of fifty-four.

85.18 Man, therefore, was not made for himself alone] Echoing a famous construction from Cicero's *De officiis* (Bk. I, cap. xxii), which was itself a translation from Plato's Epistle to Archytas: "non nobis solum nati sumus ortusque nostri partem patria vindicat, partem amici" ("since we were not born for ourselves alone, our country and our friends have separate claims upon us," in a 1798 English translation).

85.24–25 "Existence sees him spurn her bounded reign."] Adams adapts a line from Samuel Johnson's poem, "Drury-lane Prologue Spoken by Mr. Garrick at the Opening of the Theatre in Drury-Lane, 1747."

85.26–27 a "puny insect shivering at a breeze;"] And here a line from the fourth of Alexander Pope's "Epistles to Several Persons" (1731–35), later collected as *Moral Essays*.

86.38 Proinde ituri . . . posteros cogitate.] From Tacitus, *The Life of Agricola*: "As therefore you advance to battle, look back upon your ancestors, look forward to your posterity," in a 1763 translation.

87.12 the sucklings of a wolf] In Roman mythology, the twin brothers Romulus and Remus survive abandonment as infants by being nursed by a wolf. Romulus eventually eliminates his brother and establishes the city of Rome.

87.27–28 "the better fortitude of patience and heroic martyrdom."] *Paradise Lost*, IX.31–32.

88.3 *Robinson*] English clergyman John Robinson (c. 1575–1625) moved to the Netherlands in 1609 and led the exiled Separatist congregation at Leiden that included many of the future Plymouth settlers, though he himself would not make the journey.

89.20–21 without the boundaries of their charter] In 1619, the Virginia Company, one of two joint-stock companies chartered under a 1606 royal patent to undertake the settlement of North America, granted permission to the Leiden Separatists to settle in the northern part of its Virginia claim. In the end, the site of the English settlement at Plymouth was well beyond the northern boundary of the company's territory, placing the Separatists outside of its jurisdiction.

90.13 the Batavian Government] That is, the government of the states of Holland.

90.27–33 "They were well weaned . . . again at home."] Quoting from the Separatists' application to the Virginia Company, as recorded in Hutchinson's *History of the Province of Massachusets-Bay*.

91.24 *Carver, Winslow, Bradford* and *Standish*] A roll call of Plymouth Colony leaders: Governors John Carver (d. 1621), Edward Winslow (1595–1655), and William Bradford (1590–1657), and military advisor Miles Standish (c. 1584–1656).

91.38–39 that instrument of Government] Because Plymouth fell outside the Virginia Company's charter and its guarantees that all subjects who emigrate to or are born in a colony "shall have and enjoy all Liberties, Franchises and Immunities . . . as if they had been abiding and born" in England, the settlers entered into the famous agreement signed on board the *Mayflower* on November 11, 1620 [old style], which was first referred to as the Mayflower Compact in 1793.

92.22–23 the seat of an university] As Adams knew well, having studied at the University of Leiden in his youth, 1780–81. It had been founded in 1575.

92.29–31 *Maurice* and *Barnevelt . . . Episcopius* and *Polyander*] Maurice, Prince of Orange (1567–1625), stadtholder and leader of the Dutch rebellion against Spain. He parted ways with his onetime mentor, the statesman Johan Van Oldenbarnevelt (1547–1619), when the latter signed the Twelve Years' Truce with Spain in 1609 and began to agitate for Holland's independence from the other Dutch states. This fracture was aggravated by religious discord between the Arminian and Calvinist branches of Reformed Protestantism, known in the Dutch context as Remonstrants and Counter-Remonstrants. The University of Leiden was a center of this theological conflict and Professors Simon Episcopius (1583–1643) and Johannes Polyander (1568–1646) were among the chief disputants. As Adams indicates, William Bradford, in *Of Plimouth Plantation*, notes that John Robinson participated in these theological disputes and was a friend of the Counter-Remonstrant Polyander.

92.34–37 *Grotius . . .* and his work] Dutch humanist Hugo Grotius (1583–1645), a farsighted political theorist, was a figure much admired by both Adams and his father, principally for his influential 1625 work on international relations, *De Jure Belli ac Pacis*, which was first published in English in 1654 as *The Laws of War and Peace*, and which was entitled *The Rights of War and Peace* in numerous subsequent editions.

94.22–24 We have seen the same mistake . . . a larger theater.] In the French Revolution, that is, with its optimistic vision of *liberté, égalité, fraternité*.

95.40–96.2 The spot on which they fixed . . . before their arrival.] The Pilgrims landed in Patuxet, homeland of the Wampanoag people, who, though they had suffered terribly from European infectious diseases introduced by early expeditions to the coast of what would become New England, had by no means been "totally extirpated" as Adams suggests, repeating the central self-justifying myth of the English settlement in the region.

97.5–7 a capricious and sanguinary tyrant . . . four successive monarchs] Henry VIII (r. 1509–47), whose break with Rome initiated the English Reformation, which became more avowedly Protestant during the brief reign of his son Edward VI (r. 1547–53) before being largely reversed under Edward's half sister Mary. Her reign (1553–58) was followed by that of her half sister, Elizabeth I (r. 1558–1603), whose establishment of an Anglican church incorporating both Protestant and Catholic elements was consolidated by her successor to the English throne, James VI of Scotland, who styled himself James I, king of Great Britain (r. 1603–25).

98.11 a rival settlement] The short-lived Wessagusset Colony, established in 1623 to the north of Plymouth in what is now Weymouth, Massachusetts, by London merchant Thomas Weston (1584–c. 1637).

98.13 a nest of revellers] Disaffected by strict governance of the Plymouth Colony, Thomas Morton (c. 1579–1647) moved to another settlement to the north at Mount Wollaston, in present-day Quincy, Massachusetts, in 1625, renaming it Merrymount. The new colony troubled the leaders in Plymouth, who, as Adams's comment suggests, characterized it as a den of iniquity, and they soon broke it up.

99.2–3 *Raleigh, Smith . . . Penn*, and *Oglethorpe*] A roll call of colonizers: Sir Walter Raleigh (1552–1618), founder of the ill-fated Roanoke settlement in present-day North Carolina; John Smith (1580–1631) of the Virginia Colony at Jamestown; John Winthrop (1588–1649), first governor of the Massachusetts Bay Colony; Cecil Calvert, 2nd Baron Baltimore (1605–1675) and William Penn (1644–1718), proprietors, respectively, of Maryland and Pennsylvania; and James Oglethorpe (1696–1785), founder of the province of Georgia.

99.10–12 the original founder . . . of all his posterity] In Book VIII of the *Aeneid*, Aeneas, the legendary founder of Rome, is presented with a shield forged by the god Vulcan that depicts the future of Rome from Romulus and Remus to Caesar Augustus.

99.17 the horns of the altar] Cf. 1 Kings 1:50.

99.25 "Westward the Star of empire takes its way."] From "Verses on the Prospect of Planting Arts and Learning in America," poem by Anglo-Irish philosopher George Berkeley, written in 1726 but not published until 1752. Adams will refer again to Berkeley's poem in his 1828 address at the dedication of the Chesapeake and Ohio Canal (see page 289).

6: LETTERS OF PUBLIUS VALERIUS | 1804

101.24 Publius Valerius] Publius Valerius Publicola was one of the leaders who overthrew the Roman monarchy and established the Roman republic in the late sixth century BCE. The pseudonym is thus a call back to Adams's Publicola series.

NOTES   727

105.9 the General Court] The official name of the Massachusetts state legislature is the General Court of the Commonwealth of Massachusetts.

106.14–17 the Governour of the Commonwealth . . . *the rent of the Province House*] Federalist Caleb Strong (1745–1819) was governor of Massachusetts from 1800 to 1807 and again from 1812 to 1816. His official residence was the Province House, an ancient structure built as a private home in 1679 and purchased by the colonial legislature in 1716.

106.39 Mr. Ely] Massachusetts state representative William Ely (1765–1817), a Federalist. He would later serve in the U.S. House of Representatives.

107.34–35 the famous intercepted letter of Fauchet] Jean Antoine Joseph Fauchet (1761–1834) succeeded Edmond-Charles Genêt as the French Republic's minister to the United States in 1794. Amid the controversy over Jay's Treaty in the summer of 1795, Fauchet's correspondence with Edmund Randolph, who had replaced Jefferson as Washington's secretary of state, was intercepted by the British, and eventually found its way to Philadelphia. It revealed that Randolph had been criticizing the administration's policies with respect to France and betraying its internal deliberations. (Federalists also alleged that it revealed that Randolph had solicited a bribe.) When confronted with the letter by the president on August 19, Randolph promptly resigned. Concerned about divided loyalties in his cabinet, Washington replaced him with Timothy Pickering, a staunch Federalist. The episode confirmed Washington in his decision to sign Jay's Treaty.

108.13–14 the repayment of Callender's fine] Adams offers a sarcastic litany of the Jefferson administration's "achievements" calculated to embarrass Republicans. Republican muckraker James Thomson Callender (1758–1803), best known for his exposure of Alexander Hamilton's extramarital affair with Maria Reynolds, was tried and convicted under the Sedition Act of 1798, fined, and imprisoned. Callender expected the new Jefferson administration would refund his fine and provide him with a government appointment. Jefferson, after some delay, arranged for the former through private contributions (to avoid "specious criticisms," as he explained to James Monroe) but refused the latter. An embittered Callender then revealed that Jefferson, his former patron, had engaged in a long-standing relationship with Sally Hemings, an enslaved woman at Monticello. (Adams himself, writing as "Thomas Paine," published a mocking poem about the scandal.)

108.14 the nolle prosequi, to screen Duane from punishment] William Duane (1760–1835), publisher of the Republican Philadelphia *Aurora*, was also twice charged under the Sedition Act. The second time was in 1800, when Republican senators leaked a proposed Federalist bill altering the procedure for resolving contingent presidential elections, and Duane published it, along with editorials attacking the plan. Duane was ordered to appear before the Senate and charged with "false, scandalous, defamatory, and malicious assertions." Jefferson, who as vice president presided over the Senate, granted permission for Duane to leave to consult with counsel. When Duane failed to return, the Senate found him in contempt and a warrant was issued for his arrest. Shortly after assuming the presidency, Jefferson issued an order quashing the prosecution, and any others against Duane stemming from violations of the Sedition Act.

108.15 the squandered thousands upon the Berceau] In October 1800, after the Convention of 1800, also known as the Treaty of Mortefontaine, had been signed ending the Quasi-War with France, the U.S. frigate *Boston* captured the French corvette *Berceau* off Guadeloupe. The damaged vessel was taken to Boston, condemned as a prize, and sold to the U.S. government in January 1801. Under the Convention, captured "public ships" of either side were to be returned. The Jefferson administration requested, and Congress approved, an appropriation to cover the repairs and reimburse the French crew for lost wages. The vessel was restored at a cost of $32,800 and turned over to the French at Boston on June 22, 1801.

108.15–17 the dismission of numerous . . . of an opposite sect] Though it was the second presidential transition for the new republic, the inauguration of Thomas Jefferson marked the first in which control was transferred from one political party to another. Despite his famous inaugural avowal that "we are all republicans: we are all federalists," Jefferson set about systematically removing Federalists from government posts and replacing them with Republicans. Adams was never able to reconcile himself to the idea of a spoils system.

108.18–19 the comment . . . to the merchants of New Haven] Jefferson's housecleaning extended even to relatively minor federal officers, including Elizur Goodrich, the popular collector of customs in New Haven, Connecticut, who had been appointed by John Adams on the last day of his administration. When the local merchants requested Goodrich's reinstatement, Jefferson replied that "if the will of the nation, manifested by their various elections, calls for an administration of government according with the opinions of those elected; if, for the fulfilment of that will, displacements are necessary, with whom can they so justly begin as with persons appointed in the last moments of an administration, not for it's [sic] own aid, but to begin a career at the same time with their successors, by whom they had never been approved, and who could scarcely expect from them a cordial co-operation?" (Thomas Jefferson to the New Haven Merchants, July 12, 1801. In Barbara B. Oberg, ed., *The Papers of Thomas Jefferson*, vol. 34, 1 May–31 July 1801 [Princeton: Princeton University Press, 2007], 557.)

108.19–20 the destruction of the federal Judiciary] Stymied by the "good behavior" terms of judicial tenure under the Constitution, Republicans were especially frustrated by the Federalist domination of the federal bench and turned to the clumsy process of impeachment to try to oust judges. Eventually, they proposed a constitutional amendment allowing the president to

NOTES   729

remove judges with a simple majority of both houses of Congress, something more akin, ironically, to the British system of judicial tenure.

108.25–26 "To crook the pregnant hinges . . . follow fawning."] *Hamlet*, III.ii.61–62.

108.31 the Yazoo purchase of Georgia Lands] Adams refers to the Yazoo land fraud, a scheme by which Georgia legislators had been bribed to sell the state's western lands in present-day Alabama and Mississippi (an area including the Yazoo River) in 1795 to a consortium of land companies, only to rescind the sale a year later. Individuals who had purchased land through the companies were forced to seek redress from the federal government. Their claims were finally resolved by the Supreme Court in *Fletcher v. Peck* (1810), which ruled the 1796 Rescinding Act unconstitutional. See Chronology for 1809.

108.37 Mr. John Randolph] Virginian John Randolph (1773–1833) was an arch-Republican in the House, and one of the more colorful political actors of the age. Adams's grandson, the historian Henry Adams, wrote a memorable biography of him.

108.39 Mr. Thomas Randolph] Thomas Mann Randolph Jr. (1768–1828) was the husband of Martha Jefferson, the president's eldest daughter. He served two terms in Congress.

109.26 the great Mc'Fingal] Referring to the Scottish loyalist who is the titular antagonist of *M'Fingal: A Modern Epic Poem, or, The Town-meeting*, a 1775 mock epic by Connecticut patriot John Trumbull. Thought to be keen of vision, he could not see the writing on the wall in the imperial crisis until it was too late: "Alas! against my better light / and optics sure of second sight, / my stubborn soul, in error strong, / had faith in Hutchinson too long (Canto IV). Mc'Fingal's rival in the poem, the Whig lawyer Honorious, is thought to have been modelled on John Adams.

110.17–18 the commissioners of the sinking fund] The group charged with managing the revenue and long-term debt service of the federal government. In 1804, they were Secretary of State James Madison, Secretary of the Treasury Albert Gallatin, Attorney General Levi Lincoln, and John Brown of Kentucky, president *pro tempore* of the Senate.

110.26–27 the old six per cents] Federal bonds, carrying a 6 percent interest rate, issued from 1795 to 1798.

112.10–11 nearly three millions . . . by a convention with Great Britain] Referring to the agreement, signed at London January 8, 1802, resolving outstanding issues with both Jay's Treaty and the Treaty of Paris. It stipulated payments of £600,000 in three annual payments, converted at $4.40 per pound sterling, plus interest.

113.14–15 the Barbary War] The first Barbary War (1801–5), a conflict triggered when Americans refused to continue payment of tribute to the piratical rulers of the North African Barbary states of Algiers, Tunis, Morocco, and Tripoli.

114.8–10 Captains Bainbridge and Rogers . . . Mr. Simpson] American naval officers William Bainbridge (1774–1833) of the USS *Philadelphia* and John Rodgers (1772–1838) of the USS *John Adams*, and James Simpson (1747–1820), U.S. consul at Tangiers.

114.20 we have lost one of the best frigates in the navy] In October 1813, the *Philadelphia* was captured when it ran aground in Tripoli harbor, its captain and crew taken prisoner. On February 16, 1804, U.S. naval officer Stephen Decatur Jr. led a daring raid into Tripoli's harbor and burned the *Philadelphia* before it could be put into service by the Tripolitans.

114.28–30 We read of the Emperour Caligula . . . of the German ocean] According to Suetonius, Caligula led Roman forces to the Lower Rhine and the coast of Gaul to lay the groundwork for a planned invasion of Britain and there ordered his troops to gather seashells to be brought back to Rome to symbolize his conquest.

115.37–39 Hudibras. . . . a *non* lucendo."] *Hudibras* is a satirical poem (1663–77) by English poet Samuel Butler (1613–1680). But Adams quotes here lines 257–58 from Book II of *The Ghost*, a poem by English satirist Charles Churchill (1731–1764). A *lucus a non lucendo* is an illogical argument that holds one thing to be related to another not just despite but because it would seem to mean the opposite.

116.1 Mr. Livingston] Robert R. Livingston (1746–1813) was the U.S. minister in Paris from December 1801 to November 1804, and as such the principal negotiator of the Louisiana Purchase.

116.5 Mr. Monroe] Future president James Monroe was U.S. minister in London from 1803 to 1807.

117.20–22 a similar character . . . Commissioner of Loans] Earlier in 1804 Jefferson had appointed Boston merchant Benjamin Austin (1752–1820), who had been a fierce and vocal critic of John Adams's administration, commissioner of loans for Massachusetts, replacing Federalist Thomas Perkins, who had held the post since 1798.

117.36 "from whatever quarter of the House it may come,"] A common parliamentary expression.

117.38–39 sons in law] In addition to Thomas Mann Randolph Jr. (see note 108.39), the Virginia delegation included John Wayles Eppes (1772–1823), who was the nephew of Jefferson's late wife.

122.24–25 the amendment to the Constitution . . . last winter] The Twelfth Amendment, approved by Congress on December 9, 1803, and ratified by the requisite number of states on June 15, 1804. It replaced the language governing the Electoral College in Article II, section 1, clause 3, of the Constitution, providing for the separate elections of the president and vice president, among other reforms, including the reduction of the number of candidates eligible for consideration by the House in a contingent election (in which no candidate secures the requite number of electoral votes) from five to three, a change that would figure significantly in Adams's own election to the presidency.

122.26 Mr. Huger] Benjamin Huger (1768–1823) represented South Carolina's Third Congressional District from 1799 to 1805.

123.19 a committee of the whole] A parliamentary procedure by which the House of Representatives reconstituted itself as one large congressional committee, with lower thresholds for a quorum (100) and a forced recorded vote (25), and a streamlined process for debating amendments. It was often used as a device for expediting the passage of important bills.

126.10 the sword of Brennus] According to Livy, at the culmination of the sack of Rome in 390 BCE, as the defeated Romans amassed gold to pay off the attacking Gauls, the Gallic chieftain Brennus grew enraged when the Romans questioned the accuracy of the scales used to measure the ransom. "Vae victis! (Woe to the vanquished!)" he shouted as he threw his sword on the scale, increasing the ransom.

126.27 she has opened all her ports to that disgraceful trade] Anticipating federal action against the slave trade in 1808, the South Carolina General Assembly on December 17, 1803, passed a new slave importation law lifting a ban on human trafficking from Africa. From that date to until Congress outlawed the trade, Charleston imported more than seventy five thousand enslaved Africans.

128.13 the inhabitants beyond the mountains] That is, settlers in the region that would become West Virginia in 1863.

128.31–32 by the most distinguished character] Adams refers to Rufus King (1755–1827), a much admired figure who had served previously as a U.S. senator and as the U.S. minister in London. Noting that there was "much misconception of this section," King argued during the Massachusetts ratifying convention (January 9–February 6, 1788) in favor of the three-fifths clause, explaining that "it is a principle of the Constitution, that representation and taxation should go hand in hand." When asked who are the "three-fifths of other persons" referred to in the text of the Constitution, King replied, "these persons as the slaves. By this rule are representation and taxation to be apportioned. And it was adopted, because it was the language of all America." King spoke with authority at the ratifying convention, having been one of the state's delegates to the Constitutional Convention.

7: BOYLSTON ORATION | 1806

133.24–27 "undertaking of magnitude . . . it is presumption to ask."] *JQADI*, 136.

135.11 ἵνα τ'ἄνδρες αριπρεπέες τελέθουσι.] *The Iliad*, IX.441. "in debate where men illustrious shine," in an 1809 translation.

138.3–5 the writer, who maintained . . . the happiness of mankind] Referring, perhaps, to Rousseau, who in the second part of his "Discourse on the Arts and Sciences," better known as the "First Discourse" (1750), observed of the study of the sciences: "What dangers lurk! What false routes in an investigation of the sciences! How many errors, a thousand times more dangerous than the truth is useful, does one not have to get past to reach the truth? The disadvantage is clear, for what is false is susceptible to an infinity of combinations, but truth has only one form of being."

139.3–6 "Sure, he that made us . . . unus'd."] *Hamlet*, IV.iv.36–39.

139.23–24 the want of ELOQUENCE was pleaded by the chosen object of his ministry] Moses. See Exodus 4:10–11.

139.32–36 "Is not Aaron the Levite . . . him instead of God."] Exodus 4:14.

140.19–21 a God . . . interpreter of Olympus] Hermes, divine patron of orators.

146.1 this seminary] From its founding in 1636 until well into the nineteenth century, Harvard was primarily dedicated to the training of New England's Congregational ministry.

8: LETTER TO HARRISON GRAY OTIS | 1808

153.6 the Governor of the Commonwealth] Jurist James Sullivan (1744–1808), who had been Massachusetts's attorney general for many years, ran five times to be its governor before finally succeeding in 1807, as a Democratic-Republican.

153.29 our common constituents, the Legislature of the State] Until ratification of the Seventeenth Amendment in 1913, U.S. senators were elected by their respective state legislatures.

159.1 Mr. Rose] George H. Rose (1771–1855) had been dispatched to Washington in November 1807 as a special envoy to deal with the *Chesapeake* affair; when President Jefferson and Secretary of State Madison refused to treat the matter separately from other grievances with Britain, Rose broke off negotiations and returned to England in February 1808.

159.20 Mr. Erskine] David Montague Erskine (1776–1855) was the British minister to the United States from 1806 to 1809. He formally reported the orders in council to the U.S. government in a letter dated February 23, 1808.

161.12–13 now confirmed . . . by act of Parliament] In the Orders in Council Bill, passed by Parliament on March 28, 1808, which supplemented the orders with customs duties applied to goods when exported from Great Britain.

162.22 specially charged as a member of the executive] Under the Constitution, the U.S. Senate plays an intermediary role between the executive and legislative branches, with the vice president serving as president of the Senate, and the senators responsible for advising and consenting to certain executive appointments and ratifying treaties negotiated by the executive.

163.33 native Americans] As opposed to naturalized Americans.

164.29 the present War] The War of the Fourth Coalition, which commenced in October 1806.

165.24–25 the issue of Whitby's Court Martial has taught us] On April 20, 1806, HMS *Leander*, captained by Henry Whitby, was patrolling off New York when it accosted the American merchant ship *Richard*, firing a warning shot that killed an American sailor named John Pierce. In response, the U.S. government closed American ports to British squadrons and issued a call for Whitby's arrest. Whitby was acquitted at a court-martial in Portsmouth, England, on April 16, 1807, though he did remain without a command for three years thereafter.

165.27 put upon the yellow list] That is, forced to retire.

166.8 protections] Personal identification certificates used to prove citizenship.

167.36–37 Sir William Scott . . . War in Disguise] William Scott, 1st Baron Stowell (1745–1836), was a judge on the High Court of Admiralty. British Member of Parliament Robert Plumer Ward (1765–1846) was the author of *A Treatise of the Relative Rights and Duties of Belligerent and Neutral Powers in Maritime Affairs* (London, 1801). Published anonymously in London in 1805, and soon reprinted throughout the United States, *War in Disguise; or, The frauds of the neutral flags*, a vigorous defense of British policy with respect to neutrality, has been attributed to British lawyer James Stephens (1758–1832).

167.38–39 the Edinburg reviewers] Founded in 1802, the *Edinburgh Review* was an influential British magazine of generally Whig politics.

168.1–6 The *Answer* to War in Disguise was ascribed . . . of modern War] The anonymous rebuttal to Stephens's pamphlet, *An Answer to War in Disguise: or, Remarks upon the new doctrine of England, concerning neutral trade* (New York, 1806), was written by Gouverneur Morris (1752–1816), a framer of the Constitution who had been U.S. minister to France and a U.S. senator from New York.

168.6 Mr. Gore and Mr. Pinckney] Federalist Christopher Gore (1758–1827) of Massachusetts and Democratic-Republican William Pinkney (1764–1822) of Maryland.

168.20–21 the unanswered . . . memorial of Mr. Munroe] James Monroe was U.S. minister in London from 1803 to 1807. On September 7, 1807, in his final weeks in the post, he directed a lengthy remonstrance to British foreign secretary George Canning protesting the impressment of American seamen. Monroe was succeeded by William Pinkney.

170.3–9 Mr. Fox . . . the Cabinet which he had formed] With the death of William Pitt on January 23, 1806, Whig statesman Charles James Fox (1749–1806) became foreign secretary as part of the so-called Ministry of All Talents. Fox was a noted Francophile, reviving hopes for peace between France and Great Britain. On February 20, he was approached at the Foreign Office by a Frenchman proposing a plan to assassinate Napoleon. After consulting with the Cabinet, Fox relayed information about the plot to French foreign minister Talleyrand as a conciliatory gesture. Hopes for a more liberal policy toward America suffered a blow when Fox died just months after taking office.

170.16–17 the French decrees of Berlin and of Milan] Issued, respectively, on November 21, 1806, and December 17, 1807, these were the main struts of Napoleon's so-called Continental System, forbidding the importation of British goods to European countries allied with or controlled by France.

171.3–4 If she chastises with whips do not you chastise with Scorpions] Cf. 1 Kings 12:14.

171.12–15 It is not by the light . . . at Copenhagen] An allusion to a particularly notorious example of British aggression: for three days beginning on September 2, 1807, the Royal Navy had attacked Copenhagen in a preemptive strike to capture or destroy the Danish fleet before it could fall into French hands. The bombardment, which included the use of newly invented Congreve rockets, killed more than two thousand civilians, and destroyed almost a third of the city.

173.20–21 so satisfactory at Halifax] That is, to the British Admiralty. Halifax, in Nova Scotia, was the headquarters of the Royal Navy's North American Station.

174.17–21 the nobleman who moved . . . with respect to European sovereigns] On January 21, 1808, Admiral George Stewart, 8th Earl of Galloway (1768–1834), responded to the King's Address thus: "My lords, we must make a stand somewhere; and where can we do it better than in defence of our seamen and our trade; which they unequivocally demand? if America prefers French alliance to British connection, it is not in your lordships power to controul her choice; nor can you prevent that war, which I do not wish to see take place; but which, if it does take place, my lords, I am confident, if pursued by us with judgment and reference to the American character and situation, no man need fear."

176.19 the lord chancellor] A jurist and politician of strong Tory principles, John Scott, 1st Earl of Eldon (1751–1838) was lord chancellor from 1807 to 1827.

9: DEFENCE OF GENERAL JACKSON | 1818

181.24–32 "to repair . . . notify this department."] Recorded in *Message from the President of the United States, transmitting copies of documents referred to in his communication of the seventeenth ultimo, in relation to the Seminole War, etc.* (Washington, 1818), 33, 36.

182.3 "if the Ministry had but held up a finger."] Quoted in Richard Rush, *Memoranda of a Residence at the Court of London* (Philadelphia, 1833), 451.

182.5–11 "the subject of deliberation . . . by the Country."] *JQADI*, 445.

182.19–21 "the most important . . . as to logic and style."] Thomas Jefferson to James Monroe, January 18, 1819. In J. Jefferson Looney, ed., *The Papers of Thomas Jefferson*, Retirement Series, vol. 13, 22 April 1818–31 January 1819 (Princeton: Princeton University Press, 2016), 587.

183.14 Mr. Pizarro] José García Pizarro (1770–1835), Spain's foreign minister from 1816 to 1818.

184.18–19 the commandant of St. Marks and the Governor of Pensacola] In the effort to justify Jackson's unauthorized capture of St. Marks and Pensacola, Adams accuses José Masot, governor of Spanish West Florida, and Francisco Caso y Luengo (1761–1824), commandant of Fort San Marco, of supplying arms and other support to Seminole and Creek Indians at war with the United States.

185.21 Col. Nicholls] During the War of 1812, from his base at the mouth of the Apalachicola River, Edward Nicholls, an Irish-born major in the Royal Marines, had organized resistance to the United States among the southeastern Indian tribes. In the summer of 1815, outraged by what he saw as U.S. manipulation of the terms of the Treaty of Ghent to displace the Creek Indians, he concluded a separate treaty with the Red Stick Creeks (a faction of the Muscogee Creek Nation named for their painted war clubs) and returned to London to deliver and defend it. The British government renounced his treaty.

186.19 Col. Hawkins] Benjamin Hawkins (1754–1816), a former U.S. senator from North Carolina, was appointed a commissioner to the Creek Indians in 1796.

186.38 Mr. Baker] British diplomat Anthony St. John Baker (1785–1854), whom Adams had known at Ghent, where he was secretary to the British commission.

187.2–3 the Minister of the United States, then in England] This was Adams himself.

187.8–9 Earl Bathurst and Lord Castlereagh] Henry Bathurst, 3rd Earl Bathurst (1762–1834), the British secretary of state for war and the colonies, and Robert Stewart, Viscount Castlereagh (1769–1822), the British foreign secretary.

188.7 the Governor-General of the Havanna] The Spanish-born officer José Cienfuegos Jovellanos (1763–1825) became the governor of Cuba in early July 1816.

189.7–9 Lieutenant Scott . . . waylaid and murdered] In November 1817, several hundred Seminole and Red Stick Creek Indian warriors attacked a U.S. Army boat commanded by Lieutenant Richard W. Scott, killing Scott and some three dozen men, women, and children.

189.33–34 the officer in command, immediately before General Jackson] Late in 1817 Edmund Gaines had led an expedition into Florida, with orders to pursue Indian raiding parties but not to engage with Spanish forts.

193.32–33 Mr. Pizarro's successor] Carlos Martínez de Irujo y Tacón, 1st Marquess of Casa Irujo (1763–1824), interim Spanish foreign minister from September 1818 to September 1819.

193.37 McGregor] In June 1817 a group of filibusters led by Scottish mercenary Gregor MacGregor seized Amelia Island and proclaimed a revolutionary republic, one annexed to the Republic of Mexico. The island quickly became a base for predation on neutral shipping, including that of the U.S., and President Monroe resolved to intervene. U.S. naval and military forces assumed control over the island on December 23, 1817.

194.28 British Admiral Cockburn] Rear Admiral George Cockburn (1772–1853), commander of the British forces that had sacked Washington in 1814.

195.9 Hambly] Indian interpreter William Hambly.

195.18 Governor Cameron] Charles Cameron (1766–1828), governor of the Bahamas, 1804–20.

197.39 the late war] That is, the War of 1812, which was not commonly referred to by that name until later in the nineteenth century. Elsewhere in this volume Adams will call it "the American and English war" (198), "the last war" (246), "The war last waged with Great Britain" (356), and "the late war with Great Britain" (409).

NOTES   737

201.12 (says Vattel,)] Adams quotes from Emmerich de Vattel, *Le droit des gens* (1758; *The Law of Nations*, 1759).

10: FOURTH OF JULY ADDRESS | 1821

205.31–37 "I had made up my mind . . . the canvassing of others."] *JQADI*, 594.

206.1 "Macbeth policy"] Worthington C. Ford, ed., *Writings of John Quincy Adams* (New York: The Macmillan Company, 1917), VII.356–62.

209.34 the great charter of Runny Mead] Better known as the Magna Carta.

211.2 her Wicliffe] English dissident theologian John Wycliffe (d. 1384), whose writings anticipate many of the ideas of the Protestant Reformation.

211.25–27 like flaming sword . . . the tree of life] Cf. Genesis 3:22–24.

211.35–36 the rival crowns . . . united on the same head] In the person of James I (see note 97.5–7).

212.3 solving] In the now obsolete sense of breaking up or unbinding.

212.16–17 one Stuart . . . hurled another from his throne] Charles I (r. 1625–49), the second monarch of the Stuart dynasty, was executed by parliamentary authorities in 1649. After a short reign, his son, James II (r. 1685–88), was forced into exile in the Glorious Revolution.

212.23 "cast longing, lingering, looks behind,"] Cf. Thomas Gray, "Elegy Written in a Country Churchyard" (1751), l. 88.

213.13 whips and scorpions] Cf. 1 Kings 12:14.

214.31–33 Pharoah and Moses . . . Philip of Austria and William of Orange] A litany of oppressors and liberators: Moses led the Israelites out of Pharoah's Egypt, as recounted in the biblical book of Exodus; the Roman king Tarquinus Superbus was overthrown by his nephew Marcus Junius Brutus in the wake of the rape and suicide of the Roman matron Lucretia, as described in Livy's *History of Rome* (*Ab Urbe Condita*); the sanguinary Christian II of Denmark, who was deposed by the Swedish nobleman Gustav Vasa; and Philip II, Hapsburg king of Spain, who waged a long and ultimately unsuccessful struggle to retain control over the Netherlands in the face of an uprising led by William, Prince of Orange.

215.9–10 "moons revolve . . . its execution;"] Cf. Edmund Burke, *The Speech of Edmund Burke, Esquire, on Moving His Resolutions for Conciliation with the Colonies, March 22d, 1775* (New York, 1775), collected in Gordon S. Wood, ed., *The American Revolution: Writings from the Pamphlet Debate 1773–1776* (New York: Library of America, 2015), 529–89: "The last cause of this disobedient spirit in the colonies is hardly less powerful than the rest, as it is not merely moral, but laid deep in the natural constitution of things. Three thousand miles of ocean lie between you and them. No contrivance can prevent the effects of this distance in weakening government. Seas roll, and months pass, between the order and the execution; and the want of a speedy explanation of a single point, is enough to defeat a whole system."

215.19–21 St. James's . . . St. Stephen's Chapel] Respectively, the royal palace and the royal chapel, where the House of Commons sat until 1834.

216.16–20 "sat down by the rivers . . . forget her cunning."] Cf. Psalm 137.

217.6–9 the prime minister . . . the Island of Virginia] Frederick Lord North was said to have made this gaffe in the House of Lords.

217.9–11 even Edmund Burke . . . to the people of Bristol] Adams alludes to Burke's 1774 *Speech to the Electors of Bristol.*

217.39 Charlestown and Falmouth] During the battle of Bunker Hill, June 17, 1775, Charlestown, Massachusetts, was subjected to a British cannonade with combustible shells. (Adams recalled seeing the smoke from the ensuing conflagration with his mother Abigail Adams from atop Penn's Hill near his boyhood home in Braintree.) Falmouth, Massachusetts (now Portland, Maine), was bombarded by British ships and burnt on October 18, 1775.

217.40 the ear of the adder] Cf. Psalm 58:4.

218.1 two successive supplications to the throne] The "Petition to the King" of October 25, 1774, issued by the First Continental Congress, and the "Olive Branch Petition" of July 5, 1775, issued by the Second Continental Congress.

218.2 two successive appeals to the people of Britain] "The Address to the People of Great Britain," issued by the First Continental Congress on October 12, 1774, and "The Twelve United Colonies, by their Delegates in Congress, to the Inhabitants of Great Britain," issued by the Second Continental Congress on July 5, 1775.

218.5–7 "Nought but the noise of drums . . . To the grim idol."] Cf. *Paradise Lost*, I.394–96.

223.5 "with the years beyond the flood."] Edward Young, *Night Thoughts; or, The Complaint* (1742), "Night I, On Life, Death, and Immortality," l. 51.

223.6–7 the chastity of Lucretia . . . the child of Tell] Adams refers to the rape of Lucretia (see note 214.31–33) and to the popular fourteenth-century Swiss tale of William Tell, who was forced by his Austrian oppressors to shoot an apple off his son's head.

223.35–37 "How many ages hence . . . and accents yet unknown?"] Cf. *Julius Caesar*, III.i.111–13.

224.21 the genuine Holy Alliance] A pointed allusion to the reactionary "Holy Alliance" of Austria, Prussia, and Russia, which had been formed in 1815.

225.15 "With heaviest sound, the giant monster fell."] See note 75.14–17.

225.21–23 The Semiramis of the North . . . upon the seas] An allusion to the League of Armed Neutrality, formed in early 1780 by the empress Catherine II of Russia (r. 1762–96), whose formidable leadership skills invited comparison to the legendary princess Semiramis of Assyria.

225.33 vial of wrath] Cf. Revelation 15:7.

227.12–13 "Anarchy is found tolerable!"] From Edmund Burke, *Speech on Conciliation*, in *The American Revolution: Writings from the Pamphlet Debate, 1773–1776*, 551.

229.16 Aceldama] Literally, field of blood.

230.1–2 Ye improvers upon the sculpture of the Elgin marbles!] From 1801 to 1812, British nobleman Thomas Bruce, 7th Earl of Elgin (1766–1841), organized the removal of roughly half the friezes from the Acropolis in Athens for display in London's British Museum, where they remain today.

230.7 When Themistocles was sarcastically asked] As recorded in *Plutarch's Lives*.

230.13–14 who was the last President of your Royal Academy] Pennsylvania-born artist Benjamin West (1738–1820).

230.14–23 by whose mechanical combinations . . . He is now among yourselves] Adams alludes with cheek to a trio of American inventors and their most famous inventions: Robert Fulton (1765–1815) and the steamboat, Eli Whitney (1765–1825) and the cotton gin, and Jacob Perkins (1766–1849) and the "unforgeable" banknote.

230.33 "Excudent alii spirantia mollius æra,"] *The Aeneid*, VI.846: "Let others better mold the running mass / Of metals," in Dryden's 1697 translation.

230.35 "Tu regere *Imperio* populos"] *The Aeneid*, VI.851: "But, Rome, 't is thine alone, with awful sway, / To rule mankind, and make the world obey" (Dryden).

231.5–6 "prefers before all temples the upright heart and pure,"] Cf. *Paradise Lost*, I.17–18.

231.11 GO THOU, AND DO LIKEWISE.] Cf. Luke 10:37.

11: INAUGURAL ADDRESS | 1825

233.29–39 "He said he would tell me . . . I am at least forewarned."] David Waldstreicher, ed., *John Quincy Adams: Diaries 1721–1848* (New York: Library of America, 2017), 95–96. [Hereafter *JQAD2*.]

234.27–29 "after exchanging salutations . . . I retired from the Hall."] *JQAD2*, 97.

236.30 our commerce has whitened every ocean] With the canvas of sailing ships, that is.

239.15–16 modes of domestic life] A elliptical allusion to slavery.

242.21–22 except the Lord keep . . . waketh but in vain] Psalm 127:1.

12: FIRST ANNUAL MESSAGE | 1825

243.12–17 "efforts had been made . . . scarcely have been devised."] *JQAD2*, 99.

243.18–19 "the message became clear . . . by supporting it."] Parsons, *John Quincy Adams*, 183.

244.4–17 "Mr. Clay wished to . . . be prepared for the consequences."] *JQAD2*, 117–18.

247.20–22 a mass of claims . . . of indemnity for property taken] The U.S. had for many years tried to secure reparations from France for depredations on American shipping during the Napoleonic Wars. Adams would pursue these claims throughout his presidency and would be instrumental in their final resolution in his later career as a congressman.

247.27–28 the accession of a new Sovereign to the throne] Charles X (1757–1836) ascended to the French throne with the death of Louis XVIII on September 16, 1824.

247.31–32 our Minister at the Court of France] Appointed by Monroe, James Brown (1766–1835) was U.S. minister in Paris from 1824 to 1829.

249.12–13 the Seventh Article of the Treaty of Ghent] This established a commission to determine the northwestern boundary of the United States.

251.27 the Secretary of the Treasury] After seven years as Adams's successor at the Court of St. James's, Richard Rush (1780–1859) returned home to become his treasury secretary.

251.35–36 the Chesapeake and Delaware Canal Company] Incorporated in 1802 and reorganized in 1822 with investment from Pennsylvania, Maryland, and Delaware more than matched by federal dollars, the company was to build

NOTES 741

a fourteen-mile-long canal connecting the northern tip of Chesapeake Bay with the Delaware River. The canal finally opened in 1829 and its total cost of $3.5 million made it among the most expensive such projects of the era.

252.37–38 the Secretary of War] Former Virginia governor James Barbour (1775–1842).

253.7–9 The Military Academy at West-Point . . . superintendence] The U.S. Military Academy was founded in 1802. Its fifth superintendent, who served from 1817 to 1833, was Brigadier General Sylvanus Thayer (1785–1872), who became known as "the Father of West Point."

253.15 Fortress Monroe] A large fortification at Old Point Comfort in Hampton, Virginia, guarding the entrance to Chesapeake Bay. Construction began in 1822 and continued for nearly twenty-five years.

254.6–7 a Treaty was signed at the Indian Springs] Negotiated by commissioners of the U.S. government and a minority faction of Creek Indians led by William McIntosh, signed on February 12, 1825, and ratified by the Senate on March 7, 1825, this treaty provided for the cession of some three million acres of Creek lands under its terms. A large majority of Creek chiefs and warriors objected, insisting that McIntosh did not have authority to sign treaties or cede territory. Adams ratified the treaty shortly after taking office but appointed Major General Edmund P. Gaines to investigate the Creek claims. Belligerent officials in Georgia, especially the state's governor, demanded Gaines's recall and resisted all efforts to revisit the treaty's terms.

255.5–6 Lake Memphramagog] Lake Memphremagog, a large body of water straddling the border between Vermont and Quebec. It is approximately forty miles from the Connecticut River. A surveyor's report for a canal connecting the two was submitted to Congress on February 10, 1829, just before Adams left office, and never acted on (or laid on the table).

255.33–34 improvements of recent invention in the mode of construction] Adams refers to macadam, a road-building technique involving crushed stone developed within the last decade by Scottish engineer John Loudon McAdam (1756–1836).

256.32–33 The visit of General Lafayette] At the invitation of President Monroe, and in anticipation of the fiftieth anniversary of independence, the Marquis de Lafayette (1757–1834) visited the United States from July 1824 to September 1825, travelling to all twenty-four states. The triumphant tour concluded with a banquet at the Executive Mansion hosted by President Adams, in honor of Lafayette's sixty-eighth birthday.

257.22 the American Patriots] That is, the South American revolutionaries, seeking their independence from Spain.

257.38 the Islands of the Pacific] Most likely referring to the Hawaiian Islands.

258.19 Captain Warrington] Lewis Warrington (1782–1851), who had seen action in both the Barbary Wars and the War of 1812, led the so-called Mosquito Fleet patrolling the Caribbean and Gulf of Mexico in search of pirates.

259.15 the want of a Naval School] The U.S. Naval Academy at Annapolis would not be established for another twenty years.

259.28–29 the Secretary of the Navy] Samuel Southard (1787–1842) of Virginia was appointed secretary of the navy in 1823 by President Monroe and remained in the post throughout Adams's administration.

259.30 the Postmaster General] John McLean (1785–1861) of Ohio was likewise a Monroe appointee, whose services Adams retained throughout his term despite concerns among some Adams men that he was using the federal posts to advance support for Jackson.

260.39–40 first in the memory . . . first in the hearts of our country] Paraphrasing from Henry Lee's famous eulogy for George Washington, in which Lee described his friend and former commander as "First in war, first in peace, and first in the hearts of his countrymen."

261.36–37 Cook and La Perouse] Explorers James Cook (1728–1779) and Jean François de Galaup, Comte de Lapérouse (1741–1788?), both famed for their circumnavigations of the globe, and particularly for their explorations of the Pacific Ocean.

262.18–19 The River of the West . . . a countryman of our own] The Columbia River, first explored (by an individual of European descent) by American merchant Robert Gray (1755–1806) in 1792.

262.27–29 an uniform standard of Weights and Measures . . . our Constitution] See Article 1, section 8, clause 5. This was an abiding interest of Adams, who as secretary of state had prepared a lengthy, painstakingly researched *Report of Weights and Measures* (1821) that included, among other things, a detailed analysis of the metric system.

264.27–28 a predecessor in this office] James Madison, whom Adams would later memorialize in an oft-republished eulogy.

265.5–8 to promote the progress of . . . discoveries.] Article 1, section 8, clause 8, of the U.S. Constitution.

266.24 to hide in the earth the talent] Cf. Matthew 25:14–30.

267.5 a new university unfolding] The University of Virginia, brainchild of Thomas Jefferson, held its first classes on March 7, 1825.

267.8–9 the waters of our Western lakes mingle with those of the ocean] After four years of construction, the Erie Canal, which spans 363 miles in upstate New York from Lake Erie to the Hudson River, was opened on October 26, 1825.

13: MESSAGE ON PANAMA CONGRESS | 1826

269.37–38 "these resolutions . . . bear the impress of his character."] *JQAD2*, 126.

270.6–10 "With nothing connected with slavery . . . fatal to our repose."] Robert Y. Hayne, *Speech of Mr. Hayne, Delivered in the Senate of the United States, on the Mission to Panama, March, 1826* (Washington, 1826), 20.

272.15–16 The instructions prepared under his direction] As secretary of state, Adams himself had drafted these instructions.

274.18 Peace on earth and good will to man] Cf. Luke 2:14.

275.3–4 Three Commissioners, with Plenipotentiary powers] John Adams, Benjamin Franklin, and Thomas Jefferson. They received their instructions from Congress in May 1784.

275.30–31 one great and philosophical, though absolute, Sovereign] The treaty with Prussia had been concluded near the end of the reign of Frederick II (1712–1786), better known as Frederick the Great.

279.8 their acceptance of a nominal sovereignty] For two decades since its overthrow of French rule in 1804, the "Black Republic" of Haiti had been recognized by no other nation. In 1825, Charles X of France agreed to do so in exchange for 150 million francs. Widespread recognition from other countries followed, but not from the United States due to southern opposition. The U.S. would refuse recognition until Abraham Lincoln took the step on July 12, 1862, when southern resistance in Congress was no longer an issue.

279.24–25 the peculiar composition of their population] In the 1820s some 30 percent of Cuba's population and 10 percent of Puerto Rico's were enslaved.

279.27–28 some European Power, other than Spain] Adams and others were particularly concerned that Great Britain would use a revolutionary assault on Cuba and Puerto Rico as a pretense to seize the islands.

14: C&O CANAL DEDICATION | 1828

287.9–17 "infamous Slander . . . their talent for intrigue."] *JQAD2*, 162.

288.12–25 "It happened that . . . hesitation of a deficient memory."] *JQAD2*, 184–85.

288.27–32 "If only he would lend himself . . . simple, unostentatious, and unassuming."] Quoted in Parsons, *John Quincy Adams*, 185.

289.3–6 Berkeley . . . "Time's noblest empire is the last."] See note 99.25.

290.20 The project contemplates a conquest over physical nature] Among other feats, the Chesapeake & Ohio Canal allowed for the circumvention of the Great Falls of the Potomac, an impressive series of cascading rapids and waterfalls that span a seventy-six-foot-drop in elevation in less than a mile.

290.39–40 be fruitful, and multiply . . . *and subdue it*] Genesis 1:28.

292.22 he was one of the first projectors] In 1784, George Washington encouraged Maryland and Virginia's legislatures to establish a company to improve navigation on the Potomac by building a canal from the Potomac's headwaters to Georgetown. The Patowmack Canal Company was incorporated on May 17, 1785, and Washington was its first president.

292.35–36 is commencing from a neighboring city] The opening of the Erie Canal posed a significant challenge to the burgeoning city of Baltimore, threatening to divert trade from the Midwest that had been serviced by the National Road. The city's leaders responded by chartering the Baltimore & Ohio Railway Company in 1827. Charles Carroll of Carrollton, the last surviving signer of the Declaration of Independence, laid the "first stone" for the track construction on the same day as Adams's C&O Canal dedication.

292.40–293.2 every valley shall be exalted . . . the rough places plain] Cf. Isaiah 40:4.

15: FOURTH OF JULY ORATION | 1831

295.12–14 "the limitations as well as the extent of . . . its authority.'] *Andrew Jackson's Inaugural Address, on being sworn into office, as President of the United States, March 4th, 1829* (Washington, D.C., 1829).

295.18–20 "Every thing looks to decay . . . not of building up."] *JQAD2*, 222.

295.33–37 "I had in that respect no scruple . . . by the People."] *JQAD2*, 234.

296.1–2 "No election . . . gave me so much pleasure."] *JQAD2*, 238.

300.3 "shaking from its horrid hair, pestilence and war."] Cf. *Paradise Lost*, II.710–11.

300.36–39 The first of the charters. . . . The most recent of them] The first permanent English settlement in North America, at Jamestown in 1607, was established by the Virginia Company, which had been chartered by James I the year before; the last, Georgia, through a royal patent granted by George II in 1732.

NOTES   745

301.26–27 whether an egg . . . at the little end] A reference to the Big-Endian/Little-Endian controversy, an absurd schism among Lilliputians in Jonathan Swift's *Gulliver's Travels* (1726), meant as a satire on religious sectarianism.

301.31 polished perturbation and golden care] Cf. *2 Henry IV*, IV.v.23.

302.4–7 twice brought to the decision . . . his life] See note 212.16–17.

302.28–29 a royal prerogative in which the Parliament had no agency] Adams neatly summarizes the patriot position during the imperial controversy of the 1760s and '70s. For British polemicists this was a fundamental misunderstanding of the nature of sovereignty in Britain, and least in the wake of the Glorious Revolution, when it was expressly lodged with the "King-in-Parliament."

302.35–36 an English Chancellor of the Exchequer] Whig politician George Grenville (1712–1770) held that post from April 1763 to July 1765, during which time he engineered passage in Parliament of the Stamp Act, which levied a tax on legal documents, newspapers, and nearly every form of paper used in the colonies. The tax quickly became a matter of constitutional principle for the colonists, and protests and boycotts erupted up and down the Atlantic coast.

302.39–40 the Knight of La Mancha . . . his Squire] Adams read Tobias Smollett's 1782 translation of *Don Quixote* while stationed at Berlin in 1798.

303.1–2 John Hambden and ship-money] Among the financial devices Charles I exploited to raise revenues during the Personal Rule (a period when he had prorogued a defiant Parliament) was "ship money," a traditional rate charged to the gentry in coastal counties for naval defense in times of emergency, which Charles now extended to those in inland communities in times of peace. Several gentlemen resisted this novelty, which, they argued, opened the door for the king to tax his people at will and without their consent. Among them was John Hampden (1594–1643), a wealthy member of Parliament who forced the case to trial before the King's Bench. Hampden lost, but the case proved a Pyrrhic victory for the king, who suffered badly in popular opinion.

303.21 at the same time to *declare*] Significant civil unrest in the colonies led Parliament to repeal the Stamp Act less than a year after it was enacted, though as a face-saving gesture it at the same time passed the Declaratory Act, which asserted Parliament's authority to legislate for the colonies "in all cases whatsoever."

303.34 "To point a moral, or adorn a tale."] Samuel Johnson, *The Vanity of Human Wishes: The Tenth Satire of Juvenal Imitated* (1749), l. 222.

303.38–304.9 "There is, and *must be* . . . of the British kingdoms."] Adams quotes from William Blackstone's *Commentaries on the Laws of England*.

304.27 as Burke expresses it] Cf. Edmund Burke, *Speech on Conciliation*, in *The American Revolution: Writings from the Pamphlet Debate, 1773–1776*, 549.

306.1–3 whom David Hume . . . acknowledges] In *The History of England, from the Invasion of Julius Cæsar to the Revolution in 1688* (8 vols., London, 1767).

306.26 "This is *my own*, my *native* land."] Sir Walter Scott, *Lay of the Last Minstrel* (1802), canto VI, l. 3.

306.28–29 Carver and Bradford . . . Endicott and Winthrop] For Carver and Bradford, see note 91.24. John Endicott (c. 1588–1664) and John Winthrop (1588–1649) were the first two governors of the Massachusetts Bay Colony.

306.35 your Quincy, and your Hancock] Massachusetts patriot leaders Josiah Quincy II (1744–1775) and John Hancock.

307.25 this Commonwealth] Massachusetts.

309.4–5 line of battle ships in disguise] The pro-ministry *Courier and Morning Post* so described the American navy's frigates by way of explaining their stunning success against larger British vessels during the War of 1812.

309.26 a crown of imperishable glory!] Cf. Simonides, "On the Lacedaemonian Dead at Plataea."

310.19–21 In our own Commonwealth . . . of her children] An allusion to Shays's Rebellion and its aftermath. See pages 3–4 in this volume.

311.15–18 at one time in Virginia and Kentucky . . . and again in the warmer regions of the South] Adams recounts various appeals to state sovereignty in the nation's young history: first, the Kentucky and Virginia Resolutions (1798/1799) drafted by Thomas Jefferson and James Madison, respectively, which advocated for the states' power to "interpose" against the Alien and Sedition acts; second, the opposition to the embargo among New England Federalists, which culminated in the Hartford Convention in 1815; third, the controversy in Pennsylvania that culminated in the Supreme Court case *United States v. Peters* (1809), in which Chief Justice Marshall, writing for the majority, held that a state cannot annul the judgments or limit the jurisdiction of federal courts; and, finally, the nullification crisis in South Carolina.

311.38 *Lord Bacon] Adams paraphrases from the 1607 essay "Of Sedition and Troubles" by English philosopher Francis Bacon (1561–1626).

313.24–26 In some of the States . . . by their charters] Connecticut did not adopt a new constitution until 1818, and Rhode Island not until 1842.

313.26–30 In one . . . now rectified] North Carolina's constitution was adopted by its provincial congress on December 18, 1776, and never submitted to the people for ratification. After much agitation, a new constitution would finally be approved in 1835.

314.36–38 Pennsylvania was told . . . in opposite directions] This critique of bicameralism has been attributed to Benjamin Franklin.

315.1 a European philosophical statesman] Adams is likely referring to the French cleric Emmanuel Joseph Sieyès (1748–1836), a staunch advocate of unicameralism.

315.25 two apparent changes of principle] That is, first, in 1801, the transfer from John Adams's Federalist administration to Thomas Jefferson's Republican one, and second, at the previous election, from Adams's own National Republican administration to Jackson's Democratic one.

315.37 stretched to their extremest tension] An allusion to the Louisiana Purchase and the embargo, among other acts under Republican administrations that ran counter to a small-government ethos.

316.17–19 an insurrection in arms . . . a convict for treason] Adams refers to the Whiskey Rebellion of 1794, an antitax uprising in western Pennsylvania. The "convict" was John Fries (1750–1818), a Federalist militia captain who had helped suppress the rebellion but then turned against the Federalists when they enacted the house tax and became the leader of a resistance campaign among Pennsylvania Germans known as Fries' Rebellion. On March 7, 1799, he and a group of 140 men forced the release of prisoners who had been jailed for tax evasion. Fries's uprising concluded without a shot and he and thirty others were apprehended and charged with many crimes, including treason. After Fries and two of his associates had been convicted and sentenced to hang, President John Adams, forty-eight hours before the scheduled execution, pardoned the three condemned men and issued a general amnesty for all who had taken part in the rebellion. This action infuriated Alexander Hamilton and his High Federalist followers.

316.33 "We angry lovers mean not half we say."] From James Hammond, *The Love Elegies* (1743), Elegy V, l. 12.

318.26–27 the god of boundaries] Hermes.

320.38–39 "Ate, hot from Hell . . . the dogs of war."] *Julius Caesar*, III.i.272–73.

321.19–22 "came to the House of God . . . lacking in Israel?"] Judges 21:2–3.

321.22–23 The other was a successful example of resistance] Jeroboam's Revolt, recounted in 1 Kings and the 2 Chronicles.

321.32–33 "the most despised portion of their slaves."] Adams quotes from the fifteenth chapter of Edward Gibbon's *History of the Decline and Fall of the Roman Empire* (1776–83).

322.34–37 "Thy spirit, *Independence*, let me share . . . along the sky."] From Tobias Smollett's *Ode to Independence* (1773).

323.9–10 INDEPENDENCE AND UNION FOREVER!] Adams here adapts the famous toast his father had offered just days before his death on July 4, 1826, as recounted in the diary of his fellow townsman George Whitney: "Spent a few minutes with him in conversation, and took from him a toast, to be presented on the Fourth of July as coming from him. I should have liked a longer one; but as it is, this will be acceptable. 'I will give you,' said he, 'Independence forever!' He was asked if he would not add any thing to it, and he replied, 'not a word.'"

16: REPORT OF THE MINORITY | 1833

325.17–19 "Far from the line of occupation . . . estimate of its difficulties."] *JQAD2*, 279.

325.29–30 "share in the accomplishment . . . was humble and secondary."] From an August 3, 1832, letter to Richard Rush, quoted in Bemis, *John Quincy Adams and the Union*, 246.

326.37–41 "recommends a total change in . . . the nullifiers of South-Carolina."] *JQAD2*, 297–98.

330.17 Mr. Verplanck's Submission Bill] So called by its critics, this tariff bill was presented to the House by Congressman Gulian C. Verplanck (1786–1870) of New York—a Van Buren ally—on January 8, 1833, a week before Jackson sent the Force Bill to Congress. The two bills were meant to be complementary: the first would essentially replace the Adams Tariff before it had even had a chance to take effect by reducing tariffs on a more aggressive schedule (and hence "submitting" to the wishes of nullifiers) while the second allocated funds for the president to execute the tariff and suppress nullification by force if necessary.

337.2 by one of themselves] By the time he became president, Andrew Jackson enslaved nearly one hundred individuals on his plantations. An estate inventory after his death in 1845 included 161 enslaved men, women, and children.

337.23 denunciation] Here in the now antiquated sense of a formal announcement.

342.37–343.3 effectively urges upon Congress to refrain from . . . doubtful powers] Adams is responding here to this proposal in Jackson's message:

> If the propriety of the proposed [internal improvement] be not sufficiently apparent to command the assent of 3/4 of the States, the best possible reason why the power should not be assumed on doubtful authority is afforded; for if more than one quarter of the States are unwilling to make the grant its exercise will be productive of discontents which will far over-balance any advantages that could be derived from it. All must admit that there is nothing so worthy of the constant solicitude of this Government as the harmony and union of the people.
>
> Being solemnly impressed with the conviction that the extension of the power to make internal improvements beyond the limit I have suggested, even if it be deemed constitutional, is subversive of the best interests of our country, I earnestly recommend to Congress to refrain from its exercise in doubtful cases, except in relation to improvements already begun, unless they shall first procure from the States such an amendment of the Constitution as will define its character and prescribe its bounds.

344.14 the dog-in-manger disposition] Alluding to the fable of Aesop, which propounds the moral that we often selfishly deny others that which we cannot enjoy ourselves.

345.9–14 "whoever gives preference . . . scarcely any favorers of ALL."] This is likely Adams's own translation of Cicero's *De officiis*, Book I, caption xxv.

352.26 the State of Tennessee] Jackson's home state, of course.

356.35 laid up in ordinary] Mothballed, in more contemporary parlance.

364.9 "All are but parts of one stupendous whole."] Alexander Pope, *An Essay on Man* (1733), I.260.

364.22 the baseless fabric of a vision] Cf. *The Tempest*, IV.i.151.

373.34 their living machinery] Adams was familiar with the work of the Welsh manufacturer and social reformer Robert Owen, who popularized the term "living machinery" in his 1813 work *A New View of Society: Or, Essays on the Formation of Human Character, and the Application of the Principle to Practice*, which sought to ameliorate the conditions of industrial workers.

375.20–23 At this moment . . . of the united republic.] Respectively, President Andrew Jackson of Tennessee; Vice President John C. Calhoun of South Carolina, who enslaved more than seventy individuals at his Fort Hill plantation; Speaker of the House Andrew Stevenson of Virginia, who enslaved sixty-three on his plantation in Albemarle County; and Chief Justice John Marshall of Virginia, who at the time of his death held nearly two hundred individuals in bondage.

377.26–27 the attempt of the Titans to scale the throne of Heaven] In Greek mythology, the Titans were the gods preceding the Olympians. They attempted to scale heaven by piling mountains one on top of another.

377.27–28 the project of the builders on the plain of Shinar] The Tower of Babel (see Genesis 11:1–9.)

377.32 the worse than Gorgon shield] Cf. John Milton, *Comus*, I.447.

378.29–30 honors the Governor of Virginia with eleven votes] Andrew Jackson rolled to reelection in 1832, soundly defeating Henry Clay, but he did not receive the votes of South Carolina, which were awarded by the state's legislature to Virginia governor John Floyd (1783–1837), who ran as a nullifier.

381.3–4 "the SOVEREIGN'ST thing . . . Is parmacity for an inward bruise,"] *1 Henry IV*, I.iii.57–58.

381.22 *brutum fulmen*] Latin: a senseless thunderbolt. In legal terms, an empty threat.

381.32–33 "in spirit and in truth."] South Carolina attorney Thomas Smith Grimké (1786–1834) led opposition within the state to the Nullification Ordinance, particularly the test oath.

384.2 "close ambition varnished o'er with zeal."] *Paradise Lost*, II.485.

385.28 exploded] Here in a now obsolete sense of "to drive out disgracefully" (*Johnson's Dictionary*).

391.12 To solve] See note 212.3.

392.23–27 the county of Mecklenburg is metamorphosed . . . utterly groundless] The so-called Mecklenburg Declaration of Independence was first published on April 30, 1819, in a Raleigh, North Carolina, newspaper. It was purportedly written on May 20, 1775, by a patriot committee alarmed by the news of the fighting at Lexington and Concord the month before. The text appears to have some basis in fact—the county did issue resolves supporting the Massachusetts patriots—but the idea of a full-throated declaration of independence in the late spring of 1775, especially one that mirrored much of the language of the Declaration of Independence that Congress would propound more than a year later, appears doubtful. An aged John Adams was surprised when he first read of the discovery of this lost "declaration" in a Boston paper, and he forwarded the article to Thomas Jefferson, who thought the document must be a fake, professing that "I shall believe it such until positive and solemn proof of its authenticity shall be produced." It is worth noting that unlike the Declaration of Independence, the Mecklenburg "imposture" makes an explicit claim of "sovereignty."

NOTES   751

393.33–35 It has been said . . . by some sublime philosopher.] This has been attributed to Cicero.

17: SPEECH ON JOINT RESOLUTION | 1836

399.20–23 "Mr. Adams chose wisely . . . and loves the *melee.*"] William H. Oilman and J. E. Parsons, eds., *Ralph Waldo Emerson: Journals* (Cambridge: Harvard University Press, 1970), VII.339.

400.13–16 "under the necessity . . . to the northern men with southern principles,"] Adams to Charles Francis Adams, May 2, 1836, quoted in Kaplan, *John Quincy Adams: American Visionary*, 490.

400.24–27 "the Resolution was carried . . . and soon sought my bed."] *JQAD2*, 383.

403.20–21 Committee of the Whole on the State of the Union] See note 123.19. In this particular case, Abijah Mann Jr. (1793–1868), Democrat of New York, served as chair.

404.26 *common defence and general welfare*] See Article I, section 8, clause 1, of the U.S. Constitution.

405.19 the gentleman from Alabama] Joab Lawler (1796–1838), a Jacksonian, represented Alabama's Third District.

405.27 the *war power*] Article I, section 8, clause 11, of the U.S. Constitution grants Congress the power "to declare War, grant Letters of Marque and Reprisal, and make Rules concerning Captures on Land and Water."

406.21–24 I was not permitted to give this morning . . . the abolition petitions] As Adams recounts in his diary entry for May 25, 1836: "At the House, the motion of Robertson, to recommit Pinckney's Slavery Report, with Instructions to report a Resolution, declaring that Congress has no Constitutional Authority to abolish Slavery in the District of Columbia, as an amendment to the motion for printing an extra number of the report was first considered—Robertson finished his Speech which was vehement, and he read the Letter from Mr. Van Buren on the subject of the Power of Congress to abolish Slavery in the District, and he charged him with evading the question. I asked that so much of the Letter as he had referred to should be read and it was—immediately after the conclusion of Robertson's speech I addressed the Speaker, but he gave the floor to Owens of Georgia, one of the signing members of the Committee, who moved the previous question, and refused to withdraw it—It was seconded and carried by yeas and nays 110 to 89—I asked what the main question would be—the Speaker decided that it would be the adoption of the Resolutions of the Committee, which have not been in the slightest degree discussed—I appealed from the decision which the house confirmed.—The question on the first Resolution was taken 168 to 9.—Glascock asked to be excused from voting—I required that the reasons for excusing him should be entered on the Journal—The Speaker was doubtful." *JQAD2*, 382–83.

406.32 Mr. OWENS, of Georgia] George Welshman Owens (1786–1856), a Democrat, serving the first of two terms in Congress.

406.34 Mr. GLASCOCK] Thomas Glascock (1790–1841), also a Democrat, was chairman of the Committee on Militia.

407.1 the Speaker of this House is a slaveholder] Democrat James K. Polk (1795–1849) of Tennessee was the House Speaker from 1835 to 1839. The number of enslaved individuals on his plantation in Mississippi ranged from thirty to fifty-five over the course of his political career.

407.8 Mr. A. H. SHEPPERD] Augustine Henry Shepperd (1792–1864) of North Carolina was chairman of the Committee on Expenditures in the Department of State.

407.24–25 two gentlemen . . . of Maryland] Democrat Francis Thomas (1799–1866), who had previously served as Speaker, and Whig Daniel Jenifer (1791–1855).

407.36–37 an honorable member from Tennessee] Polk.

408.16 the slavery committee] Adams's deliberately provocative name for the select committee on the subject of antislavery petitions, which had been created in January with Pinckney as its chair.

409.36–410.2 It is well known . . . was successfully maintained.] Especially to Adams, who as U.S. minister to Great Britain in the years after the War of 1812, had been tireless in seeking restitution for slaveholders for the enslaved individuals evacuated by the British at the war's conclusion.

410.17–19 suppose Congress were called . . . to suppress a servile insurrection] Adams's speech came less than five years after Nathaniel "Nat" Turner (1800–1831), an enslaved man in Southampton County, Virginia, led one of the most violent and consequential slave rebellions in U.S. history. More than fifty white men, women, and children perished in the uprising, and over one hundred African Americans were indiscriminately killed during the suppression of the revolt. Turner and twenty others were executed by hanging.

410.32–35 public rumor . . . General Gaines to invade the Mexican territory] There were allegations that Jackson had provided assurances to Sam Houston (1793–1863), president of the newly established Republic of Texas, that federal troops in Louisiana would come to the Texans' aid if Mexican forces crossed the Trinity River. Edmund Gaines, who commanded the southwest military

NOTES   753

division of the United States, was highly sympathetic to the Texans, referring to them in one official communication as "our Texians."

411.14–19 Santa Ana, has been defeated . . . of the victorious Texian army] Mexican leader Antonio López de Santa Anna (1794–1876) had been captured at the battle of San Jacinto (April 21, 1836) by Texian forces under Houston.

412.31–34 That State . . . into the Union] Congress was at this time arbitrating a protracted boundary dispute between the state of Ohio and the Michigan Territory, which delayed the latter's admission to statehood. That matter would finally be resolved in early 1837, and Michigan became the twenty-sixth state in the union.

413.15–16 we have rumors . . . even before his defeat] Santa Anna, who was held captive by the Texians for several weeks and made to sign a treaty recognizing Texas, returned to Mexico City (after a brief sojourn to Washington—see note 613.35–36) to discover that he had been deposed in his absence.

413.24–25 intelligence from Peru tells of one who has fallen] Felipe Salaverry (b. 1805), who had become supreme chief of Peru in February 1835, was deposed in a coup d'état and executed on February 18, 1836.

413.25–26 Yturbide, and Mina, and Guerrero] Three short-lived Mexican leaders: Agustín de Iturbide (1783–1824), emperor of Mexico from 1822 to 1823; revolutionary Francisco Javier Mina (1789–1817); and Vicente Guerrero (1782–1831), Mexico's second president, April–December 1829.

413.32 Passamaquoddy] Region in northeastern-most Maine, on the border with British Canada.

414.19–23 Is the success of your whole army . . . in your late campaign] Late in 1835 Gaines had led a force of more than a thousand regulars and volunteers from New Orleans to Florida in a fruitless effort to bring the Second Seminole War to a conclusion.

415.24–26 Great Britain has recently . . . abolished slavery] By an act of Parliament, some 750,000 enslaved people in the British West Indies gained their freedom on August 1, 1835. Adams will commemorate the occasion in the final selection in this volume.

416.30–31 the Rio del Norte] Or the Río Bravo del Norte, the original Spanish name for the Rio Grande.

416.31–32 the reasons of Mr. Monroe for accepting the Sabine] In the Transcontinental Treaty of 1819, which Adams had negotiated as secretary of state.

418.20–21 By the other *I know* that overtures were made] The restoration of the Bourbon king Ferdinand VII to the Spanish throne in 1813 was followed by a long period of instability during which most of the kingdom's

New World possessions were lost. Adams had a firsthand awareness of these events as secretary of state.

418.22–23 And I further know that secret . . . to the then President] Adams described these events at length in an August 11, 1837, letter to William Ellery Channing, who was curious about the reference. "It was in September, 1822, that the events, to which I alluded in my speech in the House of Representatives of the 25th of May, 1836, took place," Adams informed him. He went on to explain that after the Spanish government of the Cortes was overthrown by means of a French invasion, Great Britain became alarmed lest the French should claim control over Cuba. At the same time, a Cuban faction advanced a proposal to the Monroe administration suggesting that the island would declare its independence from Spain if the U.S. offered protection and the promise of admission as a state. "While this proposition was under consideration," Adams continues, "the French Minister at Washington by a verbal, irresponsible communication, not to the Secretary of State, the only medium of official intercourse between foreign ministers and the Government of the United States, but to Mr. CRAWFORD, the Secretary of the Treasury, asseverated that the French Government had secret but positive information that the British Government had deliberately determined to take possession of Cuba." After declining the Cuban proposal, Monroe and his cabinet issued a very explicit warning to the British to refrain from taking the island, to which Foreign Secretary Canning responded in kind. In the end, as Adams reported, the parties agreed that Cuba should be maintained as a Spanish possession, and the Cuban people accommodated themselves to the new regime in Madrid. He concluded his letter as follows:

> All these transactions were at the time profoundly secret. The first public allusion to them ever made was by me, in the speech of the 25th of May, 1836, to the House of Representatives. The circumstances of the times no longer required absolute secrecy. France, Spain and Britain had all undergone political revolutions, and the abolition of Slavery in the British Colonies of this hemisphere had added tenfold terrors to her occupation of Cuba, for the meditation of our Southern statesmen. I partly raised the veil, therefore, from the negotiations of 1822, to stay the frantic hand of the Southern slaveholder, rushing from the terror of an avenging conscience into the arms of sympathizing Slavery in Texas.

Adams's letter was reprinted in the *New York Times* on October 17, 1863, under the headline "How the United States Regarded the Question of Seizing Cuba in 1822—Letter from John Quincy Adams."

418.32 the Moro Castle] Castillo de los Tres Reyes Del Morro, a large fortification guarding Havana's harbor.

419.22–23 Great Britain is even now . . . for the Spanish succession] In the spring and summer of 1836, the British government mobilized a volunteer force of ten thousand men, called the British Auxiliary Legion, to support Isabella II, the eldest daughter of Ferdinand VII, whose succession was challenged by her uncle Infante Carlos and his Carlist followers.

422.25 Mr. LEWIS] Dixon Hall Lewis (1802–1848), a staunch Democrat.

422.26 Mr. THOMPSON] Waddy Thompson Jr. (1798–1868), Adams's frequent foe on the House floor.

422.32–34 Georgia . . . first set the example] See note 254.6–7.

423.2–3 innocent, pious ministers] Congregational minister Samuel Austin Worcester (1798–1859) and missionaries from several other denominations were arrested, mistreated, convicted, and sentenced to prison terms of several years each for violating an 1830 Georgia statute prohibiting whites from living among the state's Native tribes without a license. The convictions were overturned by the Supreme Court in *Worcester v. Georgia* (1832), which established the principle of tribal sovereignty within the United States.

423.16 *peine forte et dure*] French: strong and harsh punishment.

18: LETTERS TO HIS CONSTITUENTS | 1837

426.25–26 "the subject of Slavery . . . is absorbing all my faculties."] *JQAD2*, 399.

429.10–11 John Quincy Adams belongs to neither of the prominent political parties] By the late 1830s, the Whig Party had coalesced in opposition to the ruling Democratic Party. Both were national, transsectional coalitions. Though he would grow increasingly aligned with the Whigs, Adams remained largely independent. The reaction to his speech on the Joint Resolution, which he recorded in his diary on June 2, 1836, offers a small example of his singularity: "My Speech on the distribution of rations to the fugitives from Indian hostilities in Alabama and Georgia was published in the National Intelligencer of this morning, and a subscription paper was circulated in the House for printing it in a pamphlet, for which Gales told me there were 2,500 copies ordered—Several members of the House of both parties spoke of it to me; some with strong dissent." *JQAD2*, 385.

429.28 Junius-like] Referring to the pseudonymous writer, possibly British pamphleteer Philip Francis, who penned withering letters critical of the government of George III in London newspapers from January 1769 to January 1772. Popular in America, *The Letters of Junius* were issued in numerous editions throughout the late eighteenth and early nineteenth centuries.

429.29–30 O'Connell's celebrated letters] Irish reformer Daniel O'Connell (1775–1847)—known as "The Liberator" for his successful advocacy of Catholic emancipation, which allowed him to become a member of

Parliament—published in the 1830s a series of influential letters advocating for the dissolution of the union with Great Britain and other reforms.

430.2 "odious peculiarities"] Whittier quotes from the famous passage in *Notes on the State of Virginia* (1785) in which Thomas Jefferson reflects on the effects of slavery on the master class: "The whole commerce between master and slave is a perpetual exercise of the most boisterous passions, the most unremitting despotism on the one part, and degrading submissions on the other. Our children see this, and learn to imitate it; for man is an imitative animal. . . . The parent storms, the child looks on, catches the lineaments of wrath, puts on the same airs in the circle of smaller slaves, gives a loose to his worst of passions, and thus nursed, educated, and daily exercised in tyranny, cannot but be stamped by it with odious peculiarities."

430.7 "gray, discrowned head"] Quoting from "Majesty in Misery, or An Imploration to the King of Kings; Written by His Late Majesty King Charles the First, in his Durance at Carisbrook Castle, 1648."

431.9 the National Intelligencer] The nation's leading Whig paper. Joseph Gales Jr. and his brother-in-law William Winston Seaton were its publishers and for many years the official printers to Congress.

431.18 Mr. Cushman] Democrat Samuel Cushman (1783–1851), whom Adams once referred to as "the man of previous questions" because of his frequent resort to the parliamentary procedure to close debate and call for a vote. *JQAD2*, 407.

431.18–19 the Globe] A Washington weekly published by Francis P. Blair (1791–1876), President Jackson's nephew and informal advisor, part of his "kitchen cabinet."

432.34–36 Van Buren and Rives . . . Benton and Amos Kendall] The "pure coinage" refers to Jackson's designated successor, Martin Van Buren, and William Cabell Rives (1793–1868), who had been Jackson's minister to France and Van Buren's first choice as a running mate in 1836, though he did not secure the nomination. The "counterfeit currency" to Senator Thomas Hart Benton (1782–1858) of Missouri, Jackson's onetime rival turned congressional manager, and Postmaster General Amos Kendall (1789–1869), whom Adams thought the "ruling mind" of the Jackson and Van Buren administrations.

432.36 The Albany Argus] A Democratic semiweekly and longtime organ of the "Albany Regency" of Martin Van Buren.

435.25 Mr. Haynes, of Georgia] Democrat Charles Eaton Haynes (1784–1841). In his diary Adams recalled once appealing to Haynes's "candour, and generosity and also to his State rights principles" during floor debate. *JQAD2*, 431.

436.35 Mr. Thompson, of South Carolina] See note 422.26.

437.7–9 Mr. Jefferson has observed . . . degrading passions] See note 430.2.

437.33 Mr. Lewis, of Alabama] See note 422.25.

438.36–439.1 A slaveholding President of the United States . . . slaves to insurrection."] President Jackson made this recommendation in his 1835 annual message.

440.35–36 Mr. Mann . . . of New York] Democrat Abijah Mann Jr. (1793–1868), in his second term representing a large district in rural upstate New York.

441.37 Mr. Cambreleng] North Carolina native Churchill Caldom Cambreleng (1786–1862), another New York Democrat, and another one of Adams's recurring adversaries in floor debate.

442.34–35 Mr. Jenifer . . . from Maryland] See note 407.24–25.

443.15 borne to trouble, as the sparks fly upward] Job 5:7.

443.34–35 "For earthly power doth . . . mercy seasons justice."] *The Merchant of Venice*, IV.i.196–97.

444.9–10 Mr. Dromgoole, of Virginia] Democrat George Coke Dromgoole (1797–1847), one of the chief defenders of the gag rule on the House floor.

445.10–11 Mr. Robertson, of Virginia] John Robertson (1787–1873), a Whig, had previously served as Virginia's attorney general.

445.37 Mr. Bynum, of North Carolina] Jesse Atherton Bynum (1797–1868), a Democrat.

447.3 Mr. Graves, of Kentucky] William Jordan Graves (1805–1848), a Whig, who the following year would participate in a duel with Democrat Representative Jonathan Cilley of Maine, killing his fellow congressman.

447.28–30 Governor Lincoln . . . in a pamphlet] Former Massachusetts governor Levi Lincoln (1782–1868) served in the House from 1834 to 1841. His speech in defense of Adams was published in several editions.

447.35 Mr. Phillips] Massachusetts Whig Stephen Clarendon Phillips (1801–1857).

451.31 Mr. Cushing] Massachusetts Whig Caleb Cushing (1800–1879).

452.1 Mr. French, of Kentucky] Democrat Richard French (1792–1854), a former circuit court judge.

452.7 Mr. Milligan . . . from Delaware] John Jones Milligan (1795–1875), a Whig, was his state's lone representative in the House.

452.10 Mr. Evans, of Maine] Adams thought George Evans (1797–1867), a Whig, was "one of the ablest men, and most eloquent Orators in Congress." *JQAD2*, 409.

453.12 Mr. Vanderpool, of New York] Democrat Aaron Vanderpoel (1799–1870) hailed from Kinderhook, New York, hometown of Martin Van Buren.

454.3 the President elect] Van Buren, who would be sworn in on March 4, 1837.

455.14 the rod of Aaron in the Ark] See Numbers 17:10–11.

456.20–25 "The saints may do the same .. and wicked vary."] Samuel Butler, *Hudibras* (1663), II.ii.235–40.

456.26–27 Mr. Pickens] Francis Wilkinson Pickens (1805–1869) of South Carolina, a nullifier and future secessionist.

457.21–22 the dark spirit of slavery . . . by the governor of that commonwealth] Pennsylvania governor Joseph Ritner (1780–1869), a strident abolitionist, was deeply critical of northern Democrats like Van Buren who abetted the southern dominance of the federal government. The feeling was mutual: the following year a convention of Democrats in Lancaster County issued a series of resolutions including this one: "*Resolved*, That as Joseph Ritner has had the bare-faced impudence to tell the democracy of Pennsylvania, that 'they have basely bowed the knee to the dark spirit of slavery,' we will take the liberty of telling him in October next, that we no longer need the services of him, nor his renegade Yankees, 'who left their country for their country's good'" (as reported in the *Lancaster Intelligencer*, August 28, 1838).

457.28 Mr. Lane, of Indiana] Amos Lane (1778–1849), a Democrat.

457.30–31 Mr. Taylor, of New York, and Mr. Ingersoll, of Philadelphia] William Taylor (1791–1865), a Democrat, and Joseph Reed Ingersoll (1786–1868), a Whig.

461.12–13 the publication of Mr. Slade's letter] William Slade Jr. (1786–1859), Whig congressman from Vermont, had worked for Adams as a clerk in the State Department, and was one of his chief allies in fighting the gag rule in the House. He had frequent recourse to the *National Intelligencer* to publish the texts of speeches and petitions suppressed by the House.

461.20 if coming events cast their shadows before them] From the 1802 poem "Lochiel's Warning" by Scottish poet Thomas Campbell.

464.20 Mr. Lawrence] Massachusetts Whig Abbott Lawrence (1792–1855), with whom Adams was friendly.

466.31–32 Carver . . . and Alden] For Carver, Bradford, and Winslow, see note 91.24. John Alden (c. 1598–1687) was one of Plymouth Colony's founders and leading citizens.

467.9 the Editor of the Boston Daily Advocate] Benjamin Franklin Hallett (1797–1862). The *Daily Advocate* was an Anti-Masonic paper.

470.21 Mr. Patton, of Virginia] Democrat John Mercer Patton (1797–1858).

471.32 Mr. GLASCOCK] See note 406.34.

474.19 "O! day and night, but these are bitter words!"] Cf. *2 Henry IV*, II.iv.170–71.

475.15–16 not . . . the most devoted friend of this administration] Thompson, a staunch Whig, had long been critical of the Jacksonians and their anti-Bank policies, and in particular of Martin Van Buren, whom he regarded as a political opportunist.

478.8 Mr. UNDERWOOD, of Kentucky] Joseph Rogers Underwood (1791–1876), a Whig and a former appeals court judge.

478.17 Mr. WISE, of Virginia] Adams's nemesis Henry Alexander Wise (1806–1876), who is first mentioned in Adams's diary in the entry for February 6, 1834: "He was followed by Henry A. Wise, a new and young member from Virginia who made a very keen, satirical Speech, in favour of the restoration of the deposits and of a National Bank, and against all those who are of the same opinions—He is coming forward as a successor of John Randolph; with his tartness, his bitterness, his malignity and his Inconsistencies." John Quincy Adams Digital Diary. [Hereafter JQADD.] Courtesy of the Massachusetts Historical Society.

481.17–18 "*Sacred* to ridicule . . . some *merry* song."] Alexander Pope, *Imitations of Horace* (1733–38), II.i.79–80.

482.15–18 Was I not the first . . . the majority were most devoted?] This is likely a reference to Adams's defense of the House's honor in the *Report of the Minority of the Committee on Manufactures*, against the insinuation in Jackson's annual message that the appropriations process for internal improvements was inherently corrupting. See pages 341–42 in this volume.

482.36 the French question] See note 247.20–22. On July 4, 1831, a treaty was signed stipulating payment of 25 million francs in six annual installments. When the first payment came due, it was found that the requisite appropriation by the French Chamber of Deputies had never been made. Early in 1833, Jackson sent Edward Livingston, who had just resigned as secretary of state, to France to demand "prompt and complete fulfillment" of the treaty. The French government continued to delay, forcing Jackson to strike a more strident tone in his annual message on December 7, 1834, challenging Congress to adopt measures to preserve the national honor. The Senate Committee on Foreign Relations rejected Jackson's call to action in its January 6, 1835, report, advising a wait-and-see policy. The House Committee on Foreign Affairs was slower to respond to Jackson's challenge, a dereliction that Adams attributed to Whig efforts to turn the crisis to partisan advantage. On February 27, 1835, the committee made a contradictory report that called on the president to break off further negotiation as dishonorable but deferring any measures to prepare for hostilities to the next Congress. Adams then introduced a resolution that called for the president to continue negotiations consistent with the national honor while forestalling "any legislative measure of a hostile character or tendency towards the French nation." Adams's resolution afforded a face-saving formula for a weary Congress, and with some further modification in language it was adopted 212–0 on March 2, 1835. He considered it one of the greatest achievements of his congressional career.

19: THE JUBILEE OF THE CONSTITUTION | 1839

487.13–14 "the great questions which agitate the country,"] *JQAD2*, 320.

487.17–26 "I have determined to accept . . . a younger hand, and brighter mind."] *JQAD2*, 453.

487.30–35 "I have come to the review of . . . falling into garrulity?"] JQADD, April 6, 1839. Courtesy of the Massachusetts Historical Society.

487.35–37 "Carelessly and hastily composed . . . I know not where to abridge."] Ibid., April 12, 1839.

487.39–488.2 "The Revolutionary age and the . . . age of small men, and small things."] Ibid., April 25, 1839.

488.19–27 "I had sent a copy . . . can never be sufficiently grateful to God."] Ibid., August 6, 1839.

489.14–16 *Serit arbores* . . . non seret?] For his epigram Adams chose a passage from Cicero's Tusculan Disputations, which itself begins with a quotation from the poet Caecilius: "*One plants, what future ages shall enjoy—* . . . What has he an eye to in this, but that he is interested in posterity? Shall the industrious husbandman then plant trees, the fruit of which he shall never see? and shall not the great man found laws, institutes, a republic?" (from an 1824 translation). Adams was an avid arborist, and this quote meant a great deal to him; Charles Francis Adams placed the words ALTERI SECULO atop the memorial plaque dedicated to his parents in their church in Quincy.

491.9–14 "His hands the fatal sword . . . rising on the gold"] See note 99.10–12.

491.25–26 the chancellor of the state of New York] New York City was the nation's first capital. Because there was no Supreme Court at the time of Washington's inauguration—John Jay would not become the nation's first chief justice until September 1789—the first presidential swearing-in was administered by New York chancellor Robert R. Livingston (1746–1813), the state's highest judicial officer.

492.30–31 the revoker of the Edict of Nantes] By revoking the Edict of Nantes in 1685, Louis XIV effectively outlawed Protestantism in France, forcing many into exile.

493.22 the cause of Algernon Sidney and John Hambden] Algernon Sidney (1623–1683) was an influential republican theorist executed for treason against the government of Charles II. The text of his then-unpublished *Discourses Concerning Government* was used as evidence against him at his trial. Published posthumously in 1698, the work became very important to eighteenth-century radical Whigs. For John Hampden see note 303.1–2.

493.26–30 enacted admiralty courts . . . shut up the port of Boston] Adams refers to three of the four Coercive Acts, passed by Parliament in early 1774 in the wake of the Boston Tea Party. The Administration of Justice Act allowed for the trials of those accused of committing capital crimes while enforcing the law or collecting revenue in the colonies to be removed to admiralty courts in Britain or Nova Scotia. The Massachusetts Government Act abrogated Massachusetts's 1691 royal charter by removing the power of appointing the governor's council from the elected assembly and giving it to the king. It also gave the newly appointed royal governor, General Thomas Gage, the power to appoint (or nominate, for the king's assent) all provincial judges and sheriffs, to make the sheriffs responsible for choosing jury panels, and to severely restrict town meetings. The Boston Port Act closed Boston's harbor, effective June 1, 1774, until "peace and obedience to the laws" were restored in the town and its people paid for the destroyed tea.

494.1 Charlestown and Falmouth] See note 217.39.

495.36–496.8 In the history of England itself . . . the conspiracy against him] See note 212.16–17. The latter part of this historical survey refers to Queen Mary II (r. 1689–94), the eldest daughter of James II—who was invited to assume the throne after her father was forced into exile in the Glorious Revolution of 1688—and her husband and co-regent, William III (r. 1689–1702), the Prince of Orange.

496.11 the Great Charter of Runnymede] The Magna Carta.

499.1–2 John Dickinson . . . from Pennsylvania] Most famous as the author of the influential 1768 pamphlet *Letters from a Pennsylvania Farmer*, the conservative Dickinson (1732–1808) was John Adams's primary antagonist in the Second Continental Congress.

508.40 the first ratification of the articles of confederation] This should read the *final* ratification, which took place when Maryland approved the articles on February 2, 1781.

509.32–33 Congress borrowed money in France, in Spain, in Holland] This was historical detail with which Adams was intimately familiar, having as a boy accompanied his father to Europe where John Adams was one of the Confederation Congress's principal agents in search of foreign financial support.

510.10–13 Mutiny was suppressed . . . they were sitting.] An allusion to the Pennsylvania (or Philadelphia) Mutiny of 1783, when, on June 20, some four hundred soldiers and officers of the Continental Army marched on Philadelphia to demand settlement of their claims for back pay and bounties for their military service. After appealing to the Pennsylvania Executive Council for protection, the Congress was forced to abandon the capital for Princeton, New Jersey.

514.27 expounded in the writings of Locke] Especially John Locke's *Two Treatises of Government . . . the Latter . . . an Essay Concerning the True Original, Extent, and End of Civil-Government* (1689).

515.33 It was as the late Mr. Madison remarked to Miss Martineau] English journalist Harriet Martineau (1802–1876) recounted her 1835 visit with former president James Madison, who was then eighty-three with a little more than a year to live, at his home at Montpelier in Virginia in the very opening lines of her two-volume book *Society in America* (New York, 1837): "Mr. Madison remarked to me, that the United States had been 'useful in proving things before held impossible.'"

519.17 the father of the floods] The Mississippi River.

520.3 his friend Knox] Henry Knox (1750–1806) was then serving as the Confederation Congress's secretary of war, a post he would maintain through Washington's first term under the new Constitution.

520.30–36 "though he rendered . . . he still had an eye towards futurity."] Quoting from chapter IV of the first volume of David Hume's *History of England, from the Invasion of Julius Cæsar to the Revolution in 1688* (8 vols., London, 1767).

522.9–11 "That Shepherd, who . . . Rose out of Chaos;"] *Paradise Lost*, I.8–10. Milton is referring to Moses.

522.38 the queen of the world] Cf. Pascal, *Pensées*, V.iii: "Opinion is, as it were, the queen of the world; but force is its tyrant."

523.2 which Montesquieu lays down] In *De l'esprit des loix* (1748; *The Spirit of the Laws*, 1750), III.5–8.

526.13–14 a song like that of Miriam] Cf. Exodus 15:20–21.

527.8–9 which shades the sober certainty of waking bliss] Cf. John Milton, *Comus*, I.262.

528.9–11 a very intelligent . . . foreigner, with whom I once conversed] Likely referring to Alexis de Tocqueville (1805–1859), whom Adams met at a dinner at Edward Everett's in Boston on October 1, 1831, after the Frenchman and his companion Gustave de Beaumont had completed the first leg of their investigative tour of America, through New York, the Great Lakes, and Quebec, May–September 1831. Describing the dinner in his notebooks, Tocqueville found it remarkable that Adams "was received with all the politeness due an honored guest, but that was all. Most of the guests addressed him as 'Sir,' while a few used the honorific form 'Mr. President.'" He went on to observe that "Mr. Adams is a man of sixty-two who seems still quite vigorous in mind and body. He speaks French with ease and elegance. I was seated next to him, and we had a lengthy conversation." Translation by Arthur Goldhammer from Olivier Zunz, ed., *Alexis de Tocqueville and Gustave de Beaumont in America: Their Friendship and Their Travels* (University of Virginia Press, 2010), 242–43.

532.15–17 It once accomplished . . . and then was laid aside.] That is, the transition from John Adams's administration to that of Thomas Jefferson in 1801, in the wake of the Kentucky and Virginia Resolves of 1798 and 1799.

534.3 the Institutes of Justinian] A sixth-century codification of Roman law.

538.35–37 the Secretaries . . . of their respective offices] John Jay and Henry Knox.

541.1–2 the first minister from France in her republican transformation] Edmond-Charles Genêt (1763–1834) had little regard for official diplomatic protocol, up to and including trying to recruit American volunteers after France declared war on Great Britain in 1793.

541.17–18 a minister plenipotentiary to Great Britain] This was, of course, Adams's father.

545.23 trifles lighter than air] Cf. *Othello*, III.iii.370.

546.15 an incendiary minister] Genêt.

549.5–11 the Republican plenipotentiary . . . his adopted country] Genêt's refusal to respect American neutrality in the Anglo-French war led the Washington administration to ask for his recall in August 1793, and he was replaced in February 1794. He elected to stay in the United States rather than return to France at the height of the Terror, when his party, the Girondins, suffered persecution. He married Cornelia Clinton, the daughter of the state's governor, and settled in New York's Hudson Valley.

550.2–3 the Fauxbourg Saint Antoine] The section of Paris most particularly associated with popular unrest during the French Revolution, beginning with the storming of the Bastille in 1789.

552.35–36 the godless decimal division of time of Fabre d'Eglantine] French playwright Fabre d'Églantine (1750–1794) devised the names for the French Republican calendar.

553.33–34 in part, and through a glass darkly] Cf. I Corinthians 13:12.

554.33–34 Two commissioners were appointed] William Carmichael (c. 1739–1795) of Maryland, who had been chargé d'affaires in Madrid since 1783, and William Short (1759–1849) of Virginia, who had been Jefferson's private secretary.

554.37–38 the Prince of the Peace] One of the many honorifics attaching to Spanish nobleman Manuel de Godoy y Álvarez de Faria Ríos (1767–1851).

566.14 narrated in the Holy Scriptures] In the twenty-seventh chapter of Deuteronomy.

566.21–26 bind them for signs . . . upon your gates] Cf. Deuteronomy 6:4–9.

20: SPEECH ON WAR WITH MEXICO | 1842

567.5–17 "two days since a Letter . . . before I shall retire from the world."] *JQAD2*, 503–4.

568.1–3 "a political sectarian . . . Principled against all improvement."] *JQAD2*, 505.

568.43–569.5 "They are alarmed . . . how to meet and counteract it."] *JQAD2*, 520.

571.14 Mr. Linn] Archibald Ladley Linn (1802–1857), a Whig, was chairman of the Committee on Public Expenditures.

571.22 Mr. Slade] See note 461.12–13.

571.29 Mr. W.] Wise will be referred to as such and speak in the first person somewhat interchangeably in the text that follows.

572.9 The tyrant of Mexico] Santa Anna had been restored to power in October 1841.

572.16–17 the individual selected to occupy that post] Waddy Thompson (see note 422.26).

572.32 Mr. Steenrod] Democrat Lewis Steenrod (1810–1862) of Virginia.

574.1 Mr. Poinsett] Joel Roberts Poinsett (1779–1851) of South Carolina was U.S. minister to Mexico during Adams's presidency, serving from June 1825 to October 1829.

574.11–12 our great Western mart] New Orleans.

577.13 fanaticism] This was a common shorthand for abolitionism among critics of the movement both in the North and the South.

580.21–22 the story of Captain Boyle] The episode that Wise refers to here occurred during the War of 1812, not the Revolutionary War. Thomas Boyle (1775–1825), an experienced mariner from Marblehead, Massachusetts, was commissioned to command the U.S. sloop *Comet* as a privateer in June 1812, and in three cruises between then and March 1814, he prowled the West Indies and the coast of Brazil, taking some thirty prizes. In July 1814, Boyle became part owner and commander of *Chasseur* (sixteen guns), a swift and graceful clipper that *Niles' Register* would later call "the most beautiful vessel that ever floated on the ocean." *Chasseur* cleared New York on July 24 and charted her course to the coast of Great Britain to harass the enemy's merchant fleet. After capturing the first of this cruise's eighteen prizes, Boyle released the vessel, sending it back to port with a mock proclamation of blockade, which he ordered be hung on the front door of Lloyd's of London, Britain's foremost maritime insurance company. Americans had long complained of Britain's use of so-called paper blockades; here, at last, was a fitting riposte.

580.37 booted loafers] In the nineteenth century, the term "loafers" could be used to describe a class of reckless adventurers, men "who live upon excitement," as Sam Houston referred to them.

581.5 600 American troops under Fanning] Georgia native James Walker Fannin Jr. (1804–1836) was expelled from West Point for dueling and eventually settled in the Mexican province of Tejas, where he was a plantation owner and slave trader. He joined the Texian army in 1834, rising to the rank of colonel. At the battle of Coletto Creek (March 19, 1836), he fought a protracted defense against a much larger Mexican force before finally surrendering the next day. Mexican casualties were perhaps ten times greater than those suffered by the Texians.

581.16 Mr. Cushing] See note 451.31.

581.20–21 a "foeman worthy of our steel."] Cf. Walter Scott, *The Lady of the Lake*, V.x.12.

581.30 He would risk all the blue lights] A derogatory term suggesting treasonous sympathy with Great Britain. It arose from alleged instances during the War of 1812 of New England Federalists using blue lights to alert British ships that an American vessel was going to attempt to run their blockade.

582.18–19 They remember the fate of those . . . who suffered political death] Wise alludes to the Hartford Convention of December 1814–January 1815, a meeting of New England Federalists convened to draft resolutions protesting the War of 1812 and the Madison administration's handling of it; its resolutions reached Washington almost simultaneously with the news of the signing of the Treaty of Ghent ending the war and of Jackson's triumph at New Orleans, a disastrous coincidence that proved devastating to the political fortunes of the Federalist Party.

582.29 Accomac] Wise was from Accomack County in Virginia, on the Eastern Shore of Chesapeake Bay.

583.9–10 There had come . . . an envoy extraordinary from Great Britain] Alexander Baring, 1st Baron Ashburton (1774–1848), whose arrival Adams recorded in his diary on April 3, 1842: "As we were returning home we met a carriage laden with two travelling trunks; part of the baggage of Lord Ashburton, once Alexander Baring, who arrived last Evening in the Warspite from England—whence he now comes as Envoy Extraordinary and Minister Plenipotentiary upon a special mission" (JQADD, Courtesy of the Massachusetts Historical Society). Ashburton and Secretary of State Daniel Webster would negotiate a treaty, signed on August 9, resolving the most pressing outstanding issues between the two nations.

584.14–15 the two vessels now arrived . . . the sound of his voice] The USS *Missouri* and the USS *Mississippi* had arrived in Washington with much fanfare the day before. They were among the first steamships in the U.S. Navy, with engines capable of generating six hundred horsepower.

584.39–40 Canning called the spirit of freedom] In his oft-reprinted *Speech . . . Delivered at the Liverpool Dinner, Given in Celebration of his Re-Election, March 18, 1820.*

585.40 the correspondence of Mr. Stevenson] Former Speaker Andrew Stevenson (1784–1857) was the U.S. minister in London from 1836 to 1841.

585.40–586.1 the pamphlet of Mr. Cass] While serving the U.S. minister in Paris, Lewis Cass had been vocal in his opposition to the Quintuple Treaty (December 20, 1841), an agreement among Austria, France, Prussia, Russia, and Great Britain that declared the slave trade to be piracy and granted the mutual right of search to suppress it. Cass likewise opposed the Webster-Ashburton Treaty, having staked his ground during its negotiation with the publication in Paris of a pamphlet entitled *An Examination of the Question, Now in Discussion, Between the American and British Governments, Concerning the Right of Search.* Angered that the final treaty ignored the maritime issues that concerned him, Cass resigned his post and returned to the United States to continue his dispute with Webster through published letters in the newspapers.

587.32 what the gentleman said last summer] Throughout the summer of 1841 the House had engaged in intermittent, somewhat desultory debate over a resolution by John Gelston Floyd of New York calling on the Tyler administration to release any official correspondence related to the *Caroline* affair. Adams delivered a speech on the topic on September 4, which was published as a pamphlet despite his evident misgivings about its value: "I had been urged by several members to speak on this question, and had hesitated whether I would or not, down till I entered the house this morning—In my hesitation I had made no preparation to speak, and had not one line, noting the topics to be touched upon . . . I then rambled through a Speech with out method or compass till the Speaker's hammer came down announcing that my hour was out—several motions were made for permission to me to proceed, but I declined—I scarcely know what I said." JQADD, September 4, 1841. Courtesy of the Massachusetts Historical Society.

588.40 quite equal to "the admirable Crichton,"] James Crichton (1560–1582) was a Scottish prodigy known especially for his facility with languages. His life story, which ended with his murder in Italy, was popularized by fellow Scotsman, the translator Thomas Urquhart (1611–1660), in a 1652 book called *The Jewel*.

590.40 Mr. Wilberforce] British abolitionist William Wilberforce (1759–1833).

592.17 a distinguished gentleman of Virginia] Charles Fenton Mercer (1778–1858), who served in Congress from 1817 to 1839, first as a Federalist and later as a Whig. In February 1823 he secured the adoption of the following joint resolution:

> *Resolved*, That the President of the United States be requested to enter upon and to prosecute from time to time such negotiations with the maritime powers of Europe and America as he may deem expedient for the effectual abolition of the African slave trade and its ultimate denunciation as Piracy under the laws of Nations by the consent of the civilized world.

592.20 another gentleman of Virginia] Alexander Smyth (1765–1830), a Crawford supporter, was a member of the Virginia delegation in the House along with Mercer. In his diary, then–Secretary of State Adams records a long conversation with Mercer on the slave trade and right of search, during which "Mercer spoke also of Alexander Smyth's attacks upon me as being a favourer of the Slave-trade; of his hand-bill detailing their private conversations, and mine with Mercer; and of his own relations with Crawford; which he said had not been intimate." JQADD, May 27, 1824. Courtesy of the Massachusetts Historical Society.

592.23–25 That address, and my reply to it, are in existence . . . now in this house] Adams replied to Smyth's "hand-bill" to the citizens of Virginia's Twenty-Second Congressional District with one of his own, which is excerpted in Josiah Quincy, *Memoir of the Life of John Quincy Adams* (Boston, 1858), 131–32. It is not clear to whom Adams refers as having the reply in his possession.

596.9 a declaration of Sir William Scott] Scott (1745–1836), a judge of the High Court of Admiralty, ruled in 1816 that the French ship *Louis* had been illegally seized by HMS *Queen Charlotte* off the West African coast, stating that "no nation can exercise a right of visitation and search on the common and unappropriated parts of the sea, save only on the belligerent claim."

596.14 declaration of Sir William Grant] Grant (1752–1832) was master of the rolls, or chief judge of the civil division of the British courts. In the case of the *Amedie*, an American slave trader captured by a British cruiser in 1810, he ruled on appeal that because the slave trade had been declared unjust and unlawful, "a claimant could have no right, upon principles of universal law, to claim restitution in a prize Court, of human beings carried as his slaves."

596.23–24 the case of the Swedish convoy] In 1810 the Swedish slave trader *Diana* was captured and condemned in the British Court of Vice Admiralty in Sierra Leone. This decision was reversed by Scott, who wrote, "the condemnation also took place on a principle which this Court cannot in any manner recognise, inasmuch as the sentence affirms, 'that the slave trade, from motives of humanity, hath been abolished by most civilized nations, *and is not, at the present time, legally authorized by any.*' This appears to me to be an assertion by no means sustainable." Scott ordered that the ship and cargo be restored, on the principle that the trade was allowed by the laws of Sweden.

599.6–7 one of our most celebrated naval officers] This toast is most often attributed to Stephen Decatur, the hero of Tripoli (see note 114.20).

601.12 it happened in what was called the Syrian question] On July 15, 1840, Great Britain, Austria, Russia, and Prussia signed a treaty in London pledging to support the Ottoman sultan in Constantinople against his rebellious vassal in Egypt, who had moved against Syria to gain the upper hand. France not only refused to join in the treaty but began to make military preparation to signal its opposition, before soon thinking better of it. When the Egyptians refused to relinquish their gains in the Levant, decisive actions by British and Austrian naval forces brought them to the table.

602.6 M. Guizot] François-Pierre Guizot (1787–1874), French minister of foreign affairs from 1840 to 1848.

603.31 a speech for Buncombe] Buncombe, or bunk or bunkum, a popular term for windy, nonsensical political speech, originated with Congressman Felix Walker of North Carolina, whose district in the western part of the state included Buncombe County. When he faced criticism for a long and blustering speech delivered during the Missouri Crisis in 1820, he defended himself by saying he had been "speaking . . . to Buncombe."

604.6–7 There was, I believe, a certain report] Adams alludes to the saber-rattling June 13, 1812, report of the Committee of Foreign Relations, drafted by John C. Calhoun, which suggested that the crisis that would result in Congress's declaration of war against Great Britain four days later had been rendered "formidable only by [the Americans'] love of peace." Stationed in St. Petersburg as U.S. minister, Adams was far removed from the events that led to the War of 1812.

NOTES   769

605.10 Mr. Snyder, of Pennsylvania] Democrat John Snyder (1793–1850) was a veteran of the War of 1812.

605.30–31 "Perish commerce, perish credit,"] Democrat Samuel Beardsley (1790–1860) of New York was a staunch supporter of the Jacksonian war on the Bank of the United States. "Sooner than extend the existence of the bank of the United States let it perish, and in its fall carry down every bank in the Union," he famously said, lending a scorched-earth catchphrase to the movement: "I say for one perish credit, perish commerce, perish the State institutions; give us a broken, decayed, worthless currency rather than the ignoble and corrupt tyranny of an irresponsible corporation."

605.36 John Bull] A popular personification of England, like Uncle Sam for the United States.

605.37–39 Rodney . . . Nelson . . . Wellington] Three honored British military leaders: Admirals George Rodney (1718–1792), hero of the battle of the Saintes, the last major naval engagement with the French in the War of American Independence, and Horatio Nelson (1758–1805), victor at Trafalgar; and General Arthur Wellesley, Duke of Wellington (1769–1852), who defeated Napoleon at Waterloo.

606.1 "sots or cowards;"] Cf. Pope, *An Essay on Man* (1734), IV.205.

606.4–5 There is one name . . . that of Byng] British vice admiral John Byng (1704–1757) was tried and executed by firing squad for failing to relieve British forces on Minorca during the Seven Years' War.

607.2 the present composition of that committee] The Committee on Foreign Relations comprised fifteen members, among them nine Whigs and six Democrats, including two former nullifiers from South Carolina. Eight members were from the North, seven from the South and West. Wise and Ingersoll both served on the committee, as did future president Millard Fillmore of New York.

609.18–19 "the Five Points,"] A densely populated, notoriously lawless neighborhood in lower Manhattan, home to the city's poorest residents, including many recently emancipated African Americans and newly arrived Irish immigrants.

610.3–4 "With three frigates . . . but defeat and disgrace?"] Ingersoll paraphrases a passage from a November 15, 1814, letter Adams sent to Levett Harris, U.S. consul at St. Petersburg, from Ghent, in the wake of at best mixed news from America about the course of the War of 1812: "Divided among ourselves, more in passions than interest, with half the nation sold by their prejudice and their ignorance to our enemy, with a feeble and penurious government, with five frigates for a navy and scarcely five efficient regiments for an army, how can it be expected that we should resist the mass of force which that gigantic power has collected to crush us at a blow?" (Ingersoll neglected to mention the letter's final line: "I trust in God we shall rise in triumph over it all; but the first shock is the most terrible part of the process, and it is that which we are now enduring.") Worthington C. Ford, ed., *Writings of John Quincy Adams* (New York: The Macmillan Company, 1915), V.186–88.

610.26 *qui capit ille facit*] Latin proverb roughly equivalent to the English "if the shoe fits. . . ."

610.28–29 in a letter from Governor Clement C. Clay] Former Alabama governor Clement Comer Clay (1789–1866) had resigned his seat in the U.S. Senate on November 12, 1841. His resignation letter, which was published in the newspapers and to which Adams alludes here, asserted that "to insure the permanent ascendancy of democratic principles, it is only necessary for the people of this quarter of the union to understand and appreciate the prophetic truth of Mr. Jefferson's declaration, that 'the democracy of the north is the natural ally of the south.'"

610.32–611.2 And the gentleman is the representative . . . the Bank of the United States] In this ad hominem passage, Adams makes several sly allusions to Ingersoll's family and personal history. Ingersoll's grandfather, Jared Ingersoll (1722–1781), had been a loyalist in the Revolution; his father, Jared Ingersoll Jr. (1749–1822), had been a member of the Constitutional Convention and a leading Federalist. Charles had begun his political career as a War Hawk in the Thirteenth Congress, a staunch advocate for protective tariffs and the National Bank. After failing to secure reelection, he returned to Philadelphia where he served as the U.S. attorney for Pennsylvania from 1815 to 1829, appointed by President James Madison. By the time he returned to Congress in 1841, he had become a doctrinaire Democrat, committed to the final demise of the bank he had earlier championed. Adams's contempt for Ingersoll was not new. Years earlier, in his diary, he described Ingersoll as "now a Sychophant of Van Buren, as he was late a sycophant of Jackson who turned him out of the Office of District Attorney at Philadelphia, and a demagogue of the school of Clodius and Vatinius.—Those three brothers, sons of Jared Ingersoll are all men of fine talents, and of no moral principle—Edward has absconded from the eye of honest Society, for detected forgery—Joseph came into the last Congress as worthy of being the successor of Horace Binney, and went out of it the tool of Waddy Thompson, and the scorn of every freeman in the House—Charles has spent his life in hoarding riches screwed by extortion from the poor, and in boxing his political compass to every change of the wind—Federalist, Democrat, Tory, Jacobin, Tariffite, Bankite, Anti-tariff, Anti-Bank, black, white, gray, any colour any shape that the interest, and the popular breath of the moment required, but always under every shape and colour a rapacious extortioner, and an unblushing Sycophant. His talents, with his sycophancy keep him above water, in spite of an universal distrust of his integrity—Parties want him to do their dirty work, and they at once sustain and despise him. There are many such characters in this free republic." JQADD, September 14, 1837. Courtesy of the Massachusetts Historical Society.

612.33 Thiers] French statesman Adolphe Thiers (1797–1877) had been prime minister during the Syria crisis. As tensions rose, he warned the British that an ultimatum on Egypt would compel France to act, and to underscore the point he ordered the construction of a new ring of fortifications around Paris, which now mark the city's limits.

613.30 General Hamilton] South Carolinian James Hamilton (1786–1857) had led the Jacksonian opposition in Congress during Adams's administration and then became his state's governor and chief advocate for nullification, 1830–32. After his governorship he moved to Texas, where he was offered but declined command of the Texian Army, instead becoming the fledgling republic's loan commissioner, travelling to Washington and to various European capitals in search of financial support and diplomatic recognition. He secured promises of both in London, along with an offer from the foreign secretary, Lord Palmerston, of mediation with Mexico, which Hamilton had also been pursuing, including through direct communications with Santa Anna. He returned home to Texas only to learn that newly reelected Texas president Sam Houston had terminated his services.

613.35–36 his negotiations here at the White House] After his capture in Texas and before his return to Mexico City (see note 413.15–16), Santa Anna spent some weeks in Washington, D.C.—arriving on January 17, 1837, and departing in early February—meeting at least twice with President Jackson at the Executive Mansion. In the run-up to the meetings the *Richmond Enquirer* wrote that "the visit of Santa Anna to Washington is shrouded in some mystery," and it largely remains so today.

614.2–3 a letter of President Houston] Adams refers to the just published *Letter of General Sam Houston to General Santa Anna* (Washington, D.C.: Printed at the Congressional Globe Office, March 21, 1842), which includes the following passage: "So far as I was concerned in preserving your life and your subsequent liberation [after capture at the battle of San Jacinto], I was only influenced by considerations of mercy, humanity and the establishment of a national character. . . . Your liberation was induced by principles such as these; and, though you tendered pledges, doubtless to facilitate and procure your release, they were received but not accepted as a condition. I believed that pledges made in duress were not obligatory upon the person making them, and if you intended to exercise the influence that you declared you would do, that unconditional liberty extended to you would interpose no obstacle to their fulfillment. Without any advertence to any treaty stipulations which you had made with the cabinet of Texas, I gave you entire liberty, and safe conduct to the city of Washington."

614.9–10 descend to the tomb of the Capulets] The site where Paris, Romeo, and Juliet meet their tragic, senseless ends in the last act of Shakespeare's play.

616.15 M. BILLAULT] Adolphe Billault (1805–1863), a member of the opposition in the Chamber of Deputies during Thier's premiership.

616.31–33 "The heart used to be . . . on the right side."] Adams quotes from Act II, scene vi, of Molière's 1666 farce *Le Médecin malgré lui* (*The Doctor in Spite of Himself*).

617.3–4 M. Jacques Lefebvre] Of opposition leader Lefebvre (1773–1856), Louis Philippe was reported (by Victor Hugo) to have said, "Mr. Guizot is not afraid of the opposition, nor of the press, nor of the radicals, nor of the Carlists, nor of the dynastics, nor of the hundred thousand howlers of the hundred thousand crossroads from France, he is afraid of Jacques Lefebvre."

621.8 a letter from the Governor of Mississippi] Alexander Gallatin McNutt (1802–1848) was inaugurated as governor of Mississippi in January 1838, as the state was entering a severe economic downturn resulting from the Panic of 1837. Despite his reservations about banks, he signed into law a bill creating a quasi-official state institution, the Union Bank, in hope of stabilizing credit in the state. When the bank failed in 1839, McNutt insisted he had no choice but to repudiate the state bonds that had been invested in it, causing further economic distress.

621.37–38 GWINN and THOMPSON] Democrats William McKendree Gwin (1805–1885) and Jacob Thompson (1810–1885).

623.14–15 one American citizen, a son of General Combs] Franklin Combs, a son of General Leslie Combs (1793–1881) of Kentucky, wrote a narrative of the ill-fated Santa Fe expedition during his imprisonment in Mexico City, and after his release had it printed in *Niles' National Register* of March 5, 1842.

623.15–16 the Minister of the United States] During Martin Van Buren's administration the United States was represented in Mexico City by former U.S. senator Powhatan Ellis (1790–1863) of Mississippi. He was replaced in February 1842 by Waddy Thompson, whom Adams will move on to discuss.

625.8 Mr. W. C. Johnson] Whig William Cost Johnson (1806–1860).

625.9 that execrable 21st rule] The gag rule.

625.18–19 my excellent friend from Vermont] See note 461.12–13.

625.21 threatened me with the penitentiary once] As publicized in *Letters from John Quincy Adams to his Constituents* (1837). See page 477 in this volume.

627.15–16 "had not the time to make it shorter."] It was Pascal who first made this quip, in the sixteenth of his *Lettres provinciales* (1656–57).

627.30–31 the case of . . . of Arbuthnot and Ambrister] Recounted at length in the present volume (see pages 181–204).

628.21–22 If I had but lifted my finger] See note 182.3.

630.4 a distinguished gentleman now in my eye] Henry Clay, presumably viewing Adams's speech from the gallery. Clay had resigned from the Senate just two weeks earlier.

631.1–2 a sort of a Boon] Alluding to the famed frontiersman Daniel Boone (1734–1820).

634.1–2 the resolutions proposed by . . . (Mr. Giddings,)] On March 21, 1842, some three weeks before Adams's speech, Joshua Reed Giddings (1795–1864) of Ohio, a Whig, had offered a series of resolutions in defense of the enslaved mutineers in the *Creole* case. "After much turbulence and confusion," as Adams records in his diary, "Giddings withdrew the Resolutions," but he was promptly hit by a motion of censure under the gag rule. The next day, the motion was passed, and Giddings, not having been afforded an opportunity to speak in his own defense, resigned. "I can find no language to express my feelings at the consummation of this act," Adams wrote in his diary. "Immediately after the second vote, Giddings rose from his seat, came over to mine; shook cordially my hand; and took leave—I had a voice only to say—I hope we shall soon have you back again. He made no reply, but passed to the seats of other members, his friends, and took leave of them as he had done of me—I saw him shake hands with Arnold, who voted against him. He then left the house, and this evening the City" (*JQAD2*, 534–35). Adams would get his wish, when Giddings was soon returned to the House by his outraged constituents.

634.34 the Spanish General Morillo] Pablo Morillo (1775–1837), as captain general of Venezuela, offered freedom to enslaved men who would fight on behalf of the crown against Bolívar's revolutionaries.

635.2–3 You are about passing a grant to refund Gen. Jackson] To the defense of New Orleans during the waning months of the War of 1812 Jackson brought all the tireless energy and ruthless single-mindedness that would make him the dominant political figure of his age. On December 16, 1814, some two weeks after his arrival there, he declared martial law, commandeering men and supplies as needed and jailing anyone who would dissent, including a state senator who wrote a newspaper article critical of Jackson's policies and a federal judge who attempted to intervene. After the British invasion was successfully repulsed, and martial law was after some delay lifted, Domenick A. Hall, the judge whom Jackson had had arrested, fined the general $1,000 for contempt of court, which Jackson quietly paid. A full refund of the fine, with interest, was finally appropriated by Congress and signed by President Tyler in January 1844.

635.12–13 Governor Rabun] William Rabun (1771–1819) was governor of Georgia from 1817 until his death. (See the "Appendix" to this speech on pages 639–40.)

635.21 Mr. Warren, of Georgia] Lott Warren (1797–1861), a Whig.

637.31 Tamerlane and Ghengis Khan] Famed conquerors of the Asian steppes: the first, the fourteenth-century Turkic leader whose name, Timer Lenk, was Anglicized as Tamerlane, and the twelfth-century founder of the Mongol Empire.

21: LETTER ON ABOLITION | 1843

641.8–9 "the acutest, the astutest, the archest enemy . . . that ever existed,"] From Barton H. Wise, *The Life of Henry A. Wise of Virginia* (New York, 1899), 61–62: "When a candidate for governor of Virginia, in 1855, Wise declared from the hustings: 'I have had a very severe training in collision with the acutest, the astutest, the archest enemy of Southern slavery that ever existed. I mean the "Old Man Eloquent," John Quincy Adams. I must have been a dull boy indeed if I had not learned my lessons thoroughly on that subject. And let me tell you that again and again I had reason to know and to feel the wisdom and sagacity of that departed man. Again and again, in the lobby, on the floor, he told me vauntingly that the pulpit would preach, and the school would teach, and the press would print, among the people who had no tie and no association with slavery, until, would not only be reached the slave-trade between the States, the slave-trade in the District of Columbia, slavery in the District, slavery in the Territories, but slavery in the States. Again and again he said that he would not abolish slavery in the District of Columbia if he could; for he would retain it as a bone of contention,—a fulcrum of the lever for agitation, agitation, agitation, until slavery in the States was shaken from its base. And his prophecies have been fulfilled—fulfilled far faster and more fearfully, certainly, than ever he anticipated, before he died.'"

641.13 "fanatical associations."] *JQAD1*, 486.

641.33–37 "occasioned a long debate . . . on this subject."] *JQAD1*, 138.

642.1–10 "the Missouri Question . . . my duty equally clear to give my opinion."] *JQAD1*, 524.

642.12–18 "Oh! if but one man could arise . . . an Angel upon Earth."] *JQAD1*, 529.

642.28–32 "the real question now convulsing this Union . . . was Slavery."] *JQAD2*, 300.

642.35–643.27 I answered a Letter from John G. Whittier . . . and put my trust in God.] *JQAD2*, 402–3.

646.24 Vergennes had plotted with Gustavus of Sweden] Before he became the foreign minister of Louis XVI's government and the official with whom John Adams, Benjamin Franklin, and the other American commissioners most had to deal during the American Revolution, Charles Gravier, Comte de Vergennes (1717–1787), was the French ambassador to Sweden, 1771–74, where he abetted King Gustav III in his coup d'état over the Swedish nobility.

646.25 Turgot] Anne-Robert-Jacques Turgot, Baron de Laune (1727–1781), finance minister at the court of Louis XVI.

646.26 the surrender of Burgoyne] After a series of defeats, British general John Burgoyne surrendered an army of five thousand men to the Americans at Saratoga, New York, on October 17, 1777, a victory that bolstered American efforts to secure French aid.

647.15–16 slavery within the Commonwealth] At the time of the adoption of the Massachusetts constitution, in 1780, and for four decades thereafter, the state encompassed the territory that is today the state of Maine.

647.30–32 his grandson and executor . . . in the edition] In 1829, Thomas Jefferson Randolph (1792–1875) published *Memoir, Correspondence, and Miscellanies from the Papers of Thomas Jefferson*, a four-volume edition of his grandfather's writings. Adams was fascinated by the collection, which revealed new dimensions both of the man and of the historical events that had shaped Adams's political life and that of his father. He was also appalled by what he read. "It shews his craft and duplicity in very glaring colours," he noted in his diary on August 29, 1836. The edition included a facsimile reproduction of the manuscript draft of the Declaration of Independence, including the famous strike-through of the grievance about slavery.

648.10 Urim and Thummim] Ancient Israelite priestly garb, especially a breastplate, symbolically associated with light and truth. See Exodus 28:30.

648.18–20 Anthony Benezet . . . Granville Sharp] Antislavery activists Benezet (1713–1784) and Sharp (1735–1813) founded pioneering advocacy groups in Philadelphia (1775) and London (1787), respectively. Sharp's group, the Society for Effecting the Abolition of the Slave Trade, was cofounded by Thomas Clarkson (1760–1846).

648.39 "Sweet are the uses of adversity"] *As You Like It*, II.i.12.

648.39–40 "in the day of adversity *consider*,"] Ecclesiastes 7:14.

649.19 Clarkson himself has written the history] Clarkson published his *History of the Abolition of the Slave Trade* in 1808, the year after Parliament outlawed the trade.

650.20–22 Has the unction of our eloquence moved . . . the holy pontiff] Nearly four centuries after it began, the international slave trade was finally condemned by the Holy See in 1839 when Pope Gregory XVI issued the bull "In Supremo Apostolatus" at the request of Great Britain.

650.24–25 Have we softened the heart of the fiery Mussulman of Tunis] Ahmad Bey, the tenth Husaynid ruler of Tunis (r. 1837–55), abolished slavery in Tunisia in January 1846, in part in response to pressure from British consul Thomas Reade.

651.12 is it not yet inexorably suppressed?] Adams would finally succeed in overturning the gag rule on December 3, 1844.

651.16–17 In cold-blooded defiance . . . of the Union?] In 1822, in the wake of the abortive slave uprising planned by the formerly enslaved Denmark Vesey in Charleston, South Carolina, the state passed the Negro Seaman Act. Because Vesey's "rebellion" was alleged to have involved "foreign" Black sailors, the act called for the incarceration of visiting free Black sailors from other states or countries in local jails while their vessel remained in Charleston. The next year, Associate Supreme Court Justice William Johnson Jr. (1771–1834), a South Carolina native, presiding in circuit over the South Carolina District Court, ruled the law unconstitutional, though it continued to be enforced locally for many years thereafter.

651.26–27 a sworn Post-Master General, formally avow] In 1835 the American Antislavery Society launched a concerted campaign to flood the South with abolitionist literature through the mails. Southern states responded by seizing and destroying the material, in violation of federal law. Andrew Jackson's newly appointed postmaster-general, Amos Kendall (1789–1869), refused to condemn the seizures, arguing that while postal agents had an obligation to follow the laws, they owed a "higher" duty to their communities, and "if the former be perverted to destroy the latter, it is patriotism to disregard them."

651.31–32 Have we not seen printing presses destroyed] Among many such instances the most infamous was the murder of Elijah Parish Lovejoy (1802–1837), an abolitionist newspaper editor and journalist who was killed when a proslavery mob attacked and destroyed his printing office in Alton, Illinois, on November 6, 1837.

651.32–33 halls erected . . . consumed by fire] On May 17, 1838, just three days after it opened, Pennsylvania Hall, the new meetinghouse of the Pennsylvania Anti-Slavery Society, was torched by a white supremacist mob. Adams had sent a letter to be read at the building's dedication ceremony on May 14: "I rejoice that, in the city of Philadelphia, the friends of free discussion have erected a Hall for its unrestrained exercise. My fervent wishes are, that Pennsylvania Hall may fulfill its destination, by demonstrative proof, that freedom of speech in the city of Penn shall no longer be an abstraction."

651.39 the Enterprise and the Creole] In February 1835 the American slave trader *Enterprise*, sailing from Alexandria, Virginia, to Charleston, South Carolina, was blown off course by a storm and forced to put in at the port of Hamilton in Bermuda, where its unmanifested "cargo" of seventy-five enslaved people were ordered brought ashore by British customs officials and ultimately awarded their freedom. In October 1841 the brig *Creole*, engaged in the coastal slave trade from Virginia to Louisiana, was redirected to the British colony of Nassau, Bahamas, after the 135 enslaved people on board revolted under the leadership of Madison Washington. Both incidents led to repeated calls in Congress for restitution.

653.12–18 "*Tum ab certo* . . . delightful to them as Liberty."] Livy, *The History of Rome*, Book XXXIII, chapter 32.

Index

Aaron, 139–40, 146
Abolitionism, 425–26, 445, 454, 465, 577, 582, 641–43, 647–53
Abolition petitions to Congress, 425–26, 429–86, 577
Accomac, VA, 582
Act Prohibiting the Importation of Slaves, 594–95, 641
Adams, Abigail (mother), 67–68, 149
Adams, Charles Francis (son), 288, 400, 488
Adams, George Washington (son), 295
Adams, John (father), 4–5, 12, 67, 323; diplomatic missions of, 3, 181, 275, 541–42; "Discourses on Davila," 11; election of 1796, 561; election of 1800, 81, 126, 561–63; nomination of John Marshall as chief justice, 234; as president, 101, 110, 149, 163, 166, 176, 316, 527, 562; as signer of Declaration of Independence, 206; as vice president, 11, 50, 68, 547
Adams, John, II (son), 287
Adams, Louisa Catherine Johnson (wife), 234, 288
Adams, Samuel, 77
Addison, Joseph, 648; *Cato*, 74
Aeneas, 87, 99, 491, 522
Aesop, 344
Africa, 178, 412, 459; Barbary states, 113–14, 257, 259, 419, 463, 487, 536–37, 562, 650; slave trade, 241, 256, 258, 278, 578, 585, 590–92, 594–97, 608, 614–18, 641, 648–49, 652–53
Agricola, 85–86
Agriculture, 155, 169, 326, 345, 357, 359, 366, 423; cotton, 230, 364–65, 387, 392–93, 461, 578; independent farmers, 334–39, 346, 349, 352, 356, 363; noted in JQA's Annual Message (1825), 266; noted in JQA's Inaugural Address, 233, 236; protection of, 360, 372, 378, 390, 395; rice, 392; and slavery, 335–36, 346, 372, 384–85, 387–88; tobacco, 216, 392; wealthy landowners, 336–39, 346, 349, 354, 356, 361, 363, 384–85, 390, 392–93, 396–97
Ahmad Bey, 650
Alabama, 437; cotton production in, 393; Indians in, 399, 401, 403, 405, 414, 420, 422–23; slavery in, 610, 614
Alba Longa, 8
Albany Argus, 432–33
Albaroni, Giulio, 549
Alden, John, 466
Alexandria, DC (now VA), 290, 525
Alfred, King of England, 496
Algiers, 113, 257, 259, 419, 463, 487, 536–37, 562
Ambrister, Robert Chrystie, 181, 184–85, 190, 193, 195, 197–99, 202–3, 627–28
Amelia Island, 181, 197
American exceptionalism, 67, 322
Amistad (Spanish slaver), 567–68, 597
Amphictyonic League, 319
Anderson, Richard C., 269–70, 272, 280, 284
Anglicans, 96–98
Anglo-Saxons, 411–13, 415–16, 481, 496, 646
Angoulême, duc d' (Louis-Antoine), 418
Annapolis, MD, 512

INDEX

Annual Message, 1823 (Monroe), 282–83
Annual Message, 1825 (JQA), 243–67
Annual Message, 1832 (Jackson), 326–27, 330–97
Annual Message, 1835 (Jackson), 438–39
Antifederalists, 524, 545, 549
Anti-Masonic Party, 567
Anti-Slave Trade Convention. *See* Quintuple Treaty
Apalachicola River, 185–86, 196
Appropriations, 45, 407–8, 535, 554; for army, 250–51; for commerce, 341–42; for diplomatic missions, 571, 606–7; for fugitives from Indian hostilities, 403–5, 422; for navy, 250–51, 258–59; for negotiating Indian treaties, 253, 557; for Panama Congress, 269–71, 284; for public debt, 109–12; for public works, 254, 338–42, 344–45, 347, 353, 355, 364
Arabia, 14
Arbitrary power, 17, 28, 35, 37, 64, 73, 78–79, 213, 300–301, 303–4, 320, 348, 354, 381–82
Arbuthnot, Alexander, 181, 184, 188, 190, 193, 195–96, 198–200, 202–3, 627–28
Argentina, 271–73, 276, 280, 284
Aristocracy, 11–12, 16, 21, 24, 28, 41–42, 50–52, 336, 383, 523
Aristotle, 146, 226
Arkansas, 255, 411, 414, 572, 582
Arkansas River, 417, 424, 574–76
Armies, standing, 51, 113, 416
Army, British, 75, 81, 213, 409–10, 493
Army, Continental, 75, 292, 505–6, 510, 512, 526
Army, French, 547
Army, Mexican, 579, 581
Army, Texan, 466, 581
Army, U.S., 610; appropriations for, 250–51; discipline in, 252–53; and Indians, 181, 355–56, 420, 424, 461; in peacetime, 361, 364; and possible war with Mexico, 410, 414, 416, 579, 581; in Seminole Wars, 181–85, 189–94, 197, 200–203, 635–36, 639–40; United States Military Academy, 240, 253–54, 259, 261; in War of 1812, 181, 197–98, 635
Army Corps of Engineers, 254–55
Articles of Confederation, 104, 318, 374, 527, 532; cessions of state territory, 504, 508; and commerce, 25, 104, 228, 508–12, 536–37; creation of, 498–504, 565; and Declaration of Independence, 228, 312, 498–502, 508–17, 531; defects of, 11, 24, 76, 312, 315, 347, 494–95, 510–12, 515, 524, 536, 555, 558, 565; need to replace, 512–14; no executive power under, 495, 535, 538; Northwest Ordinance, 508, 538–39, 557; proportional representation under, 503–4; and public debt, 509, 511–12, 541; relationship to state governments, 310, 312, 316, 499–500, 503–4, 509, 511, 513; taxation and revenue under, 25, 129, 503, 508–9, 511, 529; and treaty negotiations, 228, 275, 508, 541, 554; war powers under, 508. *See also* Congress, Confederation
Artificial democracy, 41
Ashburton, Baron (Alexander Baring), 583–89, 597, 603–5, 611, 613, 619
Asia, 165, 217, 536
Assyria, ancient, 289, 321
Astronomical observatory, 263
Atheism, 552
Athens, ancient, 141–42, 229, 562
Augustus, 491
Austin, Benjamin, 117
Austin, Moses, 630
Austin, Stephen F., 630

Austria, 214; and Quintuple Treaty, 568; U.S. diplomatic mission to, 571, 583, 587, 589, 606, 610; war with French Republic, 544

Bacon, Francis: "Of Sedition and Troubles," 311
Bagot, Charles, 195
Bahamas, 188, 195, 197–200, 465, 568
Bainbridge, William, 114
Baker, Anthony St. John, 186
Balance of powers, 37–38, 45
Baltic Sea, 536
Baltimore, Baron (Cecil Calvert), 99
Baltimore, MD, 168, 292
Baltimore & Ohio Railway, 292
Bangor, ME: JQA's letter to antislavery group in, 641–66
Bank of the United States, 326, 337–38, 364, 384, 390, 395, 559–60, 602
Bankruptcy, 24, 40, 61, 249–50
Barbary States. *See* Algiers; Morocco; Tripoli; Tunis
Barbary Wars, 113–14, 259, 536–37
Barbour, James, 252
Barron, James, 149
Bastille, storming of, 26–27
Bathurst, Henry, 187, 195
Beardsley, Samuel, 605
Belknap, Jeremy, 4; *American Biography*, 84
Benezet, Anthony, 648
Benton, Thomas Hart, 432
Berceau (French corvette), 108
Berkeley, George (admiral), 149, 159, 171, 173–76
Berkeley, George (philosopher): "Verses on the Prospect of Planting Arts and Learning in America," 99, 289, 293
Berlin, Germany, 589, 606, 610
Berlin Decree, 170, 177
Bermuda, 175, 465

Bible, 86, 214, 227, 423; Chronicles, 321; Corinthians, 553; Deuteronomy, 566; Ecclesiastes, 648; Exodus, 139–40, 214, 526, 565; Genesis, 211, 290, 377; Isaiah, 64, 73, 292–93; Job, 443; Joshua, 565–66; Judges, 74, 321; Kings, 99, 213, 321; Luke, 231; Matthew, 44, 58, 266; Numbers, 455; Psalms, 216–17, 242; Revelation, 225; Samuel, 75, 225
Bicameralism, 314–15, 527
Billaut, Adolphe, 615–16
Bill of Rights, U.S., 25, 517–18, 557–58
Black Sea, 537
Blackstone, William: *Commentaries on the Laws of England*, 33, 303–4, 310, 317, 320
Blockades, 169, 257, 275–77, 580, 624
Blunt, Joseph, 490
Bolívar, Simón, 269, 634
Boone, Daniel, 631
Boston, MA, 4, 11, 53, 67, 69–70, 83, 101, 133–36, 145, 149, 151, 153, 295, 297, 307, 325, 329, 425, 427, 567; during American Revolution, 81, 217, 493–94; merchants in, 163, 168–69, 537; New England Anti-Slavery Convention in, 642; public works in, 255
Boston Daily Advocate, 453, 467
Boston Massacre, 67
Boundary negotiations, 82; along Great Lakes, 542; Maine–Canada border, 543, 568, 583, 585; with Mexico, 574–76, 579–80; Oregon Country, 538, 583, 585
Bourbon dynasty, 540
Boyle, Thomas, 580
Boylston, Nicholas, 145
Boylston family, 133, 145
Boylston Professorship of Rhetorick and Oratory, 133–36, 145
Bradford, William, 91, 99, 306, 466; *Of Plimouth Plantation*, 93

Brazil, 571
Brazos River, 574
Brennus, 126
Brissot, Jacques-Pierre, 550
Bristol, England, 217
Britain, 85, 97, 112, 153, 206, 210, 229–31, 261–63, 279, 309, 336, 405, 429, 487, 510, 533, 536–37; abolition of slavery by, 415, 419–20, 465–66, 578, 596–97, 641, 645, 649, 652–53; and American Revolution, 8, 59–60, 74–77, 213–14, 217–18, 222, 225, 227, 300, 304, 307, 493–94, 496–98, 513, 518, 584, 646–49; boundary negotiations with, 542–43, 568, 583, 585; *Chesapeake–Leopard* affair, 149, 159, 163, 171–76; Civil War and Commonwealth, 301–2, 305–6, 495–96; colonial policy of, 24, 72–74, 161, 169–70, 213, 215–17, 302–7, 310, 493, 535–36; common law in, 12, 20; Constitution, 11–12, 16–22, 25–27, 29–34, 36, 38–39, 43–45, 51–52, 525, 548, 604; disputes with U.S. (1840s), 583–90, 593–606, 608–9, 611–13, 618–22, 638; elections in, 42; foreign relations with Washington administration, 541–55, 561; game laws in, 42–43; Glorious Revolution, 4, 11, 17–18, 212, 301–2, 495–96; Gordon Riots, 28; impressment of American seamen, 116, 162–67, 172, 174, 176, 547–48, 550; Indian policy of, 201, 493; interests in Florida, 181–82, 184–90, 193–99, 201–2, 628; interests in West Indies, 417–19; Jacobite rebellion in, 38; Jay's Treaty, 168, 366, 551–55; Magna Carta, 209, 226, 493, 496; monopolies in, 42–43; Napoleonic Wars, 115–16, 149–50, 158–67, 170–71, 176–78, 620; and neutral commerce, 167–71, 176–78, 546–48, 554; Norman Conquest, 20–21, 32–33; Orders in Council, 149, 158–61, 171, 176, 178; political parties in, 175–76; proposed commercial treaty with, 541–43; Reformation in, 211; and settlement of New England, 88–90, 92–93, 95, 97–98, 212, 216, 305–6; Seven Years' War, 72, 169–70, 493, 605; and slave trade, 568, 590–92, 594–97, 632; taxation by 72, 158, 161, 170, 176, 178, 213, 300, 302–3, 305, 307, 310, 493, 647; Treaty of Ghent, 82, 181, 185–87, 238, 610; Treaty of Paris, 55–56, 59–60, 225–26, 289, 493, 541–44; and U.S. war with Mexico, 415–20, 571–75, 578–83, 619, 637; War of 1812, 82, 181, 197–98, 237, 246, 249, 259, 309, 315, 356, 409–10, 563, 580, 582, 584; Wars of the Roses, 301; war with French Republic, 53, 55–61, 63–64, 545–48, 562, 620. *See also* Parliament (Britain)
Brown, James, 247
Brown, John, 110–12
Brutus, Marcus Junius, 214
Buenos Ayres Republic. *See* Argentina
Bunker Hill, battle of, 217
Burgoyne, John, 646
Burke, Edmund, 215, 217, 227; *Reflections on the Revolution in France*, 11, 13–14, 16–17, 43–44; *Speech on Conciliation*, 304
Butler, Samuel: *Hudibras*, 115, 456
Byng, John, 606
Bynum, Jesse A., 445–48, 453, 455

Caecilius, 489
Calhoun, John C., 269, 604; and election of 1824, 205, 233; *Exposition and Protest*, 296; and nullification, 296, 331; as secretary of war, 181, 205; as U.S. senator, 326; as vice president, 233, 243, 296, 375

INDEX 783

California, 573, 580–81
Caligula, 114
Callender, James Thomson, 108
Calvin, John, 97
Cambreleng, Churchill C., 441–42
Cameron, Charles, 195, 198–99
Campbell, Thomas: "Lochiel's Warning," 461
Canada, 173, 175, 256, 542–43, 568, 583–85
Canals, 243, 251, 254–55, 260, 267, 287–93, 390
Canning, George, 168, 171–72, 418, 584, 593, 618
Caracas, Venezuela, 405
Carmichael, William, 554
Carney, Eliza A., 200
Caroline (steamboat), 568, 583, 585, 587
Cartagena, Colombia, 270
Carthage, ancient, 8, 276
Carver, John, 91, 99, 306, 466
Caso y Luengo, Francisco, 184, 190, 192, 196–97, 199, 202
Cass, Lewis, 568, 586, 594, 600–602, 615
Castlereagh, Viscount (Robert Stewart), 182, 187, 628
Catherine II, Empress of Russia, 225
Catholics, 28, 96–97, 211, 579–80, 637, 650, 652
Census, 123; of *1790*, 263, 519; of *1820*, 263, 388; of *1830*, 386, 388; of *1840*, 519
Central America, 206, 240, 249, 264, 637; and Panama Congress, 269–85
Cervantes, Miguel de: *Don Quixote*, 302
Cessions of state territory, 350–51, 504, 507–8
Chaldea, ancient, 321
Chamber of Deputies (France), 346–47, 601–2, 612, 614–15, 617–18
Charles I, King of England, 212, 302–3, 306, 430, 495–96

Charles II, King of England, 306, 496
Charles II, King of Navarre, 37
Charles IV, King of Spain, 545
Charles X, King of France, 247, 279, 318, 612
Charleston, SC, 168, 259, 460
Charlestown, MA, 217, 494
Charters, colonial 20, 89, 92, 95, 212–13, 300, 302–3, 306, 313, 493–94, 499
Cherokees, 424
Chesapeake, U.S.S., 149, 159, 163, 171–76
Chesapeake and Delaware Canal, 251
Chesapeake and Ohio Canal, 254–55; JQA's speech at dedication of, 287–93
Chile, 257, 271–73, 280, 284
Chimborazo (volcano), 548
China, 137, 178, 257, 290, 305, 537, 650
Chippewas (Ojibwe), 253
Choctaws, 424, 639
Christian II, King of Denmark, 214
Christianity, 58, 81, 85, 87, 96–98, 143, 170, 209, 227, 245, 257, 274, 305, 309, 317, 423, 536, 552, 577, 585, 645, 648–50, 652
Churchill, Charles: *The Ghost*, 116
Church of England, 96–98
Cicero, 47, 69, 138, 142, 146, 345, 393; *De Officiis*, 85; *Tusculan Disputations*, 489
Cienfuegos, José, 188, 195–97
Citizenship, 164–66, 426, 651
Civil rights, 335, 478, 480
Civil society, dissolution of, 26–27, 30, 316, 371
Civil war, 25, 29, 62–63, 209, 296, 301, 305, 334, 337, 343, 345, 354, 405, 411, 417, 419–20, 494, 634, 636–37
Clarke, Archibald, 200

Clarkson, Thomas: *History of the Abolition of the Slave Trade*, 649
Clay, Clement C., 610
Clay, Henry, 244; and election of 1824, 233–34; as negotiator in Ghent, 233; as secretary of state, 233, 269, 271, 573–76, 630; as Speaker of the House, 205, 233, 269; as U.S. representative, 641
Coahuila, 413, 415
Cochin-China, 217
Cockburn, George, 194
Colman, Samuel (publisher), 487
Colombia, 248–49, 269, 271–74, 276, 278–80, 284, 634
Colonialism, 161–62, 214–15, 217, 248, 277, 302, 305, 536, 548
Colorado River, 574, 576
Columbia College, 488
Columbian Centinel (Boston), 11, 13, 53, 55
Columbian Magazine or Monthly Miscellany (Philadelphia), 3–4
Columbia Rediviva (American merchant ship), 537–38
Columbia River, 262, 537
Columbus, Christopher, 89, 210
Comanches, 580
Combs, Franklin, 623
Combs, Leslie, 623
Commerce, 4–5, 9, 61, 63, 116, 338, 357, 560–61, 604–5, 624; appropriations for, 341–42; under Articles of Confederation, 25, 104, 228, 508–12, 536–37, 541; colonial, 72, 89, 213, 216, 493, 535; and Embargo Act, 149–50, 153–54, 156, 158–62, 172, 177, 296; and neutrality, 53, 55–57, 60, 149, 160, 163, 167–71, 176–78, 225, 257, 269, 275–77, 281–82, 365, 546–48, 554; New England merchants, 108, 163, 168–69, 537; noted in JQA's Annual Message (1825), 246–48, 257–58, 262; noted in JQA's Inaugural Address, 233, 236; protection of, 114, 257, 296, 356, 360–61, 364, 369, 390, 395, 562; and right of search, 583, 587; and slavery, 385; treaties of, 55–57, 59–60, 228, 275, 284–85, 366, 541–43; in U.S. Constitution, 266, 319
Commercial states. *See* New England *and individual states*
Committee of Ways and Means (U.S. House of Representatives), 365, 370, 386, 442
Committee on Foreign Affairs (U.S. House of Representatives), 568, 570, 604, 606–7
Committee on Manufactures (U.S. House of Representatives), 325–97
Common law, 12, 20
Condict, Lewis, 327, 329, 397
Congress, Confederation, 542, 551, 555, 557; cessions of state territory, 504; and commerce, 508, 510; and Constitutional Convention, 312, 513–14; delegated powers of, 501, 503; executive power of, 538; and public debt, 511–12, 541; restrictions on, 494–95; and revenue, 509, 511, 529; and state legislatures, 310, 499–500, 503–4, 509, 511–12; term of service in, 515; and treaty negotiations, 275, 508, 541, 554; voting in, 503–4; war operations of, 310, 508; war powers of, 508
Congress, Continental: First, 20, 218, 493, 500, 538, 551; Second, 218, 227, 300, 497–98, 500–502, 506, 508, 538
Congress, U.S., 55, 155, 239–40, 243–44, 327, 330, 338–39, 342, 348, 363, 519–20, 524, 526, 543, 557, 561, 563, 567–68; Act Prohibiting the Importation of Slaves, 594–95, 641; authority over District of Columbia, 266, 447, 472–73; authorization of

Chesapeake and Ohio Canal, 287, 290; and constitutional amendments, 127; constitutional role of, 36, 527–28, 534–35, 538–39; Embargo Act, 149–50, 153–54, 156, 158–62, 172, 177, 296; Indian Removal Act, 399; Joint Resolution for Distributing Rations to the Distressed Fugitives from Indian Hostilities, 399–424; JQA's Annual Message (1825) to, 245–67; and judiciary, 528, 538, 541; and Louisiana Purchase, 562; and manufacturing, 358–59; and Nullification Crisis, 320, 325, 367, 369–71, 383, 393–94; and public debt, 110; and public land, 351–52, 354; and public works, 241, 287, 290, 340–41, 344–45, 347, 355; representation in, 52, 103–4, 129, 374, 378–79, 386, 388–89; Revenue Collection Act, 594–95; and Seminole Wars, 197, 200; and slavery, 399–400, 406–10, 420–21, 425, 429–86, 626–27, 633–34; and state sovereignty, 529–32; Tariff of 1828, 296, 325; taxation and revenue acts of, 319, 325, 367, 369–71, 383, 394, 556, 559, 594–95; war powers of, 49, 405–6, 408–10, 420, 604, 628–29, 634. *See also* House of Representatives, U.S.; Senate, U.S.

Connecticut, 226, 311, 350, 454, 473, 479, 507

Connecticut colony, 309

Connecticut River, 255

Constantinople, Ottoman Empire, 305, 470

Constituent Assembly (France), 62

Constituent communications, 425

Constituent sovereignty. *See* Sovereignty, popular

Constitution, British, 11–12, 16–22, 25–27, 29–34, 36, 38–39, 43–49, 51–52, 302, 304–5, 525, 548, 604

Constitution, French, 12, 18, 23, 31, 33–34, 36, 39–49, 51–52, 54, 63, 317

Constitution, Maryland, 407–8

Constitution, Massachusetts, 22, 36–37, 647

Constitution, New Jersey, 313

Constitution, North Carolina, 313

Constitution, South Carolina, 382

Constitution, U.S., 76, 104, 127, 153–54, 228, 289, 307, 316, 318, 338, 346–48, 363, 375, 384, 391, 397, 403, 425, 492, 512–13, 518–19, 525, 529–33, 536–37, 543, 545, 550, 555–56, 559, 636; and agriculture, 266; and business, 326; and commerce, 266, 319; constitutional roles of three branches, 36, 516, 527–28, 534–35, 538–39; democratic principles in, 522–23, 563; and elections, 120–22; and *The Federalist*, 551, 558, 560; and foreign alliances, 269, 280; formation of, 3, 11–12, 18–20, 22, 25, 36, 51–52; as fulfillment of Declaration of Independence, 292, 450, 488, 495, 514–15, 521, 523, 565–66; and Indian hostilities, 404–6, 408–9, 421–23; and inventions, 265; JQA's discourse on jubilee of, 487–566; and judiciary, 264; and Louisiana Purchase, 115, 315, 553, 560, 562, 576; Madison and Hamilton as authors of, 558; and manufacturing, 266, 367, 372, 389–90; noted in JQA's Annual Message (1825), 243–44, 249, 253, 262, 264–66; noted in JQA's Inaugural Address, 235–37, 240–41; and nullification, 296, 311, 313–14, 319–21, 343, 370–71, 377, 381–83, 389, 392–94; as paramount to state constitutions, 517; and public debt, 334; and public lands, 350–51, 354; and public works, 243, 260, 339–41, 344–45;

Constitution (*continued*)
  and representation, 125–26, 374, 377, 385; republican principles in, 236–37, 373, 522–23, 527; and right of debate, 454; and right of petition, 446, 448–51, 455, 458–60, 462–63, 468–69; separation of powers, 382; and slavery, 126, 374, 378–79, 385, 400, 420, 454, 460, 468–69, 650; state ratifying conventions, 11, 128–29, 312–13, 514, 524, 558; taxation and revenue in, 319, 376; three-fifths clause, 101, 107, 125–28, 460; and treaties, 55, 253; war powers in, 49–50, 52, 604, 629, 634
Constitutional amendments, 38, 127, 348, 454; Bill of Rights, 25, 517–18, 557–58; on choosing electors (proposed), 122–23; eliminating three-fifths clause (proposed), 101–2, 106–7, 124–25, 128–31; Twelfth, 122
Constitutional Convention, 4, 11, 228, 312, 495, 512–14, 516–18, 529, 537, 541, 543
Constitutionalism, 11–12, 22, 33–34, 157, 488
Constitutions, 19–20; South American, 318, 320; state, 18–22, 41, 43, 49–50, 52, 312–13, 318–19, 346, 382, 501, 515, 517, 527
Contraband of war, 169, 275, 277, 363, 365–66, 554, 617–18
Contracts, 3, 7–9, 59–60, 62, 249, 348, 367, 369, 371, 377, 380, 382–83, 393, 533
Cook, James, 261
Cook, Peter B., 200
Cooper, William, 70
Copenhagen, Denmark, 171
Corruption, 26, 44, 50–51, 73, 101, 116, 118, 120, 141, 143, 157, 160, 341–42, 482, 582
Cortés, Hernán, 413
Cossacks, 318

Cotton, 230, 364–65, 387, 392–93, 461, 578
Crawford, William H., 205, 233
Creeks, 181, 186, 188–89, 195, 202, 254, 269, 414, 424
Creole (American coastal slaver), 568, 583, 585, 587–88, 651–52
Crichton, James, 588–89
Cuba, 188, 196–97, 279, 417–19, 573
Cumberland Road, 241, 243, 255
Currency, 390, 461, 505–6, 509, 559–60, 580
Cushing, Caleb, 451, 469, 568, 581
Cushman, Samuel, 431

Daniels, Edward, 200
Danton, Georges, 550
David, 75, 225, 321
Davis, John M., 639
Davis and Force (publisher), 205, 207
Debate, freedom of, 320, 400, 406–8, 421–22, 425–26, 431, 435, 438, 445, 447, 449, 452, 454, 461, 467, 472, 479, 483, 625, 627, 633, 651
Decatur, Stephen, 599
Declaration and Resolves of 1774 (Continental Congress), 20
Declaration of Independence, 74, 236, 261, 270, 284, 289, 299–300, 305, 307–8, 310, 314, 320–21, 336, 345, 370, 373, 412, 492, 496–97, 504–5, 507, 518, 521, 525, 529, 532–33, 536, 548, 564–65, 645–46; and Articles of Confederation, 228, 312, 498–502, 508–17, 531; as fulfilled by U.S. Constitution, 292, 450, 488, 495, 514–15, 521, 523, 565–66; influence in France, 317–18, 540; Jefferson as author of, 24, 558, 647; JQA's address celebrating American independence, 205–31; republican principles in, 309; and Revolutionary War, 222–24,

494; text of, 218–22; and Treaty of Paris, 226
Declaration of the Rights of Man and of the Citizen, 54, 58
Deism, 348, 552
Delaware, 226, 452, 454, 507
Delegated powers, 23–25, 34–35, 38, 43, 47–48, 260, 313, 320, 343–45, 347, 354, 494, 501, 503, 513, 515–16
Democracy, 21, 42, 420; artificial, 41; distrust of, 17, 53, 234, 522–23; and factions, 124, 549–50; in France, 39, 317, 540, 544, 549–50, 612; in Latin American revolutions, 206; natural, 41; representative, 234, 238; in state governments, 309; and U.S. Constitution, 522–23, 563
Democratic Party, 296, 315–16, 429, 610–11; and annexation of Texas, 572, 581; election of 1832, 326; election of 1836, 451, 464; election of 1840, 567–68; and slavery, 399, 432, 642–43
Demosthenes, 138
Denmark, 171, 214, 247–48, 306, 585
Despotism. *See* Tyranny
Dickinson, John, 499
Diplomacy, 49–50, 68, 272–75, 325, 571, 606–7
Directory (France), 552–53
Direct taxes, 109, 111, 129, 376, 378–79, 385–88
District of Columbia: and Chesapeake and Ohio Canal, 287, 290–92; congressional authority over, 266, 447, 472–73; Georgetown in, 290, 525; grand jury in, 438, 477–80, 483; slavery in, 399–400, 432, 437, 442, 447, 455, 459–60, 462–64, 466, 471–73, 631–32. *See also* Washington, DC
Dorchester, MA, 107
Dromgoole, George C., 444, 475

Duane, William, 108
Dunkerque (Dunkirk), France, 537

Eastburn, John H. (publisher), 325, 329
East Florida, 181, 240, 352, 417
East Indies, 165
Edes, Benjamin, 67–69
Edict of Nantes, 492
Edinburgh Review, 167
Edward VI, King of England, 97
Egypt, 601, 613; ancient, 32, 139–40, 214, 290, 305
Eldon, Baron (John Scott), 176
Election of 1796, 561
Election of 1800, 81, 126, 561–63
Election of 1804, 101, 103, 106, 118, 122, 130, 561–63
Election of 1808, 150, 154
Election of 1820, 205, 233
Election of 1824, 205–6, 233–34, 242–43, 592
Election of 1828, 233, 287, 295, 375
Election of 1832, 326
Election of 1836, 451, 454, 464
Election of 1840, 567–68
Election of 1844, 568
Elections, 40–42, 104, 118–24, 157, 238, 314, 374–75, 425, 563
Electoral College, 101, 118–24, 205, 233, 374–75, 378, 385–86, 516
11th Congressional District (Massachusetts), 295–96
Elizabeth I, Queen of England, 97
Elizabethtown Point (now Elizabeth), NJ, 525–26
Ely, William, 101, 106, 124–25
Emancipation, 432–33, 436, 454, 477, 577–78, 597, 599, 634–36, 650, 653
Emancipator, The (Boston), 567–68, 640
Embargo Act, 149–50, 153–54, 156, 158–62, 172, 177, 296
Emerson, Ralph Waldo, 399

"Empty land" argument, 81–82, 95–96
Endicott, John, 306
England. *See* Britain
Enslaved people, 412; cheap woolen clothing for, 325, 387; emancipation of, 432–33, 436, 454, 477, 577–78, 597, 599, 634–36, 650, 653; fugitive, 187, 194, 199, 460, 477; human rights of, 430, 450–51, 459; impressed seamen as, 166; indemnity claims regarding, 247–49, 409–10, 420, 465; as outlaws in Florida, 183, 185–94, 196–200, 202–3; petitions from, 426, 432–63, 467–77, 482–85; population of, 376, 386, 388–89, 393, 459; taken by British in War of 1812, 249, 409–10; in war with Mexico, 412–16, 420
Enterprise (American coastal slaver), 651–52
Episcopius, Simon, 92–93
Eppes, John Wayles, 117
Equality, 39, 42, 60; natural, 514, 645–48; political, 79; of rights, 24, 36, 40, 123, 128–30, 229, 236–37, 240, 336–38, 345, 352; social, 72, 79, 227
Equal representation, 42, 503, 506
Equity, 6–7, 45, 55, 58, 60, 341, 386
Erie Canal, 267
Erskine, David Montague, 159
Erving, George, 182
Escambia River, 191
Etna (volcano), 548
Evans, George, 452, 475
Excise taxes, 109, 111, 376
Executive branch. *See* President, U.S.
Expansionism, 81, 101, 114–15, 181, 236, 240–41, 263–64, 399
Exposition and Protest (Calhoun), 296

Fabre d'Églantine, Philippe-François, 552

Faction, 11, 33, 50, 54, 94, 101, 105, 110, 116, 118–19, 122–24, 130, 147, 345, 380, 455, 524, 549–50, 642
Falmouth, MA (now Portland, ME), 217, 494
Fannin, James W., Jr., 581
Fauchet, Jean-Antoine-Joseph, 107
Federalism, 11, 76, 155, 234, 239, 292, 516, 560
Federalist, The, 551, 558, 560
Federalist Party, 11, 67, 117, 121, 123, 129, 237, 296, 524–25; election of 1800, 81, 126, 562–63; election of 1804, 101, 106, 118, 122, 130, 562–63; election of 1808, 150; election of 1820, 205; and Hartford Convention, 582; in Massachusetts, 101, 105, 130, 149; pro-British, 53, 315, 582
Federation of Central America, 280
Ferdinand VII, King of Spain, 183–84, 192–94, 199, 202, 418
Feudalism, 78, 142, 308, 336, 377, 648
Findlay, James, 642
First Barbary War, 113–14
First Continental Congress, 20, 218, 493, 500, 538, 551
Fisheries, 256–57, 361, 510, 561
Five Points (New York City), 609–10
Flaminius, Gaius, 653
Flanders, 420
Florida (Spanish): acquisition of, 182, 240, 352, 417, 576; Seminole Wars in, 181–204, 627–28, 635, 639–40
Florida Territory, 240, 255, 259, 350, 404–5, 416, 420
Floyd, John, 378
Floyd, John Gelston, 587
Forefathers' Day, JQA's oration on, 81–89
Fort Barracas, 183–85, 192, 194
Fortress Monroe, 253
Fort San Marco, 181, 183, 189–90, 192–93, 196–99, 202–3

Fox, Charles James, 170
Foxes, 253
France, 8, 29, 67, 107, 109, 246–47, 261–63, 318, 336, 411, 418, 487, 509, 536, 571, 581, 585, 596, 600–603, 611–18, 652; and American Revolution, 8, 53, 55, 59–60, 64, 77, 225, 228, 537, 646–47; Chamber of Deputies, 346–47, 601–2, 612, 614–15, 617–18; colonies of, 61–64, 417, 548; constitutions of, 12, 18, 23, 31, 33–34, 36, 39–49, 51–52, 54, 63; Declaration of the Rights of Man and of the Citizen, 54, 58; democracy in, 39, 317, 540, 544, 549–50, 612; Directory, 552–53; foreign relations with Washington administration, 539–41, 544–55, 561; Louisiana Purchase from, 101, 112, 114–15, 117, 149, 315, 352, 417, 553, 555, 560–62, 576; Napoleonic Wars, 115–16, 149–50, 158–67, 170–71, 176–78, 482, 620; National Assembly, 13, 16, 18, 21–23, 28, 31, 33–34, 39–44, 47, 49–52, 54, 57, 552; National Convention, 54, 58, 62, 545, 547, 552; republicanism in, 39, 54, 107, 541, 549, 553; Seven Years' War, 72, 169–70, 493, 605; and slave trade, 568; treaties with U.S., 53, 55–56, 59–65, 228, 275, 284, 366, 545–48, 554; and U.S. war with Mexico, 415–20; war with Britain, 53, 55–61, 63–64, 545–48, 562, 620
Francis II, Holy Roman Emperor, 57
Franklin, Benjamin, 275, 501–2, 516
Frederick I, King of Prussia, 309
Frederick II, King of Prussia, 57, 275
Fredericksburg, VA, 432, 434, 436, 439, 448, 470–71
Freedom. *See* Liberty
Free labor, protection of, 372, 376, 378–79

Free persons of color, petitions from, 432, 436, 446, 450, 455, 470, 472
French, Richard, 452, 468
French and Indian War, 72, 493, 605
French Republic, 54, 62–64, 540–41, 546, 549–50
French Revolution, 11–12, 16, 19, 26–27, 53–54, 67, 78, 94, 107–8, 238, 317, 487, 540, 544–50, 552, 558, 596, 602, 647
Fries, John, 316
Fugitives from slavery, 187, 194, 199, 460, 477
Fulton, Robert, 230

Gag Rule, 400, 425–26, 625, 651
Gaines, Edmund P., 181, 189, 200, 410, 414, 416
Gallatin, Albert, 110–12
Galloway, Earl of (George Stewart), 174
Gama, Vasco da, 210
Game laws, 42–43, 52
Garret, Mr. and Mrs. (of Georgia), 200
Gates, Seth, 568–69
Gazette of the United States (Philadelphia), 11
General Court. *See* Legislature, Massachusetts
Genêt, Édmond-Charles, 53, 541, 546, 549
Genghis Khan, 637–38
George II, King of England, 300
George III, King of England, 56, 64, 73, 163–64, 171–72, 174, 214, 218, 222, 225–27, 302–3, 308–9, 493, 499, 518, 520–21, 542, 545, 547, 646–47
Georgetown (in District of Columbia), 290, 525
Georgia, 128, 205, 226, 435, 471; under Articles of Confederation, 507; cession of territory by, 350; Indian hostilities in, 399, 401,

Georgia (*continued*)
403, 406, 414, 420, 422–23; public works in, 259; and Seminole Wars, 181, 185, 189, 191, 194, 200, 635, 639–40; tax payment default by, 129; Treaty with Creek Indians, 186, 188, 269; Yazoo land fraud in, 108, 117–18

Georgia colony, 99, 300

Germany, 57, 210–11, 246, 306, 336. *See also* Prussia

Gessler, Albrecht, 214

Ghent (Gent), Flanders (now Belgium), 82, 181, 233, 610

Gibbon, Edward: *History of the Decline and Fall of the Roman Empire*, 321

Giddings, Joshua R., 634, 636

Glascock, Thomas, 406, 471

Glorious Revolution, 11, 17–18, 212, 301–2, 495–96

Godoy, Manuel de, 554

Gordon, George, 28

Gore, Christopher, 168

Goths, 87

Grant, William, 596–97

Graves, William J., 447, 472–73

Gray, Robert, 262, 537

Gray, Thomas: "Elegy Written in a Country Churchyard," 212

Great Lakes, 542

Greece, 206, 257; ancient, 7, 133, 137–38, 140–44, 146, 229–30, 289–90, 309, 319, 345, 377, 522, 562, 653

Greek language, 133–34, 142

Gregory XVI, Pope, 650

Grenville, George, 302

Grimké, Thomas Smith, 381

Grotius, Hugo: *Laws of War and Peace*, 92

Guerrero, Vicente, 413

Guinea, 615

Guizot, François-Pierre, 600, 602, 617–18

Gulf of Mexico, 259, 416, 419, 573

Gustav III, King of Sweden, 646

Gwinn, William M., 621

Habeas corpus, 465, 493, 651

Haiti (Saint-Domingue), 63–64, 270, 278–79

Halifax, Nova Scotia, 173, 175

Hamathli Micco, 200

Hambly, William, 195–96

Hamilton, Alexander, 562; author of *The Federalist*, 551, 558, 560; in Confederation Congress, 511; military service during Revolutionary War, 558; and national bank, 559–60; and public debt, 559; *Report on Manufactures*, 559–60; as secretary of the Treasury, 149, 557–61; and U.S. Constitution, 519, 558–60

Hamilton, James, 613–14, 633

Hammond, George, 544

Hammond, John: *The Love Elegies*, 316

Hampden, John, 303, 493

Hancock, John, 6, 77, 306–7

Hanover dynasty, 300–302, 306

Hanseatic League, 246

Harold II, King of England, 32–33

Harrison, William Henry, 567–68

Hartford Convention, 582

Hartley, David, 544

Harvard University, 3–4, 133–34, 144–46; JQA's Boylston oration at, 135–47; JQA's commencement oration at, 5–10

Hastings, battle of, 33

Havana, Cuba, 188, 196–97, 418

Hawkins, Benjamin, 186

Hayne, Robert Y., 270

Haynes, Charles E., 435–37, 442, 444–45, 467, 474–75

Henry VIII, King of England, 97

Hermes, 140–41, 318

Herod, 305

Heroism, 74, 76–77, 86–87, 91, 222, 224, 257, 262, 302, 652

Hillis Hadjo (Prophet Francis), 186–89, 199
Hoffman, Michael, 642
Holy Alliance, 206, 224
Holy Roman Empire, 57
Homer, 144, 522; *Iliad*, 135, 140; *Odyssey*, 140
Horace, 14, 59
House of Representatives, Massachusetts, 106–7, 119, 122, 130
House of Representatives, U.S., 81, 108–9, 123, 153, 160, 206, 235, 245, 560; abolition petitions in, 399, 406, 425–26, 431–86, 577; appropriation of funds by, 269–70, 272, 284, 535, 554; Committee of Ways and Means, 270, 365, 370, 386, 442; Committee on Foreign Affairs, 568, 570, 604, 606–7; Committee on Manufactures, JQA's report of, 325–97; constitutional role of, 516, 528, 534–35; and election of 1824, 233; election to, 117–18, 120–21; and Electoral College, 118; Gag Rule, 400, 425–26, 625; impeachment of president by, 535; JQA's service in, 295–96, 425, 487; JQA's speech on abolition petitions, 425, 427, 430, 453, 467–86; JQA's speech on war with Mexico, 567, 569, 571, 586–638; and Panama Congress, 269–72, 274, 278, 282, 284–85; representation in, 101, 103–4, 264, 373–78, 386, 388, 392, 429, 435–36, 452, 460, 468–69; resolution on public credit, 559; taxation and revenue measures by, 319, 555–56. *See also* Congress, U.S.
Houston, Sam, 614, 623–24, 637
Hudson Bay, 256
Huger, Benjamin, 122–23
Human rights, 16, 28, 52, 58, 60, 127, 209, 213, 217, 228–29, 237, 305, 318, 337, 430, 450–51, 459, 469, 480, 493. 495, 498, 512, 514, 521, 646–49, 652
Hume, David: *The History of England*, 306, 520
Humphreys, Salusbury Pryce, 174–75
Humphries, David, 4
Hus, Jan, 211
Hutchinson, Thomas: *History of the Province of Massachusets-Bay*, 84, 90

Illinois, 479
Immigration, 72, 352, 532
Impeachment, 535
Implied powers, 558
Impressment of seamen, 116, 162–67, 172, 174, 176, 547–48, 550
Inaugural Address (JQA), 233–42
Inaugural Address (Van Buren), 455, 466
Indemnity, claims of, 247–49, 410, 420, 465
Independence Day (1793), oration by JQA, 67–79
Independence Day (1821), oration by JQA, 205–31
Independence Day (1828), speech by JQA, 287–93
Independence Day (1831), oration by JQA, 295–323
Independent farmers, 334–39, 346, 349, 352, 356, 363
India, 210, 225, 578, 584, 650
Indiana, 454, 457, 464, 479
Indian Removal Act, 399
Indians, 89, 98, 212, 416, 487, 536, 542, 562, 582, 637; efforts to "civilize," 240–41, 346, 433; hostilities in Alabama and Georgia, 399, 401, 403–6, 409–10, 420–24; Mexican, 412–13, 580; purchase of land from, 251, 254, 269; resettlement of, 414, 424; right of possession by, 81–82, 94–96; Seminole Wars, 183–203,

Indians (*continued*)
399, 414, 420–24, 627–28, 635, 639–40; treaties with, 186–88, 253–54, 349, 356, 406, 409, 422–24, 461, 556–57; and U.S. Army, 181, 355–56, 420, 424, 461; in war with Mexico, 412–16, 420. *See also individual tribes*

Indian Territory, 424

Ingersoll, Charles J., 567, 569, 583–88, 591, 593–94, 597–605, 608–11, 613, 617–20, 622, 638

Ingersoll, Joseph R., 457–63

Interior Department, U.S., 264

Internal improvements, 641; appropriations for, 254, 338–42, 344–45, 347, 353, 355, 364; Chesapeake and Ohio Canal, 254–55, 287–98; noted in JQA's Annual Message (1825), 243–44, 251–52, 254–55, 260, 266–67; noted in JQA's Inaugural Address, 233, 240–41; noted in JQA's *Report of the Minority of the Committee on Manufactures*, 325–26, 331, 337–42, 344–45, 347, 353, 355, 364, 384–85, 390, 395

International law. *See* Laws of nations

Interposition. *See* Nullification

Intolerable Acts, 24, 161, 305, 493

Inventions, 210, 228, 230

Ireland, 584

Iron, 365–66, 370, 387

Islam, 14, 536, 650

Israelites, ancient, 74–75, 139–40, 214, 216, 305, 321, 377, 522, 565–66, 648

Italy, 210, 309

Iturbide, Agustín de, 413

Jackson, Andrew, 269, 399, 611; and acquisition of Florida, 417; Annual Message (1832), 326–27, 330–97; Annual Message (1835), 438–39; at battle of New Orleans, 181, 635; election of 1824, 205; election of 1828, 233, 287, 295, 375; election of 1832, 326; as general in Seminole Wars, 181–82, 189, 191–94, 197, 201–3, 628, 635, 639–40; JQA's defense of, 183–204; policy toward Mexico, 410, 613, 630; as president, 315, 527; Proclamation Regarding Nullification, 326, 369–72, 379–81; and resolution to aid fugitives from Indian hostilities, 403, 423

Jackson, MS, 621

Jacobite rebellion, 38

Jamaica, 418

James I, King of England, 88, 90, 98, 211, 300

James II, King of England, 212, 302, 495–96

Jamestown settlement, 89, 94, 99, 300

Japan, 217

Jay, John, 511, 538, 540–41, 550–51

Jay's Treaty, 168, 366, 551–55

Jefferson, Thomas, 12, 15, 51, 182; and Barbary Wars, 113–14; Declaration of Independence by, 24, 558, 647; diplomatic missions of, 275; election of 1796, 561; election of 1800, 81, 126, 561–63; election of 1804, 101, 103, 106, 118, 122, 130, 561–63; and Embargo Act, 158–59, 172; and Indian treaties, 423; as leader of Virginia faction, 101, 106, 109, 118, 123, 129–30; and Louisiana Purchase, 112, 114–15, 149, 553, 560, 562; at Monticello, 182, 561; and neutrality, 600; *Notes on the State of Virginia*, 430, 437; as president, 81, 101, 103, 108, 110–15, 117–18, 122–23, 126, 149, 153, 158–59, 161, 163, 166, 172, 176, 181, 527, 552–53, 561–63; and public debt, 110–11; republicanism of, 553; as secretary of state, 11, 14, 36, 205, 541, 547, 557, 560; and slavery, 568, 647; and

University of Virginia, 267; as vice president, 562
Jenifer, Daniel, 407–8, 442–44
Jeroboam, 321
Jesus, 58, 143, 209, 305, 522
Johnson, Cave, 464
Johnson, Samuel: "Drury-lane Prologue Spoken by Mr. Garrick," 85; *The Vanity of Human Wishes*, 303
Johnson, William C., 625
Joint Resolution for Distributing Rations to the Distressed Fugitives from Indian Hostilities, JQA's speech on, 399–424
Joshua, 565–66
Jubilee of the Constitution, JQA's discourse, 487–566
Judicial branch. *See* Supreme Court, U.S.
Judicial tenure, 108, 116, 130, 243
Junius (Philip Francis), 429
Jury trials, 32, 465, 493, 651
Justice, 6–7, 16, 45, 55, 57–58, 60, 64–65, 72, 77, 81, 87, 94, 116–17, 127–28, 142, 146, 215, 229, 341, 386, 430, 534–36
Justinian: *Institutes*, 534

Kendall, Amos, 432, 651
Kentucky, 205, 269, 410, 447, 452, 454, 468, 472–73, 478, 641
Kentucky Resolves, 296, 311
King, Rufus, 128
Knapp, Isaac (publisher), 425, 427
Knox, Henry, 4, 520, 538, 547, 557

Labrador, 256
Lady Washington (American merchant ship), 537
Lafayette, Marie-Joseph du Motier de, 256, 287
Lake Erie, 542
Lake Memphramagog, 255
Lake Ontario, 542
Land fraud, 108, 117–18

Landholders, wealthy, 336–39, 346, 349, 354, 356, 361, 363, 384–85, 390, 392–93, 396–97
Lane, Amos, 457
Lapérouse, Comte de (Jean-François de Galaup), 261
La Salle, Sieur de (René-Robert Cavelier), 417
Latin America. *See* Central America; Mexico; South America
Latin language, 133–34, 142
Lawler, Joab, 405
Law of nature, 65, 94–95, 182, 192, 258, 305, 307–9, 496–97, 585, 646
Lawrence, Abbott, 464
Laws of nations, 60, 62, 163, 165, 169, 182, 190, 192, 257, 280, 305, 309, 365, 406, 408–9, 534, 536, 546, 588, 590, 596–97, 600, 617, 635–36
Laws of war, 190, 634–36
League of Armed Neutrality, 225
Leander, H.M.S., 165
Leavitt, Joshua, 568–69, 641
Leeds, Duke of (Francis Osborne), 543
Lefebvre, Jacques, 617
Legislative branch. *See* Congress, U.S.
Legislature, Maryland, 407–8
Legislature, Massachusetts (General Court), 37, 81, 101, 105–9, 117–24, 127, 130–31, 149–51, 153–54, 156–57, 161, 430
Legislature, Mississippi, 621–22
Legislature, New York, 123
Legislature, South Carolina, 325, 368–69, 382, 478
Legislature, Virginia, 512
Legislatures, state, 22, 36, 52, 122, 150, 154–55, 161, 296, 310–15, 339, 499–500, 503–6, 509, 511–14, 563
Leiden, Netherlands, 89, 92–93
Leopard, H.M.S., 149, 159, 171–76
Lewis, Dixon H., 422, 437–38, 440, 474–76

Lexington, battle of, 217, 493
Liberal constructionists, 558
Liberty, 6, 8–9, 13–17, 19, 21, 24, 27–28, 32–33, 36, 39, 42, 50, 58–60, 63–65, 67–68, 71–75, 77–79, 88, 90, 127–28, 130, 142, 161, 206, 209, 212–13, 229–30, 236–37, 266, 275, 345, 348, 352, 420, 430, 466, 492–93, 616, 653
Lincoln, Levi, 110–12, 447
Linn, Archibald L., 571–73
Liverpool, England, 158
Livingston, Robert R., 116, 491
Livy: *History of Rome*, 61, 83, 126, 214, 653
Locke, John, 514, 648
London, England, 194, 215, 580; abolitionists in, 648; American diplomats in, 4, 164, 166, 168, 181, 590, 593; citizens of, 26–28; Gordon Riots, 28; newspapers in, 158, 196, 199; and possible U.S. war with Britain, 584, 586, 589–90, 598–99, 604, 609
Loomis, Jairus, 200
Louis (French slaver), 596–97
Louis XVI, King of France, 31, 54, 61–64, 78, 540, 544–46, 646–47
Louisiana, 181, 347, 411, 568, 635; cotton production in, 393; in possible war with Mexico, 414, 572–75, 582; public land in, 350
Louisiana (French), 417
Louisiana (Spanish), 347, 411, 546, 554–55, 559–61
Louisiana Purchase, 117, 149, 417, 555; and public debt, 112; and public lands, 352; and sectionalism, 101, 114–15; and U.S. Constitution, 315, 553, 560, 562, 576
Louis-Philippe, King of France, 601, 611–15
Lovejoy, Elijah Parish, 651
Loyalists, 542, 610
Lucretia, 223
Luther, Martin, 211

Lynching, 582, 651

MacGregor, Gregor, 193, 195, 197–98, 202–3
Madison, James, 12, 515; author of *The Federalist*, 551, 558, 560; in Confederation Congress, 511; as president, 150, 168, 181, 527; and public debt, 110–12; on revenue, 555–56; as secretary of state, 205; and U.S. Constitution, 264, 519, 558, 560; as U.S. representative, 555–56, 560–61
Madrid, Spain, 181–82, 194, 554
Magna Carta, 209, 226, 493, 496
Maine, 452, 454, 464, 473, 475, 479, 543, 568, 581, 583, 585
Majority rights, 51–52, 314, 531
Mann, Abijah, Jr., 440–41
Manufactures, Minority Report of the House Committee on, 325–97
Manufacturing, 9, 337–38, 392, 461, 509, 511; noted in JQA's Annual Message (1825), 266; noted in JQA's Inaugural Address, 233; protection of, 333, 355–67, 370, 372, 376–78, 384, 389–90, 393, 395–97, 556; *Report on Manufactures* (Hamilton), 559–60; and slavery, 385
Marcellus (JQA), letters of, 53–65, 67
Marie-Antoinette, Queen of France, 544
Marshall, John, 234, 375, 526
Martineau, Harriet, 515
Martínez de Irujo y Tacón, Carlos, 193
Mary I, Queen of England, 97
Mary II, Queen of England, 495–96
Maryland, 226, 442, 625; under Articles of Confederation, 507–8; and Chesapeake and Ohio Canal, 255, 287, 290; constitution of, 407–8; legislature of, 407–8
Maryland colony, 99

INDEX

Masot, José, 187–92, 194
Massachusetts, 103, 110, 166, 226, 291, 346, 356, 399, 429, 432, 436–37, 441–42, 458, 467, 473; abolition of slavery in, 636, 647; abolition petitions from, 464; during American Revolution, 77, 104, 217, 294, 310; under Articles of Confederation, 507, 510; cession of territory by, 350; constitution of, 22, 36–37, 647; 11th Congressional District, 295–96; Federalist Party in, 101, 105, 130, 149; game laws in, 43; and Hartford Convention, 582; legislature of, 37, 81, 101, 105–9, 117–24, 127, 130–31, 149–51, 153–54, 156–57, 161, 430; monopolies in, 43; public works in, 255; ratifying convention, 11, 128–29; Shays's Rebellion in, 3–5, 25, 495; state sovereignty in, 311; Supreme Court, 647; 12th Congressional District, 425–66, 642
Massachusetts Anti-Slavery Society, 642
Massachusetts Centinel (Boston), 4
Massachusetts colony, 99, 305–6, 308, 493
Maurice, Prince of Orange, 92
Mayflower, 91, 212
Mayflower Compact, 91–93, 212
McLane, Louis, 386
McLean, John, 259
McLeod, Alexander, 568
McNutt, Alexander G., 621–22
Mediterranean Sea, 114, 256–57, 536–37, 561, 604
Menominees, 253
Mercer, Charles F., 592–93
Merry, Anthony, 116
Merry, Robert: "Elegy, Written on the Plain of Fonteroy," 57
Merrymount settlement, 98
Mexico, 255; agitation for U.S. war with, 399, 410–17, 419–21, 424, 568–69, 571–83, 606, 608, 613–14, 619–20, 622–23, 636–38, 652; boundary negotiations, 574–76, 579–80; at Panama Congress, 249, 272–73, 279–80; Santa Anna as leader of, 411–14, 572, 579, 613–14, 619, 629; slavery abolished in, 411–13, 415, 419, 631–32, 652; U.S. citizens held in, 568, 623–24, 628; war with Texas Republic, 411–13, 572–73, 579–82, 613–14, 619, 623–24, 627, 629, 652
Mexico City, 412, 579–80, 623–24, 637
Michigan, 412, 479
Michigan Territory, 255
Middle Ages, 142
Milan Decree, 170, 177
Militia, 4, 249–50, 414
Milligan, John J., 452
Milton, John: *Comus*, 377, 527; *Paradise Lost*, 87, 218, 231, 300, 384, 522
Mina, Francisco Javier, 413
Ministry, preparation for, 134, 146
Mint, U.S., 559
Missionaries, 423, 577
Mississippi, 411, 414; cotton production in, 393; legislature of, 621–22; slavery in, 614
Mississippi, U.S.S., 584, 589
Mississippi River, 181, 236, 253, 416–17, 424, 493, 504, 519, 537, 553–54, 573, 579, 581–82, 624, 637
Missouri, 253, 255, 411, 414, 454
Missouri, U.S.S., 584, 589
Missouri Crisis, 641–42
Missouri River, 424
Mobs, 27–28, 602
Molière (Jean-Baptiste Poquelin): *Le Médecin malgré lui*, 616
Monarchy, 11, 16–17, 21–22, 24, 26–27, 33, 47, 50–54, 58, 62–63, 67, 73, 78, 93, 209–10, 212, 301–2, 308–9, 317, 462, 479, 523, 545
Monopolies, 42–43, 52, 72, 95

Monroe, James: Annual Message (1823), 282–83; diplomatic missions of, 54, 116, 168, 172, 554; Latin American policy of, 270, 272, 277–78, 282–83; military service during Revolutionary War, 550; as president, 181–82, 240–41, 254, 262, 418, 527, 591–93, 630; as secretary of state, 186–87, 205, 416–17; and Seminole Wars, 183, 192, 197, 200, 202–3; as U.S. senator, 550–51
Monroe Doctrine, 270, 277–78, 283
Montesquieu, Baron de (Charles-Louis de Secondat), 314, 523, 648
Montezuma, 580
Morality, 16, 39, 48, 55–56, 64, 79, 94–95, 126–27, 129, 137, 141, 143, 215, 227, 305, 599–600, 622, 641
Morillo, Pablo, 634
Morocco, 113–14, 257, 259, 536–37
Morris, Gouverneur, 168, 541–43
Morton, Perez, 101, 107–12, 114–18
Morton, Thomas, 98
Moses, 139–40, 214, 565–66
Mount Wollaston settlement, 98
Moustier, Élie de, 539–40
Muhammad, Prophet, 14, 650
Mulattoes, 432, 470
Munroe and Francis (publisher), 133, 135
Muslims, 536, 650

Nantucket, 537, 581
Naples, Kingdom of, 247–48
Napoléon Bonaparte, 160, 170, 309, 552–53
Napoleonic Wars, 115–16, 149–50, 158–67, 170–71, 176–78, 237–38, 276, 317, 482, 620
Nassau, Bahamas, 197, 200
National Assembly (France), 13, 16, 18, 21–23, 28, 31, 33–34, 39–44, 47, 49–52, 54, 57, 317, 552
National bank. *See* Bank of the United States
National Convention (France), 54, 58, 62, 545, 547, 552
National credit. *See* Public credit
National debt. *See* Public debt
National Intelligencer (Washington, DC), 158, 181, 233, 269, 331, 399, 401, 431, 453, 461, 476–77, 484, 621, 630
National Journal (Washington, DC), 243, 287
National Republican Party, 237, 315–16; congressional election of 1830, 295; election of 1820, 205; and Whig Party, 567
National roads, 241, 243, 254–55, 260, 390
National sovereignty. *See* Sovereignty, national
National university, 244, 261, 263
Nations. *See* Laws of nations; Rights of a nation
Natural democracy, 41
Natural equality, 514, 645–48
Naturalization, 164
Natural law, 63, 65, 94–95, 182, 192, 258, 305, 307–8, 496–97, 585, 646
Natural rights, 18, 21, 41–42, 51, 62, 304–5, 494, 497, 505, 507, 512, 647, 649
Navy, British, 259, 554, 573, 580, 584; during American Revolution, 75, 213, 493, 605; *Chesapeake–Leopard* affair, 149, 162–66, 171–76; famous admirals of, 605–6; and foreign slave trade, 568, 578, 591, 615, 618; impressment of seamen by, 116, 162–67, 172, 174, 176, 547–48, 550; and possible U.S. war with Britain, 602, 605; and possible U.S. war with Mexico, 416–17; and right of search, 591, 594, 615, 618; and Seminole Wars, 185, 194, 197; during War of 1812, 309, 409–10
Navy, Continental, 505–6, 510
Navy, French, 116, 418, 584, 602

Navy, Spanish, 257
Navy, U.S., 188, 264, 538, 610; appropriations for, 250–51, 258–59; in Barbary Wars, 113–14, 259, 536–37; *Chesapeake–Leopard* affair, 149, 160, 171–76; and foreign slave trade, 240–41, 256, 258, 618, 653; Mediterranean squadron, 257, 604; new steamships in, 584, 589; Pacific squadron, 256–57; in peacetime, 361, 364; and possible war with Britain, 584, 586, 589, 599, 602, 604–5; protection of commerce by, 356; and right of search, 594, 618; United States Naval Academy (proposed), 259; in War of 1812, 259, 309; West Indies squadron, 258

Navy Department, U.S., 259, 264, 538

Negro Seaman Act (South Carolina), 651

Nelson, Horatio, 605

Netherlands, 214, 246–47; and American Revolution, 8, 225, 509, 646; colonies of, 178, 302; commerce with, 536; loans from, 509; during Napoleonic Wars, 170; Separatists in, 89–90, 92–93; Treaty of Amity and Commerce with, 55–56, 59–60, 228, 275; war with French Republic, 546; William III from, 17

Neutrality, 58–59; and commerce, 53, 55–57, 60, 149, 160, 163, 167–71, 176–78, 225, 257, 269, 275–77, 281–82, 365, 546–48, 554; and impressment of seamen, 162–67, 176, 547–48; and Latin America, 249, 283; and right of search, 586–87, 596, 600; and Seminole Wars, 185, 188, 190, 203

New Brunswick, NJ, 525

Newburyport, MA, 168

New England, 91, 101, 105, 115, 127, 233, 296, 465, 479

New England Anti-Slavery Society, 642

New Hampshire, 226, 233, 386, 388–89, 431, 454, 464, 473, 479, 507, 581

New Haven, CT, 108, 168

New Jersey, 226, 327, 356, 479, 507, 525–26; constitution of, 313

New Mexico (part of Mexico), 253

New Orleans, battle of, 181, 635

New Orleans, LA, 255, 417, 554–55, 571, 574–75

Newport, RI, 168

New Providence Island, 188, 195, 197–200

New Spain, 182

New states, 236, 263–64, 349, 352–53, 504, 519, 531, 560, 631

New York, 226, 233, 269, 440, 453–54, 457, 473, 479, 549, 551, 568, 571, 642; abolition petitions from, 464; under Articles of Confederation, 507; cession of territory by, 350; Erie Canal in, 267; Federalist Party in, 123; legislature of, 123; population of, 519; ratifying convention, 558; Republican Party in, 121

New York City: Five Points, 609–10; JQA's *Jubilee of the Constitution* discourse in, 487–89, 519, 525–26; merchants in, 168; population of, 343, 377, 519; and possible war with Britain, 584, 589, 598–99

New York colony, 308

New-York Historical Society, 487–91

Nicholls, Edward, 185–88, 193–99, 202–3

Norfolk, VA, 168, 176

Norman Conquest, 20–21, 32–33, 87, 209–10

North, Lord (Frederick North), 217

North Carolina, 128, 226, 392, 407, 445, 464, 507, 529–31; constitution of, 313

Northwest Ordinance, 508, 538–39, 557
Nullification, 150, 154–55, 169, 176, 296, 311, 313, 319–21, 325–26, 330–31, 338, 340, 343, 367–73, 375, 377–84, 389, 392–94, 422, 457, 488, 529, 532

O'Connell, Daniel, 429
Oglethorpe, James, 99
Ohio, 347, 412, 454, 464, 479, 567, 634, 642
Oldenbarnevelt, Johan van, 92
Oldenburg, Grand Duchy of, 246
"Olive Branch Petition" (Continental Congress), 218, 493
Oliver and Munroe (publisher), 149, 151
Onís, Luis de, 181, 183, 187
Ontario, 568
Oratory, 133, 139–47
Orders in Council, British, 149, 158–61, 171, 176, 178
Oregon Country, 240, 262, 277, 537–38, 583, 585, 587
Orléans, Duc d' (Ferdinand-Philippe), 614
Otis, Harrison Gray, 149, 488; JQA's letter to, 151–79
Ottoman Empire, 257, 601, 613
Owen, Robert, 373
Owens, George W., 406

Pacific Ocean, 182, 240, 252, 256–57, 262, 417, 537–38, 573, 575–76, 579–80
Paine, Thomas: *The American Crisis*, 6; *Common Sense*, 11, 14; *Rights of Man*, 11–23, 26–27, 29–36, 38–40, 42–52, 54
Pakenham, Richard, 619
Palestine, 214
Palmerston, Viscount (Henry John Temple), 633
Panama, 269–71, 413, 637

Panama Congress, 249; JQA's Message on, 269–85
Papacy, 15, 552, 650
Paris, France, 109, 275, 305, 418, 602, 612, 620; during French Revolution, 26–27, 54, 550, 552
Parliament (Britain), 26–28, 39, 47, 245, 304, 314, 346, 494, 605; abolition of slavery by, 649; colonial policy of, 215, 217, 302–3, 305, 307, 493, 646; and Constitution, 21–22, 29–31, 33–34, 38; and elections, 40, 42; exclusions from, 45–46; freedom of speech in, 454, 479, 481; and Glorious Revolution, 17–18; omnipotence of, 493, 507, 646; and Orders in Council, 149, 158–61, 171, 176, 178; representation in, 52, 647; and right of search, 174, 591; Stamp Act, 73, 303, 305; taxation by, 161, 213, 303, 305, 307, 310, 647
Parthenon ("Elgin") marbles, 229
Partisanship, 53, 81, 101–3, 107, 118, 123, 130, 205, 234, 429, 561
Pascal, Blaise: *Lettres provinciales*, 627; *Pensées*, 522, 627
Passamaquoddy River, 413
Patent Office, U.S., 244, 265
Patowmack Canal, 292
Patriotism, 4–6, 8–9, 19, 28, 67, 74, 77, 90, 105–6, 124–25, 145, 173, 192, 199, 206–7, 237, 241, 257, 265, 270, 285, 290, 302, 306, 312, 322, 331, 334, 345, 368, 390, 412, 494, 504, 506, 517, 524, 526, 557, 624
Patronage. *See* Spoils system
Patterson, Daniel T., 200
Patton, John M., 436–37, 439–40, 448, 451–53, 455, 457, 470–71, 482, 485
Patuxet, 95
Pausanias, 140

Peace powers, 46–50, 52, 406, 408–9, 508
Penn, William, 99, 460–61
Pennsylvania, 174, 226, 269, 314, 346, 356, 457, 479, 499, 525–26, 648; abolition petitions from, 399, 464; under Articles of Confederation, 507; and Chesapeake and Ohio Canal, 290; public creditors in, 558–59; Republican Party in, 121; state sovereignty in, 311; Whiskey Rebellion in, 316, 495
Pennsylvania Anti-Slavery Society, 651
Pennsylvania colony, 99
Pennsylvania Mutiny, 510
Pensacola, FL, 181–85, 189–93, 202–3
Pensioners, 9, 44–45, 52, 240, 250, 255–56, 360, 557
Perkins, Jacob, 230
Persia, ancient, 7, 289
Peru, 257, 413
Petitions to abolish slavery, 399, 406, 651; JQA's letters to constituents on, 425–66; JQA's speech in House of Representatives on, 425, 427, 430, 453, 467–86
"Petition to the King" (Continental Congress) 218, 493
Philadelphia, PA, 3–4, 14, 525–26, 603, 609–11; abolitionists in, 648; anti-abolition sentiment in, 457, 460–61, 651; Constitutional Convention in, 11, 512–13, 517, 529, 537, 541; merchants in, 168; as seat of national government, 68, 493
Philadelphia, U.S.S., 114
Philip II, King of Spain, 214
Philip of Macedon, 319
Phillips, Stephen C., 447
Pickens, Francis W., 456, 479
Pickering, Timothy, 149–51, 153–54, 156–59, 161–63, 168–69, 176

Pilgrims, 81, 87–99, 212, 464, 466
Pinckney, Henry Laurens, 400, 425, 460
Pinckney, Thomas, 168, 171, 554
Piracy, 53, 55–57, 113–14, 185, 257–58, 466, 510, 568, 590, 618, 651
Pitt, William (the Younger), 543
Pius VII, Pope, 552
Pizarro, Francisco, 413
Pizarro, José García, 183–84, 193–94, 202
Plato, 138, 345; *Republic*, 93
Plutarch, 230, 653
Plymouth, MA, 81, 83, 91, 255
Plymouth colony, 84, 89–99, 212, 464, 466
Poinsett, Joel R., 573–76, 631
Poland, 336, 462
Political equality, 79
Political parties, 239, 315
Political rights, 335
Polk, James K., 406–7, 422, 426, 431, 433–35, 437–40, 443, 446–48, 452, 454–55, 458, 463–64, 467, 469, 474, 479–81, 483–86
Polyander, Johannes, 92
Pope, Alexander: *An Essay on Man*, 364, 606; *Imitations of Horace*, 481; *Moral Essays*, 85
Popular representation, 39–41, 317, 373, 377, 393
Popular sovereignty. *See* Sovereignty, popular
Portugal, 210, 487, 536–37
Post Office Department, U.S., 259–60, 539, 556, 651
President, U.S.: accumulation of power by, 545; appointments of, 243, 539; constitutional role of, 534–35, 539; and diplomacy, 542; election of, 516; impeachment of, 535; peace power of, 49; term of office, 563; and treaties, 49; veto power of, 339, 382, 528; and war powers, 534–35, 604, 628–29

Press, freedom of, 238, 383, 438–39, 461, 465, 612, 651
Price, Richard: *Discourse on the Love of Our Country*, 17
Prince, Thomas: *Chronological History of New England*, 84
Privateers, 53, 55–57, 257, 275–77, 510, 546
Prize money, 113–14
Proclamation Regarding Nullification (Jackson), 326, 369–72, 379–81
Property rights, 28, 41, 81, 93–96, 349–51, 354, 525
Proportional representation, 101–2, 107, 125–28, 373–78, 386, 388, 392, 429, 435–36, 452, 460, 468–69, 503, 506, 511
Protection, 371, 377, 391, 394, 466, 536; of agriculture, 360, 372, 378, 390, 395; of commerce, 114, 257, 296, 356, 360–61, 364, 369, 390, 395, 562; of free labor, 372, 376, 378–79; from Indian hostilities, 356; of inhabitants of Florida Territory, 404–5; of manufacturing, 333, 355–67, 370, 372, 376–78, 384, 389–90, 393, 395–97, 556
Protestants, 96–98, 492
Prussia, 246, 309, 585; and Quintuple Treaty, 568, 602; Treaty of Amity and Commerce with, 56–57, 59–60, 275, 284–85; U.S. diplomatic mission to, 571, 583, 587, 589, 606, 610; war with French Republic, 544
Public credit, 4, 6–7, 9, 24, 252, 505–6, 509, 512, 555, 558–60, 562
Public debt, 8, 61, 541, 562; appropriations for, 109–12; under Articles of Confederation, 509, 511–12; final discharge of, 325, 334, 349, 352; noted in JQA's Annual Message (1825), 250–52; noted in JQA's Inaugural Address, 240; taxation for, 3–4, 104, 109, 111–12, 240, 250–51, 556, 559
Public faith, 3–4, 6–8, 25, 104, 334, 509, 512. *See also* Public credit
Public lands, 252, 326, 337, 349–54, 358, 364, 384, 390, 395
Publicola, Publius Valerius, 11, 101
Publicola (JQA), letters of, 11–53
Public opinion, 41, 49, 239, 241, 415, 429, 465, 522–23, 539, 549, 561, 563, 643
Public service, 124, 133, 242, 252–53, 261–62, 264, 295
Public virtue, 77
Public works, *see* Internal improvements
Publius Valerius (JQA), letters of, 101–31
Puerto Rico, 279, 418–19
Purchas, Samuel: *Purchas his pilgrimage*, 84
Puritans, 305–6

Quakers, 537, 648–49
Quincy, Josiah, 306–7
Quincy, MA, 295–98, 307, 645
Quincy Patriot, 429, 453, 641
Quintilian, 146
Quintuple Treaty, 568, 600–602, 612, 614–15, 618, 652

Rabun, William, 635, 639–40
Railroads, 292
Raleigh, Walter, 99
Randolph, John, 108–9, 117
Randolph, Thomas, 108–9
Randolph, Thomas Jefferson, 647
Randolph, Thomas Mann, Jr., 117
Ratford, Jenkin, 174
Ratifying conventions, state, 11, 128–29, 312–13, 514, 524, 558
Raynal, Guillaume-Thomas-François, 648
Red River, 575–76
Red Sticks (Creeks), 186, 188

Reformation, 97, 210–11
Reign of Terror, 54, 317, 549–50
Religion, 39, 42; freedom of, 42, 88–90, 96–98, 209, 212, 238, 279–80, 383, 459, 527; missionaries, 423, 577; preparation for ministry, 133–34, 143, 146. *See also individual faiths*
Renaissance, 142
Reparations, 171–73, 175, 276, 482
Repertory, The (Boston), 101
Report of the Minority of the Committee on Manufactures (JQA), 325–97
Report on Manufactures (Hamilton), 559–60
Representation, 17–18, 52, 314, 342; of enslaved population, 374, 376, 378; equal, 42, 503, 506; exclusions from, 44–45; legislative, 264; popular, 39–41, 317, 373, 377, 393; of property, 374, 378; proportional, 101–2, 107, 125–28, 373–78, 386, 388, 392, 429, 435–36, 452, 460, 468–69, 503, 506, 511; and taxation, 102, 125, 129, 213, 303, 307, 378
Representative democracy, 234, 238
Republicanism, 9, 39, 58, 76, 93, 94, 128, 134, 147, 157, 228, 584, 641; and Declaration of Independence, 309; in France, 39, 54, 107, 541, 549, 553; of Jefferson, 553; in Netherlands, 302; in Poland, 462; in state constitutions, 313–14, 380–81, 383; and U.S. Constitution, 236–37, 373, 522–23, 527
Republican Party, 11–12, 110, 120–21, 124, 129, 296, 524; election of 1800, 81, 126, 562–63; election of 1804, 101, 106, 118, 122, 130, 562–63; election of 1808, 150; in Massachusetts, 105–7, 117, 130, 149; and National Republican Party, 205, 237, 295, 315–16,
567; pro-French, 53, 315, 552–53; and state sovereignty, 315
Revenue. *See* Taxation and revenue
Revenue Collection Act, 594–95
Revenue cutters, 594–95
Revolutionary War, 6, 12, 14, 19–20, 25, 67, 74–76, 78, 104, 161, 214, 227, 265, 270, 274, 285, 299, 304, 307–8, 353–54, 492, 507, 515, 518, 545, 548, 550–51, 558–59, 584, 648–49; battle of Bunker Hill, 217; battle of Lexington, 217, 493; battle of Saratoga, 646; British army and navy in, 213, 493; burning of Charlestown, 217, 494; Continental Army in, 75, 292, 505–6, 510, 512, 526; Continental Navy in, 505–6, 510; and Declaration of Independence, 222–24, 494; Dutch alliance, 8, 225, 509, 646; French alliance, 8, 53, 55, 59–60, 64, 77, 225, 228, 537, 646–47; loyalists, 542, 610; operations under Articles of Confederation, 310, 508; pensioners, 9, 44–45, 52, 240, 250, 255–56, 360, 557; petitions to George III, 218, 493; Spanish alliance, 8, 225, 509, 545, 646; Treaty of Paris, 55–56, 59–60, 225–26, 289, 499, 541–44; Washington as commander-in-chief, 4, 77, 292, 510–12, 516
Rhetoric, 133, 137–38, 140, 144–45, 288
Rhode Island, 226, 473, 479, 507, 509, 529–31
Rhode Island colony, 309
Rice, 392
Richardson, Lord and Holbrook (publisher), 295, 297
Richmond Enquirer, 621
Right of visitation and search, 173–74, 568, 583, 585–87, 589–97, 600–602, 611–12, 615–18, 632, 652

Rights: civil, 335, 478, 480; equal, 24, 36, 40, 123, 128–30, 229, 236–37, 240, 336–38, 345, 352; human, 16, 28, 52, 58, 60, 127, 209, 213, 217, 228–29, 237, 305, 318, 337, 430, 450–51, 459, 469, 480, 493, 495, 498, 512, 514, 521, 646–49, 652; natural, 18, 21, 41–42, 51, 62, 304–5, 494, 497, 505, 507, 512, 647, 649; of petition, 399, 425–26, 429–35, 443–64, 467–77, 482–85, 651; political, 335; of possession, 81–82, 94–96, 424; property, 28, 41, 81, 93–96, 349–51, 354, 525; states', 239, 296, 311, 524, 532, 560, 635

Rights of a nation, 16–17, 21, 23–24, 51, 58, 596

Right to life, 304–5

Rio Grande (Río Bravo del Norte), 415–17, 419, 574–75, 580, 623, 630

Ritner, Joseph, 457

Rives, William Cabell, 432–33

Roads. See National roads

Robert II, Duke of Normandy, 32

Robertson, John, 445, 447, 472–73

Robespierre, Maximilien-François de, 107, 550, 552

Robinson, John, 88, 93

Rochester, William B., 269

Rocky Mountains, 412, 519

Rodgers, John, 114

Rodney, George, 605

Rome, ancient, 7–8, 53, 81, 85–87, 99, 114, 133, 137–38, 141–44, 146, 214, 223, 230, 241, 276, 289, 305, 345, 396, 491, 522, 653

Rome, Italy, 97

Rose, George H., 159, 171–72

Rousseau, Jean-Jacques, 138, 648; *The Social Contract*, 21–22, 39, 48, 93

Rush, Richard, 182, 251, 593, 628

Russell, Benjamin, 13, 15, 19, 23, 27, 31, 34, 39, 42, 46, 50, 55, 58, 61

Russell and Cutler (publisher), 81, 83

Russia, 7, 246, 261, 277, 416, 585; and American Revolution, 225; feudalism in, 336; and Quintuple Treaty, 568, 602; U.S. diplomatic mission to, 181, 571

Sabine River, 416–17, 419, 572–75, 629–30

Sacs, 253

St. Augustine, FL, 195

St. Croix River, 543

Saint-Domingue. See Haiti

St. Marys River, 259

Salaverry, Felipe, 413

Salem, MA, 168

Salic law of descent, 52

Samson, 74

Sandwich Islands (Hawaiian Islands), 257, 537

San Jacinto, battle of, 579

Santa Anna, Antonio López de, 411–14, 572, 579, 613–14, 619, 629

Santa Fe (part of Mexico), 415, 417, 568, 575–76, 623–24, 628

Saratoga, battle of, 646

Sardinia, 246

Scheldt River, 62

Scotland, 306. See also Britain

Scott, Richard W., 189, 200

Scott, Walter: *The Lady of the Lake*, 581; *Lay of the Last Minstrel*, 306

Scott, William, 596–97

Seas, freedom of, 616–18

Secession, 307, 321, 369–70, 377, 488, 529–30, 532–33

Second Continental Congress, 218, 227, 300, 497–98, 500–502, 506, 508, 538, 564

Sectionalism, 81, 101–2, 105, 114–15, 155, 205, 237, 239, 316, 372, 375, 384, 391–92, 399, 461, 553, 563, 577, 641, 651

Seminoles, 181, 183–84, 186, 188, 202, 414, 424, 627

Seminole Wars, 183–203, 399, 414, 420–24, 627–28, 635–36, 639–40
Senate, Massachusetts, 81, 119–20, 122, 131, 149, 151, 157
Senate, U.S., 106, 117, 123, 153, 156, 160, 243, 245, 326; advice and consent on appointments, 269–70, 272, 284, 535, 539; advice and consent on treaties, 49, 253–54, 278, 535, 543; constitutional role of, 516, 528, 534–35, 539; and Electoral College, 122; JQA's service in, 101–2, 133, 149–50, 157, 162, 591; and Panama Congress, 269–70, 272, 278, 284–85; representation in, 103–4, 264; resolution on neutrality, 168. *See also* Congress, U.S.
Separation of powers, 46, 48, 314, 382, 528
Separatists. *See* Pilgrims
Sergeant, John, 269–70, 280, 284
Seven Years' War, 72, 169–70, 493, 605
Shakespeare, William: *As You Like It*, 648; *Hamlet*, 108, 139; *1 Henry IV*, 381; *2 Henry IV*, 301, 474; *Julius Caesar*, 78, 223, 320; *King John*, 57; *Macbeth*, 206, 295; *The Merchant of Venice*, 443; *Othello*, 545; *Romeo and Juliet*, 614; *The Tempest*, 364
Sharp, Granville, 648
Shays's Rebellion, 3–5, 25, 495
Shepperd, Augustine H., 407
Sherman, Roger, 516
Short, William, 554
Sidney, Algernon, 493
Sieyès, Emmanuel-Joseph, 315
Simonides, 309
Simpson, James, 114
Sioux, 253
Slade, William, 461, 571–73, 625–26
Slaveholders, 346, 372–76, 378–79, 384–89, 397, 399–400, 407, 431, 433, 436–38, 441, 445, 450, 452, 462–63, 471, 478, 573, 578, 592, 646–47, 651–52
Slave insurrections, 337, 410, 438–39, 476, 584, 634, 636–37
Slave labor versus free labor, 372, 376, 378–79
Slavery, 239, 332, 608, 617, 645; abolished by Britain, 415, 419–20, 465–66, 578, 596–97, 641, 645, 649, 652–53; abolished in Mexico, 411–13, 415, 419, 631–32, 652; and abolitionism, 425–26, 445, 454, 465, 577, 582, 641–43, 647–53; abolition of, 399–400, 406, 416; and agriculture, 335–36, 346, 372, 384–85, 387–88; *Amistad* case, 567–68, 597; and commerce, 385; and Congress, 399–400, 406–10, 420–21, 425, 429–86, 626–27, 633–34; in District of Columbia, 399–400, 432, 437, 442, 447, 455, 459–60, 462–64, 466, 471–73, 631–32; effect on nation, 465–66; in Haiti, 63–64, 270; and manufacturing, 385; in Texas, 411, 413, 419, 466, 572–73, 577–79, 631–33, 652; and three-fifths clause, 101–2, 107, 125–29, 460; in U.S. Constitution, 460, 650
Slaves, *see* Enslaved people
Slave trade: in District of Columbia, 399, 432; domestic, 399–400, 432, 469, 568, 594–95, 651–53; foreign, 126, 240–41, 256, 258, 269, 278, 406, 416, 568, 578, 585, 590–92, 594–97, 608, 614–18, 641, 648–49, 652–53
Smith, John, 99
Smollett, Tobias: "Ode to Independence," 322
Smyth, Alexander, 592
Snyder, John, 605
Social compact, 4, 19, 21–23, 32, 48, 65, 85, 92, 157, 212, 215–16, 223, 235, 260, 300, 302, 304, 307–8, 335, 346, 361–63, 371, 389–91, 515

Social equality, 72, 79, 227
Socrates, 138
Solomon, 321
Solon, 562
Sophists, 138
Soto, José de, 184
South America, 199, 206, 240, 248–49, 256, 264, 606, 634, 637; constitutions in, 318, 320; independence from Spain, 257–58, 269, 271, 279, 283–84; and Panama Congress, 269–85; treaties with, 272, 276, 278, 280
Southard, Samuel L., 259
South Carolina, 205, 226, 270, 388, 400, 422, 479, 636; under Articles of Confederation, 507; cession of territory by, 350; constitution of, 382; cotton production in, 393; enslaved population in, 376; foreign slave trade in, 126; legislature of, 325, 368–69, 382–83, 478; Negro Seaman Act, 651; nullification convention in, 325–26, 331, 367–70, 372–73, 377–84, 389, 394; public works in, 259; slavery in, 466; state sovereignty in, 311, 343; tax payment default by, 129
Sovereign power, 304–5, 310–11, 313, 317, 320–21, 500, 507–8, 523, 641, 646
Sovereignty: national, 17–18, 48, 62, 150, 167, 178, 218, 222–23, 227, 277, 312; nominal, 279; popular, 53, 78, 500, 503, 507, 511–14, 516–17, 531, 533, 565; of the seas, 616–17; state, 238, 308, 310–13, 315–16, 319–20, 326, 343, 367–70, 377, 379–83, 389, 391–92, 394, 488, 500, 503–17, 524, 527, 529–30, 532, 560, 562, 565–66
Spain, 37, 92, 210, 247, 487, 493, 561; and American Revolution, 8, 225, 509, 646; colonies of, 178; commerce with, 536; feudalism in, 336; Florida as colony of, 181–204, 240, 352, 417, 576, 627–28, 635, 639–40; and independence of Latin American nations, 257–58, 269, 271, 279, 283–84, 412–13, 417, 419; loans from, 509; Louisiana as colony of, 347, 411, 546, 554–55, 559–60; Napoleonic Wars, 159, 170–71, 178; Transcontinental Treaty, 182, 240, 352, 416–17, 576, 630; Treaty of San Lorenzo, 554–55; U.S. diplomatic mission to, 571; war with French Republic, 545–46; West Indies colonies of, 188, 196–97, 279, 417–19, 573
Sparta, ancient, 309
Speech, freedom of, 320, 383, 400, 406–8, 421–22, 425–26, 431, 435, 438, 445, 447, 449, 452–54, 461, 465, 467, 472, 479–80, 483, 625, 627, 633, 651
Spoils system, 108, 116, 130, 243, 295, 461, 463
Stamp Act, 73–74, 161, 303, 305
Standing armies, 51, 113, 416
Standish, Miles, 91
State constitutions. *See* Constitutions, state
State debts, 560, 579, 584, 586, 605, 609, 620–22
State Department, U.S., 164–65, 181–83, 205, 213, 233–34, 236, 264, 538–41, 551, 556–57, 573, 606–7
State legislatures. *See* Legislatures, state
State ratifying conventions. *See* Ratifying conventions, state
State sovereignty. *See* Sovereignty, state
States' rights, 239, 296, 311, 524, 532, 560, 635
Steenrod, Lewis, 572
Stephens, James: *War in Disguise*, 167–68
Sterne, Laurence, 648

Stevenson, Andrew, 330, 375, 585, 590, 611, 618
Stock, federal government disposal of, 338, 348
Stowell, Baron (William Scott), 167
Strict constructionists, 326, 330, 559–60
Strong, Caleb, 106–7
Stuart dynasty, 300–302, 306
Sulayman bin Muhammad, Sultan of Morocco, 113–14
Sullivan, George, 233
Sullivan, James, 149, 151, 153, 157
Supreme Court, Massachusetts, 647
Supreme Court, U.S.: *Amistad* case, 567, 597; decisions regarding Indian tribes, 422–23; establishment of, 538–39; John Jay as chief justice, 541, 551; John Marshall as chief justice, 234, 375; prize cases, 590
Suwahuee, 184
Sweden, 214, 246–48, 585, 596, 646
Swift, Jonathan: *Gulliver's Travels*, 301
Switzerland, 214
Syria, 601, 613

Tacitus, 321; *Life of Agricola*, 86
Tamaulipas, 415
Tamerlane (Timur), 637–38
Tampa Bay, 197–98
Tanner, Henry S., 575
Tariff of 1828, 296, 325
Tariffs, 233, 296, 325–27, 330, 369, 393–94, 396
Tarquinus, 214, 223
Tartars, 137, 346
Taxation and revenue, 113, 321, 333, 337–38, 395–96; under Articles of Confederation, 25, 129, 503, 508–9, 511, 529; by British government, 72, 158, 161, 170, 176, 178, 213, 300, 302–3, 305, 307, 310, 493, 647; direct taxes, 109, 111, 129, 376, 378–79, 385–88; excise taxes, 109, 111, 376; in France, 40; noted in JQA's Annual Message (1825), 250–52; noted in JQA's Inaugural Address, 238, 240; for protection of manufacturing, 355–59, 361–67, 370, 372, 376–78; and public debt, 3–4, 104, 109, 111–12, 240, 250–51, 556, 559; and representation, 102, 125, 129, 213, 303, 307, 378; Revenue Collection Act, 594–95; sale of public lands, 252, 349, 352–53; in South Carolina, 380, 383, 394; in U.S. Constitution, 319; during Washington administration, 555–56, 559–60
Taylor, William, 457–58, 462–63
Tea Act, 161, 305
Tell, William, 214, 223
Ten Commandments, 566
Tennessee, 205, 352, 407, 464
Texas, 585; annexation of, 399, 415–17, 419, 466, 568–69, 572, 577–78, 619, 629, 632–33, 636–37; army of, 411, 581; battle of San Jacinto, 579; boundary of, 412, 574–76, 578, 630; independence of, 412–13, 415; settlement of, 630–31; slavery in, 411, 413, 419, 466, 572–73, 577–79, 631–33, 652; war with Mexico, 411–13, 572–73, 579–82, 613–14, 619, 623–24, 627, 629, 652
Thayer, Sylvanus, 253
Themistocles, 230
Theseus, 140
Thiers, Adolphe, 612, 614–16
Thomas, Francis, 407–8
Thomas, James: "Winter," 69
Thompson, Jacob, 621–22
Thompson, Waddy, Jr., 422, 436–42, 444–45, 448, 453, 456, 458, 474–81, 483, 571–72, 622–30
Three-fifths clause, 101–2, 107, 125–29, 460
Tippecanoe, battle of, 567
Tobacco, 216, 392

Tocqueville, Alexis de, 528
Tory Party (Britain), 170, 175–76
Transcontinental Treaty with Spain, 182, 240, 352, 416–17, 576, 630
Treason, 50, 310, 316, 320–21, 448–49, 453, 474, 478
Treasury, U.S., 111, 129, 250–52, 260, 348, 352–53, 396, 403–5, 422, 424, 511, 555, 624
Treasury Department, U.S., 236, 556–57
Treaties, 19, 49, 51, 62–63, 236, 365–66, 408, 505–6, 508, 511, 585; with Indian tribes, 186–88, 253–54, 269, 349, 356, 406, 409, 422–24, 461, 556–57; with Latin American nations, 272, 276, 278, 280
Treaty of Alliance with France, 53, 55, 59–65, 545–48, 554
Treaty of Amity and Commerce with France, 55–56, 59–60, 228, 275, 284, 366
Treaty of Amity and Commerce with the Netherlands, 55–56, 59–60, 228, 275
Treaty of Amity and Commerce with Prussia, 56–57, 59–60, 275, 284–85
Treaty of Ghent, 82, 181, 185–87, 233, 238, 249, 409, 610
Treaty of Indian Springs, 254
Treaty of Paris, 55–56, 59–60, 225–26, 289, 499, 541–44
Treaty of San Lorenzo, 554–55
Treaty with Creek Indians, 186, 188, 269
Treaty with Morocco, 113–14
Trenton, NJ, 525–26
Tripoli, 113–14, 257, 259, 463, 536–37
Trojan War, 87, 140
Trumbull, John: *M'Fingal*, 109
Tunis, 113, 257, 259, 463, 536–37, 650
Turgot, Anne-Robert-Jacques, 646

Turkey. *See* Ottoman Empire
Twelfth Amendment, 122
12th Congressional District (Massachusetts), JQA's letters to constituents, 425–66
Tyler, John, 567, 573, 585, 601; and annexation of Texas, 568, 572, 577; and slavery, 652; and war with Mexico, 569, 582, 604
Tyranny, 6, 13, 17, 21–24, 28, 30, 32, 63–64, 71, 73–75, 77–78, 141, 209–10, 214, 304, 311, 317, 320–21, 345, 348, 383, 389, 430, 446

Underwood, Joseph R., 478
United States Military Academy (West Point), 240, 253–54, 259, 261
United States Naval Academy (proposed), 259
University of Leiden, 92
University of Virginia, 267

Van Buren, Martin, 269, 457, 475, 601, 630; and abolition petitions, 432–33, 454, 462, 464; Inaugural Address, 455, 466; as president, 464–66, 481, 527; and slavery, 465–66; and Tariff of 1828, 296; as vice president, 326
Vandals, 87
Vanderpoel, Aaron, 453
Vasa, Gustav, 214
Vattel, Emmerich de: *The Law of Nations*, 201
Venezuela, 405, 634
Veracruz, Mexico, 417, 624
Vergennes, Comte de (Charles Gravier), 646
Vermont, 378–79, 386, 388–89, 464, 473, 479, 571
Verplanck, Gulian C., 330
Versailles, France, 109
Vesuvius (volcano), 548
Veto power, 339, 382, 464–65, 528

INDEX

Vice presidency, U.S., 375
Vienna, Austria, 589, 606, 610
Virgil: *Aeneid*, 99, 230, 491, 522; *Eclogues*, 58
Virginia, 149, 166, 226, 444–45, 550, 567–68; abolition petitions from, 432, 434, 436, 439, 448, 470–71; under Articles of Confederation, 507, 509–10; cession of territory by, 350; and Chesapeake and Ohio Canal, 255, 290; factions in, 101, 104, 106, 109, 118, 123, 127–30; legislature of, 512; Republican Party in, 121; slavery in, 632, 647; state sovereignty in, 311, 509; University of Virginia, 267
Virginia colony, 89, 94, 99, 300, 308
Virginia Resolves, 296, 311
Voltaire (François-Marie Arouet), 109, 648
Voluntary association, 93, 95, 212, 307, 318, 530–31

Walker, Robert J., 621
Walsh's National Gazette (Washington, D.C.), 331
Wampanoags, 95–96
Ward, Robert Plumer, 167
War Department, U.S., 181, 236, 252, 538, 556–57
War of 1812, 237, 246, 315, 563, 580, 584; battle of New Orleans, 181, 635; cost of, 356; Hartford Convention, 582; indemnities for enslaved carried away by British, 247–49, 409–10, 420; Treaty of Ghent, 82, 181, 185–87, 233, 238, 249, 409, 610; U.S. Army in, 181, 197–98, 635; U.S. Navy in, 259, 309
War powers, 46–50, 52, 400, 405–6, 408–10, 420, 508, 604, 628–29, 634
Warren, Lott, 635, 639–40
Warrington, Lewis, 258

Wars of the Roses, 301
Washington, DC, 101, 108–9, 116, 153, 172, 181, 183, 186, 205, 207–8, 234, 240, 243, 254–55, 261, 265–66, 271, 287, 290, 369, 399, 401, 431, 435, 439, 455, 461, 576, 627. *See also* District of Columbia
Washington, George, 68, 182, 205, 222, 265, 395; and census of 1790, 263; as commander-in-chief, 4, 77, 292, 510–12, 516; at Constitutional Convention, 312, 495, 516, 522, 530; Farewell Address, 269, 281–82, 600; inauguration of, 487, 491–92, 525–27, 534, 545; and Indian treaties, 423; and manufacturing, 358–59; at Mount Vernon, 512, 525; and neutrality, 53, 600; as president, 11, 53, 67, 163, 166, 316, 358–59, 423, 519–25, 527, 535, 538–62; and public works, 260–61; retirement of, 563; and slavery, 647; and Whiskey Rebellion, 316
Washington, Madison, 652
Washington Globe, 431, 443
Washingtonian, 433
Washington Monument, 265
Webster, Daniel, 81, 482
Webster–Ashburton Treaty, 583
Weights and measures, 262–63, 561
Wellington, Duke of (Arthur Wellesley), 605
Wessagusset settlement, 99
West, Benjamin, 230
West Florida, 181, 240, 352, 417
West Indies, 61–64, 149, 165, 175, 256, 258, 417–18, 545, 548, 573; British abolition of slavery in, 415, 419–20, 578, 596–97, 641, 645, 652–53; Cuba, 188, 196–97, 279, 417–19, 573; Haiti, 63–64, 270, 278–79; Jamaica, 418; and Panama Congress, 269–85; Puerto Rico, 279, 418–19; U.S. Navy squadron in, 258

Weston, Thomas, 98
Whaling, 257, 537, 581
Whig Party (Britain), 11, 20, 170, 175–76
Whig Party (United States), 429, 457; election of 1840, 567–68; and slavery, 643
Whiskey Rebellion, 316, 495
Whitby, Henry, 165
White, Hugh Lawson, 375
Whitney, Eli, 230, 461
Whittier, John Greenleaf, 425–26, 429–30, 642
Wilberforce, William, 590–91
Wilderness, 72, 88–89, 95, 98, 215, 224, 412, 417, 565, 630–31
Willard, Joseph, 3
William, Prince of Orange (1533–1584), 214
William, Prince of Orange (1650–1702). *See* William III, King of England

William I (the Conqueror), King of England, 20, 32–33, 87, 520–21
William II, King of England, 32
William III, King of England, 17, 306, 495–96
Winslow, Edward, 91, 466
Winthrop, John, 99, 306
Wise, Henry A., 478–79, 567, 569, 571–83, 604, 608, 613, 619–20, 622–27, 629–31, 633, 637–38, 641
Witenagemot, 496
Women: abolition petitions from, 432, 436, 439–40, 448, 470–71; public spirit of, 8
Woodbine, George, 185, 193–94, 197–99, 202–3
Wool, 325, 364–65, 387
Worcester, Samuel Austin, 423
Wright, Obed, 639
Wycliffe, John, 211

Yazoo land fraud, 108, 117–18
Young, Edward: *Night Thoughts*, 223

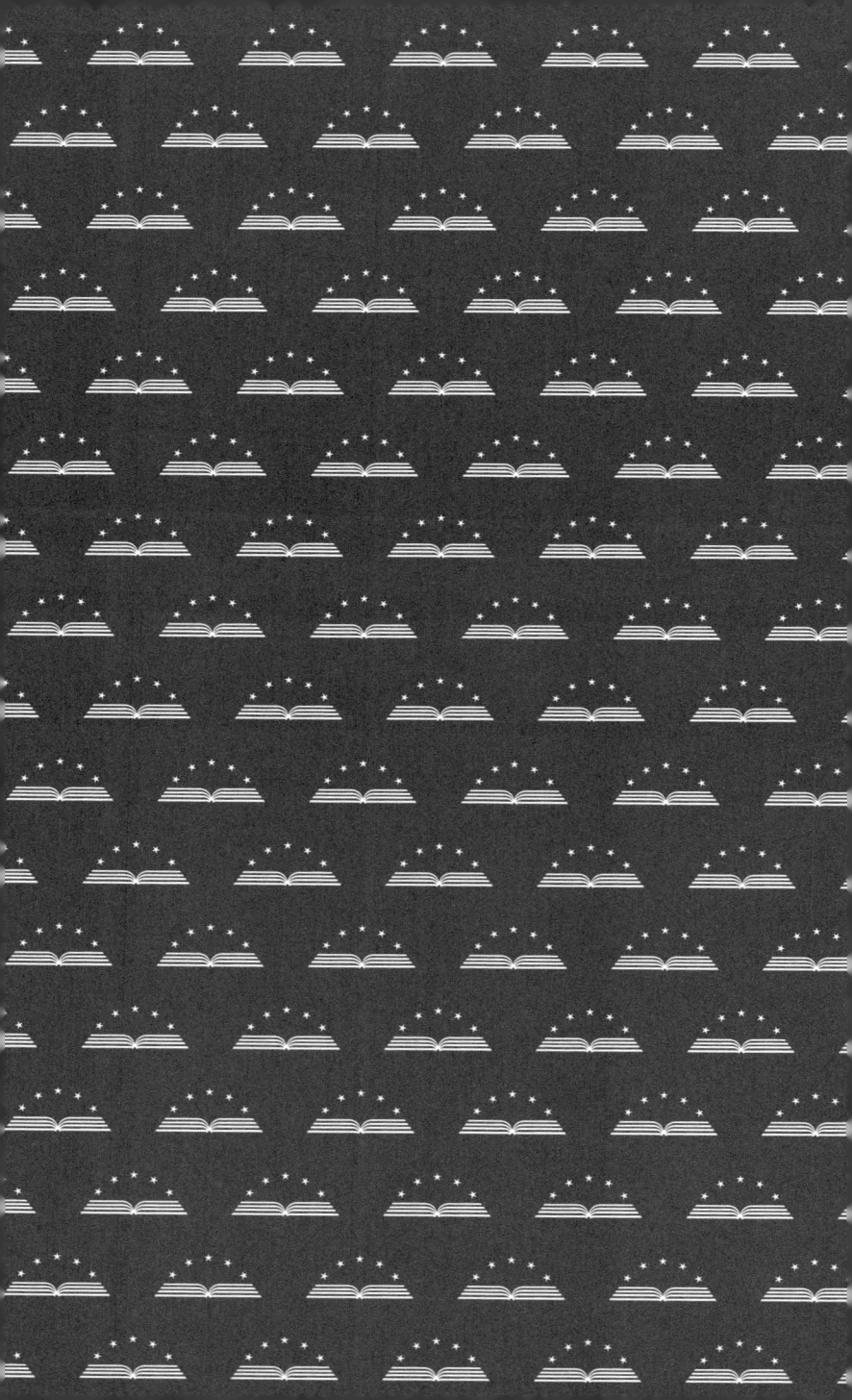